MUAY TIM—THE ART OF 8 TOOLS

(SEE PAGE 116)

TIM FERRISS
FORMER NON-COOK

The 4-Hour
CHEF

PUBLISHER'S DISCLAIMER

The material in this book is for informational purposes only. Since each individual situation is unique, you should use proper discretion, in consultation with a health-care practitioner, before undertaking the diet and exercise techniques described in this book. The author and publisher expressly disclaim responsibility for any adverse effects that may result from the use or application of the information contained in this book.

NOTICE ON FOOD HANDLING

This book is about cooking; it's not a food processing and handling manual. I strongly encourage you to read and follow the established safe food processing and handling guidelines available through the USDA, FDA, and Department of Health and Human Services, including:

foodsafety.gov
fsis.usda.gov
fda.gov/food/foodsafety

NOTICE ON INTERNET RESOURCES

My full curriculum is within the covers of this book. For those of you who want to "go beyond" in your research, I have provided links to Internet resources. My team and I have worked to check that these links are accurate and point to resources available when this book was released for publication. But Internet resources change frequently, and other confounding variables beyond my control intervene. So, for various reasons, the links may not direct you to the resource I had intended. In many cases, you will likely be able to use your favorite search engine to locate the correct link. Where links to a good resource are not working, and avid readers among you let me know, we will work to provide updated and corrected links in posts or pages at fourhourblog.com.

NOTICE ON HAND WASHING

When in doubt, wash your hands. Touched meat? Wash your hands. Rinsed spinach? Wash your hands. Saw a shooting star? Yep, wash your hands. Do it more than you think necessary.

For information about permission to reproduce selections from this book, write to Permissions, Houghton Mifflin Harcourt Publishing Company, 215 Park Avenue South, New York, NY 10003.

hmhbooks.com

ISBN-13: 978-0-547-88459-2
ISBN-10: 0-547-88459-1

Photo, illustration, and text credits, which constitute an extension of this copyright page, appear on page 668.

Library of Congress Control Number: 2012948325

Printed in the United States of America
MM 10 9 8 7 6 5 4 3 2 1

Melcher Media strives to use environmentally responsible suppliers and materials whenever possible in the production of its books. For this book, that includes the use of SFI-certified interior paper stock.

SUSTAINABLE FORESTRY INITIATIVE

The 4-Hour CHEF

THE SIMPLE PATH TO COOKING LIKE A PRO,
LEARNING ANYTHING,
AND LIVING THE GOOD LIFE

TIMOTHY FERRISS

Published by

NEW HARVEST
Houghton Mifflin Harcourt
Boston | New York
2012

Produced by

MELCHER MEDIA

Dedication

For my parents, who taught a little hellion that marching to a different drummer was a good thing. I love you both and owe you everything. Mom, sorry about all the ridiculous diets and experiments.

For Mark Twain, who had a great mustache and put it best:

"Whenever you find yourself on the side of the majority, it's time to pause and reflect."

For leekspin.com, the most ridiculous site on the web. You helped me finish this book.

And for those who defend sustainable agriculture and promote truly good food. Ten percent of all author royalties are donated to rock-star nonprofits, such as American Farmland Trust (farmland.org) and the Careers through Culinary Arts Program (ccapinc.org).

6 REASONS TO READ THIS BOOK, EVEN IF YOU HATE COOKING (AS I DID)

The 4-Hour Chef (*4HC*) isn't a cookbook, per se, though it might look like one. Just as *Zen and the Art of Motorcycle Maintenance* isn't about changing oil, this book isn't quite what it appears.

Even if you hate cooking, here are six reasons you should read at least the first few chapters of this book:

#1
YOU WILL LEARN HOW TO BECOME WORLD-CLASS IN ANY SKILL IN RECORD TIME.

Whether you want to learn how to speak a new language in three months, how to shoot a three-pointer in one weekend, or how to memorize a deck of cards in less than a minute, the true "recipe" of this book is exactly that: a process for acquiring any skill. The vehicle I chose is cooking. Yes, I'll teach you all the most flexible techniques of culinary school using 14 strategically chosen meals, all with four or fewer ingredients, and all taking 5–20 minutes to prepare (literally, *The 4-Hour Chef*). But I wrote this book to make you a master student of all things.

#2
EATING (AND LIFE) WILL BECOME HIGH-DEFINITION.

In China, a common greeting is *"Chi le, mei you?"* or "Have you eaten?" This is the universal check-in. So I pose the question to you: have you *really* eaten? I now realize that before writing *4HC*, I hadn't. Back then, food was either good or bad, hot or cold, spicy or not. Now, it's a million colors, and I can pick out the subtleties: the cilantro or tarragon, the umami savoriness, or the lack of vinegar. It's like going from a 7" black-and-white TV to HD. Before *4HC*, much of my **life** was in black and white. As you'll see, the awareness we build in the kitchen and in related adventures will affect everything. Life itself becomes high-definition.

#3
YOU WILL GET INTO THE BEST SHAPE OF YOUR LIFE.

The dishes you'll learn, apart from desserts for "cheat day," are all compliant with the Slow-Carb Diet®, which has become a global phenomenon (page 74). Fat loss of 20 pounds in the first month is not uncommon. If you follow this book, you won't have to think of following a diet, since it's built in. If you ever decide to follow another diet, you'll be twice as effective, because you'll understand how to manipulate and maximize food.

#4
IT DOESN'T TAKE MUCH TO BECOME IMPRESSIVE.

In the first 24 hours, I'll take you from burning scrambled eggs to osso buco, one of the most expensive menu items in the world. If 28% of Americans can't cook at all,‡ and if another third are on some variation of mac and cheese, having even one seemingly difficult meal up your sleeve puts you in rare company. Make that two bulletproof meals and you can host impressive dinner parties for the rest of your life.

#5
COOKING IS THE MATING ADVANTAGE.

If you're looking to dramatically improve your sex life, or to catch and keep "the one," cooking is the force multiplier. Food has a crucial role in well-planned seduction for both sexes, whether in long-term relationships ("MLBJ," page 234) or on first dates (Sexy-Time Steak, page 186). For real romantic superpowers, learn how to teach the skill of tasting (Learning to "Taste," page 50).

#6
BECAUSE IT'S FUN.

The "practical" fails more than we'd like to admit. I'll take breaks in this book as often as necessary to keep you amused. Food marathons? Check (page 468). Hysterical kitchen lore anecdotes? Tons. Eating 14,000 calories in 20 minutes (page 454)? Why not?

This isn't a textbook. Think of it as a choose-your-own-adventure book.

As Bruce Lee said, "Adapt what is useful, reject what is useless, and add what is specifically your own."

THE EDUCATION OF A CULINARY IDIOT

1979, AGE TWO
I eat my first handful of crickets à la front yard. Life is good.

DECEMBER 1980
I stop eating crickets, to my mother's delight. Now I'm tall enough to chomp on Christmas ornaments.

1989
As a rat-tailed townie in East Hampton, New York, I start working part-time in restaurants. The small collection of Long Island towns known as the Hamptons doubles as a playground for the rich and famous, while also serving as the hometown for landscapers, fishermen, and alcoholics who loathe the rich and famous. As a busboy, I worked at some of the highest-volume (The Lobster Roll) and highest-priced (Maidstone Arms) restaurants. For every Billy Joel, who smiled and tipped $20 for coffee, there were 20 wannabes in polo shirts with popped collars asking, "Do you know who I am?" I learned to hate restaurants and, by extension, cooking.

1999
While on the no-carb Cyclical Ketogenic Diet (CKD), I develop an insatiable desire for anything crunchy and start experimenting with low-glycemic baking. Pacing up and down the aisles at Safeway, I'm unable to find baking powder and conclude it must be the same as baking soda, which I grab. The chocolate-and-macadamia-nut cookies come out looking incredible, just in time for my friends to return from work. As manimals do, they each eat three cookies in seconds, promptly followed by power chucking on the lawn.

2000
To avoid starvation, I buy my first microwave.

2001
Subsisting on microwavable Lean Cuisines, I start watching the Food Network for 1–2 hours a night to decompress from my start-up. Half-asleep one evening, I overhear Bobby Flay say, "Take risks and you'll get the payoffs. Learn from your mistakes until you succeed. It's that simple." I type this up and put it on my desk for moral support during moments of self-doubt. There would be many.

2007
The 4-Hour Workweek is published after being turned down by 26 publishers. I'm still enjoying the Food Network six years later, and I still haven't made a single dish.

2008
I become YouTube-famous for microwaving egg whites in plastic containers, which earns me the scorn of foodies worldwide. My follow-up act is a how-to video on "how to peel eggs without peeling them," which gets more than 4 million views. Being too lazy to cook is apparently popular.

JANUARY 2010
My friend Jesse Jacobs wants to catch up on business and insists we cook dinner at my place. I respond that *he'll* cook and *I'll* handle wine. Unbeknownst to me, Jesse was a sous-chef (second in command) at a top restaurant in a former life. He insists on walking me through the meal. Pointing at a large Le Creuset pot he brought, he begins:

"Put those chicken pieces in the pot." Check.

"Put in the veggies and potatoes. No need to cut them." Ten seconds later, check.

"Pour in some olive oil and salt and pepper, and mix everything around with your hands to coat it. You don't need to measure anything." Ten seconds later, check.

"Now, put them in the oven." Check.

"We're done."

I can't believe it. "That's it?" I ask, incredulous.

"Let's catch up for two hours and drink some wine," he says. It's one of the most delicious meals I've had in years. Inspired, I decide to give cooking another chance.

JUNE 2010
My enthusiasm dies a quiet death. Overwhelmed by contradictory advice, poorly organized cookbooks, and unhelpful instructions (e.g., "Cook until done"), I throw in the towel yet again.

APRIL 2011
I meet my girlfriend, Natasha, who learned how to cook by imitating her grandmother. She didn't do this as a child, but when she was in her mid-20s. She decides to teach me how:

"Smell this. Now smell this. Do they go together?"

"No. Gross."

"OK, now smell this and this. Do they go together?"

"Yep."

"Great. That's cooking."

Great sex ensues, and I decide I've been unfair to cooking. Groundhog Day.

AUGUST 2011
I commit to writing a book on learning, using cooking as the vehicle. Fun! My girlfriend can help!

SEPTEMBER 2011
Over the course of one week, I ask my girlfriend, "Is this basil?" 20 times. I want to punch myself in the face 20 times. Crisis of meaning. Revisit Bobby Flay quote.

OCTOBER 2011
After four weeks of nervous breakdowns and practically zero progress, I land in Chicago. Two days later, I replicate a two-Michelin-star entrée (sea bass, Ibérico ham, watercress, butter, and olive oil) in my hotel bathroom sink with next to nothing: scalding-hot tap water, Ziploc bags, and a cheap Polder thermometer. It's ready 20 minutes later and finished with a gorgeous crust, courtesy of the iron in the closet. I had learned the technique by watching a chef's eight-year-old son. All is not lost.

NOVEMBER 2011
I hit the inflection point. Sitting at the Polaris Grill in Bellevue, Washington, I am suddenly able to see food in HD—as if someone had handed me prescription glasses and corrected lifelong blurred vision. All the random pieces come together; I can clearly "see" pairing through taste and smell (e.g., orange and fennel), I can tell if the steak is 100% grass-fed or grain-finished by the waxiness on the palate, I correctly guess the origins of the Dungeness crab, wine, and oysters (three types), and the cooking methods for the scallops, pork chops, and more. The waiter asks me if I'm a chef (answer: no), and the executive chef comes out to introduce himself. It is otherworldly.

NOVEMBER 24, 2011
I cook Thanksgiving dinner for four people. Graduation day. For a lifelong noncook, I feel on top of the world.

JANUARY 2012
I start eating crickets again, this time roasted. I've rediscovered the wonder of food . . . and the childlike curiosity I thought I'd lost.

CONTENTS

META

DOM

WILD

CONTENTS (CONTINUED)

PRO
474 THE PROFESSIONAL

APX
566 APPENDIX

ON THE SHOULDERS OF GIANTS

I am not an expert, nor am I a master chef.

I'm just the guide and explorer. If you find anything amazing in this book, it's thanks to the brilliant minds who acted as resources, critics, contributors, proofreaders, and references. If you find anything ridiculous in this book, it's because I didn't heed their advice.

Though indebted to hundreds of people, I wish to thank a few of them up front, here listed in alphabetical order (see more in the Acknowledgments on page 640):

Chef Grant Achatz
Steve Alcairo
David Amick
Chef Tim Anderson
Marc Andreessen
Corey Arnold
Chef Blake Avery
Chef Ryan Baker
Marcie Barnes
Dr. John Berardi
Patrick Bertoletti
Mark Bittman
Chef Heston Blumenthal
Chad Bourdon
Daniel Burka
Chef Marco Canora
Phil Caravaggio
Chef Mehdi Chellaoui
Jules Clancy
Ed Cooke
Chef Chris Cosentino
Chef Erik Cosselmon
Erik "The Red" Denmark
Chef Matthew Dolan
Chef Andrew Dornenburg
Michael Ellsberg
Kevin "Feral Kevin" Feinstein
Chef Mark Garcia
Brad Gerlach
Paul Grieco
Alan Grogono
Jude H.
Cliff Hodges
Ryan Holiday
Kirsten Incorvaia
Jesse Jacobs
Sarah Jay
Chef Samuel Kass
kitchit.com
Chef Dan Kluger
Nick Kokonas
Matt Krisiloff
Terry Laughlin
Karen Leibowitz
Martin Lindsay
Doug McAfee
Christopher Miller
Molecule-R
Elissa Molino
Harley Morenstein
Stephen Morrissey
Nathan Myhrvold
Chef Anthony Myint
Ayako N.
Natasha
Babak Nivi
Chef Sisha Ortúzar
Karen Page
Marcia Pelchat, PhD
Chef Georgia Pellegrini
Darya Pino
Jeff Potter
Kevin Reeve
Tracy Reifkind
Steven Rinella
John "Roman" Romaniello
Kevin Rose
Barry Ross
Mike Roussell
Blake Royer
Anthony Rudolf III
Ian Scalzo
Chef Craig Schoettler
Maneesh Sethi
Chef James Simpkins
Naveen Sinha
Chef Joshua Skenes
Bonnie Slotnick
Chef Damon Stainbrook
Leslie Stein, PhD
Neil Strauss
Dean Sylvester
Tinywino
Rick Torbett
Gary Vay-ner-chuk
"Victor"
Josh Viertel
Robb Wolf
Chef Chris Young
Jeffrey Zurofsky

Central Kitchen, San Francisco.

"Take risks and you'll get the payoffs. Learn from your mistakes until you succeed. It's that simple."
-Bobby Flay
#1 World-Famous Host,
Food Network

The quote I've had on my desk since 2001.

HOW TO USE THIS BOOK: CONFESSIONS, PROMISES, AND GETTING TO 20 MILLION

12 NOON, RIVERPARK RESTAURANT AS A GUEST

"Doesn't it taste like acorns?"

It did. Mangalitsa acorn-finished woolly boar tasted *just* like acorns. I was chewing on fall, clear as crystal, in a sliver of cured ham.

The clouds parted, and our plates were bathed in summer sunshine. Resting my elbows on the teak table, I looked out over the East River. Sunday brunch at 29th and First was off to a picturesque start.

Drinking albariño white wine with me were two friends: Josh Viertel, then president of Slow Food USA, and serial restaurateur "Z,"[1] whom I'd helped kick caffeine withdrawal the week before. I'd given him an l-tyrosine cocktail and, in exchange, he and Josh were teaching me the inside baseball of the food world.

"Check out the Bocuse d'Or—it's the Olympics of cooking."

"If you want a really funny story, you should include how Thomas Keller, as an expert witness in a trial, analyzed a fried egg as evidence."

"Visit Craft sometime. Leather covers the walls for acoustics. It distributes all the noise to the front and back corners, where the bathrooms—*not* diners—are."

"Did you know *sauté* actually comes from the French 'to jump'? To train the proper technique, you can put dried kidney beans in a skillet and mimic this motion while kneeling on a carpet. . . ." Demos ensued.

It was all new. I had never successfully cooked before, and that's why I was there—to learn.

4 P.M., BACK OF HOUSE AS A TRAINEE

"Is this clean?" I asked.

"No. See this dirt, all over the stems? That's not clean. Use a bowl instead of holding it under the faucet. Rinse three times."

"Thank you. Sorry about that," I said with a sigh. I didn't know how to *rinse* basil, let alone distinguish it from the two herbs next to it.

I was trailing a prep cook, whose job is to prepare the basics—chopped onions, sorted microgreens, etc.—before dinner, when the line cooks assemble and plate everything for guests. She'd been told to give me something idiotproof.

"How's the micro-basil coming?" she asked over her shoulder.

I wasn't one-tenth through the container I was supposed to sort. I simply couldn't combine accuracy and speed. Now I was more than an inconvenience; I was jamming up her station.

After 30 minutes of fumbling, I was relieved of duty. It would be observation only for the rest of the night. As a spectator, I jotted down dozens of finer points I'd somehow missed the first 10 times through.

Why couldn't I get it right?

---

1 To be unveiled later.

At 6 p.m. I hung up my chef's whites, looking like Eeyore from *Winnie-the-Pooh*. I had failed.

The team at Riverpark had been awesome, unbelievably forgiving, and, to my eyes, superhuman. Once dinner got rolling, I noticed that the line cooks' forearms looked like they'd been dragged through hot coals and barbed wire.

Sixty minutes into the dinner rush, when I was convinced nothing could move faster, the chef de cuisine announced, "Look happy, boys. We have 42 open menus!" That meant 42 people were looking at menus at the same time, which meant 42 orders would hit two line cooks at the same time. Chino, one of the two, kicked into high gear, moving fire and food for dozens of orders like Doctor Octopus on fast-forward.

They were completely unfazed. Another day at the office. Me? Decimated by washing a handful of leaves.

When I walked outside and back into civilian life, I hugged a new bible under one arm: *The Silver Spoon*, the best-selling Italian cookbook of the last 50 years. To me, it was like holding the *Necronomicon*. Sisha, the Chilean chef-partner, had given it to me when I first toured the kitchen earlier that day. It was his copy, and he'd insisted I take it after I commented on its beauty.

Now, I felt guilty for taking it.

I edged alongside Riverpark's outdoor farm, keeping out of frame of a car commercial being filmed in the traffic circle 30 feet away. As I jogged past an extra to catch a cab, he looked at the bundle under my arm and asked with a smile, "Future chef?"

I looked back and returned the smile as best I could.

"Yeah."

DIGITAL DEPRESSION AND THE PUZZLE OF COOKING

In 2011, a slow-growing malaise came to a head.

It hit me like acid reflux, a dull ache every time I closed my laptop with nothing to show for my effort besides invisible bits and bytes. One reflective weekend, I decided that I wanted to try woodworking: to *make* something. I needed to use my hands to *create* something. Swinging a tennis racket or lifting weights, as physical as they were, didn't cut it.

Sadly, life got in the way. The Oakland woodworking studio was too far away, I couldn't commit to a fixed time each week, I didn't have space for what I'd make—the usual list of I'm-busy-being-busy excuses.

Then, one evening, I took my girlfriend to the mecca of Northern California cooking, the world-famous Chez Panisse in Berkeley. Despite a decade in the Bay Area, I'd never been, partially because I still behaved like a cash-poor recent grad (remedied in this case by a gift certificate). Shelves of *The Art of Simple Food* by Chez Panisse founder Alice Waters lined the wall behind the bar. I skimmed a red-spined copy while we sipped wine and waited to be seated. I ended up engrossed and, much to the chagrin of my girl, took notes while we ate. As I half-watched the bustle in the open kitchen, and assured the server that I'd buy the book, I underlined two passages in particular:

"When you have the best and tastiest ingredients, you can cook very simply and the food will be extraordinary because it tastes like what it is." And: "Good cooking is no mystery. You don't need years of culinary training, or rare and costly foodstuffs, or an encyclopedic knowledge of world cuisines. You need only your own five senses."

By the time the bill came, I was practically bouncing in my seat. "Babe, I think I could actually do this!"

Cooking would become my tool for reclaiming the physical world. It was time to use my opposable thumbs for something besides the space bar.

SCD: photos + recipes from genre rest. in SF
"Gear" by budget ($50, 100, $250, $1,000)
Knife handling (29)
Recipes: simple, still simple, shmancy

CHAPT: Close Cousins: Effective Variants of SCD
(organize by both food ("staple") and meal
(cross-reference table)

[redacted] smelling approach

differences (p. 11), types (13),
TF tossing the 'bachelor rack'
CPR

(5) Herbs + Spice + Everything Nice (or "How to Cheat")

(29) Make broth w carcass (66) — complex 68

p. 6 TF: Plant a garden
Kill chicken, hog
Live w/ farmers
(Kenya?)

pot or 2 of herbs on window sill

'Myths + Microwaves'
(BPA, cans, microw. etc.)

('Slow-Carb Wines'
(my faves) + Nor-Cal

Reprint labeling post

"Cheat day:
crazy or conservative?"
→ give real examples w/ caloric counts

Sidebar: Bean Flour and Almond Milk: Form affects function (61, etc.)

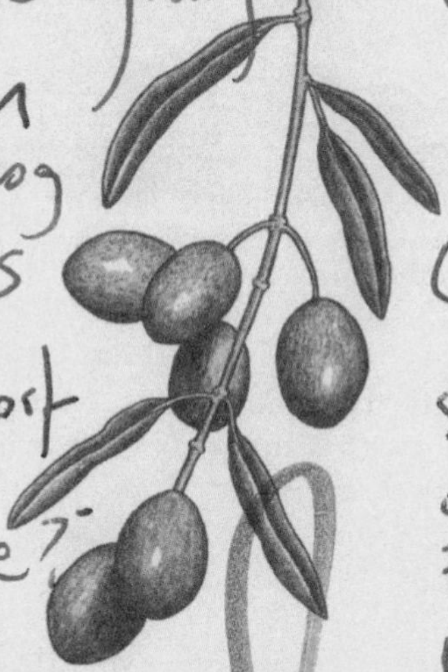

Sweet Sin: Sweet pot., Yams, taro, etc.

The Milky Way: Goat vs. Cow vs. Raw

Slow-Food Chapter + contribution
Culinary map of SF

My very first notes in *The Art of Simple Food*. The beginning.

MEKANISM
Culinary Artistry

The starting point: hundreds of books, filtered by overlaying survey results, average Amazon reviews, and Nielsen Bookscan sales numbers.

Cooking wasn't the first skill I'd tackled. In fact, I'm somewhat obsessed with accumulating strange credentials, ranging from a Guinness World Record in tango to a gold medal at the 1999 Chinese national kickboxing championships.

Given this, why had cooking kicked my ass so many times?

- There's an overabundance of information. No other subject matter I've encountered comes close. It's a full-time job just to find the best place to start.

- Cookbooks are often formatted for the writers, I discovered, not for the readers. A logical grouping for the writer is rarely a logical progression for the student. Who's going to cook six chicken dishes in a row?

- Cooking practice can be expensive and impractical. If you have the time, you can practice your tennis serve a thousand times a day for a few dollars. Making a thousand omelets a day? That's a different story.

So, what to do?

WHY YOU'LL SUCCEED—TWO PRINCIPLES

I eventually learned to cook by focusing on two principles. Both of them apply to all learning and will be your constant companions throughout this book: **failure points** and **the margin of safety.**

FAILURE POINTS—THE POWER OF PRACTICAL PESSIMISM

I don't care why people pick up cookbooks. I'm much more interested in why they put them down.

The hypothesis: if I can address the primary, but often ignored, tripping points, I should be able to increase the number of people who eventually become master chefs. To develop a list of failure points—the reasons people put cookbooks down—I polled more than 100,000 of my fans on Facebook (64% male, 36% female) and looked for patterns. Here are a few:

- Too many ingredients (and therefore too much shopping and prep).
- Intimidating knife skills, introduced too early in cookbooks.
- Too many tools, pots, and pans, which are expensive and require too much cleanup.
- Food spoilage.
- Different dishes finishing at different times, leading to cold food, undercooked food, burned food, etc.
- Dishes that require constant tending, stirring, and watching.

Saying I can create more master chefs doesn't mean I'm a master chef, even if I've improved 100-fold (which I have).

Nor does it mean that this book alone will make you a master chef. It simply means that no master chef exists who hasn't overcome the above problem areas, so addressing them should be a novice cookbook's *primary* goal, not an afterthought.

This book aims to systematically overcome all of the above failure points, step-by-step.

THE MARGIN OF SAFETY—IF WARREN BUFFETT DESIGNED MENUS

Most cookbooks ignore how unreliable recipes can be.

As scientist Nathan Myhrvold points out, even if you follow the exact same recipe using identical equipment and ingredients, humidity and altitude alone can create totally different outcomes. If a cookbook author is testing a recipe in Tahoe during the winter and you try to replicate it in San Diego in July heat, you might fail, even though you follow it perfectly. Rather than hope your environment is the same as mine, I looked for bulletproof recipes.

This is where the **margin of safety** applies.

Warren Buffett is the most successful investor of the 20th century and a self-described "value investor." He aims to buy stocks at a discount (below intrinsic value) so that even with a worst-case scenario, he can do well. This discount is referred to as the "margin of safety," and it's the bedrock principle of some of the brightest minds in the investing world (e.g., Joel Greenblatt). It doesn't guarantee a good investment, but it allows room for error.[2]

In the world of cooking, I'll apply the margin of safety as follows: how badly can you mangle the recipe and still get something incredible? In real estate, the adage is, "You make your profit when you buy the property, not when you sell it." In cooking, it could be, "You guarantee a good meal by picking the recipes well, not by following recipes well."

Early wins are critical for momentum, so we'll guarantee them.

THE PROGRESSION—DOM, WILD, SCI, PRO

There are five sections in this book. After META-LEARNING, the progression is color coded for difficulty, just like jujitsu: blue, purple, brown, and black.

From the science of el Bulli, the famed Spanish restaurant that was harder to get into than Harvard,[3] to the fish markets of Kolkata to the backcountry of South Carolina, no stone was left unturned in search of powerful simplicity.

Turn the page to see what our journey together will look like.

2 This principle applies outside of investing. In childbirth, for instance, research reports have concluded that long forceps are safer than suction or a C-section. Veteran ob-gyns, however, disagree. Why? Because forceps are safe *if* you can maintain no more than 2 lbs of squeezing pressure *and* no more than 40 lbs of pull, and only *if* you can repeat this under stressful conditions every time. One of my close friends, who is now a professor at Stanford Medical School, suffered brain damage and hemorrhaging when he was delivered because the doctor used too much pressure. Forceps have a low margin of safety—no wiggle room for mistakes.

3 On a single day in the fall of each year, the restaurant booked the next year's reservations, accepting approximately 8,000 seats from a reported 2 million requests.

the Menu

L'ANTIPASTO

META-LEARNING

(META)

This is where I introduce every important principle I've discovered about accelerating learning.

It starts with smart drug self-experimentation at Princeton (inhaling hormones, anyone?), progresses to language learning, and branches off into everything imaginable: sports, memorizing numbers, "learning" smells, deconstructing food, even cramming six months of culinary school into 48 hours.

If you're only interested in cooking, you can skip this section, but I highly suggest you give it a read at some point. It is the backbone of this book.

IL PRIMO

THE DOMESTIC

(DOM)

DOM is where we learn the building blocks of cooking. These are the ABCs that can take you from the simplest words to Shakespeare.

The goal of this section is ambitious: to deliver all the fundamental building blocks of culinary school in four hours of total prep time: 14 core dishes x 5–20 minutes. This is the literal portion of *The 4-Hour Chef*. Here, we also *begin* to answer the question that Sherry Yard, the executive pastry chef of Spago in Beverly Hills, put to me when I explained the premise of the book: "How do you cut time without cutting corners?"

The secret is in sequencing.

If you stop reading here, you will know "how to cook" for all intents and purposes and will earn back the price of this book manyfold.

IL SECONDO

THE WILD

(WILD)

WILD is where you will become not only good *with* your hands, but also self-sufficient *in* your own hands. If you've ever wondered about urban foraging, fermentation, hunting, or pigeons as food, this will probably be your favorite section.

IL CONTORNO

THE SCIENTIST

(SCI)

If WILD is the die-hard pragmatist, SCI is the mad scientist and modernist painter wrapped into one.

Rather than preparing you for spartan minimalism, this section is about rediscovering whimsy and wonder, two ingredients sorely lacking past childhood.

IL DOLCE

THE PROFESSIONAL

(PRO)

Swaraj, a term usually associated with Mahatma Gandhi, can be translated as "self-rule." Think of it as charting your own path.

In PRO, we'll look at how the best in the world *become* the best in the world, and how you can evolve far beyond this book. There's much more to cooking besides food. Take Chef Grant Achatz "plating" your table, which is covered in gray latex, by dropping and shattering a dark-chocolate piñata full of assorted desserts. It's texture, theater, and so much more, all wrapped into one.

We'll finish up with tools for perfecting your own creative powerhouse.

THE MICRO GOAL—ON BECOMING A "CHEF"

Julia Child wasn't always Julia Child. In fact, she could barely boil an egg when she got married.

Late in her career, she became a chef—and changed how the English-speaking world viewed cooking.

In restaurants, the distinction between *cook* and *chef* is important: someone who can cook is a cook, whereas someone who can create a menu and run a kitchen is a chef. Calling yourself the latter when you're the former, as many TV hosts do, is a no-no. In some circles, the cook is a technician, however good, and the chef is the conductor. The former is the bricklayer, the latter the architect of the cathedral.

In *The 4-Hour Chef*, I use *chef* in the most literal sense, like the Spanish *jefe*. Derived from the Latin term for "head," it signifies boss or leader. This book aims to make you self-reliant, whether in the kitchen or in life: to wrestle control from chaos, to feel like a director instead of an actor, and perhaps to create something bigger than yourself.

In their wonderful book *Culinary Artistry*, Andrew Dornenburg and Karen Page provide a table with three hypothetical categories of chefs (see below).

My goal is to move you from the far left to the right, and the customer quotes will be your own. The most important part of all is that *you* finish *your* meals with the bottom-right sentiment. Even if you end your journey at burgers—damn fine burgers, mind you—life can and should be wonderful.

We'll use training *in* the kitchen as training for everything *outside* of the kitchen.

THREE TYPES OF CHEFS—THE PROGRESSION

COURTESY: *CULINARY ARTISTRY*

	TYPE OF CHEF		
	TRADE	CRAFT	ART
CATEGORY	"Burger-flippers"	"Accomplished chefs"	"Culinary artists"
CUSTOMER GOAL	Survival	Enjoyment	Entertainment
CHEF'S INTENTION	Fill/feed	Satisfy/please	Transcend/transport
PRICE OF LUNCH	Movie ticket	Off-Broadway theater ticket	Broadway orchestra ticket
WHO DETERMINES MEAL	Customer ("Have it your way")	Customer/chef	Chef (tasting menu)
CHEF'S PRIMARY REPERTOIRE	Hamburgers	Classic dishes	Chef's own dishes
NUMBER OF SENSES AFFECTED	Five	Five	Six
CUSTOMERS LEAVE SAYING	"I'm full."	"That was delicious."	"Life is wonderful."

THE MACRO GOAL—20 MILLION PEOPLE

I'd never had coffee-cup envy before. But this was one hell of a coffee cup:

"Can I get one of those?" I asked.

"Probably not," Sam replied.

Well, it was worth a try.

Sam Kass honed his culinary skills at Avec restaurant in Chicago. Then he became a private chef and started cooking for an up-and-coming senator named Barack Obama. Now, as assistant White House chef and food initiative coordinator, Sam is one of the first family's go-to experts in all things culinary. This spans from national food policy to replacing pesticides in their backyard with crab meal and ladybugs.

When Sam and I met in Washington, D.C., I explained my background in publishing and tech, mentioned the acquisition of this book by Amazon Publishing, and politely asked his advice:

"I have a platform to reach millions of people, and I don't want to screw up this opportunity. I might not get it again. How should I be thinking about the bigger picture of food?"

SEAL OF THE PRESIDENT OF THE UNITED STATES

His answers paralleled what I'd read and heard from Mark Bittman, the great *New York Times Magazine* food writer: in effect, that we are at a deciding fork in the road, and the next 10 years (perhaps less) will decide the future of food production in the United States.

Here are a few of my notes, from multiple sources:

- In the U.S., the last generation of career farmers is retiring. Specifically, more than 50% are set to retire in the next 10 years. Their farmland will be up for grabs. Will it go to an industrial agro-corp like Monsanto, and therefore most likely lead to monocrops (wheat, corn, soy, etc.) that decimate ecosystems? Will it be strip malls? Or might it become a collection of smaller food producers? The last option is the only one that's environmentally sustainable. It's also the tastiest. As Michael Pollan would say: how you vote three times a day (with the meals you eat) will determine the outcome.

- Going small can amount to big economic stimulus. Let's look at the economic argument for shifting from a few huge producers to many smaller producers: by diversifying crops beyond corn and soybeans in just six agricultural states, the net economic gain would be $882 million in sales and 9,300 jobs, according to the Leopold Center for Sustainable Agriculture at Iowa State University.

- Environmental impact? Converting the U.S.'s 160 million corn and soybean acres to organic production would sequester enough carbon to satisfy 73% of the Kyoto targets for CO_2 reduction in the U.S.

In other words, the fun you have in this book will do a lot of good beyond you and your family. In many ways, our eating behavior in the next few years will decide the future of the entire country.

The magic number and my target is 20 million people. It is the tipping point: 20 million people can create a supertrend.

To dodge the submerged iceberg of industrial-scale food production and its side effects, to alter the course of this country and reinvigorate the economy, all I need to do is make you more *interested* in food. In total, we need to make 20 million people more *aware* of eating.

This will lead to changes, starting with breakfast. Then the snowball of consonant decisions takes care of the rest.

Stranger things have happened.

LET US BEGIN WITH BEGINNER'S MIND

Mise en place, called *meez* in kitchen slang, means everything in its place. Commit this term to memory. It refers to your workplace. In this book, it also refers to your mind, your business, and your life.

One of Anthony Bourdain's former chef colleagues had a habit of walking up to frazzled cooks in his kitchen, pressing his hand into their cutting boards, and lifting his palm to their faces. As he showed them the detritus embedded in his skin, he'd say, "You see this? That's what the inside of your head looks like now."

What does *your* mind look like?

We'll find out, and we will make it orderly.

While in Kolkata, India, for this book, I stayed at the iconic Oberoi Grand. The concierge explained to me the hotel's hiring philosophy: "You can't bend mature bamboo. But if you get it as a young shoot, you can bend it, mold it. We hire them between the ages of 18 and 21 so we can mold them." The concierge was one of only 15 double golden key (Clef d'Or) concierges in India, and he knew that sometimes having no experience is a huge advantage. Age doesn't matter; an open mind does.

This book isn't baptism by fire. It's a series of small experiments, with the occasional off-color joke and *Calvin and Hobbes* cartoon to keep you interested. The only part I consider mandatory reading, DOMESTIC, is fewer than 150 pages! Skip around and have fun.

This book is not *the* truth, but it contains many truths as I've found them, and—even if they're not your truths—the process I teach can help you find yours.

May all of your creations have just the right flavor, and may the joy of discovery be your guide.

Pura vida,

Tim Ferriss
San Francisco, California
August 24, 2012

Meta

Meta-Learning

META is where you'll learn to mimic the world's fastest learners.

It *is* possible to become world-class in just about anything in six months or less. Armed with the right framework, you can seemingly perform miracles, whether with Spanish, swimming, or anything in between.

Ed Cooke can memorize a shuffled deck of playing cards in 45 seconds, a feat accomplished purely through training. Ed became famous in ***Moonwalking with Einstein*** for coaching Joshua Foer to become the 2006 U.S.A. Memory Champion.

Daniel "Brain Man" Tammet learned to speak Icelandic in seven days.

"BILL GATES WALKS INTO A BAR . . .": THE POWER OF OUTLIERS

"A good teacher must know the rules; a good pupil, the exceptions."
—MARTIN H. FISCHER, PHYSICIAN AND AUTHOR

Smart Design became one of the top industrial design firms in the world by being (you guessed it) smart.

With locations in New York, San Francisco, and Barcelona, Smart Design represents clients ranging from Burton Snowboards to Starbucks. The company has also been strategic partners with OXO International since 1989. That ubiquitous line of Good Grips kitchenware with the comfy black handles? The ones that cover an entire wall at *Bed Bath & Beyond*? They made 'em.

In the documentary *Objectified,* Dan Formosa, PhD, then with Smart Design's research department, explained one of the first steps in its innovation process:

"We have clients come to us and say, 'Here is our average customer.' For instance, 'Female, she is 34 years old, she has 2.3 kids,' and we listen politely and say, 'Well, that's great, but we don't care . . . about *that* person.' What we really need to do, to design, is look at the extremes. The weakest, or the person with arthritis, or the athlete, or the strongest, the fastest person, because if we understand what the extremes are, the middle will take care of itself."

In other words, the extremes inform the mean, but not vice versa.

That "average user" can be deceptive or even meaningless, just as all averages[1] can be. Here's a statistician joke for your next hot date:

Person A: What happens when Bill Gates walks into a bar of 55 people?

Person B: I don't know. What?

Person A: The "average" net worth jumps to more than a billion dollars![2]

Buahaha! Not exactly Chris Rock, but the joke makes an important point: sometimes it pays to model the outliers, not flatten them into averages. This isn't limited to business.

Take, for instance, this seemingly average 132-lb girl who ended up anything but:

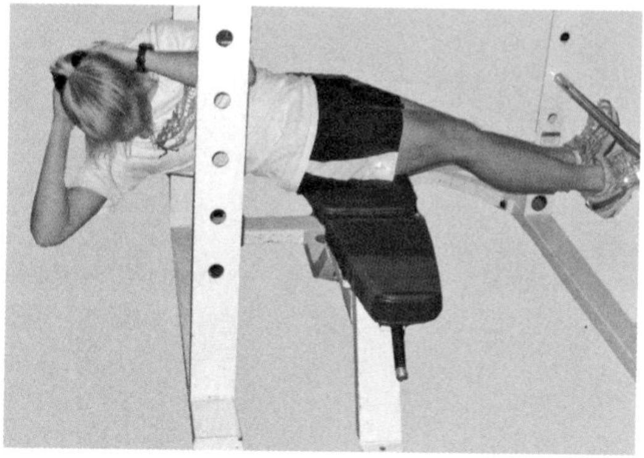

The girl next door . . . kind of.

1 Technically, arithmetic mean.

2 Bill Gates's estimated net worth as of March 2012 was $61 billion.

275-lb Mark Bell sumo dead-lifting 325 lbs, plus 160 lbs of band tension and chains at the top, for a 485-lb total. He has pulled 766 lbs in competition.

CREDIT: JIM MCDONALD, SUPERTRAINING.TV

Her picture was sent to me by Barry Ross, a sprint coach who creates world-record-breaking athletes, to illustrate an ab exercise called the torture twist. He nonchalantly added on the phone: "Oh, and she dead-lifts more than 400 lbs for repetitions."

What?!? For those of you not familiar with the dead lift, take a look at the sequence at left.

Even more impressive, she developed this otherworldly power the "wrong" way:

- Rather than train the conventional full range of motion, she utilized only the weakest range of motion, lifting the bar to knee height and then lowering it.
- Total muscular tension (actual weight lifting) was limited to five minutes per week.

This all makes our average-looking high-schooler *extreme*.

But was she an *exception*?

In the outside world, absolutely. Even in track and field, she was a freak. Had she been thrown into a study with 40 randomly selected female sprinters, she would have been a ridiculous exception. "Must have been a measurement error!" Then the baby would get thrown out with the bathwater.

But WWWBS? That is: What Would Warren Buffett Say? I suspect the Oracle of Omaha would repeat what he said at Columbia University in 1984 when mocking proponents of the efficient-market hypothesis.

First, he pointed out that, yes, value investors (devotees of Benjamin Graham and David Dodd) who consistently beat the market are outliers. Then he posed a question, which I've condensed:

> What if there were a nationwide competition in coin flipping, 225 million flippers total [then the population of the USA], each flipping once per morning, and we found a select few [say, 215 people] who'd flipped 20 straight winning flips [flips where the result was guessed correctly] on 20 mornings?

He then continued (bolding is mine):

> "Some business school professor will probably be rude enough to bring up the fact that if 225 million orangutans had engaged in a similar exercise, the results would be much the same—215 egotistical orangutans with 20 straight winning flips.
>
> There are some important differences in the examples [of value investors] I am going to present. For one thing, if a) you had taken 225 million orangutans distributed roughly as the U.S. population is; if b) 215 winners were left after 20 days; and **if c) you found that 40 came from a particular zoo in Omaha, you would be pretty sure you were on to something.** So you would probably go out and ask the zookeeper about what he's feeding them, whether they had special exercises, what books they read, and who knows what else. **That is, if you found any really extraordinary concentrations of success, you might want to see if you could identify concentrations of unusual characteristics that might be causal factors.**"‡

Our sprint coach, Barry Ross, has a most unusual zoo. In fact, he can engineer mutants at will.

His best female distance runner has dead-lifted 415 lbs at a body weight of 132 lbs.

His youngest male lifter, 11 years old, has dead-lifted 225 lbs at a body weight of 108 lbs.

Our *extreme* high-schooler is the standard in his gym.

This naturally led me to ask: could I, a nonelite runner and an *average*, possibly replicate her results? I tried, and . . . it worked flawlessly.

In less than 12 weeks, *sans* coach and following a printout from Barry, I went from a max dead lift of 300 lbs to more than 650 lbs.[3]

BEING THE BEST VS. BECOMING THE BEST

As I write this, the two most-viewed freestyle swimming videos in the world are of:

1. Michael Phelps
2. Shinji Takeuchi

Michael Phelps freestyle multi angle camera
yuzik
Subscribe
97 videos
0:17 / 1:46
Like
Share
2,864,979
Uploaded by yuzik on Mar 21, 2006
Michael Phelps freestyle multi angle camera
3,818 likes, 105 dislikes
As Seen On:
Rival Soul

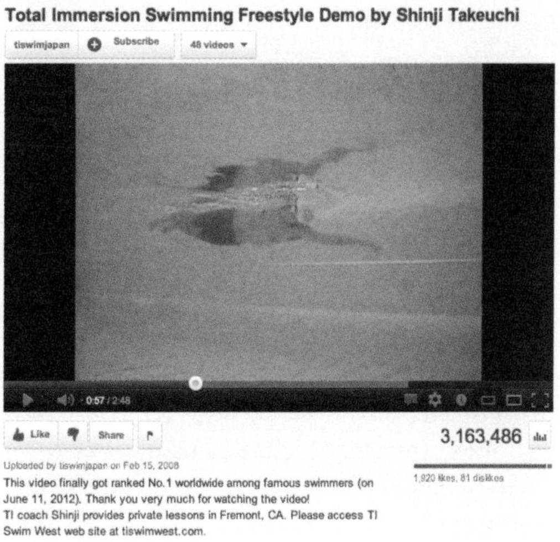
Total Immersion Swimming Freestyle Demo by Shinji Takeuchi
tiswimjapan
Subscribe
48 videos
0:57 / 2:48
Like
Share
3,163,486
Uploaded by tiswimjapan on Feb 15, 2008
This video finally got ranked No.1 worldwide among famous swimmers (on June 11, 2012). Thank you very much for watching the video!
TI coach Shinji provides private lessons in Fremont, CA. Please access TI Swim West web site at tiswimwest.com.
1,920 likes, 81 dislikes

3 Pulling from the knees using a double-overhand grip (not hook) without wrist wraps. I could then do 475 from the floor for repetitions. See "Effortless Superhuman" in *The 4-Hour Body* for the full program description.

Phelps makes sense, but . . . who the hell is Shinji Takeuchi?

Phelps learned to swim at the tender age of seven. Shinji learned to swim at the well-ripened age of 37. More interesting to me, Shinji learned to swim by doing practically the opposite of Phelps:

- Shinji drives his lead arm forward, almost two feet beneath the water, rather than "grabbing" near the surface and pulling.
- Rather than focus on kicking, Shinji appears to eliminate it altogether. No paddleboard workouts to be found.
- Shinji often trains freestyle stroke with closed fists, or by pointing his index finger forward and keeping the arms entirely underwater.

Phelps looks like he's attached to an outboard motor. It's a heroic output of horsepower. Shinji has been watched millions of times because he offers the flip side: effortless propulsion.

So who would you rather have as a teacher: Phelps or Shinji?

Arthur Jones, founder of Nautilus, when asked how to gain muscular mass quickly, recommended the following (I paraphrase): Approach the biggest bodybuilder at your gym, ideally a ripped 250–300-lb professional, and politely ask him for detailed advice. Then do precisely the opposite. If the T-Rex–size meathead recommends 10 sets, do one set; if he recommends post-workout protein, consume pre-workout protein, etc.

Jones's tongue-in-cheek parable was used to highlight one of the dangers of hero worship:

The top 1% often succeed *despite* how they train, not because of it. Superior genetics, or a luxurious full-time schedule, make up for a lot.

This is not to say that Phelps isn't technical. Everything needs to be flawless to win 18 gold medals. It's the people a few rungs down—the best you realistically have access to—whom you need to be wary of.

And then there is the second danger of hero worship:

Career specialists can't externalize what they've internalized. Second nature is hard to teach.

This is true across industries.

As Erik Cosselmon, executive chef at Kokkari, my favorite Greek restaurant in San Francisco, said to me amid my novice questioning: "The problem with me is I've always been a cook. I don't remember ever wanting to be something else."

Daniel Burka, a designer at Google and the cofounder of tech start-up Milk, echoes the sentiment: "I don't think I'd be particularly good at teaching the basics of CSS [a language used for the look and formatting of web pages[4]]. Now I do 12 things at once and they all make sense. I can't remember which of those was confusing when I was just starting out."

These top 0.01%, who've spent a lifetime honing their craft, are invaluable in later stages, but they're not ideal if you want to rocket off the ground floor. The Shinji Takeuchis, on the other hand—the rare anomalies who've gone from zero to the global top 5% in record time, despite mediocre raw materials—are worth their weight in gold.

I've spent the last 15 years finding the Shinjis of the world and trying to model them.

4 Yes, I realize this is a vastly simplified definition.

INHALING HORMONES: WHAT COULD GO WRONG?

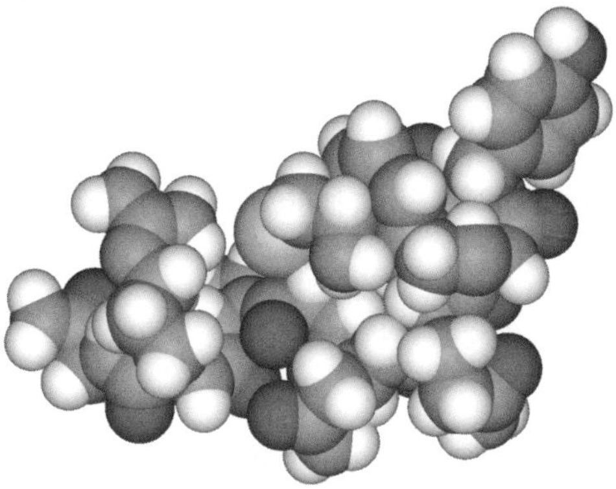

My old friend desmopressin.

My interest in accelerating learning started at a biochemical level.

In 1996, as a planned neuroscience major at Princeton University, I began experimenting with a panoply of smart drugs (nootropics) I'd imported to the U.S. under the FDA personal importation policy.[5]

After four weeks, I'd fine-tuned a routine for Mandarin Chinese character quizzes: 15 minutes prior to class, I would administer two hits of vaporized desmopressin in each nostril. Desmopressin is a synthetic version of vasopressin, a naturally occurring anti-diuretic and peptide hormone. As a nasal spray, it is often prescribed for children who bed-wet past a certain age. I was more interested in its off-label applications for short-term memory.

Putting theory into practice, it looked like this:

1. Two hits of desmopressin in each nostril.
2. Flip through characters in *Chinese Primer: Character Text* almost as quickly as I could turn the pages.
3. Score 100% on the quiz 5–10 minutes later.[6]

It was fantastically reliable.

But after a few months of testing Hydergine, oxiracetam, and combinations of dozens of other drugs, headaches set in and a thought occurred: perhaps snorting anti-diuretic hormones isn't the best long-term strategy? My dorm bathroom had also started to resemble a meth lab, which was repelling girls.

So I shifted my obsession from molecules to process.

Was it possible to develop a sequence, or a blueprint, that would allow one to learn *anything* faster? Any subject, any sport, anything at all?

I suspected so.

I'd glimpsed one piece of the puzzle four years earlier, in 1992.

MATERIAL BEATS METHOD

In 1992, I was 15 years old and had landed in Japan for my first extended trip abroad. I would be an exchange student at Seikei Gakuen high school for one year.

On the first day of classes, I reported to the faculty lounge in my required navy-blue uniform, looking like a West Point cadet. I nervously awaited my student chaperone, who would be taking me to my "home class," the group of 40 or so students I'd be spending most of my time with. One of the faculty members noticed me sitting in the corner and approached:

"*Ah, Timu-kun!*" he said with a wave. *Kun* is like *-san* but used to address male inferiors.

"*Kore wa . . .*" *This is . . .* he said as he pointed at a mysterious piece of paper. I could barely manage greetings, so he hailed an English teacher to explain the document. The page, written entirely in characters I couldn't read, detailed my daily schedule, as it turned out.

5 Not something I recommend. One mistake and you're illegally trafficking drugs, which the *Federales* frown upon.

6 If you'd like the opposite effect, go binge drinking. Excessive alcohol inhibits vasopressin release, which explains the peeing every 10 minutes followed by time travel (i.e., blacking out or forgetting everything).

The English teacher translated: "Physics, mathematics, world history, *kōbun*—ah . . . traditional Japanese," and on it went.

Panic set in. I'd only had a few months of rudimentary Japanese prior to arrival, and my teachers in the U.S. had reassured me with: "Don't worry, you'll have plenty of Japanese classes!"

Now irretrievably in Tokyo, I realized I was dealing with a major *Lost in Translation* screwup. "Japanese classes" hadn't meant language classes. For the entire year ahead, I was to attend normal Japanese high school classes alongside 5,000 Japanese students prepping for university exams! This is when I pooped my Pampers.

I proceeded to flounder horribly, just as I'd failed with Spanish in junior high. Sadly, it seemed I was simply "bad at languages." Six months into my exchange, I was ready to go home.

Then Lady Luck smiled upon me. I stumbled upon a poster (see opposite) while looking for *The Book of Five Rings* in the Kinokuniya bookstore in Shinjuku.

This poster, which I still have on my wall 20 years later, contains all 1,945 of the *jōyō kanji* (常用漢字), the characters designated for basic literacy by the Japanese Ministry of Education. Most newspapers and magazines limit themselves to the *jōyō kanji*. For all practical purposes, this means that if you know the meaning-rich characters on the poster, you know Japanese, including all the most important verbs.

Japanese on one page! Holy shit!

Language is infinitely expansive (much like cooking) and therefore horribly overwhelming if unfiltered.

This poster was a revelation. It brought to light the most important lesson of language learning: *what* you study is more important than *how* you study.

Students are subordinate to materials, much like novice cooks are subordinate to recipes. If you select the wrong material, the wrong textbook, the wrong group of words, it doesn't matter how much (or how well) you study. It doesn't matter how good your teacher is. One must find the highest-frequency material.

Material beats method.

THE GRAMMAR OF JUDO: TRANSFER

If you have no interest in politics, will you enjoy a language course that uses political articles? Of course not. You'll get bored and quit.

The authors of most Japanese language books appeared to think that reading the *Asahi Shimbun* (Asahi Newspaper) was the only litmus test for Japanese mastery. For a high school student, and even now, reading the *Asahi Shimbun* is about as interesting as watching paint dry.

Fortunately, as long as you hit the highest-frequency material, I learned that content matters very little.

My panacea, it turned out, was judo textbooks.

Though the vocabulary (think, *ingredients*) was highly specialized, I eclipsed the grammatical ability of four- and five-year students of Japanese after two months of studying judo. Why? Because the grammar (think, *cooking methods*) was universal.

The principles transferred to everything.

常用漢字表

新学習指導要領準拠

●緑色の漢字は、教育漢字を示し、各漢字の右下の数字はその漢字を学習する学年を示す。

あ	亜	哀	愛	悪	握	圧	扱	安	案	暗	い	以	衣	位	囲	医	依	委	威	胃	為	尉	異	移	偉	意	違	維	慰	遺	緯	域	育	一
壱	逸	芋	引	印	因	姻	員	院	陰	飲	隠	韻	う	右	宇	羽	雨	運	雲	え	永	泳	英	映	栄	営	詠	影	鋭	衛	易	疫	益	液
駅	悦	越	謁	閲	円	延	沿	炎	宴	援	園	煙	猿	遠	鉛	塩	演	縁	お	汚	王	凹	央	応	往	押	欧	殴	桜	翁	奥	横	屋	億
憶	虞	乙	卸	音	恩	温	穏	か	下	化	火	加	可	仮	何	花	佳	価	果	河	科	架	夏	家	荷	華	菓	貨	渦	過	嫁	暇	禍	靴
寡	歌	箇	稼	課	蚊	我	画	芽	賀	雅	餓	介	回	灰	会	快	戒	改	怪	拐	悔	海	界	皆	械	絵	開	階	解	塊	壊	懐	貝	外
劾	害	涯	街	慨	該	概	垣	各	角	拡	革	格	核	殻	郭	覚	較	隔	閣	確	獲	嚇	穫	学	岳	楽	額	掛	潟	括	活	喝	渇	割
滑	褐	轄	且	株	刈	干	刊	甘	汗	缶	完	肝	官	冠	巻	看	陥	乾	勘	患	貫	寒	喚	堪	換	敢	棺	款	間	閑	勧	寛	幹	感
漢	慣	管	関	歓	監	緩	憾	還	館	環	簡	観	艦	鑑	丸	含	岸	岩	眼	頑	顔	願	き	企	危	机	気	岐	希	忌	汽	奇	祈	季
紀	軌	既	記	起	飢	鬼	帰	基	寄	規	喜	幾	揮	期	棋	貴	棄	旗	器	輝	機	騎	技	宜	偽	欺	義	疑	儀	戯	擬	犠	議	菊
吉	喫	詰	却	客	脚	逆	虐	九	久	及	弓	丘	旧	休	吸	朽	求	究	泣	急	級	糾	宮	救	球	給	窮	牛	去	巨	居	拒	拠	挙
虚	許	距	魚	御	漁	凶	共	叫	狂	京	享	供	協	況	峡	挟	狭	恐	恭	胸	脅	強	教	郷	境	橋	矯	鏡	競	響	驚	仰	暁	業
凝	曲	局	極	玉	斤	均	近	金	菌	勤	琴	筋	禁	緊	謹	襟	吟	銀	く	区	句	苦	駆	具	愚	空	偶	遇	隅	屈	掘	繰	君	訓
勲	薫	軍	郡	群	け	兄	刑	形	系	径	茎	係	型	契	計	恵	啓	掲	渓	経	蛍	敬	景	軽	傾	携	継	慶	憩	警	鶏	芸	迎	鯨
劇	撃	激	欠	穴	血	決	結	傑	潔	月	犬	件	見	券	肩	建	研	県	倹	兼	剣	軒	健	険	圏	堅	検	嫌	献	絹	遣	権	憲	賢
謙	繭	顕	験	懸	元	幻	玄	言	弦	限	原	現	減	源	厳	こ	己	戸	古	呼	固	孤	弧	故	枯	個	庫	湖	雇	誇	鼓	顧	五	互
午	呉	後	娯	悟	碁	語	誤	護	口	工	公	孔	功	巧	広	甲	交	光	向	后	好	江	考	行	坑	孝	抗	攻	更	効	幸	拘	肯	侯
厚	恒	洪	皇	紅	荒	郊	香	候	校	耕	航	貢	降	高	康	控	黄	慌	港	硬	絞	項	溝	鉱	構	綱	酵	稿	興	衡	鋼	講	購	号
合	拷	剛	豪	克	告	谷	刻	国	黒	穀	酷	獄	骨	込	今	困	昆	恨	根	婚	混	紺	魂	墾	懇	さ	左	佐	査	砂	唆	差	詐	鎖
座	才	再	災	妻	砕	宰	栽	彩	採	済	祭	斎	細	菜	最	裁	債	催	歳	載	際	在	材	剤	財	罪	崎	作	削	昨	索	策	酢	搾
錯	咲	冊	札	刷	殺	察	撮	擦	雑	皿	三	山	参	桟	蚕	惨	産	傘	散	算	酸	賛	残	暫	し	士	子	支	止	氏	仕	史	司	四
市	矢	旨	死	糸	至	伺	志	私	使	刺	始	姉	枝	祉	肢	姿	思	指	施	師	紙	脂	視	紫	詞	歯	嗣	試	詩	資	飼	誌	雌	賜
諮	示	字	寺	次	耳	自	似	児	事	侍	治	持	時	滋	慈	辞	磁	璽	式	識	軸	七	失	室	疾	執	湿	漆	質	実	芝	写	社	車
舎	者	射	捨	赦	斜	煮	遮	謝	邪	蛇	勺	尺	借	酌	釈	爵	若	弱	寂	手	主	守	朱	取	狩	首	殊	珠	酒	種	趣	寿	受	授
需	儒	樹	収	囚	州	舟	秀	周	宗	拾	秋	臭	修	終	習	週	就	衆	集	愁	酬	醜	襲	十	汁	充	住	柔	重	従	渋	銃	獣	縦
叔	祝	宿	淑	粛	縮	塾	熟	出	述	術	俊	春	瞬	旬	巡	盾	准	殉	純	循	順	準	潤	遵	処	初	所	書	庶	暑	署	緒	諸	女
如	助	序	叙	徐	除	小	升	少	召	匠	床	抄	肖	尚	招	承	昇	松	沼	昭	宵	将	消	症	祥	称	笑	唱	商	渉	章	紹	訟	勝
掌	晶	焼	焦	硝	粧	詔	証	象	傷	奨	照	詳	彰	障	衝	賞	償	礁	鐘	上	丈	冗	条	状	乗	城	浄	剰	常	情	場	畳	蒸	縄
壌	嬢	錠	譲	醸	色	食	植	殖	飾	触	嘱	織	職	辱	心	申	伸	臣	身	辛	侵	信	津	神	唇	娠	振	浸	真	針	深	紳	進	森
診	寝	慎	新	審	震	薪	親	人	刃	仁	尽	迅	甚	陣	尋	す	図	水	吹	垂	炊	帥	粋	衰	推	酔	遂	睡	穂	錘	随	髄	枢	崇
数	据	杉	寸	せ	畝	瀬	是	井	世	正	生	成	西	声	制	姓	征	性	青	斉	政	星	牲	省	逝	清	盛	婿	晴	勢	聖	誠	精	製
誓	静	請	整	税	夕	斥	石	赤	昔	析	隻	席	惜	責	跡	積	績	籍	切	折	拙	窃	接	設	雪	摂	節	説	舌	絶	千	川	仙	占
先	宣	専	泉	浅	洗	染	扇	栓	旋	船	戦	践	銭	銑	潜	線	遷	選	薦	繊	鮮	全	前	善	然	禅	漸	繕	そ	阻	祖	租	素	措
粗	組	疎	訴	塑	礎	双	壮	早	争	走	奏	相	荘	草	送	倉	捜	挿	桑	掃	曹	巣	窓	創	喪	葬	装	僧	想	層	総	遭	槽	操
燥	霜	騒	藻	造	像	増	憎	蔵	贈	臓	即	束	足	促	則	息	速	側	測	俗	族	属	賊	続	卒	率	存	村	孫	尊	損	た	他	多
打	妥	堕	惰	駄	太	対	体	耐	待	怠	胎	退	帯	泰	袋	逮	替	貸	隊	滞	態	大	代	台	第	題	滝	宅	択	沢	卓	拓	託	濯
諾	濁	但	達	脱	奪	棚	丹	担	単	炭	胆	探	淡	短	嘆	端	誕	鍛	団	男	段	断	弾	暖	談	壇	ち	地	池	知	値	恥	致	遅
痴	稚	置	竹	畜	逐	蓄	築	秩	窒	茶	着	嫡	中	仲	虫	沖	宙	忠	抽	注	昼	柱	衷	鋳	駐	著	貯	丁	弔	庁	兆	町	長	挑
帳	張	彫	眺	釣	頂	鳥	朝	脹	超	腸	跳	徴	潮	澄	調	聴	懲	直	勅	沈	珍	朕	陳	賃	鎮	つ	追	墜	通	痛	塚	漬	坪	て
低	呈	廷	弟	定	底	抵	邸	亭	貞	帝	訂	庭	逓	停	偵	堤	提	程	艇	締	泥	的	笛	摘	滴	適	敵	迭	哲	鉄	徹	撤	天	典
店	点	展	添	転	田	伝	殿	電	と	斗	吐	徒	途	都	渡	塗	土	奴	努	度	怒	刀	冬	灯	当	投	豆	東	到	逃	倒	凍	唐	島
桃	討	透	党	悼	盗	陶	塔	搭	棟	湯	痘	登	答	等	筒	統	稲	踏	糖	頭	謄	闘	騰	同	洞	胴	動	堂	童	道	働	銅	導	峠
匿	特	得	督	徳	篤	毒	独	読	凸	突	届	屯	豚	鈍	曇	な	内	南	軟	難	に	二	尼	弐	肉	日	入	乳	尿	任	妊	忍	認	ね
寧	熱	年	念	粘	燃	の	悩	納	能	脳	農	濃	は	把	波	派	破	覇	馬	婆	拝	杯	背	肺	俳	配	排	敗	廃	輩	売	倍	梅	培
陪	媒	買	賠	白	伯	拍	泊	迫	舶	博	薄	麦	漠	縛	爆	箱	畑	肌	八	鉢	発	髪	伐	抜	罰	閥	反	半	犯	帆	伴	判	坂	板
版	班	畔	般	販	飯	搬	煩	頒	範	繁	藩	晩	番	蛮	盤	ひ	比	皮	妃	否	批	彼	披	肥	非	卑	飛	疲	秘	被	悲	扉	費	碑
罷	避	尾	美	備	微	鼻	匹	必	泌	筆	姫	百	氷	表	俵	票	評	漂	標	苗	秒	病	描	猫	品	浜	貧	賓	頻	敏	瓶	ふ	不	夫
父	付	布	扶	府	怖	附	負	赴	浮	婦	符	富	普	腐	敷	膚	賦	譜	侮	武	部	舞	封	風	伏	服	副	幅	復	福	腹	複	覆	払
沸	仏	物	粉	紛	雰	噴	墳	憤	奮	分	文	聞	へ	丙	平	兵	併	並	柄	陛	閉	塀	幣	弊	米	壁	癖	別	片	辺	返	変	偏	遍
編	弁	便	勉	ほ	歩	保	捕	浦	補	舗	母	募	墓	慕	暮	簿	方	包	芳	邦	奉	宝	抱	放	法	泡	胞	俸	倣	峰	砲	崩	訪	報
豊	飽	褒	縫	亡	乏	忙	坊	妨	忘	防	房	肪	某	冒	剖	紡	望	傍	帽	棒	貿	暴	膨	謀	北	木	朴	牧	僕	墨	撲	没	堀	本
奔	翻	凡	盆	ま	麻	摩	磨	魔	毎	妹	枚	埋	幕	膜	又	末	抹	万	満	慢	漫	み	未	味	魅	岬	密	脈	妙	民	眠	む	矛	務
無	夢	霧	娘	め	名	命	明	迷	盟	銘	鳴	滅	免	面	綿	も	茂	模	毛	妄	盲	耗	猛	網	目	黙	門	紋	問	匁	や	夜	野	厄
役	約	訳	薬	躍	ゆ	由	油	愉	諭	輸	癒	唯	友	有	勇	幽	悠	郵	猶	裕	遊	雄	誘	憂	融	優	よ	与	予	余	誉	預	幼	用
羊	洋	要	容	庸	揚	揺	葉	陽	溶	腰	様	踊	窯	養	擁	謡	曜	抑	浴	欲	翌	翼	ら	裸	羅	来	雷	頼	絡	落	酪	乱	卵	覧
濫	欄	り	吏	利	里	理	痢	裏	履	離	陸	立	律	略	柳	流	留	竜	粒	隆	硫	旅	虜	慮	了	両	良	料	涼	猟	陵	量	僚	領
寮	療	糧	力	緑	林	厘	倫	輪	隣	臨	る	涙	累	塁	類	れ	令	礼	冷	励	戻	例	鈴	零	霊	隷	齢	麗	暦	歴	列	劣	烈	裂
恋	連	廉	練	錬	ろ	炉	路	露	老	労	郎	朗	浪	廊	楼	漏	六	録	論	わ	和	話	賄	惑	枠	湾	腕							

明朝体活字と筆写の楷書との関係について

1 明朝体活字に特徴的な表現の仕方があるもの

衣－衣 人－人 芝－芝 八－八 子－子 辶－辶
去－去 家－家 入－入 手－手 ⺮－⺮
玄－玄 北－北 史－史 了－了 心－心

2 筆写の楷書では、いろいろな書き方があるもの

雨－雨雨 風－風風 糸－糸糸 主－主主 又－又又 文－文文 奥－奥奥 骨－骨骨 切－切切切 陸－陸陸陸 木－木木 来－来来 令－令令
無－無無 仰－仰仰 ネ－ネネ 年－年年 月－月月 角－角角 酒－酒酒 牛－牛牛 女－女女
戸－戸戸戸 比－比比 衤－衤衤 言－言言 条－条条 保－保保 公－公公 改－改改改 環－環環 外－外外外

全教図

投技編
バイタル柔道
岡野 功・佐藤哲也 共著

Vital Judo: My grammar teacher.

THE MAKING OF A METHOD: 1999–2010

I came back to the U.S. after Tokyo and scored higher on the Japanese SAT II than a friend who was a native speaker. By high school graduation in 1995, I'd developed two simple lenses through which I viewed language-learning methods, and learning in general:

Is the method effective? Have you narrowed down your material to the highest frequency?

Is the method sustainable? Have you chosen a schedule and subject matter that you can stick with (or at least put up with) until reaching fluency? Will you actually swallow the pill you've prescribed yourself?

Alas, there was still one missing piece: efficiency. If effectiveness is *doing the right things*, efficiency is *doing things right*. Martin Luther King, Jr., famously remarked that "justice too long delayed is justice denied." Learning is similar—speed determines the value. Even with the best material, if your time-to-fluency is 20 years, the return on investment (ROI) is terrible.

Though 1996 heralded itself with vasopressin and its cousins, taking me to the biochemical level for immediate payoff, it wasn't until 1999 that I returned to the hardest part, the most slippery element of the puzzle: the *method*.

The catalyst came serendipitously one evening on Witherspoon Street in downtown Princeton. I was heads-down working on my senior thesis, a sexy tome entitled *Acquisition of Japanese Kanji: Conventional Practice and Mnemonic Supplementation*, and I'd developed a phone friendship with Dr. Bernie Feria, then director of curriculum and development at the world headquarters of Berlitz International, conveniently located only miles from campus. He invited me out to a jacket-and-tie dinner, and I put on my fanciest: corduroys, an ill-fitting sports coat, and a counterfeit Polo shirt.

It was a glorious feast, and Bernie was a gracious host. He knew his languages, and the red wine flowed. We shared war stories from the linguistic trenches: lessons learned, comedic mistakes, and cultural faux pas. Bernie shared his French adventures, and I told him about the time I asked my Japanese host mother to rape me at 8 a.m. the next morning. Ah, just one vowel off! But *okasu* (to rape) was not *okosu* (to wake). You've never seen such a confused Japanese woman.

He roared. By the time dessert came around, Bernie paused and said, "You know, it's a shame you're not graduating earlier, as we have a project starting soon that you'd be perfect for."

The "project" was helping redesign their introductory Japanese curriculum, which doubled as an opportunity to revisit their English curriculum, which then accounted for 70% of their roughly 5 million lessons a year at 320 language centers around the globe.[‡]

Imagine wandering into your local guitar shop and approaching the high school intern behind the counter: "Hey, kid, how would you like to tune the London Philharmonic Orchestra? They have a live gig in Central Park next week and it'll be broadcast into 50 countries. You in?" I felt like that kid.

I left Princeton in the middle of my senior year, just months before graduation, to pursue this love of language. I worked for Berlitz, then—itching to test new ideas immediately—traveled to Taiwan, where many of the pieces started to fall into place for "DiSSS" (coming next page).

Then I did something odd. I applied the same DiSSS process to learning kickboxing and, less than two months later, won the Chinese national kickboxing championships at 165 lbs.

Flash forward to 2005.

I had spent six years testing different approaches to natural languages. Here's what my language acquisition times looked like in order, using standardized testing for all but Chinese:

JAPANESE
ONE YEAR
MANDARIN CHINESE
SIX MONTHS
GERMAN
THREE MONTHS
SPANISH
EIGHT WEEKS

Recall that, at age 15, I'd failed to learn enough Spanish to hold a basic conversation.

Now people were lauding me for being "good at languages" or congratulating me on being "gifted." It was hysterical. I just had a better instruction manual.

In 2005, I traveled the world as a digital nomad, an experience later chronicled in *The 4-Hour Workweek*. I focused on language to conquer loneliness: Irish Gaelic, Norwegian, German, Spanish (including Lunfardo dialect in Argentina), anything I came into contact with. The refinement continued through 2010 and to the present. I've vetted the process on Turkish, Greek, Xhosa, and other languages over shorter 1–2-week periods.

The DiSSS process I used was effective for acquiring *declarative* "facts and figures" knowledge (e.g., memorizing serial numbers, remembering where your car is parked). It also worked incredibly well for *procedural* "action" knowledge (e.g., practicing judo, riding a bike, driving a car). It even worked for hybrids (e.g., writing Chinese characters).

None of this is said to impress you. It's said to impress upon you that there *is* a *repeatable process*, and that hundreds of readers have replicated my results.

It is possible to become world-class, enter the top 5% of performers in the world, in almost any subject within 6–12 months, or even 6–12 weeks.

There is a recipe, the *real* recipe in this book, and that is DiSSS. Turn the page to learn the formula.

DiSSS

The recipe for learning any skill is encapsulated in this acronym.

HOW TO REMEMBER IT: Ah, the 1980s cultural contribution to modern English: *diss*. Just remember *diss* with an extra *s*: DiSSS. If you're a gamer and know PS3 (PlayStation 3), just think of DS3.

Here's the sequence:

D

DECONSTRUCTION

What are the minimal learnable units, the LEGO blocks, I should be starting with?

S

SELECTION

Which 20% of the blocks should I focus on for 80% or more of the outcome I want?

S

SEQUENCING

In what order should I learn the blocks?

S

STAKES

How do I set up stakes to create real consequences and guarantee I follow the program?

CaFE

There are several secondary principles that, while very helpful (I use all three constantly), are not required. Here, *CaFE* is the acronym:

C

COMPRESSION

Can I encapsulate the most important 20% into an easily graspable one-pager?

F

FREQUENCY

How frequently should I practice? Can I cram, and what should my schedule look like? What growing pains can I predict? What is the minimum effective dose (MED) for volume?

E

ENCODING

How do I anchor the new material to what I already know for rapid recall? Acronyms like *DiSSS* and *CaFE* are examples of encoding.

TWO NOTES BEFORE WE PROCEED

First, I've incorporated DiSSS and CaFE into this book, so you don't have to worry about them. If you're eager to get cooking, feel free to read Stakes (page 68) and Compression (page 70), and then jump straight to DOMESTIC on page 102.

Second, and most important, if anything gets too dense in META (and it might), jump to Stakes, read Compression, then skip to DOMESTIC. DOM will take you from making scrambled eggs to making $30 restaurant entrées in 24 hours. You can always come back to META later, after a few early wins and high fives.

There's no rush, and feel free to jump around. You don't have to understand how the engine works (cognition) to drive the car (in this case, cook).

For those brave souls who dare enter here, turn the page to see how deep my favorite rabbit hole goes.

Di S S S DECONSTRUCTION: EXPLORING THE GREAT UNKNOWN

> "Whenever you find yourself on the side of the majority, it is time to pause and reflect."
> —MARK TWAIN

> "Writing a novel [or learning] is like driving at night in the fog. You can see only as far as your headlights, but you can make the whole trip that way."
> —E. L. DOCTOROW, AUTHOR

Deconstruction is best thought of as exploration. This is where we throw a lot on the wall to see what sticks, where we flip things upside down and look at what the outliers are doing differently (and what they're not doing at all).

First and foremost, it is where we answer the question: how do I break this amorphous "skill" into small, manageable pieces?

Just as with literal deconstruction—taking a building apart, for example—you need the right tool for the job. Sometimes that is a hammer, sometimes it's a saw, sometimes it's both. In this chapter, we'll look at four primary tools. Each will be explained using real-world skills for context:

Reducing: How to learn 1,945 Japanese[7] characters.
Interviewing: How to shoot a basketball 3-pointer.
Reversal: How to build unparalleled fires.
Translating: How to dissect the grammar of any language in 1–2 hours.

Photo of "deconstructed" cheesecake, where diners can see the separate ingredients. Though I prefer the traditional version for eating, this version is far better for learning.

7 These characters, *kanji*, are actually borrowed from the Chinese. In 1981, there were 1,945 characters; since 2010, there are 2,136.

REDUCING: JAPANESE CHARACTERS

The ecstasy of finding my *jōyō kanji* poster was followed by the crushing task of learning, well, 1,945 characters.

That's more than 81 times the English (Roman) alphabet, and we're not talking about ABCs. The most complicated letters in English, like *E* and *W*, have four strokes. Many Japanese characters have more than **15 strokes**:

The above *gi* of *gisei* (meaning "sacrifice"[8]) has 17, and it just gets worse. Each stroke has to be in a specific order, so that you can write (and, more important, read) the equivalent of cursive. These 1,945, though finite, quickly become overwhelming.[9]

Fortunately, I was required to take a *shodō* (calligraphy) class, and I learned that each character can be broken into components: far left, top, middle, etc. These LEGO pieces, referred to as *radicals,* form the building blocks from which all *kanji* are made.

There are 214 radicals. They provide clues to both meaning and pronunciation, killing two birds with one stone. Radicals are also always written in one order: left to right and top to bottom. This all turns an impossible task—learning 1,945 characters—into one that some people can complete in less than two months.

Take, for instance, the radicals found in the character *ai,* which means love, as in *"Ai shite iru!"* (I love you):

1
2
3
4

To remember how to write this character, one might imagine "clawing" (1) through a "roof" (2) to get to a "heart" (3) that's "running away" (4)—ah, *c'est l'amour!*

The key was peppering my calligraphy teacher with questions, which leads us to the next complementary tool: interviewing.

8 Which I learned in judo's "sacrifice throw."

9 In the world of cooking, such paralysis is most often induced by herbs and spices.

INTERVIEWING: SHOOTING BASKETBALL 3-POINTERS

"You're doing a terrible job on your drink."

Start-up veteran Babak "Nivi" Nivi was finishing his sake as I took my first sip.

We were well en route to inebriated at Eiji, a tiny Japanese restaurant tucked in between the Castro and Mission districts of San Francisco.[10] Daiginjo was the perfect fuel for our discussion of odd skills and physical tracking. He had recently picked up Olympic lifting for fun, and I had a glucose monitor implanted in my side to track spikes in blood sugar. At one point, Nivi randomly offered:

"If you ever want to deconstruct basketball, I have the DVD for you: *Better Basketball.*"

Ever since my seventh grade PE teacher told me I dribbled like a caveman (I did), I'd written basketball off. So "thanks, but no thanks" was my answer to Nivi.

But lo! Three years later I found myself watching a Lakers game with my friend Kevin Rose and his fiancée, Darya, a Lakers fanatic. Their dog even had a Lakers jersey on.

I had an epiphany:

Even if I have zero *interest in playing basketball, perhaps learning the fundamentals over a weekend would allow me to love watching it.*[11] After all, it is the third most popular sport in the U.S.

That's when I asked Nivi to point me to the master: Rick Torbett, the founder of Better Basketball.

Rick has coached entire teams to shoot better than 40% for three consecutive seasons. To put that in perspective, in the last decade, only one NBA team—the Phoenix Suns—came close to 40% from the 3-point line.

To dissect his unusual success, I started by e-mailing him interview questions, the answers to which I'll share with you shortly. But let's start with the general process.

FIRST, CREATE A LIST OF PEOPLE TO INTERVIEW

If you're going for high-level athletics, for instance:

1. Use Wikipedia to find out who was the best (or second best, which is often ideal) in the world 5–10 years ago, or 2–4 Olympics ago, since those currently in the limelight are less likely to respond.

2. Search Google for "[My closest city] [sport] [Olympian or world champion or world record]." Hypothetically, I might look for "San Francisco bobsled Olympian," which gets me to a team doctor—perfect for a first lead.

NEXT, MAKE FIRST CONTACT AND PROVIDE CONTEXT

"Do me a favor" is not a compelling pitch. The proposed interview should somehow benefit your contact.

The path of least resistance is to freelance write for a blog, newsletter, or local newspaper and do a piece on this person and his/her methods, or to quote him/her on a related topic as an expert ("Expert Predictions for Winter Olympics," for instance). Once you're in the door, ask your expert all the questions you'd like. Are you terrible at writing? No problem. Make it a Q&A format and simply print the relevant questions and answers.[12]

LAST, ASK YOUR QUESTIONS

When I was looking into ultra-endurance for *The 4-Hour Body,* I sent different combinations of the below questions to people like the

---

10 For any vegetarians who might land there, the oboro tofu is incredible.

11 This logic reiterates the benefit of this book: even if you never cook, you'll increase your enjoyment of meals.

12 If they coach and do hourly consultations, you could also just pay for a telephone or Skype session.

legendary Scott Jurek, who won the Western States 100, a mountainous 100-mile race, a record seven times.

- "Who is good at ultra-running despite being poorly built for it? Who's good at this who shouldn't be?"
- "Who are the most controversial or unorthodox runners or trainers? Why? What do you think of them?"
- "Who are the most impressive lesser-known teachers?"
- "What makes you different? Who trained you or influenced you?"
- "Have you trained others to do this? Have they replicated your results?"
- "What are the biggest mistakes and myths you see in ultra-running training? What are the biggest wastes of time?"
- "What are your favorite instructional books or resources on the subject? If people had to teach themselves, what would you suggest they use?"
- "If you were to train me for four weeks for a [fill in the blank] competition and had a million dollars on the line, what would the training look like? What if I trained for eight weeks?"

In the case of basketball, I started by sending Rick four questions related to shooting:

1. First, what are the biggest mistakes novices make when shooting or practicing shooting? What are the biggest misuses of time?
2. Even at the pro level, what mistakes are most common?
3. What are your key principles for better, more consistent shooting? What are they for foul shots (free throws) vs. 3-pointers?
4. What does the progression of exercises look like?

I received his e-mail responses and, two days later, hit nine out of 10 free throws for the first time in my life. Then, on Christmas Eve, I went bowling and realized that many of the same principles applied. I scored 124, my first time over 100 and an Everest above my usual 50–70.[13] Upon returning home, I immediately went outside and sunk the first two 3-pointers of my life. For Lakers games with the Roses, I now see a ballet of kinesthetic beauty that was invisible before. That's a hell of a lot of fun.

For those interested, see Rick's 3-pointer tutorial in the Appendix on page 596.

13 Strangely, the basketball principles later produced a quantum leap in my handgun marksmanship—most important, that you should solve left-right deviation before worrying about long-short adjustments.

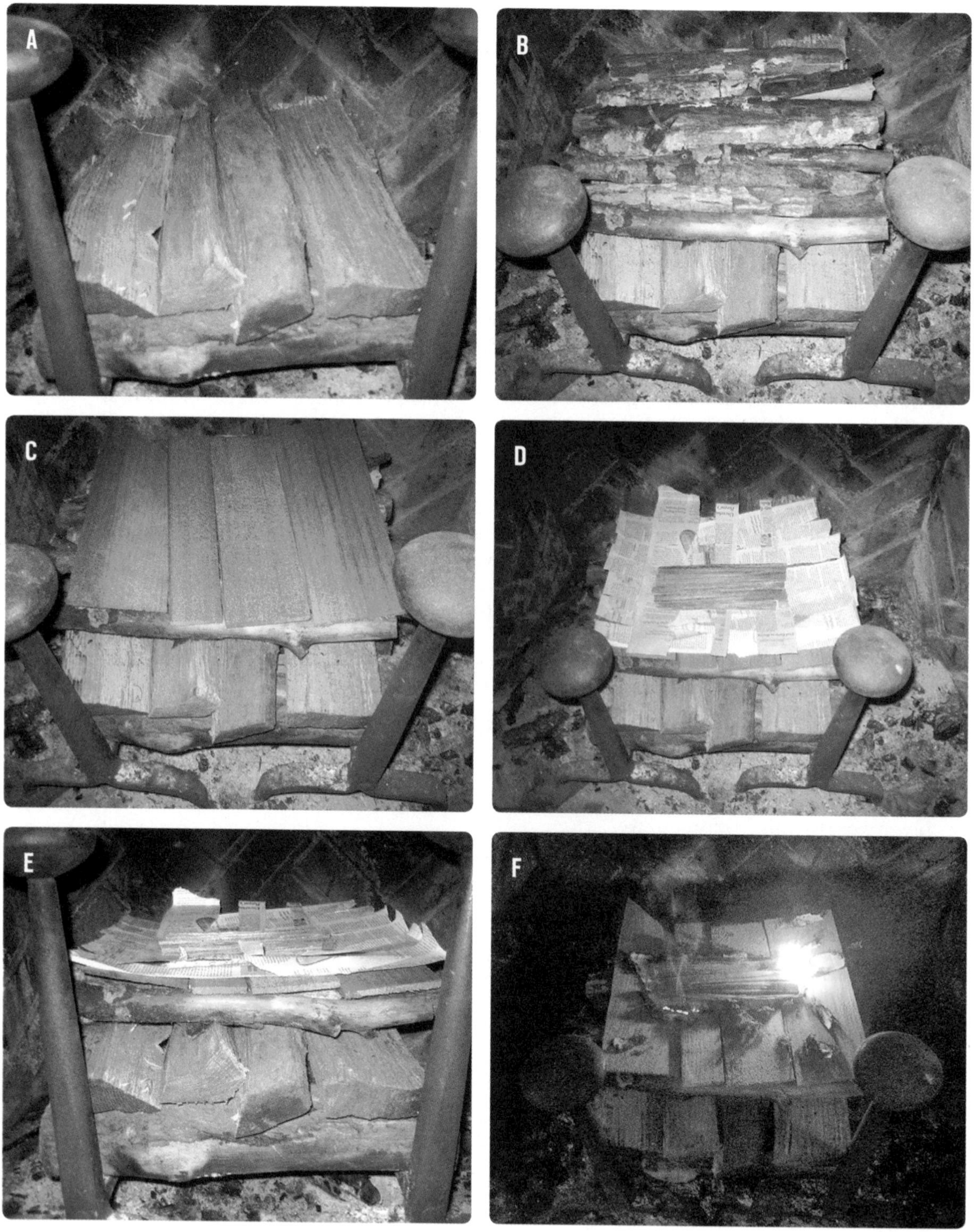
A
B
C
D
E
F

Here's what the process looks like in photos, which were taken on Christmas Day 2008. The embers this fire produces are unlike anything I've ever seen.

REVERSAL: BUILDING BETTER FIRES

How would you like to light a fire perfectly and have it burn for 3–7 hours without adding more wood? It requires forgetting everything you've learned about starting fires.

Now, I can make a raging furnace of epic proportions, a crackling and screaming banshee of life-giving heat... but it lasts for a euphoric five minutes. Then the real fun begins: the fiddling and fussing, poking and prodding every five minutes thereafter for the next hour to keep the charred remains clinging to life.

I was in the Boy Scouts and learned the ropes: tons of paper and tinder at the bottom, building upward like a tepee with the smallest kindling at the bottom and the biggest logs at the top. It's how fires are built, right?

Let's call this the "tepee" fire.

The alternative is the "upside-down" fire.

To learn the manliest of the manly arts, I looked to one of my most feminine readers, Marcie. She was seeking the best method of starting fires at her mountainside cabin, and the final result was as odd as it is effective.

The method is simplicity itself: do exactly the opposite of the tepee method.

1. Put the largest logs at the bottom, ensuring there is no space between them whatsoever.

2. Lay a second perpendicular layer of smaller logs on top of the largest, again ensuring there are no spaces between them.

3. Repeat with perpendicular layers until you get to the top, where you will put strips of crumpled paper and—at the very top—3–5 fire-starter squares (my preference) or fire-starter oil sticks. From bottom to top, I like to use large logs (unsplit), split logs, sapling wood, cedar shingle wood, then paper and fire-starting squares.

The finished appearance.

Prepare for much more heat. Once about 75% of the shingle wood is burned, the fire will start to give off a *lot* of heat. The flame from the top warms the air in the flue and creates a more efficient current of air for cross-ventilation, and there is little warmth wasted.

Three more benefits:

No smoke or minimal smoke. This is related to the thermodynamics of the flue air being heated faster, based on explanations I've read.[14] No backdraft smoke into the house.

No management. Assuming you don't have gaps between logs, the fire will burn beautifully for 3–7 hours, depending on the amount of wood used. This alludes to one potential drawback: you must start with a substantial amount of wood.

No ashes. This amazed me. It all burns down to nothing. No waste at all, as nearly every fiber is converted into heat. It's beautiful, in fact.

There are some things to keep in mind:

1. The upside-down fire won't look like much for about 20 minutes. Be patient. The goal is to create embers that then fall to the layer below, which is why there

14 Even for tepee-style fires, you can ensure a smoke-free start by lighting the end of a rolled up newspaper and holding it up the chimney for 10–15 seconds before lighting the fire.

cannot be any spaces between logs. Real flames take a while.

2. Ensure that the paper strips are bent or otherwise prop up the fire-starting squares/sticks so they don't lie flat on the shingles or the layer below. If you don't have this slight spacing for the fire-starting material to catch, you will have trouble lighting the fire and get frustrated. This is the only place where a little space is good.

Sometimes, whether in the world of fire-making or cooking, finding the path of least resistance is as easy as Googling "backward," "upside-down," or "reverse," plus whatever skill you're deconstructing.

TRANSLATING: THE GRAMMAR OF ANY LANGUAGE

(If the language stuff gets too dense, skip to Learning to "Taste" on page 50.)

"*Wer fremde Sprachen nicht kennt, weiß nichts von seiner eigenen.*"

"He who doesn't know foreign languages knows nothing of his own."

—Johann Wolfgang von Goethe

Cardinal Giuseppe Mezzofanti, born 1774, was called "the Devil" on many occasions.

The charming Italian could speak at least 39 languages and, by some accounts, had been tested in 72. As arguably the world's most famous hyperpolyglot, he was also systematic.

First, he learned languages in families.

Second, and related to deconstruction: Instead of using grammar books, he had native speakers of each language recite the Lord's Prayer. This short passage gave him an overview of nearly all important grammatical structures (direct object, indirect object, noun cases, possessives, etc.):

Our Father, who art in heaven,
Hallowed be Thy Name.
Thy Kingdom come.
Thy will be done
On Earth as it is in heaven.
Give us this day our daily bread.
And forgive us our trespasses,
As we forgive those who trespass against us.
And lead us not into temptation,
But deliver us from evil.[15]

I have used a nearly identical approach for decades: a 12-sentence audit.

By simply asking, "How do you say [sentence] in your language? Would you mind writing that down?" I can uncover the soul of a language and estimate how long it would take me to learn it. Pictures A and B on the opposite page tell the story of a Ukrainian woman who taught me Cyrillic in 30 minutes, and the whole conversation was two hours long.

Here are the 12 sentences, the "Deconstruction Dozen":

The apple is red.
It is John's apple.
I give John the apple.
We give him the apple.

He gives it to John.
She gives it to him.

Is the apple red?
The apples are red.

I must give it to him.
I want to give it to her.
I'm going to know tomorrow.
(I have eaten the apple.)[16]
I can't eat the apple.

The benefits of these few lines can be astonishing.

---

15 Prayer edited to reflect the Catholic version as it would have been in the 18th and 19th century (though translated into English).

16 This is a bonus 13th, to be explained later.

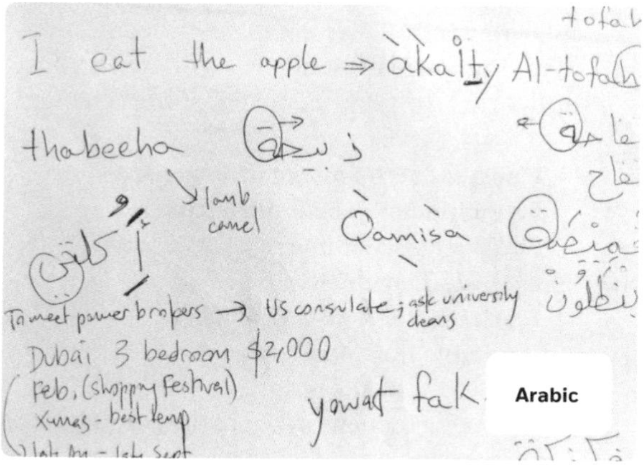
I eat the apple ⇒ àkalty Al-tofah
thabeeha
lamb
camel
Qamisa
To meet power brokers → US consulate; ask university deans
Dubai 3 bedroom $2,000
Feb. (shopping festival)
Xmas - best temp
yowat fak
Arabic

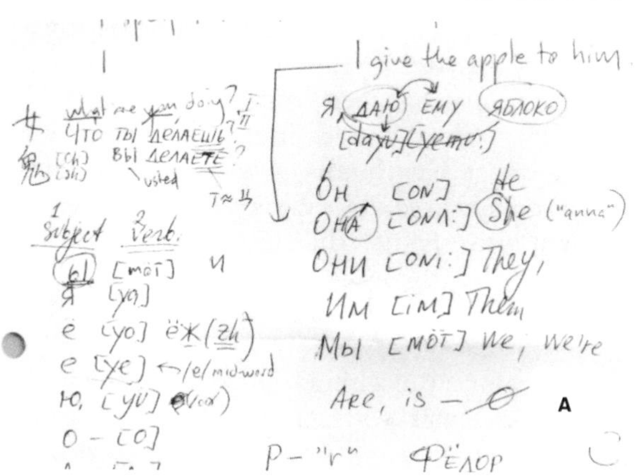
I give the apple to him.
Я ДАЮ ЕМУ ЯБЛОКО
Что ты делаешь?
Вы делаете?
Subject Verb.
Он [ON] He
ОНА [ONA:] She ("anna")
ОНИ [ONi:] They,
ИМ [iM] Them
Мы [MŌT] We, We're
Are, is - Ø
A

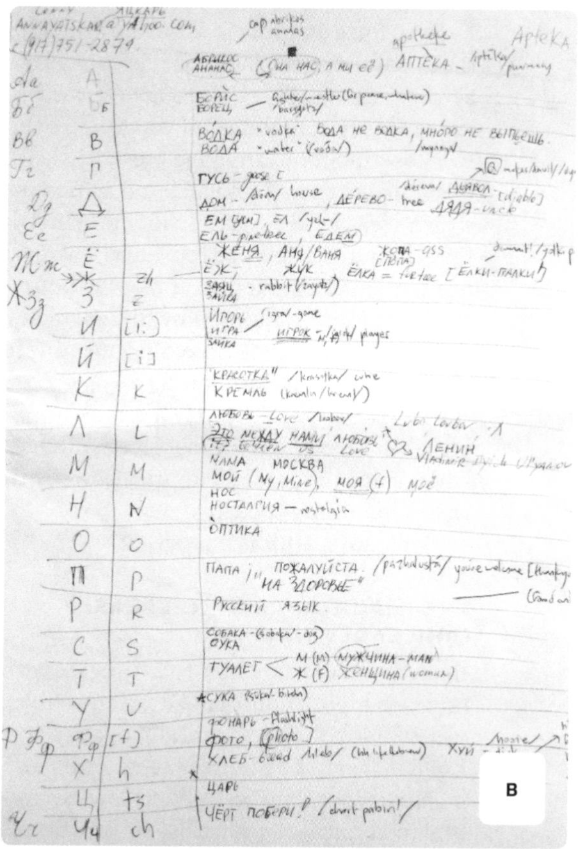
АПТЕКА
ВОДКА "vodka"
ВОДА "water"
ГУСЬ - goose
ДОМ - /dom/ house, ДЕРЕВО - tree
КРЕМЛЬ
ЛЮБОВЬ - Love
ЛЕНИН
МОСКВА
НОСТАЛГИЯ - nostalgia
ОПТИКА
ПАПА
ПОЖАЛУЙСТА
НА ЗДОРОВЬЕ
РУССКИЙ ЯЗЫК
СОБАКА
ТУАЛЕТ
МУЖЧИНА - MAN
ЖЕНЩИНА (woman)
ФОТО, [photo]
ХЛЕБ - bread
ЦАРЬ
ЧЁРТ ПОБЕРИ!
B

Greek

Deconstructing Arabic, Russian, and Greek using sentences on the opposite page. Imperfect but highly effective.

I was once en route to Istanbul and did the 12-sentence audit with a friendly Turk across the aisle. There was a layover before my connecting flight, and I wandered over to a Rosetta Stone language kiosk. I asked if I could try their Turkish demo, which the woman was kind enough to let me test-drive for 15 minutes. I skipped to a Level 3 test, which is intended to be taken after 120–150 hours of study, and scored more than 80% correct. In addition to saving me time, that 30-minute, 12-sentence audit saved me $399.

Not bad, right? Keeping things as simple as possible, I'll explain the last five sentences, which have the greatest application to other fields, including cooking.

Get ready . . . this is important.

THE IMPORTANCE OF HELPERS (AND EARLY WINS)

Remember learning how to conjugate verb tables in high school? I do. It was horrible.

Let's look at one example: "To eat." The English "I eat, she eats, we eat" is "*mangio, mangia, mangiamo*" in Italian. Now expand that to a typical 2–4-page list of variations (one measly verb out of thousands!) and it feels like an insurmountable task.

In reality, most people aren't "bad" at languages. They're bad, like me, at memorizing boring, zero-gratification tables that make DMV forms look sexy.

This is where helping verbs (auxiliary verbs) come in. Thank God. If I hadn't discovered them, I never would have learned any languages. They're the ultimate cheat.

By memorizing a few verbs in a few tenses, you get access to *all* verbs. It opens up the entire language in a matter of 1–2 weeks.

To illustrate, let's look at simplified versions of my four primary sentences with Italian. Just notice that the verb (*mangiare*) doesn't change:

I must eat. → ***Ho bisogno di mangiare.***
I want to eat. → ***Voglio mangiare.***
I'm going to eat tomorrow. → ***Vado a mangiare domani.***
I can't eat. → ***Non posso mangiare.***
[Literally: I am unable to eat.]

All I need to memorize are the conjugations for a few verbs—to have, to want, to need, etc.—and I can slap the infinitive or *to* form of any other verb on the end (I want *to eat*, I'm going *to read*, I need *to drink* water, etc.).[17]

If you learn the auxiliary verbs in your target language, plus the all-important *to be, to have, to do*, and *to go*, you can very quickly express any idea.[18] Just see the chart at right.

Imagine me teaching you soccer through books. I insist you memorize the physics of each possible shot, over 1–2 years, before we get on the field. How will you do? Well, first, you'll likely quit before you ever touch a ball. Second, when you get on the field, you'll have to start from scratch, turning that paper knowledge into practical knowledge.

Looking for the helping (auxiliary) verbs in any skill—those magical crutches that allow you to kick the ball as early as possible—is fundamental to becoming a learning machine.

The grammar of cooking, as we'll see in the next chapter, has exactly three "helping verbs" that will put everything into hyperdrive.

---

17 I can't hold back on one more tip: to start, you can just learn the *I* and *you* (first- and second-person) conjugations, as you will be using those more than 80% of the time.

18 FOR NERDS: What about that bonus line in parentheses? It was: *I have eaten the apple*. The present tense of "to have" is particularly important, as it also buys us a simple version of the past tense. For example: **I have eaten.** → ***Ho mangiato.*** Once I know even *ho* (I have) and *hai* (you have), I can ask and answer almost any past-tense question. For instance: Did you understand? *Hai capito?* In "*Hai capito?*" *capito* (from *capire*, to understand) is called the *past participle*, and you can learn the rules for these in an afternoon—*voilà*, past tense for all verbs! To practice this all-important "to have" as much as possible, I customized another one of my helper sentences. There are quite a few ways to translate "I must eat" in Italian, but I selected one that includes "to have"—"I have need of eating/to eat."

KICK-STARTING NINE LANGUAGES WITH FOUR SENTENCES

	I MUST EAT.	I WANT TO EAT.	I'M GOING TO EAT TOMORROW.	I CAN'T EAT.
SPANISH	Tengo que comer. *I-have that to-eat.*	Quiero comer. *I-want to-eat.*	Voy a comer mañana. *I-go to to-eat tomorrow.*	No puedo comer. *I cannot to-eat.*
GERMAN	Ich muss essen. *I must to-eat.*	Ich möchte essen. *I want to-eat.*	Ich werde morgen essen. *I going tomorrow to-eat.*	Ich kann nicht essen. *I can not to-eat.*
FRENCH	Je dois manger. *I must to-eat.*	Je veux manger. *I want to-eat.*	Je vais manger demain. *I will to-eat tomorrow.*	Je ne peux pas manger. *I no can't to-eat.*
JAPANESE	Taberu hitsuyoo ga aru. 食べる必要がある。 *To-eat necessity there is.*	Tabetai. 食べたい。 *Want-to-eat.*	Ashita taberu. 明日食べる。 *Tomorrow to-eat.*	Taberu koto ga dekinai. 食べることができない。 *To-eat thing cannot.*
CHINESE (MANDARIN)	Wǒ yào chī. 我要吃 *I must eat.*	Wǒ xiǎng chī. 我想吃 *I want eat.*	Wǒ míngtiān huì chī. 我明天会吃 *I tomorrow will eat.*	Wǒ bù néng chī. 我不能吃 *I not can eat.*
CHINESE (CANTONESE)	Ngoh yat ding yiu sik. 我一定要食。 *I must eat.*	Ngoh seung sik. 我想食。 *I think eat.*	Ngoh jyen bei ting yat sik. 我準備聽日食。 *I plan tomorrow eat.*	Ngoh mh neng gau sik. 我唔能夠食。 *I can't eat.*
RUSSIAN	Ya doljen yest. Я должен есть. *I must to-eat* (male). Ya doljna yest. Я должна есть. *I must to-eat* (female).	Ya hochu yest. Я хочу есть. *I want to-eat.*	Ya budu yest zavtra. Я буду есть завтра. *I going to-eat tomorrow.*	Ya ne mogu yest. Я не могу есть. *I not can to-eat.*
ARABIC	Min al-lâzim an âkula. من اللازم أن آكل *It is imperative that I eat.*	Urîdu an âkula. أريد أن آكل *I want to eat.*	Sa-âkulu ghadan. سآكل غدا *I will eat tomorrow.*	Lâ astatî u an âkula. لا أستطيع أن آكل *I cannot eat.*
DOTHRAKI	Anha'th adakhak. *I must to-eat.*	Anha zalak adakhat. *I want to-eat.*	Anha vadakhak silokh. *I will-eat tomorrow.*	Anha laz vos adakhok. *I can not to-eat.*

ASSIGNMENT: LEARNING TO "TASTE"

"Nothing would be more tiresome than eating and drinking if God had not made them a pleasure as well as a necessity."

—VOLTAIRE

"Is this basil?"
"No."

"This is . . . basil?"
"No."

"What is this?"
"C'mon, you know this."
"No, I don't."
"It's basil."

Basil. I must have asked my girlfriend 20 times on 20 occasions if the herb I was eating was basil. I just couldn't remember the goddamn plant. Smell it, taste it, draw it—nothing worked. She found it rather amusing, cute even, kinda like that kid in *Jerry Maguire*. "Did you know the human head weighs eight poundthz?!" Ha.

I found it infuriating.

Like many people, I'd watched the Food Network for 1–2 hours a night after work to unwind, but I'd never made a single dish. Now that I was going to be *using* ingredients, I needed to be able to recall them like song lyrics. I needed a *working* vocabulary.

I started with the most basic of basics, which, I'll admit, I had to look up.

Herbs? Herbs are from the leaves and stems of plants.

Spices, on the other hand, are from the root, bark, and seeds.[19]

Looking for data to soothe my ego, I found out that I wasn't alone. Flavor illiterates are everywhere. In 1986, *National Geographic* sent out scratch-and-sniff samples to subscribers, asking them to categorize six common odors, and 1.4 million people responded. The *best* performers—young adults—averaged barely over 50% correct. Women scored slightly higher than men, but everyone was piss poor.

19 Bonus: Nuts are fruits from trees, except peanuts, which are seeds from underground legumes.

WHAT WORKED FOR ME

Out of dozens of approaches I tried, there were only a few that actually helped me learn flavors. I suggest the following in order, but feel free to dabble:

1. **Smell food like a dog.**
2. **Literally deconstruct your food.**
3. **Leverage non-tongue taste.**
4. **Isolate the basics.**
5. **Try unusual food combinations.**

1. SMELL FOOD LIKE A DOG

Let's try an experiment. Get a few jelly beans of different flavors: cherry, root beer, coffee, whatever. Avoid anything with strong sour or hot characteristics. Now close your eyes, pinch your nose shut, and eat them one at a time. Try to guess the flavors.

If you prefer, get two glasses of wine, one white and one red, and repeat the drill.

Either way, it will be very, very hard.

As scientists at the Oxford Symposium on Food and Cookery put it in 2000:

> Although there is disagreement on the exact number of taste qualities, everyone acknowledges that the number is small. The usual list includes sweet, sour, bitter, salty, and umami (*Physiology and Behavior*, 1991). So, if taste were synonymous with flavour, the number of flavour experiences would be limited as well. Beef would be interchangeable with lamb. In terms of taste alone, raspberry, mango, grape, and peach would all be sweet, tart, and difficult to distinguish from one another. It is the odor component that makes their flavours unique and gives a seemingly endless variety of flavour experiences.‡

Flavor is, counterintuitively, less than 10% taste and more than 90% smell. The numbers tell the story:

Taste qualities = five

Scents = 10,000+

Of the taste qualities, you might not recognize *umami,* sometimes called *savory* or *brothy.* Professor Kikunae Ikeda of Tokyo Imperial University isolated umami as glutamic acid while studying kombu, giant Japanese sea kelp. He commercialized this finding as monosodium glutamate (MSG), but you need not eat headache powder to taste the wonder (and healthfulness, when organic) of umami. Tomatoes, parmesan, and chicken broth all have high glutamate content. There are also mimics: shiitake mushrooms have umami-like nucleotides that allow them to impart a similar taste.

But back to scents:

1. Before you scarf down your food like a hyena, pause and sniff a few inches above each item on your plate. For bonus points, open your mouth slightly as you do so to engage the *retronasal* pathway.[20] Smell each forkful, if you prefer, but I find that the face-in-the-plate approach provides more clarity.

2. If you tend to have a stuffed nose or chronic sinus infections, as I did for years, start using a ceramic neti pot before bed and upon waking.

Even if you never cook, smelling your food before eating it will radically change how you experience flavor.

20 "To be perceived, flavour molecules need to reach the olfactory epithelium, located in the nasal cavity. This can be achieved through orthonasal (sniff) or retronasal (mouth) airways." *Flavour and Fragrance Journal.* 2004; 19: 499–504.

2. LITERALLY DECONSTRUCT YOUR FOOD

I used to collect comic books. Perhaps you collected baseball cards or stamps. Now you need to start collecting flavors. The problem: dishes do not isolate flavors.

The solution is to break them down.

I did this for the first time at ABC Kitchen in NYC. After perusing the menu and asking the server, as I always do, "What have you had for lunch the last three days?" I chose a few appetizers based on her responses. Next—and this was the new part—I asked her to bring out a small amount, even a single leaf, of any unfamiliar ingredients, to taste alone before having them in complete dishes.

This is what she brought:

- Anise hyssop (from a dish of raw diver scallops with chiles and lime).
- Sage (from a chicken liver dish—fried in soy and salt, I later learned).
- Chervil (from the beet and yogurt salad).
- Nasturtium, an edible flower (from a vinaigrette used with steamed hake—a dish I didn't order, but after polite pleading the server kindly brought me the flower).

Each pinch arrived on a small, circular bread plate. It was no sweat for the kitchen, but it signified a *huge* leap forward for me. Then, I *layered* my tasting of each dish. This is a critical concept. For instance, I tasted the chicken liver in a progression of increasing complexity, in this order:

- Sage leaf by itself (as it was my highest-priority flavor to isolate).
- A small dab of chicken liver pâté by itself.
- Chicken liver on a small piece of the bread.
- All of it together.
- Salt alone, pepper alone, then salt and pepper added to the above. (Never salt your food before tasting it.)

Though it reads like a lot, it took place within a square foot and required less than two minutes. If you can't identify a mysterious flavor, as I couldn't with the soy coating on the sage, ask your server. They like people who care.

Deconstructing in this fashion was like pressing fast-forward on developing a palate.

Suddenly, the vague blend of flotsam and jetsam that I'd enjoyed as "meals" in the past, perhaps as "chicken cacciatore" or a similar label, became combinations of line items. **For each target flavor (usually an herb), I collected an *anchor* dish.** I couldn't really remember an herb in isolation (e.g., *This is the flavor of rosemary*), but I could perfectly remember the flavor of the herb if I associated it in my mind with a single representative dish (e.g., *This is rosemary, the flavor you had with rack of lamb*). Cilantro? Vietnamese pho noodles. Chives? Sour-cream-and-chive potato chips. Cloves? Christmas tea. And so on.

Despite my great success with deconstruction, there were really tough items, like basil, that required one more technique: non-tongue taste.

3. LEVERAGE NON-TONGUE TASTE

This epiphany took place at the Oberoi Grand, in Kolkata, India.

I had taken a Bengali cooking class the day before, and I was having an existential crisis over my iced tea. Why the hell couldn't I isolate and remember a few key ingredients, like turmeric, cardamom, and cumin? I asked the waiter if he could bring out a side dish with two pinches of each; I'd try deconstruction again.

It didn't work. To escape this frustration, I went to my e-mail in-box, where I found a note from researchers at the Monell Chemical Senses Center, in Philadelphia, who'd been introduced to me by my friend and fellow experimenter A.J. Jacobs. Leslie Stein, PhD, and Marcia Pelchat, PhD, had once again proven invaluable. In their message, I found a few choice lines:

"Not all taste buds are located on the tongue. Some are found on the roof of the mouth and in the throat.... Taste receptors are also found in the lining of the intestine, suggesting that our concept of the sense of taste should include these chemical-sensing systems."

This is when the lightbulb went on. Jumping online, I started digging and found more: There are taste cells and receptors in the small intestine. And in 2006, glutamate receptors were identified in the stomach.

Maybe doing what I had been doing—rolling herbs in my fingers, smelling them, moving them around my mouth—was akin to listening to your favorite song with one ear and no bass. Perhaps I wasn't flavor-deaf. Perhaps I wasn't using enough of my body.

So I waved down a waiter to help me test Plan B:

- I asked for one cup of hot water for tea, and three extra cups.
- I cut or smashed the target herbs and spices into little bits, keeping them separate.
- I put each small pile in its own cup.
- I started with the usual: roll in the fingers, smell, taste on tongue.
- Then I poured a little hot water (about ¼ c) into each cup and swirled it around. I let things steep for a few minutes.
- Last, I took small sips of each, swishing it around my mouth like fine wine, even aerating it (that annoying air-sucking sound wine drinkers make), and finally swallowing it.

It worked like a charm. For the first time, I "got" a few spices on their own. The volume is turned down with water, but you hit more areas—like stereo sound versus mono—so I found the resolution higher.

If you are tackling a tough flavor, throw your whole body into tasting. The tongue is just one part of the equation.

4. ISOLATE THE BASICS: TASTES, SENSATIONS, FLAVOR PROFILES

Combine one cup of water with each of the below, and sip to better identify the different taste qualities:

Tastes:

Sweet — Table sugar or other sweetener.

Sour — Ideally, "sour salt" (citric acid),[21] as it's odorless, but lemon juice or vinegar will do the job.

Bitter — Tonic water (quinine).

Salty — Various types of salt: table salt, kosher salt, sea salt.

Umami — Human breast milk.

What's that? You don't have human breast milk on hand? A little MSG will work. Barring that, try dashi (or its constituent parts, kombu seaweed or bonito flakes), mushrooms, or the little white crystals on good ol' Parmigiano-Reggiano.

Sensations:

Astringency — Think of this, for now, as synonymous with "tannins." It's the cottonmouth feeling you know. Try sipping overbrewed black tea (two packets steeping for 15 minutes) or eating underripe persimmons.

Hotness — Try Anaheim peppers or, if you're macho, jalapeño. If you're straight-up masochistic, chomp habañero.

I was once invited to a rather fancy cocktail party in San Francisco, held at a billionaire's house. The front walkway was flanked by an Aston Martin and an Audi S5 with a modified Lamborghini engine inside. I rolled up to the valet in my supa' fly 2004 Volkswagen Golf and bounced out with a bottle of pickled vegetables under one arm and a carrot in my mouth (I was starving and had bought them en route). "Hello, gents!" I said to the linebacker-like security guards, who, after much confusion, led me inside.

---

21 Available at GNC, it can be used in place of lemon juice on food, to prevent fruit from browning, or to keep your glasses clear in the dishwasher (1 T should do it).

Now among three-piece suits, I mingled and had a jolly ol' time, wine in one hand, pickled veggies in the other.[22] Then, mid-conversation, I felt a little funny. Suddenly, I felt a lot funny. Looking down at my hand, I saw a half-eaten habañero, which I'd chomped and swallowed without looking. "I gotta go," I said to my unnamed drinking partner, and made a beeline through the kitchen doors. As I barged in, the caterers stood bewildered, staring at me. Tears were streaming out of my eyes. "I . . . need . . . whole milk! Please!!!" I stammered, dropping the habañero on the counter as evidence. Then, without a word, I pulled open the fridge and started chugging 2% milk. The mouthful of cream I drank next sealed the deal and got me back to normal within five minutes.

All that is to say: use fat, not water, to counter hotness. Capsaicin is fat-soluble.

Flavor profiles:

Last, play with foodpairing.be, which is based on the Volatile Compounds in Food (VCF) database. The objective is to start thinking about how to mix and match foods based on similar *characteristics.*

Don't have saffron? On their site, you'll learn that you can replace it with, oddly enough, tarragon. Ran out of sage? No problem; use rosemary instead. Both contain eucalyptol, so your dish should turn out similarly. Wondering what the hell will go with the leftover cucumber and grapes? Try the various cucumber soup recipes they have links to. Ran out of lemongrass, or don't want to bother buying it in the first place? Type it in and you'll learn that you can combine a little lemon peel, ginger, and basil to reconstruct the basic lemongrass flavor. Pretty damn cool.

5. TRY UNUSUAL FOOD COMBINATIONS. ASK "WHY DOES IT WORK?"

There's a concept in Zen Buddhism called "beginner eyes," which means to look at something as if you're seeing it for the first time. No matter how many times you've eaten meatloaf or sweet-and-sour chicken, picking out the specifics takes practice. Does it need more salt? A little acid? What?

As a cook, you'll have to start asking, "Why does this work?" or "Why doesn't this work?" a lot.

I found this hard to do with dishes I'd eaten dozens of times. My taste buds were too close to the problem. It was a lot easier with combos I had no reference point for. This became clear when an Indian friend suggested mango with cayenne pepper. It sounded disgusting until she walked me through it (this progression should look familiar):

"Try the mango alone." (Delicious.)

"Shake on some cayenne powder and try again." (Wow, even more delicious.)

"Now put on some sea salt." (Incredible and by far the best.)

This sharpened my perception of hotness as it contrasted with sweetness, and the use of salt to bring out flavors. I needed something weird to get me there. The oddness also made this anchor meal nearly impossible to forget.

Here are some unusual combos to start with. Why do they work?

- Cinnamon and chile powder on vanilla ice cream.
- Olive oil on chocolate ice cream (bonus point: put an olive oil–fried sage leaf on top).
- Cinnamon on bacon.
- Almond butter on hamburger.
- Black pepper on watermelon.
- Mustard on black-eyed peas.
- Cinnamon on grilled pineapple (a favorite in *churrascaria,* grilled meat restaurants in Brazil).

---

22 Yes, I know this isn't normal.

Once you've tested the odd, you can introduce traditional taste pairings, like beef and horseradish or orange and fennel.

Adding to the flavor collection: turkey testicle soup, courtesy of Hillside Supper Club.

ZE HERBS — A SHORT LIST

> "Marjoram, [Mario Batali] said on another occasion, has the oily perfume of a woman's body: 'It is the sexiest of the herbs.'"
>
> —BILL BUFORD, *HEAT*

In *Culinary Artistry*, authors Andrew Dornenburg and Karen Page asked a number of famous chefs the question, "If you could only take 10 ingredients with you to a desert island, which would they be?" Below are some of their herb-specific answers, as well as responses from chefs I asked the same question of. Those without attribution are ones that showed up more than a few times:

- **Rosemary** (Alice Waters)
- **Smoked paprika** (Mark Bittman, Erik Cosselmon)
- **Thyme** (considered the most versatile by many chefs; one of the most universally liked by diners)
- **Chiles** (Jean-Georges Vongerichten)
- Basil (Gary Danko, Bradley Ogden)
- Marjoram (Mario Batali; this one also pairs well with brains, if that's someday relevant to you. Use sparingly.)
- Chives (my favorite green garnish)
- Lemongrass (Personally, I think the choking hazard isn't worth the flavor. Ditto with bay leaves.)
- Chervil (Odd fact: can be smoked like marijuana for similar effects, or so I've been told.)

Those bolded above are my personal favorites. Rosemary and thyme can be steeped in hot water for delicious tea, so I don't have to watch leftovers decompose. Smoked paprika is canned and will last forever.

DiSSS SELECTION: 80/20 AND MED

"Do as little as needed, not as much as possible."

—HENK KRAAIJENHOF, COACH OF MERLENE JOYCE "QUEEN OF THE TRACK" OTTEY, WHO WON 23 COMBINED MEDALS AT THE OLYMPIC GAMES AND WORLD CHAMPIONSHIPS

"That's it?" my dad had asked me.

"That's it," I replied with a smirk. My recommendation seemed too simple to work: eat 30 grams of protein within 30 minutes of waking up, no more. I suggested—actually, insisted—that he make no other changes to his diet or exercise.

After four weeks, we tallied the results. His average monthly fat loss had gone from roughly 5 lbs to 18.75 lbs, a 275% increase. He'd tripled his fat loss by spending less than two minutes consuming a protein shake each morning. Astonishing? Not really. I'd seen the pattern in the data across hundreds of people: simple works, complex fails.

The lowest volume, the lowest frequency, the fewest changes that get us our desired result is what I label the **minimal effective dose (MED).** It's a broad concept that applies to almost any field. Here are a few eclectic but tested examples:

- Fat loss MED = consume 30 g of protein within 30 minutes of waking up. Dozens of readers have lost 100+ lbs each; thousands more have lost 10–100 lbs.

- To overcome female weight-loss plateaus, MED = five minutes of kettlebell swings, three times per week. Tracy Reifkind, for example, lost 120+ lbs as a 40-something mother of two.

- To gain 10–30 lbs of lean tissue in one month, MED = 90–120 seconds of tension for most muscles. Slow-cadence lifting (five seconds up, five seconds down) with these parameters helped me add 34 lbs of lean mass in 28 days.[23]

- Master conversational fluency in any language, MED = learn 1,200 words, focusing on highest frequency.

- The marketing MED = Read Kevin Kelly's article "1,000 True Fans."

To reiterate what we've already covered: material beats method.

The 20-volume *Oxford English Dictionary, Second Edition,* contains full entries for 171,476 words in current use. If we include colloquial and derivative terms, the word count easily tops 250,000. Crikey. At the end of this chapter, I've listed the 100 most common words in written English. It's a drop in the bucket, a mere .06%, or 6/100ths of 1%, of the 171,476 total.

Yet the first 25 words on my list make up roughly 33% of all printed material in English.

23 See "From Geek to Freak" in *The 4-Hour Body.*

The first 100 comprise 50% of all written material. If we were to expand the list to the top 300, they would make up about 65% of all written material in English.

What you need to remember: 100 *well-selected* words give you 50% of the practical use of 171,476 words.

So, do you work from A to Z through 250,000 words over 25+ years, or do you master this high-frequency 100-word list in less than a week, then decide on next steps? Clearly, you do the second.

We should remember the warning of the wise Grail knight in *Indiana Jones and the Last Crusade*:

"You must choose, but choose wisely, for as the true Grail will bring you life, the false Grail will take it from you."

Choose the highest-yield material and you can be an idiot and enjoy stunning success.

Choose poorly and, as the Grail knight implied, you're screwed no matter what. You'll chase your own tail for years.

How do we choose wisely for cooking?

THE MED OF COOKING: TECHNIQUE OVER RECIPES

Remember our helper (auxiliary) verbs (page 48)?

Roughly 14% of the 171,476 words listed in the full *Oxford English Dictionary* are verbs.‡ This means there are approximately 24,007 verbs in English, which can be unlocked with 6–12 helper verbs.

In the same way that auxiliary verbs give access to all verbs and unlock the grammar of language, a few cooking methods unlock all ingredients and cuisines.

In their wonderful book *Culinary Artistry*, Karen Page and Andrew Dornenburg asked several dozen world-class chefs which three cooking techniques they'd choose if they were limited to those three for the rest of their lives.

For cooking methods, the most popular (as also confirmed by my interviews) were as follows:

1. Grilling
2. Sautéing
3. Braising

These become your auxiliary verbs. Next, we evaluate each through the lens of Buffett's "margin of safety" and reorder them. The method that is most forgiving—braising—goes first, because early wins are paramount.

The order of learning then becomes:

1. Braising
2. Sautéing
3. Grilling

These will be taught as universal principles that apply:

- Make one braise and you can make them all.
- Sauté one dish and you can sauté them all.
- Grill one fish and you can, to a degree (get it?), wing it and get it right.

DISTILLING TO THE FEWEST MOVING PIECES

Braising, as our first example, typically involves the following steps:

1. Brown the outside of the meat, then remove.
2. Sauté mirepoix (carrots, onions, celery) in the same pan.
3. Return meat to pan.
4. Add enough liquid to cover ⅓–⅔ of the meat.

Much like Toyota removed steps to make "lean manufacturing" a groundbreaking new standard in car production, we can eliminate steps one and two. If we choose our recipes well, we'll still end up with delicious results. This takes us from 7–10 discrete tasks (cutting prep, browning, moving ingredients between pans, etc.) to 1–4 tasks and reduces all of our "tripping points": time, cleaning, and overall beginner stress.

This simplification should at least double our *compliance rate*: the percentage of people who make this dish more than once.

Whenever I read a "simple" recipe, my first question is: can I use half the ingredients and half the steps and get something some people will not just love, but perhaps even *prefer*?

Sure. For one thing, you can afford better ingredients if you're buying fewer of them. Reduction, much like with sauces, can concentrate flavor. In comic book penciling, there's an expression, "When in doubt, black it out." Here, the same applies: when confused and overwhelmed, remove ingredients or steps.

The best method for you is the method you'll use more than once. The best method is the one you use many times because it's easy, the same method you'd recommend to friends to help them reduce stress.

You don't need more recipes. You need to learn to cook without them.

THE 100 MOST COMMON WORDS IN WRITTEN ENGLISH‡

Dr. Seuss (Theodor Seuss Geisel) wrote *The Cat in the Hat* using only 236 different words. Later, to win a bet with his editor, he wrote *Green Eggs and Ham* using just 50 words.

What can you do with the below 100?

1. the
2. be
3. to
4. of
5. and
6. a
7. in
8. that
9. have
10. I
11. it
12. for
13. not
14. on
15. with
16. he
17. as
18. you
19. do
20. at
21. this
22. but
23. his
24. by
25. from
26. they
27. we
28. say
29. her
30. she
31. or
32. an
33. will
34. my
35. one
36. all
37. would
38. there
39. their
40. what
41. so
42. up
43. out
44. if
45. about
46. who
47. get
48. which
49. go
50. me
51. when
52. make
53. can
54. like
55. time
56. no
57. just
58. him
59. know
60. take
61. people
62. into
63. year
64. your
65. good
66. some
67. could
68. them
69. see
70. other
71. than
72. then
73. now
74. look
75. only
76. come
77. its
78. over
79. think
80. also
81. back
82. after
83. use
84. two
85. how
86. our
87. work
88. first
89. well
90. way
91. even
92. new
93. want
94. because
95. any
96. these
97. give
98. day
99. most
100. us

DiSSS SEQUENCING: THE MAGIC OF PROPER ORDERING

"His first question when we sat down to lunch was, 'When you go to pee in a restaurant urinal, do you wash your hands before or after you pee?'

I was stunned. 'Afterwards, sir.'

He looked at me sourly. 'That's the wrong answer. You're a conventional thinker and not rational. I always wash before rather than after.'"

—BARTON BIGGS, INVESTOR, IN *HEDGEHOGGING*[24]

My first visit to the American Kickboxing Academy to train with Dave Camarillo was memorable.

Not because his technical abilities are amazing (which they are), and not because elite judoka fear him on the ground and top jujitsu players fear him on his feet (both true), but because his students were uniformly difficult to deal with.

Sure, you have the UFC champions like Cain Velasquez and soon-to-be champions, who travel to San Jose, California, from around the world to be engineered by the Camarillo machine and the magic touch of Javier Mendez.

But I found the lesser mortals even more impressive.

Blue belts, with far less experience than me, were throwing arm bars from angles I'd never seen and exhausting me from postures I couldn't break. At first, I assumed it was one or two standouts. No such luck. I began to spot patterns—first principles—that his disciples had wired into their DNA, like marines reassembling guns blindfolded. The positions were the same, pressure was applied in the same places, and each input was paired with its desired output. The 230-lb guys weren't brute forcing things like I expected—they were attempting to fine-tune in the same way that the 130-lb players had to. Something here was different.

His students were infuriatingly *reliable*.

In contrast, most world-famous black belts, often world-class athletes, teach a hodgepodge of random techniques. Daily classes are submissions du jour that leave students to assemble the puzzle themselves. Some succeed, but the vast majority fail. At the very least, students plateau for months or years at a time.

There is no system, no clear progression.

Dave had what other coaches didn't: **a logical sequence**.

THE (NEGLECTED) FINE ART OF SEQUENCING

Stan Utley, a short-game (think: putting) golf guru, explains the first distinction we'll make:

"*Form* refers to things like grip, stance, and balance. *Sequence* refers to the order the

24 Biggs is recounting his 1964 interview with the legendary hedge-fund manager Alfred Jones. Jones had, at that time, averaged 28% compounded annual returns for nearly a decade.

parts move in. A lot of times, people will think they have poor form, when in fact it's their sequencing that's off."‡

Nowhere is this truer than in a fluid movement like swimming. Despite having grown up five minutes from the beach, I could never swim more than two laps in a pool. This was a lifelong embarrassment until I turned 31, when two catalysts changed everything.

At the end of January 2008, a friend issued me a New Year's resolution challenge: he would go the rest of 2008 without coffee or stimulants if I trained and finished an open-water 1-km race that same year. That created **stakes,** which I'll explain in the next chapter.

Months after this handshake agreement, after many failed swimming lessons and on the cusp of conceding defeat, a former non-swimmer, Chris Sacca, introduced me to Total Immersion (TI). You might recall this as Shinji Takeuchi's preferred method. Total Immersion offered one thing no other method appeared to, just as Dave Camarillo differentiated himself: a well-designed progression.

Each exercise built upon the previous, and failure points like kickboards were completely avoided.

The first sessions might include kicking off a wall in 4 feet-deep water and practicing gliding in a streamlined position for 5–10 feet, at which point you simply stand up. Practicing breathing came much, much later; and learners of TI, by design, dodge that panic-inducing bullet when they most need to: in the beginning. The progression won't *allow* you to fail in the early stages. There is no stress.

The skills are layered, one at a time, until you can swim on autopilot.

In my first instructor-less workout, I cut my drag and water resistance at least 50%, swimming more laps than ever before. By the fourth workout, I had gone from 25+ strokes per 20-yard length to an average of 11 strokes per 20-yard length. In other words, I was covering more than twice the distance with the same number of strokes, expending less than half the effort.

For the first time in my life, I felt better after leaving the pool than before getting in. Unbelievable.

Within 10 days, I had gone from a two-length (18.39 m/2 x 20 yards) maximum to swimming more than 40 lengths per workout in sets of two and four.

Several months later, having never met a coach, I drove to my childhood beach after a cup of coffee and a light breakfast. I calmly walked into the ocean, well past my former fear-of-death distance, and effortlessly swam just over 1 mile—roughly 1.8 km—parallel to the shore. I only stopped because I'd passed my distance landmark, a beachfront house. There was no fatigue, no panic, no fear—nothing but the electricity of doing something I'd thought impossible.

I felt like Superman.

That's *exactly* how I want you to feel with any skill you tackle, including cooking.

HOTLINES AND MAYONNAISE: WHEN SIMPLE ISN'T SIMPLE

Let's learn a phone number. Start with this: 305-503-0846.

Now, try it again with 267-436-5128, but simultaneously pat your head and rub your stomach while a friend lists off random numbers.

Harder, right? This is an illustration of pushing *working memory*, which is taxed by tasks that "require the goal-oriented active monitoring . . . of information . . . in the face of interfering processes and distractions."‡ Think of it as your RAM. Too many applications at once and your computer freezes.

This is where mayonnaise, a cookbook staple, is relevant. It's perfectly slow-carb and I love the stuff, but it's problematic.

Cookbooks introduce mayo with good intentions: *Look how simple it is! You're making something you've always bought at the supermarket . . . just imagine the possibilities!* Now, if you rate difficulty based on number of ingredients, a chimpanzee could make mayo. Four ingredients: eggs, olive oil, lemon juice, and a bit of salt.

THE TI FREESTYLE STROKE

A

Notice how far below the water the lead hand is. Rather than pulling from the surface, Terry Laughlin, founder of Total Immersion, is focused on pushing his arm into fuselage left position.

B

A slight flick of the left leg, initiated here, is used only to rotate his hips. Otherwise, the legs are kept tight together so they can draft behind your upper body, much like a small car can draft behind a bus. There is no flutter kicking.

C

Notice the entry point of his hand, just in front of his head and angled down 45 degrees.

D

The left hand travels straight back under the body simultaneously, fingers slightly spread, and we reach. . . .

E

Fuselage right, where we glide as far as possible before repeating the steps, from the opposite side. This is how you go from converting only 3% of your energy into forward motion (the norm for human swimmers) to effortlessly gliding.

On paper, all is well. In practice, it goes more like the following. I've put my novice thoughts in brackets. The bolded instructions are taken from a real recipe:

Just add A, then a bit of B . . . but don't break the emulsion, whatever you do! [What is an "emulsion," and how do I avoid "breaking" it? But first of all, how on earth do I hold the bowl and whisk while pouring something at the same time?]

Be sure to secure your bowl, ideally a heavy pot, lined with a damp dish towel. [Lined? How and where?]

Add olive oil 1 drop at a time and continue . . . [How do I pour 1 drop at a time out of a spout . . . especially while reading the next step?] **adding roughly 1 c per 20 seconds.** [How do I time that?]

If it breaks, stop, do Y, then repeat steps L and M. Again, not too fast! [I hate you, cookbook. . . .]

If it's too thin, just add a splash [How much is a "splash"?] **of water and mix again.**

Footnote: If that doesn't achieve the desired consistency [And how do I know what that is?], **add some Dijon mustard** [What?! . . . wish I'd known that beforehand.]

Our dear mayonnaise, treated like the ABCs in the first pages of many wonderful books, overloads our circuits with variable pacing, performing multiple new skills ambidextrously and simultaneously, and much more. It's an interference hail storm.

And so we learn a lesson: it's the burden on working memory that makes something easy or hard.

No wonder so many people give up on cooking! You throw in the towel after asking: "Why bother trying if I can't even handle the basics, the ABCs?" The good news is that it's not your fault. You're being forced to do the CABs, and that makes no sense.

It's time to reorder things.

KINGS AND PAWNS: STARTING WITH THE ENDGAME FIRST

I first met Josh Waitzkin at a coffee shop in Manhattan. Having just read his second book, *The Art of Learning,* I was as giddy as a schoolgirl at the prospect of meeting him.

About 15 minutes into sipping coffee and getting acquainted, I was thrilled to realize that he dropped f-bombs as much as I did. He was no Rain Man, and I felt silly for half expecting him to be.

If you've seen the movie *Searching for Bobby Fischer,* then you know of Josh. Wandering through Washington Square Park with his mom at age six, he became fascinated with the "blitz chess" that the street hustlers played at warp speed. He watched and absorbed. Then he begged his mom to let him give it a shot. Just once! Soon thereafter, dressed in OshKosh overalls, he was king of the hustlers.

Labeled a prodigy (a term he dislikes[25]), Josh proceeded to dominate the world chess scene and become the only person to win the National Primary, Elementary, Junior High School, Senior High School, U.S. Cadet, and U.S. Junior Closed chess championships before the age of 16. He could easily play "simuls," in which 20–50 chessboards were set up with opponents in a large banquet hall, requiring him to walk from table to table playing all of the games simultaneously in his head.

Bruce Pandolfini, Josh's original chess teacher, started their first class by taking him in reverse. The board was empty, except for three pieces in an endgame scenario: king and pawn against king.

---

25 The term *prodigy* shouldn't apply to Josh because *prodigy* is used with a single modifier in front of it, as in "Josh is a chess prodigy." Josh defies pigeonholing. He tackled t'ai chi ch'uan after leaving the chess world behind. Thirteen Push Hands National Championships and two World Championship titles later, he decided to train in Brazilian jujitsu. Now, a few short years later, he's a black belt training with phenom Marcelo Garcia for—this should sound familiar—the World Championships. I have no doubt he'll win. If not in 2013, then in 2014. He is the meta-learner's meta-learner.

Through the *micro*, positions of reduced complexity, Josh was forced to learn the *macro*: principles. He learned the power of empty space, opposition, and setting an opponent up for *zugzwang* (a position where any move he makes will destroy his position). All from a near-empty board. By limiting himself to a few simple pieces, he mastered something limitless: high-level concepts he could apply anytime against anyone. Josh explains further:

"Most of my rivals, on the other hand, began by studying opening variations. At first thought, it seems logical for a novice to study positions that he or she will see all the time at the outset of games. Why not begin from the beginning, especially if it leads to instant success? The answer is quicksand. Once you start with openings, there is no way out. Lifetimes can be spent memorizing and keeping up with the evolving Encyclopedia of Chess Openings (ECO). They are an addiction, with perilous psychological effects.

"It is a little like developing the habit of stealing the test from your teacher's desk instead of learning how to do the math. You may pass the test, but you learn absolutely nothing—and, most critically, you don't gain an appreciation for the value or beauty of learning itself."‡

Always relying on recipes is a lot like stealing the test from your teacher's desk. But if tackling a new skill, how might you uncover the key techniques and order them?

ARGENTINE TANGO: A CASE STUDY

After living my life in 15-minute Outlook increments from 2000 to mid-2004, I decided to travel the world with no structure, no schedule, and no return date.

The only plan was to go where the wind took me. Juan Manuel, a Panamanian I'd befriended in January 2005, acted as a gust of wind that would change my life: "Argentina has the best wine in the world, the best steak, the most beautiful women, and you can live like a king for pennies on the dollar."

And that's how I ended up in Buenos Aires in February, taking a tango class to escape the oppressive heat.

Carolina, an assistant instructor, was my first tango partner and none too happy about it. She was 5'4", 23 years old, and dressed in what appeared to be—no exaggeration—a black latex catsuit. Imagine Catherine Zeta-Jones from *Entrapment*.[26]

Her opener was charming: "C'mon, I don't have all day. I have my own practice. Just grab me and let's get this over with."

Looking at other men and imitating as best I could, I tentatively placed one hand in hers and delicately wrapped my other forearm around her back.

Not good enough.

She spat out "Ugh!" as if I'd just taken a dump on the floor, and she threw her arms down in disgust. It knocked me off balance and almost forced my megahead to butt her like a ram. Hands placed on her hips, she *yelled* over the music as an announcement to the group:

"This guy's built like a goddamn mountain . . . and he's grabbing me like a fucking Frenchman!!!"

Everyone broke into hysterical laughter. This lasted several minutes. Carolina then turned around to face me, expressionless: "Let's go. I still have to help the others."

Humiliated and angry, my Spanish inadequate, I resorted to playground tactics: I crushed her. I had no master plan, besides squeezing her until her eyes popped out like a stress doll or she let out a little yelp. Instead, she looked up at me in slow motion. Her mouth broke into the first smile I'd seen: "Now that's . . . *much*, much better."

Thirty minutes later, I bought tickets for another 10 classes.

---

26 Catherine has played a lot of Latinas, but she's Welsh.

Roughly six months later, I set a Guinness World Record in tango and made the semifinals of the World Championships.

How?

First, I started off backward, much like Josh did with chess.

I looked at what some male pros did later in their careers: they learned the female role. I made it a point to do this at the beginning. Understanding the female "follow" first allowed me to subsequently learn an effective "lead" (*la marca*) much faster. It also forced me to focus on footwork—the equivalent of Josh's three pieces on the chessboard—through which I learned the macro principles: proper posture, foot position, weight shifting, etc. This seemingly reverse approach was actually common in the late 1800s, when men practicing with men was the norm.[27]

Second, I did an inventory, separating *implicit* from *explicit*.

As soon as I recruited Alicia Monti (later my teacher) to compete in the Buenos Aires World Tango Championships,[28] I began to collect and categorize tango video, much like George Carlin categorized his jokes and ideas. From Pepito Avellaneda to Miguel Angel Zotto, from black-and-white bootleg VHS to broadcast video of the World Championships, I went over tapes like a boxer researching the greats. What did the maestros have in common, and what did they rely on when the stakes were highest?

Next, I met the greats in person, since most of them taught in Buenos Aires. I invited them to coffee, or went to their classes, and asked all of my usual questions (see "Deconstruction"): what did they recommend I do or not do?

There was clearly *explicit expertise* (what they told me to do) and *implicit expertise* (what they did under pressure that they weren't aware of or couldn't verbalize).

Third, I identified what I could become good at quickly if I leveraged past experience.

Given my background in wrestling and breakdancing, were there facets of tango I could learn faster than other people?

In short, I looked for the answers to three questions:

1. What are commonalities among the best competitors?

2. Which of these aren't being actively taught (i.e., *implicit*) in most classes?

3. Which neglected skills (answers to #2) could I get good at abnormally quickly?

The sweet spots were the places where all the answers overlapped like the center of a Venn diagram. If you're competing against people with 20–30 years of experience, and if you have four months to train for the Buenos Aires Championships, followed by a short 6–8 weeks to train for the World Championships, you need to be surgically precise.

I ended up focusing on three skills, ordered by *margin of safety*:

1. Large, elegant steps.

2. Creative pivots, especially when moving in straight lines.

3. Variable speed—using fast and slow movements together—particularly in sequences assumed to be exclusively fast.

---

27 To see a fantastic contemporary example, check out Los Hermanos Macana, two brothers who perform together as a pair. Their brand of "power tango" is a violent spectacle.

28 Pure chance. We passed a flyer after post-training espressos and I asked her, "Want to give this a shot?" She was so amused, believing it to be a joke, that she said yes.

Gabriel Missé and Alejandra Mantiñan dance the tango.

Then Alicia helped me choose, after many auditions in paid classes, one world-class teacher who could teach all three together: the inimitable wunderkind Gabriel Missé.

Loved by old veterans and avant-garde dancers alike (unheard of in the divisive world of tango), Gabriel offered two additional advantages: he'd judged competitions before, and he led primarily with his forearm, not his chest. Men who lead with their chests, the standard, need to develop incredible strength in their toes to maintain a strong forward lean.

I didn't have time to develop a lot of attributes, so Gabriel was perfect: a pure technician.

The entire process worked, and a similar sequence can work for you, whether you're training for a job interview or Cirque du Soleil.

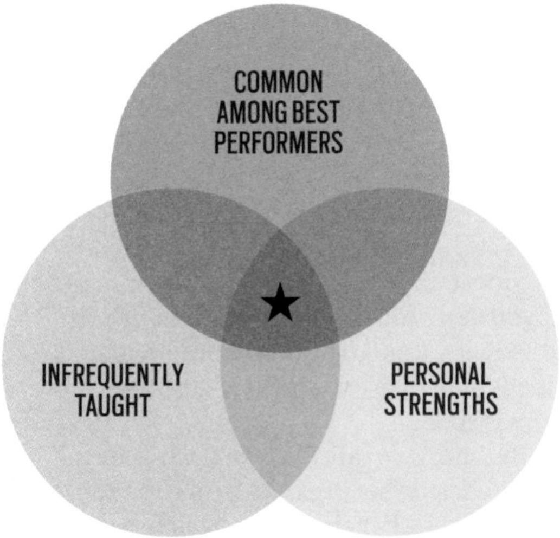
COMMON AMONG BEST PERFORMERS
INFREQUENTLY TAUGHT
PERSONAL STRENGTHS

The sweet spot.

DiSSS STAKES: THE CARROT AND THE STICKK

> "It's not because things are difficult that we dare not venture. It's because we dare not venture that they are difficult."
> —SENECA, ROMAN PHILOSOPHER

If you were to sum up the last 50 years of behavioral psychology in two words, it would be: "logic fails."

No matter how good a plan is, how thorough a book is, or how sincere our intentions, humans are horrible at self-discipline. No one is immune. The smartest, richest, and most dedicated people abandon commitments with disgusting regularity.

But what if you *truly* want to get something done? In this book, your goal will be cooking dinner twice a week. Is there a way to create an Odysseus Contract, so named because Odysseus had his sailors tie him to a mast to resist the temptation of the Sirens? Can you failure-proof your decision?

For hints, we can look at auction behavior.

BIDDING WARS, WINNING PERSONAL BETS

Answer me this: would you work harder to earn $100 or avoid losing $100? The smiley optimist says the former, but if research from the Center for Experimental Social Science at New York University is any indication, fear of loss is the home-run winner.

Experimental groups given $15 and then told the $15 would be rescinded if they lost a subsequent auction routinely overbid the most. Groups offered $15 if they won weren't nearly as "committed." Participating economist Eric Schotter explained the results:

> Economists typically attribute excessive bidding to risk aversion, or the joy of winning. What we found is that the actual cause of overbidding is a fear of losing, a completely new theory from past investigations.

Coming back to our cooking resolution, we can use technology to our advantage: stickK.

Dean Karlan, an economics professor at Yale, came up with the idea of opening an online "commitment store" in 2006. This evolved into stickK, which he cofounded based on the principle that creating incentives and assigning accountability are the two most important keys to achieving a goal. If you don't fulfill your commitment with stickK, it automatically tells your friends and opens you up to endless mockery. Peer pressure is good!

But that's not all. You can also set up an "anti-charity," an organization you so despise that you'd rather slam your head in a car door than donate to them. If you don't fulfill your commitment, your funds are wired automatically. Based on stickK's goal completion percentages from 2008–2011, we find that the success rate with no stakes is 33.5%. Once we add stakes like an anti-charity, that success rate more than doubles to 72.8%!

Ah, loss aversion. How I love thee.

The upshot: you gotta put your money (or reputation) where your mouth is. This works well beyond auctions. Everything from weight loss to quitting smoking is fair game.

A goal without real consequences is wishful thinking. Good follow-through doesn't depend on the right intentions. It depends on the right incentives.

Set up the stickK, and I'll provide the carrots.

HOW CAN YOU USE THIS?

In this book, we build in accountability with group dinners. If you'd like additional insurance, which I suggest, here's what to do:

1. Sign up for stickK or a similar service like egOnomics Lab, and introduce cash stakes before starting. "If I don't hit [goal], I'll mail a check" doesn't cut it. Your commitment is cooking just two meals per week!

2. Pick your "anti-charity." If you prefer the tried and true, the top-yielding anti-charities on stickK, in descending order, are:

    1. The George W. Bush Presidential Library and Museum
    2. Americans United for Life
    3. NRA Foundation
    4. Institute for Marriage and Public Policy
    5. NARAL Pro-Choice America Foundation

    I have no political association with any of the above. Them's just the facts, ma'am. Feel free to pick anything that gets your knickers in a twist.

3. Choose an amount that is painful to lose. If you're serious, at least 1% of your annual pretax income is a good starting point. This means:

    - $50,000 → wager $500 or more.
    - $75,000 → $750 or more.
    - $100,000 → $1,000 or more.
    - $1,000,000+ → send a check for at least $10,000, made out to "The Tim Ferriss Post-FMOF[29] Lifestyle Assurance Foundation," directly to: 123 Smith St., c/o Santa Claus, North Pole, Arctic Circle, FIN-96930. I'll hold on to those for safekeeping.

The good news: if you don't perform, most of the charitable donations are tax-deductible.

29 Fifteen Minutes Of Fame.

Ca F E COMPRESSION: CHEAT SHEETS FOR ANYTHING

"I am sorry for the length of my letter, but I had not the time to write a short one."

—BLAISE PASCAL, FRENCH MATHEMATICIAN, PHYSICIST, AND INVENTOR

"Thirty years ago my older brother, who was 10 years old at the time, was trying to get a report on birds written that he'd had three months to write. It was due the next day. We were out at our family cabin in Bolinas, and he was at the kitchen table close to tears, surrounded by binder paper and pencils and unopened books on birds, immobilized by the hugeness of the task ahead. Then my father sat down beside him, put his arm around my brother's shoulder, and said, 'Bird by bird, buddy. Just take it bird by bird.'"

—ANNE LAMOTT, *BIRD BY BIRD: SOME INSTRUCTIONS ON WRITING AND LIFE*

Any subject can be overwhelming.

Magazines have to fill editorial space month after month with "new" recommendations, the 24/7 news cycle of the web needs garbage to plug the voids, and the result is predictable: clashing recommendations, uncertainty, information deluge, and opting out.

To stem the tide, I have a constant checkpoint posted over the walkway into my atrium: Simplify.

Above the sign rests the beautiful and brutal Nepalese *khukuri*, a curved knife symbolic of the legendary Gurkha military regiments. Field marshal Sam Manekshaw, former chief of staff of the Indian Army, was quoted as saying: "If a man says he is not afraid of dying, he is either lying or is a Gurkha." Famous for withstanding hardship with laughter, for recognizing that perfect conditions are impossible, the Gurkha war cry was *"Jai Mahakali, Ayo Gorkhali!"* ("Glory be to the Goddess Kali [the Hindu goddess of power], here come the Gurkhas!")

The blade is in my home to remind me of the importance of *decision*. The word *decision*, closely related to *incision*, derives from the meaning "a cutting off."

Making effective decisions—and learning effectively—requires massive elimination and the removal of options.

SIMPLIFY

THE HOLY GRAIL OF THE ONE-PAGER

The easiest way to avoid being overwhelmed is to create positive constraints: put up walls that dramatically restrict whatever it is that you're trying to do.

In the world of work, a task will swell in complexity to fill *the time* you allot it, a phenomenon often referred to as Parkinson's Law. How does so much get done just before you leave for holidays? All the items lingering on your to-do list for weeks or months? It's the power of the clear and imminent deadline.

Though vastly simplified, in the world of cooking, Le Chatelier's Principle is invoked to remember that a gas will expand to fill the size of its container.

So . . . all we have to do is create a tiny container: the wonderful one-pager.

The goal here is to make something intimidating unintimidating, so you don't quit. You have the rest of your life to seek out and master the exceptions, to be comprehensive, if you want.

I use two different types of one-pagers:

1. The first is the **Prescriptive One-Pager,** which lists principles that help you generate real-world examples. In short: "Here are the rules."[30]

2. The second is the **Practice One-Pager,** which lists real-world examples to practice that indirectly teach the principles.[31]

Both of these are tremendously valuable, and we'll look at each in turn.

First, let's create a prescriptive one-pager for almost all of the recipes in this book. Ready?

Just turn the page.

30 This is known as a *deductive* approach to teaching. I explain the rules of grammar, and you create the sentences, for example. Think of "dead" grammar, presented out of context, to remember *deductive*.

31 This is known as an *inductive* approach to teaching. I give you the real-world examples (sample sentences), and you pick up the principles (grammar) by spotting patterns.

GEORGE GERMON ON THE POWER OF SIMPLICITY

George Germon (co-owner of the famed Al Forno restaurant) recounts an experience that he says he'll never forget.

"I was visiting some people in England who had a four- or five-year-old daughter. They weren't around, but I was in the kitchen and the little girl pulled a chair over to the stove and started heating up a pan, saying she was going to make tomato soup," he remembers.

After getting the little girl's assurance that her parents allowed her to do so, Germon says he watched her heat some butter in the pan, then take out a knife and cutting board and chop some tomatoes. She cooked the tomatoes in the butter for about 3 minutes, and then added a little salt and a little cream. "Would you like some?" she asked Germon, who politely replied, "Sure!" Once he tasted it, Germon says he was absolutely floored. "It was unbelievable," he says. "I couldn't believe that something tasted as good as it did with so few ingredients."

Al Forno's menu features a potato soup that's equally simple. "It has just four ingredients: potatoes, onions, butter, and water. That's it," says Germon. "And when our cooks first made it, they kept asking, 'What's the next step?'" Johanne Killeen remembers, "They found it impossible to believe that anything wonderful could result from four ingredients!"

PRESCRIPTIVE ONE-PAGER FOR COOKING

Just follow these rules:

PROBE IT

Use a probe thermometer for just about everything. You'll never need to guess if something is done or not again. Whether the perfect cup of coffee or the best steak you've ever had, this is your key to the kingdom. (page 186)

350

Set the oven at 350°F (180°C). But what about roast chicken, squash, or brownies? Doesn't matter. Setting the oven at 350 will work more than 90% of the time. Just use the probe thermometer and cook all proteins (steak, chicken, etc.) until the internal temperature reaches 140°F (60°C), and yank 'em when the alarm goes off.

TOP IT OFF

For entertainment or conversational value, offer one of the following as a topping at the table:

- Edible green tea leaves (eatgreentea.com)
- Lemon or "Buddha's hand" zest (using Microplane)
- Crickets, roasted and placed in a pepper grinder; they taste nutty. (page 306)

HERB PAIRINGS

For each type of protein, there is a spice or herb that will never fail you. (Don't forget to add Maldon sea salt.)

- Fish → fennel or dill
- Beef → rosemary
- Pork or lamb → rosemary
- Lamb → mint
- Eggs → tarragon (tarragon goes with little else, but it's miraculous on eggs)
- Non-protein bonus: tomatoes → basil

GO COLD

If you need an appetizer for a group and want to minimize stress, always go cold: make gazpacho in advance (takes 10 minutes) and leave in the fridge until ready. (page 208)

ADD INSURANCE

Add one or more of the following to make anything delicious:

- Montreal steak rub
- Prosciutto—it's already cooked, unlike bacon
- Guacamole
- Ghee
- Thyme

JUST STEAM IT

Just steam vegetables: Put ½" of water in a pot, throw in the veggies, cover, and leave for 15 minutes on a burner set to high. Squeeze lemon juice on them just before serving. Note: Almost all vegetables are done when you can slide a fork, held between thumb and index finger, into them easily.

MAKE IT PRETTY

To make your served food look pretty and "restaurant-made":

- Sprinkle sliced almonds (they should look like flakes, not chippings), *pepitas* (pumpkin seeds), or chopped chives on top. Beeea-utiful.
- Stack things atop or against each other on the plate: make the food look tall. You can cheat by cutting a paper coffee cup in half around the equator and using the top half as a cylinder: put food in, press down slightly, then remove the coffee cup.
- Buy or make pesto (page 212) and follow photos on the opposite page before "plating" your food (putting cooked food on the plate).

AND . . . THAT'S IT

You'll make awesome stuff, and nothing should be overcooked or undercooked. Congrats! You are now cooking better than at least 50% of the people in the entire U.S.!

If you ever feel overwhelmed while reading this book, just return here.

CUT HERE

PRACTICE ONE-PAGER FOR KNIFE SKILLS

When you are an autodidact—learning a subject solo—practice one-pagers are wonderful for self-testing and keeping motivated.

Knife skills are a major failure point for aspiring cooks. Blades are scary, and most how-to guides make using a knife seem like cardiac surgery. I have an entire shelf of books dedicated to cutting techniques, from mincing to julienning (oh, and the French again!). It's enough to make anyone throw in the towel.

Instead, I'll point you to a single recipe that takes 10 minutes to cook, such as Moules Marinière on page 324. Take a peek at it. As you flatten the book out, I put an arm around your shoulder and say, "See this? *This* is your goal for knife skills. Once you can make this one recipe, you're set for millions of recipes! In fact, unless you want to get really fancy, you won't need additional knife skills for the rest of your life!"

Cool, right? Reassuring and confidence building? Absolutely. It's a clear target, achievable and easily flipped to when things seem complicated. Having that finite brass ring in mind is why you'll succeed where 99 out of 100 fail. You are not flailing through a rain forest of information with a machete; you are a sniper with a single bull's-eye in the crosshairs: mussels.

But, as Mr. Miyagi would say, "Afta, afta. . . ." We'll get you there in due time.

Just remember ABC—Always Be Compressing. It's the key to low-stress, high-speed learning.

BONUS: HOW TO MAKE A PRETTY PLATE

Plop a circular dollop on the side of a plate.

Use the back of the spoon to smear the pesto across in one motion and one line. It should look something like a comet.

Put your food on top of, or on either side of, the comet. Serve.

RELEVANT: THE SLOW-CARB DIET ONE-PAGER

THE SLOW-CARB DIET HAS HUNDREDS OF THOUSANDS OF FOLLOWERS WORLDWIDE

The 4-Hour Body, which debuted at #1 on the *New York Times* Best Sellers List, launched it into the mainstream. Almost all of the restaurants I visited for this book had at least one chef on the SCD, and devotees include everyone from A-list actors to Super Bowl NFL players. Even the staff of the hit show *Intervention* has used it to lose hundreds of collective pounds.

If you follow the SCD for the next month, it's not unreasonable to expect to lose 10–20 lbs of fat. This is true even without exercise. As one follower put it, "You lose ounces in the gym, but you lose pounds in the kitchen."

To give you a nudge, nearly all of the recipes in this book are 100% slow-carb compliant. Besides cheat day delights, of course (see Rule #5).

THE FIVE RULES OF THE SLOW-CARB DIET

RULE #1

Avoid "white" starchy carbohydrates (or those that can be white). This means no bread, pasta, rice, potatoes, or grains.

RULE #2

Eat the same few meals over and over again, especially for breakfast and lunch. You already do this; you're just picking new default meals.

RULE #3

Don't drink calories. Exception: 1–2 glasses of dry red wine per night is allowed.

RULE #4

Don't eat fruit. Generally speaking: Fructose → glycerol phosphate → more body fat. Five hundred years ago, your ancestors probably didn't eat oranges in December. Get vitamin C from your veggies.

RULE #5

Take one day off per week and go nuts. I recommend Saturday, often nicknamed "Faturday" by followers.

THE MEALS

Build each of your meals from the list below, picking one item from each of the three groups. I've underlined the choices that produce the fastest fat loss for me:

PROTEINS

<u>Eggs</u>

<u>Chicken</u> (breast or thigh)

<u>Fish</u>

Beef (preferably grass-fed)

Pork

Lamb

LEGUMES

<u>Lentils</u>

Black beans

Pinto beans

Red beans

Soybeans

VEGETABLES

<u>Spinach</u>

<u>Mixed vegetables</u> (including broccoli, cauliflower, or any other cruciferous vegetables)

Sauerkraut, kimchi (I typically eat a few forkfuls first thing in the morning before cooking my eggs.)

Asparagus

Peas

Broccoli

Green beans

CUT HERE

CUT HERE

KEEP IT SIMPLE

Eat as much as you like. There is **no** calorie counting whatsoever on the SCD. And **keep it simple:** pick three or four meals and repeat them for at least the first two weeks. Here are a few of my recurring meals:

BREAKFAST (HOME)

Three scrambled whole eggs, lentils, and spinach (microwaved or steamed).

LUNCH (MEXICAN RESTAURANT)

Grass-fed organic beef, pinto beans, mixed vegetables, and extra guacamole.

DINNER (HOME)

Salmon (from Trader Joe's), asparagus (or lentils), and Coconut Cauliflower Curry Mash (page 154).

TIPS AND TRICKS

Still having trouble? The below will fix at least 75% of all starting and stalling problems:

Try the "30 in 30" rule.
Eat 30 g of protein within 30 minutes of waking up. Recall that my dad was prone to skipping breakfast. Once he implemented "30 in 30," his monthly fat loss more than tripled, from 5.5 lbs/month to 18.75 lbs/month(!). For fat loss, my favorite breakfast is whole eggs, spinach, and lentils. If you're in a rush, unflavored whey protein (which I mix with Athletic Greens) or a less-than-ideal Myoplex (which my dad used) will still do the trick.

Eat more protein.
Get *at least* 20 g of protein per meal. This is most critical at breakfast.

Drink more water.
If your liver is burdened with dehydration, it won't metabolize body fat well. Down more agua and/or unsweetened iced tea.

If you have to ask, don't eat it.
"But, but . . . can I eat plantains?" No. "But, but . . . what about Ezekiel bread or steel-cut oats?" Nope. Stop stalling. If you eat the way that made you fat, you will remain fat—period. Don't use incomplete information as an excuse for inaction.

EXTRA CREDIT

For detailed fine-tuning (ideal meal spacing, managing diet soft drinks, etc.) related to the SCD, refer to *The 4-Hour Body*, which covers it all.

To read case studies of individuals who've lost 150+ lbs, see fourhourchef.com/100.

The 4HBTalk forum at 4hbtalk.com is also active and helpful. Join the discussion and share your experiences.

And when you lose more than a few clothing sizes, just remember to put on a bit of Gotu Kola cream to minimize stretch marks, as Olympic strength coach Charles Poliquin recommends.

RICARDO

Before: 410 lbs. After: 246 lbs.

MARIE-PIER

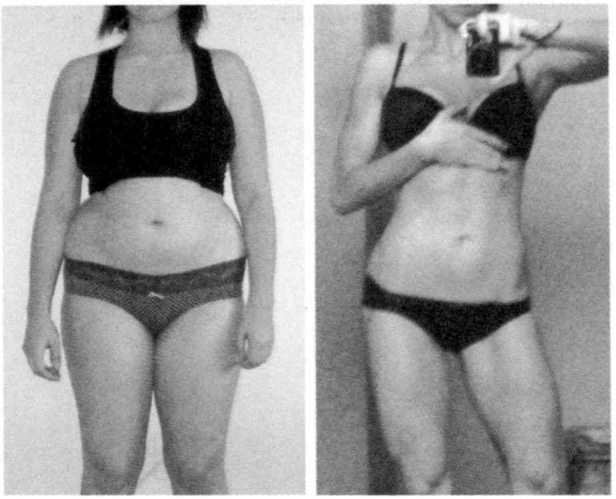

Before: 34% body fat. After: <20% body fat.

MARIA

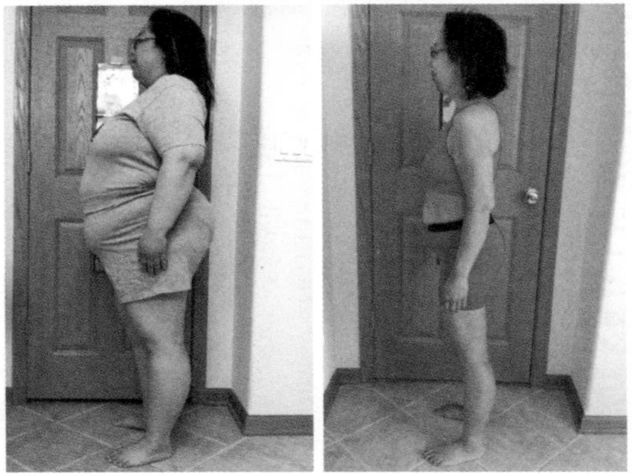

Before: Size 24+. After: Size 4 petite (125+ lbs lost).

24 SKILLS YOU CAN ACQUIRE IN 48 HOURS

"Acquire" in this context means learning the fundamentals and having fun doing so.

Think video is best for physical skills, anything involving motion? Maybe. But there are cases where the static word forces the teacher to *think* about logical progression more than a casual YouTuber.

For you to compare different media and your own learning style, the 24 skills are broken down into:

- One book (a must-read, even if you have no interest in the subject matter).
- Eight videos.
- Four step-by-step lessons from Instructables (text and pictures).
- Eleven multimedia lessons from me (all across the board).

Enjoy.

ONE BOOK—GOLF SWING

1) *Ben Hogan's Five Lessons: The Modern Fundamentals of Golf* by Ben Hogan
fourhourchef.com/ben-hogan

The most perfect how-to book I've ever read, and I don't play golf! I still reread this short 128-page book at least once a year to refine my teaching. It was a godsend when I injured my Achilles tendon years ago and ended up immobilized at a driving range. This is how I aspire to teach.

EIGHT VIDEOS

In each video, consider: What makes its approach helpful or confusing? How is the sequencing helpful, and what is omitted that shouldn't be? When do words (spoken or written) help or hurt?

2) How to Fold a T-Shirt in Two Seconds
fourhourchef.com/fold-shirt

3) How to Juggle Three Balls
(Note the isolation and sequencing)
fourhourchef.com/juggle

4) How to Make a Rose Out of a Napkin
(This is pure gold on dates. Wait for your companion to head to the bathroom and present this upon his or her return.)
fourhourchef.com/napkin-folding

5) How to Throw a Knife (or Fork, or Anything Sharp)
fourhourchef.com/knife-throwing
(Just to get you interested)
fourhourchef.com/knife-throwing2
(Technical breakdown)

6) How to Fold a Fitted Sheet and Impress Your Mom
fourhourchef.com/fitted-sheet

7) How to Learn the First 100 Signs in American Sign Language (ASL)
fourhourchef.com/sign-language
(Random: did you know that people learn foreign vocabulary faster when they are simultaneously learning sign language?)

8) How to Do the *Bloodsport*/Kung Fu Coin Grab
fourhourchef.com/coin-grab

9) How to Perform the Poco Card Sequence
fourhourchef.com/card-sequence

FOUR STEP-BY-STEP INSTRUCTABLES

10) How to Make DIY Shot Glasses Out of Ice (Blue!)
fourhourchef.com/shot-glasses

11) How to Peel a Banana Like a Monkey
fourhourchef.com/banana

12) How to Create a Vegan "Egg"
(A foreshadowing of SCI, inspired by Wylie Dufresne)
fourhourchef.com/vegan-egg

13) How to Make a Cardboard Moose-Head Wall Hanging (A foreshadowing of WILD)
fourhourchef.com/moose-head

ELEVEN FROM ME

14) How to Read 300% Faster in 20 Minutes
fourhourchef.com/speed-read

15) How to Tie the Perfect Tie Every Time
fourhourchef.com/tie

16) Basics of Pen Tricks, à la Japanese High-Schooler
fourhourchef.com/pen-tricks

17) How to Perform the Kettlebell Swing—One Move for Maximum Fat Loss
fourhourchef.com/kettlebell-swing

18) How to Travel the World with 10 lbs or Less
fourhourchef.com/travel-light

19) How to Hack Your Sleep in Five Steps
fourhourchef.com/sleep-hack

20) Public Speaking—How I Prepare Every Time
fourhourchef.com/public-speaking

21) Prepping for Warren Buffett—The Art of the Elevator Pitch
fourhourchef.com/elevator-pitch

22) How to Ski Powder—15 Tips for Learning in 24 Hours
fourhourchef.com/ski-powder

23) How to Design a Million-Dollar Business in a Weekend (Really)
fourhourchef.com/business

24) How to Create a Global Phenomenon for Less Than $10,000
fourhourchef.com/global

Ca F E FREQUENCY: CRAMMING SIX MONTHS OF CULINARY SCHOOL INTO 48 HOURS

"Tell me and I'll forget; show me and I may remember; involve me and I'll understand."

—CHINESE PROVERB

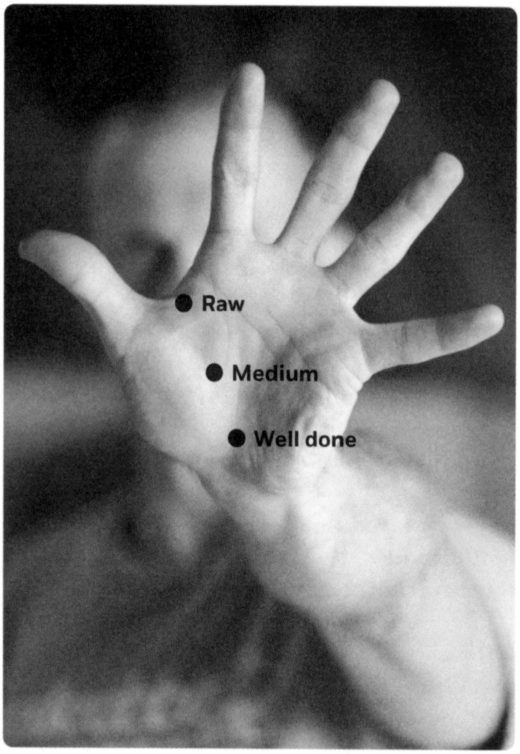
Raw
Medium
Well done

The points on the hand that, when poked, correspond to different levels of doneness.

"At FCI,[32] we always said 'raw,' 'medium,' and 'well done.'" JZ smiled: "A rule of thumb."

Holding a Peltex fish spatula in one hand, he used its handle to illustrate on his other hand.

As he did this, he watched consommé on the stove. I was prepping salsa verde. The next task for me was juicing a few lemons, and JZ looked over his shoulder: "Make sure you roll them out by hand first. You'll get twice as much juice." Sure enough, he was right. We were also using sherry vinegar instead of balsamic vinegar, which he recommends to all of his noncook friends for general use: "Most vinegar sold as 'balsamic' isn't even 'balsamic.' It's sweet, fake BS." Genuine balsamic vinegar is aged for decades in a succession of barrels, each made of a different wood. The real McCoy is sold for as much as equally aged Scotch and in containers not much bigger than a perfume bottle.

JZ—better known as Jeffrey Zurofsky[33]—worked in the kitchens of Chapel Hill, North Carolina, through college, after which he moved to Manhattan to study at the French Culinary Institute. He then honed his craft in some of the most prestigious kitchens in the U.S., including Lespinasse and Union Square Cafe. Now, as partner and cofounder of 'wichcraft, he wears nearly all hats for 16 restaurants and counting.

32 The International Culinary Center, formerly known as the French Culinary Institute.

33 Also the serial restaurateur "Z" from the Introduction.

In the week prior to our current meeting, he'd checked off 60+ hours of air travel, six beds, three airlines, two continents, and one president of a country (Chile, where he was invited to discuss entrepreneurship). As you'd expect of someone this driven, he's methodical: to teach employees to eyeball 2 oz of sweet potato puree, he modeled the training after Toyota manufacturing, having each person measure the exact amount 10 times with electronic scales in between estimates.

On top of this, he'd used the Slow-Carb Diet to transform his blood work and lose close to 20 lbs of fat:

MAY 2011—BEFORE	
TOTAL CHOLESTEROL	234
TRIGLYCERIDES	215
HDL	52
LDL	139

JANUARY 2012—AFTER	
TOTAL CHOLESTEROL	180
TRIGLYCERIDES	135
HDL	63
LDL	90

For all of these reasons, he was the perfect architect for my latest experiment: attempting to compress six months of culinary school into 48 hours.

Here's how our rough schedule looked:

FRIDAY NIGHT

7 p.m.: Meet JZ in San Francisco, head to 'wichcraft's downtown location on Mission Street to pick up the many, many fish tubs (imagine gigantic Tupperware) full of food we would need for our avalanche of activity.
8 p.m.: Unpack it all, and practically drop-kick the supplies into my inadequate civilian refrigerator.

SATURDAY

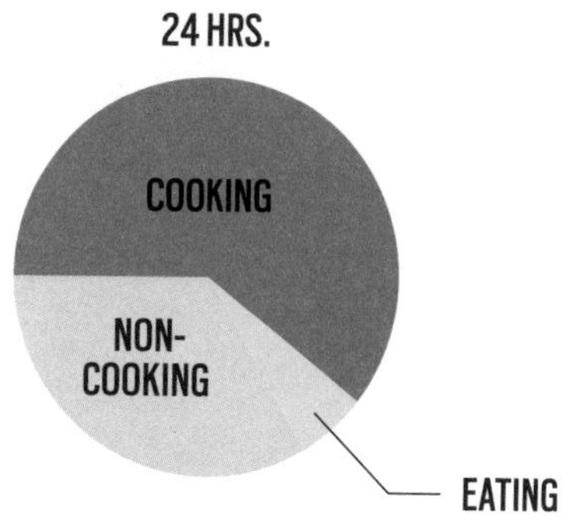
24 HRS.
COOKING
NON-COOKING
EATING

8:30 a.m.–12:30 a.m.: Sixteen hours of cooking and eating (90/10 split), with a six-person dinner party hosted at 8 p.m. On each day, we aimed to cook four courses for each of three meals. My personal goal was to internalize the principles, not the recipes.

SUNDAY

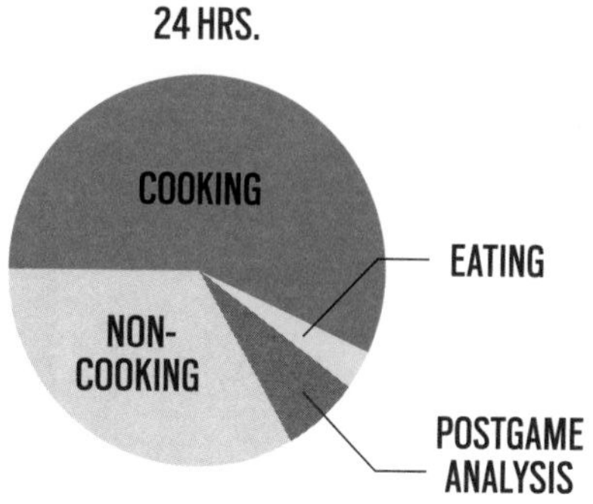
24 HRS.
COOKING
EATING
NON-COOKING
POSTGAME ANALYSIS

10 a.m.–2 a.m.: Sixteen hours of cooking, eating, and postgame analysis (85/5/10), with another six-person dinner party hosted at 8 p.m.

By Sunday morning, both JZ and I had Frankenstein hands. From grabbing salt and washing our hands every 5–10 minutes, they were swollen to 150% of their normal size. Looking at my puffy mitts, wiped endlessly with blue chef's towels, I could vaguely see my heart beating. It was *Looney Toons* meets Emeril Lagasse. From wrist to fingertip, we were covered with dozens of visible and invisible nicks.

We couldn't have been happier.

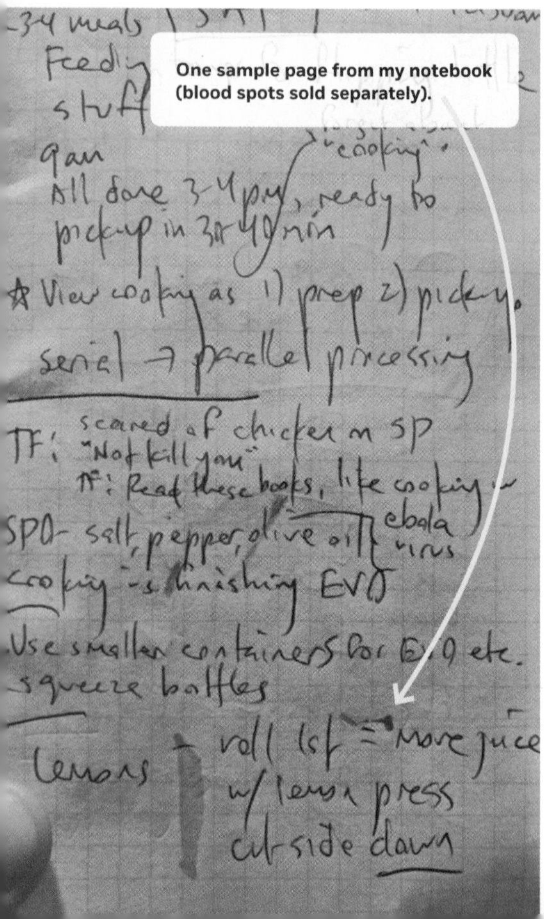
3-4 meals
Feeding
stuff
9am
All done 3-4pm, ready to
pickup in 30-40 min
"cooking"
View cooking as 1) prep 2) pickup.
serial → parallel processing
TF: scared of chicken in SP
"Not kill you"
TF: Read these books, like cooking
ebola
virus
SPO - salt, pepper, olive oil
cooking - finishing EVO
Use smaller containers for EVO etc.
squeeze bottles
roll 1st = more juice
lemons
w/ lemon press
cut side down
One sample page from my notebook (blood spots sold separately).

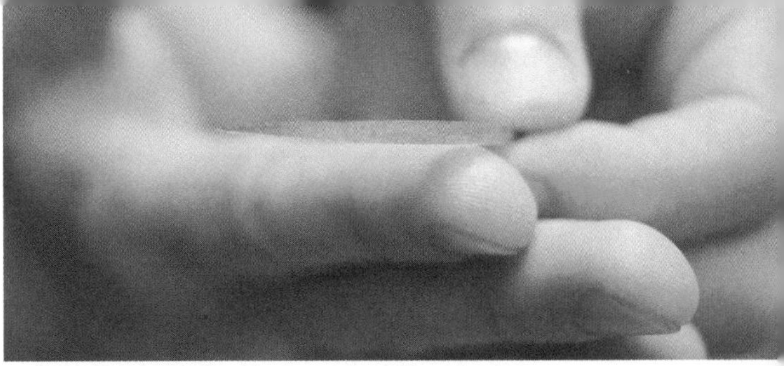

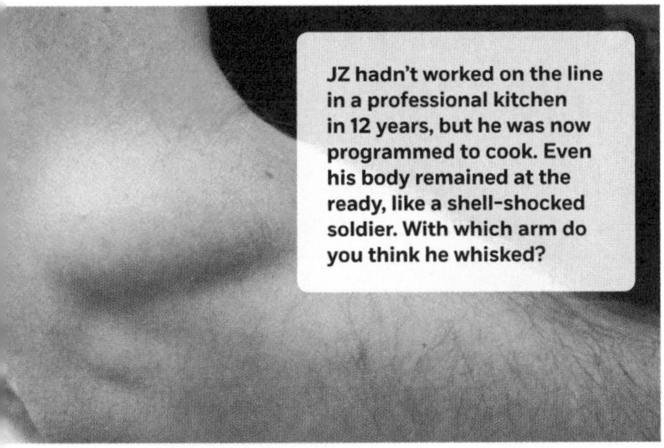

JZ hadn't worked on the line in a professional kitchen in 12 years, but he was now programmed to cook. Even his body remained at the ready, like a shell-shocked soldier. With which arm do you think he whisked?

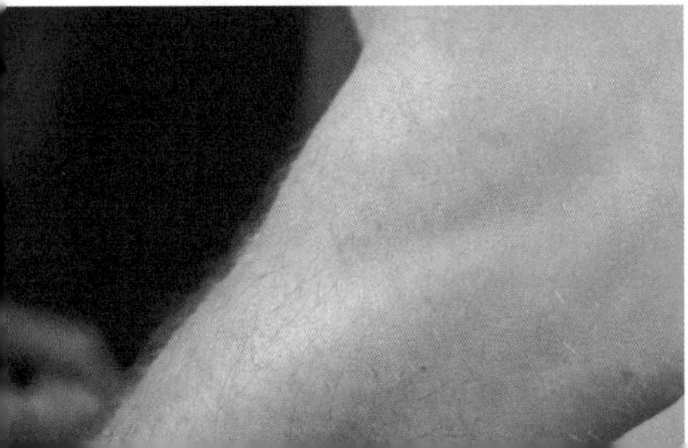

LITTLE DETAILS, BIG RESULTS

How you do *anything* is how you will do *everything*. John Wooden, legendary UCLA basketball coach, had his players learn how to put their socks on—step-by-step—during their first all-team meeting of the season. As surgeon Atul Gawande explained in *The New Yorker*:

"He had two purposes in doing this. First, wrinkles cause blisters. Blisters cost games. Second, he wanted his players to learn how crucial seemingly trivial details could be. 'Details create success' was the creed of a coach who won 10 NCAA men's basketball championships."[‡]

Below are some of the details acquired over my cramming weekend with JZ. This list alone made the trial well worth it.

These are included to give you a taste of things to come, so don't struggle to memorize them. The most important ones will be woven throughout this book in hands-on lessons. As JZ's wife likes to say: "Practice makes permanent."

Micro-

- The reason to use cold water instead of hot water for cooking at home is not because things boil faster or slower. Hot water runs through a hot water heater, which can taint the taste.

- For a makeshift spatula, and delicious infused taste, put a clove of garlic on the end of a fork. This is perfect for moving around anything you're sautéing, like spinach. JZ picked this up courtesy of chef Dan Kluger on his first day at Union Square Cafe.

- Salt beans after cooking. If you salt them during cooking, they take longer to cook.

- When adding dressing to salad, drizzle it around the outside of the bowl, not on the leaves, then hand-mix. This prevents the bulk of the dressing from getting stuck on a few leaves.

- If you need to truss (tie up) a chicken so it cooks evenly, but you realize you're out of kitchen twine, you can poke holes in the rearmost fat and stick the legs through the holes so they're crossed, then fold the wings underneath.

- When ladling, remember two points. First, "double dip, no drip." To avoid dripping everywhere, ladle up whatever you need, then tap the very bottom of the ladle onto the surface to remove any excess liquid or sauce. Second, always tip the ladle toward you to pour.

- Have pesky bubbles or film on top of your consommé (filtered stock)? Just drag a folded paper towel across the top to clean it up.

- When frying in oil, always place a food's closest edge down first, so you don't *Phantom of the Opera* yourself. JZ taught me this technique when it technically didn't matter, which is a point that matters: "This won't hurt you, but you need to build the right habits."

Macro-

- Setting up your *mise en place* (or *meez*) is #1: everything must be ready and in its place before you start.

- Good cooking, especially French cooking, is about economy of movement. Keep your elbows close to your sides. If you move your elbows away from your sides or up toward shoulder height, you'll need to move your feet. If you move your feet, you'll make mistakes. The same principle is taught to surgeons and even wrestlers.

- If you're doing a lot of cooking, put staples like olive oil and salt in smaller containers for ease of use. We used plastic Chinese takeout soup containers, which also conveniently doubled as measuring cups for 2-cup and 4-cup portions.

- **CRITICAL:** Forget about "cooking" as one activity. Think of it henceforth as 1) prep and 2) pickup. In our case, we aimed to have everything cooked, or within 10% of cooked, by 3–4 p.m, before our 8 p.m. dinner. This would allow us to put in 30 minutes of "pickup" later to serve four courses in perfect condition—no racing or nervous breakdowns required. For example, we would cook our pork roast in the afternoon to an internal temperature of 125°F, say, if our just-before-dinner goal was 135°F. Then we'd throw it in a 400°F oven when we'd sit down to eat appetizers with our guests. Five to 10 minutes later, it's done. No stress, no mess.

- Chefs use kitchen towels for everything, and so should you. I suggest you have one for drying hands (damp) and another for handling hot metal (dry). Don't use the wet one for grabbing anything hot; if you do, you'll Chinese dumpling (steam cook) your palm.

- Good chefs always keep their dry towel well folded in their apron waist string, so that it's automatically folded over when they grab it. Amateurs tend to haphazardly tuck towels, which inevitably leads to grabbing something that's 400°F with a single layer of cloth, which, you guessed it, doesn't feel good.

- Grab all pan handles from underneath for more control, never from the top.

- The magic number for stove-top frying is 350°F. You can use less than that to make things soggy and more than that for a fast fry (crisping the outside). For cooking perfect French fries, we used both in succession: lower to cook, then higher to crisp.

- Nothing wet goes on your cutting boards. Use a paper towel to dry off fish, chicken, etc. Moist objects slide, and we don't want to chop off those pretty little fingers.

- Always sear the "presentation" side (the side that will be faceup for diners) first, as the second side you cook is most likely to stick.

- For almost any protein cooked on a stovetop at medium or higher heat, about four minutes per inch will get you to done. So, if it's 1" thick, cook two minutes on each side. If it's 1½" thick, three minutes on each side, and so on. This rule applies up to about 2" thickness.

CULINARY CRAM SCHOOL—THE BLUEPRINT

We'll work on the most central techniques throughout this book, but if you want to replicate our madness, here's the blueprint. Find a chef coach to lead the way.

INVENTORY/INGREDIENTS

QTY	UNIT	DESCRIPTION
2	NA	3–5-lb (1.4–1.8-kg) whole chickens
1	NA	Bone-in pork loin
2	lb	Flatiron steak
1	NA	Whole striped bass
2	lb	Haricots verts
2	lb	Turnips
5	lb	Russet potatoes
2	lb	Veal for stew
5	lb	Veal bones
1	head	Cauliflower
7	lb	Leeks
5	lb	White onions
1	lb	Garlic
2	lb	Zucchini
3	lb	Carrots
2	bunch	Basil
1	flat	Eggs
1	qt	Red wine vinegar

CULINARY CRAM SCHOOL—LESSON PLAN

NUMBER	TECHNIQUE	DESCRIPTION	DISH
1	Butchery	Chicken, trussed[34]	Roast chicken
2	Butchery	Chicken, quartered	Lemon-olive chicken
3	Butchery	Pork roast	Pork roast
4	Butchery	Whole fish	Various
5	Cooking	Blanching	Tuna Niçoise (haricots verts)
6	Cooking	Étuve	Turnips
7	Cooking	Fried potato	French fries
8	Cooking	Concentration, roast chicken	Roast chicken
9	Cooking	Concentration, pork roast	Pork roast
10	Cooking	Mixte, braised chicken	Lemon-olive chicken
11	Cooking	Consommé	Consommé
12	Cooking	Pureed soup	Cauliflower soup
13	Cooking	Searing, fish	Tuna Niçoise
14	Cooking	Grilling, fish	Composed plate
15	Cooking	Poaching, fish	Composed plate
16	Cooking	Steaming, fish	Composed plate
17	Cutting	Peeling with paring knife	Various
18	Cutting	Dice onion	Various
19	Cutting	Slice garlic	Various

2	lb	Arugula
10	NA	Lemons
2	bunch	Thyme
1	bunch	Rosemary
1	can	Olive oil
1	qt	Whole milk
½	lb	Flour
½	lb	Shallots
2	lb	Butter

20	Cutting	Mince garlic	Various
21	Cutting	Jardiniere	Zucchini sauté
22	Cutting	Julienne	Pickled vegetables
23	Cutting	Macédoine	Various
24	Cutting	Brunoise	Various
25	Cutting	Chiffonade	Various
26	Egg Cookery	Poached	Eggs Zurofsky
27	Egg Cookery	Soft-boiled	Tuna Niçoise
28	Egg Cookery	En cocotte	Eggs en cocotte
29	Egg Cookery	Rolled omelet	Omelet
30	Egg Cookery	Scrambled	Scrambled
31	Garde Manger	Basic vinaigrette	Various
32	Garde Manger	Dijon vinaigrette	Tuna Niçoise
33	Garde Manger	Simple salad	Simple salad
34	Garde Manger	Mixed salad	Mixed salad
35	Garde Manger	Composed salad	Tuna Niçoise
36	Sauce Making	Chicken stock	Various
37	Sauce Making	Velouté	Poached fish
38	Sauce Making	Veal stock	Various
39	Sauce Making	Bordelaise	Various
40	Sauce Making	Fish fumét	Various
41	Sauce Making	Hollandaise	Eggs Zurofsky
42	Sauce Making	Mayonnaise	Various
43	Sauce Making	Beurre blanc or rouge	Various

34 Trussing, while not technically butchering, is a technique performed by most butchers in restaurants.

LONGER-TERM LEARNING SUGGESTIONS

Y Combinator, quietly tucked away off highway 101 just miles from Google headquarters, is named after one of the coolest ideas in computer science: a program that runs programs.

Cofounded in 2005 by Paul Graham, Robert Morris, Trevor Blackwell, and Jessica Livingston, YC offers small amounts of capital ($14,000–$20,000) to founders in exchange for, on average, 6% of each company. Thousands of applications flow in for dozens of spots in each "class," leading to an acceptance rate of 2.5–3.5%. The chosen few move to Silicon Valley, refine their companies 24/7 for three months, and then pitch investors at Demo Day. This is where you might find Ashton Kutcher sitting next to a partner from the blue-chip venture capital firm Sequoia.

In name, YC is an early-stage or seed-stage investment fund. In reality, it has built something more like a SEAL Team 6 meets Harvard[35] of start-up cram schools. The system works: YC-backed start-ups have an average valuation of $22.4 million. Some get to the billions within a few years of graduation: DropBox and Airbnb, for instance. Others sell for hundreds of millions, like Heroku ($212 million in cash). Brian Chesky, cofounder of Airbnb, says of Paul Graham, the godfather of YC: "Just as [legendary music producer, John] Hammond found Bob Dylan when he was a bad singer no one knew, Graham can spot potential."

If Graham can spot potential, the question I had was: how does he do it?

The answer: YC has funded more than 450 start-ups since 2005. They have a far better sample size than most venture capitalists.

I vividly remember my first visit to Y Combinator Demo Day. The only photograph I took was of a graph labeled "The Process" on a whiteboard, reflective of a good data set (below, at left).

For many reasons, it fascinated and amused me. First and foremost, I'd sketched out an eerily similar graph for language learning in 2005 (below, at right).

This sketch, covering roughly eight months, represented my Japanese learning curve from 1992. Why did I draw it in 2005? Because in 2005, I noticed the same ups, downs, and plateaus, in the same exact order, for my German over three months in Berlin!

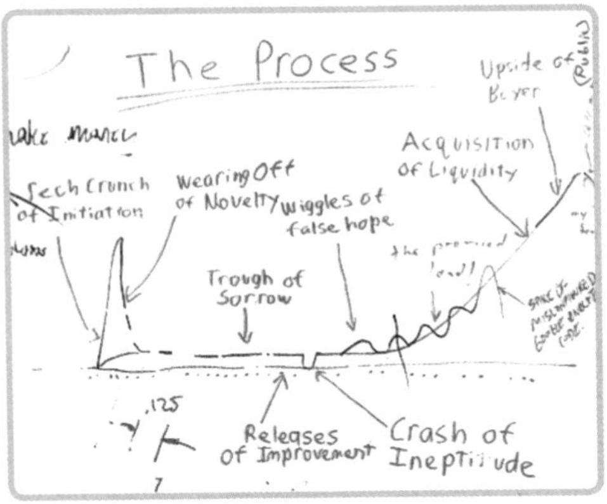
The Process
Upside of Buyer
Acquisition of Liquidity
Wearing Off of Novelty
Wiggles of false hope
Trough of Sorrow
Releases of Improvement
Crash of Ineptitude

The YC start-up "process."

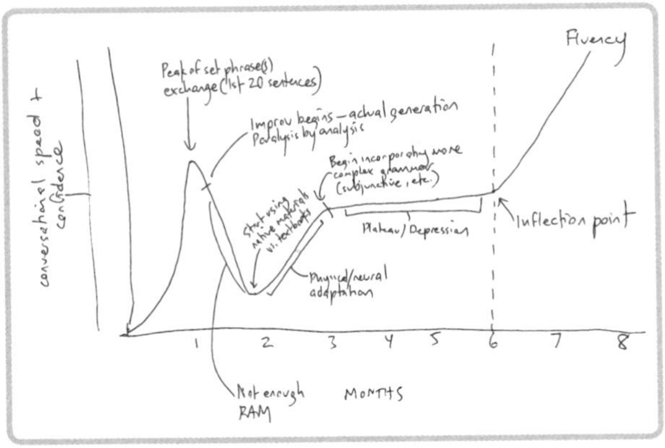
Fluency
Peak of set phrase(s) exchange (1st 20 sentences)
Improv begins—actual generation
Paralysis by analysis
Begin incorporating more complex grammar (subjunctive, etc.)
Start using native materials vs. textbooks
Plateau/Depression
Inflection point
Physical/neural adaptation
conversational speed + confidence
1
2
3
4
5
6
7
8
Not enough RAM
MONTHS

My sketch of how languages are learned, since refined. See chart, opposite.

35 Though, in 2011, YC was twice as hard to get into.

MY LANGUAGE LEARNING PROCESS: A BIPOLAR LEARNING GRAPH

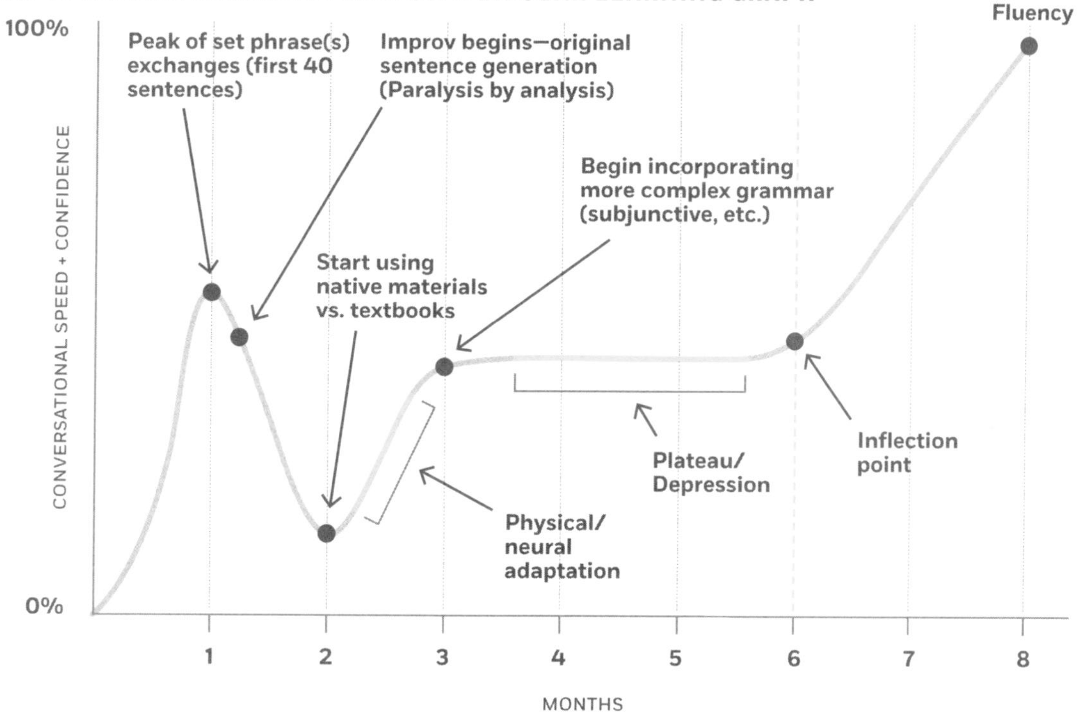
100%
0%
CONVERSATIONAL SPEED + CONFIDENCE
Peak of set phrase(s) exchanges (first 40 sentences)
Improv begins—original sentence generation (Paralysis by analysis)
Start using native materials vs. textbooks
Begin incorporating more complex grammar (subjunctive, etc.)
Physical/ neural adaptation
Plateau/ Depression
Inflection point
Fluency
1
2
3
4
5
6
7
8
MONTHS

For Spanish, later tackled over eight weeks, again the same pattern emerged. For complex physical skills, whether over one week, one month, or one year, it was nearly identical. To me, this suggested a few things:

- It is possible to vastly compress most learning. In a surprising number of cases, it is possible to do something in 1–10 months that is assumed to take 1–10 years.

- The more you compress things, the more physical limiters become a bottleneck. **All learning is physically limited.** The brain is dependent on finite quantities of neurotransmitters, memories require REM and non-REM (NREM) sleep for consolidation, etc. The learning graph is not unlike the stress-recovery-hyper-adaptation curves of weight training.

- The more extreme your ambition, just as in sports, the more you need performance enhancement via unusual schedules, diet, drugs, etc.

- **Most important: due to the bipolar nature of the learning process, you can forecast setbacks.** If you don't, you increase the likelihood of losing morale and quitting before the inflection point.

Based on all I've seen, it's possible to roughly forecast your progress on the back of a napkin. The process, which is optional, is the following. Skip if you find it dense:

1. Pick your world-class (top 5%) objective, and set your timeline. For this example, we'll use Spanish in one month (28 days).

2. Use deconstruction, 80/20, and everything in META-LEARNING to nail your materials, determine your sequence, and map out your calendar.

3. To forecast different milestones, work backward from your total allotted time of 28 days.

First, we divide our total time units by eight, to reflect the monthly units (eight) needed on my graph to reach fluency. Our progress unit is therefore **3.5** (28 days divided by eight).

Next, we look at the graph and multiply out, based on the location of milestones. We round up, so:

- **Sugar high** @ 1 unit = sugar high @ 3.5 days (3.5 x 1), so rounding up, expect a sugar high @ day 4 of 28 days.

- Followed by **immediate drop and low point** @ day 7 (3.5 x 2 units).

- Rapid progress after the low point, followed by **plateau** @ day 10.5 (3.5 x 3), so day 11.

- **Inflection point** @ day 21 (3.5 x 6).

- **Fluency** @ day 28 (3.5 x 8).

This forecast is subject to you nailing every other step in Meta-Learning, of course, and it's a tool of estimation. That said, it can be surprisingly accurate, especially for attempts that last longer than two months.

And keep in mind that, even if you feel like you've failed, you can win. Google cofounder Larry Page once said, "Even if you fail at your ambitious thing, it's very hard to fail completely. That's the thing that people don't get." Cramming isn't pass-fail. Let's say you attempt culinary cram school—cramming six months into 48 hours—as I did. Let's then say that you retain only 40% of what was taught. If you develop the motor patterns to continue practicing *correctly*, which is exactly what happened to me, did you fail? Of course not! Even 40% of six months means that you absorbed 2.4 months of skills in 48 hours!

To keep things practical for most readers, I've set up this book to avoid cramming.

You'll cook just twice per week, which is just enough practice to keep skills persistent from one session to the next.

For those who want to consider cramming, we'll finish this chapter with a "total immersion" menu and a few cognitive tricks for making crash courses work. Some weirdos, like me, love the high-concentration, high-reward sprint. Others will find it masochistic, preferring a Zen-like tempo.

Both speeds work.

THE VALUE OF 5–10-MINUTE BREAKS

The *serial position effect* refers to improved recall observed at the beginnings and ends of lists. Separately, these are called the *primacy effect* and *recency effect*, respectively. Memorizing a hypothetical list of 20 words, your recall might look something like this:

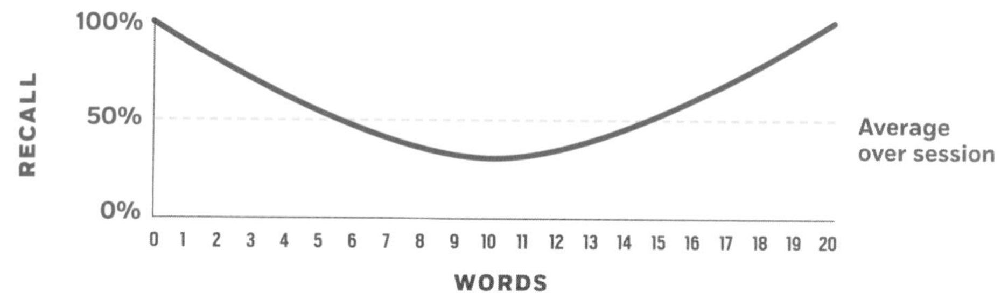
100%
50%
0%
RECALL
0 1 2 3 4 5 6 7 8 9 10 11 12 13 14 15 16 17 18 19 20
WORDS
Average over session

This mid-list dip can be observed in study sessions as well, so a 90-minute session might resemble the below graph:

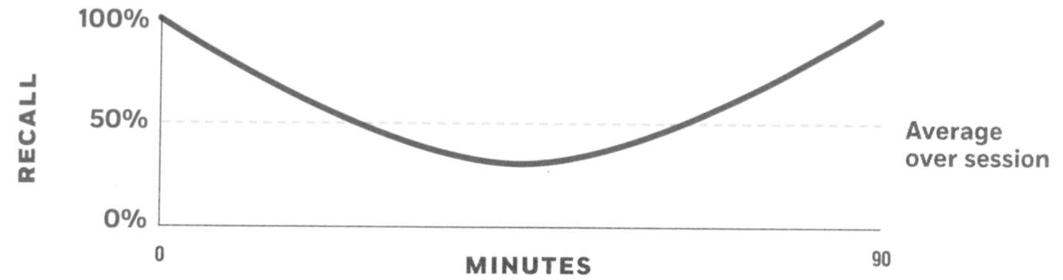
100%
50%
0%
RECALL
0
90
MINUTES
Average over session

We can dramatically improve recall by splitting that single session into two sessions of 45 minutes with a 10-minute break in between.

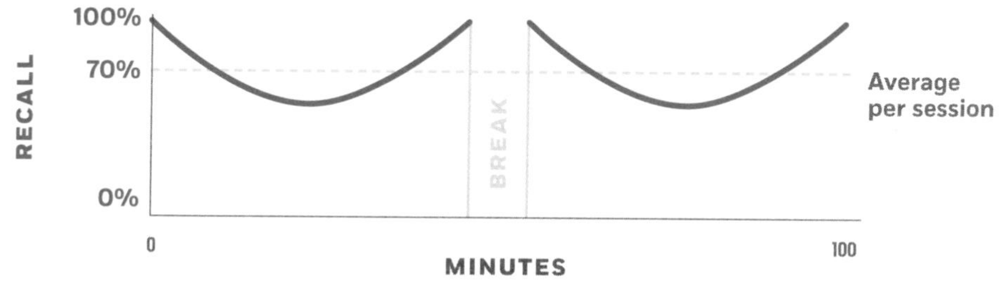
100%
70%
0%
RECALL
BREAK
0
100
MINUTES
Average per session

Two smaller dips vs. one big dip

TOTAL CULINARY IMMERSION RESOURCES

To maximize learning-by-osmosis while writing *The 4-Hour Chef*, I went all-in with 24/7 immersion.

What follows are some of the tools that kept me excited about cooking and that steepened the learning curve (not always both).

Find all links here: fourhourchef.com/immersion

SHORT TV

I use Roku and Amazon Prime to stream when I can:

- *Escape to River Cottage* and *Return to River Cottage*—This is by far my favorite food series, and *Escape to River Cottage* is the strongest. Absolutely wonderful.

- Heston Blumenthal's "In Search of Perfection" on YouTube.

- *Top Chef* season 6, episode 13: "Goodbye to Vegas"—Features Thomas Keller; Jerome Bocuse, son of Paul Bocuse; and a simulated Bocuse d'Or, the "Olympics of Food."

- *After Hours with Daniel* (Daniel Boulud)—If you've ever wondered what chefs talk about over drinks late at night, this is the series for you.

- *A Day in the Life* (Morgan Spurlock series, free on hulu.com)—What does a typical day look like in the lives of Mario Batali or Stephanie Izard? The former is now a celebrity chef, and the latter is the first female winner of *Top Chef*, who is still focused on creating the perfect restaurant. These 30-minute profiles are perfect pre-bed snacks. (For those interested, I also have a profile, which was filmed while writing this book.)

MOVIES

I suggest alternating between fiction and documentaries.

Documentaries

- *Jiro Dreams of Sushi* (Japan)—The most beautifully shot food film I've ever seen. During my last trip to Tokyo, I ate at the younger brother's restaurant, where he was the consummate host.

- *A Matter of Taste: Serving Up Paul Liebrandt* (USA)—The perfect introduction to the trials and tribulations of being a chef, even (or, perhaps, especially) a brilliant one.

- *Pressure Cooker* (USA)—This is the only real tearjerker, a life-affirming story of a culinary teacher in Philadelphia who trains students to win full scholarships.

- *Garlic Is as Good as Ten Mothers* (USA)—Les Blank's incredible (and funny) movie about one ingredient: garlic. Features wonderful vintage footage of Alice Waters and early-era Chez Panisse.

- *Kings of Pastry* (France, Netherlands, United Kingdom)—Who knew pastry could be a full-contact sport? Just as in *Pressure Cooker*, you'll notice that all the coaches are awesomely brutal.

- *Le Cirque: A Table in Heaven* (USA)—Before you open that restaurant you've always dreamed of, watch this and *The Restaurateur*. These are the troubles that even the best in the world have, so consider yourself forewarned.

- *The Restaurateur* (USA)—Follow Danny Meyer through the opening of Eleven Madison Park. Be sure to watch the epilogue in the Special Features section.

- *Eat This New York* (USA)—A cautionary tale of opening a restaurant when you're not ready for it. My favorite part is the chef interviews in the DVD extras.

- *El pollo, el pez, y el cangrejo real* (The Chicken, the Fish, and the King Crab) (Spain)—This covers the training of one Spanish competitor invited to the 2006 Bocuse d'Or.

Non-documentaries

- *Ratatouille* (USA)— Pixar rules. 'Nuff said.

- *Julie & Julia* (USA)—Though a controversial film among foodies, it is a must-see for any new cooking student, in my opinion.

- *Eat Drink Man Woman* (Taiwan, USA)—This wonderful movie is worth watching just for the intro sequence. I *love* Taiwan and Taiwanese food.

- *Tampopo* (Japan)—A Japanese *Amélie* that predates *Amélie*. Watch this on a Friday night prior to cheat day, since you'll immediately want to eat ramen.

- *Babette's Feast* (Denmark)—Very somber, but the ending makes it awesome. You won't forget the punch line.

- *Like Water for Chocolate* (Mexico)—Sexy, sexy, sexy. Great date movie.

- *Perfume: The Story of a Murderer* (France, Germany, Spain)—This is not technically about food, but about smell.

- *Big Night* (USA)—One of the most quotable food movies of all time. Chefs like this one, probably because Tony Shalhoub (*Monk*) loves food and hates his dumb-ass customers.

- *The God of Cookery* (Hong Kong)—The most ridiculous of the bunch. Have some "brownies" (wink, wink) and enjoy this Stephen Chow (*Shaolin Soccer, Kung Fu Hustle*) delight. The broken English subtitles make it twice as funny.

MAGAZINES

There are many wonderful food magazines, but here are three you might not see on local newsstands:

- *Cook's Illustrated*—cooksillustrated.com
- *The Art of Eating*—artofeating.com
- *Gastronomica*—gastronomica.org

TRAVEL COOKING KIT

While traveling, I checked a Polder probe thermometer and timer, a 6" chef's knife with a blade guard, and a small plastic cutting board, so I could conduct experiments in hotel rooms.

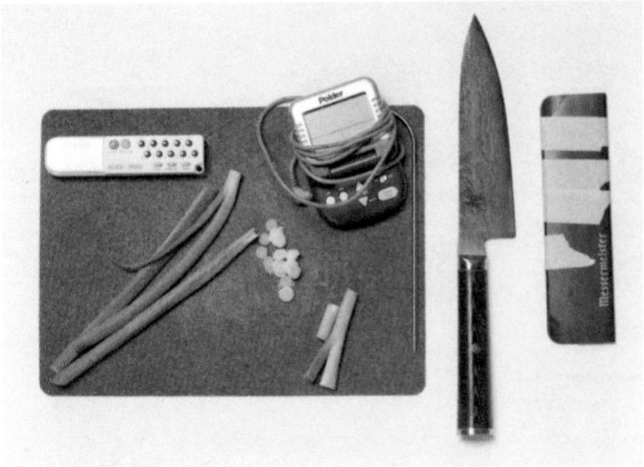
Polder
Messermeister

BOOKS

- *Becoming a Chef* (Andrew Dornenburg, Karen Page)
- *Mission Street Food* (Anthony Myint, Karen Leibowitz)
- *The Whole Beast: Nose to Tail Eating* (Fergus Henderson)
- *White Heat* (Marco Pierre White)
- *The River Cottage Meat Book* (Hugh Fearnley-Whittingstall)
- *La Technique* (Jacques Pepin)
- *The River Cafe Cookbook* and variants (Rose Gray, Ruth Rogers)
- *Culinary Artistry* (Andrew Dornenburg, Karen Page)
- *The Kitchen Diaries: A Year in the Kitchen with Nigel Slater* (Nigel Slater)

THE VON RESTORFF EFFECT

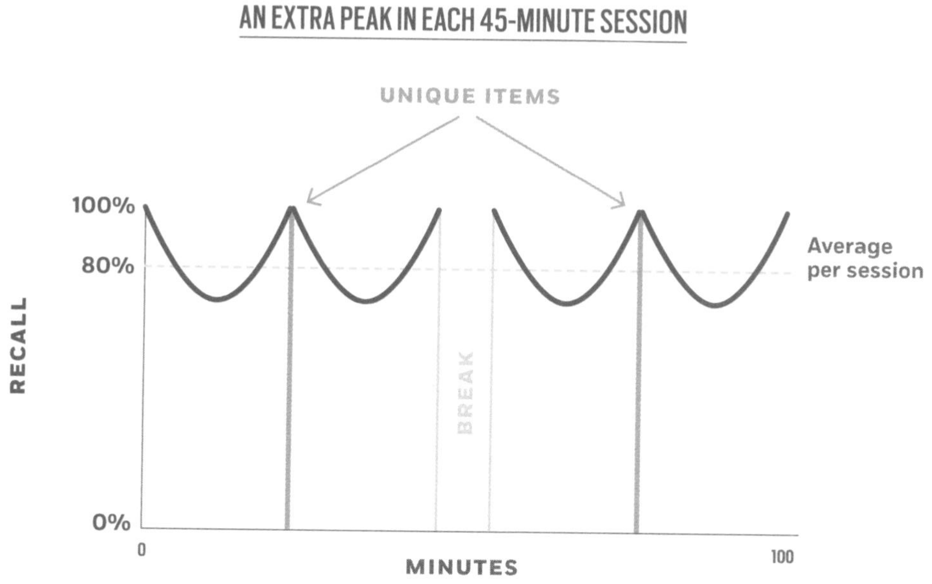
AN EXTRA PEAK IN EACH 45-MINUTE SESSION
UNIQUE ITEMS
100%
80%
0%
RECALL
BREAK
Average
per session
0
100
MINUTES

The Von Restorff effect, also called the *novel popout effect*,* correlates unique items in a list to better recall. For example, if the fifth item in a word list uses a unique color or a larger font size, it will be better remembered than others. This is perhaps obvious. What isn't obvious is that planting odd material in the middle of a session can produce a macro–Von Restorff effect.

Let's assume we have a list of 100 plain-Jane, high-frequency words, split into 50 words per 45-minute session. The recall will look just as it did in the primacy and recency effect graph on page 89.

Now we spike the punch in the middle of each 45-minute session, injecting 2–4 idiomatic phrases that are sexually related from minutes 20–25. There are two content changes: the sexual content and, almost as important, the word-to-phrase shift. In my experience, the memory curves can then morph into the above graph.

Instead of averaging out at 60%–70% recall over a week, say, we can get well over 80%. Furthermore, it's a more sustainable and pleasant learning approach. This is the approach I used with the Linkword method to achieve more than 85% retention of 350 Italian words 72 hours after cramming them into 12 hours.

BUT WHAT ABOUT THE 10,000-HOUR RULE?

For those not on the bandwagon, the so-called 10,000-Hour Rule is based on a study by K. Anders Ericsson and was popularized by the Malcolm Gladwell book *Outliers*. It dictates, in simple terms, that becoming world-class at something requires 10,000 hours of deliberate practice. This number has been correlated with top violinists and aviators, and Malcolm extended this theory to well-known greats like the Beatles and Bill Gates.

Accumulating 10,000 hours requires 20 hours a week for 10 years. So how can I claim that becoming "world-class" is attainable within six months? There are a few reasons, most of which I think Malcolm would agree with:

- First, I define *world-class* very specifically: The top 5% in a given field. For Japanese, let's say, it's having greater conversational fluency than 95 out of 100 people who study Japanese. For the dead lift, a 650-lb pull from the knees at a body weight of 165 lbs puts me above 95 out of 100 male gym members. That said, I'd be laughed off the platform by competitive power lifters. But these power lifters are in the top 0.5%, and we're aiming for the top 5%.[36]

- Correlation (e.g., A and B are found together) doesn't mean causation (A causes B). The fact that 10 out of 10 top violinists practiced 10,000 hours over a certain period of time doesn't mean that this volume is what made them world-class. Imagine all of them are Asian. Does being Asian automatically make you a good violinist? Of course not. There are too many variables. It's nearly impossible to show cause and effect with observational (versus experimental) data.

- Training method can have an exponential impact on per-hour yield. My before-and-after experience with Spanish proves this, as have my readers' experiences in dozens of areas.

- People who are singularly focused on a career in a highly competitive field (e.g., concert violinist) are incentivized to practice as much as possible. In other words, if your professional future depends 100% on one skill, you'll put in as many hours as your body (and schedule) will tolerate. This doesn't mean 10,000+ hours are required, but if this is your one ticket in life, are you going to take the risk by doing less? No. Once again, correlation does not equal causation.

- Patterns can be meaningful, but so can anomalies. If we look at the Olympics from 1920 to 1967, most high-jump medalists used a straddle technique or scissor jump

---

36 Some might criticize this bar, calling me a jack-of-all-trades. Shouldn't I focus on being the best at one thing instead of merely good at many? To them, I'd point out:

- If you're capable of becoming a Tiger Woods or a Yo Yo Ma, you'll know early in life. Tiger Woods wasn't drawing pirate ships as a kid, he was literally drawing trajectories of golf balls hit with different irons. He broke 80 for the first time at age eight.
- Being a generalist can be powerful. Steve Jobs was not a specialist nor a technician; he was a conductor who could connect dots others couldn't.
- It's more fun for me to imagine being in the top 5% in the world in dozens of things, as opposed to in the top 1% for one or, at most, two things.
- I'm actually aiming to be the best in the world at one thing: meta-learning.

to clear the bar. In 1968, Dick Fosbury, to the laughter of spectators, went over backward in what was nicknamed the "Fosbury Flop." He laughed last and won the gold medal. Now, almost 100% of competitors use some variation of his technique. Had we stopped our data collection at 1968, we would have considered him nothing more than a statistical outlier and removed him from the calculus. The Fosburys of the world matter.

- Technology also matters. How did Fosbury make his breakthrough? Partially, it was because the landing surface changed in the mid-1960s from a hard surface (sand, hay, and sawdust) that required a feet-first landing to a soft cushion that allowed for new experimentation. Today, $100 30-frame-per-second cameras and the Internet, to name just two advances, improve both access to expertise and the speed of the feedback loop.

Take, for instance, how I learned to pop up on a surfboard. Prior to a planned trip to Costa Rica, I found myself in Berlin, with no beach or pool in sight. I connected via Skype video with Brad Gerlach, formerly the #1-ranked surfer in the world. In 2006, he won the prestigious Billabong XXL by successfully riding a 68-foot wave in Todos Santos, Mexico. Now, he's turned his mind to teaching. To start, he forced himself to surf "switch stance" (opposite foot forward) just so he could better communicate the mechanics. From inside a rainy apartment in Germany, I watched him demonstrate technique in Los Angeles, after which I turned the camera on myself and listened to his coaching.

The tools of learning are not fixed, nor is the amount of time needed to become world-class.

bradley gerlach

bradley gerlach

bradley gerlach

Ca F E ENCODING: MAKING SLIPPERY IDEAS STICK

> **"At my age, the only problem is with remembering names. When I call everyone 'darling,' it has damn all to do with passionately adoring them, but I know I'm safe calling them that. Although, of course, I adore them too."**
>
> —RICHARD ATTENBOROUGH, BELOVED BRITISH ACTOR, BEST KNOWN FOR PLAYING KRIS KRINGLE IN *MIRACLE ON 34TH STREET*

PALO ALTO, CALIFORNIA

"Oh, ah . . . ha-ha . . . is that *your* water?" the woman next to me asked. I'd grabbed the wrong water. Once again, I'd somehow ended up at a dinner with assigned seating, penguin suits, and polished fake laughter. At my last outing, I thought a beauty at the table was flirting with me—that coy smile! It turned out that I'd just splattered tomato sauce all over my white shirt.

Elbows on the table? Check. Stealing the wrong bread? Way ahead of you.

What's a simple Long Island boy to do?

Just a year ago, I learned three memory devices that have prevented my brutish manners from making me look like a complete animal.

B and D—Make the "OK" sign with both hands, touching index fingers to thumbs. The left hand now looks like a lowercase "b" and your right hand looks like a lowercase "d." This tells you where your "b"read is (left side) and where your "d"rink is (right side). Sure, it's a little weird making hand signals under the table, but I've never made a mistake again. I still do this more often than I'd like to admit.

LEFT has four letters; RIGHT has five letters—The FORK (four letters) goes to the LEFT (four letters) of the plate. The KNIFE and SPOON (each five letters) both go to the right of the plate.

Work from the outside in—If faced with a Swiss Army knife collection of silverware around your plate, work from the outside in (furthest from the plate to the closest). This also tells you where to put the spoon relative to the knife on the RIGHT side: on the outside.

Et voilà! Problem solved. All of these are examples of smart encoding.

Encoding is a term used in computing and physiology,[37] but in the context of memory, I'll use it to mean one thing:

Converting the unfamiliar and unwieldy into the familiar and manageable.

Mnemonics (pronounced "nuh-MON-ics"), named after the personification of memory

37 For instance, when a pinprick is converted into a nerve signal, something the brain can interpret.

in Greek mythology, Mnemosyne,[38] are a form of encoding. These memory devices come in several common shapes and sizes.

Some are *acronyms*, which use letters to encode words. U.S. elementary school students use ROY G. BIV to memorize the colors of the rainbow:[39]

- Red
- Orange
- Yellow
- Green
- Blue
- Indigo
- Violet

Others are precisely the opposite. *Acrostics* use words to encode letters. Flashing back again to elementary school, "Every Good Boy Deserves Fudge" is used to memorize the basic musical scale: EGBDF. Others, like "work from the outside in" are simply memorable rules of thumb, but you can call them *heuristics* when you sip Limonata and hang out at the Harvard Club.

Lost for witty party trivia? Try *chunking*, or grouping bits of data to make them more memorable. How tall is Mount Fuji? It's 12,365 feet, of course—12 months in a year, 365 days in a year.

To illustrate how far you can take encoding, we'll look at how you handle really difficult material. The first technique can also be used to increase your IQ, a ridiculous metric that's fun to game.

The second technique is out of this world.

Think of both techniques as your Practice One-Pagers for encoding.

This is where the imagery gets weird, and you can lock anything into place. NOTE: if you're not a superdork who loves mental tail-chasing, I *strongly* encourage you to jump to the velvety smooth DOM on page 102.

Still here? OK then, my precious, you asked for it.

OF SAVANTS AND SOROBAN—SLIPPERY NUMBERS

I remember sitting on a freezing *tatami* in 1992. Roughly an hour outside Tokyo, my high school's high-altitude judo camp (*gasshuku*) had started, and the entire team woke up at 7 a.m. to rub their eyes, shake off the frost, and train. In between workouts and before bed, my classmates and I would sit cross-legged, drink hot green tea, and play a wonderful Japanese card game called *hanafuda*.

One night, I had a lucky streak and demolished my buddies without a shred of skill. Recognizing that it would never happen again,[40] I immediately folded my hand and started smack talking. The back-and-forth devolved into a competition of stupid human tricks. "But can you do *this*?" Rolling the tongue. "That's nothing. How about this?" The Vulcan hand sign. Then my friend Tanaka called over one of our classmates, Nakajima. Tanaka looked at me: "Oh, yeah? How about this? Nakajima, what's 287 times 965?"

Nakajima, still standing, locked his eyes upward and to the right. His index finger danced in the air, and after a few seconds, he hurriedly spit out the answer, as if afraid to lose it:

"276,955."

I was speechless, and Tanaka laughed. He turned back to Nakajima: "How about 156 times 643?" Nakajima returned to the trance, his fingers darting around within a 6" imaginary circle. He didn't even look at his frenetic hand:

"100,308."

I looked at Tanaka and stuttered out in worse-than-usual Japanese: "Wha . . . How . . . I mean . . . Huh?"

---

38 Trivia: she also slept with Zeus for nine nights to create the nine muses. Zeus must have been using pine pollen (page 186).

39 The parts of the electromagnetic light spectrum visible to the human eye.

40 "*Saisho de saigo*," as the Japanese would say—"the first time and the last time."

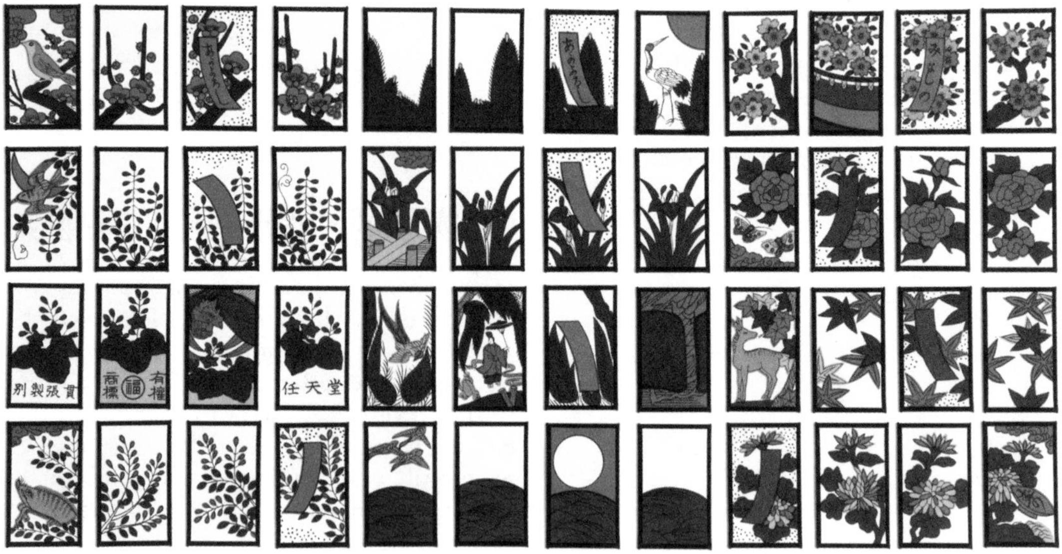

A *hanafuda* set. One of the pioneer manufacturers? Nintendo. That's a real gaming company.

He held back for a minute, enjoying my confusion, then gave in: "*Soroban da yo.*" In effect: "An abacus, dude." Nakajima had used an abacus so extensively in primary school that he no longer needed it to compute. He simply visualized using it, which explained the air waving.

Nakajima wasn't particularly smart, nor was he unique. Many Japanese schoolkids can do the same thing. Becoming a human calculator was just a matter of internalizing the age-old abacus.

PARTYING LIKE IT'S 1999

By 1999, I'd played with the abacus multiple times and finally given up. It was too time-consuming. But by synchronicity, I came across yet another Japanese phenomenon at this breaking point: Hideaki Tomoyori. Hideaki memorized pi to 40,000 digits in 1987. In 2006, researchers conducted a barrage of routine numerical and verbal tests to find the secret sauce. Their conclusion: Hideaki has no superior memorization abilities whatsoever. It was all technique.

My routine became memorizing the serial numbers on 3–4 bills in my wallet immediately upon waking. I timed myself with a stopwatch and aimed to beat my average time every week. For a bill to be considered "successful," I needed to be able to recite the numbers and letters both forward and backward, as well as recall the denomination.

To do this quickly enough to pull off over drinks, I combined the *consonant system mnemonic* with the *loci mnemonic*.

(Warning again for non-nerds: Boring paragraphs ensue for four pages.)

The *consonant system mnemonic* (also called the *Major System*) encodes numbers zero through nine as consonants of the English language. These consonants are then converted into nouns, then images. Vowels have no value, nor do *w*, *h*, or *y*. These are just used as filler for creating words. Clear as mud? Great. Not to worry. Read on and the examples will help.

The table opposite shows the pairings I used, with recommendations for remembering them in parentheses. In a few cases, examples are given to show that what matters is the consonant *sound*, not the spelling:

Using the below table, 8209 could equal "fan" (82) and "soap" (09), thus a fan made of soap. Remember: numbers are converted to words by the phonetics (sounds), and spelling is unimportant. Thus: 8762 = FKSHN = fikshun = fiction = image: a clear fiction character, like Alice from *Alice in Wonderland*. But 8762 could just as easily be VKCHN = "vac" "chin" = image: vacuum on a chin. Use whichever vowels you want.

Repeated letters are represented by a single number unless two separate sounds are made: 3230 = MNMS = Minnie Mouse ("nn" is represented by the single 2).

Let's memorize 16 numbers so you can see what I mean. Here they are: 9265358979323846. I've chosen specific nouns to illustrate rules of the system:

9265 — **Bo**n**e** and **Sh**e**ll** → Image: a huge bone bouncing up and down, smashing a shell.

3589 — **M**o**le** and **FB**I (notice how an acronym is fair game) → Image: a mole looking like a Secret Service agent, with sunglasses and a black suit, flashing an FBI badge.

7932 — **C**ow**b**oy and **M**oo**n** (notice how *w* and *y* have no value) → Image: a cowboy roping a moon.

3846 — **M**a**f**ia and **R**a**sh** → Image: The Godfather, Marlon Brando, with a rash on his head.

Hang in there—you'll like the payoff.

Next, we're going to incorporate the *loci system* to keep it all straight.

The loci system, also called the *memory palace technique*, uses places[41] to hold images. Cicero was famous for using this technique to remember his talking points when addressing the Roman senate during marathon sessions, and it's just as useful today. There are two primary ways you can peg locations.

First, you can memorize stops or landmarks on a familiar route, say 20 spots in your home or 50 spots on the walk from your home to downtown. This route is used over and over again. Having a longer route is very useful for high-volume recall and speed-based competition.

Second, and this is what we'll try now, you can peg items to things in your immediate surroundings, such as inside a room.

I did this with my serial numbers and still like to do it with short lists, especially as a party trick. Why? Because then I have different places and clear, independent lists. No overlap, in other words. In college, during my serial-number experiments, I'd have someone mark the bills I memorized with a pen and keep them in his or her wallet. I'd ask that person not to spend them until we next met. Then, perhaps a week later, I'd see the person

THE CONSONANT SYSTEM MNEMONIC

1=	T (also TH) or D (single downstroke)
2=	N (two downstrokes)
3=	M (three downstrokes)
4=	R (the last letter of *four* is *r*)
5=	L (you have five fingers on your left hand; make an *L* with your index finger and thumb)
6=	J, CH, soft G, SH (*J* is a near mirror image of 6) (e.g., Jelly, CHips, garaGe, SHoe)
7=	K, hard G, hard C (7 side-by-side with a mirror image form a sideways *K*) (e.g., Kite, Goat, Cat)
8=	F, V, PH (8 is similar to the lowercase cursive *f*) (e.g., Flame, Vest, graPH)
9=	P or B (9 is a mirror image of *P*)
0=	Z, S, soft C (O or *zero*) (e.g., Zipper, Scarf, iCe)

41 Literally *loci* in Latin, plural of *locus*, meaning place.

and ask, "Want to see if I still remember those serial numbers?" I could think back to the room where we were originally sitting and pull up all the images, with almost 100% accuracy, forward and backward. I could do this for multiple people.

Let's try it out.

Right now I'm on a farm in Victoria, Canada, sitting behind a wooden desk and looking out through enormous bay windows. I see the ocean and mountains in the distance, I'm drinking Pu-Erh tea, and a dog is lying down by my side. All is right in the world. Scanning from left to right around the room, I'll pick four spots for our four sets of numbers. In order, I'll choose the telescope, sewing machine, mannequin, and rocking chair. Here are the images, then:

On the telescope, I imagine a huge bone bouncing up and down, smashing a shell.

On the sewing machine, I imagine a crouched mole looking like a Secret Service agent, with sunglasses and a black suit, flashing an FBI badge at me.

Balanced atop the mannequin, I imagine a cowboy roping a moon.

On the rocking chair sits the Mafia (*The Godfather,* Marlon Brando) with a huge, red rash on his head.

Pick four locations around you, in scanning order, and try it yourself. Or just imagine my room and go for it. Try this, please, before continuing. Do it 1–3 times through.

Now, guess what?

Tag the 3.1415 on the front, and you've just memorized pi to 20 decimal places! If you really want to get laid at the math bar down the street, recite them backward.

BIG-GIRL PANTS AND MOVING TO COOKING

But let's say you want to go a step further and become a Memory Grand Master, joining fewer than 100 people in the world with that title. You'll need to put your big-girl pants on for a bigger test: a deck of cards.

This is also more involved, and therefore outlined in the Appendix on page 606. For those up for a challenge, there is a $10,000 prize involved.

Now, shall we get you kicking ass in the kitchen?

LOCKED AND LOADED: A LITTLE MATRIX

If you're willing to invest a little time, you can become a speed demon. Just once, memorize the below matrix, which I use.[42] Lock in one preset image for each possible pair of numbers and you won't have to generate your own.

00	Suzie (a friend), SOS
01	Seed
02	Sun
03	Sam (Uncle Sam)
04	Zero
05	Seal
06	Sash (red kung fu sash)
07	Sack (yes, that kind)
08	Sofa
09	Sap
10	Toes
11	Tit, Dad
12	Tin (Tin man), dune
13	Tim, dime
14	Tire, deer
15	Tail (German shepherd), tile
16	Dish, tush (ass)
17	Duck
18	TV, dove
19	Tuba, tape (VHS)
20	Nose
21	Net (basketball)
22	Nun
23	Nemo (*Finding Nemo*)
24	Nero (imagine a Caesar-type figure), NR (choose something obscene from a Not-Rated movie)
25	Nail
26	NJ, nudge, ENGine
27	Nike (swoosh), neck, nookie
28	Knife (chef's knife), Na'vi
29	Knob (doorknob)
30	Mouse (Mickey Mouse)
31	Moat, mat (wrestling mat)
32	Moon
33	Mom
34	Mario (Super Mario), mower
35	Mail (envelope), mule
36	*M*A*S*H* (Alan Alda in Army fatigues), match
37	Mic, mug (coffee mug)
38	Muff (earmuffs)
39	Map
40	Rose
41	Rat
42	Rain
43	Ram
44	Roar (tiger)
45	Rail
46	Rash
47	Rock
48	Roof
49	Rope
50	Lace
51	Light (lightbulb), loot
52	Lion
53	Lime
54	Lure (fishing lure)
55	Lily, LOLcatz
56	Leech, leash
57	Lake, log
58	Lava
59	Lip
60	Cheese
61	Sheet (bedsheet)
62	Shin
63	Jam (berry jam)
64	Cherry
65	Jell-O
66	Judge
67	Chalk, shake (milkshake)
68	Chef, Jeff (a friend)
69	Ship (sailboat)
70	Gas (gas tub)
71	Cat
72	Cane, cone
73	Comb
74	Car
75	Coal, cola
76	Cage, kosher (salt)
77	Cake (ice-cream cake)
78	Cave, café
79	Cape (like Superman)
80	Foos/Fooz/ (Foosball)
81	Foot
82	Fan (standing fan)
83	Foam
84	Fairy (Tinkerbell), fire
85	File, fly
86	Fish
87	Fog
88	Five (fingers on a hand)
89	FBI
90	Bus (school bus)
91	Bat
92	Bone
93	Bamm-Bamm (from *The Flintstones*)
94	Bear
95	Bell, bale (of hay)
96	Bush (GW)
97	Book, bike
98	Beef
99	Pipe

42 Mostly a combination of pegs found at litemind.com/major-system and rememberg.com/peg-list-1000, plus a few of my own. Keep in mind that not all images are created equal. Let's take the number 71 to illustrate this. It could be encoded as dozens of words, but consider two of them: cat and cot. Which is better? Ask yourself: if I showed a picture of each to 10 people and asked them what it was, what would they say? A cat is a cat—end of story. But if shown a picture of a cot, most would likely call it a bed. In the long term, so will you, and that will produce a mistake. When possible, choose single-label images or you'll have retrieval errors later. Nouns are easier than verbs, and both are better than adjectives.

ДОМ

THE DOMESTIC

DOM is the mother lode.

As you complete 14 core lessons, each taking no more than 20 minutes of prep (for our total of roughly 4 hours), you will learn the principles needed to cook thousands of dishes. Furthermore, “gear” (pots, pans, etc.) is severely restricted and introduced slowly, making costs gradual. As chef Tom Colicchio, famed restaurateur and head judge on *Top Chef*, has said: almost anyone can become a great cook with unlimited time and budget.

We’ll constrain both and learn to do the absolute most with the least. What follows are the 80/20 keys to the culinary kingdom.

Practice cooking without cooking (clockwise from top left): sautéing dry beans, hotel cutting practice, watching "the pass" in restaurants.

RETHINKING RECIPES

> **"Do you really believe the Babbo cookbook when it tells you that a linguine with eels takes four garlic cloves, that a lobster spaghettini takes two, and that the chitarra takes three? No. It's the same for each: a small pinch."**
> —BILL BUFORD, *HEAT*

> **"Do not be afraid of cooking, as your ingredients will know and misbehave. Enjoy your cooking and the food will behave."**
> —FERGUS HENDERSON, CHEF/CO-OWNER OF ST. JOHN[1]

Imagine that you are driving, which requires serious multitasking.

Now imagine that you are handed the below driving directions to read while avoiding telephone poles, old ladies, and people texting on iPhones:

> First, put the transmission into first gear. On a standard "H" manual transmission, it's to the top left. Facing northwest, look into your left mirror to ensure there's no oncoming traffic, and pull out of the parking lot at no more than 15 miles per hour onto Bosworth Road, taking a 90-degree right-hand turn. Past the Osha Thai restaurant, look for your first right-hand turn after the BART subway station, which will be an entrance ramp for Interstate 280 South. Entering this ramp, you will accelerate gradually, keeping right, to 55 miles per hour and . . . [it continues]

Now, in contrast, consider the following, where (R) is "right" and (L) is "left":

> 280S
> (R) N De Anza[2]
> (L) Mariani Ave.
> (L) Infinite Loop[3]

Which set of directions is easier to follow and less stressful? Something closer to the second, of course.

Recipes, alas, are often written like the first set of driving instructions. This is how you end up standing at your counter, rereading a Godzilla 'graph for each step, smelling burning on the stove, and shaking a fist at the sky.[4]

In this DOMESTIC section, we will start with in-depth instructions, all intended to teach principles and vocabulary. As you

---

1 Voted "Best British Restaurant"; Henderson originally trained as an architect.

2 Note that this automatically means you exit on De Anza Boulevard.

3 These short driving directions are from San Francisco to Apple World Headquarters in Cupertino. It's the only place you can find official Apple swag: limited-edition gear and products. Japanese tourists, among others, make the pilgrimage by bus precisely for this reason. Save it for your next trip to Nor-Cal.

4 Here is a real-world single step, taken from a source that shall remain nameless. I've removed the ingredients: *In a large saucepan, melt 2 tablespoons of butter. Add the A, B, C, diced D and E and cook over moderate heat, stirring occasionally, until the vegetables are lightly browned, about 5 minutes. Add the F and cook, stirring, for about 2 minutes. Add the G and cook, stirring occasionally, until completely absorbed, about 5 minutes. Add half of the broth and cook, stirring occasionally, until completely absorbed, about 12 minutes. Season with salt and pepper. Add the remaining X and cook, stirring occasionally, until completely absorbed, about 12 minutes longer. Discard the Y. Stir in the Z along with the Q and the remaining 2 tablespoons of. . . .* And it *continues!* One step, my ass.

progress to subsequent sections and internalize things (just like [R] for "right" on the previous page), the instructions will be compressed. By the end of the book, instead of 3–5 pages of explanation, all you will need to create delicious dishes is shorthand like this:

> Cauliflower Bites: toss cauliflrflorets/3T olvoil/2t cumin&garlc/T currypdr/s+p. Roast on bkgsheet~20m@400F; turn1x.[5]

Once you graduate to this, you'll be ready to tackle practically any cookbook and any recipe in the world, including our Appendix of nearly 200 shorthand recipes: one flagship dish for every country of the world.

Cool, right?

THE FORMAT

Each recipe in DOMESTIC will teach you broadly applicable skills. Even if you don't make every dish (which you should), you should read all of them. They are intended to help you win victories and conquer fears in a logical progression. Here's a sample of what you'll cover:

- Cooking technique (braising, roasting, mashing, steaming, etc.).
- Tools (knives, Polder thermometer, Dutch oven, etc.).
- Herbs, spices, and flavor fluency.
- Phobia fixers (knives, liver, anchovies, bitter tastes, etc.).
- Tricks to impress your friends (uncommon proteins like eel, professional presentation tips, etc.).

All without trying very hard, quite frankly! Some important notes on recipe format:

- **Each recipe in DOMESTIC will have no more than four ingredients,** though there are a few staples we don't count. *Wheel of Fortune*–style, you get free letters. In our culinary alphabet, they are: salt[6] and pepper (S+P), garlic, extra-virgin olive (or grapeseed) oil, and vinegar.

- **Mirroring professional chefs, the steps for each recipe are broken into two parts: prep and pickup.** I don't want you to think of "cooking" as one activity. Think of it as "prep," things that can be done hours/days in advance, and "pickup," or what you do when you decide it's time to eat. This will greatly reduce feeling rushed. So remember: it's no longer *cooking*, it's *prep* and *pickup*.

- **Measurements are shown in both metric and the U.S.-favored Imperial.** Metric is magical for reasons we'll cover. As chef James Simpkins put it: "The day people stop measuring in cups is the day American cooking goes to the moon." I'll ease you into this, so don't get short of breath when you see grams, for instance.

- **Don't freak out about "total time."** For each dish, I'll list "hands-on time," which is your *active* time requirement, and "total time," which is how long you'll have to wait to eat.

THE RULES—READ THRICE

- **Read each recipe from start to finish *before* buying ingredients or trying anything.** Absorb the principles before putting them into action. This is critical.

- **When you make each dish, you have a choice: follow the longer directions step-by-step, or refer to the nutshell**

---

5 Recipe by the brilliant Maureen Evans of eat-tweet.com.

6 Or liquid salt, like tamari.

version at the start. When you make anything a second or third time, try to follow the shorthand, which is faster and removes the training wheels.

- **Don't worry about being exact unless I tell you to.** I want to teach you to eyeball amounts, so you'll see measurements like "2-finger pinch" (between index and thumb) and "3-finger pinch" (index finger, middle finger, and thumb). If I don't provide an exact amount, or if a quantity seems vague, it's to keep you unattached to gadgets and measuring spoons. We'll use tools to get you cooking well, but eyeballing is used to get you cooking without recipes.

- **How you make the recipe the first time is the "lesson"; how you make it after that is up to you.** Since I'm teaching skills, some recipes will seem very long, since they're "lessons" first and "recipes" second. This is especially true here in DOMESTIC. Follow it verbatim the first time through. The second time, just follow the shorthand and omit anything time-consuming.

THE INSURANCE POLICY

Whether you're looking to quit smoking, lose 20 lbs of fat, learn Arabic, or cook twice a week, the rules of behavioral change are the same. Here is the formula:

- **Make it small and temporary.** Plan on cooking twice per week for the next three weeks, which means six meals. This is achievable and enough to cement a new behavior, according to Nike+ designers, who found five sessions to be the minimal magic number after looking at more than 1.2 million users:

> If someone uploads only a couple of runs to the site, they might just be trying it out. But once they hit five runs, they're massively more likely to keep running and uploading data. At five runs, they've gotten hooked on what their data tells them about themselves.‡

So consider six meals a complete victory. If you want to cook more than twice a week, go for it, but just remember, you aren't "failing" if you're not cooking a ton—twice a week is all that's required to win.

- **Make it measurable, make it a game.** Each meal ("lesson") is worth points. Different recipes have different points (max 100), as do bonuses and variations. Keep track of your total on the inside back cover. The final assignment at the end of each month is a dinner party for four people. They're worth a lot! Peter Drucker, management theorist and recipient of the Presidential Medal of Freedom, put it best: "What gets measured gets managed."

- **Make it competitive.** To ensure your two-times-weekly cooking commitment, follow the directions in the "Stakes" chapter from META-LEARNING (page 68), or simply compete with a friend on points. If you want to up the ante, recruit four people (including you). Each person puts $50–$100 into a betting pool; each person then hosts a dinner for the four-person group at the end of the month, using recipes exclusively from DOM. After the last group dinner, you all vote on who had the best taste, texture, presentation, and ambience. Drink, debate, name-call, and have a good ol' time with it. The grand winner takes home the betting pool.

- **Take pictures of it all.** This is your version of Nike+ uploading. Take photographs of your meals and share them, whether through Facebook, Twitter, or e-mail. Tracking begets feedback, which begets more tracking. This virtuous cycle will dramatically accelerate your learning and results.

- **In the beginning, focus on convenience.** Don't be in a rush to save the planet. Thinking long-term, I'm going to give you permission to be wasteful when you first start cooking: paper cups, paper plates, paper towels, etc. This isn't required, of course, but if you historically hate doing dishes and let them pile up, load up on enough disposables to last you six meals. Ecologically sound brands include Wasara, Bambu, and VerTerra, but even simple paper is OK.

  Then, instead of quitting cooking after three meals, you can quit disposables after three weeks and cook without waste for a lifetime. Of course, the environmental ROI of the latter dwarfs the former.

LAST, EXPECT LITTLE HICCUPS AND CTFO

I am the king of freaking out in the kitchen. Think Cornholio meets Woody Allen. This is why I dodged cooking at all costs for decades. In retrospect, I was a stress case because I never had a Plan B. The first and last rule of *The 4-Hour Chef* is this: if you fuck it all up, you can always order takeout.

Get a few delivery menus for nearby slow-carb-compliant food—Thai or Mexican—and pick your backup dishes in case things go sideways. Program the restaurant numbers into your phone, and start your "lessons" a good hour before they stop taking orders. Problem solved. Still upset you wasted ingredients? Relax. View the cost as a very inexpensive cooking class.

As you stumble and learn, stumble and learn again, resolve to talk to yourself as if you were your best friend. So no "What a #?%&@ idiot!" when your BFF smashes an egg on the floor, m'kay? Be cool, like the Fonz.

My goal is to train you to be unshakable, not unlike quarterback Joe Montana, who was MVP in three of his four Super Bowls. ESPN covered his Zen-like mastery of high performance:

> Take the 1989 Super Bowl against the Cincinnati Bengals. The San Francisco 49ers were down by three points with 3:20 left when Montana spotted—no, not an open receiver—but a personality. "There, in the stands, standing near the exit ramp," Montana said to tackle Harris Barton. "Isn't that John Candy?" And then he led the 49ers 92 yards, throwing for the winning touchdown with 34 seconds left. This was one of Montana's 31 fourth-quarter comebacks in the NFL.[‡]

Your training in the kitchen will transfer to your world outside it.

CTFO! This is all play, not homework.

THE 80/20 PANTRY: ALL YOU NEED

> "I fear not the man who has practiced 10,000 kicks once, but I fear the man who has practiced one kick 10,000 times."
>
> —BRUCE LEE

If Guillaume Tirel, alias Taillevent, who wrote the seminal French cookbook *Le Viandier* in 1380, could make do with primarily ginger, pepper, saffron, and cinnamon, then you can create masterpieces with a handful of well-chosen *flavor enhancers.*

Why don't I say "herbs and spices"? Because getting confused by herbs and spices early on causes novices to quit. If you *never* use any herbs and spices, you can still make incredible food that makes people ask, "What did you put in this?!" We'll get to herbs and spices, but not yet.

Sophisticated can be simple. We'll approach cooking the way the Thais approach fighting. Thai kickboxing—Muay Thai—is nicknamed the "art of eight limbs" for its use of kicks, punches, elbows, and knees on both sides. It's a simple art with maybe a dozen principal techniques. And yet, it's simultaneously one of the most brutally effective martial arts in the world. Thai boxers spend the majority of their training time on what matters far more than fancy technique: timing, speed, and power. **In other words, the masterful application of their purposefully limited tools.**

Instead of stocking your kitchen full of "just in case" food and seeing undone homework every time you open the refrigerator, master a few staples. Buy everything else "just in time." Everything in this section will keep almost forever, which is important if you travel often and unpredictably, as I do. Nothing here will prompt anyone to ask, "What is that smell?" Links for everything can be found at **fourhourchef.com/pantry,** but please note: you do *not* need to buy all of these at once. Feel free to acquire ingredients as dishes call for them, which will spread out your costs.

EXTRA-VIRGIN OLIVE OIL (EVOO)

There's no need to go overboard here, at least not now. EVOO doesn't play well with light, so ixnay on clear glass or plastic containers. Go for metal or dark glass.

For cooking, I buy cheaper Partanna Asaro EVOO in bulk, which is common in restaurants.

For fancier "finishing" (topping food just before eating), none of my favorites is from Italy, surprisingly. I prefer the olive oils from Spain and North Africa (Algeria). If you really want to splurge, my faves are:

- **In Situ EVOO from Chile**. This one is hard to get, but I have to mention it. I found it on a ski trip when our group visited a small winery in San Esteban. Everyone was impressed with the red wine but went home with the olive oil. Uh-mazing. I stuffed bottles in my luggage and can practically drink the stuff. Truly a breed apart.
- **McEvoy Ranch Organic EVOO from California**. Every time I go to the home of an outstanding Californian chef, this is what comes out.

GHEE

Called *sman* in Middle Eastern cooking, ghee is common shorthand for clarified butter. Clarified means the milk solids have been removed, making ghee slow-carb, rich, and butterlike in taste. It's also able to withstand higher heat (normal butter is easy to burn and therefore perfect for ruining dishes). This is win-win-win. In Hindu food practices, ghee is categorized as a Sattvic food: "balancing to the body, purifying to the mind, and calming to the spirit."‡ What's not to like?

I purchase ghee at the grocery store, but if you'd like to make it from regular butter with a slow cooker, here's how you do it:

Put 2–3 lbs of butter in a slow cooker.

Cook on low for 1–2 hours until the solids float.

Skim them off (a folded paper towel works).

Filter the remaining liquid through cheesecloth.

UNREFINED VIRGIN COCONUT OIL

Coconut oil is the Swiss Army knife of oils. My girlfriend uses it to wash her face, one of my good buddies at Google uses it on his hair and swears it's regrown his locks, and it's a fantastic cooking oil. I started using it after taking the Cadillac of blood tests through start-up WellnessFX (**wellnessfx.com**). In the lipid profile, which goes miles beyond total cholesterol, HDL, and LDL, I noticed I was low in myristic acid, a saturated fatty acid that's abundant in sperm whale oil and coconut oil.

Since I'd run out of sperm whale oil, I opted for the latter. I started downing a heaping tablespoon each morning. Within three days, I felt reborn. Fixing my myristic acid deficiency gave me as much energy as two cups of coffee, fixing chronic morning fatigue with a snap of the fingers. Get thine blood tested, ladies and gents. It pays.

GRAPESEED OIL

If I'm searing meats at high heat, I always use this neutral-flavored (essentially flavorless) oil. It will show up a lot in this book for just about everything.

MACADAMIA NUT OIL

Some athletes consider macadamia nut oil the new and improved olive oil. I alternate the two for variety.

Unlike EVOO, macadamia nut oil tastes almost like butter and has a high smoking point (413°F/210°C), making it more versatile for stove-top cooking. Macadamia nut oil is also more stable than olive oil when exposed to light. Some industry analysts estimate that more than 50% of all mass-produced olive oil is spoiled when consumed.

Last but not least, the fat in macadamia nut oil contains the lowest concentration of omega-6 fatty acids of all common cooking oils. I purchase mine from **oilsofaloha.com**, and I favor their unflavored oils for learning to cook.

SMOKING/BURNING POINTS

FAT	SMOKE POINT‡
Butter	**250–300°F/ 121–149°C**
Coconut Oil (Unrefined Virgin)	**350°F/177°C**
EVOO	**375°F/191°C**
Virgin Olive Oil	**391°F/199°C**
Macadamia Nut Oil	**413°F/210°C**
Grapeseed Oil	**420°F/216°C**
Almond Oil	**420°F/216°C**
Extra-Light Olive Oil	**468°F/242°C**
Ghee	**485°F/252°C**
Avocado Oil	**520°F/271°C**

THE ORIGINAL
Maldon
SEA SALT
FLAKES
SEASONING WITH SUBSTANCE

SALT
(DIAMOND CRYSTAL KOSHER + MALDON)

In the heyday of the Roman empire, workers were sometimes paid in salt, hence the word *salary* in English.[7]

Most chefs agree that salt is the most important ingredient in the kitchen, so don't cut corners here. Diamond kosher salt is a restaurant staple and will be your workhorse, used before or during cooking. Maldon sea salt (this changed my life) is your "finishing" salt; again, put it on food just before eating. Erik Cosselmon, the executive chef at Kokkari and Evvia, the late Steve Jobs's favorite restaurant, loves to sit down and eat tomato slices seasoned with nothing but Maldon. I've started doing the same with avocados.

Salt isn't only used to change flavor. It can remove moisture, change texture (think Parma ham, prosciutto), counter bitterness (try it on dark chocolate), or help you wash salad greens more easily. (I could not find a good scientific explanation for the latter, but Heston Blumenthal agrees.)

TAMARI

Tamari has little or no wheat, and is therefore slow-carb-compliant soy sauce. We'll use it for anything Asian-ish, and it can be treated like liquid salt in many cuisines.

LEMONS

If something is missing, if the flavors don't quite pop, the easiest way to fix it is with a little acid. As chef Mehdi Chellaoui says, "I use lemon like I use salt." Mario Batali would agree: if something is missing, it's probably acid.

TELLICHERRY
PEPPER

PEPPER
(PEPPERCORNS)

Buy peppercorns in bulk bags so you can smell them. If they're musty like corked wine, don't buy 'em. Marcella Hazan, the godmother of Italian cooking, favors the Tellicherry variety, so I follow suit. For grinding, any mill will do a decent job, but I use a Unicorn peppermill.

SHERRY VINEGAR + CHAMPAGNE VINEGAR

Since most "balsamic" vinegars are impostors, I suggest switching to this dynamic duo. Much like lemon, both can be used to "brighten" with acid. Try the sherry vinegar anywhere you'd use balsamic, or on top of fatty meat dishes (the change is remarkable). Use champagne vinegar for anything you don't want to stain (chicken, cauliflower, etc.) or for variety. I love to use it on steamed vegetables like broccolini. Play and experiment. Just remember to put your thumb over the spout to control flow. A tablespoon is magic, but ½ cup is more like a culinary punch in the face.

7 For a great look at the history of salt, read *Salt* by Mark Kurlansky.

BUYING PRODUCE BY THE NUMBERS

LOOK FOR NUMBER 9

When you buy your lemons or any other produce, look for a stickered number (PLU number) that starts with 9. This signifies that it was grown organically.

This is most important when consuming the so-called "Dirty Dozen," which have the highest levels of industrial chemicals when grown conventionally (nonorganically).

Eating any five of the below 12 will give you a liver-spanking 14 pesticides. Here are the bad boys for 2012, listed in descending order:

1. Apples (92% contain two or more pesticides)
2. Celery
3. Sweet bell peppers
4. Peaches ("As a category, peaches have been treated with more pesticides than any other produce, registering combinations of up to 57 different chemicals.")
5. Strawberries
6. Nectarines (imported)
7. Grapes
8. Spinach
9. Lettuce
10. Cucumbers
11. Blueberries (domestic)
12. Potatoes

THE CLEAN 15

Conversely, eating from this list, even if the produce is conventionally grown, will cut your pesticide intake up to 90%.

1. Onions
2. Sweet corn
3. Pineapples
4. Avocados
5. Cabbage
6. Sweet peas
7. Asparagus
8. Mangoes
9. Eggplant
10. Kiwi
11. Cantaloupe (domestic)
12. Sweet potatoes
13. Grapefruit
14. Watermelon
15. Mushrooms

These two lists are compiled by the Environmental Working Group (EWG) and updated yearly. You can download them at ewg.org/foodnews/guide.

If you want to go the extra mile to remove pesticides, make a 3:1 (three parts to one part) mixture of water and acids (cider or distilled white vinegar, or lemon juice) in a spray bottle and spritz the veggies. Let them sit for a minute, rinse as usual, and go about your merry way.

GARLIC

Most good chefs believe there is no such thing as too much garlic. If you're a novice, I strongly suggest starting with garlic powder (sacrilege!). The real stuff can be challenging until we uncomplicate it. In the beginning, keep it convenient.

SLICED ALMONDS

These are my go-to garnish (decoration) and can make almost anything look like a $30 entrée. Definitely optional, but a simple addition to the kitchen that, worst-case, can be eaten as a slow-carb snack.

TRADER JOE'S
Product of Dijon, France
Moutarde de Dijon
DIJON MUSTARD
with White Wine
NET WT. 13 OZ (369g)

MUSTARD

Mustard is one of French cuisine's secrets. It can be used for dipping, making mixes, even creating the illusion of something battered and deep-fried (just coat and cook). Much like salt and EVOO, we want a basic mustard for cooking and a fancier mustard for dipping or finishing. This can add up, so just start with the former. Special thanks to Olivia Fox Cabane for her mustard (and chocolate, opposite page) recommendations.

Cooking: Trader Joe's Dijon Mustard

Finishing or dipping (can be mixed into guacamole too):

- Tarragon Mustard by Edmond Fallot or Delouis Fils
- Plantin Black Truffle Mustard or Fauchon Truffle Mustard

EDEN ORGANIC
BLACK BEANS
POMODORO PELATI • WHOLE PEELED TOMATOES
San Marzano
WESTBRAE NATURAL
VEGETARIAN
Organic
LENTIL BEANS
USDA ORGANIC

CANNED TOMATOES, LENTILS, BEANS

Let's get something straight: canned doesn't mean less fresh. In fact, quite the opposite can be true, and ditto for frozen. Tomatoes canned at the height of their prime will be superior to flash-ripened "fresh" tomatoes shipped out of season.

Since tomatoes go bad quickly, I buy San Marzano canned tomatoes, ideally diced, 2–10 cans at a time. Lentils and beans are slow-carb staples that I always have on hand. Pick a drawer, then store them and forget them. They'll be there when you need 'em. Many a late-night hunger tantrum has been prevented by lentils.

now
vegetable
glycerine

GLYCERIN/GLYCEROL

I use this to add sweetness or moisture to baking without sugar, or for adding more body to wine (again, sacrilege!). It is a natural by-product of wine making and gives wine its "tears" or "legs" that streak down the glass. Don't add much. If 3–4 T before bottling is enough, a tiny dash will do. There is one more application. Some elite cyclists use it to "hyper-hydrate" before long races, and I've used it to rehydrate for kickboxing post-weigh-ins. In all cases, just be sure to get "food grade." Don't consume any industrial versions or hand moisturizers, please.

MICHEL
CLUIZEL
NOIR
INFINI 99%

CHOCOLATE

How could I leave out chocolate? These aren't really for cooking per se. More for eating on cheat day with great friends. I say "great friends," because these aren't Hershey's bars. If you've never ventured above 80% cacao (cocoa solids) before, prepare yourself. Just 5 g of these two will satisfy you in a way that would require 50 g of a less-intense chocolate.

Michel Cluizel Noir Infini 99% Cacao. Incredibly smooth and intense. It will make you a chocolate snob for the rest of your life.

Francois Pralus Le 100% Tablette. Buttery smooth, a hint of a lemon finish. Less bold than the Cluizel but just as good.

ALICE IN WONDERLAND

Want to get fancy or simply fantasize? The below books have pantry lists that will blow your mind (and sometimes your budget).

Mission Street Food
(Myint & Leibowitz)

The pantry list that opened my eyes more than any other. One of the following will make almost anything better:

- Miso
- Herbs on fruit and desserts: cilantro, mint, basil, marjoram, tarragon, oregano (the last three for fruits)
- Goat cheese (Laura Chenel's is cost-effective)
- Smoked salt and fish sauce
- Squid ink
- Spanish chorizo
- Macadamia nuts
- Stock dashi (just add kombu and bonito flakes)
- Nori (blend into powder)
- Really good bacon (the smokiest is from Benton's Smoky Mountain Country Hams in Madisonville, Tennessee)

Alinea (Achatz)

This book explains what you need to cook à la chef Grant Achatz, from agar-agar to invert sugars and xanthan gum. Imagine Mr. Science or Alton Brown on steroids.

TOP GEAR: FROM SURGICAL TOWELS TO BIG GREEN EGGS

"Economy is a distributive virtue and consists not in saving, but in selection."

—*LETTERS TO A NOBLE LORD*, EDMUND BURKE, 1796

Don't you love it when cookbooks give you a 30-item equipment list as a starting point?

Imagine picking up a book on casual cycling that starts with "Want to see if you like cycling? Fantastic! Before we get started, go buy a custom-fitted carbon-fiber road bike, then pick out your uniform and competition clip-in shoes . . ." You'd close the book, precisely as I did with cookbooks my entire life. When I ran the numbers on these "essentials," totals of $1,200–$2,000 weren't uncommon.

Aside from cost, the "more is less" ethos that we aim to cultivate (for problem solving in general) is undermined if you splurge on equipment. Spending like a drunken sailor is no way to sharpen your brain. It also won't help you much.

Give a billiards pro a broomstick and he'll beat an amateur with the latest $1,000 wonder stick. Similarly, give a mediocre line cook who's survived six months in New York City restaurants two thinnish $20 cast-iron skillets. Match him dish-for-dish against an enthusiastic novice armed with a $3,000 seven-ply 12-piece set. The latter will get demolished.

My recommendations for "must-have" items are different from most cookbooks'. The goal is to get you through this book, not the entire world of cooking. I had a few criteria:

OUT-OF-THE-BOX LEARNING CURVE

Apple is famous for its intuitive "out-of-the-box" experience. I aimed for this, because a lot of "simple" cooking gear is misleading. Take, for instance, the following instructions for "dry beans and peas," which accompany a Presto-brand pressure cooker:

"Quick method: Clean and rinse beans; cover with three times as much water as beans. Bring beans to a boil and boil for two minutes. Remove from heat, cover, and let stand for 1–2 hours. Drain." And it continues from there.

Quick?

My assistant, Charlie, needed 20 minutes and 30 seconds just to get started after opening the manual. We timed it. It then took roughly 20 minutes to pressurize, 20 minutes to cook, and 20 minutes of attempting to depressurize before food could be served. Charlie is a *very* smart cookie, and this "quick" method totally demotivated him. Sure, pressure cookers can be great, especially for concentrating flavor in stocks, but I won't recommend them until the very end. They're totally unnecessary for the "undergrad" portions of this book.

COUNTING THE UNCOUNTED TIME

If cooking flank steak in a certain brand of griddle pan requires just five minutes, but the cleanup takes 20 minutes of repeated wire brushing with rock salt, it is not a five-minute meal. It is a pain-in-the-ass meal. The tool is therefore disqualified.

SPACE AND MULTIPLE USES

I sought out the people who do the most with the least: chefs like Jehangir Mehta, of Graffiti in New York City, which has a broom closet–size kitchen; food-truck operators; and caterers, who need to build a new kitchen at each gig. What are the lightweight and low-cost tools that serve as their Swiss Army knives? How do Susan Feniger and her team replicate street food en masse at their restaurant Street in L.A.? How the hell did Dan Kluger of ABC Kitchen produce 24,000 plates per day at the Formula 1 Singapore Grand Prix?!

Oh, there are secrets.

As you look at the following lists, don't forget to repurpose what you already have. Gray Kunz of four-star Lespinasse used to grind spices in his restaurant using a coffee grinder, so why can't you?[8] Do you have a French press for coffee? If it's one liter or larger, you can use it for straining stock and filtering all sorts of goodies. That was introduced to me by an accomplished chef who made me swear I wouldn't put his name in this sentence.

But unlike the books that so frustrated me, I don't want to assume you have anything, so I'll start from zero. Since practically no cookbooks price out their recommendations, you may still get a twinge of sticker shock, even in the $150 range. I don't blame you, but we're going absolutely bare bones. And if you still think $12 is too much to spend on towels . . .

Julia Child made the case for equipment by comparing them to the food itself: "a large enameled skillet can be bought for the price of a leg of lamb . . . a fine paring knife may cost less than two small lamb chops."[‡] These tools are investments in a lifelong skill, so don't balk and then spend $40 on drinks this weekend.

Now, on to the lists. Descriptions follow picture spreads.

NOTE: Though you might enjoy this section, you don't have to read it line by line. Feel free to jump to page 132 and refer back only when recipes call for gear you don't have.

---

8 Just don't grind cloves or allspice, as they can cloud plastics.

THE BASICS—WEEKS 1–8 (MANY ARE EITHER/OR)

1
2
LODGE
3
PANSAVER
Multi-Use Cooking Bags/Liners
- Slow Cooker Liners
- Oven Dish & Roaster Liners
- Steamer Bags
One Product Does It All!
400°F
25 Liners & Nylon Ties
4
5
6
7
8
9
10
11

12
13
14
15
16
17
18
Polder
19
DeLonghi
20

WEEKS 1–2

1. Lint-Free Surgical Huck Towels
2. Lodge LCC3 Logic Pre-Seasoned Combo Cooker
3. PanSaver EZ Clean Multi-Use Cooking Bags/Liners
4. Rada Cutlery Chef's Dicer
5. Tramontina Old Colony Stainless-Steel 6" Household Meat Cleaver
6. Dexa Small Grippmats
7. Bialetti Aeternum 10¼" Sauté Pan
8. OXO Good Grips 5-lb Food Scale with Pull-Out Display
9. Star Peeler from Zena Swiss
10. Kuhn Rikon Original Swiss Peeler
11. Silicone Spatulas

WEEKS 3–4

12. OXO Good Grips Locking Tongs with Nylon Heads, 12"
13. Kuhn Rikon SoftEdge Slotted 12" Spatula
14. Gray Kunz Sauce Spoons
15. Stainless-Steel Mixing Bowls
16. Chrome-Plated Steel-Footed Wire Plate Cake Rack
17. Microplane Classic Zester/Grater
18. Polder THM360/365 Digital In-Oven Thermometer/Timer

WEEKS 5–8

19. DeLonghi 380-Watt Tri-Blade 2-Speed Hand Blender
20. Winware 24-qt Professional Aluminum Stockpot

For links to all gear, visit FOURHOURCHEF.COM/GEAR The page includes up-to-date alternatives. Needless to say, prices and availability may change.

THE BASICS

WEEKS 1–2[9] ($143–$184)

TOWELS

Lint-Free Surgical Huck Towels

$12/dozen ($1 each)

$57/100 ($.57 each)

Forget about oven mitts and pot holders. The pros use folded towels for just about everything, and using them will teach you a lot.

How do you tell the veterans from the newbs? The former have a neatly stacked pile of cooking towels, crisply folded at the edges and tucked into their aprons. The latter have sloppy messes pushed through string. In a world of high-speed repetitive action, the little things *are* the big things. Suffice it to say, if you grab something hot with a single layer of a damp towel, your hands will be cooked like dumplings. (Not to worry: it's easy to avoid.)

Ever since my first visit to Riverpark restaurant, I wanted to get a stack of blue chef's towels. They were incredible for drying hands, easy to fold, and had no lint or fuzz whatsoever. But—no one sold them! The linen company that rents towels to Riverpark wouldn't give up their top-secret vendor.

One fateful evening, my friend Jacob came over for dinner and I shared my plight. He kept eating and casually said, "Oh, you mean lint-free surgical towels? My dad was a doctor. Yeah, they're great." Bingo.

I suggest ordering a dozen from Amazon to start. If you want something close, but—in my opinion—inferior, the long, narrow IKEA towels with red stripes will suffice.

RAW OR FINISHED CAST-IRON DUTCH OVEN AND SKILLET COMBINATION (COMBI)

Lodge LCC3 Logic Pre-Seasoned Combo Cooker

$30

Francis Mallmann, the most famous chef in South America, has classical French training, which involves using high-end copper pots and pans. He still prefers cast-iron, because nothing transfers heat more uniformly.

I've tried every possible cast-iron cooking vessel, and the combination Dutch oven and skillet is your best bang for the buck. Confession: I didn't know that a Dutch oven was a piece of cookware. I knew it only in its more, ahem, biological capacity: farting under the covers and then trapping someone beneath the covers. Commence bowing head in shame.

My favorite combination model for value is the Lodge LCC3.

If you'd like to cook tomatoes, baked beans, or other acidic foods in raw, or unenameled, cast-iron (which is what I use most often), you have two options: use a cooker liner (next item) or season the pan over the course of 6–12 meals first. I'll suggest the former, but let's look at the latter. "Seasoning" helps the iron absorb a protective coat of oil so that acids don't react with the surface and cause a metallic taste or black coloring. Since we're not going to take our time over 6–12 meals to season our tool, here's how to do it in an evening:

- Coat the pan in oil (flaxseed is ideal; look for it in health food stores among refrigerated nutritional supplements) by spreading it all over the inside surface with a folded paper towel.
- Bake the skillet and Dutch oven upside down in your oven, on the top rack, at 350°F (180°C) for 1 hour, then turn off the heat, open the door, and allow the pan to cool for 30 minutes.
- Rinse with warm water (no soap), towel dry immediately, and repeat five more times.

Too much hassle?

Just get a cheap skillet for tomatoes, eggs, and acidic stuff. My recommendation is the Aeternum, which is on the opposite page.

If you have the dough, you can buy enameled (finished) cast-iron skillets and Dutch ovens separately (Lodge brand: $100–$200; Le Creuset: $300+).

COOKER LINERS

PanSaver EZ Clean Cooking Bags/Liners

$11 for 25

These are typically used in slow cookers, skillets, and other cookware to prevent food from sticking. I often use them in the Lodge combi if I'm cooking acidic foods.

CLEAVER

Rada Cutlery Chef's Dicer

$7

OR

Tramontina Old Colony 6" Meat Cleaver

$35

The Rada Cutlery Chef's Dicer has a 5¼" blade and a lifetime warranty against defects. The Tramontina Old Colony cleaver, which I bought in a hardware store, is also great. Choose one to begin your knife journey.

"But," some accomplished cooks might gasp, "how can you recommend such junk? You should buy the best knife you can afford!" I respectfully disagree. As a novice, you'll end up buying the most expensive knife a salesperson can sell you. Why not buy the cheapest knife that helps you learn knife skills? Of everything I've tested, that is the Rada.

The Rada is less intimidating than a normal chef's knife, as it lacks a point and has a rounded front corner, but it still offers the proper elevation of the "bolster" (thus the proper knuckle clearance). This means the Rada prepares you for any good chef's knife. With the $70–$200 you save by starting with the Rada, you can buy far more helpful non-knife gear.

---

9 Based on the two-meals-per-week plan.

THE ANATOMY OF A KNIFE

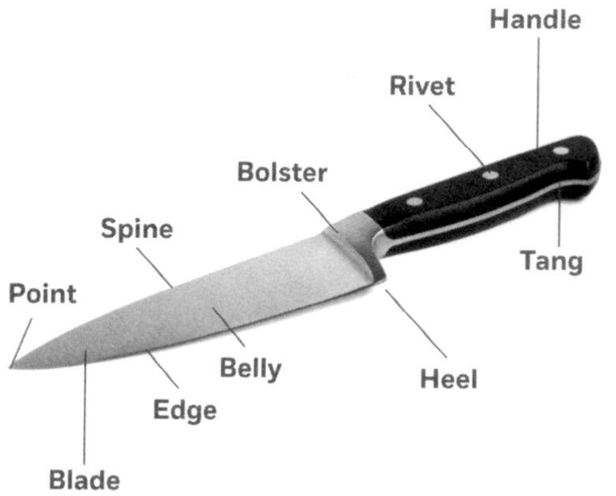
Handle
Rivet
Bolster
Spine
Tang
Point
Belly
Heel
Edge
Blade

INEXPENSIVE, FLEXIBLE CUTTING BOARDS

Dexa Small Grippmats
$10 (set of 4)

These are my favorite inexpensive cutting boards, which I also use for practicing knife skills on the road.

OR

NOT PICTURED
MIU Flexible Cutting Boards
$10 (set of 5)

I have also used and like the MIU Flexible Cutting Boards, which are easier to find online than the Dexa and come in a set of five. What do you do with the extra two or three that you never use? Sell them to friends, or use them as boot tubes—curl them and place them in boots to help the boots dry.

My philosophy for cutting boards is the same as my philosophy for knives: don't hesitate to start cheap, then invest if you're committed. If you have a few extra dollars (even $10) and want something awesome that will last, though, skip to page 124 for OXO or Boos. I'd still suggest the small cutting boards for travel purposes.

NONSTICK SAUTÉ PAN

Bialetti Aeternum 10¼" Sauté Pan
$25

This is the pan I use for cooking eggs.

Health concerns aside, the environmental effects of Teflon production are horrific. This led me to the gorgeously designed Aeternum, which I saw *the* man (Jacques Pépin) use once.

The interior features a water-based coating made of titanium and suspended silicate microparticles (the main component of glass), one of the most ecological, nondamaging materials usable for this purpose. Even though the packaging says "scratch-resistant," I don't recommend using metal against the surface. Stick to your silicone spatula.

Technically, a sauté pan should have straight, vertical sides and be deeper than a skillet, which has sloped sides. Practically, many chefs and manufacturers use the terms interchangeably, so I will.

If you want higher-end nonstick, I also like the Scanpan line from Denmark, recommended to me by Dr. Andrew Weil.

DIGITAL SCALE

OXO Good Grips Food Scale with Pull-Out Display
$30

Imagine measuring out one cup of feathers. Depending on how they fall, it might total 15 feathers or 10 feathers. Measuring cups and spoons (volume) can trick you. Errors of more than 25% are common when measuring flour, for instance.

To fix this, get a decent electric scale, weigh everything in grams (mass), and never have a problem again.

This is a must-have, and I prefer the OXO scale with pull-out display. Mixing bowls will often cover the display otherwise. If you have the moolah, get the 11-lb-capacity model instead of the 5-lb-capacity model, though both work wonderfully for all recipes in this book.

VEGETABLE PEELER

Star Peeler from Zena Swiss
$16 (set of 3)

OR

Kuhn Rikon Original Swiss Peeler
$11 (set of 3)

Joe Ades (may he rest in peace) made a fortune selling $5 Swiss-made peelers in New York City's Union Square. He even taught his daughter the art of the pitch, and she put herself through Columbia University by selling children's books on the street.

The Zena Swiss may be the original, but the Kuhn Rikon version is cheaper and easier to clean. The latter was one of two items (the other a Microplane) an executive chef recommended when I asked, "What do professionals use all the time that home cooks don't?"

I *hate* peeling, and this gadget makes it a cinch. Don't need three peelers? Well, for a thundering $11, you just handled two sweet Christmas gifts.

SILICONE SPATULAS

NOT PICTURED
Wilton Easy Flex 3-Piece Silicone Spatula Set
$7

OR

NOT PICTURED
Rachael Ray 3-Piece Spoonula Set
$15

I use a silicone spatula for stirring or moving food. It's flexible enough to reach every crevice of a container, but it's heat resistant and won't scratch your pans. Try it for scrambled eggs and you'll never go back to a normal spatula.

If you purchase a version with a plastic handle, don't leave it leaning on the edge of a hot pan. It'll melt.

THE OBSESSIVE WORLD OF KNIVES

Learning to properly wield a knife is one of life's great pleasures.

If you want the best knives in the world, you might look to the NFL Combine of bladesmith testing: the Master Smith Test, designed by the American Bladesmith Society. It holds court over the land of the razor's edge, and knives must successfully:

- Cut through a free-hanging rope, 1" or greater in diameter, in one strike.
- Chop through a wooden two-by-four twice. Any nicks to the blade result in failure.
- Shave hair off the arm of the knife-smith contestant (the one wielding the knife) to show edge retention after the chopping test.
- Be bent 90 degrees in a vise without snapping, the focal point of the bend being 3" from the tip.

It's all very impressive, but you don't need impressive anytime soon.

Don't worry about carbon steel vs. stainless vs. Damascus vs. adamantium. Similarly, the "[metal X] will hold an edge for six months" comments often assume *professional* use and hours of daily abuse, not prepping vegetables for 10–20 minutes a few nights a week.

Stick with steel (not ceramic), and find something you're comfortable with. In the top Thai restaurant in all of India, the executive chef uses a Victorinox chef's knife you could buy at Walmart for $15. Some outstanding Chinese chefs squat down and sharpen their all-purpose cleavers on brick floors.

I tried everything you can imagine. I even traveled around the world with a 6" Miyabi Kaizen (**2,** $120), a 6" Tramontina cleaver, and Grippmat cutting boards. From hotel room to hotel room, I'd slice and dice celery, carrots, and onions. In between "sets," I'd study videos, my favorites being from *Yan Can Cook* and Gordon Ramsay, which we'll cover later.

Each time I was within a 15-minute drive of Sur la Table, I would visit and test everything they had in stock.

Ultimately, after butchering all the cucumbers in several stores, I settled on the Wüsthof Santoku as my favorite all-purpose knife:

1
2
3
4

1.

Wüsthof Classic Hollow-Ground Santoku, 7"

$98

I simply found this knife easy to use. Much later, I found out that Rachael Ray, before her endorsement deals, also used this as her default knife. Santoku, mistakenly called "santuko" at Bed, Bath & Beyond among other places, literally means "three [*san*] virtues/specialties [*toku*]" and refers to cutting fish, meat, and vegetables. In Japan, it's considered the homemaker's savior, a culinary chameleon for all purposes.

Though this Wüsthof is my favorite recommendation for novices, there are a few other knives I really like. Some are slightly longer, which you'll only enjoy once you are 100% comfortable with something 6"–7" long.

3.

MAC MTH-80 8" Professional Series Chef's Knife with Dimples

$120

This was recommended by the private chef of UFC fighter Georges St-Pierre. It's also the top recommended chef's knife on the site Cooking for Engineers, authored by Michael Chu, who subjected knives to extensive vegetable testing (fourhourchef.com/chef-knives-rated).

4.

Shun Classic 8" Chef's Knife

$170

I now use this knife as much as the Wüsthof, but it took me a few months to get comfortable with the longer blade.

Last, if you really want to blow your paycheck on a work of art, consider a Japanese knife from Korin Trading Company in New York City or a handmade Berti knife from Italy.

WEEKS 3–4 ($75–$90)

SOFT-HEADED TONGS, PELTEX, OR SAUCE SPOON

You have three options for turning things. You'll need to buy the first two. Chefs don't pierce their food like savages, spilling all the juices that should remain inside.

OXO Good Grips Locking Tongs, 12"
$10

AND

Kuhn Rikon SoftEdge Slotted 12" Spatula (Peltex)
$18

OPTIONAL EXTRA

Gray Kunz Sauce Spoon
$10

Tongs with tips that don't scratch, like the OXO nylon-tipped tongs, will be the easiest to use. Real chefs end up using a "Peltex," which is a brand name but generically refers to a slotted fish turner. I use "fish turner" and "Peltex" interchangeably in this book. The better the cook, the fewer tools required, and you'll find that many of the best use a 1- or 2-oz sauce spoon for spatula duty.

These days I use the Kuhn Rikon most often, as it has silicone edges and can also effectively replace silicone spatulas. For our lessons, you'll want both tongs and a Peltex.

MIXING BOWLS

Stainless-Steel Mixing Bowls
$10

I use my set of stainless-steel mixing bowls for almost every meal, as:

- Prep bowls, garbage bowls
- Rinsing bowls for vegetables
- Warm-water containers for thawing meats

J. Kenji López-Alt, the brilliant author of "The Food Lab" on the blog Serious Eats,‡ recommends the ABC Valueline brand of cheaper mixing bowls. These are more than sufficient and might cost $10 for a set of three. Regardless of the brand, start with at least 2-, 3-, and 5-qt bowls, as Kenji suggests.

CAKE RACK

Steel-Footed Wire Plate Cake Rack
$7

A cake rack is typically used for cooling cakes or pies. I don't use mine for either. I place it at the bottom of my cast-iron Dutch oven and I use it to steam anything: vegetables, chicken, and more. I find it much easier to clean than the steamer baskets that open and close like a flower. A few companies have caught on and now offer "steel-footed wire steam racks," which are elevated to allow more water underneath.

RASP GRATER OR ZESTER

Microplane Classic Zester/Grater
$11

Generically called a "rasp grater" or "zester," we'll use the Microplane primarily for lime and lemon zesting; you'll shave off flakes of the skin for flavor. It can be used for garlic, it works wonders for ginger, and it can make short work of shallots. This underrated utensil can be found in nearly any professional kitchen.

There are a ton of off-label uses. Looking for that beautiful dusting of sugar on top of brownies? Usually bakers would use a "sugar shaker," but you can just pour sugar on top of your Microplane and give it a few taps. You can grate cinnamon sticks and nutmeg with it, too.

DIGITAL IN-OVEN PROBE THERMOMETER

NOT PICTURED

ThermoWorks The Original Cooking Thermometer/Timer
$19

OR

Polder THM360/365 Digital In-Oven Thermometer/Timer
$24

I use a ThermoWorks or Polder probe thermometer almost every day. I also throw one in my luggage any time I travel. This is the easiest way to never over- or undercook anything ever again. No more checking on doneness, no more "Sorry it's so tough." Nothing but wonderful food. This tool is absolutely required.

WEEKS 5–8 ($85)

IMMERSION BLENDER

DeLonghi 380-Watt 2-Speed Hand Blender
$50

OR

Breville Control Grip
$100

I started using immersion blenders to reduce cleanup. I could, for example, blend tomatoes into tomato soup right in a saucepan.

Later, I had an epiphany: if you get a model with a 2–3 cup "chopper" attachment, you have a mini food processor that's easier to clean than full-size processors!

One chef joked that we should write a book called *The Immersion Blender Cookbook*. Get the chopper attachment and you can do just about anything: grind hamburger meat, make mayonnaise in seconds, blitz gazpacho in no time, create foams, and more.

I love the Breville but often use the cordless Braun Multiquick 7. I've tested the less expensive DeLonghi, which absolutely works.

STOCKPOT

Winware 24-qt Professional Aluminum Stockpot
$35 (lid sold separately)

My go-to option for stovetop sous-vide (explained later), and my preferred vessel for makeshift smoking.

EXTRAS AND UPGRADES

1. **OXO Good Grips Cutting Board (15" x 21")**
2. **John Boos Reversible Maple Cutting Board (18" x 24")**
3. **Kuhn Rikon Epicurean Garlic Press**
4. **Grapefruit Seed Extract**
5. **Isopropyl Alcohol**
6. **Tolco Empty Spray Bottle (8 oz)**
7. **Unicorn Magnum Pepper Mill**
8. **OXO Salad Spinner**

SHOPPING SPREE

9. **MIU France Stainless-Steel Magnetic Knife Holder (20")**
10. **Anchor Purity Wrap**
11. **Cuisipro Stainless-Steel Measuring Spoon Set**
12. **Fissler Magic Smooth-Edge Can Opener**
13. **iSi Silicone Scraper Spatula**
14. **Proctor Silex 1.7-L Automatic Electric Kettle**
15. **Zoo Med Laboratories Stainless-Steel Feeding Tongs (10")**
16. **Amco Enameled Aluminum Lemon Squeezer**
17. **Kinetic Glasslock 3-Piece Square Glass Food Storage Set with Locking Lids**
18. **Hamilton Beach 8-Cup Food Processor**
19. **Back to Basics SE3000 Smoothie Express Lifestyle 26-oz Smoothie Maker**
20. **DUXTOP 1800-Watt Portable Induction Cooktop**
21. **Vitamix 5200**
22. **SousVide Supreme Sous-Vide Water Oven**

EXTRAS AND UPGRADES

OPTIONAL BUT RECOMMENDED WHEN YOU CAN

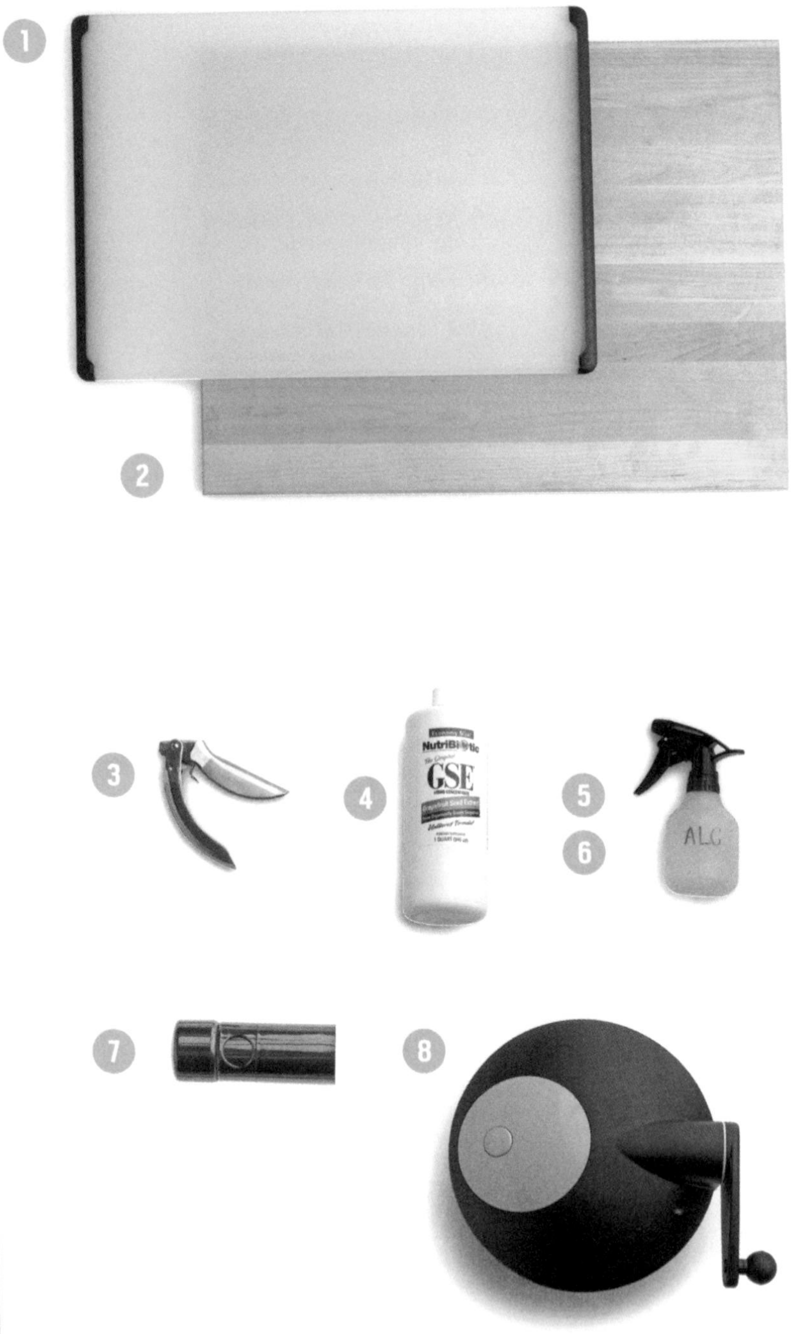
1
2
3
4
GSE
5
6
ALC
7
8

SHOPPING SPREE

THINGS I ENJOY

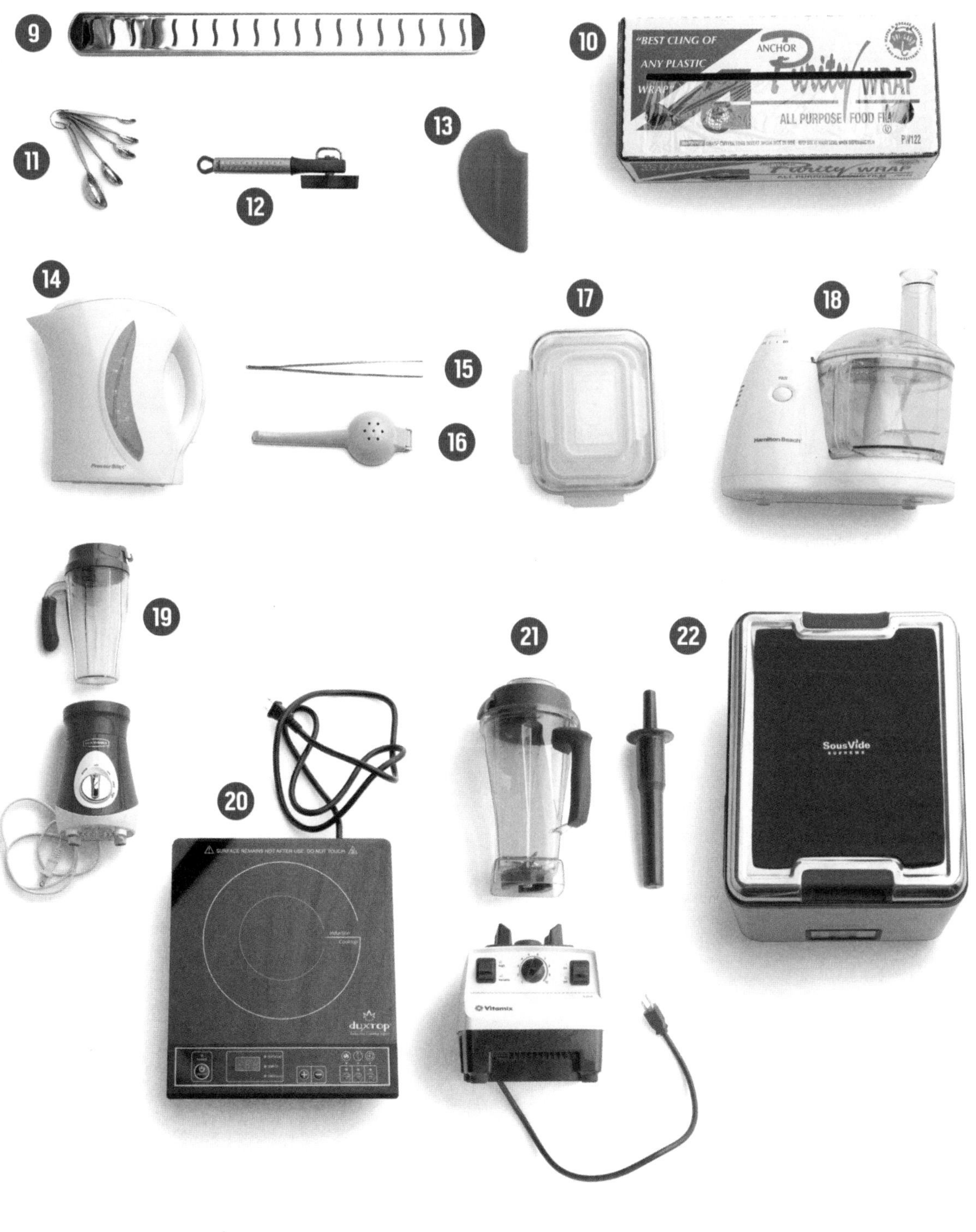
9
10
"BEST CLING OF ANY PLASTIC WRAP"
ANCHOR
Purity WRAP
ALL PURPOSE FOOD FILM
11
12
13
14
15
16
17
18
Hamilton Beach
19
20
duxtop
21
Vitamix
22
SousVide SUPREME

EXTRAS AND UPGRADES

OPTIONAL BUT RECOMMENDED WHEN YOU CAN ($133–$203)

CUTTING BOARDS

OXO Good Grips Cutting Board (15" x 21")
$25

OR

John Boos Reversible Maple Cutting Board (18" x 24")
$90

The OXO can fit (barely) into my dishwasher and has grooves to catch juices. The maple Boos is gorgeous, stable, and a mainstay in professional kitchens around the world. It's wonderful to work on. It's suggested that you oil it once a month to prevent warping or bending.

If you'd like wood but want a thinner cutting board, teak comes recommended, because it contains tectoquinones, which make it more resistant to moisture than other woods.

GARLIC PRESS

Kuhn Rikon Epicurean Garlic Press
$38

The Epicurean press does a *better* job of pressing garlic when you keep the skin *on*! Read that sentence again—it's a big deal! No more peeling, no more cutting, no more pain-in-the-ass cleanup of a poorly designed press. I've tried them all, and this press is the one press to rule them all. Yes, it's expensive . . . and totally worth it.

GERM KILLER: ALCOHOL OR GRAPEFRUIT SEED EXTRACT (GSE)

Isopropyl Alcohol
$4 (16 oz)

OR

Grapefruit Seed Extract
$8 (2 oz)

(MULTI-USE SPRAY BOTTLE)
Tolco Empty Spray Bottle (8 oz)
$2

More than a few chefs, even former French Laundry hotshots, use rubbing alcohol (isopropyl alcohol) to disinfect cutting boards and utensils at home. They'll only use bleach (in a 1:100 ratio of bleach to water) to meet code at events where an inspector might show up. Alcohol won't eat your fingers, and it dries quickly. I use the Tolco 8-oz bottles, but any spray bottle will work.

In addition to alcohol, I use grapefruit seed extract (GSE) to disinfect heavier jobs, especially if I'm cooking with a lot of chicken. A component of GSE, naringenin, is a potent antiviral and antibacterial agent; it also extends the effect of caffeine (see *The 4-Hour Body*). Add in hesperidin, also in GSE, and you can reduce everything from hepatitis C and *E. coli* to methicillin-resistant staph bacteria.‡ I travel with a small bottle of GSE. If I think something tastes off, I put a few drops in water and down the hatch it goes.

PEPPER MILL

Unicorn Magnum Pepper Mill
$35

I never thought this mill could live up to its hype. Once I tried it, I immediately purchased a second one for my momma. It's that good.

SALAD SPINNER

OXO Salad Spinner
$30

This doubles as a colander, and it's my preferred tool for washing vegetables and salad. Wet greens don't hold dressing.

SHOPPING SPREE

THINGS I ENJOY ($1,506–$4,101)

MAGNETIC KNIFE STRIP

MIU France Stainless-Steel Magnetic Knife Holder (20")
$28

OR

NOT PICTURED
Messermeister Bamboo Knife Magnet Block (16½")
$120

The ubiquitous wooden knife block, nicknamed the "bacteria hotel" by some chefs, is far inferior to a simple magnetic wall strip.

I use the MIU France magnetic knife holder, but *Cook's Illustrated* recommends the Messermeister bamboo knife magnet. This is because the wood is supposedly gentle on blades. I save the blade edge by putting the spine of the knife on the magnet first, then slowly rotating the blade on.

PLASTIC WRAP

Anchor Purity Wrap
$13

Plastic wrap, such as Saran Wrap, is a headache. It gets stuck to itself, it won't cling to whatever you want it to, and you wonder: why the hell even bother?

Anchor Purity is the industrial solution (what the pros use), and you can get 2,000 feet for a mere $13, which will last you forever. Easier to use, faster to use, no mess, and it just works.

METAL CART AND HOOKS

NOT PICTURED
Whitmor Supreme Cart
$37 (3-tier)

AND

NOT PICTURED
Cuisinart Chef's Classic Cookware Universal Pot Rack Hooks
$8 (set of 6)

These were both game changers for me. They allowed me to double the amount of gear I tested while decluttering at the same time. My flat surfaces were clear for the first time in years.

For $37, I expected very little, but these chrome racks support an incredible amount of weight. One of mine holds six cast-iron pots for starters, and it's easily rolled around. I now have three racks and don't know how I lived without them. Do your TV and microwave need to go somewhere more convenient? These will work.

To increase the loading capacity of each, I added a few S-hooks to the sides (pot rack hooks are even better), from which I can hang pans, towels, and so on. Even if you quit cooking, these can remake your house.

MEASURING SPOONS

Cuisipro Stainless-Steel Measuring Spoon Set
$11

If you must use measuring spoons, use spoon-shaped versions, which are easier to insert into spice jars and other containers.

CAN OPENER

Fissler Magic Smooth-Edge Can Opener
$30

OR

NOT PICTURED
Rösle Can Opener
$37

In the can-opening world, the equivalent of the Epicurean press is the Fissler Magic Smooth-Edge Can Opener. It cuts around the *side* of the can, leaving no sharp edges and a lid that can be put back on. As one chef asked me upon seeing it, "Why did it take 100+ years for someone to think of that?"

If you can't find the Fissler, manufacturer Rösle seems to have caught on with its own 8" version.

PASTRY SCRAPER

iSi Silicone Scraper Spatula
$6

I didn't buy this for pastries. I use it for picking up chopped bits of anything on my cutting board. If I'm doing a bunch of cooking, it will sit in my back pocket like a switchblade comb from *The Outsiders*, ready for action. If you have a hardware store nearby, any flexible scraper for home improvement will work. Just ensure it's at least 4" wide at the blade.

WATER BOILER

Proctor Silex 1.7-L Automatic Electric Kettle
$22

OR

NOT PICTURED
Hamilton Beach 10-Cup Stainless-Steel Electric Kettle
$30

I never use pots to heat water for tea or coffee. My go-to device is the Proctor Silex. If you get the 1.7-L version, you can also use it to help you peel vegetables. Just score an X on both sides of each tomato (or shallot, etc.) with a knife and drop them in the boiling water. Take them out after 30 seconds and peel from the Xs.

If heating water in plastic bothers you, a glass or steel equivalent like the Hamilton Beach can be used.

FEEDING TONGS

Zoo Med Laboratories Stainless-Steel Feeding Tongs (10")
$8

Ever seen dishes come out looking like a MoMA piece? These feeding tongs, intended for feeding insects to pet lizards, are perfect for "tweezer cuisine." They're also perfect for turning over small pieces of fish or vegetables in a skillet. If you get bored with using them for food, they're useful for saving things from drains and pulling paper jams out of printers.

CITRUS SQUEEZER

Amco Enameled Aluminum Lemon Squeezer

$9

If you start using acid like you use salt—an approach I recommend—this tool is invaluable. It's not a must-have from the outset, but I use this every time I squeeze juice from a lemon or lime. It's the difference between getting 50% of the juice and 80% of the juice.

STORAGE

Kinetic Glasslock 3-Piece Square Glass Food Storage Set with Locking Lids

$32

I want to single-handedly wipe out round plastic storage containers, which are optimized to waste space. The goddamn lids roll everywhere, too.

I prefer the Kinetic Glasslock storage set, which comes with locking lids. "3-piece" means what it should: three separate boxes that nest inside one another. Many manufacturers will count a lid as a "piece," so look out for this con job. It's just like the occasional Chinese restaurant that serves oily food and asks, "Oh, you want rice with that?" and then charges you extra. *Psshhht.*

FOOD PROCESSOR

Hamilton Beach 8-Cup Food Processor

$34

OR

NOT PICTURED

Hamilton Beach 500-Watt Food Processor

$35

For fast cutting or dicing in really high volume, you'll want a food processor or a mandoline. The latter, especially the Japanese Benriner model (*benri* means "convenient" in Japanese), is found in all restaurants worth their salt. It's also very "convenient" for chopping fingertips off.

I use an 8-c food processor instead, but the 500-watt, 10-c model has a higher average review on Amazon.

TRAVEL BLENDER

Back to Basics SE3000 Smoothie Express Lifestyle 26-oz Smoothie Maker

$25

OR

NOT PICTURED

Hamilton Beach Single-Serve Blender with Travel Lid

$15

I have one friend, EP, who makes his smoothies with an enormous Vitamix blender. He's as faithful to "Vittie" as a Labrador to his master. EP checks separate luggage for his Vitamix, powders, and potions when he travels. That, ladies and gentlemen, is dedication. Me? Too lazy. During my travel experiments with knife skills, I bought the Back to Basics Smoothie Express. It's small enough to fit in a suitcase with the rest of my clothing, and it can liquefy well-chopped veggies (with some liquid added). Be forewarned: it's not strong enough for blending really hard foods, and I wouldn't mess with anything frozen.

As of this writing, the Hamilton Beach single-serve blender has been getting better reviews.

INDUCTION BURNER

NOT PICTURED

Cooktek Heritage Single Countertop Induction Cooktop

$805

DUXTOP 1800-Watt Portable Induction Cooktop

$75

I clearly remember my first encounter with an induction burner. Nick Kokonas, co-owner of Alinea restaurant, brought me to the side wall of their incredible kitchen. It has a surprisingly small oven range but dozens of induction burners that can be moved or stored as needed. The readout on the Cooktek burner was 500°F.

"Put your palm on it," he suggested.

"Nah, I think I'll pass," I said.

So Nick, after removing his wedding ring, placed his hand on the burner and smiled at me. I then did the same: nothing. Normal gas burners have an efficiency of less than 40% (energy purchased vs. energy deposited into food). Induction, on the other hand, is well over 80% efficient, but it can only heat materials a magnet will stick to. Cast-iron and All-Clad steel will work, but 100% aluminum or copper will not. Even though the latter are more conductive, they are not ferromagnetic. The induction burner uses a magnetic field to create electrical current: almost all the heat goes directly into the vessel. If you're in a rush to boil water, induction is the way to go.

These extra-lightweight burners can be used just about anywhere and are popular in food trucks.

The nicer versions, like the Cooktek Heritage, cost $800, but cheaper models, like the DUXTOP, cost just $75. The latter will, curiously, heat up a little. Hmmm. . . .

BLENDER

NOT PICTURED

Vitamix Vita-Prep 3

$520

OR

Vitamix 5200

$449

The Vita-Prep is industrial, and the 5200, which I own, is a high-end home unit. Both could probably blend rocks. I use mine to demolish anything (including vegetables) that resists my less powerful devices. If you're going to make a lot of smoothies or soups and have the budget, this is your Ferrari.

Just be cautious, as you should with any blender, about hot liquids. They can shoot out the top like a volcano, literally hitting the ceiling. If you're blending hot soups, take the stopper out of the top and lightly cover with a towel. This will allow steam to escape and prevent *Double Dare*–like catastrophes.

SOUS-VIDE

SousVide Supreme Sous-Vide Water Oven

$429

This allows more controlled low-temp cooking experiments, like the 72-Hour Beef Short Ribs we'll see later.

It's also a shortcut to zero-cleanup meals for 6–10 people.

OR

NOT PICTURED

PolyScience Standard Immersion Circulator

$1,705

The sous-vide standard for the professionals. PolyScience makes some of the coolest cutting-edge gadgets for cooking, but you might need a credit increase on your AMEX.

BBQ GRILLS AND SMOKERS

NOT PICTURED

Big Green Egg Smoker

$700+

This *kamado*-style grill and smoker has a cult following. Devotees call themselves "EGGheads," and there is even an annual "EGGtoberfest" each October at the manufacturer's Georgia headquarters. It draws 1,500+ people from around the world. But $700?! As one user says, "I can cold-smoke salmon at 100°F, and I can sear steaks at 1,200°F. They're as versatile as anything on the market."‡

OR

NOT PICTURED

Weber Smokey Mountain Cooker 18½" Smoker

$300

The highest-rated cooker and smoker on Amazon, by light years. Of 220+ reviews, all are four or five stars, 200+ being five stars at the time of this writing.

THE NOVICE NINE

TOTALLY OPTIONAL

bodum
PAVINA

THE NOVICE NINE

1. **Sur La Table French Onion Soup Bowl**
2. **Himalayan Salt Block**
3. **Mexican Fajita Sizzler Platter Set**
4. **Terra-Cotta Cazuela**
5. **Medium Triangle Bowl**
6. **Staub 2.25" Round Cocotte**
7. **Bodum Pavina Double-Wall Thermo Glasses**
8. **Ramekins**
9. **Beaker Assortment**

THE NOVICE NINE

The novice nine are my go-to serviceware and make you look better than you are. All nine of them hide functionality in sex appeal. Unless you have an unlimited budget, form should follow function. Those terra-cotta dishes? They can dramatically cut down on cleanup. Those sizzler platters? They allow you to serve oven-to-table without additional plates. The UFO-like triangle dishes that can be used as plates or bowls? These multipurpose cost savers are space savers in your cupboard.

Most can be found for less than $20, and all but one cost less than $50. I've starred the ones I use most. Most can be found at Sur La Table, but it's great fun to search for stranger (and still cheap) pieces at Chinese supply stores like Mei-wa in SF or Pearl River Mart in NYC.

★ Sur La Table French Onion Soup Bowl

$13

This soup bowl is made from high-fired stoneware and is finished with non-porous enamel to prevent cracks or chips. French onion soup is traditionally served in bowls like this with an easy-grip handle. I use it for everything.

Himalayan Salt Block

$47

Himalayan salt blocks are not only beautiful, but they also serve a variety of purposes. Used as a platter for sashimi, you can see fish being cured by the salt. Or, my favorite, cook steak on it in the oven and bring it straight to the table.

Mexican Fajita Sizzler Platter Set

$27

Cast-iron, as mentioned, retains heat much better than most other cookware materials. The slanted sides of this pan keep liquid in the center to create steam and intensify flavors.

★ Terra-Cotta Cazuela

$15

This traditionally Spanish cooking vessel insulates the sides and bottom, effectively cooking from the top only. It is easy to clean and often one-tenth the cost of Staub (below). I use these for cooking and holding salt and herbs.

★ Sur La Table Triangle Bowl

$10

Made of restaurant-quality porcelain, this bowl is both dishwasher and microwave safe. Because of its corners, it also works great for dips.

Staub 2.25" Round Cocotte

$150

Cooks faster than terra-cotta and from all directions.

★ Bodum Pavina Double-Wall Thermo Glasses

$17

Great for hot and cold drinks, the borosilicate-glass double wall prevents condensation.

Ramekins

$11

These 4-oz ramekins are made from dishwasher-, microwave-, and oven-safe porcelain. With a classic style, they are perfect for serving individual soufflés, custards, or even dipping sauces. Place directly on plates, if you like.

★ Beaker Assortment

$27

This set of beakers includes 50 ml, 100 ml, 250 ml, 600 ml, and 1 liter. I use them for serving wine and blending things.

For convenience, links to the "novice nine" can be found at FOURHOURCHEF.COM/SERVICEWARE

LESSON CALENDAR

DECEMBER 2012[10]

MON	TUES	WED	THURS	FRI	SAT	SUN
OK, ready to rock and roll? Do some jumping jacks, and get in a karate stance. Here's the curriculum of DOM. I've sketched out eight hypothetical weeks of cooking twice per week. I like Wednesday and Sunday for many reasons, but feel free to choose whichever days you like. No need to memorize this; you'll flip back to it often. **Be sure to see your scorecard on the inside back cover.**					1	2 OSSO "BUKO"
3	4	5 SCRAMBLED EGGS	6	7	8	9 COCONUT CAULIFLOWER CURRY MASH
10	11	12 UNION SQUARE ZUCCHINI	13	14	15	16 HARISSA CRAB CAKES
17	18	19 BITTMAN CHINESE CHICKEN	20	21	22	23 ARUGULA, AVOCADO, AND ROMA SALAD
24	25	26 SEXY-TIME STEAK	27	28	29	30 DINNER PARTY
31						

10 These are the first two months following this book's pub date. All you need to know: I suggest cooking Wednesday and Sunday.

LESSON CALENDAR

JANUARY 2013

MON	TUES	WED	THURS	FRI	SAT	SUN
	1	2 ROASTED GARLIC AND GAZPACHO	3	4	5	6 IMMERSION SAUCES
7	8	9 ROCK 'N' EEL	10	11	12	13 SOUS-VIDE CHICKEN BREAST
14	15	16 SEARED SCALLOPS	17	18	19	20 CHICKEN HIGADO PÂTÉ
21	22	23 "MLBJ"	24	25	26 SURPRISE! BLOCK OUT EVENING	27 SECOND DINNER PARTY
28	29	30	31			

LESSON 01 +12

SKILLS

BRAISING, BLADE GRIP

OSSO "BUKO"

SHORTHAND

350F 2hr: Cook lamb, 1 bunch halved carrot, 1 can whole tom, 5 minced garlic cloves, 2T EVOO, 1¾c white wine, S+P

HANDS-ON TIME

5 minutes

TOTAL TIME

2 hours 5 minutes

GEAR

- Knife + cutting board
- Raw or finished cast-iron Dutch oven
- If using raw cast-iron, optional but suggested: PanSaver

OPTIONAL PAIRINGS

"Don't Sweat the Technique" by Eric B. & Rakim

Anti-angiogenesis blended tea (see page 140)

Want flavor but 50–75% less caffeine? Just steep tea leaves in boiling water for 10–15 seconds, discard the water, and proceed as normal. Simple and effective. This is how I can drink various teas at dinner without staying up all night.

> "Fucking delicious. Honestly, one of the easier things I've ever cooked. You were right to give this the #1 placement."
>
> —RYAN HOLIDAY, NON-COOK RECIPE TESTER FOR *THE 4-HOUR CHEF*

Even if you've screwed up scrambled eggs in the past, you can get to haute cuisine in a day and acquire an amazing standby dish that will never fail you. This is that dish.

Good marketing is important in the food world. When's the last time you had Patagonian toothfish? Not recently, right? That's because savvy spin doctors know you'll eat more of it with a sexy rebranding: Chilean sea bass!

But sometimes there's more meaning behind a name. This version of osso buco, for instance, is called Osso "Buko," not unlike the "Adidems" (think: Adidas) I bought in Beijing. It's not 100% faithful to the purists, but it's more idiotproof, your guests will love it, and some will even prefer the black-market version! First off, we won't brown the meat. Second, we'll use lamb shanks instead of the traditional veal shanks. A bone hole is a bone hole,[11] after all, and even turkey drumsticks sawed in half by your butcher can work beautifully.[12] Furthermore, as author P. J. O'Rourke puts it: "Veal is a very young beef and, like a very young girlfriend, it's cute but boring and expensive."

The Osso "Buko" you're about to make prompted one friend of mine, author Michael Ellsberg, to put down his fork and suggest, "You should start the Tim Ferriss restaurant!" When I laughed and explained how simple it was, he responded with "*This is simple?!*" as if I'd insisted Santa Claus were real.

Enjoy this beauty, and remember: read it all through before starting.

---

11 *Osso buco* literally means "bone hole" in Italian.

12 Check them after about 1½ hours; they should be succulent, and the meat will have pulled back from the ends of the bones. Lulzim Rexhepi used turkey at the famed Kittichai in New York City.

This is what my first Osso "Buko" looked like. Shanks uncut.

And this is a later attempt. Bones cut.

ABBREVIATIONS YOU'LL SEE THROUGHOUT THIS BOOK

t	teaspoon
T	tablespoon
EVOO	extra-virgin olive oil
S+P	salt + pepper
c	cups
qt	quarts
oz	ounces
lb	pounds
g	grams
≈	approximately

NOTE:

Grams and milliliters are, for all intents and purposes, equivalent in the kitchen. If I give something in ml, you can weigh it in g.

COPPOLA
Partanna

INGREDIENTS	TO SERVE 4
Lamb shanks (even if cooking for 2, I suggest making enough for 4. Think leftovers.)	**4** (12 oz/ 340 g each)
Carrots	**1 bunch**
Canned whole San Marzano tomatoes (ideally a can with a pull tab; otherwise, you'll need a can opener)	**1 can** (15 oz/ 425 g)
Garlic powder, or garlic cloves pushed through a garlic press (if the latter, keep the skins on in the presser)	**3-finger pinch of powder, or 5 cloves**
EVOO	**2 T**
White wine (just about anything dry will work, and cheap is fine[13])	**About ⅓ bottle**
S+P	**To taste**

PREP

00 At least 1 hour prior to cook time, thaw the frozen lamb shanks. I put the plastic-bagged shanks in a large mixing bowl full of the hottest tap water I can muster, and I weigh them down with an upside-down plate or bowl.

01 Scrub the carrots with a vegetable brush or coarse sponge (I peel as few things as possible), and chop off the ends. Roughly break by hand into halves.

02 Get your *meez* ready—that is, get everything you will use in one place.

PICKUP[14]

00 Preheat the oven to 350°F (180°C). Place a PanSaver, if using, in the Dutch oven.

01 Place the carrots in the pot to create a bed for the meat to rest on.

02 Add the 4 lamb shanks.

03 Open the tomato can and squish the tomatoes with one hand (beware of squirting juice—poke a thumb through first) as you drop them into the Dutch oven, along with their juice.

04 Sprinkle in the 3-finger pinch of garlic powder or 5 cloves of raw garlic.

05 Drizzle in about 2 T EVOO. Don't sweat the precision. A decent "glug" is approximately 2 T.

13 Nothing sweet like Gruner or Riesling. Ideal is an Italian table wine, like Trebbiano. I tend to use whatever I have.

14 Attention, professionals: I realize I'm using "pickup" more flexibly than in the "finished cooking to plating" industry sense.

A

B

C

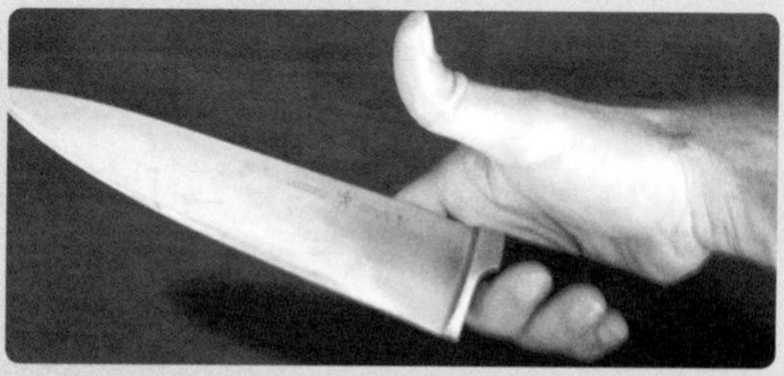

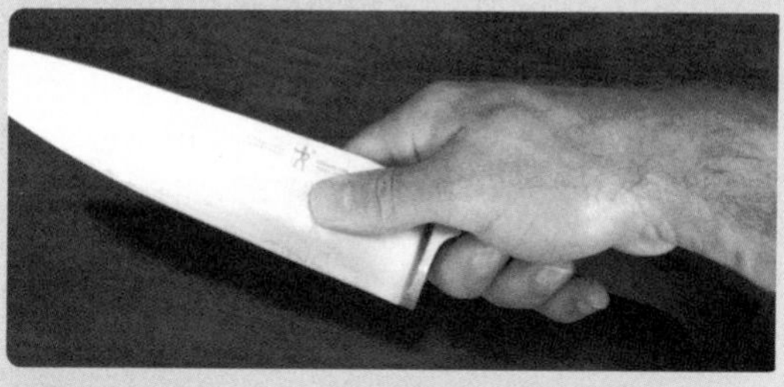

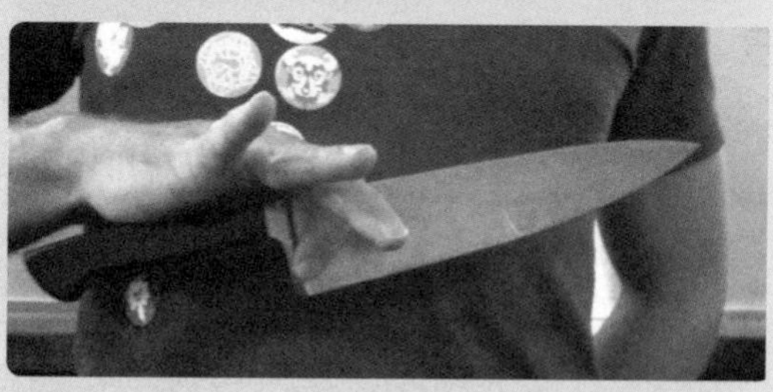

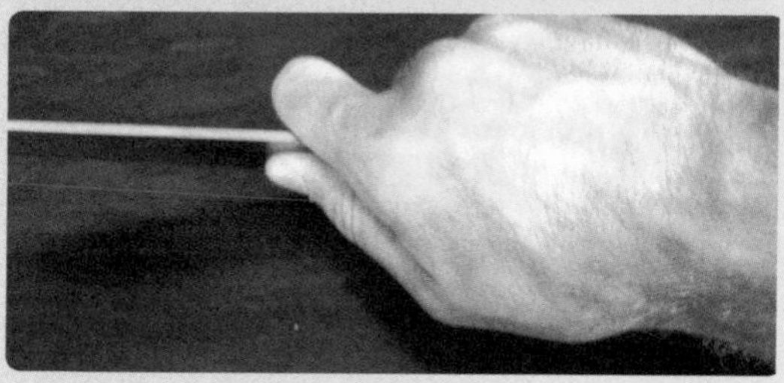

How to Hold Your Blade

To chop off the ends of the carrots, hold the knife like a chef. It's best described as holding the *blade*. The thumb and pad of the index finger pinch the base of the blade. The bottom of the index finger's top knuckle applies pressure and never leaves contact. It's similar to how one holds a golf club.

06 Add enough white wine to cover ½–¾ of the meat. Don't cover it completely.

07 Grind 10 hard turns of pepper onto your shanks (add more than you think you need), and add two 3-finger pinches of kosher salt, sprinkling from a height of 12" (30 cm). This will create an even spread and prevent clumps of salt.

08 Cover the pot, put it in the oven, and come back 2 hours later.

09 Serve on VerTerra pressed-leaf disposable plates, or whatever you have. Gracefully accept lavish praise from guests.

10 If you've used a PanSaver, here's the great part: just bunch up the edges so you have the leftovers in a bag, and put it in the fridge in a pan or dispose of it. No cleaning other than your silverware! One Michelin three-star chef believes braised meats taste best 3 days after cooking.

ON BRAISING: Braising—long cooking, partially submerged—is incredibly forgiving. Forgot the timer and "overcooked" by 30 minutes? No problem. Things will still be amazing. Braising turns tough cuts into choice cuts. These working muscles—which the animal uses to move around or hold itself up—are also the cheapest, as they tend to have a lot of tough connective tissue. Braise those bad boys for a few hours and they become wonderfully moist. This is thanks to collagen, connective tissue that turns into a Jell-O-like consistency. If you've ever had amazing brisket or baby back ribs, it's thanks to this transformation.

The exact braising method for Osso "Buko" could be used for even fancier-sounding *boeuf braisé aux carottes*, *coq au vin*, or *carbonnade flamande*. Jude's Chuck Roast (opposite) is a variation for another time.

BONUS POINTS +2

ZESTING

Use your Microplane to zest a lemon or, if you are feeling exotic, Buddha's hand, onto your Osso "Buko" before serving. This is a training-wheels version of one of the most famous of all Italian garnishes, gremolata, a mixture of lemon zest, parsley, and garlic.

BONUS POINTS +2

LEARNING TO "SIMMER"

While the meal is cooking, boil water in your nonstick skillet (or other container) with a probe thermometer in the water. Turn the heat down to maintain a "simmer," where there is just slight turbulence, like it's threatening to boil, and note the temperature: what's the degree range for low simmering?[15] This type of technique practice outside of a meal is what we'll call "no-stakes practice."

15 It should be between 180°F and 190°F (82°C and 88°C) at sea level.

VARIATION +2

JUDE'S CHUCK ROAST

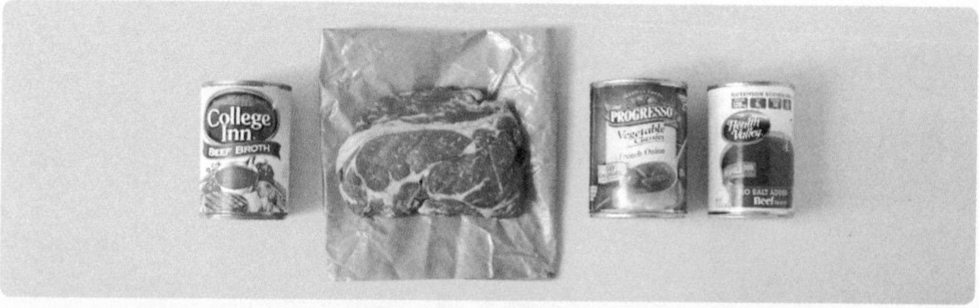
College Inn
BEEF BROTH
PROGRESSO
Vegetable Classics
French Onion
Beef

Here's an even easier braise.

If you'd like to relabel this to impress any shallow friends, the French might call it *boeuf à la cuillère* (spoon beef), because it's tender enough to eat with a spoon.

SHORTHAND

350F 2½–3hr: Cook 2½lb chuck, 1 can beef broth, 1 can French onion soup, 1 can consommé

HANDS-ON TIME

5 minutes

TOTAL TIME

5 minutes, plus 8–10 hours slow cooking (or 2½–3 hours oven-braising)

GEAR

- 6–8-qt slow cooker, or raw or finished cast-iron Dutch oven

INGREDIENTS	TO SERVE 4
Boneless chuck or rump roast	**1** (2½ lb/1 kg)
Beef broth	**1 can** (15 oz/ 425 g)
French onion soup (beware: this often contains sugar) or another 1 can beef broth plus 3 T dried, minced, or chopped onions	**1 can** (15 oz/ 425 g)
Beef consommé	**1 can** (15 oz/ 425 g)

Jude is a smart, busy, slow-carbing mom. This is one of her go-to recipes.

The first time I made it, I couldn't find beef consommé and omitted it. It still turned out amazing.

Also, don't worry about can sizes too much. You can use the smaller cans of condensed broth or the larger cans equally well.

Jude uses a Crock-Pot for this (any slow cooker will work), but you can also use your Dutch oven. Here are both options.

IF USING A SLOW COOKER

PREP + PICKUP

00 Place the roast in the slow cooker.

01 Pour 1 can each of broth, soup, and consommé over the meat.

02 Cover, set to low, and come back 8–10 hours later. Done!

IF USING A CAST-IRON DUTCH OVEN:

PREP

00 Preheat the oven to 350°F (180°C).

PICKUP

00 Place the roast in the Dutch oven.

01 Pour 1 can each of broth, soup, and consommé over the meat.

02 Cover and bake for 2½–3 hours. Done!

BONUS POINTS +2

CIPOLLINI

In step 01, since I had the ingredients, I added three halved cloves of garlic (a few shakes of garlic powder will also work fine) and 10 peeled cipollini onions. Cipollini onions, much neglected, are the deliciously sweet bite-size variety. I dropped them into boiling water first to speed up the peeling process.

TEA PAIRING

ANTI-ANGIOGENESIS TEA

"Virtually 100% of us have microscopic cancers by the time we're 70 years old."

While at the annual TED Conference in 2010, I learned that two close friends had been diagnosed with cancer. By chance, the event was simultaneously abuzz about Dr. William Li's presentation about anti-angiogenesis therapy: in this case, how to starve cancers of blood.

Cancer is common. With 19 billion capillaries in our bodies, on average, virtually 100% of us have microscopic cancers by the time we're 70 years old, more than 40% of us by age 40. There's a good chance you have pinhead-size cancers in your body right now.

These "cancers without disease" aren't typically a problem, as they can't grow larger than 0.5 mm without a blood supply. Therein lies the key. Dr. Li specializes in anti-angiogenesis (blood-vessel growth inhibition) therapies that keep abnormal growth in check. The simplest "drug" he recommended was tea. Drinking a daily blend of white tea (specifically Dragon Pearl jasmine) and green tea (Japanese sencha), which are both available from Harney & Sons (fourhourchef.com/harney), can specifically inhibit blood-vessel growth to tumors. The Earl Grey in your cupboard is a close second to the blend.

Don't boil the tea leaves. Boil the water first, then let it cool for 2–3 minutes, to about 175°F (80°C), then steep the tea (leave the tea leaves in the hot water) for 4–5 minutes. The bioactive elements remain active even if the liquid cools, so feel free to make popsicles if you like.

Tea isn't the only ingestible with anti-angiogenesis properties. For the geeks and Dr. Weston Price fans out there, foods rich in vitamin K2 (menaquinones) are particularly promising in anti-cancer applications. If you need another reason to eat our Osso "Buko," here you go: in a 20-year study of almost 79,000 men, those who consumed cooked tomatoes 2–3 times per week had up to a 50% reduction in advanced prostate cancer risk, as inversely correlated to malignant angiogenesis.

In DOMESTIC, I've added "pairings," but not the normal kind. As you've noticed, instead of wine, I'm offering music and tea. None are mandatory. **Links to all the songs can be found at fourhourchef.com/music-pairings.** The teas were carefully selected (and described) with the help of Jesse Jacobs, former sous-chef and founder of Samovar Tea Lounges, and Kevin "Man Stems" Rose, STI-certified tea master. All paired teas can be found through two sources:

samovarlife.com
redblossomtea.com

The simplified steps of brewing:

1. Boil water.
2. Add ≈12 oz (1½ c) of boiling water to 1–2 T of tea. Yes, 1–2 entire tablespoons.
3. Brew for ≈30 seconds. Yes, only 30 seconds. If it's good and fresh tea, that's enough for the first *infusion* (the term for multiple steeps).

My suggestion is to start experimenting with one or two teas whose descriptions really fascinate you. No need to buy a collection.

SOME OF MY FAVORITE TEAS AND TOOLS

Large compressed disc of *pu-erh* tea, a variety of post-fermented tea from Yunnan, China. It's good for fat loss and tastes like barnyard clippings.

Self-filtering porcelain teacup

Purified *pu-erh* amber—hard to get outside of China, but a small chip will yield as much as a quarter of the above cake

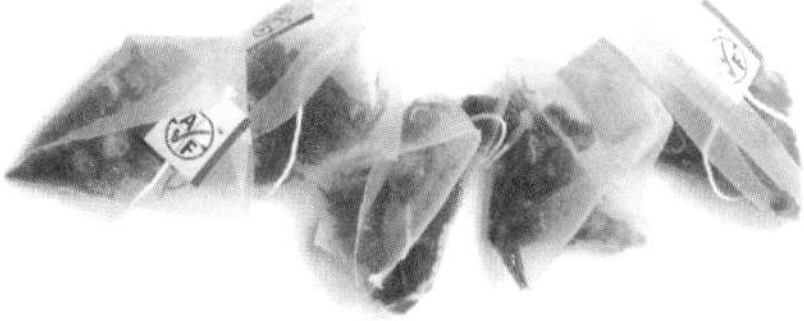

Anti-angiogenesis tea

I use this tea filter basket (tea strainer) for *pu-erh.*

Tea infuser spoon

Blomus teastick

These filters for steeping tea eliminate the need to filter tea leaves through your teeth like a plankton-eating whale. See **fourhourchef.com/tea.**

可以興茶莊

Non-Godzilla-size *pu-erh* cake, wrapped in tea condom

LESSON 02 +8

SKILL
FLAVOR COMBINATIONS

NORTHEAST AFRICAN (OR MIDDLE EASTERN)
SCRAMBLED EGGS

SHORTHAND
Scramble 4 yolks, 2 whites, S+P, 1T grapeseed oil over low heat till fluffy & moist. Add herbs & spices; cook gently till solid but shiny.

HANDS-ON TIME
5 minutes

TOTAL TIME
10 minutes

GEAR
- Nonstick skillet
- Short glass or other small storage container for egg whites (I use my whiskey glass, a tumbler.)
- Silicone spatula

OPTIONAL PAIRINGS
"Pa' Bailar (Siempre Quiero Más)" by Bajofondo

Masala chai black tea

This is an awesome coffee alternative: dark, creamy, and richly complex. Brewed at home, it can be made sweet or unsweetened, or you can add whole raw milk (as Jesse does), almond milk, or coconut milk (as I do). Its subtle notes include cardamom, cinnamon, and cloves.

"It is a poor figure of a man who will say that eggs are fit only to be eaten at breakfast."
—M. F. K. FISHER, *HOW TO COOK A WOLF*

"Tomatoes and oregano make it Italian; wine and tarragon make it French. Sour cream makes it Russian; lemon and cinnamon make it Greek. Soy sauce makes it Chinese; garlic makes it good."
—ALICE MAY BROCK, MADE FAMOUS IN ARLO GUTHRIE'S SONG "ALICE'S RESTAURANT"

Now that you have Osso "Buko" to cover any dinner party for up to four people, let's expand your vocabulary. In fact, let's open up all of the world's cuisines.

Eggs will be our vehicle. Simple combinations of 2–3 herbs and spices can help you create the flavors you associate with dining out. To jump from one ethnicity to another often requires one simple substitution. As if by the wave of a magic wand, your meal is transformed. For example, here's how you jump from:

NEPALESE
chile, lime, ginger

TO

MEXICAN
scallions, chile, lime

TO

THAI
scallions, ginger, chile, cilantro

TO

CHINESE OR "ASIAN"
scallions, ginger, tamari[16]

To cover all four, the only ingredients you need are scallions, ginger, chile, lime, cilantro, and soy sauce or tamari. They can be applied to *anything*—chicken, beef, pork, and vegetables of all types—giving you dozens, if not hundreds, of dishes at your fingertips.

This, ladies and gentlemen, was an epiphany (perhaps *the* epiphany) for me: knowing vastly simplified flavor pairings, you can use a few ingredients to unlock the world.

The table on page 148 was inspired by *Ethnic Cuisine,* by Elisabeth Rozin, a brilliant book that never got the attention it deserved. It will give you

16 Remember that I use *tamari* to refer to wheat-free tamari. Feel free to use the more traditional soy sauce if you're not avoiding gluten.

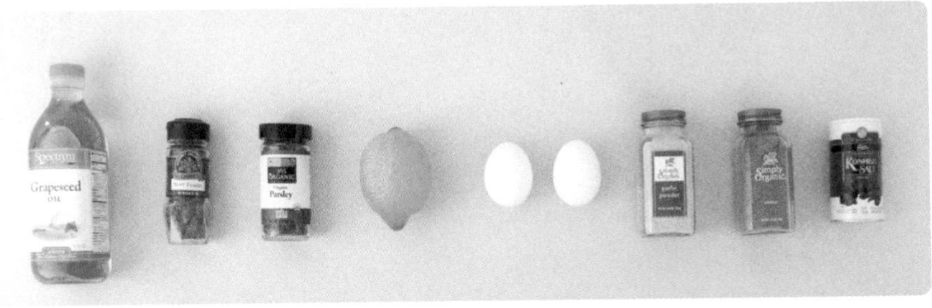
Grapeseed
Parsley

INGREDIENTS	TO SERVE 2–4
Eggs	2–4
Grapeseed oil	1 T
S+P	To taste
FOR NORTHEAST AFRICAN	
Powdered garlic	3-finger pinch
Ground cumin	3-finger pinch
Dried mint	3-finger pinch
FOR MIDDLE EASTERN	
Dried parsley	3-finger pinch
Lemon	1

near infinite options for the rest of your life. **We'll start with an assignment: for the next two weeks, eat eggs in the mornings as often as possible (remember our slow-carb 30-within-30 guideline?), experimenting with a different flavor combination each time.** Eggs have a counterintuitively neutral flavor that offers the perfect palette for this testing.

If you're a beginner, I *highly* suggest you use dried herbs and preground spices instead of cutting or grinding your own.

We'll start with your choice of northeast African or Middle Eastern scrambled eggs.

Pick one combo from the ingredients list above.

PREP

00 Take the eggs out of the fridge, run them under hot water for 20 seconds, and then leave them on the counter to warm up to room temperature. I typically do this before getting my morning tea in order. Getting foods to room temperature is referred to as "tempering" and is critical to good cooking, especially when working with meats. As a general rule, never cook cold or cool food, as you'll burn the outside and leave the inside undercooked.

The key to perfect scrambled eggs is using twice as many yolks as whites (2:1 ratio). This will give you a delicious, creamy consistency that would otherwise require the addition of milk or cream. We'll save the egg whites for another use.

For the opposite effect—a fluffy, light omelet, for instance—you'd flip the ratio and use more whites. For this first experiment, try the recipe verbatim. Next

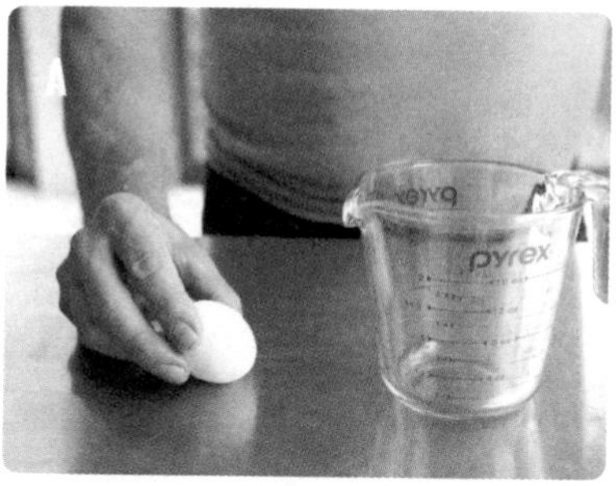
A

B

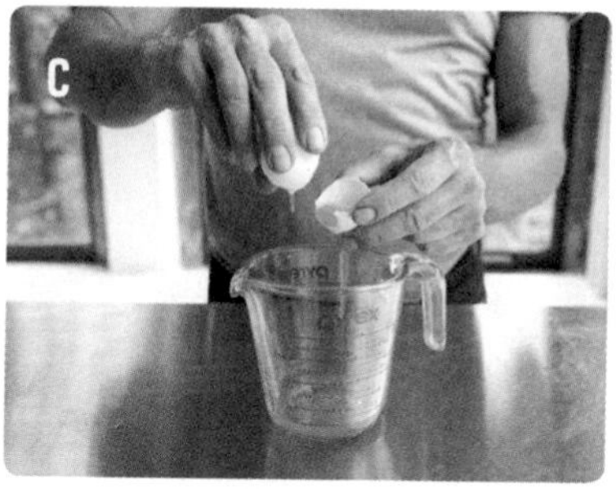
C

time, adjust egg whites up or down based on your preference.

01 Get your *meez* and flavor combo ingredients ready.

02 If you've chosen to make the Middle Eastern version, roll your lemon on a flat surface and cut a small slit in the side. Rolling it allows you to easily get twice as much juice out (an alternate trick is to microwave it on high for 15 seconds). Cutting a slit instead of cutting it in half allows you to squeeze out only what you need, and store the lemon in the fridge without a bag.

PICKUP

00 Place the nonstick skillet on a burner and turn the heat to low.

01 Pour in 1 T (about a 4"/10-cm diameter circle) of grapeseed oil, which is neutral-flavored. This makes it a great oil when you want flavors of the other ingredients to come through clearly.

02 Get a compost or garbage bag ready for the eggshells. I break my eggs directly into the skillet to avoid extra cleanup, but if you try this and it gets messy, you can scramble your eggs in a bowl.

03 Crack your first egg. To avoid pushing shell fragments into your eggs, crack them on a flat surface instead of on the edge of the pan.

04 Add exactly half of your eggs to the skillet (e.g., if using 4 eggs, add 2.)

05 Now place just the whites of the remaining eggs in your glass or container (see above pics). Crack each egg, and swap the yolk from one shell half to the other until the white slides out into the glass. Add the yolk(s) to the skillet, and put the whites in the fridge.

06 Using your silicone spatula, give the eggs a stir. Add 3–5 twists of pepper and a 3-finger pinch of kosher salt (grab between your thumb, index, and middle fingers). If the eggs aren't cooking at all, turn the heat up to low-medium, but no higher. For good scrambled eggs and omelets, you'll want to cook them slowly and pull them off earlier than usual. The French use the word *baveuse* to refer to the desirable "snotty" consistency in the middle of a good omelet. Yummers!

07 Stir in your herbs and spices. For northeast African: powdered garlic, cumin, and mint. For Middle Eastern: dried parsley (save the lemon for later).

A

B
GARLIC POWDER
CALIFORNIA

C

Start with a 3-finger pinch of each, and add more after cooking if you like. This eyeballing is part of training you to cook without recipes.

08 Stir every minute or so until the eggs are mostly solid but still reflect light and look moist. At this point, lift the pan about 12" (30 cm) over the heat and keep stirring. The eggs will usually finish cooking, and you're ready to eat. If you think they're not finished, return to a low heat and repeat.

09 If going Middle Eastern, squeeze on the lemon juice and mix just before eating.

10 Enjoy! I suggest using paper plates in the beginning, since cleanup angst is multiplied in the morning. If you prefer, you can eat directly out of the skillet like a savage (me). Use a small plastic or wooden spoon, never metal, on coated nonstick surfaces.

Q&A

You might have a few questions:

Q: Do I have to use this 2:1 yolk to egg white ratio all the time?
A: No. I just want you to taste the difference in texture. Feel free to use whole eggs for the rest of your flavor experiments, which is my default.

Q: How do I know if I've been robbed by a "pasture-raised" con artist?
A: If the white is really runny or clear, the egg has come from a battery-raised chicken stuck in a cage. The tastiest eggs will also have yolks closer in color to red or orange instead of yellow, which Italians refer to as *il rosso*.

Q: What the hell do I do with these extra egg whites?
A: There are many options. This is your introduction to food storage.

Option 1 (recommended):

Make scrambled eggs tomorrow or the day after with the same herbs/spices (to keep that variable fixed), but add the extra egg whites. You'll then experience the opposite textural effect. This is precisely what chefs do to make omelets "fluffy." Bakers use egg whites for a similar airy effect in pastries.

Option 2

You will need an extra egg white when you make crab cakes (see page 172). Egg whites will last 2–4 days in the fridge. How do I know they'll last 2–4 days? Because I searched for "egg whites" on stilltasty.com, which will tell you how long almost anything will keep. It's my most frequently used online food resource.

Option 3

Freeze one white in each compartment of an ice cube tray. These will keep practically indefinitely.

Option 4

Make egg white–based hair conditioner. Combine 2 egg whites and 5 T (75 g) full-fat plain yogurt. Plain Greek yogurt is ideal. Apply the mixture to your hair, and, if you have long hair, let it sit in a towel turban for 30 minutes. Then rinse it out, dry your locks, and get cast in a slow-motion Pantene commercial.

AROUND THE WORLD IN 44 FLAVOR COMBINATIONS

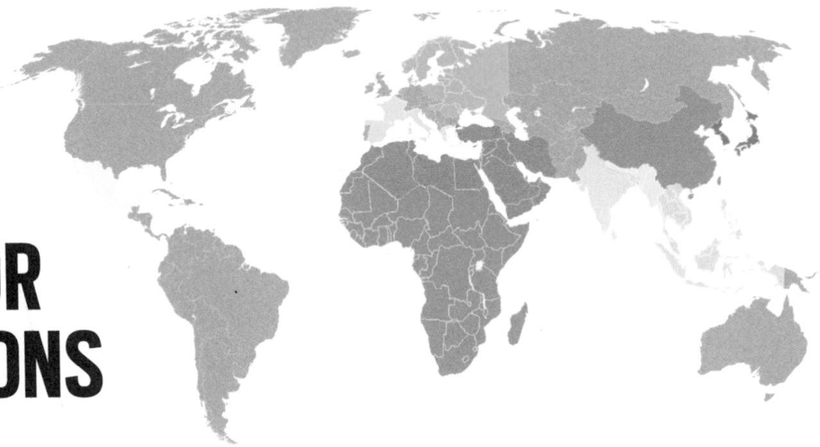

Let the morning egg experiments begin!

For the purposes of learning, try and stick with the "to learn" column. Think of these as your traditional primary colors—red, blue, and yellow—from which you can create almost any dish.

The "to cheat" column features shortcuts for when you are in a rush. The two columns will not taste identical, as the blends (shortcuts) often have 5+ ingredients.

Below is your starter menu of flavor options, with my novice favorites bolded and starred.

CUISINE	TO LEARN	TO CHEAT
Mexico	★ **lime, chile**	taco seasoning + chili powder
	tomato, chile	
Yucatán	sour orange, garlic, achiote	
India	★ **curry**	curry powder
Northern India	★ **cumin, ginger, garlic, and variations**	garam masala
Southern India	mustard seed (oil OK), coconut, tamarind, chile, and variations	
Bengal	cumin, chile, coriander, turmeric	panch phoron
Middle East/North Africa	★ **lemon, parsley**	*za'atar* (general Arab) or *baharat* (Levant)
	cumin, cilantro	
Morocco	cumin, coriander, cinnamon, ginger, and onion and/or tomato and/or fruit	ras el hanout

CUISINE	TO LEARN	TO CHEAT
East Africa	chile, garlic, ginger, fenugreek, cloves	berbere
West Africa	tomato, peanut, chile	
North East Africa	★ **garlic, cumin, mint**	
Greece	★ **olive oil, lemon, oregano**	
Italy, France	★ **olive oil, garlic, basil**	
France	wine, herbs	*fines herbes* or *herbes de Provence* or *quatre épices*
	butter and/or cream and/or cheese + wine and/or stock	
Normandy	apple, cider, Calvados	
Northern Italy	wine vinegar, garlic	
Southern Italy, Southern France	★ **olive oil, garlic, parsley and/or anchovy**	
	(optional: tomato)	
Provence	olive oil, thyme, rosemary, marjoram, sage	
	(optional: tomato)	
Spain	olive oil, garlic, almond	
	olive oil, onion, pepper	
Hungary	★ **onion, lard, paprika**	
Eastern European Jewish	onion, chicken fat	
Northern and Eastern Europe	sour cream, dill or paprika or allspice or caraway	
Central Asia	cinnamon, fruit, pistachio or walnut or pine nut	
Burma	onion, ginger, garlic, turmeric, chile	
Nepal	★ **lime, ginger, chile**[17]	
Thailand	ginger, scallions, cilantro	red or green curry paste
	★ **fish sauce, curry, chile**	
	ginger, cilantro, chile	
Vietnam	★ **fish sauce, lemon**	
Laos	★ **fish sauce, coconut**[18]	
Indonesia	tamari, brown sugar, peanut, chile	
Japan	tamari, sake, sugar	
Korea	tamari, brown sugar, sesame, chile	
China	tamari, rice wine, ginger	5-spice powder
	★ **tamari, scallions, ginger**[19]	
+ Beijing	miso and/or garlic and/or sesame	
+ Szechuan	sweet, sour, hot	
+ Canton	black beans, garlic	

17 Example: *choyela*, which is grilled beef tenderloin with lime, ginger, chiles, and spices. Serve chilled, with red onion and cilantro.
18 Feel free to use coconut oil in place of grapeseed oil to make this easier.
19 We'll use this on chicken a little later.

SLOW-CARB WINES: THE TOP 10 LISTS

"I cook with wine.
Sometimes I even add it to the food."
—W. C. FIELDS

Rather than clog this book with different wine pairings for every dish (who buys that much wine?), I asked three wine experts to assemble all-star favorite lists of slow-carb wines: five white and five red.

Chris Miller is the wine director at Spago in Beverly Hills. *Wine Spectator* bestowed its Grand Award on Chris's wine list, the highest honor possible for such a list.

Gary Vaynerchuk, listed in *Decanter* magazine's "Power 40" for wine, transformed his parents' corner liquor store into Winelibrary TV, a $45+ million-per-year behemoth. He's been called the most influential wine critic in the United States besides Robert Parker.

Paul Grieco is co-owner of Terroir in NYC and won the James Beard award for wine service when he was at Gramercy Tavern in 2002.

Each of the wines has world-class taste but a low residual sugar (RS) level, making it perfect for your 1–2 glasses a night. They're also listed in ascending order of cost, so you can find a fit for your budget. The "best" for you may not be the priciest you can afford; one of the best white wines I've ever had was a $4 bottle I bought on clearance at Trader Joe's.

But pay attention to the varietals (grape type). If you can't find the exact Italian pinot grigio listed, for example, a substitute Italian pinot grigio will also likely have low RS.

Links for all can be found at fourhourchef.com/wines. Of course, prices and availability change.

Chardonnay
DRY WHITE WINE
1997

CHRIS MILLER'S PICKS

WHITES/ROSÉS

Schloss Gobelsburg Grüner Veltliner
2011, Austria ($15)
Terrific savory wine, with a flavor combination between pinot grigio, dry Riesling, and a dash of sauvignon blanc. Hints of celery root, green apple, lemon peel, and white pepper. Great as an aperitif or with food.

Scarpetta Pinot Grigio
2010, Italy ($20)
Made in Italy by a sommelier and a chef from Colorado who really know what they're doing. As a general rule, just about any Italian white is safe—most are low-to-average in alcohol and very few (other than mass-market pinot grigio) carry any RS at all.

Domaine du Bagnol Cassis Rosé
2011, France ($25)
Likely my favorite rosé in the world. Perfectly dry and balanced, delicate, and worth the struggle to find—it won't be easy. I know the importer personally, and I only got 12 bottles last year.

Paul Lato "Le Souvenir" Chardonnay
2009, California ($50)
In my opinion, maybe the best oaky, buttery chardonnay made in the United States. If you want to drink a big, tropical chardonnay or rich, dark-fruit pinot noir, it's hard to get better than this guy without paying a small fortune.

Larmandier-Bernier "Blanc de Blancs" Extra-Brut
Champagne, France ($56)
Champagne is usually loaded with calories. Producers often dump in a ton of sugar (called the "dosage") to balance out the high acid in the wine. All you have to do is look for the term Extra Brut, Brut Zero, or Brut Sauvage. This means that almost no extra sugar was added. Just in case you needed an excuse to pop a bottle.

REDS

Domaine de la Chapelle des Bois Beaujolais
2010, France ($16)
It's almost impossible to beat the French for cheap, dry, inexpensive, flavorful reds. Beaujolais often gets a bad rap from the large-scale production wines that flood the market, but the smaller producers make incredible wines on the cheap. Ask your wine guy for a "Cru Beaujolais," the highest ranking. For an extra $5 or so, it's a huge step up in quality.

Melville "Estate" Pinot Noir
2009, California ($34)
One of the best values in pinot noir on the planet. Made in Santa Rita Hills, this wine so overdelivers it's really not fair to the other producers in the area.

Montevertine Le Pergole TorteToscana Rosso (Sangiovese)
2007, Italy ($76)
Chianti has come a long way in the past 10 years and has regained its status as one of the great wines of the world. Always superdry and begging for food.

Marqués de Murrieta Rioja Gran Reserva
2001, Spain ($50)
Spain can be tricky because so many areas are very warm. Rioja is usually a safe bet, though, and is truly a special place for wine. In the right hands, you get the nuance and flavors of Burgundy, the punch of savory tones of Châteauneuf-du-Pape, and a fruitiness bordering on zinfandel. All in a dry, moderate-alcohol wine. This producer also makes a rare, delicious white wine.

Abreu Rothwell Hyde Cabernet Sauvignon
2007, California ($150+)
Big, bold, and beautiful. When nothing less than a blockbuster will do. One of the great cabernet-blend producers in the world. Hard to find and very, very expensive, but an experience everyone should have at least once.

THE NOT-TO-DRINK LIST

As a general rule, the following wines are classic and utterly delicious, but they're also a few of the worst RS offenders:

White: Dessert wines, wines from Alsace and Germany, a lot of popular, high-end U.S. chardonnays, viognier, most French chenin blanc, and most popular brands of champagne.

Red: Dessert wines, amarone, wines from Australia, zinfandel, and grenache from Australia or California.

How to Flash-Cool Wine

Oops! Forgot to chill the white wine and people are showing up? Forget the fridge. It's time to flash-cool and pretend like you know what you're doing. Here are two options for bringing your white wine to life:

1. Wrap the wine bottle in a damp towel and put it in the freezer for 10–15 minutes. The towel will cool much faster than the glass. If the towel freezes, run it under hot water until it unleashes the death grip.

2. If you have ice on hand, you can accelerate things further. Fill a cooler or sink basin with ice, add water, and thoroughly mix salt in. Stick the wine bottle in this salty Siberia and check it again in five minutes. The salt lowers the freezing point of water, and you'll be astounded at how quickly this takes effect.

Cold.

GARY VAY-NER-CHUK'S PICKS

WHITES

Eradus Sauvignon Blanc, 2009, New Zealand (<$22)

André Neveu Sancerre Les Monts Damnes, 2009, Loire (<$30)

Marimar Estate La Masia Chardonnay, 2007, California (<$31)

Oliver Leflaive Meursault, 2009, Burgundy (<$34)

Jean-Louis Chave Hermitage Blanc, 2005, Rhône (unlimited budget)

REDS

Luigi Bosca Cabernet Sauvignon, 2007, Argentina (<$20)

Franciscan Cabernet Sauvignon, 2009, California (<$23)

Château Gloria, 2008, Bordeaux (<$50)

Massolino Barolo, 2007, Italy (<$37)

Vincent Girardin Chambertin, 2005, Burgundy (unlimited budget)

Hawt!

PAUL GRIECO'S PICKS

All of Paul's picks have less than 14 g of RS per bottle. His e-mail signature also has, after his phone number, "Carrier Pigeon: Stanley," which is listed above his *American Idol* contestant number. He's a total lunatic.

If you ever visit Terroir in New York (tag line: "The Elitist Wine Bar for Everyone!"), take time to read the wine list. Part Vonnegut and part ransom letter, it's the only wine list I've ever read cover to cover.

Of his descriptions below, my favorite is the South African red.

WHITES

Goldwater Sauvignon Blanc, 2010, New Zealand (<$20): Purity of apple and grapefruit notes and zingy acidity will bring a smile to your face.

Abbazia di Novacella Sylvaner, 2009, Italy (<$20): Slightly restrained and shy, but it certainly makes a lingering impression.

Alice & Olivier De Moor Chablis Bel Air, 2009, France (<$30): Minerals, minerals, minerals, and a smack in the face of chalkiness . . . like a Le Corbusier building.

Alzinger Riesling Federspiel Dürnsteiner, 2010, Austria (<$50): A bracing shock of life force . . . you must be wide awake to relish this. If not, it will awake you from your slumber![20]

Georges Vernay Condrieu, Coteau du Vernon, 2009, France (unlimited budget): Initially discreet and disarming, but the wine just goes and goes and goes. You will understand why Gaia is our matron.

REDS

Allegrini Palazzo della Torre Veronese, 2008, Italy (<$30): Cherries and violets and cool red fruits, with the brightness of a cloudy fall morning.

Au Bon Climat Santa Barbara County Pinot Noir, 2009, California (<$30): A silk dress, covering a strawberry and raspberry tart. You cannot stop eating . . . I mean drinking.

Kanonkop Paul Sauer, 2006, South Africa (<$50): Earth-toned and powerful and all-knowing, but not confrontational . . . like a conversation with your guidance counselor in high school.

Bonny Doon Le Cigare Volant, 2007, California (<$40): A perfect example of why we drink wine: balance in moderation with equal parts of everything.

Chateau Musar, 2002, Lebanon (<$50): A little bit salvation and damnation. Wine isn't supposed to taste like this, but more wines should absolutely taste like this. Do you know what a life force feels like?!

---

20 Paul is a true Riesling fanatic, and not in the overused, watered-down version of fanatic. For multiple summers at Terroir, he's offered only one white wine by the glass: hyperlocalized versions of Riesling. He says, "I think that more people should drink Riesling—they'd be better people if they did."

Don't Want to Be the Dork Ordering Pinot at the Club?

Here are a few non-wine slow-carb options.

NORCAL MARGARITA

The "NorCal Margarita," introduced to me by Paleo demigod Robb Wolf, is my go-to slow-carb cocktail.

• 2 shots tequila
Preferably Añejo. If you want super-high-end, try my favorite sipping tequila, Casa Dragones.

• Juice of 1 lime
Don't skimp here! Lime juice helps blunt insulin release. If anything, I'll add more lime juice, always freshly squeezed.

• Splash of soda water to taste

This simple cocktail offers an economical route to oblivion, as Robb explains: "The bubbles in the soda water act as a nonpolar solvent, to naturally extract the ethanol out of that aqueous matrix. When those bubbles interact with your gut lining, it releases the ethanol in your system faster, so you get drunk quicker." For a spicy version, muddle a serrano chili in the tequila, then follow the basic recipe.

WHISKEY GOODNESS

I've hated whiskey and all dark liquors for my entire life.

In 2007, Drew Curtis, founder of fark.com, invited me to Kentucky and force-fed me dozens of variations of bourbon. It produced a series of twisted faces, headaches, and "no, thank-you"s until we chanced upon Bulleit Bourbon. I fell in love. Its high rye content (28% of the mash bill) made it unique, as did the fact that I enjoyed it.

Nothing tickled my fancy for five more years. Then, one night in 2011, Marc Andreessen introduced me to a series of winners over dinner. At the time, his kitchen featured a walk-in whiskey library stocked with a fit for every palate, each scored from 1–4 (4 being best). If you've ever used the Internet, you probably have Marc to thank. Coauthor of Mosaic, the first widely used web browser, Marc has a résumé that's something else: cofounder of Netscape Communications (acquired by AOL for $4.2 billion), chairman of Opsware (acquired by HP for $1.6 billion), board member at Facebook, eBay, and much more. He also knows his whiskeys.

I asked Marc to kindly share his top four picks that aren't impossible to find, and here they are, in his words:

1. Highland Park 18 Year: My go-to whiskey for friends and relaxation. Scales down nicely to the 12 year for casual drinking and to the 25 year for very special occasions.

2. Johnnie Walker Black: To paraphrase the immortal words of Christopher Hitchens, "breakfast of champions, beloved by dictators the world over."

3. Leopold Brothers American Small Batch Whiskey: The best of the new American distillers and astonishingly tasty, both by itself and in an old-fashioned.

4. Amrut Fusion: Unbelievably delicious whiskey from India (!)—it's just like Scotch, and exploding with flavor.

LESSON
03
+6

SKILL
MASH ANYTHING
COCONUT CAULIFLOWER CURRY MASH

SHORTHAND
Bring 1 head cauliflower, ¾c coconut milk, ¼c cashews, salt, 2T H2O to boil; simmer covered 20min. Mash, + ¼t curry powder, cinnamon to taste

HANDS-ON TIME
15 minutes

TOTAL TIME
35 minutes

GEAR
- Towel
- Knife + cutting board
- Digital kitchen scale
- Raw or finished cast-iron Dutch oven
- If using raw cast-iron, optional but suggested: PanSaver
- Optional: silicone spatula
- Large dinner bowl or medium mixing bowl

OPTIONAL PAIRINGS
"Supreme Illusion (Nickodemus Remix)" by Thievery Corporation

Iron Goddess of Mercy oolong tea
This tea is creamy, slightly vegetal, and nutty at the same time. It pairs beautifully with the buttery quality of cauliflower, whether steamed with ghee or in a rich curry sauce.

> "Cauliflower is nothing but cabbage with a college education."
> —MARK TWAIN

When the carb demons curse me with sugar cravings, there are two things I do to prevent unscheduled cheating:

1. Take 8–12 g of Branched-Chain Amino Acids (most commonly sold as "BCAAs"), which your liver can convert into just enough blood glucose[21] to make your brain tantrum stop but not enough to slow fat loss. During fasting periods, BCAAs also help prevent or minimize muscle loss.

2. Consume fake carbs that look and feel like real carbs.

For a mashed potato mouthfeel without the guilt, the following quick dish is the answer. The recipe was developed by Dr. John Berardi, chief science officer of Precision Nutrition. This dish is also our introduction to the all-important digital kitchen scale.

Two brands of BCAAs I've used.

BodyTech
Instantized
BCAA
POWDER
Unflavored
5 g of Branched Chain Amino Acids Per Serving
200
BCAA
1000 CAPS
ON

21 A process called gluconeogenesis.

The Curry Illusion: Mythical "Ethnic" Foods

Just as there are no "French fries" in France, did you know you can't buy "curry powder" at legitimate markets in India? Turmeric, yes. Cumin, yes. But the blend the rest of the world knows as *curry*? Nope. Rumor has it that even the venerated chicken tikka masala,[22] the #1-selling dish in the U.K., doesn't exist in its spiritual homeland. According to some in the House of Commons, it was created in Glasgow, Scotland.

None of this surprises me. In Beijing there are chains and restaurants specializing in "California beef noodles." The most popular, California Beef Noodle King U.S.A., had hundreds of locations in northeastern China. As a Californian, I can tell you: it tastes a hell of a lot like Chinese food.

22 *Masala* means "spice blend" in Hindi. If you'd like to attempt your own with an Indian flair, just combine the Cs from your spice and herb drawer: cinnamon, cardamom, cumin, cloves, coriander seed, caraway, cilantro, or (of course) curry.

simply Organic
curry powder
THAI KITCHEN
Coconut Milk
KOSHER SALT

INGREDIENTS	TO SERVE 4 LITTLE PEOPLE OR 2 BIG BOYS
Cauliflower	**1 small head, to yield ≈3 c florets (≈1½ lb/680 g) Don't worry if not exact**
Cashews (I use roasted unsalted)	**¼ c (1¼ oz/35 g)**
Unsweetened coconut milk (I use Thai Kitchen brand)	**½ can (6 oz/≈180 ml)**
Salt	**Two 3-finger pinches**
Curry powder	**3-finger pinch**
OPTIONAL BUT RECOMMENDED	
Ground cinnamon, ideally Saigon cinnamon	**To taste**

PREP

00 First, pull off as many leaves from the cauliflower as possible. Once it resembles a tree ("tree" of florets and "trunk" of stem), wrap it in a towel and smash the stem on your cutting board until it all breaks into pieces. Discard the now-naked stem.

01 Pull apart the florets by hand and place them on your electronic scale to approximately hit the target weight of 1½ lbs (680 g). Put the florets in the Dutch oven. If you want the feeling of some "potato skins" later, keep a few cauliflower leaves in the mix.

02 Place the mixing bowl or large dinner bowl on the electronic scale, hit "tare" or "zero" to zero it out, and add cashews until you have ¼ c (35 g). If they're uncrushed, you can then crush them in your hands directly into the bowl. This is how Chuck Norris does it.

03 Hit "tare" again. Mix the coconut milk with a spoon and add 180 ml. Since the can (and most similar-looking cans) is roughly 400 ml, it'll be just less than half.

You can eyeball all this next time, but we're learning how to measure properly. It'll help you later.

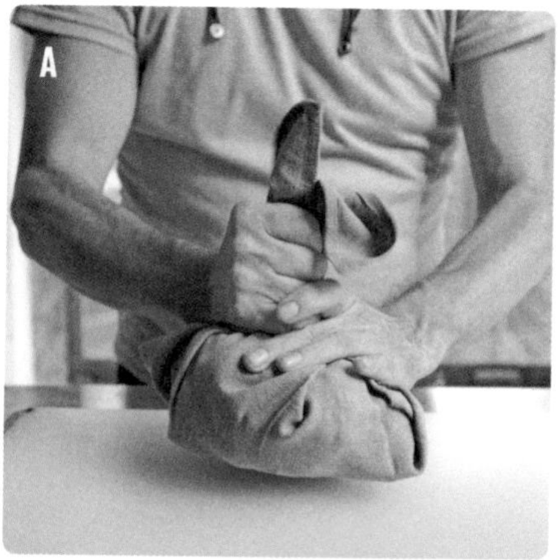
A

B

C

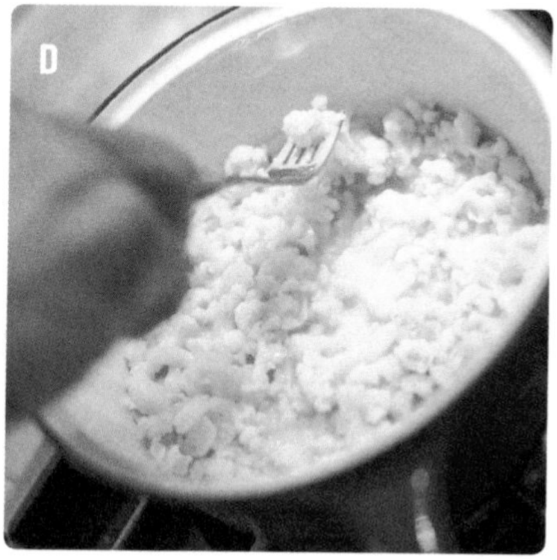
D

Mashing Variations

Now that you "own" mashing, try other root vegetables.

How about a Mexican-style sweet potato mash with chiles and EVOO (omit the coconut milk), adding lime and cilantro before serving? Delicious.

Consider experimenting with unfamiliar foods, like a 50/50 (12 oz/ 340 g or so each) carrot and rutabaga mash. Use the exact same process, but omit the spices and use 2 T ghee and a glug of EVOO instead of the coconut milk.

PICKUP

00 Turn the burner to high and bring the contents to a boil. Immediately reduce to a simmer (light turbulence, as if threatening to boil), cover, and let cook for 20 minutes.

01 Remove from the heat. Sprinkle in the two 3-finger pinches of salt and 3-finger pinch of curry powder, and use a fork to mash cauliflower into a mashed potato–like consistency.

02 Transfer to a serving bowl and add more salt, if needed. It'll be delicious as is, but for a finishing touch, you can mix in a little cinnamon, which will also lower the glycemic index of the entire meal. My fave is Saigon cinnamon.

LESSON 04 +4

SKILLS

STAR PEELER, SAUTÉ

UNION SQUARE ZUCCHINI

+ VARIATION: SQUASH PAPPARDELLE

SHORTHAND

Sauté 1t chile flakes and 1T oil. Mix w speared garlic 30sec; + 2 sliced zucchini, 1t ghee, juice of ½ lemon 2min; + 2 more zucchini 2min. S+P to taste

HANDS-ON TIME

5 minutes

TOTAL TIME

10 minutes

GEAR

- Knife + cutting board
- Star or Swiss Peeler
- Cast-iron combi or nonstick skillet
- Fork

OPTIONAL PAIRINGS

How Joe Ades sold millions of dollars' worth of $5 peelers (fourhourchef.com/ades)

"Get This Right" by Nate James

Silver Needle white tea

Kevin put it thusly: "This is simply the best white tea I've ever had." Mildly fruity with notes of muscatel (think sweet raisiny dessert wine). Great with steamed and buttered summer squash dishes, or with foods with similar characteristics, like zucchini.

"The greatest delight the fields and woods minister is the suggestion of an occult relation between man and the vegetable. I am not alone and unacknowledged. They nod to me and I to them."

—RALPH WALDO EMERSON

"You can lead a horticulture, but you can't make her think."

—DOROTHY PARKER, WHEN CHALLENGED TO USE THE WORD *HORTICULTURE* IN A GAME OF "CAN-YOU-GIVE-ME-A-SENTENCE?"

This dish is named in honor of Joe Ades, but it was inspired by one of Jamie Oliver's Fifteen Amsterdam students, while in Italy.‡ We make it faster by using the peeler in lieu of a knife, and we make it slow-carb with ghee in place of butter.

Using the Peeler

Before the recipe, let's learn how to use the peeler. To peel zucchini using the standard technique, it looks like this:

A) Place the zucchini on your cutting board. Do *not* hold the zucchini in the air.

B) Gently take strips off (notice hand position) . . .

C) . . . as you rotate the zucchini to get all sides. When finished, cut off the ends. You can also cut off the ends before peeling.

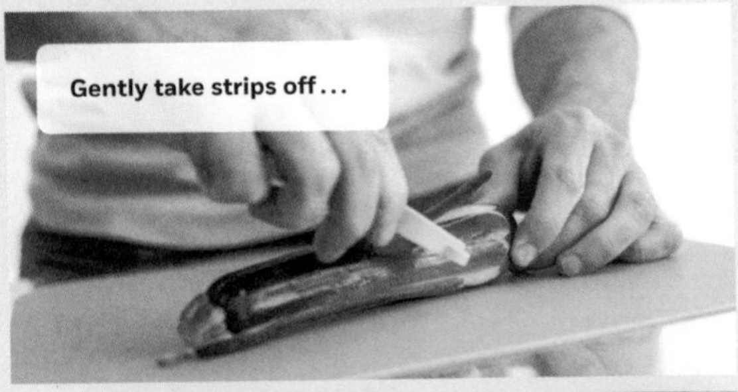

Gently take strips off . . .

. . . As you rotate the zucchini

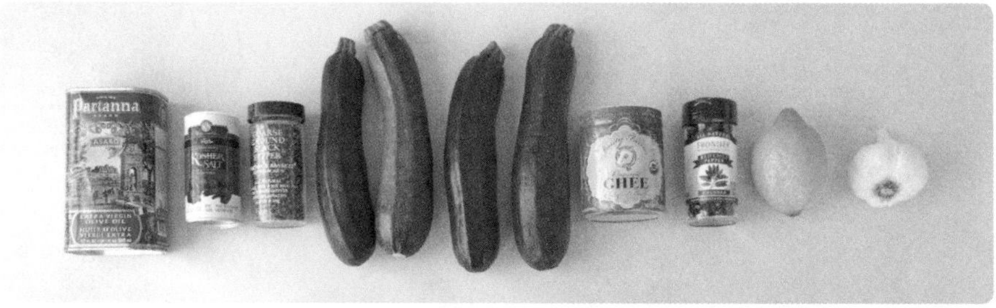
Partanna
GHEE

INGREDIENTS	TO SERVE 4
Zucchini, no wider than the Star Peeler blade (1 per person, and buy 1 extra)	**4 small (6 oz/180 g)**
EVOO or macadamia nut oil	**1 T**
Garlic, peeled but left whole	**1 clove**
Chile flakes (or red pepper flakes)	**2-finger pinch**
Ghee	**1 t**
Lemon juice	**½ lemon**
S+P	**To taste**

PREP

00 Cut just one end off each zucchini, one allotted per person.

That peeler? It's not just a peeler, *padawan*—it's an all-purpose slicing machine. Most don't exploit its full potential and use it only in the standard position (A). *We* are going to move the zucchini instead of the slicer (B). Voilà, a make-shift mandoline!

Brush the zucchini downward on top of the peeling blade, holding the end that hasn't been cut. (Don't worry about the last nub—it's not worth risking losing your fingertips.)

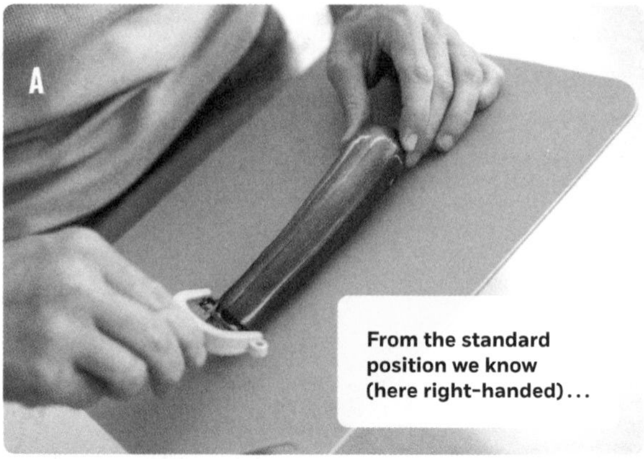
A

From the standard position we know (here right-handed) . . .

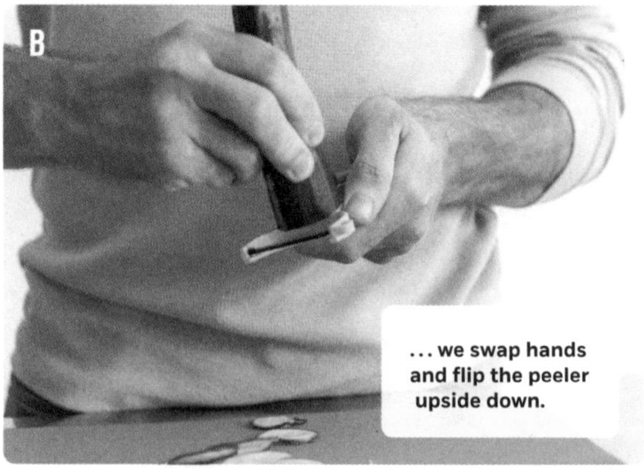
B

. . . we swap hands and flip the peeler upside down.

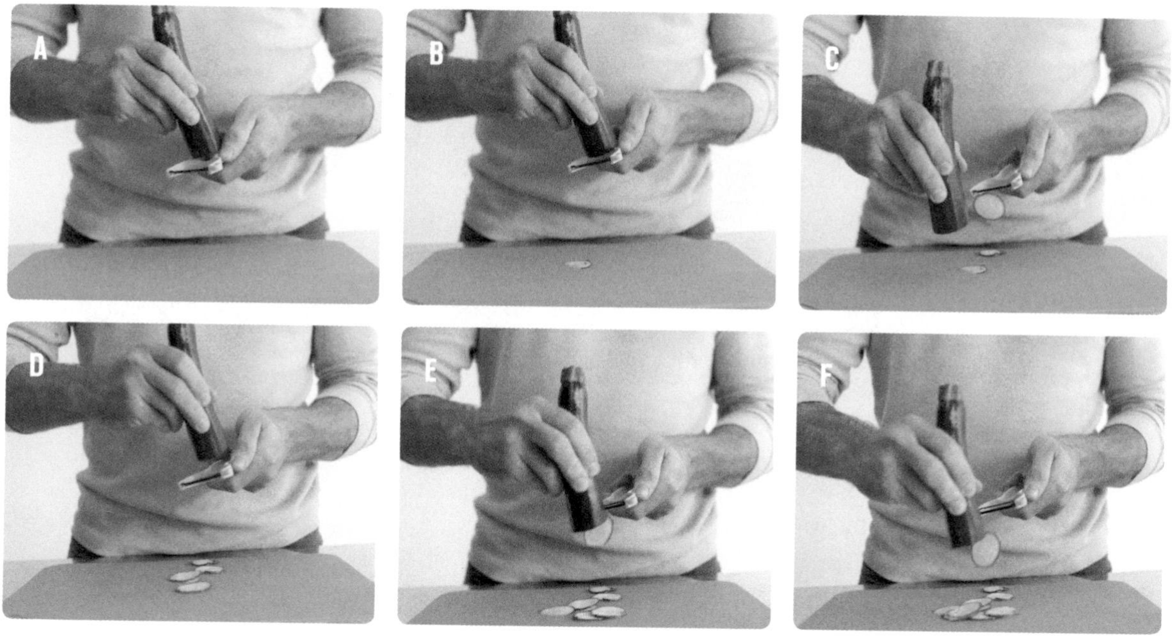
A
B
C
D
E
F

Do this for each zucchini you'll be using.

01 Pat down the zucchini slices with a paper towel for 1–2 minutes to remove as much water as possible, but don't stress over every drop.

PICKUP

00 Heat the skillet over medium-high heat.

01 When a drop of water sizzles as it hits the pan, pour in a 4" (10-cm) diameter circle of oil (≈1 T).

02 Spear the clove of garlic sideways on the end of a fork.

03 Sprinkle the chile flakes on top of the oil and wait 30 seconds. Use the garlic clove on the fork to spread them around. (This awesomely simple technique is borrowed from Chef Dan Kluger of ABC Kitchen.)

04 Add half of the zucchini slices, doing your best to spread them out no more than 3–4 slices deep. But don't get stressed if they clump together.

05 Add the 1 t of ghee (eyeballing is fine) and squeeze in the lemon juice (too much of either won't hurt you).

06 Move the zucchini around using the fork with the clove of garlic for about 2 minutes.

07 Push the cooked zucchini to the side of the skillet and add the remaining zucchini.

08 Let sit for 2 minutes, then mix everything together and remove from the skillet.

09 Try a bite, then season with S+P if needed. Heat more if you like. Enjoy!

VARIATION +2

SQUASH PAPPARDELLE

Partanna

INGREDIENTS	TO SERVE 4
Summer squash (3 squash, preferably an assortment of colors)	**1 lb (454 g)**
Garlic	**1 clove**
Fresh parsley	**½ c packed (30 g)**
EVOO	**2 T**
S+P	**To taste**
Lemon juice	**½ lemon**
OPTIONAL	
Pitted olives (choose your favorite kind; I like castelvetrano or Niçoise) **or 1 T drained capers**	**About ⅓ c (60 g)**
Pick one: Almonds, pine nuts, hazelnuts, pistachios, or hulled pumpkin seeds	**About ⅓ c (60 g)**

INSPIRED BY

Darya Pino

Karen Liebowitz

SHORTHAND

Make/refrigerate sauce up to 2hr: chop 1 clove garlic, ½c parsley, ⅓c olives & nuts. Sauté 1lb ribboned squash, 2T oil till al dente; + sauce, S+P, juice of ½ lemon.

HANDS-ON TIME

5 minutes

TOTAL TIME

10 minutes

GEAR

- Knife + cutting board
- Star Peeler
- Garlic press
- Raw or finished cast-iron Dutch oven
- Fork

The genus Cucurbita is diverse. It includes hard winter vegetables, like pumpkin and spaghetti squash, but also tender produce like zucchini and yellow squash.

No need to bake our choice, summer squash, to soften it. In fact, you could eat it raw, skin and all.

And unlike the misleadingly named spaghetti squash, summer squash can more believably replace pasta. In what may be the easiest technique in this book, we'll simply shave ribbons off the squash with a Star Peeler. The ribbons can be served at room temperature for a refreshing "pasta salad" or warm, more along the lines of a traditional pappardelle.

PREP

00 Trim the ends off the 3 squash. Lay each squash on the cutting board, and run the Star Peeler lightly and quickly from the middle toward the tip, rotating the squash as you go. Flip the squash around every 2 layers so that you can work on the other end. This kind of whittling approach lets you get the most slices out of your squash, as well as fairly even pieces. Stop when you get to the seeds in the center, and discard the seeds.[23] Set the squash slices aside.

01 Press the clove of garlic through your press. Pile the ½ c (30 g) parsley on top of the garlic, along with the ⅓ c (60 g) olives and ⅓ c (60 g) almonds or other

23 Or save for squash puree/soup.

nuts (if using), and coarsely chop them all together on the board (see pics on next page). If prepping in advance, place the squash ribbons and parsley mixture in separate bowls, cover, and refrigerate for up to 2 hours.

PICKUP

00 Heat the 2 T oil in the Dutch oven over medium-high heat until it "shimmers" like a mirage and gives off a bright, glistening appearance.

01 Add the ribbons and use a fork to toss them in the hot oil until they are just barely wilted and still *al dente* (firm), about 2 minutes. Season lightly with S+P, keeping in mind that if you're using olives or capers it'll be salty already.

02 Remove from the heat, add the parsley mixture, squeeze the lemon juice through your free hand (to catch seeds) and over everything, then toss to combine. Taste and season with more salt if necessary. Serve hot, or transfer to a bowl and let cool to room temperature before serving.

Or Just Boil 'Em

Instead of sautéing the ribbons, you can boil them. Bring a pot of water to a boil, add a few pinches of salt, and drop in the squash. Cook for just 5 seconds, then drain in a colander. Transfer to a large bowl, season with salt and lemon juice, and drizzle with the oil. Toss with the parsley mixture and serve.

THE VOCABULARY OF CUTTING

I'll try to minimize French vocab in this book, but you should be aware of a few key terms. The best way to learn them is visually, hence this graphical orgy. Don't bother memorizing them now, but take a quick peek and refer to this spread later when needed.

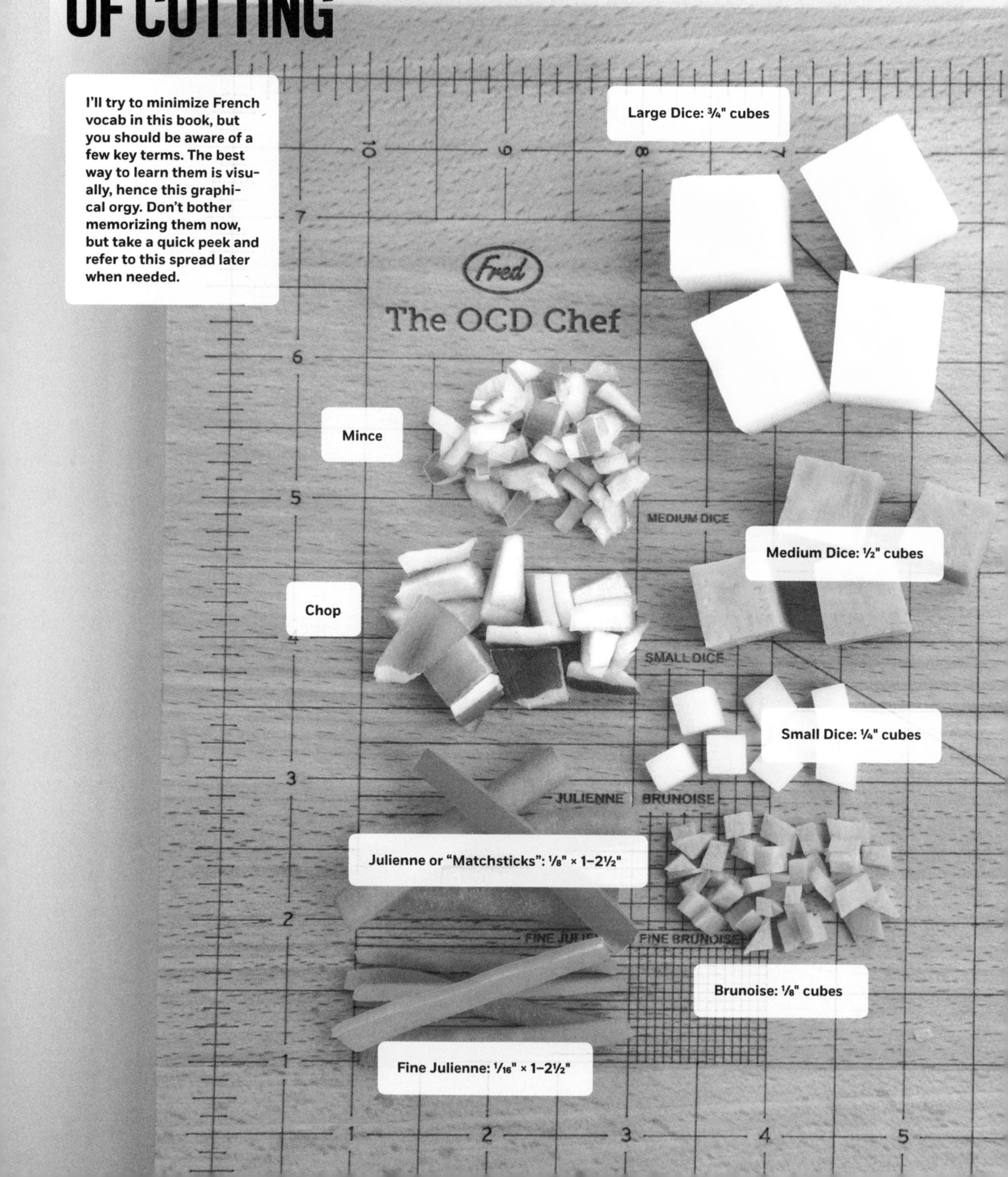
Large Dice: ¾" cubes
Fred
The OCD Chef
Mince
MEDIUM DICE
Medium Dice: ½" cubes
Chop
SMALL DICE
Small Dice: ¼" cubes
JULIENNE
BRUNOISE
Julienne or "Matchsticks": ⅛" × 1–2½"
FINE BRUNOISE
Brunoise: ⅛" cubes
Fine Julienne: 1⁄16" × 1–2½"

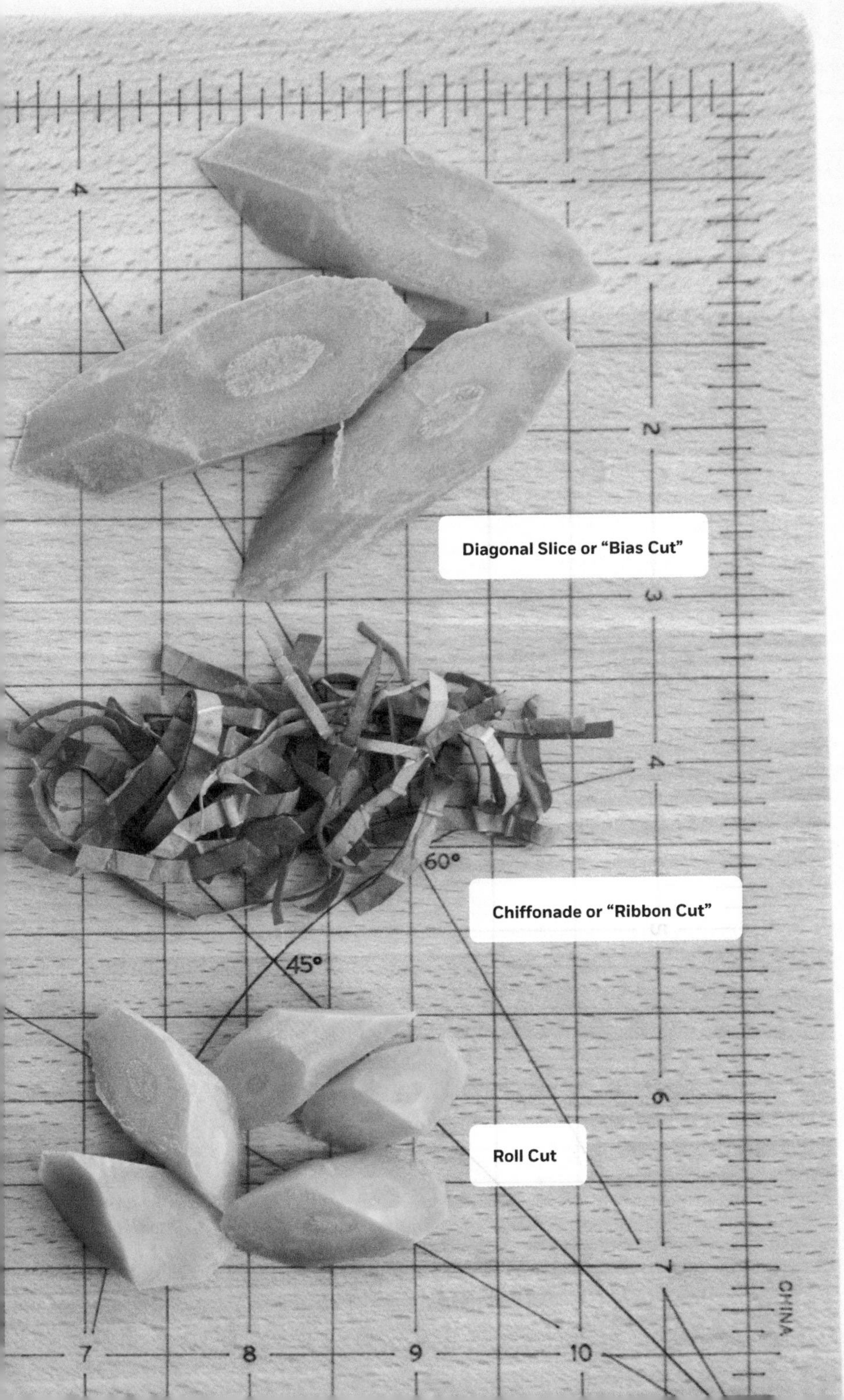
Diagonal Slice or "Bias Cut"
Chiffonade or "Ribbon Cut"
Roll Cut

HOW TO COARSELY CHOP

We can practice with some rosemary. Using your hand or the back of your knife (to avoid dulling the blade), scrape the rosemary needles into one line, as if you were going to sniff them through a dollar bill. This line will utilize the entire length of your blade.

Next, use a common chopping technique I call the "windshield wiper." Gently holding down the front of the knife with your nondominant hand, rapidly chop the knife like a paper cutter, sweeping it back and forth. After each sweep, wipe the herb bits off of the blade and back onto the board. Regather them into a line and repeat.

INTRODUCTION TO *DIM MAK*

THE MOST IMPORTANT OF KNIFE SKILLS

As Jackson asked in the awesomely bad movie *Bloodsport*: "What the hell is a *dim mak*?!?"

Dim mak, literally "press artery" in Cantonese, refers to the so-called death touch in Chinese kung fu. One of the hand positions for *dim mak* also happens to be *the* key hand position for knife skills. In a few sessions of practice, you can go from idiot to idiot savant.

This education will take 10–20 minutes. A chef is as subservient to his knife as Mario Andretti is to his car, so don't skip the next few pages.

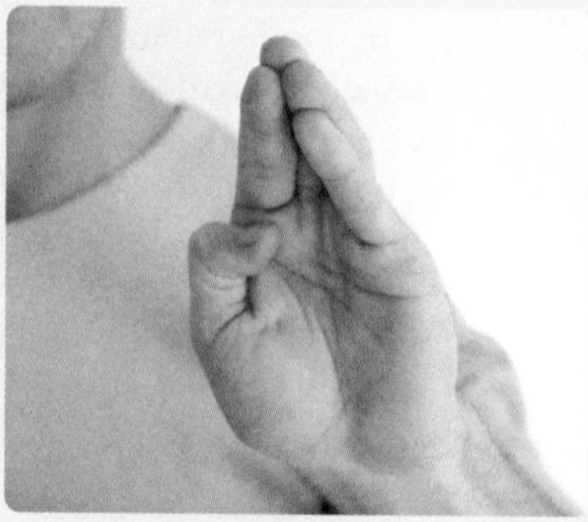

Notice the triangle formed by the index, middle, and ring fingertips. We'll call this the "triangle." For the first two weeks of practice, keep the index and ring fingers pressed together behind the middle.

In practice.

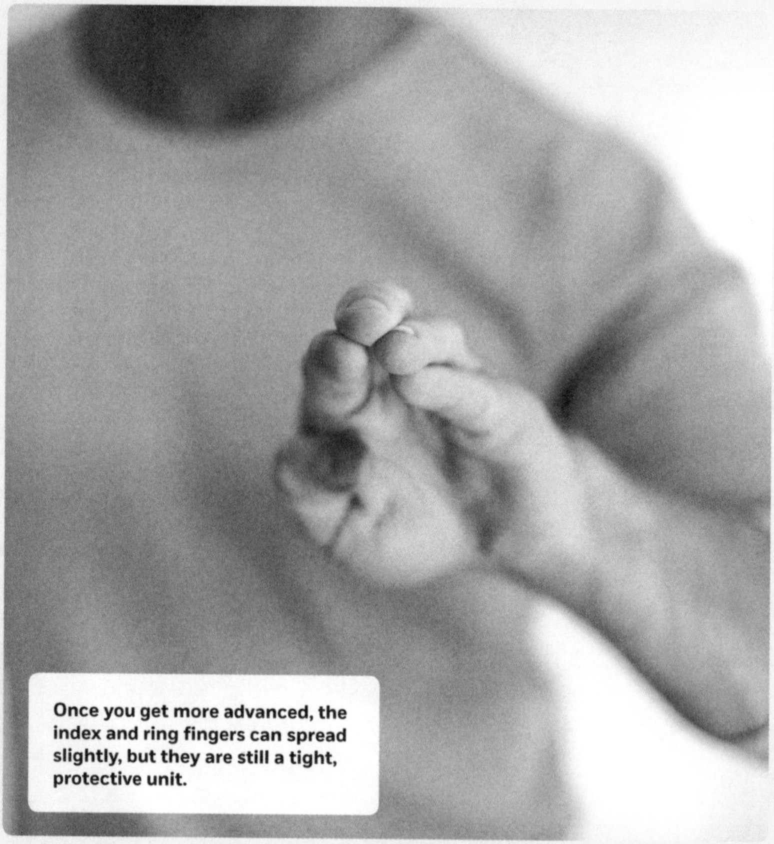

Once you get more advanced, the index and ring fingers can spread slightly, but they are still a tight, protective unit.

PLACEMENT (BODY)

Discard the unused pieces into your garbage bowl, which should be right next to your cutting board.

00 Buy some celery or scallions, which are great for eggs (and our next recipe). Rinse them if they're dirty.

01 Take 2 scallions and cut off the ends using the proper blade-holding grip. Remove about ¼" (0.6 cm) of the white and perhaps 2" (5 cm—or whatever looks nasty) of the green. Ensure both scallions are roughly the same length. Peel off any slimy bits.

Throughout this cutting, maintain proper body position relative to your cutting board: the scallions should be parallel to the edge closest to you, your feet and body angled roughly at 45 degrees, and your knife perpendicular to the board when you cut.

99.9% of the time, you rotate whatever you cut, not your body (hand, arm, feet, torso, etc.), which should remain in position per the illustration at right.

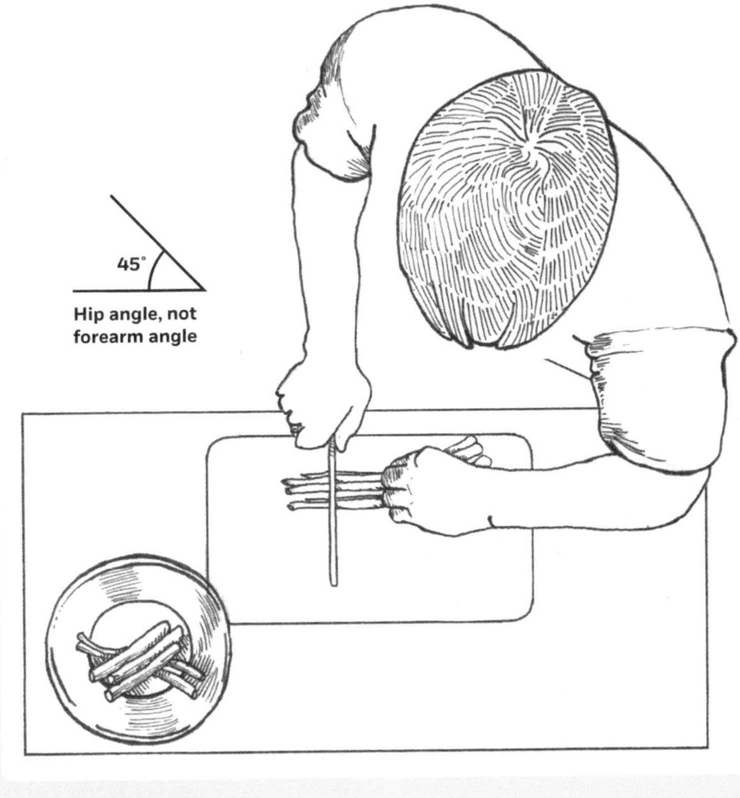
45°
Hip angle, not forearm angle

PLACEMENT (HAND)

02 To use *dim mak* properly, you have to first break longer pieces of food into manageable 2–3" (5–8-cm) pieces.

Your thumb will act as a backstop to keep the food from moving. In this case, the thumb rests on the end of the scallion. Notice how the 2–3" (5–8-cm) piece means your fingers look like they're grabbing a tennis ball, nothing larger. If your hand is too splayed out, as if grabbing a softball, you'll have no stability. So remember: tennis ball or smaller.

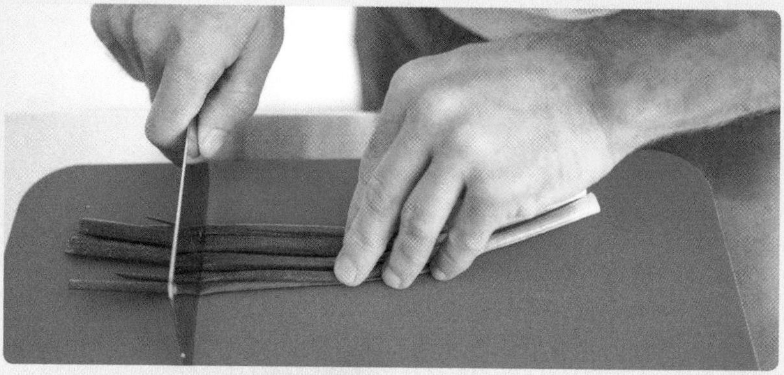

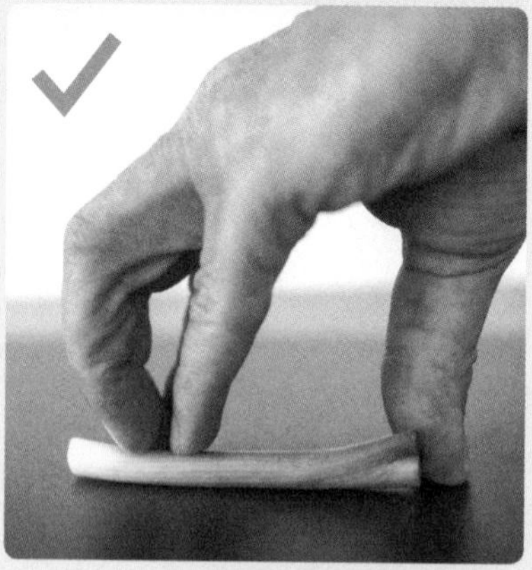

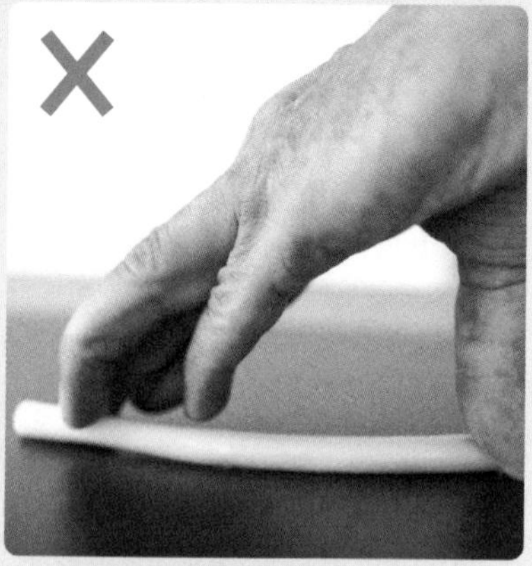

03 We apply *dim mak* for precision and protection. Practice makes perfect, so from this lesson onward, use this technique with any and all cuts possible.

So, where does the blade go? **No matter what, the blade will be in contact with your middle finger,** and this is absolutely the best way to keep your hands safe. I have never cut my hands when keeping good form, nor have any of my students.

PLACEMENT (FINGERS)

For precision, go tip to tip. This means you're cutting with the tip of the blade (or close to it), and it touches the tip of your finger (literally brushing down the fingernail).

As you cut, drag your triangle slowly toward your thumb, as if slowly pinching. Cut at the desired spacing. The thumb doesn't move, nor does the food. With the scallion, you probably won't cut all the way through. Don't sweat it. This is a rehearsal.

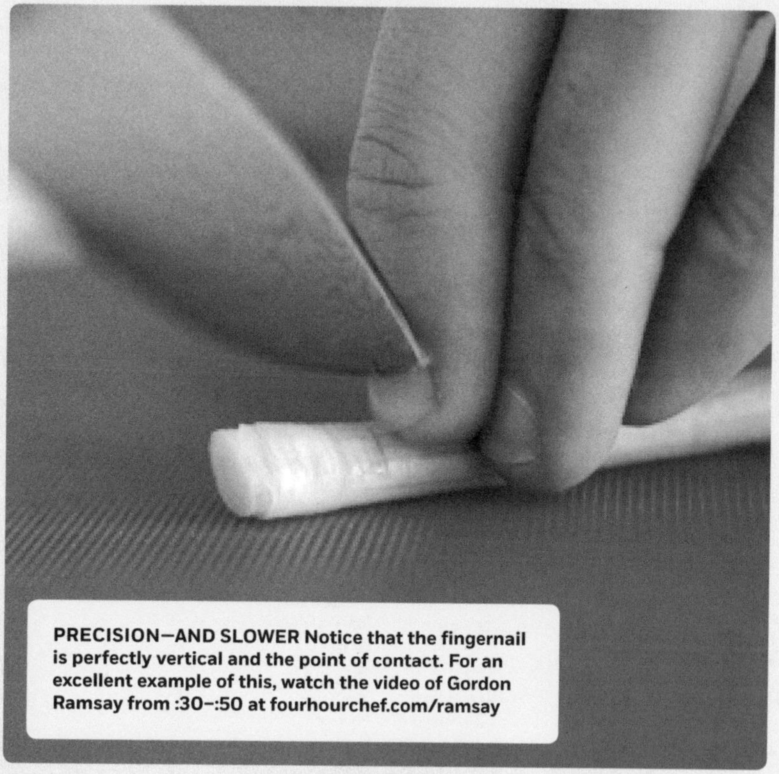

PRECISION—AND SLOWER Notice that the fingernail is perfectly vertical and the point of contact. For an excellent example of this, watch the video of Gordon Ramsay from :30–:50 at fourhourchef.com/ramsay

For speed, go mid to mid. This means you'll cut with the middle of the blade (or farther back), and the blade will touch the first or second knuckle. We'll practice using predominantly the first knuckle. The fingertips are angled in at 45 degrees, which completely prevents you from cutting your fingers. The faster I cut, the farther I curl the fingers. I use the first knuckle most often, but if rapid chopping with a heavy cleaver, I'll use the second knuckle as my point of contact.

In short, the faster you cut, the higher the contact.

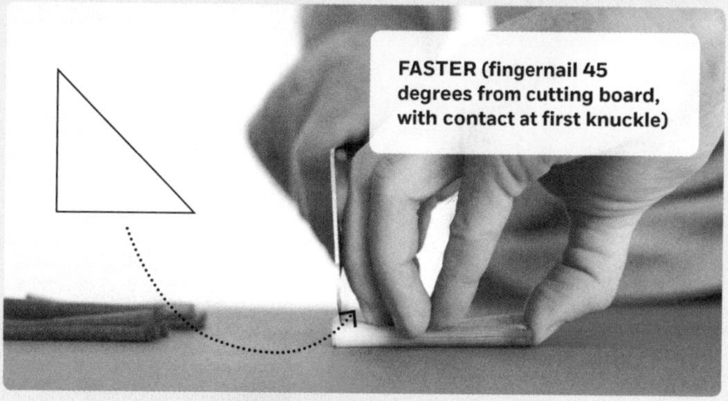

FASTER (fingernail 45 degrees from cutting board, with contact at first knuckle)

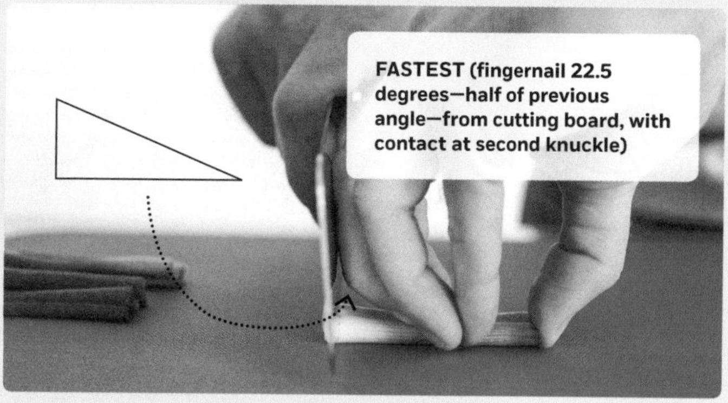

FASTEST (fingernail 22.5 degrees—half of previous angle—from cutting board, with contact at second knuckle)

PUTTING IT TOGETHER

OPTION 1—FRENCH

This is what is taught in culinary schools. It's not what I recommend, but you should know it.

If you watch French chefs cut quickly, they keep the knife tip in constant contact with the cutting board and move their elbow (and therefore the blade) in a small elliptical motion. Having the point of the blade on the board is argued as safer.

The hand "triangle" is held still, but the thumb pushes the food under the fingers and through the blade. Imagine you are cutting celery through a paper cutter, keeping your middle finger in contact with the blade, pushing the veggie through with your thumb—that is the motion. I find pushing with the thumb makes you more prone to extending your fingers. This makes it more dangerous (at least for novices) than what I'll recommend next, in my opinion. The only times I've cut myself have been when using this French approach.

Yes, I'm an amateur, but chances are... so are you.

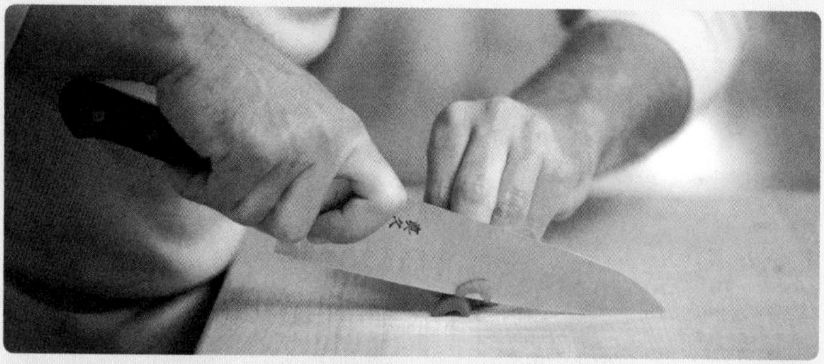

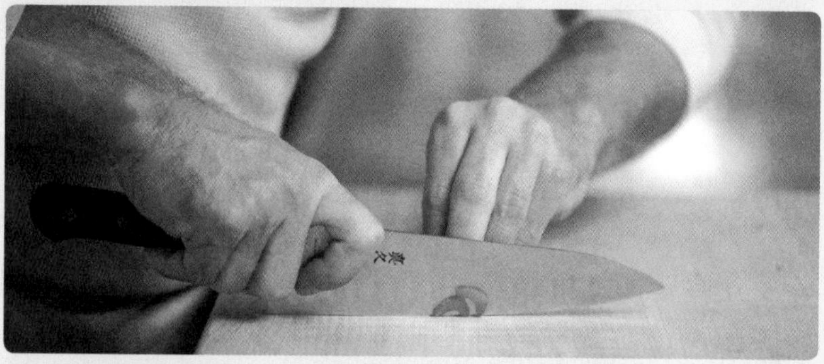

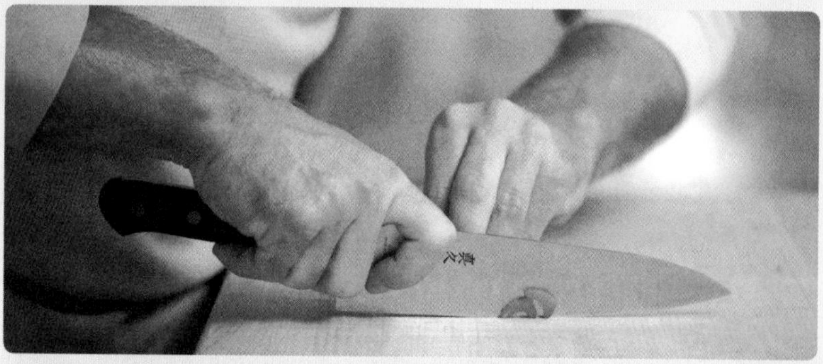

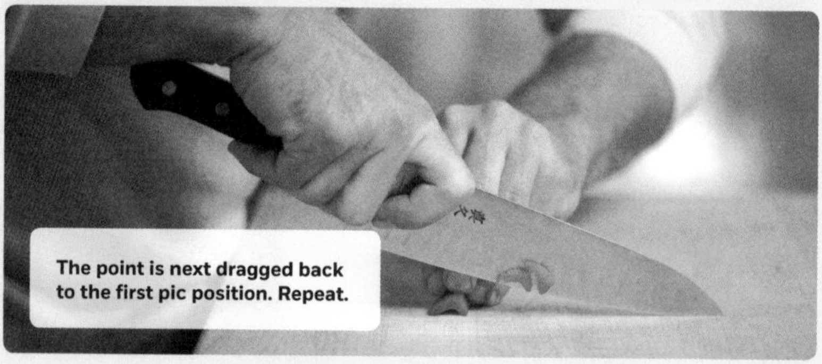

The point is next dragged back to the first pic position. Repeat.

OPTION 2—CHINESE

This is the Chinese standard, which I use most and recommend.

I discovered this approach when two things happened. First, I cut off a third of a fingernail with the French approach as I subconsciously pushed my middle finger under the blade. Second, five minutes later, I saw an astonishing YouTube video of Chef Martin Yan (**fourhourchef.com/yan**). His lightning-fast coordination (especially from 1:02 forward) showed me three things: (1) I didn't need to touch the cutting board with the knife tip to be a good chef, (2) a cleaver could work as well or better than a traditional chef's knife, and (3) the magic was in the knuckles.

Martin chops straight down in many of the video clips, as he uses a heavy cleaver. He can rely on weight for a clean cut. We'll instead slice at a diagonal. This movement lets us use the lighter cleavers I've recommended (the Rada and Tramontina). It works equally well with chef's knives.

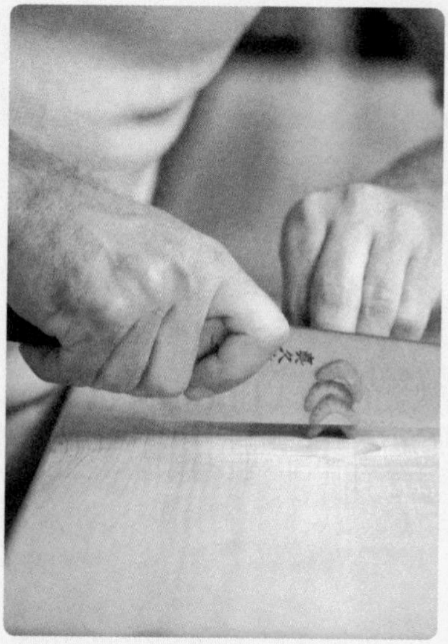

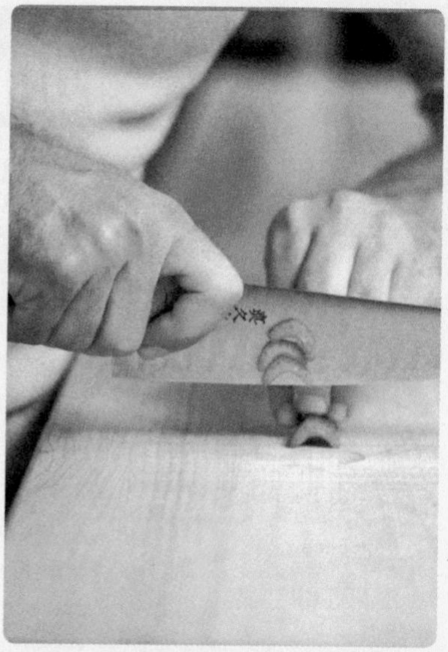

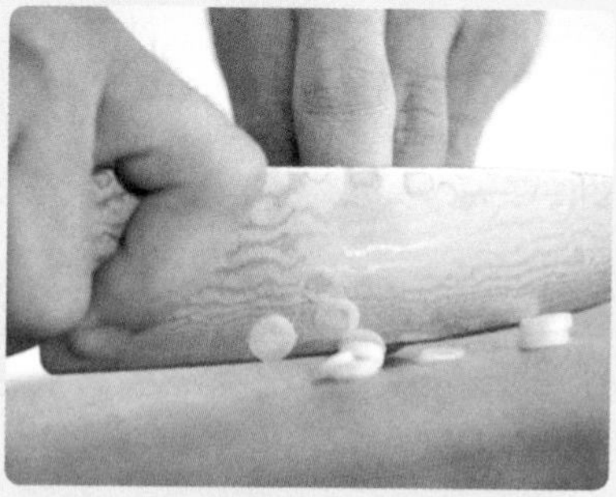

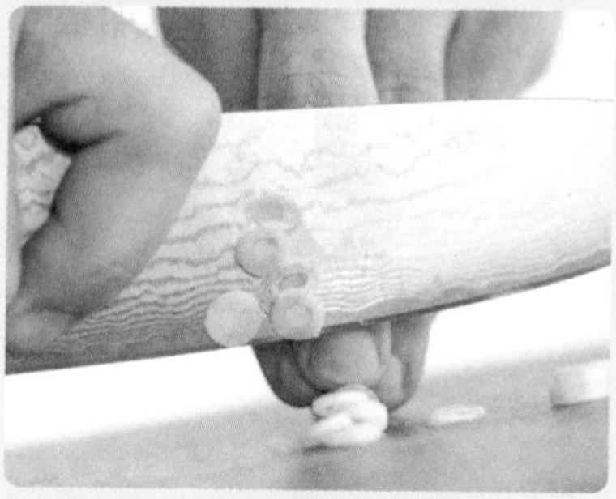

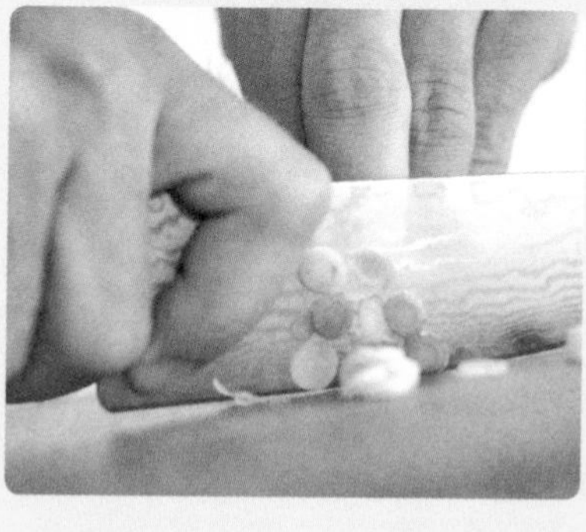

BUT ISN'T LIFTING THE KNIFE DANGEROUS?

Not from all I've seen, read, and tested.

Assuming equal knife control and sharpness, what determines the injury potential of a knife technique is **the height of the edge relative to the fingers**.

The blade should be raised no higher than necessary to cut your food. If you are cutting a carrot, both the French and Chinese approaches require *exactly* the same clearance.

The Chinese have been cooking for a few thousand years longer than the French. Granted, they dropped the ball on that gunpowder thing, but I feel confident that the Chinese cutting method is just as safe as the French if you keep the blade as low as possible.

One thing is certain: it is, without a doubt, far easier to become proficient with the Chinese method.

LESSON 05 +8

SKILLS

USING EGG WHITES, *DIM MAK*

HARISSA CRAB CAKES

SHORTHAND

Mix 1 egg white, 1 chopped scallion, 1T harissa, ¼t pepper, 8oz crab; form into 4 patties. Sauté in 2T oil 3min per side. Serve w lime juice.

HANDS-ON TIME

15 minutes

TOTAL TIME

15 minutes

GEAR

- Knife + cutting board
- Small glass
- Plastic wrap
- Large bowl
- Aeternum or similar nonstick skillet
- Peltex

OPTIONAL PAIRINGS

"Raise Your Weapon (Noisia Remix)" by Deadmau5

Matcha green tea
This is best at an early dinner, as it has the most caffeine—and nutritional content—of all the pairings. This is because you're "eating" the super-finely pulverized shade-grown leaves, which are suspended in water. Good matcha is perfect with seafood, especially raw seafood.

> "Have you ever watched a crab on the shore crawling backward in search of the Atlantic Ocean, and missing? That's the way the mind of man operates."
> —H. L. MENCKEN

One of mankind's favorite flavor combinations is sweet plus sour. It's a universal mouth pleaser. Since sweet-and-sour sauce doesn't fit the slow-carb diet, we'll substitute a lesser-sung hero: hot and sour.

Kimchi, Korea's pride and joy, pulls this off beautifully. Just pick one from each of the groups below, then add salt, for a good outcome.

In this recipe, Harissa Crab Cakes showcase chile (contained in the harissa) and lime, a dynamic duo that infuses any protein with a Mexican accent.[24] The crab cakes, which can be served as an appetizer, contrast nicely with a savory main course, like the Osso "Buko" (rich in glutamate from the tomatoes).

This lesson delivers a lot: we'll use an egg white as binder, add pan-frying to our repertoire, and use *dim mak* in a real dish.

HOT		SOUR
Chiles	+	Vinegar
OR		OR
Pepper		Citrus (lemon or lime)

24 As listed on page 148.

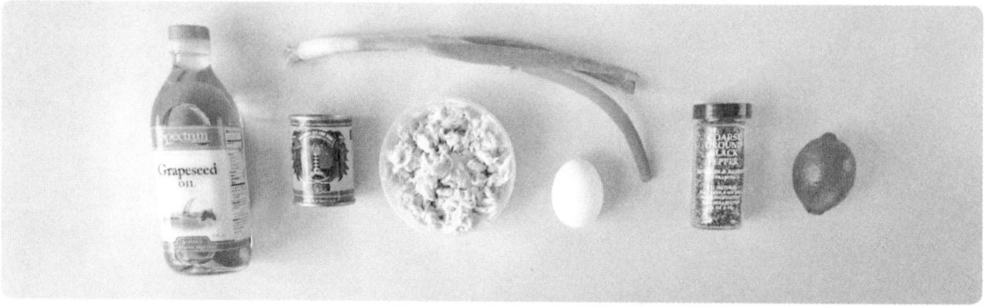

INGREDIENTS	TO SERVE 4
Scallion (green onion)	**1**
Grapeseed oil	**½ c (120 ml), plus 2 T**
Egg white	**1**
Harissa sauce, such as Shiloh's brand	**1 T**
Freshly ground black pepper	**10 turns**
Crabmeat, ideally fresh (I often keep it simple: 2 cans [each 6 oz/180 g] of Crown Prince canned lump meat)	**8 oz (227 g)**
Lime, used for serving	**1**

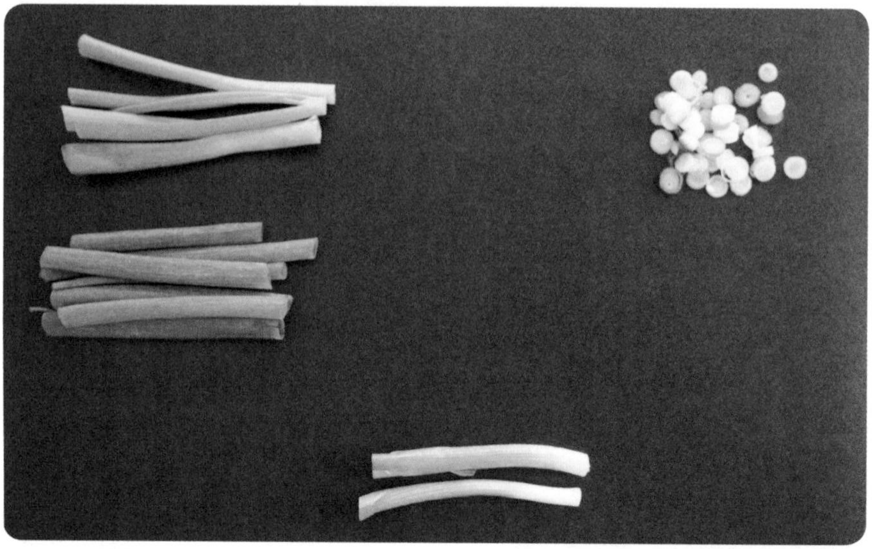

PREP

00 Organize your 2–3" (5–8-cm) pieces of scallion in the upper-left-hand corner of your cutting board. Divide into 2 groups.

01 Cut the first group nice and slowly under complete control and one at a time, using your precision fingernail contact. Cut roughly ⅛" (0.3-cm) pieces. As you finish cutting each segment, use the top of your knife blade to push them to the upper-right-hand corner of your cutting board.

02 If you're still feeling awkward, continue

Don't Be a Pan Shaker

Poking and stirring food unnecessarily pegs you as a pan shaker (yes, the term is derogatory).

Pan shaking is common among actor-chefs on TV. It goes something like this: "Aaaaaaand . . . cut! John, you gotta shuffle that shit around! This segment will be like watching paint dry otherwise. All right, buddy? Show that risotto who's boss! And . . . rolling!"

It might make good TV, but it isn't necessarily good cooking. Learning when to leave food alone is as important as learning when to manipulate it.

with precision contact for the second group. If you feel comfortable, try to cut *slightly* faster (probably still slowly) using contact at the first knuckle of your middle finger.

03 Place ½ the cut scallions in a small glass. Pour in ½ c (120 ml) oil, and use your digital scale to avoid cleanup. These will be used in our next recipe. Put plastic wrap on top and store in the fridge.

04 Place the egg white, 1 T harissa, remaining cut scallions, and 10 turns pepper in a large bowl (if you have to crack a whole egg, store the yolk in the fridge for use in your morning egg experiments).

05 Squeeze the crabmeat over the sink to remove excess water, then add to the bowl. Mix everything together.

06 Sculpt the crab cakes:

OPTION A: The pretty-uniformity-for-guests method. Form the mixture into 4 tightly packed patties about 2½" (6 cm) in diameter and ½" (1.3 cm) thick. Got that, Johnny 5?

OPTION B: The Tim-feeding-his-maw method. Make 1 little blob that kinda-sorta holds together, like a weak snowball. Squeeze out the extra liquid and put down. Repeat for 4 total.

PICKUP

00 Pour an 8" (20 cm) diameter circle of oil (about 2 T) into a large nonstick skillet over medium-high heat. As soon as it starts to shimmer, move to the next step.

01 Using the Peltex, add the crab snowballs and keep track of the order in which you added them. I place them down clockwise from 12 o'clock.

02 Don't fuss with them. Don't. Fuss. With. Them. If you move them, they will break into a hash-brown-like mess of sadness.

03 Let the crab cakes cook in peace for 3 minutes, until nicely browned on the bottom, which will hold them together. Carefully use the Peltex to turn them over in the order you put them down. Use a few fingers or a spoon on top, if needed, for control. Smoosh them down to approximately equal thickness, then cook for another 3 minutes.

04 Remove to individual serving plates or a platter and squeeze lime juice on top. Don't hold back on the lime.

05 Accidentally eat all the delicious li'l bastards before your friends get there.

Repeat process.

LESSON 06 +4

SKILLS

STEAMING, FAKE CONFIT

BITTMAN CHINESE CHICKEN WITH BOK CHOY

SHORTHAND

Make sauce overnight: 2T tamari, 1T ginger, ½c grapeseed oil, ¼c chopped scallion. Steam 2 halved chicken breasts, 2 halved baby bok choy 15min. Serve w sauce.

HANDS-ON TIME

5 minutes

TOTAL TIME

15 minutes

GEAR

- Cast-iron Dutch oven
- Cake rack or steaming basket
- Optional but recommended: Microplane and Star Peeler
- Tongs
- Spoon

OPTIONAL PAIRINGS

"Steam" by Peter Gabriel

Tien Gaun Yin oolong tea

This tea, with notes of dark chocolate and even charcoal, is Kevin's favorite dark roast. It's good for many infusions. Try roasted duck or roasted chicken to fully complement the dark, roasted flavors of this tea.

> "Food is music inside the body, and music is food inside the heart."
>
> —GREGORY DAVID ROBERTS, AUTHOR OF *SHANTARAM*

> "China is a big country, inhabited by many Chinese."
>
> —CHARLES DE GAULLE

Have you ever wondered what the *confit* in *duck confit* or *garlic confit* means? In cooking, it means cooked or stored in fat. It can be really involved. But . . . what if experts couldn't tell the difference between duck cooked in oil (duck confit) and duck simply doused with oil afterward?

Based on taste tests run by Nathan Myhrvold and his *Modernist Cuisine* team, this appears to be the case: "We performed this experiment with duck confit and pork carnitas. In each case, we prepared one batch traditionally and made a second batch by cooking the meat sous-vide or steaming it. We then anointed it with oil (duck fat for duck, pork fat for pork)."‡

Assuming the same temperature and time, the team couldn't tell the difference, and they are world-class chefs! This lesson will teach such a cheat, introduce you to Chinese flavor combinations, and it might be the best chicken you've ever had.

I was introduced to this dish by Mark Bittman, one of the funniest men I know and author of the much-missed "Minimalist" column in the *New York Times*. The first time I had it, I thought: this tastes just like perfect sous-vide chicken! (We'll cover this later.) I then learned that some restaurants, like Café du Parc, in D.C., make "perfect" sous-vide chicken and duck breasts by first bulk-steaming them in a Rational Combi-Oven Steamer ($28,387.44 list price). Their next step is reheating in an industrial sous-vide immersion circulator ($1,000) when orders come in. The breasts are finished with a quick pan sear.

The results of steaming in your covered cast-iron Dutch oven ($20!) can rival this high-end preparation. I'm not kidding.

Since you're making food for a few people, you actually have a huge advantage over professionals, who must use fancy gear to cook in volume for a commercial kitchen.

Maldon

INGREDIENTS	TO SERVE 2
Tamari (you can also use Bragg Liquid Aminos or Raw Coconut Aminos)	**2 T**
Powdered ginger or grated fresh ginger (+2 bonus points, see opposite page)	**1 T**
Grapeseed oil	**½ c (120 ml)**
Trimmed and chopped scallions, white and green parts combined (⅛" pieces; if they end up a little bigger, don't worry about it)	**¼ c (28 g)**
Boneless, skinless chicken breasts (<500 g each)	**2**
Baby bok choy	**2 heads**
Kosher or Maldon sea salt	**To taste**
OPTIONAL, WHICH I ALMOST NEVER USE	
Toasted sesame oil	**1 t**
Lemon juice	**To taste**

PREP

00 Prepare the sauce: in a small bowl on your electronic scale, combine the 2 T tamari, 1 T ginger, ½ c (20 ml) grapeseed oil, ¼ c (28 g) scallions, and 1 t sesame oil (if using).

NOTE: If you recently made the Harissa Crab Cakes (page 172), you have the scallions and grapeseed oil ready, so take the trouble to use real ginger (see opposite page). It makes a difference in taste and texture.

01 Stir this sauce for a few seconds and set aside. It's best after it sits overnight.

02 Cut the 2 chicken breasts into halves lengthwise on your cutting board, or in the store packaging to save cleanup. This will produce 4 pieces that look like big chicken tenders. Halving them increases the surface area exposed to steam and speeds up the cooking. Wash your hands.

03 Rinse the bok choy under running water, without pulling the leaves off the base. Look for dirt where they join together, and remove any disgusting wilted leaves. Cut them in half lengthwise. (See pic on previous page.)

PICKUP

00 Fill your steaming vessel (Dutch oven or stockpot) with 1" (2.5 cm) of water, up to just a hair under the cake rack or steamer

basket that you've put in it. The food should not touch the water.

01 Place the chicken on the rack or in the steamer in one layer, no overlapping. If the end tendrils of the chicken barely flop into the water, it's fine. Place the bok choy on top of the chicken and cover the pot.

Alternatively, if you have two pots, you can steam them separately.

02 Set the pot over high heat.

03 Turn off the heat after 15 minutes. Check to make sure the chicken is cooked through by cutting into the thickest part of one piece; if it's still pink inside, steam over high heat for another 2 minutes.

04 Remove the bok choy with tongs, shake off excess water, and "plate" it (arrange it on plates or a platter). Plate the chicken beside the bok choy. Sprinkle both with salt to taste. Squeeze lemon on the bok choy. Drizzle the sauce on top of all with a spoon and enjoy!

PRESENTATION TIP: If serving guests, place an odd number of chicken pieces on the plate, saving the end pieces for leftovers. For whatever *feng shui* reason, it looks dramatically better. Many restaurants follow this odd-number rule as gospel. See the glamour shot on page 177.

BONUS POINTS +2

PREP FRESH GINGER

Here's how you prepare 1 T of fresh ginger.

Peel about ⅓" (0.8 cm) of the skin off the end, using either the Star Peeler (my preference) or the traditional edge of a spoon. No need to be exact, as you can always peel more if needed. If there are knobs in the way, cut them off.

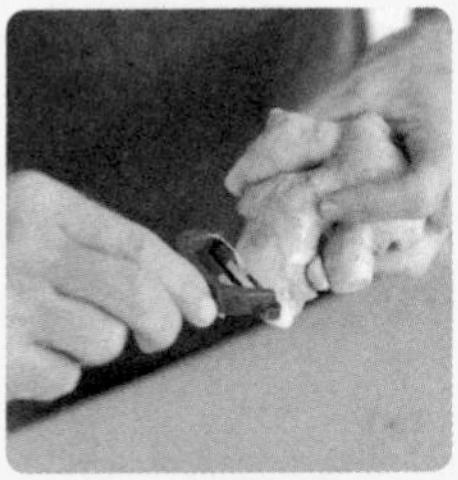

OPTION A: Set the Microplane at an angle on the cutting board and shave off what you think is 1 T. Remember to whack the Microplane on the cutting board at the end, as most of the goodies will stick to the underside. Measure it using a tablespoon if you like, but I don't bother.

OPTION B: If you're lazy (like me), you can also put the Microplane horizontally over the sauce bowl, grate directly into it, and then rap on the edges to remove any stuck ginger.

LESSON 07 +4

SKILL

SEMI-COMPOSED SALADS

ARUGULA, AVOCADO, AND ROMA SALAD

+ OPTIONAL EGGOCADO AND BOILED EGGS EXPERIMENT

SHORTHAND

Toss with oil & vinegar in bowl: 1 bunch arugula, then sliced Roma tomatoes, then ½ avocado/person. S+P to taste.

TOTAL TIME

10 minutes

GEAR

- Mixing bowl
- Knife + cutting board
- Spoon + butter knife
- Optional: salad spinner (or colander)

OPTIONAL PAIRINGS

"To Know You Is to Love You" by Greyboy (feat. Bart Davenport)

Bai Mudan white tea

Buttery in body (like the mouthfeel of avocado), slightly nutty, and wholesome, this is a full-bodied white tea with enough astringency, aroma, and taste to handle any kind of vegetarian dish, even with vinegar.

> "I could have sexual chemistry with vinegar."
> —JESSICA ALBA

In the United States, most salads suck. It's taken decades to get past iceberg lettuce and Russian dressing. In the U.K. and most of South America, it's even worse.

But . . . I've always loved caprese salad. Those thick slabs of buffalo mozzarella cheese and tomatoes, covered with basil and calorie-rich oil! Delicious.

The caprese is referred to as a *composed* salad. A composed salad is usually neatly arranged on a plate as opposed to tossed. I find the main benefit to be heft. It's a solid appetizer, not a shameful side dish. It feels like eating food instead of swallowing air.

This Arugula, Avocado, and Roma Salad is intended to give you a solid (semi-) composed salad and teach a few things:

1. We'll discuss how to properly dress salads, as well as store leftovers.

2. You'll learn that species matters. Argentina introduced me to smaller Roma (Roman) tomatoes, which are all meat with minimal juice and seeds. No more explosions of watery disgust.

For dinner parties, this salad is one of my two defaults. The other is gazpacho, coming soon.

PREP

00 Get your *meez* (all materials) in place.

01 Wash the arugula properly.

Maldon
Partanna

INGREDIENTS	TO SERVE 2–4
Arugula, ideally baby arugula (called "rocket" in the land of Posh Spice)	**1 bunch**
Roma tomatoes	**1–2 per person**
S+P	**To taste**
Sherry vinegar	**A drizzle**
EVOO	**A drizzle**
Avocado	**½ per person**

Getting the EVOO to Flow

If you have a large metal container of EVOO, use the back corner of your chef's knife to stab a hole into the back of the top lid. This will facilitate airflow. The Rada might not work for this, but a Tramontina or any standard chef's knife will do the trick.

Don't wash like this:

Do wash like this:

Place the leaves in a mixing bowl or, ideally, a salad spinner. Cover at least ¾ of it with water, then toss with your hands. Lift out the greens, discard the water, and repeat once more.

02 If you have a salad spinner, dry the arugula. The dressing won't stick well to wet leaves. If you don't have a salad spinner, go MacGyver: Place the arugula leaves in the middle of a towel, roll it up, hold both ends, and swing 10 times overhead to force some of the water into the towel.

03 Rinse, dry, and cut the Roma tomatoes into roughly ½" (1.3-cm) slices *latitudinally*—around the thinner equator, not pole to pole. (See pics on next page.)

PICKUP

00 Place the arugula in the mixing bowl. Add Maldon sea salt and a few turns of pepper to taste. Now we'll add the dressing, and you have two options:

(A) Drizzle in the vinegar, *then* the oil. Why? If you put the EVOO on first, the vinegar will slip off of the leaves and pool at the bottom. Cover the spouts of the vinegar and EVOO with your thumb to control the flow. Don't drown your salad.

OR

(B) Drizzle both the vinegar and EVOO around the perimeter of the metal mixing bowl, not on the leaves. Then . . .

01 Toss and mix the salad with your hands.

02 Place the dressed arugula in individual serving bowls.

03 Add the tomatoes to the mixing bowl and toss them in the remaining dressing; place them on top of the arugula in the serving bowls.

04 Cut open the avocado longitudinally (pole to pole) with a sharp knife and twist the halves apart like you're opening a jar of peanut butter. (See pics on page 183.)

Place the avocado half with the pit on a flat

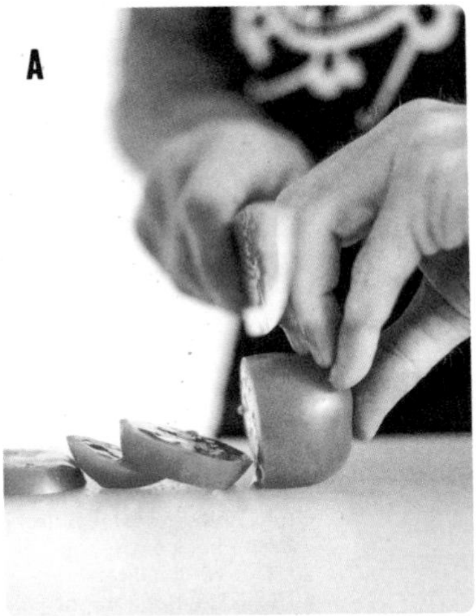
A

B

C

surface. Using the Rada or chef's knife, chop down into the middle of the pit. You're not chopping lumber, so no more than a few inches of drop is needed. Once the blade is well stuck, hold the underside of the avocado and turn the knife counterclockwise to pop the pit out. Knock the pit off the blade into the garbage with a spoon. If you store a half, squeeze some lemon juice on the cut side first. The lemon juice will lower the pH and minimize the grody browning.

05 Using a butter knife, make a grid in each avocado half. Spoon the pieces into the mixing bowl to coat with the remaining dressing. Then transfer the squares on top of your salad, in the serving bowls.

Why not mix everything in the big mixing bowl from the outset? The tomato slices and avocado pieces tend to fall to the bottom and get gross.

Now, *mangia!*

Ripening with a Paper Bag

If your avocados seem hard and unripe, introduce them to a paper bag. Putting them inside a closed bag concentrates the ethylene gas that avocados give off, which accelerates ripening. The process can be reduced from several days to overnight. This trick can be used on almost all fruits, excluding a few dissenters like pineapple.

This is what my first attempt looked like. No food stylist involved.

A

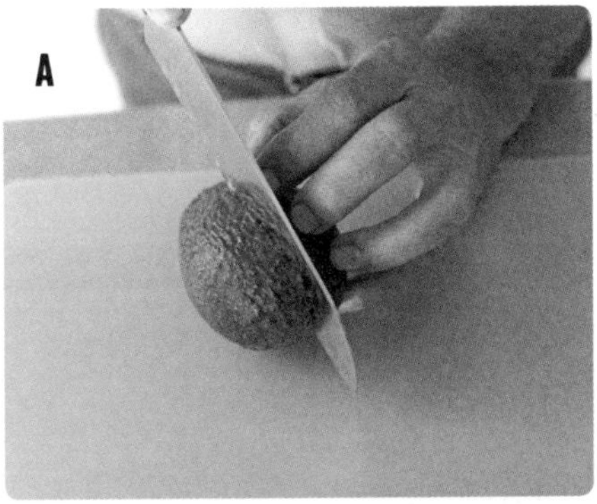

+2

B

C

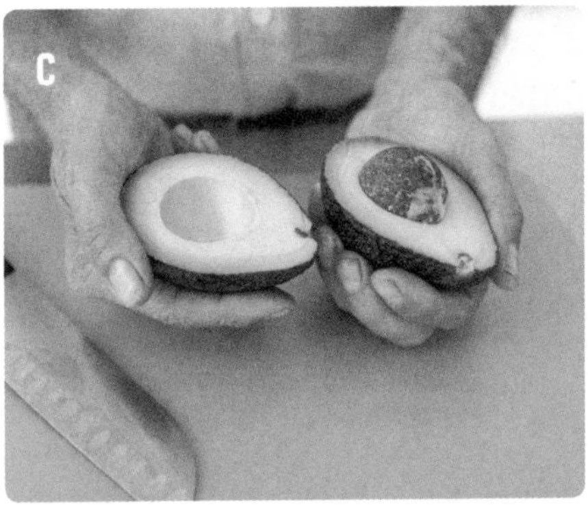

D

E

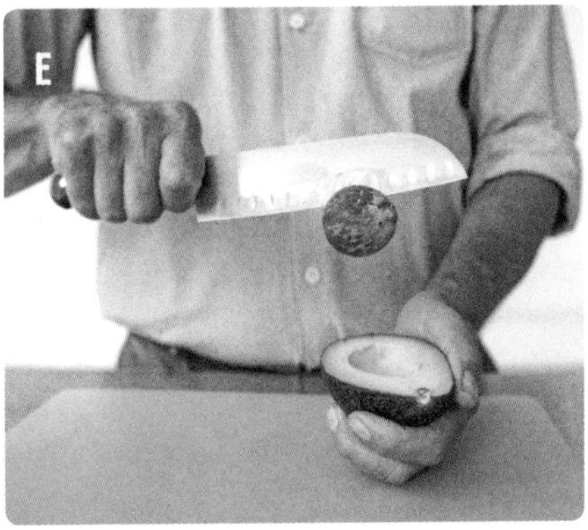

F

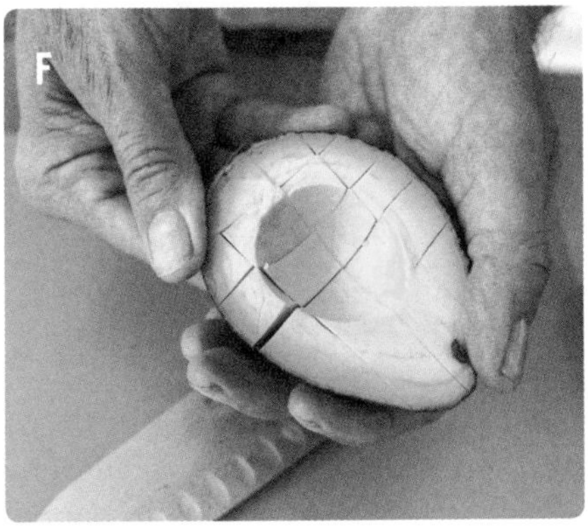

G

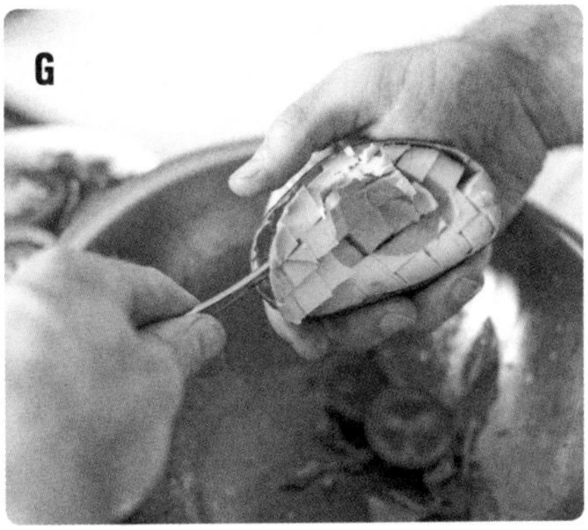

BONUS POINTS

GOING BALLS OUT: THE EGGOCADO

Need a break from scrambled eggs? Now that you've conquered the mighty avocado (derived from the Aztec word for "testicle" [*ahuacatl*], by the way), you can enjoy a no-cleanup wonder. Hat tip to Alan Henry of Lifehacker, who introduced me to this:

1. Preheat your oven to 425°F (220°C). Beat 1 egg with a fork to blend white and yolk.
2. Cut an avocado in half and de-pit as shown at left. Next, slice off a quarter's worth of each "back" so they lay flat. Sprinkle a little salt in each pit hole.
3. Place the avocado halves in an oven-safe skillet, pitted side up, propped against the side to keep them steady.
4. Pour ½ the egg into the center of each avocado half. If you're using a Hass avocado (the smaller, wrinkly, dark-skinned variety), you might need to scoop out a little flesh to make room first. Add any spices or condiments you like on top. Hot sauce, chili powder, cumin, paprika, or lemon zest all work brilliantly.
5. Carefully place the skillet in the oven and bake for 16–18 minutes, until the egg is set.
6. Devour with a spoon, then send me thank-you letters and chocolates.

BONUS POINTS +2

THE BOILED EGGS UPGRADE

TIME
15 minutes

GEAR
- Raw or finished cast-iron Dutch oven (or other pot for boiling), no lid required
- Large metal spoon
- Timer
- Sharpie pen

Conducting egg experiments at home with chef James Simpkins, whom I found on kitchit.com.

INGREDIENTS	
Baking soda, to make eggs easier to peel	1 t
Large eggs ("large" is a standard size in grocery stores, so no need to search for Paul Bunyan eggs)	3
Black truffle oil (usually $9 or so)	A drizzle
Maldon sea salt	A sprinkle

This experiment might just change your life. It takes something you think you know—hard-boiled eggs—and makes them orgasmic.

00 Pour roughly 3" (7.5 cm) of water into your Dutch oven or pot.

01 Add 1 t baking soda, which will reduce adhering of the egg white to the shell. This makes the eggs *far* easier to peel. Gently stir to mix in.

02 Set the burner to high and wait until the water boils. If you want an alert, you can set your probe thermometer to go off at 212°F (100°C), which is boiling temp at sea level.

03 Get a timer that can count up—and get your finger ready.

04 Gently add all 3 eggs to the boiling water and start your timer.

05 After 6 minutes exactly, remove 1 egg using a large metal spoon. Gently run it under cold water to lower the temperature. Place this egg in a cup. If cool enough to do so, write "6" on the egg with a Sharpie pen. Otherwise, use scrap paper.

06 After 7 minutes exactly (1 minute later), repeat with another egg.

07 After 8 minutes have elapsed, repeat with the last egg.

08 Now peel the eggs. The fresher the eggs, the harder they'll be to peel.

OPTION A, which I recommend, since the eggs are less likely to end up on the floor:

1. Tap both ends of each egg to crack them.

2. Gently roll the eggs on the counter and peel them under cold running water.

OPTION B, the party trick:

This could be called "how to peel eggs without really peeling them." I created a video of this years ago, and it's still my most popular on YouTube, with well over 4 million views. Though not the best for dinner-party hygiene, it's worth trying, assuming you've used baking soda as recommended.

1. Tap both ends of the egg and pinch off a small fragment from each. You want a small hole at either end.

2. Hold the egg in 1 hand and, keeping the other hand just behind this hand, blow the egg out of the shell. Catch it to applause and shouts of "I'll eat the other egg,

thanks!" Even if this doesn't work, it loosens the shells and makes them easier to peel.

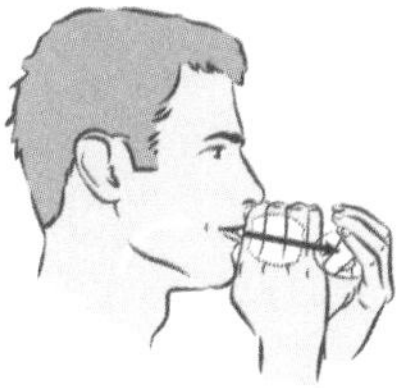

09 Cut each egg in half, being careful not to spill the contents, and do a side-by-side comparison. It should look something like the photo at right.

10 Last and most important, drizzle a little truffle oil onto all of the pieces, then sprinkle Maldon sea salt on each. Try the 6-, 7-, and 8-minute eggs by yourself or with another person. Which do you prefer? I prefer the 7-minute egg, but this is a subjective science. And that truffle-oil-and-salt combo? Brain explosion! To die for. Add your own superlative and spread the good word.

Now you know why truffle oil is considered "cheating" by experienced chefs when they see it overused.

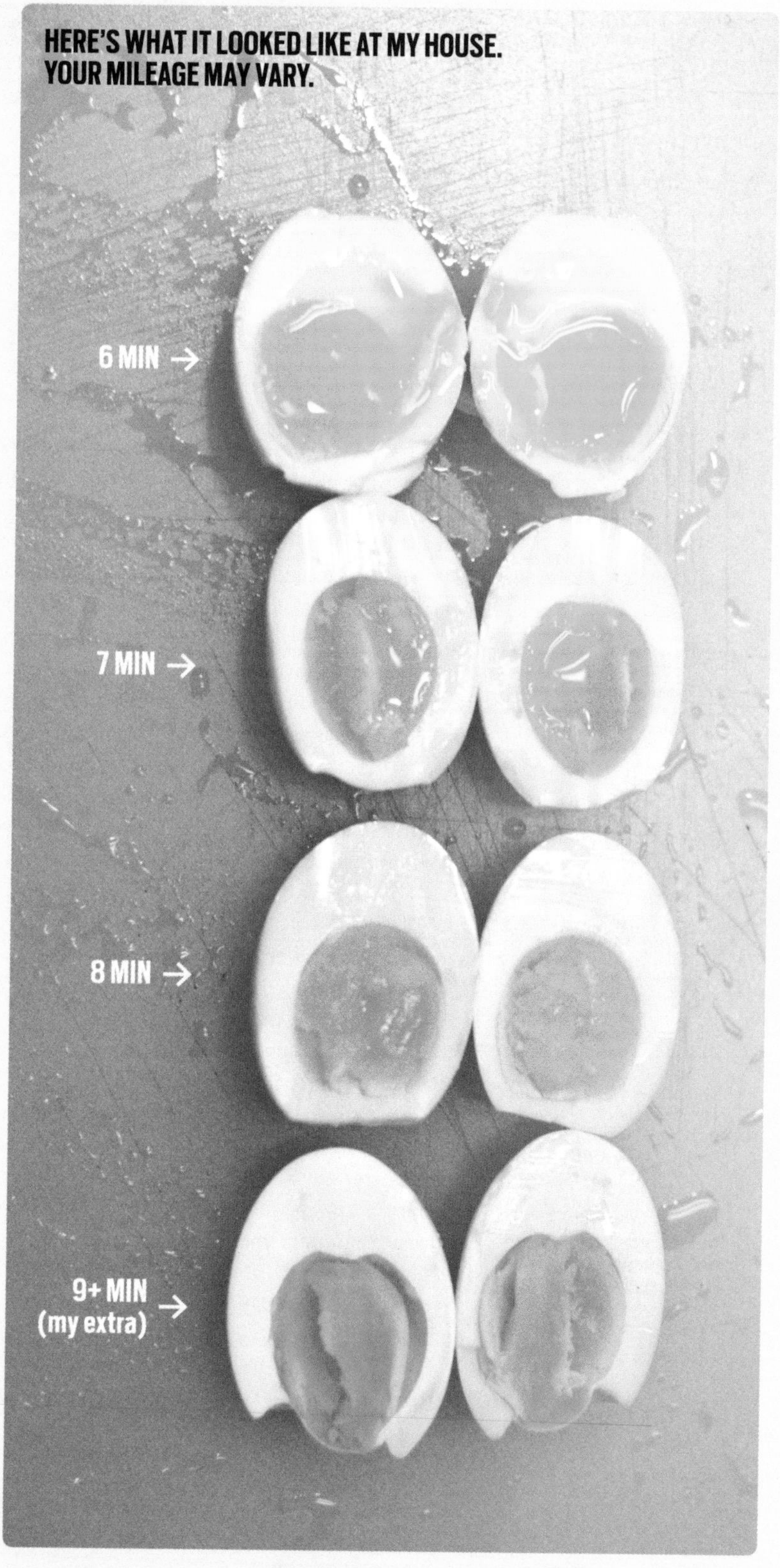
HERE'S WHAT IT LOOKED LIKE AT MY HOUSE.
YOUR MILEAGE MAY VARY.
6 MIN →
7 MIN →
8 MIN →
9+ MIN
(my extra) →

LESSON 08 +4

SKILLS

DRY BRINING, PROBE THERMOMETER

SEXY-TIME STEAK

AND PINE POLLEN COCKTAIL

INSPIRED BY

Phil Caravaggio

SHORTHAND

200F oven: Sear dry-brined, garlic-rubbed, S+P steak 1min per side, place on rosemary bed, roast 30min. Baste w skillet juices, serve.

HANDS-ON TIME

5 minutes

TOTAL TIME

35 minutes, plus hands-off brining and freezer time

GEAR

- Probe thermometer
- Cast-iron skillet
- Tongs

OPTIONAL PAIRINGS

"SexyBack" by Justin Timberlake

Maiden's Ecstasy Puerh

This is the equivalent of a heavy, rich, and dark red wine. Earthy and creamy, with notes of bittersweet coffee and even espresso, it brings out any smoky, earthy, or gamey qualities of meat.

> "If God did not intend for us to eat animals, then why did he make them out of meat?"
>
> —JOHN CLEESE

She was a pretty young thing, but not subtle. After 20 dolphin-like nose jabs to my crotch, she started trying to flip my balls, using her head like a spatula.

"I've never seen her hump anyone before," Nick Bilton said, dumbfounded. He was as puzzled as everyone else in the kitchen watching Pixel, his dog, go to town on my leg.

My test had succeeded, albeit with the wrong species.

Yellow pine pollen, originally introduced to me on a foraging trip through Golden Gate Park in San Francisco (page 298), doesn't just act as a precursor to testosterone. It *is* testosterone. Several species contain not just androstenedione (remember Mark McGwire?) but also DHEA and testosterone itself.

Combine it with a fat steak and all sorts of mischief is possible. That's what I'd done 90 minutes before heading to Nick's house.

We'll optimize this next recipe to do three things:

1. Teach you a fail-proof method for the perfect steak while emphasizing a few crucial principles.
2. Maximize post-meal sex drive (assuming 60–90 minutes for the meal).
3. Maximize sex drive roughly 24 hours later, for the following night's sexy time.

First, you need a nice, fatty cut. As covered extensively in *The 4-Hour Body*, we can cholesterol-load with saturated fat to improve testosterone production. We'll cook the classic, a rib eye, which is thick enough for probe-thermometer practice and easy to find. Ladies, no need to worry about testosterone, because you have it too, at between one-twentieth and one-tenth the levels of males.[25]

For the quick adrenaline shot of testosterone, we'll use pine pollen. It's easiest to order online (fourhourchef.com/pine).

It's best consumed when added to cold water. Not recommended for pregnant women or people with weak stomachs. If you'd like a good pre-workout performance enhancer, it'll do the trick there, too. Use in moderation, my excessive Americans, as more is not better.

This recipe is written for one steak, but you could easily use two surfaces to cook two steaks. Just double up on everything.

25 This increases with age. Forty-year-old women can have half the levels of men. Hark, the roar of the cougar!

TO TIM,
PLAY MORE
VIDEO GAMES,
AND SORRY PIXEL
WANTED TO FUCK YOU

Book inscription from Nick Bilton, lead technology writer for the *New York Times*'s "Bits" blog.

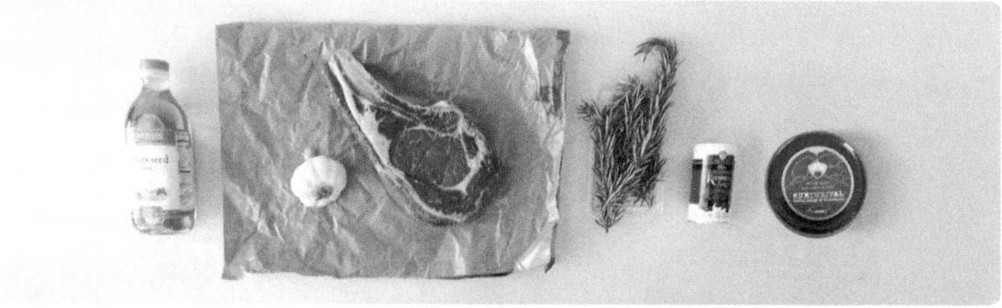

INGREDIENTS	TO SERVE 1–2
FOR THE STEAK	
Rib eye steaks (Read the entire recipe first. There are reasons to buy at least 2. Thickness is important.)	**1 or more (1–1½"/ 2.5–4 cm thick)**
S+P	**To taste**
Garlic clove	**1**
Grapeseed oil	**Enough to coat skillet**
Fresh rosemary sprigs (for another fast default steak seasoning, use Montreal steak rub)	**1 large package**
OPTIONAL	
Ghee	**1 dollop**
FOR THE PINE POLLEN COCKTAIL	
Pine pollen powder	**1 t**
Cold water	**½ c (120 ml)**
Strong stomach	**1**

PREP

00 At least a few hours before cooking your steak, "dry brine" it. I do this step the night before. Generously coat one side of your steak with kosher salt and place it, uncovered and salted side up, on a plate in the fridge. We'll rinse it off later, but in the meantime the salt will pull water out of the steak, and this salty water (brine) will form a layer on top of the steak for about 30–45 minutes before it's reabsorbed into the meat, which flavors and tenderizes it.

Unlike "wet brining," where you soak meat in saltwater, this "dry brining" doesn't risk water-logging your food. The technique was popularized by chef Judy Rodgers of Zuni Café, who uses it for prepping roast chicken. It was introduced to me by Jaden Hair, who uses it for turning "cheap 'choice' steak" into "Gucci 'prime' steak."

PICKUP

00 Roughly 90 minutes before you want to eat, rinse off the steak(s) and pat *completely* dry with paper towels. Really get 'em dry.

01 Rub both sides with a halved garlic clove and sprinkle S+P on them. If you want to

A

get all sciency, use 0.5% of your meat weight in salt, 0.25% per side. Personally, I just coat the sucker. It's hard to overdo it.

02 Put the steak in the freezer, unwrapped, for 30–45 minutes. Elevate it if possible (even on a few pencils on a paper plate), so that all surfaces are exposed to air. A cake rack works perfectly. Place a paper towel underneath to catch drippings. This freezer trick from *Cook's Illustrated* is used to evaporate any residual surface moisture, which will allow for the perfect sear. The freezer, just like Antarctica, is an unusually dry environment. Don't exceed 45 minutes, as we don't want to freeze our steak, just dry its exterior.

03 After putting the meat in the freezer, preheat your oven to 200°F (90°C). This low temperature offers a large margin for error and will cook the steak incredibly evenly.[26] To standardize how you cook your steaks, ensure the rack is set in the middle or lower third of the oven (things generally cook more slowly at the top). Heston Blumenthal cooks his "perfect steak" at 122°F (50°C), but you probably don't want to wait 24 hours, like he does.

Red Meat Alternatives

How can you cholesterol load for testosterone without red meat? First, try shrimp. A mere 3 oz (85 g) will give you 55% of your daily allowance. If you want to skip the foreplay, try a can of Rose Pork Brains, which contains 3,190 mg of cholesterol in one serving, delivering a whopping 1,063% of the daily 300 mg recommended by the American Heart Association. Eat 15 whole eggs or a slurp of canned pork brains? You decide.

26 Our default 350°F (180°C) will work for steak, but you'd use different prep. See page 194.

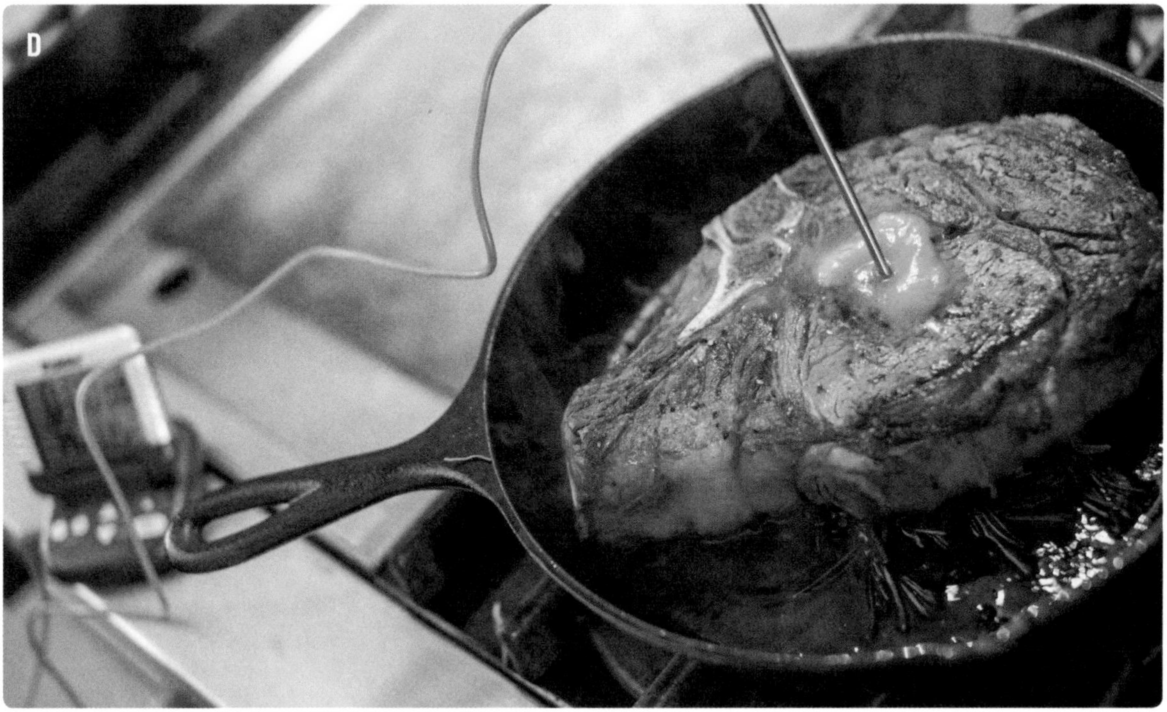
D

04 **CRUCIAL MOVE:** Get your probe thermometer ready and set the alarm for 135°F (57°C). Place it near the stovetop for easy access.

05 When your freezer time is up, set your cast-iron skillet over the highest heat and leave it alone for 5 minutes to get it scorching hot. It's hot enough when a drop of water sizzles on the surface. Turn on your exhaust fan if you have one. Things are about to get smoky.

06 Add grapeseed oil to the skillet and tilt it in a circle to coat entirely. You are about to *sear* that steaky sumnabitch. The purpose of searing isn't to lock in moisture (it doesn't), but rather to add flavor by caramelizing the exterior amino acids via the Maillard reaction (think freshly toasted bread).

07 Using tongs, carefully lay your steak down in the skillet.

08 After roughly one minute, just long enough to nicely brown the side, flip it over to sear the other side for one minute. Brown the edges if you'd like to sharpen your tong-ninja skills.

09 Once done searing, pick up the steak with tongs and place several (6 or so) full rosemary sprigs in the pan. Lay the steak back down on top of this bedding, which will both flavor the steak and help prevent it from overcooking on that side.

10 Optional for the decadent: Place a dollop of ghee on top of the steak.

11 Turn off the burner. Insert the probe thermometer straight down into the center of the steak. If it leans over like the Leaning Tower of Pisa, that's fine, but it shouldn't touch the rim of the skillet.

12 Place the pan in the oven, uncovered, and forget about it until the alarm goes off; this should take about 30 minutes.

13 Move the steak to a cutting board or platter (see pic on next page). Grab a rosemary sprig (fresh or from the pan) and use it to mop up juices in the skillet and to "paint" the top of the steak. Flip and repeat. (This painting technique can be done with other woody herbs, such as thyme, for a different flavor.)

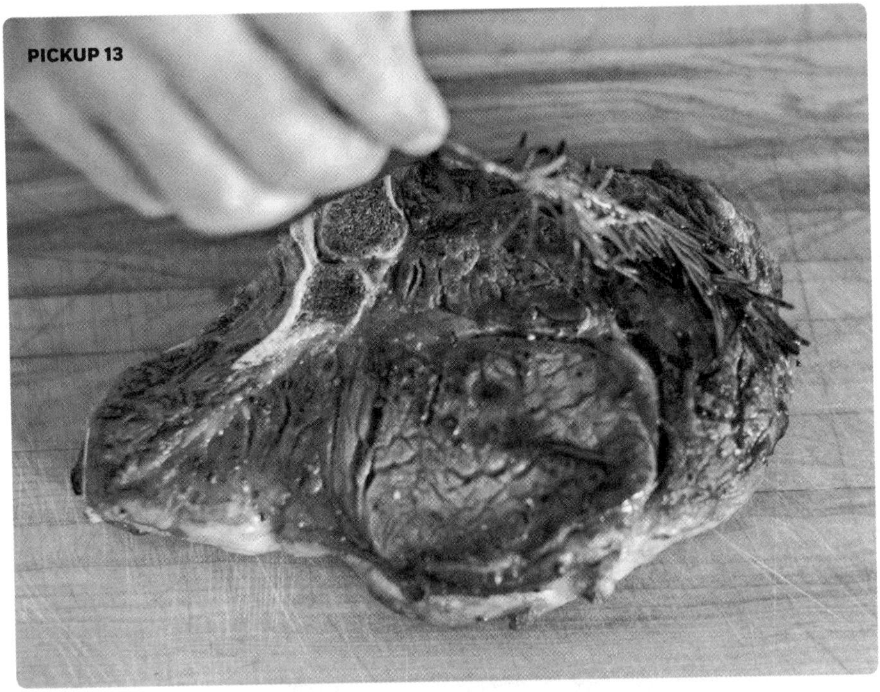
PICKUP 13

14 Serve, bite, turn to a friend, and moan like a camel with an ulcer. That's the sound people make when they eat perfectly cooked cow bits.

15 Now, for that cocktail. Fill a drinking glass ½ full of water, add ½ of the pollen, and mix. Add the rest of the pollen, then more water, and mix again. Now it's ready to drink/vomit!

16 Two to 3 days later, repeat the recipe with one or more remaining steaks, which have now been deliciously aged (see opposite page).

Beef-on-Beef and Other Tricks

Instead of using grapeseed oil, you can cut off some of the beef fat and allow that to melt as oil. Using an animal's fat to cook its meat is a favorite technique of Anthony Myint of Commonwealth restaurant in San Francisco. Beef-on-beef, pork-on-pork, duck-on-duck... you get the idea.

Instead of rosemary or Montreal steak seasoning, you can also coat the steak with good, grainy Dijon mustard (or even miso paste) before cooking.

Taking your raw meat on an extended backpacking trip? Try brushing it with finely ground white pepper before setting off. Pulitzer Prize–winning author John McPhee tested this during canoe trips after doing research for his incredible *New Yorker* piece "Brigade de Cuisine."

BONUS POINTS +2

MULTITASKING: ANABOLIC STEAMING

This is your last meal before the first dinner party, so why not give 100%? If you dare, try multitasking with two "active pots" for the first time.

When you put the steak in the oven, set up your now uncovered Dutch oven for steaming, just as you did with the Bittman Chinese Chicken (page 176): a bit of water, cake rack, and so on.

Throw in some mustard greens that you've cut into 1" strips using proper knife holding, and turn the burner to medium-high. Cover it with the rounded bottom of your nonstick skillet or a baking sheet, if you have one. Warning: don't use one of your plastic cutting boards—melted plastic isn't delicious.

Leave it for about 10 minutes, at which point you should test a strip of the greens. If it seems edible, turn off the heat and leave it until you're ready to serve it with the meat. If not, cook it for a few more minutes until done.

Mustard greens contain 28 homobrassinolide (HB), a plant steroid shown in preliminary studies to facilitate muscular adaptations much like anabolic steroids, minus the side effects.[*] Interestingly, HB does not appear to bind to androgen receptors (good news, unless you *want* a larger Adam's apple), and its effects are potentiated by a higher (39%+) protein diet. To mimic the study, you'll have to eat a hell of a lot of mustard greens, but it's a good excuse to get acquainted with a peppery veggie.

As Chef Joshua Skenes explained in his 2011 Best New Chefs Award profile in *Food & Wine:* "In Japan, they age fish. We all think fish should be eaten straight out of the water; it's not always true. Hanging game birds is another great method of preservation. We accidentally aged turnips from our garden in the walk-in, and they became a concentrated version of themselves."

BONUS POINTS +2

AGING

To experiment with aging, place an additional 1–2 raw steaks in the fridge, uncovered. The aging process, which you'll visibly notice 2–3 days later, is nature's flavor enhancer. This was made crystal clear to me by Joshua Skenes, of Saison, who ages everything from beef and tuna to squab (pigeon) and lamb.

What happens over 2–3 days of aging? Decomposition provokes changes in taste, texture, and appearance. I encourage you to take pictures of the meat on day 1 and day 3 for comparison—the progression can be dramatic.

Here's a mild example:

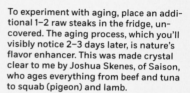

DAY 1

DAY 2

DAY 3

LAND OF CONFUSION: THE FAQs OF STEAK

ALL THE FOLLOWING APPLY TO MEATS IN GENERAL, NOT JUST STEAK

HOW SHOULD YOU THAW YOUR STEAK?

If you're anything like me, you often realize your main course is frozen when you're already starving. There's no need to let your steak sit in the fridge for eight hours to thaw. Just ask iconic food scientist Harold McGee, who described the smart way to thaw in his piece "A Hot-Water Bath for Thawing Meats." I've bolded the most actionable points, and 45–60 minutes will take care of a rib eye:

"I fill a **large pot** [or a mixing bowl] **with 125°F [52°C] water from the tap, immerse the plastic-wrapped meat, weigh it down with a slotted spoon to keep it underwater, and stir the water occasionally.** The water temperature drops, but stays above 100°F [38°C] for a half-hour or so, depending on how much food is thawing.

"Last week, I thawed 2"-thick filets mignons in an hour, whole squab in 40 minutes, a 1-lb whole fish in 20 minutes, and 1¼"-thick salmon fillets in 15 minutes. Thawing times can vary, depending on the volume, temperature, and movement of the water, as well as the food's thickness and how it's wrapped. **(A lot of plastic swaddling interferes with heat transfer. It's best to remove it and place the food in a thin, resealable plastic bag, partly immersing it to force the air out before zipping it shut.)"**‡

WHEN DO YOU "TEMPER" MEAT?

If you cook meat right out of the fridge, you typically risk having "black and blue" meat—overcooked on the outside and undercooked on the inside. Dee-sgusting.

So why *didn't* we let our rib eye come to room temp? Because we cooked it *low* and *slow*.

As a general rule, if cooking over 300°F (150°C), get the protein to room temperature first. The higher the heat (and shorter the cook time), the more important tempering to room temp is, whether it's eggs, steak, chicken, llama, or Gremlins.

If you want to try a more traditional high-temp steak recipe, see page 494 for Bistro-Style Bavette Steak.

WHY DO YOU USUALLY REST STEAK?

Meats cooked at 300°F (150°C) or above (or large pieces, like a roast) are left to rest for two reasons:

1) The semi-rare middle will continue to cook (heated, in essence, by the hotter layers around it). This is referred to as *carryover* cooking.

Let's say we'd cooked our rib eye in the oven at 350°F (180°C). We would have pulled it out of the oven when the probe thermometer hit 125°F (52°C). After 10 minutes or so of resting on the cutting board, the center temp would reach around 135°F (57°C).

2) The juices, which pool in the middle, need to redistribute. As the muscle fibers at the edges cool and relax, they reabsorb fluids.

If you were to chomp the steak straight out of the oven, the treasure juices you want in your maw would escape. Take a look at the pics below of identical steaks cut after different resting times.

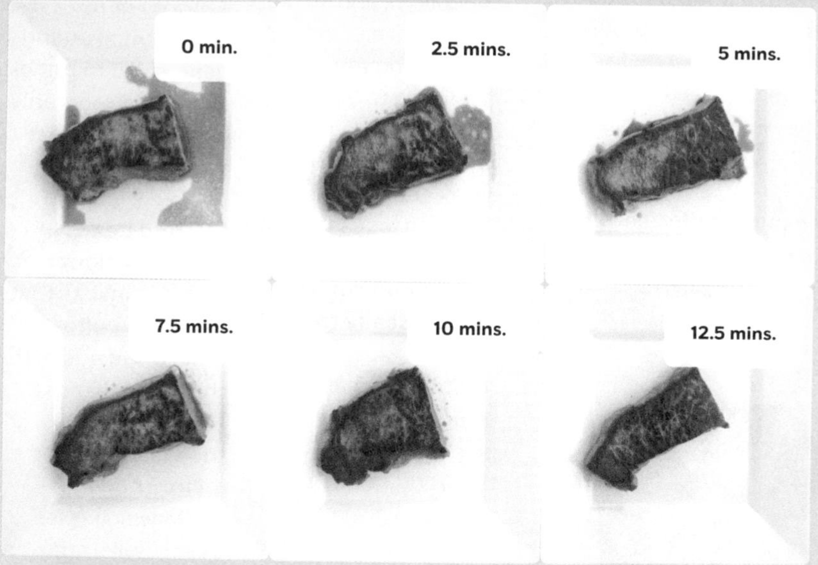
0 min.
2.5 mins.
5 mins.
7.5 mins.
10 mins.
12.5 mins.

HOW DO I UNF*CK OVERCOOKED MEAT?

Whenever possible, try to err on the side of undercooking versus overcooking, as you can always cook longer. But let's assume it's too late. You've turned your meat into shoe leather. There are at least two options for salvaging it:

1. If it's steak, mince it into hamburger-like meat and combine it with scrambled eggs. (I use a stick blender with chopper attachment for this.)

2. If you've slow-cooked something for 3+ hours and it's overcooked (which is possible, even if cooked in liquid), forge ahead. Continue cooking it for another 2 hours to turn it into a meat sauce, not unlike the amazingly simple *peposo notturno* (Google it).

IN SEARCH OF THE PERFECT CUP OF COFFEE

I was drinking the best cup of coffee I'd ever brewed, without a doubt. Even as a palate idiot, I could tell: it was magnitudes better than anything I'd made before.

My teacher, standing with a Cheshire Cat grin on his face, was a crazy Irishman: Stephen Morrissey, who now works at Intelligentsia Coffee in Chicago. In 2008, he was World Barista Champion, whittled down from a starting pool of nearly 3,000 competitors.

For 48 hours in Chicago, Stephen and I tested the entire gamut of coffee-brewing and filtering options, using every tool imaginable. Coffee is more labor-intensive than wine to produce and has three times the "complexity"—the volume of taste compounds (called organoleptic compounds). In other words, there was a lot of education to cover.

As it turns out, you can make coffee better than almost anyone in your city by following a few rules. Before we look at details, let's revisit 80/20.

DRINK COFFEE
Do Stupid Things Faster with More Energy

THE PRINCIPLES

Sure, you can go crazy, using special detergents to clean your equipment (Cafiza, JoeGlo), modifying your water for optimal hardness (4–5 grains per gallon), and so on, but there's a point of diminishing returns. According to Stephen, out of the dozens of variables you could tweak, there are three things to focus on first:

1. Buy good coffee beans, ideally freshly roasted.
As Stephen makes clear: "I'm supposed to be one of the best in the world at this shit, but if you give me bad beans, there's nothing I can do to make it taste good."

I get my beans from Intelligentsia, but there are other good roasters and distributors in the U.S., including:

- **Ritual Roasters from SF**
- **Stumptown Coffee from Portland, OR**
- **Counter Culture Coffee from Durham, NC**

For a cost-practical guideline, aim to consume beans within a month of roast date. Buy in small quantities, as you might buy expensive vegetables or bread (for cheat day, of course).

2. Grind beans in single portions
Stephen insists that "stale-ish coffee off a good grinder is better than fresh beans (within two weeks of the roast date) off a shitty grinder."

Brewing coffee beans is like cooking garlic. If you use bigger chunks of garlic, the taste is mild; if you put garlic through a press or finely dice it, the taste can be overwhelmingly

MY TOOLS

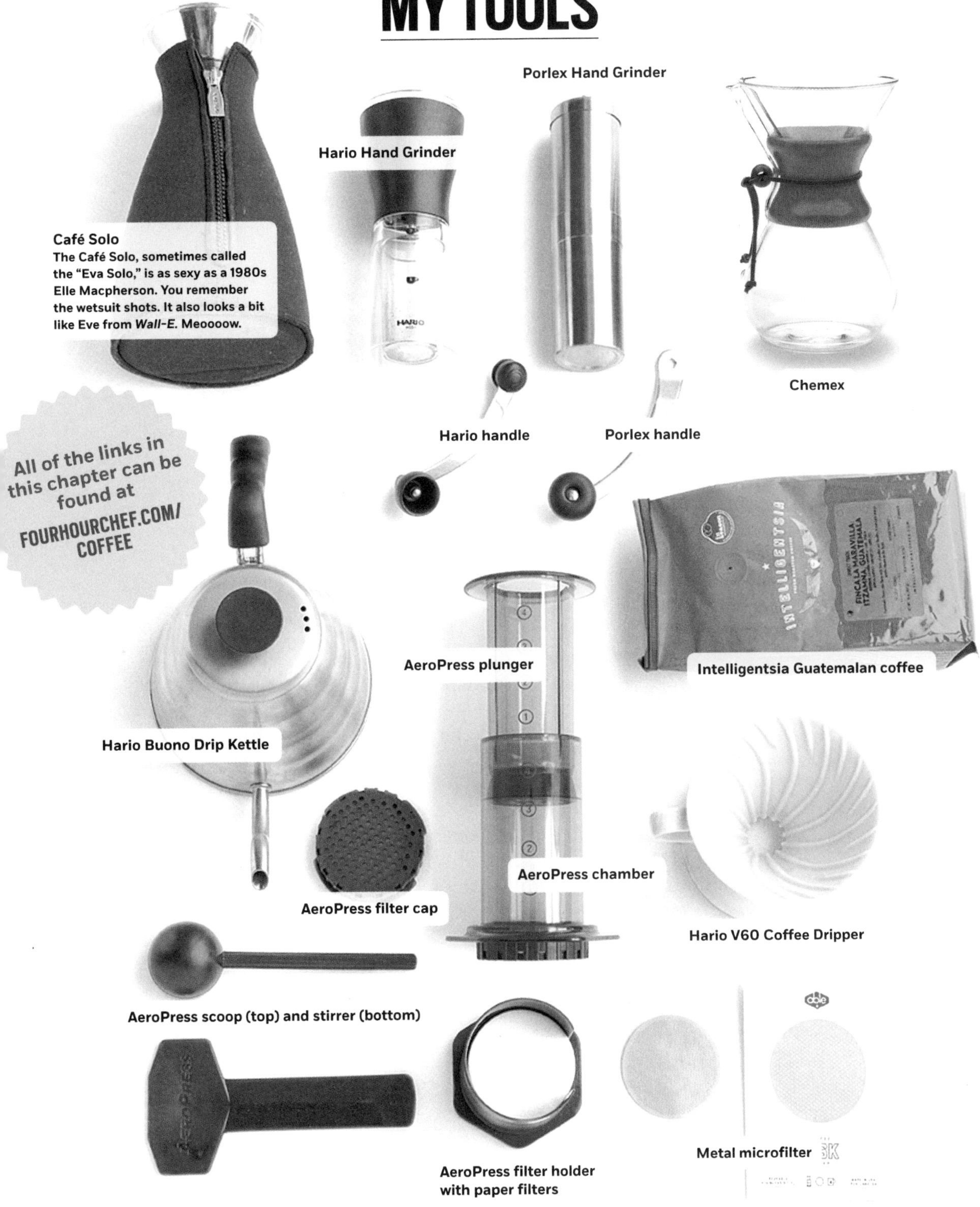
Porlex Hand Grinder
Hario Hand Grinder
Café Solo
The Café Solo, sometimes called the "Eva Solo," is as sexy as a 1980s Elle Macpherson. You remember the wetsuit shots. It also looks a bit like Eve from *Wall-E*. Meoooow.
Chemex
Hario handle
Porlex handle
All of the links in this chapter can be found at FOURHOURCHEF.COM/COFFEE
AeroPress plunger
Intelligentsia Guatemalan coffee
Hario Buono Drip Kettle
AeroPress chamber
AeroPress filter cap
Hario V60 Coffee Dripper
AeroPress scoop (top) and stirrer (bottom)
Metal microfilter
AeroPress filter holder with paper filters

powerful, even bitter. This is why chefs harp about cutting into uniform size. Coffee's no different.

"Extraction" is the dissolving of bean solids into water. If the grind is inconsistent, the brew will exhibit both sour underextraction (from the large particles) and bitter overextraction (from the smaller particles) at the same time. The solution is using a burr grinder, *not* a blade grinder. Depending on your budget and time, you can:

A) **Take your beans to a good coffee shop, which can use its commercial burr grinder to grind for you.**

B) **Use a $30–$70 hand-powered burr grinder, as we will later.**

C) **Use an electrical burr grinder, like the $200 Breville BCG800XL Smart Grinder that I use at home.**

The biggest quantum leap for me, regardless of grinding method, was **grinding a single-serve portion of beans just before making each cup.** This ensures that the oils and flavors end up in your drink and not in the air (oxidized). Again, not unlike garlic, freshly chopped is best.

If you really want to obsess on grinding, I suggest reading "The Dark Age of Grinding" **(fourhourchef.com/darkage).**

3. Weigh your coffee and water in grams.

Measuring water by weight (grams) is more reliable than measuring by volume (ounces), since the density of water changes when heated.

Using the metric system fixes the problem: 1 L = 1,000 ml = 1,000 g. The rest of the world may, in fact, be on to something!

My default recommendation for damn good coffee is 2 g per 30 ml/g, commonly translated to 2 g of coffee for every 28 g (1 oz) of water.[27]

Brewing methods for coffee can be categorized as **filtered** and **unfiltered.** Just as with sake, some people prefer the crispness of the former; others prefer the flavor depth of the latter. Filtering holds back more oils and fine particles.

Of all the brew methods, my favorites follow. I've omitted French press, my previous fave, because of its far superior close cousin. I've omitted the siphon because, while it looks amazing and it's fun to show off, the coffee produced isn't worth the hassle.

THE FINALISTS

If you're impatient, skip to the last method for the grand winner. Otherwise, each one has a good use:

Hario V60: The "pour-over" was invented in 1908. The most widely used single-cup dripper is the Melitta, but I prefer the V60 dripper from Japanese manufacturer Hario. Its large, open hole at the base maintains a constant flow, and the curved grooves facilitate an even extraction while preventing pooling. Several of the start-ups I work with opt for the Hario—it can be used cleanly in an office without a sink.

Chemex: The all-American Chemex is unique because of its thicker filters, which are 20–35% thicker than other paper filters. This means they hold back more of the lipids and sediment that can result in bitter flavors, delivering an incredibly clean, sweet cup. Stephen typically uses the Chemex for brewing coffee for more than one person at home.

Technically, his wife, Jen, makes the coffee and he makes the eggs. If he violates this sanity-saving division: "I spend the entire brewing cycle dwelling (pun intended) on variables. I wonder how much coffee I should use to purge. I wonder: Did I store the coffee properly? Will two days off-roast have a big impact? Should I let the grounds sit a little before brewing, or should I brew with hotter water? I wonder if I should boil the water in the kettle, and then decant into the Buono, or maybe bring all the water to a boil on the hob? Jen makes the coffee while checking Facebook on her phone. She doesn't fuss about it, and when I drink it, I don't think about it, and it's lovely."

Cafe Solo: The Cafe Solo, designed by Claus Jensen and Henrik Holbaek, was introduced

27 This would be considered "overdosed" by many baristas, who aim for closer to 1.8 oz/g, but I find that math more headache than benefit.

by the Eva Solo company in 2003.

This, more than any other brew method, produces a flavor profile similar to what one tastes in a *cupping*, which is like a wine tasting for coffee. In the Cafe Solo, as in the cupping, there is next to no agitation, and there is no separation of water from the grounds. The grounds settle in a bottom corner during pouring, which keeps the coffee from overextracting.

I made my first truly amazing cup of coffee using the Cafe Solo. I intended to use it as my default method forever.

And then I met the AeroPress.

AeroPress: This is now, bar none, my favorite brewing method.

Remember the Aerobie, the amazing UFO-like disc that you could throw farther than a football field, 20 times farther than a standard Frisbee? Alan Adler, a mechanical engineer and Stanford University lecturer, created it. After conquering the 1980s toy market, he began to obsess over coffee.

The result was the AeroPress, which debuted in 2006. Quickly adopted by the specialty coffee community, it offers a simple way to prepare a small amount of good coffee. Armed with an AeroPress and a tiny manual hand grinder like the Hario MSS-1B Mini Mill,[28] you can make world-class coffee on an airplane meal tray! No mess and no fuss.

In Stephen's words:

"The AeroPress has the thinnest paper filter I know of, and it's an awesome one-cup brewer. People [baristas] often use it on flights. They just held the World AeroPress Championship (WAC) in Portland, Oregon. [As cons], it isn't as sexy as the Cafe Solo and has a limited brew volume. Overall, though, the flexibility and mobility of the AeroPress makes it a win."

The paper filter removes many of the brew solids, decreasing perceived bitterness and yielding a clean, light mouthfeel. If you prefer the slightly heavier body and mouthfeel of a French press, no problem. Try the Able Brewing metal filter, which supposedly allows oils to flow through. I was introduced to this option by Brian W. Jones, a cofounder of Coffee Common who has also competed in the WAC.

---

28 Stephen prefers the Porlex hand grinder, also Japanese made, partially due to its sturdier design. I like both but favor the Hario as A) it's half the cost, and B) it has a 1-dose icon on the plastic for eyeballing, which, in my testing, weighed in at almost exactly 12 g (see the next recipe). I use the sturdier Porlex handle with the Hario body for the best of both worlds.

AMAZING COFFEE FOR LAZY PEOPLE

SHORTHAND

Pour 100ml 175F H_2O over 12g coffee in AeroPress. Stir. + 100ml H_2O. Slowly press into desired cup.

HANDS-ON TIME

5–10 minutes

TOTAL TIME

5–10 minutes

GEAR

- Kettle or other pouring container
- AeroPress
- Digital scale
- Handheld burr grinder
- Probe thermometer

INGREDIENTS	TO SERVE 1
Medium-fine ground coffee	12 g
Water (for 1 cup of coffee)	200 ml

The AeroPress instruction booklet has simple and effective instructions.

But baristas in competition have bootlegged a faster, more effective approach: using it upside down. Here's how to do it.

PICKUP

00 Heat water to a boil. I use a Proctor Silex kettle.

01 As the water is heating up, run the plunger of the AeroPress under the faucet and insert the smaller cylinder ½" into it.

02 Flip the device upside down (as in pic B, opposite) on a digital scale. Zero out (or "tare") the scale and add **exactly 12 g** of medium-fine ground coffee (ground using a handheld burr grinder).

03 Once the water is boiling, turn off the heat.

04 Pour the water into a more precise pouring container—I use a Hario V60 Coffee Drip Kettle—and insert a Polder probe thermometer.

When the temperature is a few degrees above 175°F (79°C), which the AeroPress folks recommend based on taste tests, start pouring water slowly into the AeroPress for a total of 100 ml. Most of the bitter stuff just doesn't get into the liquid if you keep the temperature below 180°F (82°C).[29]

05 **Once you hit 100 ml of water, stir to mix, then add another 100 ml for a total of 200 ml.** Stir a final time so the grounds are fully mixed in.

06 Insert the filter into the cap; secure the cap.

07 Flip the entire device over onto a cup, and slowly press out the best coffee you've ever had. Slow and steady wins the race. Aim for roughly 20 seconds of pushing.

08 Now the grand finale: cleaning. It's my favorite part! Just push another inch, and pop the thin paper filter and grinds into the garbage disposal (or compost). Rinse off the end for a millisecond and you're done.

If you want to make 2 cups: Use 24 g of coffee with the same 200 ml of water. Push it into 1 cup, then split the coffee 50/50 into 2 cups. Add hot water to each cup for your desired volume.

To get fancy: The fanatics (not a pejorative term) run hot water through 2 paper filters before starting to prevent any bleached-paper taste from leaching into the coffee.

29 Different compounds are soluble at different temperatures.

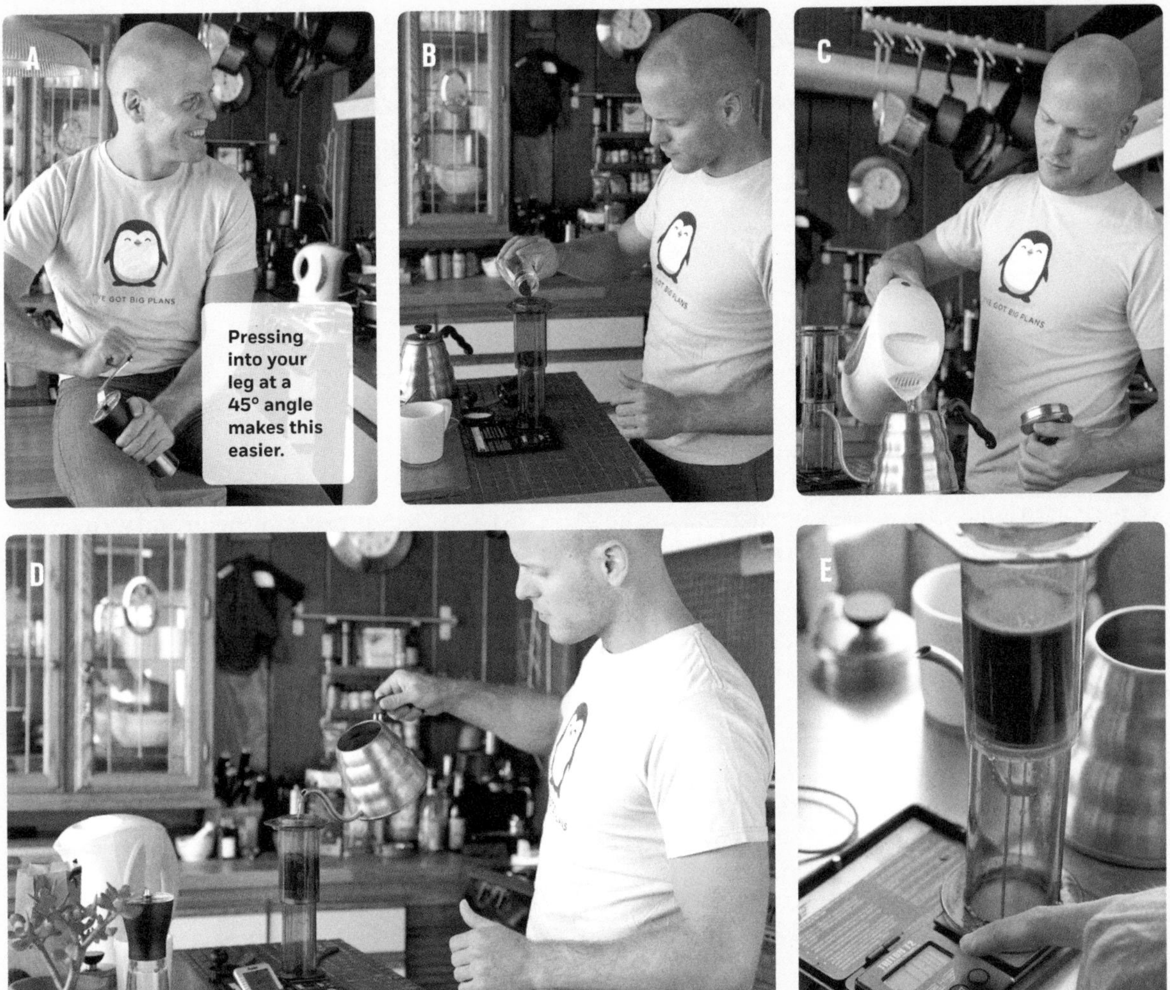
A
Pressing into your leg at a 45° angle makes this easier.
B
C
D
E
F
G
Samoa Cookhouse
SINCE 1893
Eureka, California

LESSON 09 +10

SKILL

COOKING FOR GROUPS — GAME TIME!

9TH MEAL — 4-PERSON DINNER PARTY

"Life begins at the end of your comfort zone."
—NEALE DONALD WALSCH

The goal of your first dinner party is not to dazzle people.

The success of the night depends on how *you* feel at the end of it. If you blow your guests away but end up over a sink at midnight regretting the evening, it's a failure. If, on the other hand, you screw up everything but keep the wine flowing, crack jokes with friends, and wrap up thinking, "That wasn't so bad. I should totally do this again," you win.

For starters, you should invite people who already know one another. Rather than learning how to cook for and host groups at the same time, you'll focus on one thing: cooking for peeps who can mingle without you.

People fail at dinner parties primarily for two reasons:

1. They try to do too much.
2. They expect things to go perfectly.

So we'll do the opposite: curb your ambition and budget for curveballs. In cooking—as in business and war—hope for the best but plan for the worst.

To help, I've collected three groups of suggestions:

1. For sanity (calm).
2. For presentation (cool).
3. For dodging bullets (collected).

FOR SANITY

STEP 1: Decide on your menu and write down the shopping list, dish by dish, the day before.

Of the dishes you've learned so far, you might consider one of the following meals:

- **Option 1 (my strong suggestion for novices):**
  Arugula, Avocado, and Roma Salad
  Osso "Buko"

- **Option 2:**
  Arugula, Avocado, and Roma Salad
  Osso "Buko" + Union Square Zucchini

- **Option 3:**
  Any combination you like. The Eggocado (page 183) is a crowd-pleasing appetizer.

But . . . what if you want to serve the Sexy-Time Steak at your party?

It might be too much for you to get four steaks ready with our gear (trust me). But what if you think in terms of the principles? Could you get a roast, cook it to a center temp of 125°F (52°C), let it sit for 10 minutes under aluminum foil tenting, then cut it up for four people? *Ahhh . . .* now you're thinking like a cook!

But don't push it. Make this first party easily "winnable." Do far less than you think you can.

Other suggestions, if you go with Option 3, despite my warnings:

- **Minimize dishes that need to be "ready" when people arrive.** Osso "Buko," for instance, can sit in the oven for 30 minutes at 200°F (90°C) if people are late, and it will still be delicious. The salad, likewise, is just chillin' in the fridge or at room temp. No sweat. But scrambled eggs? Gotta be cooked on demand.

- **Related to the above, don't use one cooking vessel for multiple dishes:** If I'm cooking Harissa Crab Cakes and Scrambled Eggs, I'd want to use my nonstick for both. This means I'll need to keep one warm while cooking the second, or serve one and cook again while guests are waiting, or reheat something. Don't do it.

STEP 2: Set expectations low and early.

In 2008, Denmark emerged as the world's happiest country, beating out the "Gross National Happiness"–touting Bhutan, the longtime favorite of anthropologists everywhere.

So why is the birthplace of LEGO (a contraction of *leg godt* or "play well") such a happy spot? I asked my Danish readers, and the answer was unanimous: **low expectations.**

Indeed, set expectations low and you're never disappointed. Sooo . . . set low expectations for dinner ASAP. When you invite your friends, prepare them for something slightly better than microwaved dog food. Your e-mail should read like this:

> "Guys! I'd like to invite you all to a dinner at my place [insert date]. I'm learning to cook and want to treat you to a ghetto-fabulous experiment. NOTE: I will have excellent booze and break out my fanciest paper plates. If I screw it all up, I have an awesome Thai place on speed dial and high-end ice cream in the freezer, so we're set. Who's in?"

Set them up for dry retches and they'll love even mediocre cooking.

This isn't negative thinking; it's good strategy. If you think you're the bomb-diggity, that's great. Just high-five yourself in private this time around.

STEP 3: Start setting up your *meez* at the grocery store.

Reducing stress starts while shopping.

If something can be done by others, take advantage of it. Have the butcher cut the Osso "Buko" lamb shanks, if you want to cut them at all (I don't); the same butcher can dice medallions for a separate meal, etc.

As you're checking out, put the "app" (appetizer) ingredients into one bag, the main into another, and so on to keep your dishes separate. This will save you time later and make the meal "no assembly required." This one-dish-one-bag rule becomes much more valuable as you add ingredients or guests, so get into the habit now.

STEP 4: Have a delay tactic—the "standing course."

I unnecessarily stressed myself my first few dinner parties. As the host, I felt I should be with my guests at all times.

This is silly, and I've found that having a "standing course" relaxes everyone. What is a standing course? Simple:

Grab four wineglasses (I like stemless blue glasses, which are easier to clean and harder to break), line them up on a table or counter in the kitchen, and place a bottle of wine next to them. Now you're ready for guests to arrive. If you're finishing cooking, when they ask, "Can I help with anything?" you can answer, "Yeah. Relax and pour us a glass of wine!" while handing them the corkscrew.

Rather than rushing when my guests arrive, I now enjoy it. The wine is on the kitchen island, and as each guest arrives—some 10 minutes early, some 10 minutes late—we mingle in the same space.

Dinner guests are like German shepherds. They can smell fear and get anxious if you are anxious. Give them a reassuring but confident pat on the head (wine) and relax. They'll do the same.

STEP 5: Avoid silence.

Silence can be deafening at a dinner party, especially your own.

The winningest music I've found for grooving dinners is a "Federico Aubele" station on pandora.com. If it saves you time, just visit my playlist and click on the station at pandora .com/people/timferriss.

I use a Sonos wireless sound system, which I control from my iPhone. If you want to go slightly more tech but less pricey than Sonos, try the tiny JAMBOX by Jawbone. But as long as you have an iPhone or music-playing smartphone, you can impress your guests with the "mixing-bowl amplifier."

Download the Pandora app, create a "Federico Aubele" station, and put your phone in a mixing bowl. Instead of sounding tinny and mono, like 100% treble, it will suddenly sound as if you've injected bass. It's a Christmas miracle! To kill time during your standing course, show this to the guests and ask them to pick their favorite mixing bowl (the sound is very different, depending on size).

FOR PRESENTATION

I like to ask chefs questions with constraints. One of my faves is: "If you had $100 to spend on serviceware [anything food goes on or drinks go in] and you never have to serve more than four people, what would you buy?"

Below is chef James Simpkins' answer:

"First, skip large dinner plates. Get wider bowls with a rim, so they're dual-purpose. Also, never get white. If you want that tone, get ivory. Then get four 4–6-oz ramekins, which you can use for side dishes, desserts, custards, whatever. They also fit on plates. Otherwise . . . just don't buy stuff from a place like Macy's. Look for fun pieces, whether vintage online, yard sales, etc."

Is there anything else impressive but easy?

"It's a genre called 'by the platter.' Get an oval platter so the salad isn't in a goddamn bowl where you can't see anything. My friends have asked me, 'Duuude . . . how did you do that?!?' and I say, 'I bought a $15 platter at Crate & Barrel off-season. That's how I did it.'"

This forces people to pass the platter and, a point not to be missed, serve themselves. A thing of beauty! More interaction and less labor for you. My own "Novice Nine" appear on page 130.

General plating tips from James:

"Square food (like a salmon fillet) goes with round plates. Roundish food goes with square plates. Turn up the contrasts. Use odd numbers—like five pieces of pork, even if you have six. It looks better. To clean the rim of the plate just before serving or to take off smudges and fingerprints, wet a towel, wring out, and use a damp corner. Pick a 'line' and travel around the plate. Then, hold the plate under the edges when you deliver it to the table; *don't* grab the edge and ruin your final touch by putting fingerprints back on top."

Last but not least: Set the table *before* you start cooking. Finishing up cooking when people arrive is expected, but having a messy or bare table is really junior varsity.

FOR DODGING BULLETS

Ask, "What could go wrong?" and have a damage-control plan.

There are knowns in life. For instance, the average guest consumes 4–6 hors d'oeuvres per hour.

Then there are the unknowns. Do hungry, hungry hippos really eat white marbles? Will my idiot friend show up 30 minutes late? Those kinds of things.

My nightmare of nightmares came true at one of my first dinner parties in SF.

I was cooking a beef roast, and it was 20 minutes until guests were due. I'd planned it all down to the minute, and I was watching the Polder thermometer like a hawk. The plan was to pull out the roast and let it rest while we all ate salad. By the time we were done with appetizers, the meat would be perfectly cooked and . . . standing ovation!

But a text snapped me out of this fantasy: one of my less-reliable friends was going to be 30 minutes late.

Ummm . . . now what?!? Full-blown panic, of course. I couldn't leave the roast in until he arrived, or it'd be overcooked. I couldn't pull it out at the planned time and wait for him. Or could I? What the hell could I do? I didn't know. The cookbooks don't include fuck-ups. There are no DVD outtakes.

This meltdown was 100% preventable. I could have set rules beforehand, especially for timing curveballs, as I suggest you do. Using the roast (any meat, really) as our example, my rules after that day became, in descending order of importance:

1) Late-comers eat coldish or reheated food. Sorry.
2) Pick a forgiving technique like braising whenever guests might be flaky.
3) Have a standing course. We've already covered this great insurance policy.
4) When you have to accommodate:

If you have to postpone serving time by 20 minutes or less, continue cooking as planned—do not deviate. Pull it when it's done and simply tent the roast using aluminum foil. Move it off of cast-iron; the cast-iron will overcook it.

If you have to postpone by more than 20 minutes, here's what you do:

- Pull it out earlier than planned. For instance, pull out the roast at 115°F (46°C) instead of 125°F. Then let it sit on the countertop, leaving the probe thermometer in. The cast-iron will continue to cook it a bit. No tenting.
- Crank the oven up to inferno: 500°F (260°C).
- Relax and have a glass of wine. If folks are there, serve the salads or other appetizers, take a break. When the slowpoke arrives and you're 10 minutes from wanting to eat the roast, throw it back in the oven with the probe thermometer alarm set for 130°F (54°C).
- After hitting temperature, let it rest for five minutes, cut, and serve.

Ever wonder why waiters say, "Please be careful—the plates are very hot!"? It's because the kitchen either: a) uses a plate oven/warmer, or b) cooks nearly everything beforehand and finishes food in 4–6 minutes by throwing dish and all in a scorching oven.

Whether for a phone negotiation or a dinner party, budgeting for the worst-case scenario is one of the keys to surfing the waves of life.

And remember . . . you can always order takeout if you fuck it all up! Have fun and don't take it too seriously.

WHAT DO I DO WITH EXTRAS?

Orphaned raw materials cause angst, at least for me.

More often than not, they sit in some cubbyhole in the fridge until they look like a petri dish, then you throw them out and feel guilty. This all leads to less cooking.

So what to do with that 25–75% of a bunch that's left over? Here are a few options I like:

1. Bag it and freeze it. You can freeze almost anything *once*.

2. Blend the bastards into something you can drink. Just about any veggie is fair game here. I hit upon this while traveling with my knives and cutting boards. Annihilating stalk after stalk of celery while practicing knife skills, I started to feel bad about tossing out pounds of cuttings. That's when I bought the Back to Basics SE3000 Smoothie Express mini travel blender (page 125).

I could make a tasty (maybe *invigorating* is a better word) greens drink in a few seconds. My default recipe became 3 stalks chopped celery, 1–2 T cider vinegar, the juice (not pulp) of 1 lemon, and 1 c water. Problem solved! If you want to get fancy, you can try illusionist David Blaine's Morning Juice. You might need a higher-powered Vitamix to get the job done.

Pro tip: Disgusting beverages often make incredible popsicles.

David Blaine's Morning Juice

2 cloves garlic
Bok choy
Kale
Collard greens
Spinach
½ beet
½ apple
2 lemons
Cayenne

3. Dry herbs, don't store them. Rather than watch herbs sadly decompose in the icebox, I like to dry them out on top of paper towels in a colander. It just sits on top of my fridge.

4. Store it confit-style. Food goes bad for several reasons, but oxygen is a major culprit. Storing in water, which contains oxygen, doesn't help us much here. Oil, on the other hand, does. If I have, say, two scallions left over, and I know they'll go bad in the crisper before I next use them, I'll chop them up, place them in a small cup, cover them with grapeseed oil or olive oil, and refrigerate. This will keep for at least a week, and I'd put this example in scrambled eggs. Keep it longer than a week and you run some risk of botulism.

5. Drop the extras (garlic cloves, sprigs of rosemary, etc.) into a bottle of oil or vinegar to flavor it.

6. Make delicious tea. Thyme, sage, and rosemary make wonderful nightcap teas. Rosemary is known for its antioxidant properties and is high in a variety of vitamins, including A, B_1, B_2, B_3, B_6, B_{12}, C, D, E, and K. It's now also my favorite caffeine-free option for first thing in the morning or just before bed. Place your clippings or sprigs (3–6 sprigs' worth) in the cup, pour in boiling water, and steep for 5–10 minutes. This is how I polish off the extra sprigs in a bunch over 2–3 days following a rosemary-rich recipe.

Ahhh . . . rosemary tea. My next book will be scratch-and-sniff.

LESSON 10 +8

SKILLS

ROASTING, IMMERSION BLENDER

ROASTED GARLIC AND GAZPACHO

SHORTHAND

350F 30–45min: Roast 1 head garlic, 1t oil, S+P in foil till soft. Blend 1 can diced tomato, 7oz diced & seeded bell pepper & cucumber, 5T oil, 2T vinegar, 2 cloves garlic, S+P. Garnish w sliced almonds.

HANDS-ON TIME

10 minutes

TOTAL TIME

40–55 minutes

GEAR

- Knife + cutting board
- Can opener
- Vegetable peeler
- Spoon
- Digital scale
- Immersion blender with chopper attachment
- Garlic press

OPTIONAL PAIRINGS

"Orchestrated Incident" by Gramatik

Hawaii-grown oolong tea

This isn't the most famous oolong in the world, but it is one of the most unusual. It has some of the grassiness of Japanese sencha, but it's not brothy. It's flinty and crisp with hints of evergreen.

> "There's no doubt that after you eat a lot of garlic, you just kind of feel like you are floating, you feel ultra-confident, you feel capable of going out and whipping your weight in wild cats."
>
> —LES BLANK, DOCUMENTARY FILMMAKER

Roasted garlic is part of a pantheon of special ingredients. Along with shallots and truffle oil, it's embraced by professional chefs but neglected by home cooks.

Garlic is a hard-to-peel, hard-to-cut, hard-to-rinse-off-your-hands hassle that causes neophytes to quit cooking. Leftover garlic causes similar disenchantment; you buy eight heads of garlic in a panty-hose bag, use a few cloves a week, and are left staring at wasted money. What to do with all the rest? The Mint in Victoria, Canada, was the first restaurant to give me the solution to all these problems: whole-head roasted garlic.

Even if you *hate* garlic, you will love this lesson. Cooked as I'll show you, garlic breath disappears, and all is right in the world.

Second, gazpacho, fresh and beautiful gazpacho, will become one of your favorite appetizers. Originally from the Andalucia region of Spain, it's easy to make and even easier to serve (straight out of the fridge).

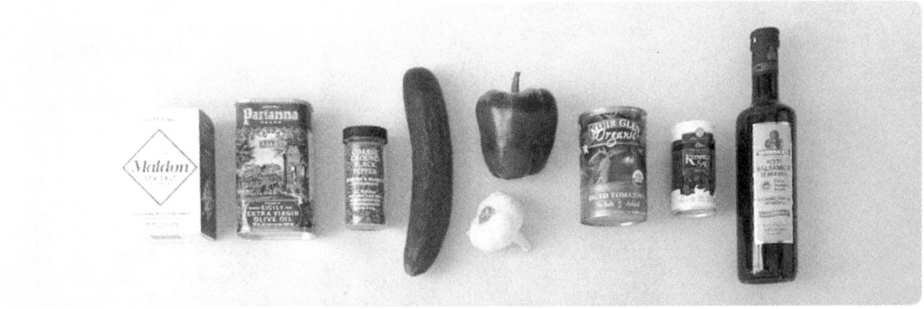

A

Shopping note[30]

INGREDIENTS	TO SERVE 4
FOR THE ROASTED GARLIC	
Garlic	**1 head**
EVOO	**A drizzle**
S+P	**To taste**
FOR THE GAZPACHO	
Diced tomatoes	**1 can (≈14 oz/396 g)**
Medium-large red bell pepper (you can use any color, but red will enhance the color of the gazpacho)	**≈7 oz/198 g**
½ large cucumber	**≈7 oz/198 g**
EVOO	**5 T (70 ml)**
Maldon sea salt	**3-finger pinch**
Black pepper	**4 turns**
Balsamic or sherry vinegar (this is *key*)	**1–2 T**
Garlic (or 1 t garlic powder)	**2 large cloves**

B

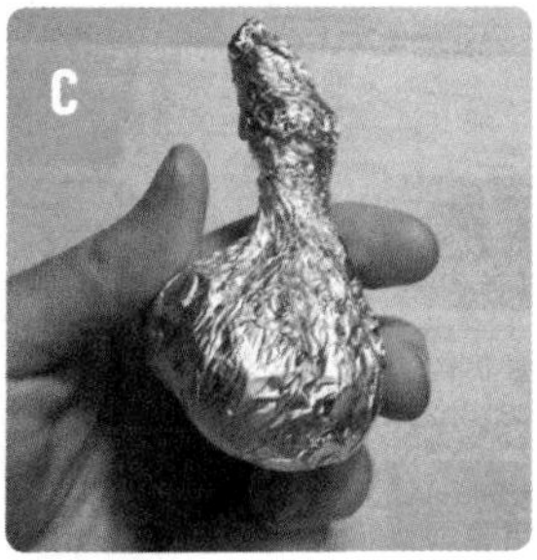
C

MAKE ROASTED GARLIC

00 Preheat the oven to 350°F (180°C). Lay out a sheet of aluminum foil on your countertop.

01 Cut off the top ⅓ of the head of garlic, keeping the rest intact. Remove any loose skin, and set the head in the center of the foil. Drizzle with a little oil, and season with a little S+P to taste. Gather up the foil into a package and seal it closed.

02 Place the package in the oven and roast for 30–45 minutes. I err on the longer side and then eat the garlic right out of the head using a butter knife or a fork.

While the garlic is roasting, make the gazpacho:

PREP

00 Open the can of tomatoes.

01 Cut the bell pepper in half and remove the seeds, stem, and white membranes. Rinse under water to remove remaining seeds, then chop.

02 Peel the ½ cucumber, remove the seeds with a spoon, then dice.

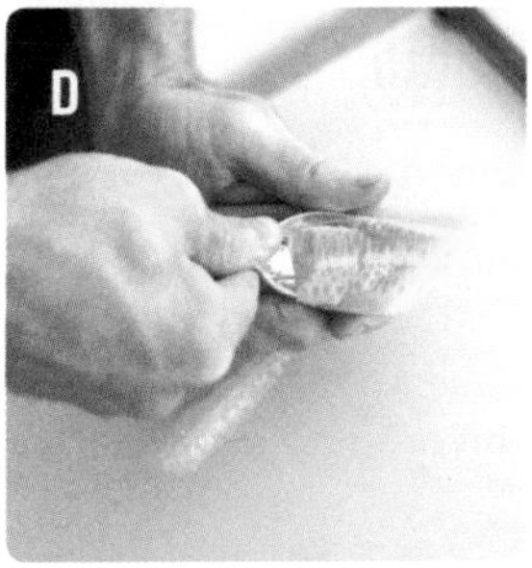
D

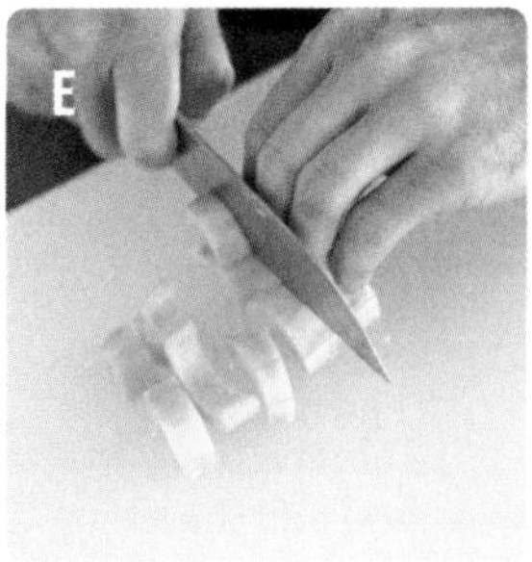
E

30 See the green inside? It means this garlic's not the freshest. Still delicious, though.

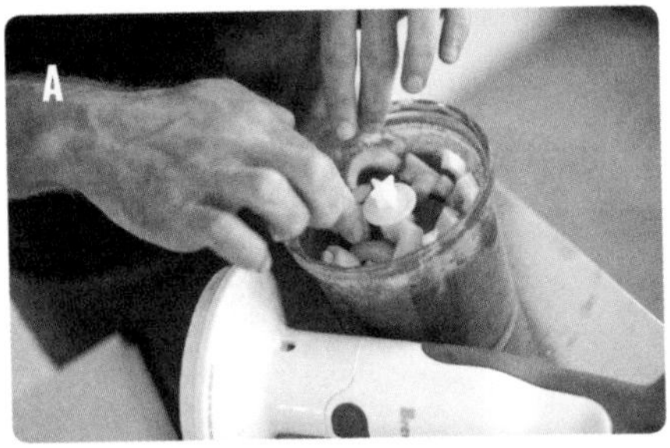
A

B

C

D

E

PICKUP

00 Place your blender chopper attachment on your digital scale and dump in the can of tomatoes.

01 Tare the scale so that it again reads zero, then add bell pepper until you've added half the weight of the tomatoes (so about 7 oz/198 g).

02 Tare the scale again and add the same amount (about 7 oz/198 g) of cucumber. If your chopper attachment is full, feel free to blend down before adding the cucumber. Work in batches, if necessary.

03 Add 5 T (70 ml) oil, a 3-finger pinch of salt, 4 turns of black pepper, and 1–2 T vinegar.

04 Push 2 cloves of garlic through the press right into the mix (or add garlic powder).

05 Attach the immersion blender and blend, until the gazpacho is nearly smooth. There will be some tiny bits and pieces, and that's fine. Texture is good! Taste and add more salt or vinegar as necessary. Pour into small bowls. Serve chilled.

+2

BONUS POINTS

GARNISH

Place a few sliced almonds in the center of each serving of gazpacho.

and/or

Serve gazpacho in green dishes for better reviews. I tested this at home after reading about Chinese cuisine's use of contrasts (sweet-sour, etc.), including opposing colors in ingredients.

The visual has a huge impact on our perception of flavor. The University of Bordeaux conducted a study involving 54 experienced wine students, who were asked to note the characteristics of two wines: a red and a white. The results came back as expected, with, for example, discussions of tannins in the red. The only problem? The "red" wine was actually white wine with red food coloring added to it.

SO YOU WANT TO TRY PEELING GARLIC?

GOOD ON YA . . .

Here are three techniques I use. I most frequently use the press, but it's good to have press-free options.

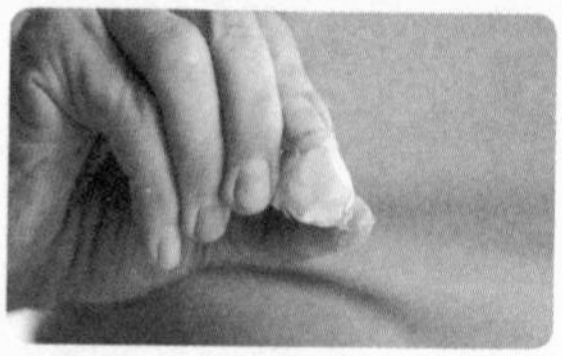

1) THE ONE-STEP METHOD

- "Pop" the skin by squeezing end-to-end like so. Remove by hand.

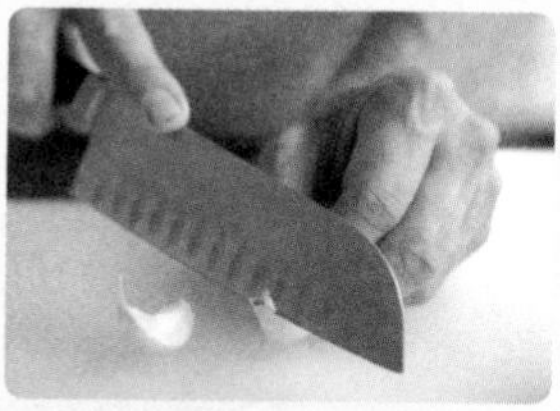

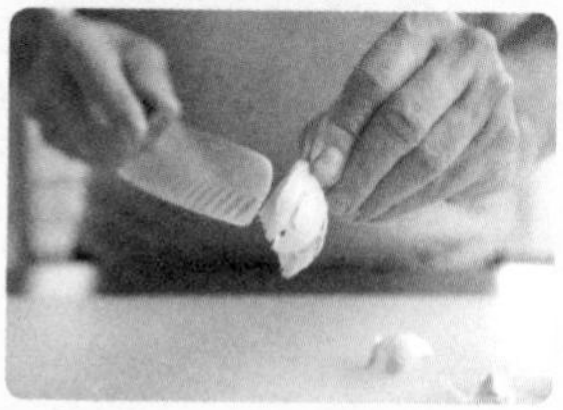

2) FROM JACQUES PÉPIN

- Break the head into cloves with a diagonal kung fu palm strike.
- Cut off the root ends of the cloves, which are the scabby parts, *not* the wispy tail ends.
- One at a time, smack each clove with the flat side of your knife a few times to loosen the skin.
- Hold each clove up by the tail and flick it with the dull side (not edge) of your knife until the meat falls out.

3) FROM TODD COLEMAN OF *SAVEUR*

How to peel an entire head in 10 seconds:

- Kung fu palm strike, as above.
- Find two large mixing bowls of roughly the same size. Sweep the cloves into one bowl and invert the second bowl on top. I've tried plastic cups (à la martini shaker), a bowl covered with a cutting board, and so on, but only mixing bowls have worked.
- Holding the bowls together tightly, shake like hell for 20–30 seconds, knocking everything loose.
- Uncover the bowl and behold: perfectly peeled cloves.
- This is helpful for our Chimichurri recipe (page 213), which uses an entire head of garlic.

LESSON 11 +4

TIM'S **TOP 4** IMMERSION SAUCES: PICK ONE

"Last Thanksgiving I made the world's worst pie. I mean, a disaster of epic proportions. My Aunt Sally was like, 'A little garnish of whipped cream and you should be good.' Then she looked at me and said, 'You know *garnish* is French for 'f*ckup,' right?' That's probably the best cooking tip I've ever heard."

—KITCHEN TOUR WITH JESSICA, A COOK IN QUINCY, MASSACHUSETTS

There are a million and one sauces you can make with your immersion blender. Here are my top four picks for novices.

This is my learning order, but pick whichever you like and make it. Save the sauce as a dipping side or topping for the next one or two dishes.

Almost all cookbooks suggest slowly dripping in the oil when blending. I've found an immersion blender works fine, as long as you:

1. Stir in the oil after blending the other ingredients.

OR

2. Use a light olive oil or mild vegetable oil (e.g., grapeseed oil) that doesn't produce the weird metallic taste that EVOO can when blended at high speed.

OR

3. My favorite: ignore all the warnings and blend everything all together. Nine out of 10 times it turns out delicious anyway.

CASHEW PESTO

(Jules Clancy)

1 c (135 g) roasted, salted cashews
½ c (120 ml) EVOO
1 c (25 g) unchopped fresh basil
2–3 cloves garlic
Squeeze of lemon juice (optional)

This variation on traditional pine nut pesto is inspired by Jules Clancy of Stonesoup. Not only are pine nuts wicked expensive, they also cause severe allergic reactions in many people. We'll use cashews instead. I blend everything at once, but for a new knife skill, chiffonade the basil immediately before blending (see pics, opposite).

I *love* this pesto and will regularly store it in the freezer in Ball or Kerr mason jars. To thaw, leave the jar in a warm-water bath for 10 minutes. This pesto is good on any protein.

Especially great on:
Salads
Eggs

GARLIC AIOLI

(Jeffrey Zurofsky)

1 large egg yolk
Juice of ½ lemon
1 T Dijon mustard
1 clove garlic
½ t kosher salt
¾ c (180 ml) grapeseed oil
½ c (120 ml) EVOO (but see details below)
Cayenne pepper to taste

Fancy mayo! This is so good that I ate nearly a liter within 24 hours of making it with JZ. We cooked more food just to dip it in extra tubs of the stuff. Traditional EVOO is listed above, but I actually prefer macadamia nut oil or, for pure decadence, almond oil.

This will keep in the fridge for up to 5 days. It's short-lived, but don't worry. You'll eat it all.

Especially great on:
Roast chicken
Broccoli
Steamed artichokes
Girlfriends

BONUS POINTS +2

HOW TO CHIFFONADE BASIL OR ANY LEAVES BIG ENOUGH

STACK LEAVES

ROLL UP LIKE A CIGAR

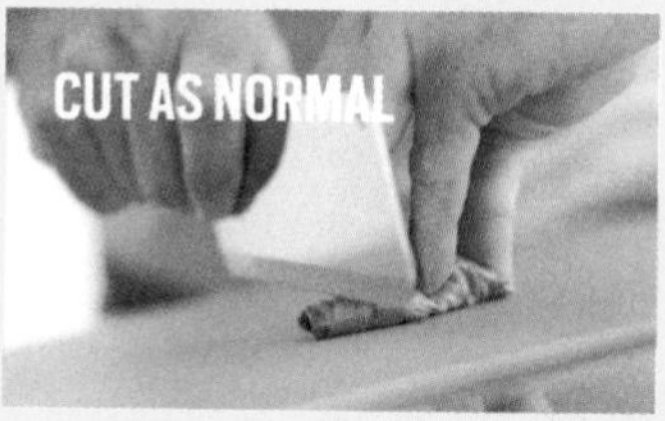
CUT AS NORMAL

UNFURL RIBBONS

SALSA VERDE

(Sisha Ortuzar)

2 bunches flat-leaf parsley

2 T white wine vinegar (potential substitution: lemon juice)

2 T kosher salt

1 t freshly ground black pepper

½ c (120 ml) EVOO (but see details below)

2 T diced shallots

1 T capers (optional)

Salsa verde is a flexible sauce that can save almost any seafood dish.

It is almost identical to an Argentine variation I call GOOP: garlic, olive oil, and parsley, with salt and pepper to taste. To convert salsa verde into North African *charmoula,* be sure to use lemon juice (instead of vinegar) and add 1 c (60 g) of freshly chopped cilantro.

Especially great on:
Chicken breast
Fish

CHIMICHURRI

(Francis Mallmann)

1 c (240 ml) water

1 T salt

1 head garlic (peeled)

1 c (2 oz/57 g fresh) flat-leaf parsley (or 1 oz/28 g dried—Mallmann uses fresh; I use dried)

1 c (2 oz/57 g fresh) oregano leaves (or 1 oz/28 g dried—he uses fresh; again, dried is fine)

2 t crushed red pepper flakes

¼ c (60 ml) red wine vinegar

½ c (120 ml) EVOO

This is one of the hallmarks of Argentine beef and the more complex cousin of salsa verde.

Even a whiff of chimichurri, ubiquitous in all Buenos Aires steak houses, takes me back to memories of tango and late-night Malbec. It is my favorite steak condiment, and it's as tough as nails—it will last 2–3 weeks in the fridge. It tastes best to me 5–7 days after making.

If it turns out watery, add more parsley and oregano in equal amounts, a little at a time, and blend until it takes on a thick consistency that doesn't drip. It shouldn't be soupy. It should be closer to chewy.

Especially great on:
Steak

LESSON 12 +6

SKILL

UNUSUAL PROTEINS

ROCK 'N' EEL

INSPIRED BY:

Anthony Myint

SHORTHAND

Broil 1 pkg eel till brown. Keep warm in oven. Sauté 1 chopped head broccoli, 2T oil till crisp; mix w 1 chopped avocado, ½ lime in bowl. Serve eel atop avocado, + salt, tamari to taste.

HANDS-ON TIME

5 minutes

TOTAL TIME

10 minutes

GEAR

- Knife + cutting board
- Immersion blender (and chopper attachment)
- Medium-size mixing bowl
- Cast-iron skillet
- Peltex

OPTIONAL PAIRINGS

"Shima Uta" by The Boom

Turmeric Spice tea

Turmeric is a potent anti-inflammatory. It's also mildly spicy, with a hint of licorice root and a sweet aftertaste. Some attribute Okinawans' long life expectancy to daily consumption of fermented turmeric tea. I'm not convinced the fermentation is necessary for health benefits.

"Do you know what that sound is, Highness? Those are the shrieking eels! . . . If you swim back now, I promise no harm will come to you. I doubt you'll get such an offer from an eel."

—VIZZINI, *THE PRINCESS BRIDE*

Eels are not attractive animals. Their snakelike bodies, their gaping mouths, their hollow eyes staring out from the aquarium tank . . . it's all rather creepy.

Eel flesh, on the other hand, is the bomb-diggity, with rich flavor and melt-in-your-mouth texture. It will be your introduction to uncommon proteins, one of the easiest ways to impress dinner guests.

Unagi, or Japanese river eel, is a staple of sushi joints across America, and if you've ever sunk your teeth into a "rock-and-roll," you know why. The unctuous combination of eel and avocado has the universal appeal of kid food, like mac and cheese for grown-ups. As an American sushi invention, rock-and-rolls succeed because they manage to have it both ways: comfort food and exotic delicacy, all wrapped into one.

We're going to capitalize on the flavor profile of the rock-and-roll, but swap out the sushi rice for tiny bits of broccoli, which take on a nutty flavor when well browned.

Who needs rice?

The first time I made this, I couldn't find eel, so I used thin cod sprinkled with Chinese five-spice instead. I just broiled for slightly longer: five minutes total. It was amazing!

The rock-and-roll you'll find in sushi restaurants.

Keep Frozen
TAMARI

INGREDIENTS	TO SERVE 4 AS APPETIZER OR 2 AS ENTRÉE
Broccoli, including the stem	**1 medium head (about 8 oz/ 227 g)**
1 small package Japanese unagi (broiled eel)	**Typically 8–12 oz/ 227–340 g**
Ripe Hass avocado	**1**
Lime juice	**½ lime**
Grapeseed oil or ghee	**2 T**
Tamari	**A splash**
OPTIONAL	
Sesame oil (strongly recommended)	**A splash**
Toasted sesame seeds	**1 t**

PREP

00 Trim away any woody or dried parts of the broccoli, then cut the rest into 1" (2.5-cm) chunks.

Using an immersion blender with a chopper attachment, pulse the broccoli repeatedly until it resembles a rough rice texture (see pics, opposite). Anything close is fine. If you enjoy manual labor, you can use a cheese grater instead, or finely chop the broccoli with your knife.

01 Thaw and rinse the eel to remove the sweet barbecue sauce that typically coats it.

Pat dry with a paper towel and cut lengthwise into 2 long fillets. Slice crosswise at a sharp diagonal to create sashimi-type slices (see pic B, opposite).

Place the eel, skin side down, on a sheet of aluminum foil and set aside, if cooking right away. If cooking hours later or the next day, wrap the slices in plastic wrap and refrigerate until you're ready to cook.

PICKUP

00 Arrange an oven rack about 6" (15 cm) from the top heat source (usually coils). Preheat the broiler to high. If there's no "high" option, just hit the "broil" button.

01 Put the eel (on aluminum foil) directly under the broiler for 1–5 minutes. Times

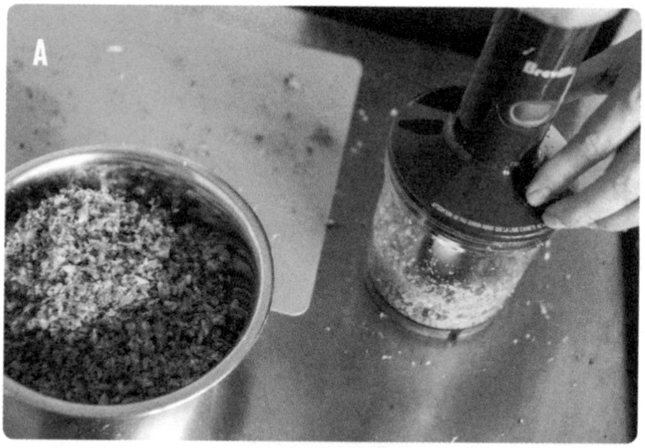
A

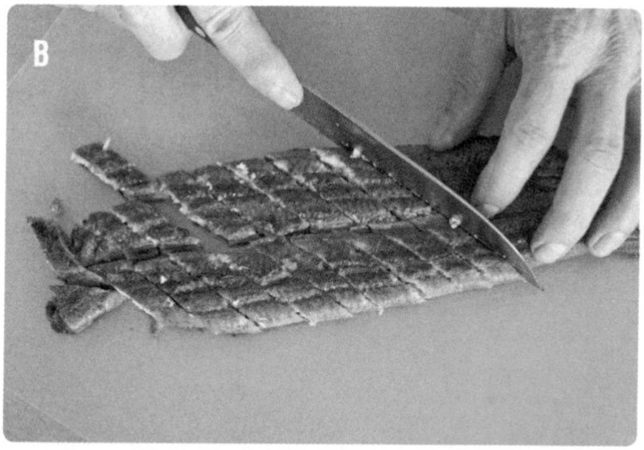
B

C

D

will depend on your oven. Once eel is browned and sizzling, turn off the broiler and leave in the oven, door closed. This will keep it warm while you do the rest.

02 Cut the avocado into roughly ¼" (0.6-cm) chunks (page 183). Place them in the mixing bowl and sprinkle with some of the lime juice.

03 Heat a cast-iron skillet over high heat and add the 2 T grapeseed oil or ghee.

04 Transfer the broccoli to the skillet and pat it into an even layer using a Peltex or silicone spatula; allow it to cook undisturbed for 1–2 minutes, until crisp on the bottom (no need to shake the skillet). Toss the broccoli as best you can, and allow the other side to lightly brown. Scrape it all into the bowl with the avocado. Toss with Peltex to combine (or use your hands, if impervious to heat).

05 To serve, top the broccoli-avocado mixture with the roasted eel and a splash of tamari (which also acts as your salt) and sesame oil and/or seeds to finish.

Deconstructed rock-and-roll!

LESSON 13 +4

SKILLS

SOUS-VIDE, MULTITASKING

SOUS-VIDE CHICKEN BREAST

WITH DINO KALE AND JAPANESE SWEET POTATO + 2 VARIATIONS

INSPIRED BY

Grant Achatz/
Nick Kokonas

SHORTHAND

350F 80m: Roast 4 foil-wrapped sweet potatoes. Simmer in bag at 145F 80min: 1 chicken breast, 1 pinch tarragon, 1T ghee, S+P. Steam 1 bunch kale 15min. Serve potato w coconut oil, chicken & kale w juice of 1 lemon.

HANDS-ON TIME

10 minutes

TOTAL TIME

1 hour 45 minutes

GEAR

- Aluminum foil
- Raw or finished cast-iron Dutch oven
- Cake rack
- Knife + cutting board
- Large stockpot
- 1 gallon-size Ziploc freezer bag per breast
- Tongs
- Probe thermometer

OPTIONAL PAIRINGS

"Slow and Low" by Beastie Boys

Nishi Sencha tea

The most balanced sencha I've tasted. It has notes of sea vegetables (also umami), is easy to brew, and pairs with nearly everything.

> "Is this chicken, what I have, or is this fish? I know it's tuna, but it says 'Chicken by the Sea.'"
>
> —JESSICA SIMPSON

Put a pinkie to your mouth like Dr. Evil. Because, dear friend, this will be your first triple-header: three simultaneous dishes in one meal.

Ready? Of course you are. The preceding lessons guarantee it.

This recipe involves almost zero cleanup and makes perfect chicken breast using a low-cost version of sous-vide cooking. *Sous-vide* translates to "under vacuum" in French, just as *sous-chef* means "under chef" (second in command). The stockpot approach we'll use was introduced to me by Grant Achatz and Nick Kokonas, both of Alinea fame. Nick uses this when cooking at home with his kids. It's that easy.

While in Chicago for the first time, I stayed at the Elysian Hotel. One night, I measured the temperature of the hot water in my bathroom sink—128°F (53°C). I then took 20 minutes to cook flawless sea bass with watercress and Iberico ham, all of which I'd bought at the downstairs restaurant, Ria (two Michelin stars), as raw materials. Like I said: easy.

Dinosaur "Dino" Kale

"Dino" kale, nutrient dense and nearly impossible to destroy, is perhaps my favorite green. It's flatter than curly kale, and both sweet and bitter. In the Campania region of Italy, where Naples is the capital, its consumption predates pasta! Now *that's* real Paleo goodness.

INGREDIENTS	TO SERVE 2–4
Japanese sweet potatoes, or any sweet potatoes or yams	**1 per person**
Dinosaur kale (lacinato or Tuscan), or any steamable greens	**½ bunch per person**
Lemon	**1**
Boneless, skinless chicken breasts	**1 per person (<17 oz/ 482 g each)**
S+P	**To taste**
Dried or fresh tarragon (or other herb of your choice)	**2-finger pinch per breast**
Ghee	**1 T per breast**
Coconut oil	**To taste**

PREP

00 Wrap the sweet potatoes in individual sheets of aluminum foil. (Remember the Roasted Garlic on page 208?)

01 Prepare the Dutch oven to steam the kale: place the cake rack in the bottom and add water to just below the rack. Have the lid ready.

02 Cut the kale into ≈¾" (2-cm)-wide strips. Cutting first makes rinsing easier.

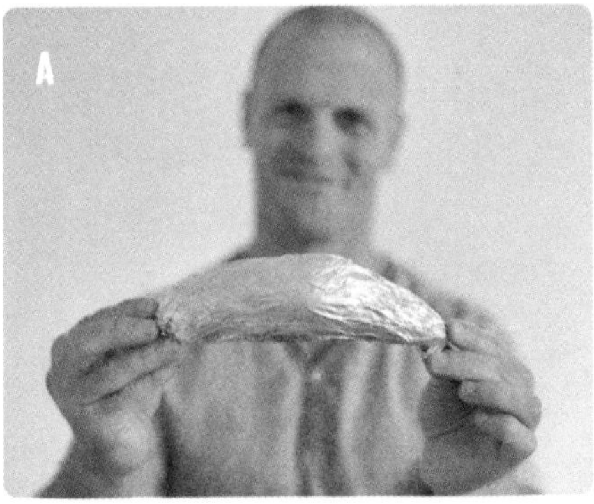
A

B

C

A

B

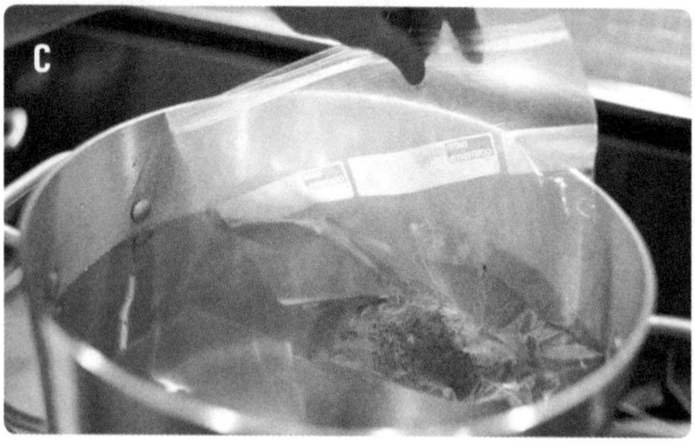
C

D

03 Rinse the kale, simultaneously massaging it (squeezing the leaves) with your hands to break down tough fibers. Set aside. No need to dry if cooking soon.

04 Roll the lemon around on the counter, then cut it in half and set aside.

05 Fill the stockpot ¾ full (I find it easiest to fill in the bathtub), and move to a stovetop burner.

06 Season 1 side of each chicken breast with salt and pepper and add a 2-finger pinch of tarragon.

Or season both sides. I typically stick with one to minimize chicken-to-peppermill cooties, but Jeffrey Zurofsky once scolded me, "It's not like you're cooking with Ebola virus!"

07 Using tongs, place each breast, along with 1 T of ghee, in individual Ziploc bags. Squeeze out as much air as possible from the bags and close the seals ¾ of the way. Do *not* put multiple chicken breasts in one bag. They'll make contact and be undercooked.

PICKUP

00 Preheat the oven to 350°F (180°C), and make sure the oven rack is set in the middle.

01 Turn the heat under the stockpot to high. Place the thermometer probe in the water with the alarm set to sound at 135°F (57°C). Cover the pot, leaving the probe inside.

02 As soon as the thermometer alarm goes off, turn the burner down to low. We're actually aiming for 145°F (63°C), and the last 10 degrees will come fast. If it overshoots, up to 155°F (68°C) is fine for the next step.

03 Holding the open top corner of one chicken bag, lower it slowly into the water until the water forms a seal around the food. In other words, the water will compress the bag and push the remaining air out.

Once the food is well submerged (it's OK if air remains in the very top portion of the bag), seal the bag completely. If the food floats for some reason, push it down with tongs or a spatula until it remains underwater and you can see proper vacuuming around the food.

Now leave it alone. Repeat with the remaining bags. Place the lid on the stockpot.

04 Immediately put the wrapped sweet potatoes on the middle rack in the oven.

05 Set an alarm for 30 minutes (when you'll check on the sous-vide temp). Watch a TED talk on ted.com. Try Elizabeth Gilbert's "On Nurturing Creativity" or Dan Gilbert's "Why Are We Happy?"

06 When the alarm goes off, adjust the heat under the stockpot as needed to maintain 145–155°F (63–68°C) and set the alarm for another 30 minutes. Read "Letter from a Birmingham Jail" or "Shooting an Elephant" if you haven't. Or watch another TED talk.

07 When the alarm sounds, revisit the sous-vide temp and set the alarm again, this time for 20 minutes. Yes, you guessed it: TED. How about Tony Robbins's "Why We Do What We Do"?

Optional: Adapting Slow Cooker to Sous-Vide

If you're adapting a slow cooker recipe for sous-vide and wondering about temperature, keep in mind that a typical slow cooker heats to 170°F (77°C) on low, around 185°F (85°C) on medium, and 200°F (93°C) or more on high. Don't use EVOO and, if using a vacuum sealer, don't use liquid or it will get ingested by the machine! Use ice cubes instead (like stock frozen in an ice-cube tray).

08 When the alarm goes off, the chicken (and sweet potatoes) will have undergone 80 minutes of cook time. Check the temperature of the sous-vide water again, and adjust to keep it within your target range.

09 Turn on the burner under the kale, cover, and set the alarm for 15 minutes.

10 When the alarm sounds this last time, turn off all heat sources—the burners under the stockpot, the burners under the Dutch oven, and the oven.

11 Take the sweet potatoes out of the oven, unwrap, split, and slather with coconut oil. Be generous and reap mouthgasm.

12 Kale next. Shake excess water off with the tongs and place greens in the middle of the plate. Squeeze a bunch of lemon juice on top.

13 Now the chicken. If you want to check doneness, just cut a breast in half lengthwise so it looks like you're cutting it for presentation. Arrange around kale opposite sweet potato (see pic on page 218) and you're finished.

Nicely done! Give yourself a well-deserved pat on the back and dig in.

Variation: Perfect French Eggs

Traditionally, making perfect "French eggs" involved standing over a bain-marie for 30-plus minutes, watching your eggs like a hawk. There's an easier, more reliable method:

Crack a couple of eggs into a quart-size Ziploc bag, seal, and cook sous-vide style in a stockpot of water at 167°F (75°C) for 15 minutes, taking the bag out at minutes 5 and 10 to massage the eggs with your hands. *Voilà!*

If you'd like soft-boiled eggs instead, try putting the eggs in the water without a bag (but in the shell, of course) at 147°F (64°C) for an hour or more.

The SousVide Supreme Machine makes this precision much easier.

VARIATION +2

THE MICHELIN 2-STAR BATHROOM SINK

My bathroom sink at the Elysian Hotel in Chicago.

Raw materials bought from Ria (thanks again, guys!).

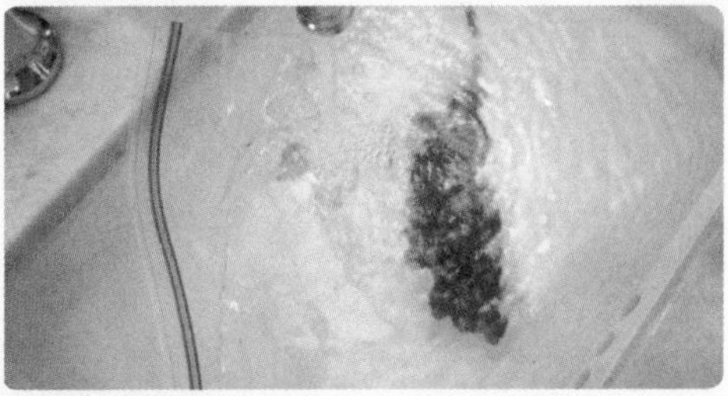

No stockpot? If you have a sink, and your hottest tap water is between 122°F and 130°F (50°C and 54°C), you're in business. It doesn't matter if the basins are dirty, since your food will be in plastic.

Get a thin fillet of salmon. Fill your sink with the hottest water possible, and use the bagging technique described in the preceding recipe. For seasoning, I like to use the Asian flavor combinations from page 149, like our familiar tamari, scallions, and ginger. If you have sesame oil, use 1 t or so of that. Grapeseed oil will also work.

Submerge the bagged salmon into the sink. If you have a small basin, you'll need to keep the hot water running to maintain a temp above 122°F (50°C). I prefer the texture at 125°F (52°C) or slightly above, but others like it as low as 115°F (46°C). Leave it alone for 20 minutes and you're done!

Maxime Bilet, coauthor of the encyclopedic *Modernist Cuisine*, recommends finishing with a quick 10–20-second sauté in butter and, among other things, using crushed hazelnuts and poppy seeds to provide a crunchy coating.

For a vastly simplified version: crush cashews beforehand using a mortar and pestle. Or put them in a sealed Ziploc bag and roll a wine bottle over them. Coat the salmon before serving.

Delicious decadence! French wine and dark Scharffen Berger chocolate, courtesy of the minibar.

VARIATION +2

KALE CHIPS

Maldon
SEA SALT
Partanna
SICILY
EXTRA VIRGIN
OLIVE OIL

INGREDIENTS	TO SERVE 4
Kale	**1 bunch**
EVOO	**A drizzle**
Maldon sea salt	**To taste**

SHORTHAND

350F 15min: Roast 1 bunch torn kale drizzled w EVOO & sea salt till crispy.

GEAR

- Baking sheet
- Parchment paper or Silpat

My girlfriend insisted I put this recipe in. Her shorthand: "kale + olive oil + sea salt = yum!"

I most enjoy making kale chips late at night, rather than at mealtime. If you really want to convert a non–kale eater, sprinkle either Parmesan cheese (use your Microplane) or nutritional yeast on these bad boys as a cheese substitute before cooking.

Nutritional yeast is typically gluten-free and high in glutamic acid. Parmigiano-Reggiano is so rich in glutamic acid that it's nicknamed "Italian MSG."

PREP

00 Preheat the oven to 350°F (180°C).

01 Tear the kale leaves into bite-size pieces, removing and discarding the thick, fibrous stems (also called ribs). No need to cut.

02 Rinse and dry the leaves completely. This is where a salad spinner is helpful. Letting them air-dry a bit makes results more consistent, but I'm usually too lazy to wait.

PICKUP

00 Spread the kale on a baking sheet, placing either parchment paper or a reusable Silpat[31] underneath. Ensure that no leaves overlap—this will lead to soggy, gross edges, crying children, and whimpering puppies.

01 Drizzle a thin stream of oil over the kale, using your thumb over the spout for control. This is what I do, but a Misto oil mister makes things easier. You can also toss them in a mixing bowl like lettuce. Whatever floats your boat.

31 A reusable, nonstick Silpat is one of the secrets of pastry chefs. It's overkill for kale chips, but it's a decent habit to develop.

02 Sprinkle salt on top. All of the following are delicious add-ons: paprika, chili powder, garlic powder, or lemon zest. *Almost* anything good on potato chips will work.

03 Place in the oven and try a piece at 15 minutes. The edges should be lightly browned but not like burned toast. If they still need more crisping, leave them in for another 5 minutes.

The perfect use of extra kale.

LESSON

14

+4

SKILLS

SEARING, LOVING BITTERNESS

SEARED SCALLOPS

WITH PROSCIUTTO, ENDIVES, AND RADICCHIO

SHORTHAND

Sauté 1 head radicchio, 4 heads endive, S+P, 2T oil till wilted. Sear 12 scallops, 1T oil 1–2min per side till brown. Wrap in 6 slices prosciutto. Serve atop veg w lemon wedge.

HANDS-ON TIME

5 minutes

TOTAL TIME

10 minutes

GEAR

- Knife + cutting board
- Cast-iron skillet
- Tongs

OPTIONAL PAIRINGS

"El Estuche" by Aterciopelados

Matcha green tea (see page 172)

> "People need to rediscover bitter as a flavor. I love frisée, cocoa nibs, black coffee. . . . In Italy, bitter greens are sought after."
>
> —MARCO CANORA

In Beijing, older people often scold the younger for not knowing how to *chī kŭ:* eat bitterness. Idiomatically, this means to endure hardship.[32] For cooking, we can take it literally. Most Americans have forgotten how delicious bitter can be.

Radicchio, endives, and escarole, all from the chicory family, fall in this category.

Bitterness is also an opportunity. Since it's neglected by nearly all home cooks, it offers a unique chance to shine. And, as with coffee, "bitter" often means that ingredients help liver detoxification.

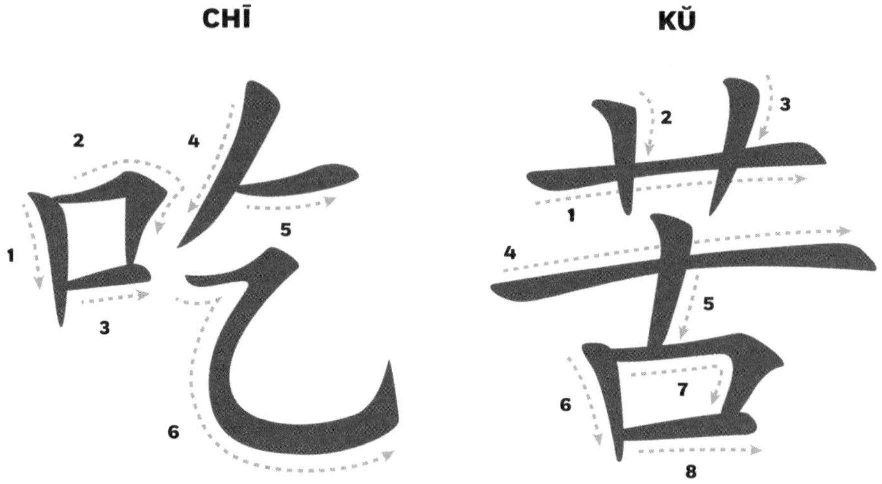
CHĪ
KŬ
1
2
3
4
5
6
1
2
3
4
5
6
7
8

Need a lower-back tattoo to regret in 10 years? Here are the characters and stroke order for "eat bitterness."

32 *Tā bù néng chī kŭ!* This means, in effect: "He/she can't do what it takes!"

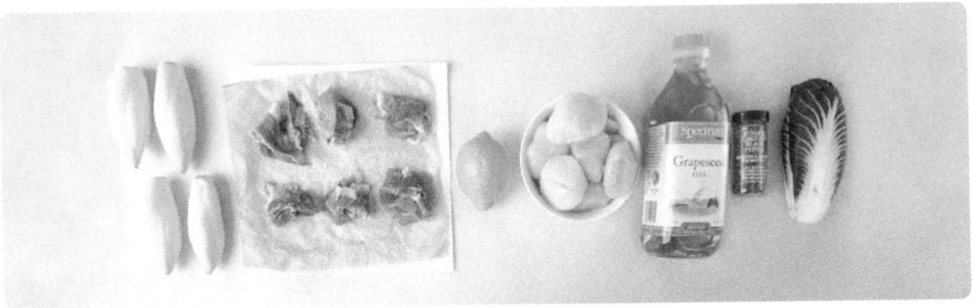

INGREDIENTS	TO SERVE 4
Radicchio	**1 large head**
Belgian endives	**4 heads**
Prosciutto	**6 slices**
Lemon	**1**
Macadamia nut oil (my fave here), ghee, or grapeseed oil	**3 T**
S+P	**To taste**
Sea scallops, preferably dry packed, tough side muscle removed, rinsed, and patted dry (ask your fishmonger)	**12 large (about 1½ lb/680 g total)**

PREP

00 Remove any browned or wilted leaves from the radicchio and endives. Rinse and pat dry. Roughly chop the radicchio and endives (see pics A and B) and set aside.

01 Cut each slice of prosciutto in half lengthwise and set aside.

02 Have 4 serving plates ready next to the stove.

03 Cut the lemon into quarters and set one on each serving plate. No need to roll beforehand.

PICKUP

00 Season the scallops very lightly with salt and pepper and set aside.

01 Heat a cast-iron skillet over high heat and add 2 T of the macadamia nut oil, ghee, or grapeseed oil. When it shimmers, add the radicchio and endives, and season with salt and pepper. Cook, tossing frequently with tongs, until just wilted, about 2 minutes. Remove to the serving plates.

02 Add the remaining 1 T oil and the scallops. Cook without touching until the scallops are well browned on the bottom—it will take only 1–2 minutes. Turn them over and brown the other side. They should still be barely translucent in the center.

03 Loosely wrap each scallop in a piece of prosciutto and arrange on top of the radicchio and endives.

04 Serve and instruct everyone to douse everything with lemon juice.

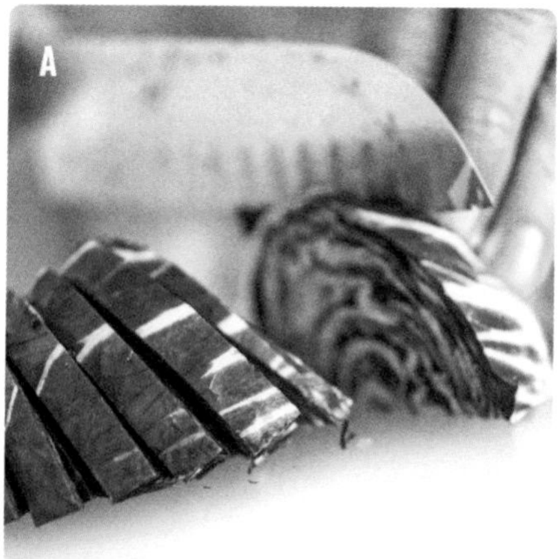

A

B

BONUS POINTS +2

BOIL DANDELION GREENS AS A SIDE

If arugula is the lightweight champion of bitter greens, dandelion greens are the heavyweight champion.

I suggest we follow Mario Batali's advice: "Much better to boil the shit out of them and then sauté them in olive oil and garlic—you can then actually chew the fuckers."‡

Place the dandelion greens in some salted water and bring it to a boil about 30 minutes before starting this meal. Once everything else is done and plated, pick up the greens with your slotted Peltex, shake off any excess water, and sauté them in the same skillet for 1–2 minutes with the remaining oil from the scallops. Plate and drizzle with sherry or balsamic vinegar.

C

D

Presentation Variation

For a more refined look, cut the endives lengthwise in half or into quarters instead of chopping them to bits.

LESSON 15 +4

SKILLS

OVERCOMING PHOBIAS, ONION CUTTING, DECEIVING FRIENDS

CHICKEN HIGADO PÂTÉ

INSPIRED BY

Tracy Reifkind

SHORTHAND

Sauté 1 onion, 1T oil till soft; + ½lb ground chicken, 1T oil till brown, + 1lb liver, 2T H2O 6min. Blend meat, 2T pan juices, 4 anchovies, 4 cloves garlic, 4T ghee. Chill.

HANDS-ON TIME

20 minutes

TOTAL TIME

20 minutes, plus 2 hours cooling

GEAR

- Knife + cutting board
- Cast-iron skillet
- Peltex
- Immersion blender with chopper attachment

OPTIONAL PAIRINGS

"Superstition" by Stevie Wonder

Pi Lo Chun green tea

Pi Lo Chun is brisk. It has notes of steamed asparagus and toasted peanuts. Cold chicken (as found steamed and chilled in Chinese restaurants) is awesome with this tea. It's Kevin's favorite all-purpose green.

> "Of all the ingredients used in Italian cooking, none produces headier flavor than anchovies. It is an exceptionally adaptable flavor that accommodates itself to any role one wishes to assign it."
>
> —MARCELLA HAZAN, *ESSENTIALS OF CLASSIC ITALIAN COOKING*

I vividly remember one evening in Beijing. It was 1996.

For the preceding two months, I'd eaten lunch every day at a restaurant across the street from my university. The family that ran it, who hailed from a rural southern province, was always welcoming. Before my transfer to another school, the owner insisted on treating me to a final meal. "I'll handle everything," he assured me with the wave of a hand. The last supper, brought out with much fanfare, was a mountainous plate of unadorned chicken livers. There were no vegetables or side dishes. "Oh . . . why . . . thank you!" I stammered. The owner stood above me, arms crossed, staring at the feast like a proud father. I gathered my white rice as a chaser, took a deep breath, and . . .

I tapped out five minutes later, less than halfway through. All I could think was: *How the hell do people eat livers?*

The following recipe helped me conquer this phobia, and it's intended to do the same for you. In fact, we'll overcome two

ANCHOVIES
Grapeseed

INGREDIENTS	TO SERVE 8
Large onion (get a sweet onion[33] if you can)	1
Ghee	4 T (56 g)
Grapeseed oil	2 T
Ground chicken (thigh meat is ideal; I used breast meat the first time I made it)	8 oz (227 g)
Chicken livers	1 lb (454 g)
Water (use chicken stock instead, if you have it)	2 T
Garlic	4 cloves
Anchovy fillets (not paste)	4
S+P	To taste
OPTIONAL	
Brandy (I use Cognac)	2 T

common revulsions at once: livers *and* anchovies. Trust me on this one.

We'll also learn the fastest method for cutting onions, a go-to technique popular among prep cooks.

The final end product is another no-stress cold app that can chill in your fridge until guests arrive.

A few tips:

1. If you have the Cognac, use it.

2. To help guests overcome liver phobia, a little white lie might be in order. The first time I served this, I told guests it was tuna with cognac, because it smells like it, looks like it, and . . . who the hell knows what tuna and cognac tastes like?

3. If you make this on a cheat day, get some good bread to spread it on. I like sliced baguette bread (≈½"/1.25 cm thickness), fried in olive oil, budgeting 1 T EVOO per slice. Nom nom livers.

PREP

00 Chop the onion. (See pics, next page.)

To minimize crying, I suggest buying a sweet onion (often yellow) if you can. There's plenty of time for sobbing later. The cutting technique, faster but less precise than most methods, is used by pro chefs when speed is paramount. Though we'll cover fine dicing

33 Ideally Vidalia or Maui.

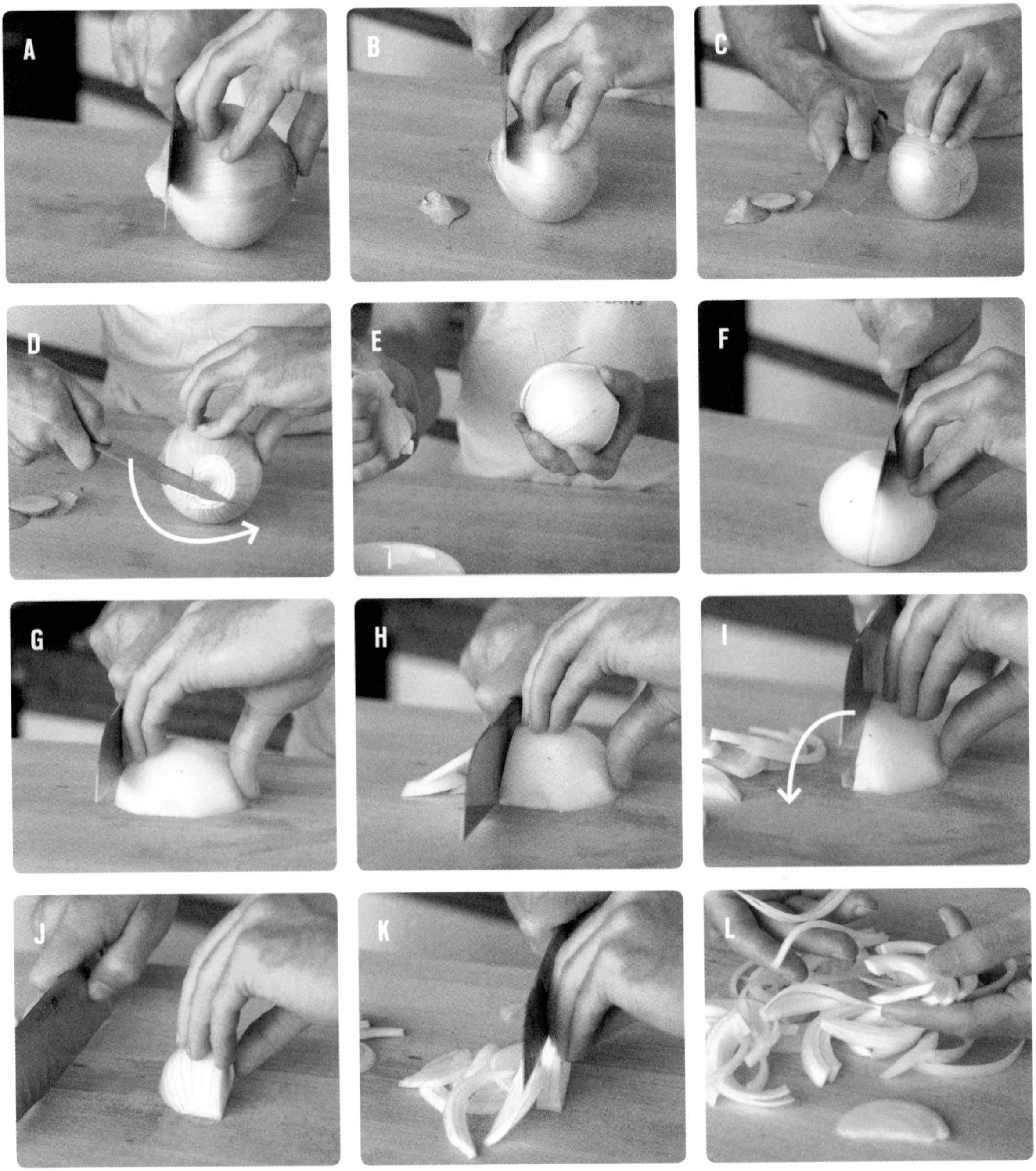
A
B
C
D
E
F
G
H
I
J
K
L

later, this is the technique I use most often:

01 Cut off both ends of the onion.

02 Roll your knife around the onion from pole to pole, to score it and cut through the top layer.

03 Peel off the outside layer and throw it into your garbage bowl.

04 With a flat end down, cut the onion in half.

05 Holding one half flat side down, cut *with* the grain (knife and lines of the onion parallel). Chop into ≈⅛" (0.3-cm) slices, slightly less than pencil width.

06 Just around the midway point, it'll get a bit wobbly. At that point, flip it down and finish. Repeat the process with the other half.

07 Bring the 4 T (56 g) ghee to room temperature, if it's been in the fridge.

PICKUP

00 Place the cast-iron skillet on the stove over medium-high heat for 3 minutes and add 1 T grapeseed oil.

01 Add the chopped onion and stir with the Peltex for roughly 3 minutes. The onions should visibly soften.

02 Push the onion to the edge of the pan and add the remaining 1 T oil to the center. Add the 8 oz (227 g) ground chicken to the cleared area and stir to break up the meat for about 4 minutes, until it's no longer pink.

OPTIONAL: If you want to use the brandy/Cognac, splash in the 2 T when you add the chicken.

03 Push the chicken and onion to the side to create another clearing. Add the 1 lb (454 g) livers and 2 T water (or chicken stock). Stir the livers frequently, until they are firm and just barely pink in the center (check by cutting into a thick piece with the Peltex or a small knife). This should take 6–8 minutes.

04 Now we blitz the whole concoction. Transfer everything into the chopper attachment, and pour in 2 T or so of the liquid from the pan. No need to be exact; just eyeball. This part is hard to screw up. Add in 4 cloves garlic (use a press, as I do, or just toss in after peeling) and the 4 anchovy fillets.

05 Blend until smooth. Add the ghee in small dollops. Taste, then season with salt and pepper to your liking. The anchovies will have added some saltiness, so taste before adding salt.

06 Cover with plastic wrap and refrigerate until chilled, at least 2 hours. It might look runny after blending, but it will firm up as it cools. To serve, either spoon into bowls and sprinkle some lemon zest on top (using the Microplane) or scoop it into 4–6 ramekins (those bowl-like dishes on page 130) and smooth down the tops with a butter knife.

Serve with cold white wine, introduce your "tuna" with big smiles, and break bread if it's a cheat meal. Luxuriate in the loveliness of phobias turned favorites.

It's delicious as leftovers, which I like to spread on endive leaves if I have them. Otherwise, I down it by the spoonful.

BONUS POINTS +2

FRIED SAGE

The second time you make this dish, put a fried sage leaf on top. This is what Dan Kluger of ABC Kitchen does for their chicken liver pâté, which was the first liver pâté I ever went gaga over.

OPTIONAL LESSON 16

SKILLS

LOAVES, THE WOMANLY ARTS

"MLBJ"

INSPIRED BY

Ayako N.

SHORTHAND

425F 60min: Mix 2lb beef, 2 eggs, 6 chopped mushrooms, 1 onion, 3 cloves garlic, 3 scallions, 4 shakes cayenne, ¼t oregano & salt. Fold around handful spinach, 3 oz goat cheese. Spread 2T tomato paste; sprinkle pepper & 1 sprig minced rosemary; bake till 150F.

HANDS-ON TIME

25 minutes

TOTAL TIME

1 hour 25 minutes

GEAR

- Large mixing bowl
- Immersion blender with chopper attachment
- Plastic wrap
- Ungreased baking dish (e.g., Pyrex)

OPTIONAL PAIRINGS

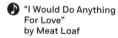

"I Would Do Anything For Love" by Meat Loaf

Breakfast Blend black tea

With its malty notes and an astringent body, it accentuates beef or veal, holding up to their earthy, gamey, roasted/burned qualities. It has a slightly peaty element that matches even rare meat.

"I regret to say that we of the FBI are powerless to act in case of oral-genital intimacy, unless it has in some way obstructed interstate commerce."

—J. EDGAR HOOVER

75¢ A Paperback Library Easy-to-Cookbook 64-320
More than 150 recipes designed to please any man
Sex Pots... And Pans
The single girl's guide to hooking her man—through cooking
By Munroe Howard

"101 ways to please your man!" *Cosmo* covers make Ayako laugh.

Ayako is the wife of a dear friend, and they've been happily married for almost five years. She has a way with words. After he went to a strip club for a friend's bachelor party, her husband asked her if the excursion bothered her. Her response: "I don't care where you build up your appetite, as long as you eat at home."

For the women who believe men need 100+ pleasure points to remain interested, she has this to say:

"Many women complicate things. I know how to keep my man happy, and keep him, period: meatloaf and blowjobs. That's it." I'm not going to provide any how-to for the latter, but it's worth learning Ayako's recipe for the former.

This "MLBJ" has more than four ingredients (and is therefore optional), but it's simple, as many things in life should be. Amen.

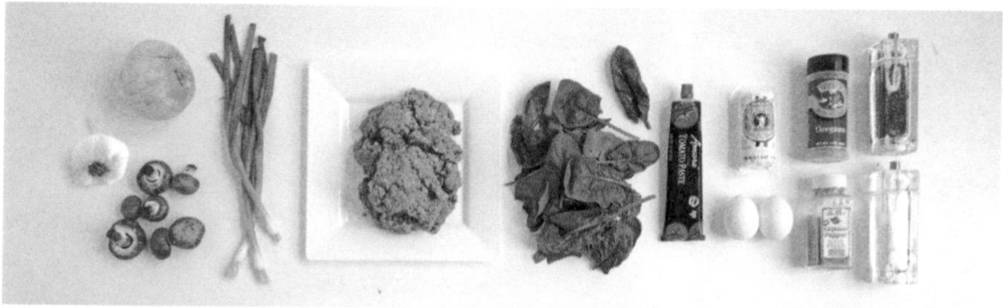

INGREDIENTS	TO SERVE 4
Fatty ground beef, ideally grass-fed	2 lbs (0.9 kg)
Whole eggs	2
Scallions	3
Large onion (any kind, but I like yellow)	1
Garlic	3 cloves (or more, if you like garlic)
Medium mushrooms (baby bellas, button) or 1 large portobello cap	6
Raw spinach, any kind (variation: kale)	Large handful
Chévre goat cheese (most "goat cheese" you find is this soft goat cheese, but it's good to confirm)	3–4 oz (75–100 g)
Tomato paste	2 T
SEASONINGS	
Cayenne pepper powder	4 shakes (light dusting)
Oregano	3-finger pinch
Salt	Two 3-finger pinches
Freshly ground black pepper	6 coarse grinds
Rosemary (1 for eating, 1 for garnish)	1 or 2 sprigs

A

B

C

D

E

F

G

H

I

Slowly flip seam-side down.

J

PREP

00 Rinse all vegetables. Peel garlic.

01 Cut scallions into thin slices (⅛" or so).

02 Chop 1 sprig of rosemary for the seasoning; save one to be used for garnish at the very end.

03 Peel and rough-cut onion.

PICKUP

00 Preheat oven to 425°F (220°C).

01 Put 2 lbs meat in mixing bowl, then 2 whole eggs. No need to mix yet. Wash hands.

02 Add scallions.

03 Using chopper attachment on immersion blender, chop the onions and garlic together. Put this in the mixing bowl on top of the rest.

04 Repeat again for the mushrooms: blend and then put in mixing bowl.

05 Now mix everything together by hand. Wash hands.

06 Add the cayenne, oregano, and S+P, trying to coat the meat somewhat evenly on top. Sprinkle from 12–18" (30–45 cm) up. Mix again. Wash hands.

07 Lay out roughly 18" (46 cm) of plastic wrap on the counter.

08 Put the meat mixture on the plastic and flatten out into a rectangle of uniform width, ensuring at least 1" (2.5 cm) of uncovered edges all around.

09 Lay out the handful of spinach leaves in the middle.

10 Put the goat cheese on one side of the spinach. Ensure both spinach and cheese reach the edges of the meat, so people who get the end pieces aren't screwed out of goodies.

11 Place your hands underneath the plastic wrap, then gently roll up the near side so the edge lands on the opposite edge of the spinach (see pic E, at left). Tuck it a bit, as if rolling a burrito or sushi. Pull back the plastic so it doesn't fold into the meat.

12 Pull up the far side and pat down the meat flaps to seal it all together.

13 Now transfer to the baking dish. This is the big moment. Follow pics G, H, and I. If it falls apart, and it might, don't panic. Just squash it roughly into the shape of a loaf and it'll turn out delicious regardless.

14 Discard the plastic. Smear the tomato paste on top and sprinkle on the rosemary.

15 Stick the whole thing in the oven uncovered. I like to use a probe thermometer and pull when the middle hits 150°F (66°C), but it should take 50–60 minutes. Since you'll be slicing to serve anyhow, I encourage you to cut it in half when you think it's ready, to double-check doneness.

16 Put a sprig of rosemary across the top to make it pretty. Eat and have loud sex.

LESSONS

17+17½

+10

SKILL

HOSTING PARTIES

THE FIRST HOSTING PARTY, THE SECOND DINNER PARTY

"I deserve good things. I am entitled to my share of happiness. I refuse to beat myself up. I am an attractive person. I am fun to be with."
— STUART SMALLEY

The next two parties (you read that right) will require that you practice entertaining others.

For the final weekend of DOM, I'm going to suggest two parties, and you should hold them in short succession. Using our sample calendar on page 132, it might look like this:

First, a wine and cheese party, let's say Saturday, Jan 26. This is to practice hosting skills alone, without cooking. You will invite people who *do not* know each other.

Second, the dinner party, let's say Sunday, Jan 27. Recall that your very first dinner party (page 202) was cooking for people who knew each other (skill: cooking only). The wine and cheese party will introduce you to hosting (skill: hosting only). Here, you combine the two.

THE WARM-UP ACT

Let's talk about the wine and cheese party.

I first hosted such a gathering on a Saturday night at 6 p.m., knowing that people would head out to dinner or parties afterward. I invited them all to swing by and watch some UFC over tons of wine and cheese as their evening warm-up act.

I called my local small grocery store and asked them if they could put together a collection of cheeses ("cheese plate") and crackers for $50, for me to pick up later that day. I told them about the party and asked them to make all the decisions. Of course, you don't have to spend $50, and much less will do, but I didn't want to worry about it and knew nothing about cheese.

If you're doing the shopping, get two soft cheeses (Brie and goat cheese contrast and work well together) and one hard cheese (Parmigiano-Reggiano is a safe bet). Then buy safe wines, such as pinot noir, Rioja, or chardonnay.

Cheese and wine set, your role as host is simple:

- Relax so others relax.
- Make fun of yourself before others do (i.e., embrace any cheesiness you associate with playing host).
- Facilitate interesting conversations.

But if it's not dinner, what do you *do*? Just sit at a table and talk? No. That'd be too weird. Instead, you choose an event as an excuse for the hangout, and as a distraction to fill voids that crop up. For me, it's usually a fight night or the UFC, hence the importance of Saturdays, but it could just as easily be another sport, an episode of a popular TV show, or a classic movie (*Ferris Bueller's Day Off* works well). Alternatively, invite people to your place for wine and cheese before all heading out together to a movie theater, bar, or other place.

Having an excuse to meet up, something to talk about, makes everyone relax.

THE FORMULA

If you've never hosted, it can be nerve-wracking. Will people talk? What if the dynamics are off? There are a few rules you should follow:

1. Introduce people to one another as they arrive, and give them one prompt. Think up one fascinating thing about each person before the party. Then, "Tom, this is Jack. Jack, Tom. I think you guys will really hit it off. Tom, didn't you study computer science at school? Jack's in tech, but I thought you guys would also connect over triathlons..." or something to that effect. If they don't take the bait, try, try again. That's what both nights are for. Practice. It's easiest to hand off the conversation when you're prepping food or drinks.

2. Don't hesitate to play up the fact that you're learning to be host. This breaks the ice and gets some laughs. After sitting everyone down somewhere (e.g., around the TV, on cushions around a coffee table), I'd say something like:

> "Well, I suppose I'm technically the host here, right? OK, some of you haven't met before, so let's do quick self-intros. But first: wine." [Make a toast and take a big swig.] "All right, here's the format: give a quick self-intro, however you like, and then, just to spice things up, mention a pet obsession of yours, or a weird interest, that most people don't know about."[34]

Then, you can let the conversation wander or you can pose more questions. The latter might seem artificial, but if the questions are good, you can learn a lot about people you think you already know. Here are a few I like:

> "If you had to choose a totally different career now, what would it be and why?"

> "What did you want to be when you were a kid? In college?"

> "Name one weird superstition you have."

In each case, you answer first and then pick someone to go next. If the above fails, you can go for the age-old dad opener: "Did you know that...?"

> "In French, someone who loves sex is called a 'hot rabbit' (*chaud lapin*)?"

> "Salumi and salami are different? Salumi refers to dry-cured meats, while salami is specifically a cured sausage made from ground pork. It's a subset of salumi."

> "Cooking gas from gas stoves is actually odorless? The smell is added to it so you can detect leaks."

> "People whose pee smells after eating asparagus have a particular type of genetic variant? It's the MTHFR gene, nicknamed the 'motherfucker' gene by some scientists."

Rinse and repeat. Eat, drink, and be ridiculous.

SUGGESTION: WHIMSY

This suggestion is short and sweet.

At the beginning of the second dinner party, consider adding an *amuse bouche* (literally "mouth amuser"). This is a preappetizer treat to whet the appetite, often brought out in fancy restaurants as "compliments of the chef."

Here are two options:

> 1. Good orange (blood orange is ideal) slices sprinkled with Maldon sea salt. Serve in small bowls or ramekins.

34 For me, that's marine biology and comic book penciling.

2. Single baklava bits, coated with cinnamon, preferably a snowlike coating (using a cinnamon stick and Microplane). Serve in small bowls or ramekins.

Chill the bowls or ramekins for added effect.

SUGGESTION: CLEANUP

Mehdi Chellaoui got his first professional cooking gig at Le Cirque, the meeting place of presidents and celebrities.

This is impressive, especially considering that he was 16. His culinary teacher at Long Island City High School convinced Jacques Torres, then executive pastry chef of Le Cirque, to give the kid a shot. *Gourmet* did a full-page story on him at age 17, and after attending the Culinary Institute of America (CIA) courtesy of nonprofit C-CAP, he went on to work at famed Jean-Georges, later acting as private chef to Sean "Diddy" Combs. Now he makes artisanal chocolates [35] and works with C-CAP to help other inner-city youth follow in his footsteps.

While working for Sean Combs, Mehdi developed his own system for cleaning dishes. I was able to cut my cleanup time by at least 50% using his process. Before this, my cleanup was haphazard and random. I'd clean and rinse a fork for the dishwasher, followed by a few glasses for the rack, followed by a few plates, etc.

Mehdi explains his approach, which assumes no dishwasher:

"In professional kitchens, every large task gets broken down into small steps. To wash dishes, we use a three-sink compartment. To the right of the sinks is a trash bin. This helps break down the dishwashing process."

Here are my suggestions for replicating this process at home in a one-basin sink:

1. Scrape food scraps into trash and put all dirty dishes in the sink.

2. Clean the countertop to the right.

3. Quickly rinse dishes [no soap] with an abrasive scrubber one by one and arrange neatly on the countertop. This step will quickly make the mess look orderly.

4. Dip a sponge into a bowl of hot, soapy water. Quickly scrub each dish and place back into sink [leaving suds on them].

5. Rinse dishes one by one and place onto rack [or laid-out towels].

Clean similar items in batches together. For instance:

1. Clean the dishes in the sink first. This assumes you keep the pots and pans (cooking vessels) on your left countertop.

2. Then silverware.

3. Then cooking utensils (spatulas, etc.).

4. Then cooking vessels (pots, pans, skillets, etc.).

Last, but not least, it's best to clean up as you go. The easiest way to conquer the Everest of dirty stuff is to avoid it. Assuming you've spiked the dinner conversation with good hosting (and perhaps copious alcohol), the two minutes you're gone won't matter to your guests, and it will definitely matter to you at the end of the night.

Keep calm and carry on. And give yourself a pat on the back. You're really cooking!

35 dorkchocolate.com

ROCK-PAPER-SCISSORS 2.0: BEAR-NINJA-COWBOY (BNC)

> **Haru: "The blackness of my belt is like the inside of a coffin on a moonless night."**
>
> **Joey: "That's pretty black, man."**
>
> —*BEVERLY HILLS NINJA*

In a pinch, how do you decide who cleans up, heads out on a beer run, or pays for dinner?

Rock-paper-scissors (known as "RPS" to the devoted) has been the gold standard for ages.

First mentioned in records from the Han Dynasty in China, it has an illustrious history. Though thought of as a kid's game, it's been used to settle a litigation dispute in Florida (not kidding). In 2005, it was also used by Japanese manufacturer Maspro Denkoh to decide whether Sotheby's or Christie's would win the contract to sell a $20 million collection of Impressionist paintings, including works by Picasso and van Gogh. Christie's won . . . based on an 11-year-old's hunch.

And therein lies the problem with RPS. Anyone can beat anyone.

For his piece titled "Four Square for Grown-Ups?" journalist Christopher Noxon took on the first winner of the $50,000 USA Rock Paper Scissors League championships in a best-of-three showdown. Chris won, and as the disillusioned champ said, "Rock-paper-scissors isn't even a sport. A sport is catching a football or getting punched in the face. This is ridiculous."

So, where do we find a more skillful game of pure chance? A more athletic test of sheer luck? A replacement?

The answer is Bear-Ninja-Cowboy. One of my friends learned the game in 2001 as a counselor at a day camp, where he became famous for having LL Cool J's daughter punch him in the nuts. Her technique was admirable: while he chatted up a female counselor, LL's daughter lined up from 20 feet away and, arm extended like a lance, sprinted straight into his testicles like a battering ram.

But I digress.

Here's how Bear-Ninja-Cowboy (BNC or "B 'n' C") works:

Each character has a pose.

- Cowboy has two guns drawn close to the hips.
- Bear has claws overhead.
- Ninja is sideways and in a karate/ninjutsu stance.

Starting back-to-back like an Old West duel, take three large steps, one person counting them off. On "three," pivot and blast your opponent with your pose of choice. See how powers measure up at right.

COWBOY BEATS BEAR

C'MON, REAL COWBOYS HUNT BEARS FOR BREAKFAST.

BEAR BEATS NINJA

NINJAS HAVE CLIMBING CLAWS. BEARS HAVE REAL CLAWS. GAME OVER.

NINJA BEATS COWBOY

SEEN THE MATRIX? YEP, INSPIRED BY NINJAS. BULLETS DON'T WORK ON NINJAS.

WILD

THE WILD

"WILD" is where we step out of the kitchen and, while learning new techniques, connect firsthand with ingredients. On a personal level, how do you go farm-to-plate or field-to-plate? Put another way, do you have what it takes to cope with an extended power outage or a long camping trip? This section is intended to make you uncomfortable. It will force you to question yourself, your limitations, and your beliefs. View it as an exercise.

To quote Lucius Annaeus Seneca, born 4 BCE:

"Set aside a certain number of days, during which you shall be content with the scantest and cheapest fare, with coarse and rough dress, saying to yourself the while: 'Is this the condition that I so feared?' . . . Let the pallet be a real one, and the cloak coarse. Let the bread be hard and grimy. Endure all this for three or four days at a time, sometimes for more, so that it may be a test of yourself instead of a mere hobby. Then, I assure you . . . you will leap for joy when filled with a penny worth of food, and you will understand that a man's peace of mind does not depend upon Fortune, for, even when angry, she grants enough for our needs."‡

There are, however, tools that help you endure, and that's where we'll start.

TOP GEAR SURVIVAL: TARPS, TRAPS, AND TACTICAL KNIVES

This gear section is offered for fun, as a collection of toys I kept after testing hundreds of options.

In other words, you don't have to buy anything. Some of the most practical items, like the survival fishing kit, will be covered later. For those interested, I had to cut more than 50 pages of gear-related craziness that answered questions like:

- What does an Armageddon-proof billionaire compound look like, based on real-world specs from hedge fund managers?
- Is it possible to purchase an "up armor" Humvee from Serbia for the cost of your Prius? (Yep.)
- If a major disaster hit cities like NYC, SF, or L.A., what are the best escape methods and vehicles?

Find these cut sections and more at fourhourchef.com/extras.[1] In the meantime, enjoy my short list, for entertainment purposes only. The most helpful tools will appear again.

STARTERS

1. Guardian Two-Person Survival Bag

$95

Hard-core survivalists won't settle for this, but if you're a busy person looking for decent disaster insurance, this is a one-click (mostly) all-in-one option. This backpack contains emergency blankets, water purification tablets, roughly 5,000 calories' worth of food bars, waterproof matches and a lighter, a first-aid kit, a waste disposal bag, and so on. I keep it at home in a closet and toss it in the car before remote road trips. The components don't last forever, so replace every five years.

2. Leatherman Surge Multitool

$70

If you had to choose one tool for indoors and outdoors, this is it. Whether fixing that stupid dresser drawer, tweezing fishing line, or breaking down a 500-lb animal, it can get the job done.

3. Coghlan's Fire Paste

$7

Odorless and tasteless paste for starting fires, even in damp conditions. Bootleg version: rub cotton balls in Vaseline and store in a film canister. Don't leave the trailhead without it.

4. Lockpick Set

(Prices vary)

Author Neil Strauss's favorite lockpicks are Eric Michaud's. SerePick, run by an ex-Marine, makes an excellent set of "Bogota" picks, as well as universal handcuff keys, Kevlar survival cord, and diamond wire blades for all your daily urban-evasion needs.

5. ThermaCELL Bug Repellant Appliance

$17

DEET- and odor-free, this small appliance heats a chemical film that creates a 15 x 15–ft bug-free zone for up to 48 hours. This will save your sanity if camping or hiking in mosquito-infested territory for several hours or days. It's not incense, so don't breathe it in.

6. Trumark Wrist-Braced Slingshot

$6

I have always loved slingshots (sorry about shooting out the car windows, Mom), and this model remains almost unchanged since 1953. Great for informal target shooting on tin cans, etc. (called "plinking"), it can also be effective at close range for small game like rabbit.

7. Daisy ¼" Slingshot Ammo

$6

You won't be taking down any charging rhinos with these. They're strictly for target practice. For getting food, you'll need rocks or at least ½" ammo.

8. Magnesium Fire-starter

$10

Magnesium shavings are less foolproof than fire paste but are a more common alternative. To use them, you will need both tinder and a blade to shave off the magnesium and strike the flint (the black edge).

9. Highgear Trail Torch Mini Lantern

This pocket-size device, which can be used as a lantern, flashlight, or beacon, has been discontinued. I love it, but reviews are all over the map. For consistent positive reviews, I recommend the Coleman MicroPacker compact lantern ($13) as an alternative.

All of these items can be found at FOURHOURCHEF.COM/WILD-GEAR

1 They'll be put up over time in a series.

1
Survival Kit
2
3
COGHLANS
Fire Paste
CAUTION
FLAMMABLE
IRRITANT
Quick Clean
Fire Starter
Squeezes on,
primes stoves,
starts campfires
and fireplaces
Net Weight: 3.75 oz. wt.
(106.5 g.)
4
5
ThermaCELL
6
Daisy
PREMIUM STEEL
SLINGSHOT AMMO
1/4 Inch Diameter
250 COUNT
TAKE PRIDE
IT'S A DAISY.
Daisy
PREMIUM STEEL
SLINGSHOT AMMO
1/4 Inch Diameter
250 COUNT
TAKE PRIDE
IT'S A DAISY.
7
ThermaCELL
8
9

1
2
10"
3
4
5
Survival Fishing Kit
Standard Version
6
7

8

1.
Self-Locking Snares
$10 (set of 3)

There are two primary types of traps for catching small game: deadfalls (think Looney Tunes rock balanced on a stick) and snares. "Body gripping" snares, which were official issue to soldiers during WWII, lock around an animal's torso or leg and, while effective, cause an agonizing and protracted death. They should never be used outside of emergency circumstances and are categorically illegal in most states. I have never used one, thankfully, but I pack them for remote trips. One professional trapper recommended survival snares from snareshop.com, which are small enough to fit in your pants pocket.

2.
Outdoor Aluminum Dutch Oven
$50+

This differs from what you bought for "DOM" in two respects: the top is flat to support coals, and it's one-third the weight of cast-iron. For hiking, consider a 2-qt version if you're cooking for 1–2 people, or a 5-qt model if feeding a small tribe. They will add 4½ lbs and 8 lbs to your payload (what you're carrying), respectively. By comparison, the combi you own has 3 qt of volume and weighs 14 lbs.

If you're not carrying the Dutch oven far, the most popular outdoor model is still a large, 8-qt–capacity cast-iron monster. It clocks in at a hernia-worthy 20 lbs.

3.
Gill Net
$22

For fishing, trapping, and more. One of the most underrated survival tools. See page 320.

4.
Conibear 110 or Duke 110 Trap
$20

Typically used for mink, muskrat, and weasel, these traps are famous for their speed and considered humane, as far as such things go. Imagine a double-sided mousetrap at 1,000 times the strength.

5.
All-In-One Fishing Survival Kit
$27

See page 321.

6.
Tannerite
$40 and up

I included this just to blow your mind. Tannerite falls in the "how can that possibly be legal?" category. Consisting of two elements that are nonexplosive when kept apart, it's considered a "binary" explosive and used for avalanche control, police applications, and target practice. Tannerite explodes when shot with a high-powered rifle, making it useful for identifying long-range hits without visual inspection. Beware: while buying Tannerite might be legal in your state, detonating it under most circumstances will put you in jail.

7.
10 x 12-ft Tarp
$20

Uses abound for the lowly tarp, making it perhaps the most valuable item on this page. Under normal circumstances, it makes the perfect picnic "blanket," as seen in Japan during cherry blossom season. For camping or survival, it can serve as a shelter roof or rainwater collector.

8.
JBL 6-ft Breakdown Travel Pole Spear
$112

Recommended to me by several friends who spearfish exclusively for food 4–8 weeks of the year, this elegantly designed pole spear is dead simple to use. The kit includes two spear points: a single rock point and a trident "paralyzer" tip. It can be broken down into sections and is small enough to fit in a backpack or suitcase. To use the pole spear, you loop your thumb through the rubber tubing and stretch it toward the opposite end, grabbing the spear toward the tip. When you open your hand, the elastic energy propels the spear through the water. Pole spears are more challenging than the similar Hawaiian sling, and much more kinesthetic than the speargun, which a friend described as "like shooting deer with an Uzi." Buy the extra "sling assembly" (backup tubing) in case of breakage. Otherwise, you might end up angry enough to punch all the lionfish in the world. And remember good goggles. My favorites are the Kaiman from Aqua Sphere.

1. .22 Caliber Starter (Blank) Pistol

$50

I bought the cheapest model I could find, despite bad reviews, and ordered no ammo. Why? Better luggage handling. See sidebar on opposite page.

2. Vortex Viper HD 10x42 Binoculars

$600

These were my first really legit binoculars. Sadly, $400–$500 is the minimum threshold for "now I get it" quality. Another entry-model option my consiglieri recommended was Cabela's Alaskan Guide, 8x42 Full-Size. If you want to get fancy, try a chest harness instead of a neck strap. This allows you to move around, or lie prone, without the binocs swinging around.

What does 8x42 or 10x42 mean? The first number is the magnification. The lower the magnification, the wider your field of view. The higher your magnification, the farther you can see. The 8s would be perfect in South Carolina, as you're hunting at closer range (typically <300 yards). Out west, where you might stalk prey (e.g., elk) from mountaintop to mountaintop (called "glassing") and then pursue, 10s are better. In that case, spotting from a distance is more important than wide field of view. The higher the magnification, the more hand shake (which is always present) will throw off the image.

The second number, the 42 of 10x42, refers to the diameter of the front lens (the *objective lens*) in millimeters. The bigger that number, the more useful the binocs are in low-light conditions, just like owl eyes.

1
VORTEX
2

TANNING BED GOGGLES[2]

2 Just kidding. Lens covers.

ONE REASON TO BUY A "GUN," EVEN IF YOU HATE GUNS

In February 2012, I landed at JFK to a rude awakening: American Airlines had lost one of my bags.

Three days and many fruitless phone calls later, I was stuck wearing a bathing suit for underwear and feeling like one grumpy sister-fucker.[3] Sitting down in my filthy pants, I delivered a rare public smackdown to @AmericanAirlines on Twitter, and my bag was miraculously found within three hours. In the meantime, one of my readers (@imchrisv) pointed me to Bruce Schneier's outstanding security blog (schneier.com), where one of his readers had a related tip:

> A "weapon" is defined as a rifle, shotgun, pistol, air gun, and *starter pistol*. Yes, starter pistols—those little guns that fire blanks at track and swim meets—are considered weapons . . . and do *not* have to be registered in any state in the United States. I have a starter pistol for all my cases. All I have to do upon check-in is tell the airline ticket agent that I have a weapon to declare . . . . I'm given a little card to sign, the card is put in the case, the case is given to a TSA official who takes my key and locks the case and gives my key back to me.
>
> That's the procedure. The case is extra-tracked . . . TSA does not want to lose a weapons case. This reduces the chance of the case being lost to virtually zero.
>
> It's a great way to travel with camera gear . . . . I've been doing this since December 2001 and have had no problems whatsoever.

Limit this trick to domestic flights, and you'll want to buy a TSA-approved lock (which they have a master key for) so they don't cut yours off.

Even if you're packing clothing instead of high-grade camera gear, $50 is a cheap insurance policy against airline dumb-assery.

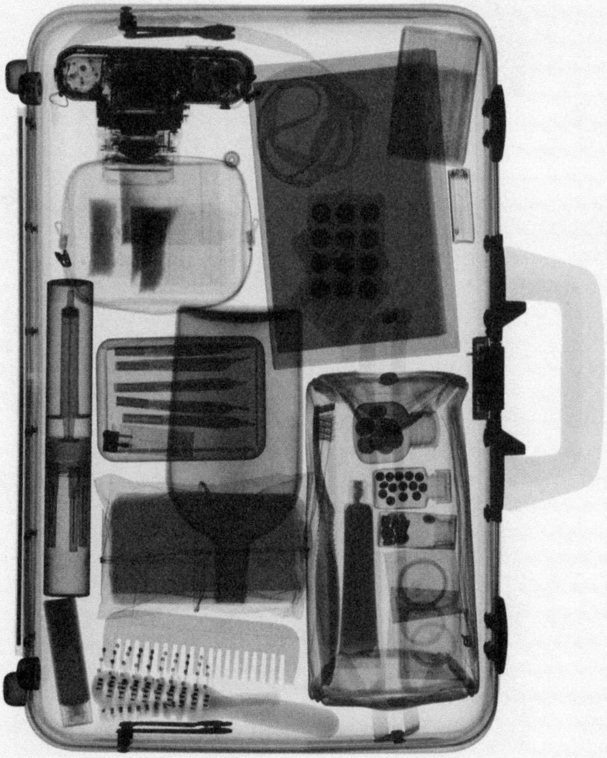

3 Since you asked, Indians and Pakistanis find "motherfucker" too unbearably vulgar, so they substitute "sisterfucker" instead. The most common spelling in English, though it depends on dialect, is *bhenchod*. May it serve you well.

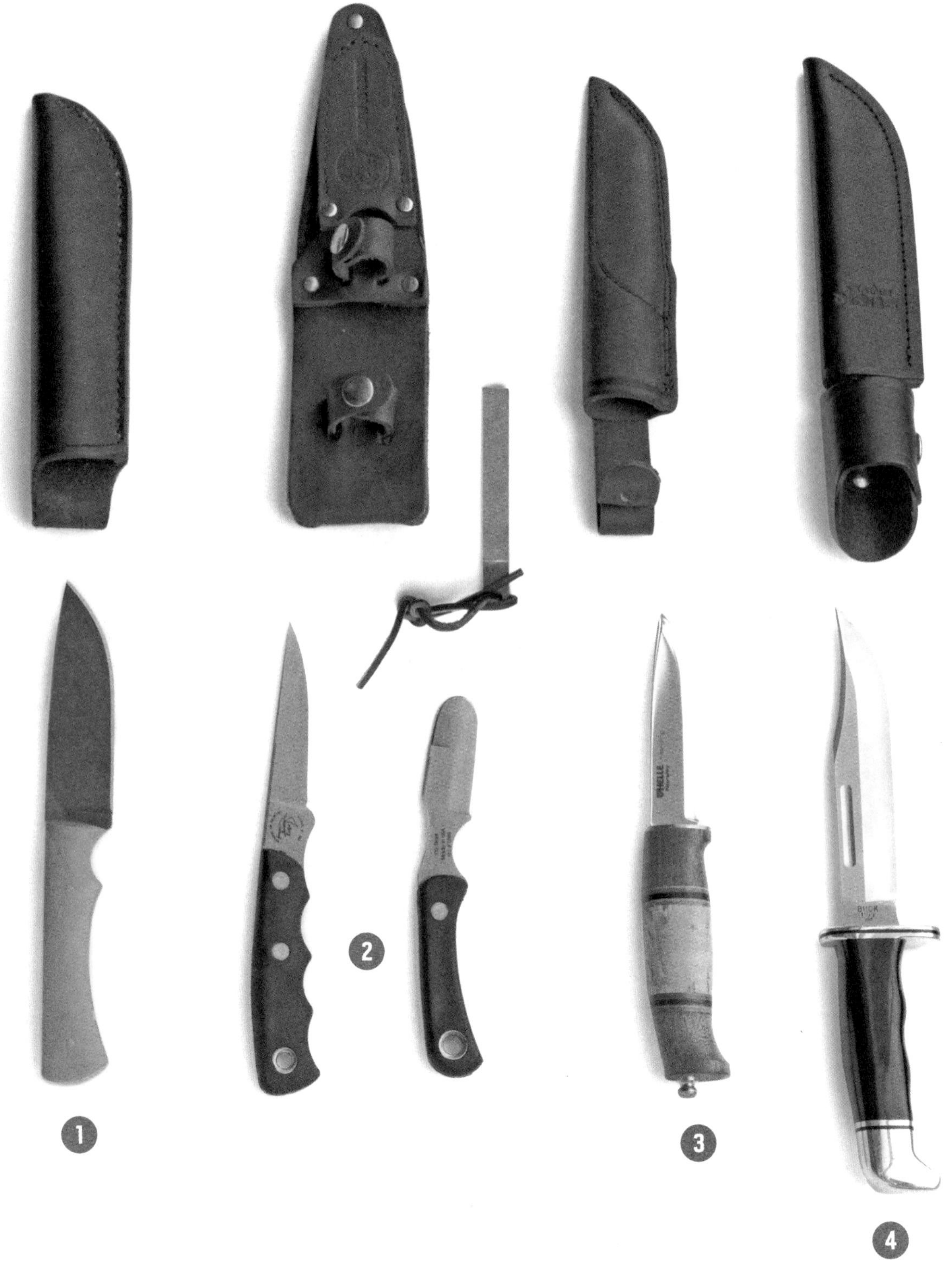
1
2
3
4

5

6

HUNTING AND RIGGING KNIVES

1.
Brian Goode "B. Goode" Utility Knife

(Prices vary)

If I had to pick one all-purpose knife, this beautiful, perfectly balanced handmade knife would give the ESEE-5 (see next spread) a run for its money. This is lighter and easier to wield.

2.
Knives of Alaska Suregrip Jaeger/ Muskrat Knife Combo

$165

If minimizing weight while hunting is a priority, this combo is best of breed. The Muskrat's double edge allows a back-and-forth motion that greatly reduces both skinning time and headache. Comes with sharpening steel.

3.
Helle Harding

$110

This Norwegian knife has the most intricate woodwork in my collection. I haven't had the heart to abuse it in the wild.

4.
Buck Knife 119 Special

$45

This is my favorite Buck knife, handcrafted by Hoyt and Al Buck almost 50 years ago and backed by an unconditional lifetime warranty. It was a gift from my mama, who introduced me to responsible knife handling on childhood camping trips.

5.
Davis Deluxe Rigging Knife

$20

This is the sailor's best friend, useful for all manner of rigging and knot tying (or untying). The blade doesn't lock, so be careful, but the marlin spike alone makes it worth the price.

6.
Havalon Piranta

$60

The Piranta is, by many orders of magnitude, the sharpest knife I have ever owned. It's better thought of as a field scalpel. The #60XT blades are replaced like razor blades rather than resharpened.

7.
AccuSharp (not pictured)

$10

For sharpening any of the double-beveled knives (besides the Havalon), I use the AccuSharp Knife and Tool Sharpener, which is pocket-size and can be used on everything from kitchen knives to axes.

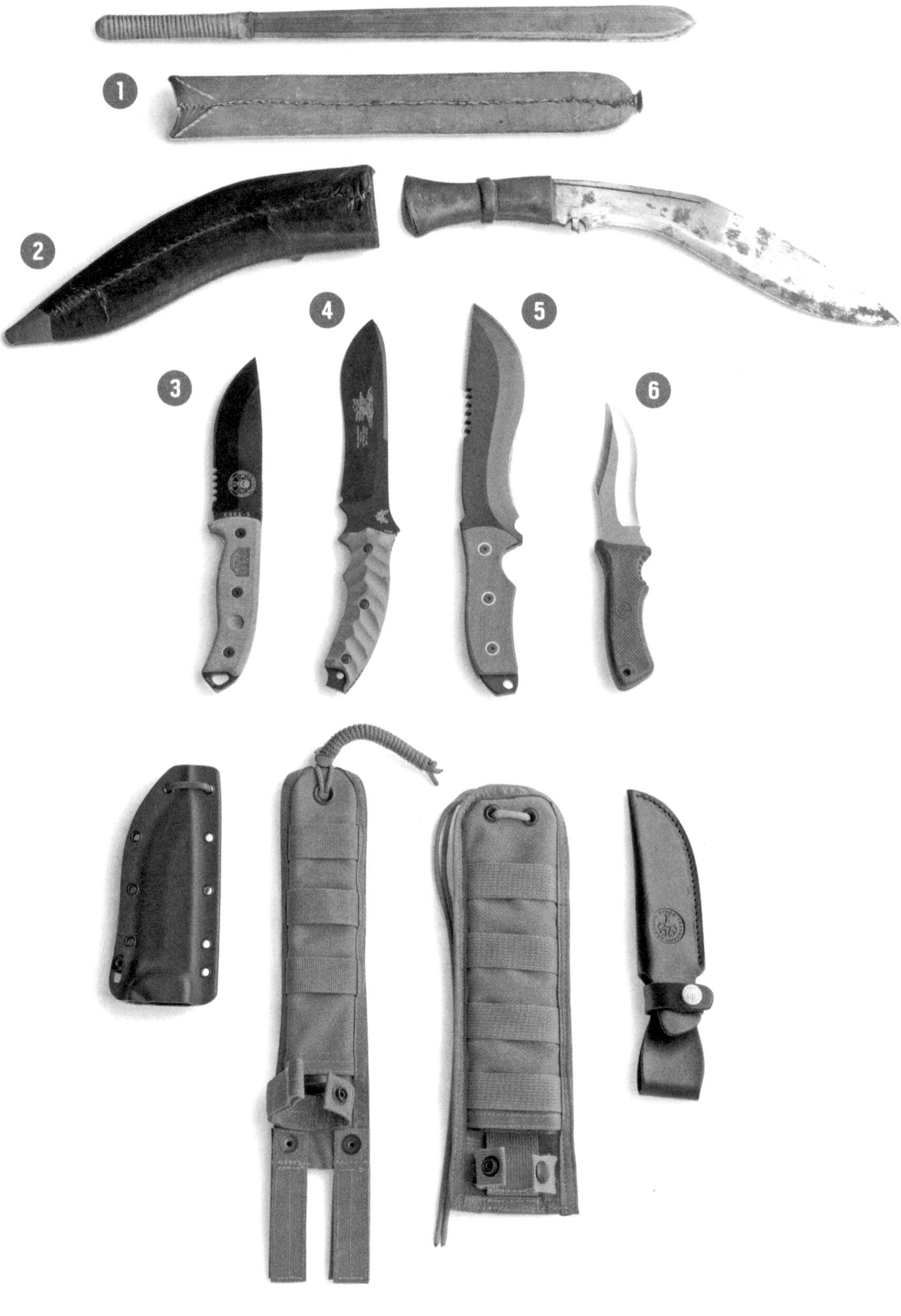
1
2
3
4
5
6

COLLECTIBLE KNIVES

1.

Maasai Warrior Sword

This sword is fashioned out of a ground-down British machete. Used ritualistically for cow sacrifice by the Maasai tribe—who subsisted on cow meat, milk, and blood for centuries—the handle and sheath are both made of cow hide. The Maasai warrior I bought this from was eager to talk, which we did for more than an hour, on topics ranging from scaring off lions (easy compared to the more dangerous hippos and elephants) to multiple wives (their culture is traditionally polyamorous). The more cattle and stature a man has, the more wives he's permitted. I asked if the men with more wives were happier. He laughed out loud and responded, "Are you kidding? How could they ever make them all happy?!" That's why polyandry is also par for the course; the ladies get multiple men.

2.

Nepalese Khukuri

Of all the knives pictured, I've had this one the longest. See page 70 for details.

"TACTICAL" KNIVES

"Tactical" generally refers to tools designed for military or law-enforcement use. My curiosity about tactical knives was piqued during evasive-driving training in Arizona with Safehouse Anti-Terrorism and Force Protection. It was there that I bumped into stacks of magazines dedicated to blade forging.

Here are a few models I took for test drives simply to answer the question: "What makes these knives so special?"

3.

ESEE-5

$200

If I could take only one knife into the unknown, this would have to be it. The ESEE-5 was designed by Air Force SERE (Survival, Evasion, Resistance, and Escape) instructors. At 16 oz, it is heavy enough to use as a makeshift axe (unlike the B. Goode knife) and also features a lanyard hole and divot for bow-drill fire making. Entirely independently, Neil Strauss declared the close cousin ESEE-3 (5 oz) to be his favorite general-purpose fixed-blade knife.

4.

Benchmade Marc Lee Knife

$245

Marc Lee was the first Navy SEAL killed in the Iraq war. This knife's handle has the best hand-feel of any I own. Oddly, the thumb release on the sheath seems to be on the wrong side for right-handers.

5.

Grayman West Nile Warrior 7.5"

$215

This knife received an incredible amount of military praise. For its size, the ease-of-use is surprising, and the sheath is the best I own. The product page online is something else. "The GRAYMAN SB West Nile Warrior is a balanced single-bevel [ground on one side only] single-edge fighter/utility knife with a dramatic recurved bolo design for optimum chopping and slashing performance. Additionally, the wide foreblade causes a disproportionately large wound channel. Now comes with working oil and exposed pounding butt." Intense.

6.

Böker Gaucho Bowie Recurve with Kraton Handle

(Prices vary)

Böker fixed-blade knives were recommended by Yvon Chouinard, founder of Patagonia, who cited Aron Ralston (of *127 Hours* fame) as a cautionary tale: if you ever have to cut off your own arm, you better have a good knife. This recurve model is now hard to find, but there are plenty of comparable options. I prefer the B. Goode.

The Importance of Rabbits.

"From 1980 to 1983, I worked in the kitchen of a small restaurant near Catskill, New York, on a patch of the Hudson River Valley so remote it didn't have an address. The 60-seat restaurant was owned by René and Paulette Macary (she remains its proprietor today). La Rive, named thus because it sat on a wide running creek, was a fruitful training ground, and New York State had extraordinary livestock. Beautiful veal came down from Utica. I found a man who raised spectacular pigeons. I began to ask these farmers for unusual items to experiment with, things like pigs' ears, cockscombs, duck testicles.

One day, I asked my rabbit purveyor to show me how to kill, skin, and eviscerate a rabbit. I had never done this, and I figured if I was going to cook rabbit, I should know it from its live state through the slaughtering, skinning and butchering, and then the cooking. The guy showed up with 12 live rabbits. He hit one over the head with a club, knocked it out, slit its throat, pinned it to a board, skinned it—the whole bit. Then he left.

I don't know what else I expected, but there I was out in the grass behind the restaurant, just me and 11 cute bunnies, all of which were on the menu that week and had to find their way into a braising pan. I clutched at the first rabbit. I had a hard time killing it. It screamed. Rabbits scream, and this one screamed loudly. Then it broke its leg trying to get away. It was terrible.

The next 10 rabbits didn't scream and I was quick with the kill, but that first screaming rabbit not only gave me a lesson in butchering, it also taught me about waste. Because killing those rabbits had been such an awful experience, I would not squander them. I would use all my powers as a chef to ensure that those rabbits were beautiful. It's very easy to go to a grocery store and buy meat, then accidentally overcook it and throw it away. A cook sautéing a rabbit loin, working the line on a Saturday night, a million pans going, plates going out the door, who took that loin a little too far, doesn't hesitate, just dumps it in the garbage and fires another. Would that cook, I wonder, have let his attention stray from that loin had he killed the rabbit himself? No. Should a cook squander anything ever?

It was a simple lesson."

—Thomas Keller,
The French Laundry Cookbook

THE MANUAL ARTS

"The noncook is in a helpless position, much like that of the car owner who can't change a tire and has to depend on mechanics to keep his automobile running."

—RAYMOND SOKOLOV, *HOW TO COOK*

"According to the map, we've only gone four inches."

—HARRY, *DUMB & DUMBER*

Is this your image of a hunter? Georgia Pellegrini, author of *Girl Hunter*.

(CREDIT: T. KRISTIAN RUSSELL)

Georgia Pellegrini didn't start off as a hunter.

She graduated from Wellesley and headed to Wall Street, which she later deserted to attend the French Culinary Institute (FCI) in New York City. In no time flat, Georgia was working alongside the best in the business at restaurants like Gramercy Tavern and Blue Hill at Stone Barns. It was at the latter that she had to slaughter her first turkey. This was a pivotal moment in her life and sparked her exploration of "field-to-table" eating.

Through Georgia, I met Doug, a lifelong Napa resident who's only been to San Francisco twice, even though it's a mere 1½ hours away.

He can tell the difference between delicious cocora mushrooms (popular with Roman emperors) and deadly nightcap mushrooms, which look nearly identical. He knows how to dive for abalone, and if deer are in season, he's in deer season. He never hunts the morning after a full moon, as the animals had been out to feed the night before. If the trout are running, he knows exactly where to find the best steelhead.

Doug hates being indoors as much as I was resigned to spending most of my life there. Rather than battle the physical world, after all, I'd chosen to master the digital, just like all of my friends.

Georgia's father jokingly refers to her (and my) generation as one of "manual illiterates." He's absolutely right:

- My dad can fix his car if something goes wrong. I cannot. Take the most basic of emergency tasks, changing a flat tire. I'd done this once or twice and long since forgotten everything. Changing the oil by myself? Forget it.

- My dad can splice wire, fix basic electronics. I cannot.

- My dad and granddad could navigate the outdoors. Nothing fancy, but the basics. I cannot. Put 10 of my closest friends from SF in the wilderness with no trails, no iPhone, and no GPS? They wouldn't stand a chance.

After two events, I realized all this could be a very serious problem.

EVENT 1: THE 12-HOUR WAKE-UP CALL

Three months after meeting Doug, I awoke on a Friday at 10 a.m. to move my car.

Standing barefoot on my doorstep, I could see that I'd beaten the meter maid. No ticket. Instead, I found a form letter from Pacific Gas and Electric (PG&E): due to construction, they were shutting off electricity and water on my street, a quaint four blocks, from 8 a.m.–6 p.m.

The lack of tap water and toilet water would be annoying, I thought, but no big deal. I had a Brita pitcher full of water, which would last me a few hours. If I needed wireless, I could always go to a café, but maybe a half-day vacation from the Internet was exactly what I needed?

Amidst these thoughts, I walked back inside to make breakfast. The gas was still on, but I had to ignite the pilot light (electrical) with a match. For this minor victory, I gave myself a hearty pat on the back. I then shuffled sideways and opened the fridge to grab eggs . . . and that's when I tilted my head like a Labrador.

Condensation was dripping off of everything. All the food, including nearly $200 worth of frozen meat, had been thawing and creeping toward room temperature for two hours. One of my good friends, Neil Strauss, had long ago told me to get a generator, and I'd dutifully put it on the "someday" nice-to-do list.

Now, "someday" had arrived. But how hard could it be for a resourceful young guy with a car, iPhone, AMEX, and no 9–5 job to get organized? Starting at 10:30 a.m., the sequence of events looked like this:

- Call Cole Hardware, which has *everything*. The line is busy after three calls, so I drive down. No generators, but they recommend a construction supply store and call ahead, confirming that generators are in stock.

- I drive to the supply store and am told they have no generators. After 90 minutes of insisting, I find one remaining unit. It's for construction sites, costs $500, and is the size of small whale shark. It takes two people 30 minutes to get the 200-lb beast into the back of my Volkswagen Golf. Just as I'm about to leave, I realize that I need a gas container (another 20 minutes of searching), and I have to stop at a gas station to purchase fuel.

- I get home close to 2:30 p.m. (four hours after starting) due to unexpected traffic. It takes me almost an hour to get the generator out of my car and up a 14-step patio flight of stairs. Resting a minute before the second leg indoors, I notice a huge sticker: "WARNING: Never use indoors. This generator produces carbon monoxide and can kill you in minutes." Fuck balls. I do not have 50-ft extension cords and concede defeat. Life: 1, Tim: 0.

- Now it's 4 p.m., and I decide to clear my head with a walk. I'm not alone. A half-dozen neighbors are doing the same, looking frustrated. Nearing the end of my block, I hear an oddly familiar "thump, thump" sound, which leads me to an open garage. There, I find a man who's done things properly. He has a small generator, easily one-fifth the size of mine, powering his refrigerator via extension cords. He's duct-taped a tube onto the exhaust release, and the carbon monoxide is going straight out a window. I strike up a conversation with "Bob" and ask him about the make and model. It is a Honda EU2000i, the preferred generator for die-hard "Burners," as he points out. Burners are attendees of the annual Burning Man event, which takes place on the Nevada salt flats and lasts more than a week. The mantra: bring everything you need, leave nothing. I'd been twice, which explained why I recognized the sound.

- By 5 p.m., two more men have discovered Bob's "thump, thump" and are asking if they can borrow it. His tool was what everyone needed and he was now the unenviable center of attention. One man became flustered and almost insistent. But how could Bob let them use it and not have his own food spoil?

He couldn't.

And that's when, fortunately for Bob and everyone else, the power went back on.

All of my refrigerated food went into the garbage, but a third of my frozen food was still usable. At the end of the day, a mere four blocks had been off the grid for less than 12 hours. It wasn't an "event," let alone an emergency, and I'd lost nearly every ounce of food, not to mention all of my potable water.

What if it had been 24 hours? 48 hours? 72 hours?

I ordered the Honda EU2000i.

EVENT 2: NERT

One fair-weather afternoon, I received the following e-mail from a friend:

> My girlfriend and I will be attending six NERT (Neighborhood Emergency Response Team) classes in the Marina from 6:30–9:30 p.m. on Mondays starting next week.
>
> At the end you get a cool vest, hat, and badge that can get you special access through checkpoints, etc., in case of an emergency, as well as a good idea of how to survive the chaos that would inevitably follow a major disaster.
>
> If anyone wants to join us, you can get more information at sfgov.org/sffdnert. If there is an earthquake in the next 30 years (as is often predicted) or any other major disaster, it could save your life. The training is free and is sure to be an interesting look at the world we live in.

NERT was created by the San Francisco Fire Department. I signed up out of curiosity. Our first session, early on a Saturday morning at Bayside Police Department, started off with a question.

"How many people live in San Francisco?" asked the instructor, a police officer, of the 50 or so volunteers.

Correct answer: "More than 800,000 residents in the city."

If we count commuters or the SF-Oakland-Fremont triangle, there are more than 4 million people. In fact, San Francisco is the second-most densely populated large city in the United States after New York City.

Next question: "How many fire trucks do we have in the city of San Francisco?"

Guesses from the crowd: "50?" "100?"

Answer: "19."[4]

The room fell silent. We were left to soak in the reality for a few seconds.

4 Somewhat freaked out by this, I found out later that there are an additional 43 fire "engines," which are equipped with hoses and water but lack the ladders, rescue equipment, and other tools of a fire "truck."

"What this means," the officer continued, "is that if there is a serious disaster like a big earthquake—let's say 6.9 or higher on the Richter scale, which is almost certain in the next 20 years—it might be a while before anyone comes to save you."

Following that, we dissected the logistics of SF as a city: how the water functions, historical fires and patterns, average deployment time for state and federal emergency teams, etc. Every fact underscored the necessity of trained civilians, and explained the existence of NERT. We could be "activated" like benevolent splinter cells via phone, walkie-talkie, or ham radio to help address chaos.

The most important realization was a sobering one: "It could take 7–10 days for a real team to get to you."

We were assigned homework for that weekend: go home and practice turning off your water and gas. Other students got more ambitious, deciding to go 24 hours without water or power. I was in the former group, and though a small step, the dress rehearsal in self-reliance felt great.

All along, I wondered: *how on earth have I not learned this stuff?*

Sometimes you go to the wild, and sometimes the wild comes to you (e.g., Hurricane Katrina).

Knowledge of basic improvised cooking is cheap insurance in a complex world. Plus, it's a blast.

Looking out your window and seeing food where other people see weeds is fun. Being ahead of the eight ball and 99% of the population? That's fun. Playing catch-and-release with pigeons at the park? Beats the hell out of *Seinfeld* reruns. Some of the skills we'll learn can be viewed like CPR: you never *want* to use them, but in the unlikely event that you *need* to use them, they're a godsend. And, not to be undervalued, you'll get outside for a change.

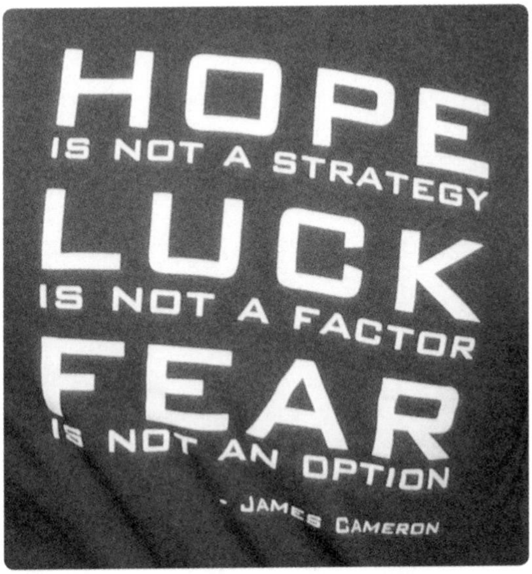
HOPE
IS NOT A STRATEGY
LUCK
IS NOT A FACTOR
FEAR
IS NOT AN OPTION
- JAMES CAMERON

The James Cameron quote I used to get through my last book deadline, which I now apply to much more. This shirt was given to all staff working on *Avatar*.

The heart of this section (in more ways than one) is a portfolio of new techniques you can use anywhere, whether in a kitchen, a forest, or a parking lot.

But before we get to food, there are a few other survival check boxes to tick. Let's start with the Rule of Threes.

THE RULE OF THREES

> "I'd rather wake up in the middle of nowhere than in any city on earth."
>
> —STEVE MCQUEEN

Calvin and Hobbes by WATTERSON
YOU KNOW, HOBBES, IT SEEMS THE ONLY TIME MOST PEOPLE GO OUTSIDE IS TO WALK TO THEIR CARS.
WE HAVE HOUSES, ELECTRICITY, PLUMBING, HEAT.... MAYBE WE'RE SO SHELTERED AND COMFORTABLE THAT WE'VE LOST TOUCH WITH THE NATURAL WORLD AND FORGOTTEN OUR PLACE IN IT. MAYBE WE'VE LOST OUR AWE OF NATURE.
THAT'S WHY I WANT TO ASK YOU, AS A TIGER, A WILD ANIMAL CLOSE TO NATURE, WHAT YOU THINK WE'RE PUT ON EARTH TO DO. WHAT'S OUR PURPOSE IN LIFE? WHY ARE WE HERE?
WE'RE HERE TO DEVOUR EACH OTHER ALIVE.
TURN ON THE LIGHTS! TURN UP THE HEAT!
1/6

"Wow, that's a big bear."

The Department of Fish and Game warden was right: 450 lbs made it a very large black bear indeed. He took the required measurements, pulled a tooth for population studies, and casually asked the hunter about the type of gun used: "What caliber?"

"Actually, it was an archery kill," Cliff Hodges responded.

"No shit? What kind of bow?"

Cliff pulled out his *self bow*—a modest-looking 5-ft-long stick, made from a single piece of wood cut from an Osage tree. As he did so, the warden stopped everything he was doing.

"I have the arrow," Cliff added, lifting a turkey feather–fletched shaft from the bed of the truck, the bloody stone point held in place with pine sap, crushed eggshell, and deer sinew.

"You . . . you killed *this* thing . . . with *that*?!" The warden's jaw dropped.

"Yup, I actually made these myself."

There were 10 long seconds of silence. The warden inspected the bow and arrow up close. He handed them back to Cliff, looked him straight in the eyes, and said, "I've been doing this for 40 years, and this is, by far, the most impressive thing I've ever seen." They stood there in silence for another minute or so. Finally, the warden asked, "Do you mind if I run inside and grab my camera? I gotta get a picture of this."

To the warden's knowledge, it was the first bear killed with a stone point in California in more than 150 years.

Cliff, as always, was all smiles.

"Hell yeah, man, knock yourself out."

The Santa Cruz Mountains are home to the oldest state park in California, Big Basin Redwoods State Park. Its 18,000+ acres are dotted with waterfalls and inhabited by fauna including black-tailed deer, foxes, bobcats, and mountain lions. Outside of the park's boundaries, the mountainous terrain continues, enveloping the 30 or so wineries that have made this region famous.

Now I found myself off the beaten path, under the canopy of giant coastal redwoods and Douglas fir.

Cliff Hodges, 32, was standing next to me in the shade.

He grew up in Santa Cruz, the son of a physician and an occupational therapist. In high school, he developed a fascination with edible plants and began to give outdoor walking tours. This was interrupted only when he was

recruited to the East Coast by MIT. As his then-roommate Kai McDonald recalls, Cliff brought an unusual touch to campus: "I remember going into the freezer one day and seeing a strange item wrapped in plastic. It was a deer brain, which he was using to tan animal hides."[‡]

Cliff graduated with bachelor's and master's degrees in electrical engineering and computer science. He returned to the Bay Area to start a job working on flash memory for consumer electronics.

It lasted barely three months. The prospect of sitting behind a screen for the rest of his adult life was akin to a slow death.

Flash forward (pun intended) to 2012. Cliff now runs two companies that keep him in motion or outside. The first is CrossFit West, the largest CrossFit facility in the western United States. The second is Adventure Out,[5] the reason for my visit. It is a school for all things outdoor, based on skills Cliff has further refined since MIT. He's traveling the world to surf the biggest waves and climb the biggest rock faces. He's traveled to Bozeman, Montana, to study under the Yoda of bow building and hunting, Bill McConnell. He's apprenticed (and then taught for) the best trackers in the United States, from the Pine Barrens to the Arizona desert.

5 adventureout.com

Cliff making handmade "cordage" (rope or string), here woven in "reverse wrap" and fashioned from palm tree raffia fibers. Anything fibrous and celery-like can work, including inner layers of tree bark.

To use his self bow for anything deer-size or larger, he must stalk to within 20 (preferably 10) yards.

(CREDIT: TOM MCELROY)

Setting a Paiute deadfall trap: for bait, Cliff has used flower buds to lure small game like rabbits and squirrels. To get even one small animal, it's a numbers game. Set 10–20 traps in the right spots (you'll need basic tracking skills) and cross your fingers.

Using anthropological studies, he's re-created artifacts from museums, and learned to produce sophisticated tools from next to nothing.

Next to nothing was exactly where my survival skills were when I landed under his care in Santa Cruz.

THE RULE OF THREES

"These skills are part of who you are . . . you've just forgotten them. None of this is hard."

Cliff was warming up the crowd; a group of ten 30-something entrepreneurs, chefs, and venture capitalists. We'd all been brought to the mountains by a vague urban malaise.

Our education began with the Rule of Threes:

Shelter — Three hours
Water — Three days
Food — Three weeks

In other words, you should assume you can survive without shelter for three hours, without water for three days, and without food for three weeks. Food, though the focus of this book, is the last priority in an emergency. Before we jump into improvised cooking, therefore, the next few lessons will cover shelter and water.

After all, it'd be pretty embarrassing to freeze to death while trying to cook Harissa Crab Cakes. You don't have to complete these lessons, but you should read them.

THE COSTCO SOLUTION

In an urban environment, the Rule of Threes still applies. The solutions are just easier to find, probably as close as your nearest Costco.[6]

At the very least, go out and purchase the following **(links to all can be found at fourhourchef.com/costco):**

Emergency blankets and sleeping bags. Make sure they're rated for the lowest recorded temperature in your area. I like Chinook bags, or the oversize 1–2-person Teton Sports Celsius XXL. In a home robbed of power, "shelter" equals warmth. If you have a chimney, get seasoned wood; if not, get a vent-free gas stove like the portable Mr. Heater F232000. Don't forget the fuel.

Two weeks' worth of water. Budget at least one gallon per person per day, and backup water purification tablets are a good idea. If you live close to the ocean, you could also buy a desalinator for turning salt water into potable water.

Two weeks' worth of food with a long shelf life. Lentils, rice, beans, canned vegetables, etc. Protein bars are a good supplement and provide some variety, as do military MREs. If you want a more unique field trip than Costco, check out an LDS (Mormon) cannery, where supplies can be purchased in #10 storage cans, which you pack yourself using their equipment.

Emergency lighting, including a few headlamps, and a ton of batteries. I ended up choosing the following:

- A 300-lumen Rayovac LED lamp.

- 3–10 stick-and-click LED lights for secondary light throughout the house.

- Hand-cranked flashlights/radios/chargers, USB port included. I bought two, the second endorsed by the American Red Cross.

First-aid kit and (for the ambitious) extra antibiotics. Ciprofloxacin (Cipro) and Azithromycin (Z-Paks), while imperfect, are good broad-spectrum antibiotics. If your doc isn't up for a 30-day scrip, how do you get them? Two options: buy them at fish supply stores (I'm serious), or do what Neil Strauss does—keep a list of what you want on your phone, then pick them up when abroad. In St. Kitts, where Neil has a home, you can get over-the-counter aspirin with codeine as a starting point.

This basic prep might seem crazy if you've never been caught in a disaster. No one in SF expected the 1989 Loma Prieta earthquake, either, but it left thousands without running water for 10 days, and without power for four days. Just remember the words of that humble genius, Anonymous, who once said:

"Procrastinating is like masturbating. It feels good at the time, but, in the end, you're just fucking yourself."

---

6 Or order their disaster kits online: fourhourchef.com/costco.

OPTIONAL LESSON 18

SKILL

BUILDING A SHELTER

HOW TO BUILD A DEBRIS HUT

TOTAL TIME

2–8 hours, depending on debris availability

GEAR

- Branches, large and small
- Smaller sticks
- Leaves and/or pine needles
- Dried grass
- Anything that trees drop

"Somewhere along the line, we seem to have confused comfort with happiness."

—DEAN KARNAZES, ULTRAMARATHONER WHO, IN 2006, RAN 50 MARATHONS IN ALL 50 U.S. STATES IN 50 CONSECUTIVE DAYS

"Generally speaking, a howling wilderness does not howl. It is the imagination of the traveler that does the howling."

—HENRY DAVID THOREAU

If you move around when lost, you're expanding the square mileage rescuers need to cover around your last known position. Statistically speaking, you're better off staying put and *not* searching for help.

Ninety-nine percent of people found alive are found within 51 hours of being reported missing.[‡] During this time, you're most likely to die of exposure, even if temperatures are in the high 50s. Though we took Cliff's word for it, this seemed impossible to our group. It had been sunny California tanning weather all day, and the evening was the epitome of mild. Many of us slept outside near the fire in sleeping bags. A few hours later, *every* person who chose to sleep outside of a tiny shelter felt like they were freezing to death.

The emergency shelter we later learned to build, the debris hut, is designed to do two things: insulate you from the outside and provide a small airspace.

If it's too big, it won't retain your body heat and you're screwed. The crawl space should be slightly bigger than a coffin or a sleeping bag. The tighter the fit, the better. This cannot be overemphasized. The most beautiful debris hut is pointless if too big. Remember: this is an emergency shelter for when you do *not* have a sleeping bag.

Built properly, a debris hut fashioned from sticks and leaves can last up to two weeks.

Needless to say, practice your skills in warmer climates first.

PICKUP

00 Find a site (5–120 minutes). When choosing the site for your debris hut, the real estate mantra "location, location, location" applies. Keep in mind three factors:

- High and dry: Find a spot that's sufficiently far from creeks that could overflow or low-lying areas where flooding could happen due to rising waters or rainfall.

- Proximity to debris: Why don't deer run until absolutely necessary? The same reason you shouldn't put your shelter on top of a hill that requires a 100-m jog for each pile of

Debris hut (almost) complete. A couple more feet of piling to go. From left to right: Theodore Agranat, Asil Toksal, me, Andrew McCormack, and Jeremy Johnson.

branches: conservation of energy. The more calories you burn, the sooner you'll need food. You'll need to collect enough debris to fill a large pickup truck, so there should be plenty of material in the immediate vicinity. Also look for a nearby rock, stump, or low tree branch for anchoring your hut.

• Safety: Use common sense: A hut set up beneath a heavy hanging branch is a bad idea, and so is choosing terrain that's susceptible to rockslides, erosion, heavy water flows, etc.

01 **Lay down the ridgepole** (20–40 minutes). It's time to select and rig the spine of your hut's skeletal structure. You'll need to find a suitable log (no rot or large breaks) that's 1–2 ft longer than your body; this ridgepole will dictate the length of the hut. Clear debris from the ground at the base of your future shelter and lay the ridgepole over an adjacent rock, stump, or branch (see illustrations on the next page), leaving no more than a foot of clearance between the inclined log and your body when lying underneath.

02 **Line the ridgepole with ribs** (30–60 minutes). The ribs—stout sticks each about as thick as a baseball bat—will define the sides of your shelter. Lean 15–30 ribs on each side of the ridgepole, evenly spaced a few inches apart. Ensure that the ribs don't jut far above

The ridgepole should be about the diameter of your calf.

Ribs should be about as thick as a baseball bat, but use what you can.

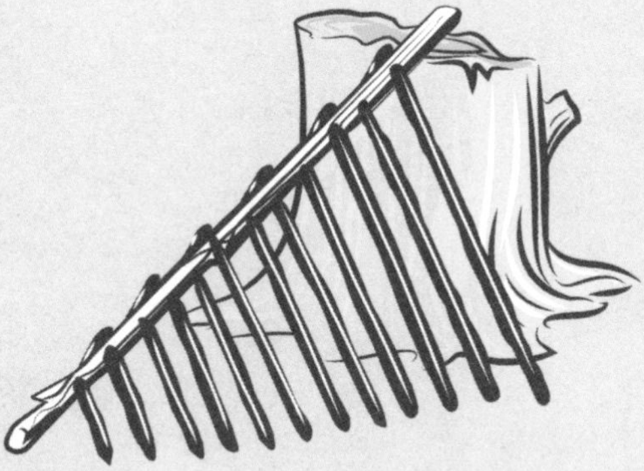

After the ribs are placed (there should be 15–30 per side, sometimes more), create a latticework of criss-crossing smaller (pinkie-size) sticks or whatever you can find. Then start piling.

For details on that funny-looking door, see the below step.

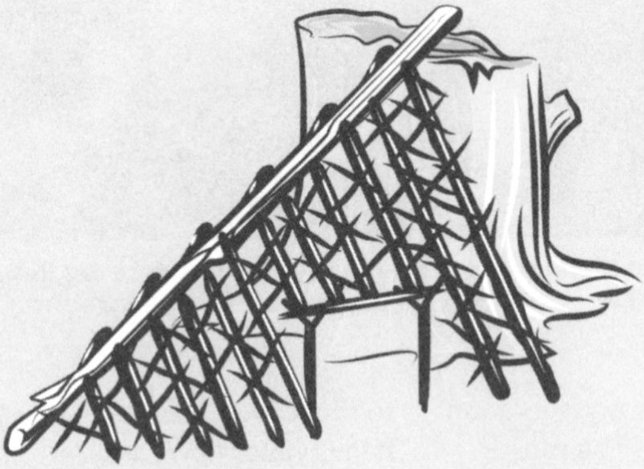

To avoid creating a huge heat-sucking door where the ridgepole meets the stump, we sealed that off and instead created a side door, just big enough for our shoulders to fit (entering feetfirst). We pounded in two Y-shaped sticks, lay two sticks in them, which we pushed through to the opposite side, then we layered sticks and debris on top as we did everywhere else.

The tunnel to our "bed" was 2–3 feet long.

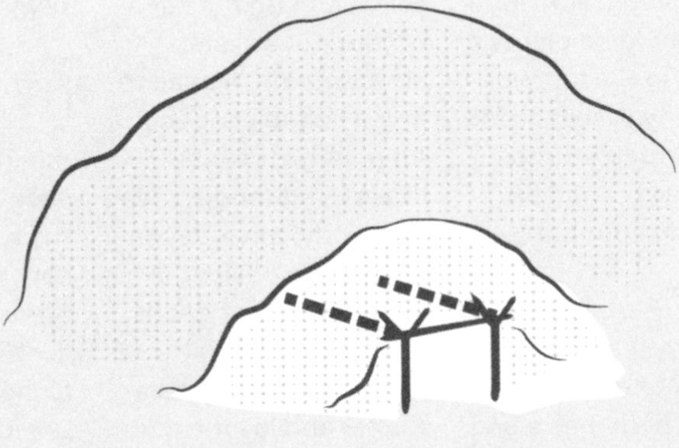

the ridgepole. If they do and it rains, they'll pull rainwater right into your "bed." Make the ribs and debris as steep as possible (while still allowing you to fit), which will help "sheet" rainwater off.

03 Create a lattice (1 hour). Lay down a latticework of small, crisscrossed sticks and twigs (pinkie size).

04 Spread debris over the frame (1–6 hours). Now it's time to insulate your hut well enough to create the dead airspace within. Scour the forest floor for pine needles, bark, leaves, grass, and other fallen plant matter.

Think you have enough debris? Put on twice as much. Aim for shoulder or head height (about 5–6 ft high); until then, it will have trouble withstanding heavy rain or wind and will not be warm enough to keep you alive in freezing temperatures.

And don't forget to insulate inside. The ground gets cold. Create a bed of needles, leaves, etc., in your hut to give you a buffer. Pack in all the extra insulation you can. If really cold, consider also packing debris inside your clothing, just as many New York City homeless people do with newspapers during the winter.

05 Create a side door entrance (30 minutes). To avoid creating a huge heat-sucking door where the ridgepole meets the stump, we sealed that off and instead created a side door, just big enough for our shoulders to fit (entering feet first). We pounded in two Y-shaped sticks, lay two sticks in them, which we pushed through to the opposite side, then we layered sticks and debris on top as we did everywhere else.

The tunnel to our "bed" was 2–3 feet long.

Leave some extra debris piled up at the tunnel entrance, so that when you slide into the hut feetfirst, you can gather the pile toward you and seal off the hut.

Sleep tight.

OPTIONAL LESSON

19

SKILL

WATER

MAKING DRINKABLE WATER

T-SHIRTS TO ROCK BOILING

HANDS-ON TIME

1–3 hours

TOTAL TIME

1–5 hours, unless you are waiting for rain, in which case it could be days.

GEAR

- Varies

> "Though it's a shame, what's been done to people these last hundred years: men turned into nothing but labour-insects, and all their manhood taken away, and all their real life."
>
> —CONNIE, *LADY CHATTERLEY'S LOVER*

Let's say you get to day two and still haven't been rescued. Going to bed, you can barely swallow due to dehydration. What do you do?

COLLECTION

If you can't find a natural "catch" (stream, pond, lake, etc.), there are a few things you can do:

A. Use the shirt off your back . . . literally. Sweep up the morning dew and wring it out into any vessel (a leaf, a jar, etc). If there's enough dew, you can easily collect a day's worth of water in an hour.

B. Build coal-burned bowls to catch rainwater. To make a coal-burned bowl, alternate between placing hot coals on the wood—I used sticks as chopsticks to rotate the coal—and digging out the charred black wood. If you have a good fire going, a bowl like the one below should take approximately 1–2 hours to make (softer wood like cedar = approximately one hour; harder wood like oak = up to 2–3 hours). How do you make the fire? See page 618 in the Appendix.

B. COAL-BURNED BOWL AND SPOON

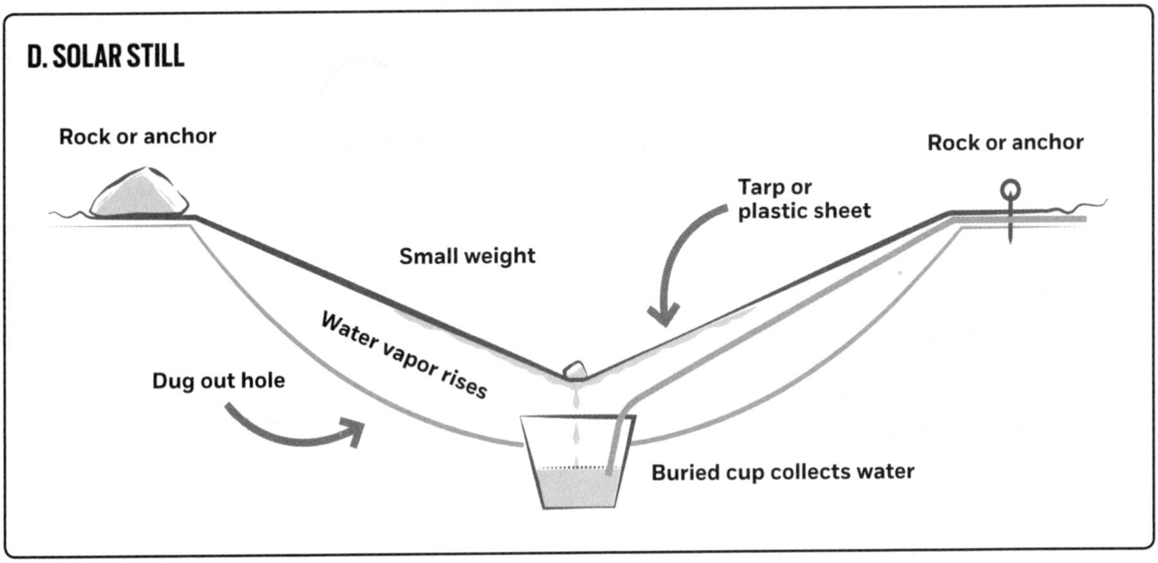
D. SOLAR STILL
Rock or anchor
Rock or anchor
Tarp or
plastic sheet
Small weight
Water vapor rises
Dug out hole
Buried cup collects water

C. Use a tarp-based catch for rainwater.
The tarp can protect you while it collects water, and the greater surface area collects far more water than bowls alone.

D. Build a solar still.
Designed by two physicians working for the U.S. Department of Agriculture in Arizona, the "solar still" is an ingenious method for both collecting and purifying (distilling) water simultaneously. If you carry a 6 x 6–ft plastic drop cloth while hiking, as commonly used under a tent, you're in business. The still can gather about a quart a day.

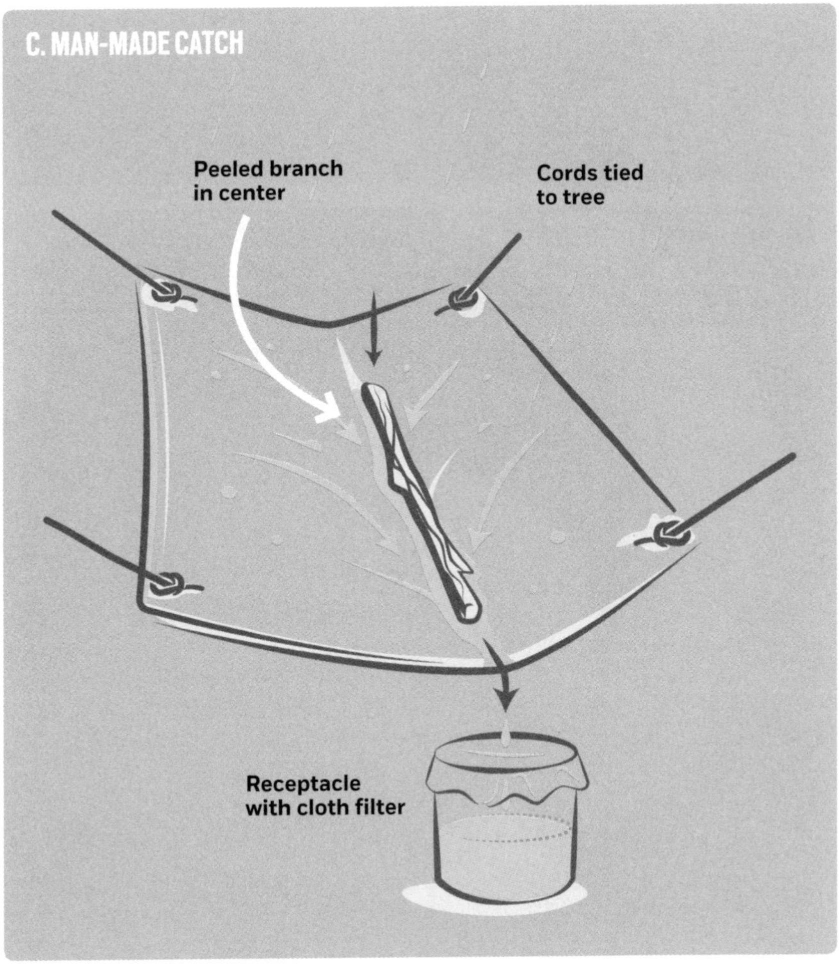
C. MAN-MADE CATCH
Peeled branch
in center
Cords tied
to tree
Receptacle
with cloth filter

1
2

The metal pot pictured above was used for convenience; in survival circumstances, another coal-burned wooden container would obviously be used.

PURIFICATION

Practically speaking, if you're suffering from severe dehydration, drinking murky water is better than dying. That said, if you have the means, you should purify before you ingest.

You can boil water, thus purifying it, using hot rocks. "Rock boiling" is Cliff's preferred method, and it can be used to purify water and cook food simultaneously.

Cooking in liquid retains all of the nutrients and calories from vegetables and meat. This is unlike spit roasting, for instance, where fats and liquids can drip off.[7]

The following assumes you've already built a decent fire.

00 First, create 2 large coal-burned bowls, as described on the previous pages, and fill them with water.

01 Put 1–2 dozen grapefruit-size rocks into your fire for 1–2 hours to heat them.

02 Remove the hot rocks from the fire, using 2 large sticks as tongs. Dunk the rocks into the first container of water for rinsing, then quickly move them to the second container for cooking and purifying water.

03 After your first 3–5 rocks lose their heat, rotate in 3–5 new rocks to keep the water boiling.

7 That said, spit roasting, which we'll cover later, is far faster. It requires neither containers nor water.

CLIFF NOTES

Feeling bitten by the bug of survival skills? There's a lot of reality-show BS out there. Cliff suggests the following resources.

BOOKS:

Survival Skills of Native California by Paul Campbell (fourhourchef.com/campbell). "Definitely the most legendary survival skills book of all time."

Bows & Arrows of the Native Americans: A Step-by-Step Guide to Wooden Bows, Sinew-backed Bows, Composite Bows, Strings, Arrows & Quivers by Jim Hamm (fourhourchef.com/hamm).

Shelter by Lloyd Kahn (fourhourchef.com/kahn). This 176-page book covers just about every shelter and terrain imaginable. Cliff describes it (and I agree) thus: "It's a large 12" x 18" book that looks like *The Anarchist's Cookbook*—old crusty photos mixed with handwritten notes. It's totally weird but totally awesome, and it discusses everything from tepees and pueblo cliff dwellings, to yurts, tree houses, and African mud shelters."

TRAINING:

Here are three outfits that pass muster:

PAST Skills Wilderness Training (MT)
pastskills.com
Founded by Bill McConnell, et al.

Roots School (VT)
rootsvt.com
Founded by Brad Salon, et al.

Adventure Out (CA)
adventureout.com
Founded by Cliff Hodges

THE ANTI-HUNTER'S FIRST HUNT

> "Subsistence hunters are among the happiest, most respectful and knowledgeable people that I have met. Needing nothing but their skills and their senses to score a good meal, they are happy because—in this respect at least—they are truly free."
>
> —*THE WILD GOURMETS: ADVENTURES IN FOOD & FREEDOM*, BY GUY GRIEVE AND THOMASINA MIERS

6 A.M., SOUTH CAROLINA

An animal's response to your shot tells you a lot.

"If you hit the lung or heart, fatal wounds, a deer will first pop up as if hearing a loud noise. If you hit the hindquarters or other innards, the deer will first drop down, which means a bad shot and a bad meal. It will run, especially if you're stupid enough to chase it. If a wounded animal flees, give it an hour to die. Stressing the animal by chasing it can lead to off-tasting meat and, sometimes, a condition known to beef processors as a 'red cutter.'"[8]

Steve Rinella's tutelage in all things hunting was encyclopedic. My 6 a.m. brain struggled to absorb a motley assortment of miscellanea:

- Deer are classified as "crepuscular"; in simple terms, they move mostly at dawn and at dusk.
- Kiefer Sutherland was once swindled in a cattle-rustling Ponzi scheme.
- If Steve could eat only one meat for the rest of his life—a monthly 50-lb allotment of any wild or domesticated animal—it would absolutely be elk. Specifically, cow elk or young bull elk.
- The original version of *The Joy of Cooking* had instructions for how to fatten a trapped opossum with milk and cereals for 10 days before slaughtering and cooking it.
- The neck of a male deer in mating mode (a "rutty buck") can double in size, making it look like a linebacker.
- Skinning a rabbit is easier than taking off your socks—grab the scruff and peel, pulling down toward the head. Eating rabbits requires caution, though, as you can die from tularemia, an infectious disease named after Tulare County in California.

Steve is as down-to-earth as you would hope any good hunter to be, but he didn't fit my stereotype. For instance, he applies physics terms to skinning. And most relevant to my food quest, as he put it: "There are far better chefs out there than me. There are far better hunters out there, too. But there aren't many who can combine the two like I do." He is a master of turning the wild into "ingredients" people recognize. In 2004, he prepared a three-day, *45-course* banquet from Escoffier's landmark 1903 classic, *Le Guide Culinaire*.[9]

8 More commonly known as "dark cutter" meat, it occurs when the animal's adrenaline level is high prior to slaughter. This changes the pH balance of the meat and makes it dark and hard.

9 Steve doesn't use "wild game cookbooks," nor does he recommend them. His favorite chef is Jacques Pépin, whom he jokingly refers to as "Jack" Pepin. His favorite book on curing meats is *Charcuterie* by Michael Ruhlman and Thomas Keller.

By "prepare," I mean that he foraged, killed, or otherwise procured every ingredient from the outdoors . . . then re-created the feast himself, which took more than a week. This experiment was chronicled in his first book, *The Scavenger's Guide to Haute Cuisine*. He started trapping for income in rural Michigan when he was 10. Now 38, he writes for a living, and his work is as likely to be seen in *The New York Times* as in *Field and Stream*.

Now, he and I were sitting 20 ft above the ground in a deer blind dressed like a ghillie suit. Semitransparent camouflage netting draped down around the four sides of our 10 x 10–ft wilderness cubicle, hung over horizontal poles that reached our chins. There was, inexplicably, a nice office chair in one corner, completely out of place and therefore appropriate for me to use.

It was a stunning vista, covered in dew and shrouded in early-morning mist. There were three wide lanes of vibrant green grass that extended in front of us and to both sides like three driving ranges. Trees comprised the borders, shooting skyward as entrances to the South Carolina forest. And so we watched the edges. I swept from right to left, the opposite of our conditioned left to right, so as not to miss any details.

Twenty minutes in, Steve nudged me with his elbow and handed me the binoculars, which were much easier to scan with than the scope atop the rifle in my hands. He pointed my eyes in the right direction, where I saw a faint shadow.

"See how he's moving in circles?" Steve whispered. "I think it's a buck working a scrape." To "work a scrape," bucks first hook an overhanging branch with their antlers and rub it against their frontal gland, on the forehead. Next, especially during the breeding season, they paw a "scrape" out of the earth and pee down their rear legs over their tarsal glands. This scenting is thought to be advertising for receptive does, and bucks might repeat the drill up to 100 times in a single square mile.

The ranch owner hosting us had requested we not shoot young bucks, those with antlers inside the ears. At 200 yards, even with binoculars, it was hard to tell what we were looking at in the pinkish haze of dawn. So we waited for the sun. Our quarry would probably wander back into the protective silhouettes of the pine trees.

The custom rifle I held was Steve's. It rested snugly, perfectly balanced like a fine knife. I had no fatigue, and the barrel didn't wobble, despite my heart-pounding nervousness. The morning light crept in slowly, brightening the greens a few degrees of resolution at a time. I scanned through the scope, my mind focused and atypically quiet; a rare vacation from my own internal noise.

Before I knew it, before I had a chance to consider or evaluate, Steve pointed to a well-lit spot within 100 yards. A beautiful doe, a female and fair game, had suddenly emerged.

"There she is. Kill that deer."

I already had the scope on her when he said it. The crosshairs were just behind the shoulder blade as Steve had instructed.

The gun bounced skyward and there was no further thought.

Did I miss? I immediately resighted as Steve said, "You got her." Her legs kicked in the air, the tall grass hiding most of her body, and I felt a wave of terror wash over me: Fuck—did I simply injure her? Everything I'd learned to hate about hunting flashed through my mind. Growing up on Long Island and watching deer struggle across our land with arrows stuck in them. Deer dying on our property because bow hunters couldn't get the job done or simply didn't care. The beer cans littered on the side of the road, next to trucks outfitted with hunting racks. I was suddenly furious with myself. I'd become one of the things I most despised.

Then, she stopped kicking.

It was all over, and no more than 10 seconds had passed.

I let out a long exhale of relief.

Unlike the assholes I'd wanted to shoot at as a kid, though I never owned a gun, this wasn't where my hunt would end.

This is where my first hunt started.

The shot, a bull's-eye. Steve turned back to me. "Eighty-seven yards." He'd confirmed the shooting distance by aiming his Leica 1600 laser range finder back at the blind.

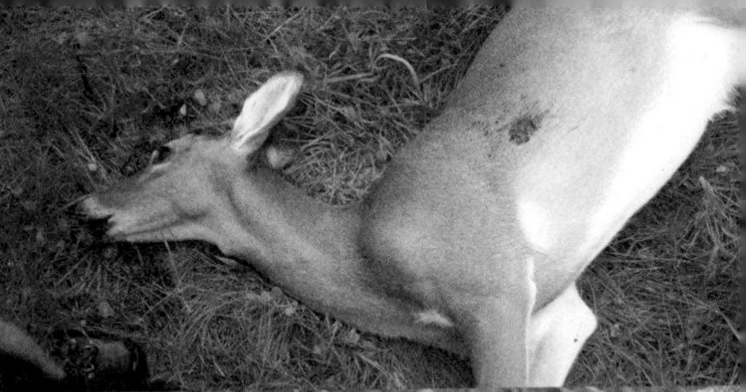

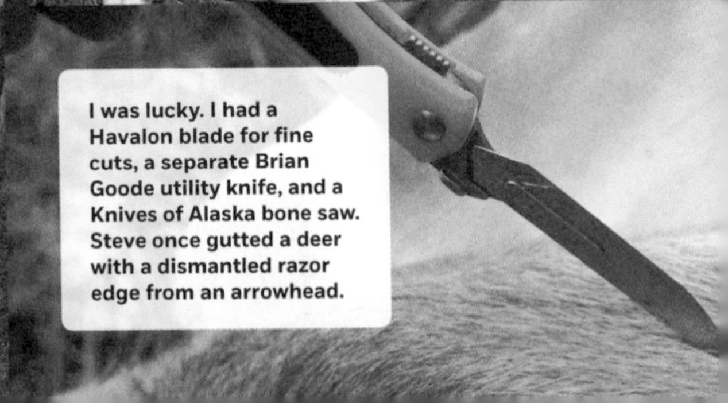

I was lucky. I had a Havalon blade for fine cuts, a separate Brian Goode utility knife, and a Knives of Alaska bone saw. Steve once gutted a deer with a dismantled razor edge from an arrowhead.

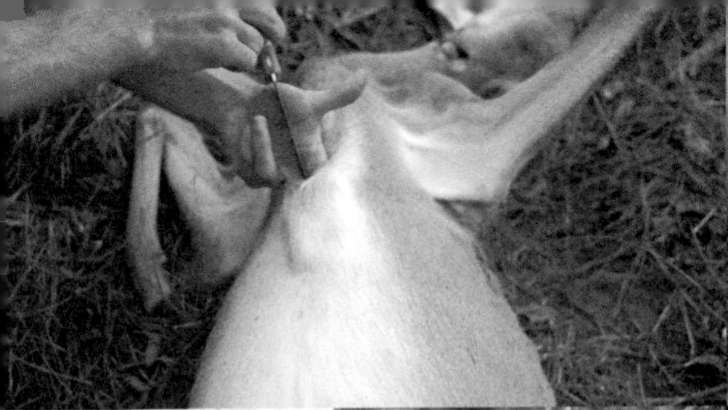

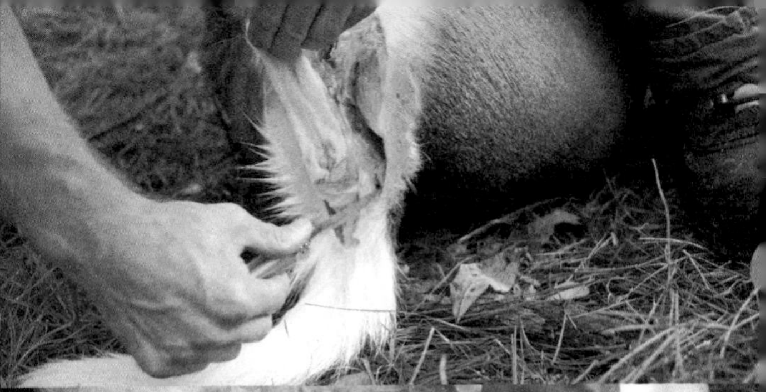

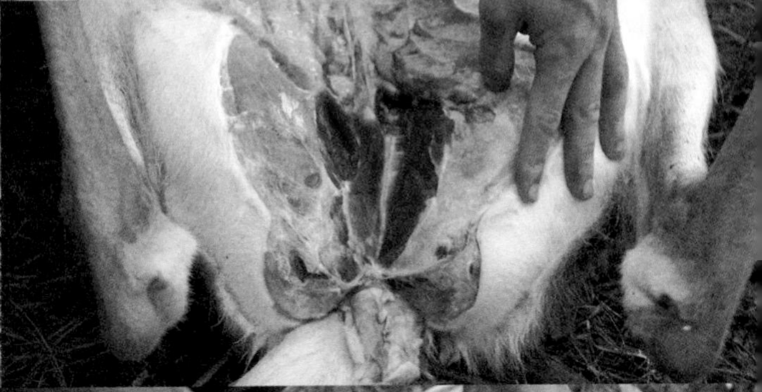

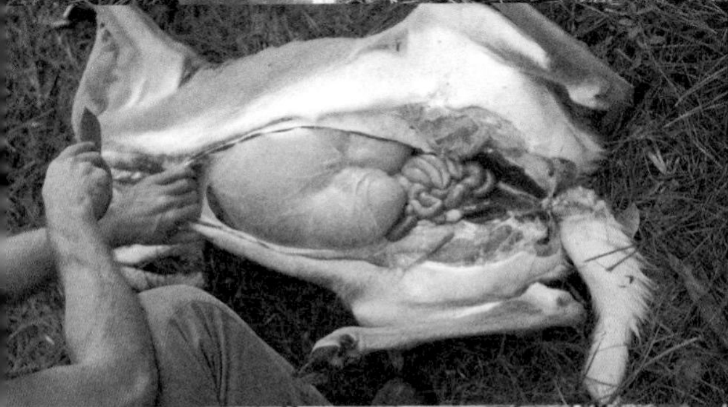

Before scheduling my hunt, I vowed not to romanticize it. I had no desire to be Hemingway, nor to glamorize killing. But something very odd did happen: 30 seconds into gutting the deer, once my hands were inside and heated, it felt like second nature. The anxiety vanished, and I was inexplicably good at it. How do any animals in isolation know how to behave, how to hunt, how to do anything? Hardwiring, I suppose. I've never experienced anything like it.

The heart is an excellent muscle to eat first, followed by the tenderloin, which has big, loose fibers. The latter gets too dried out after hanging and doesn't need to be aged for tenderness. Organ meat, as a rule, is best eaten fresh rather than frozen.

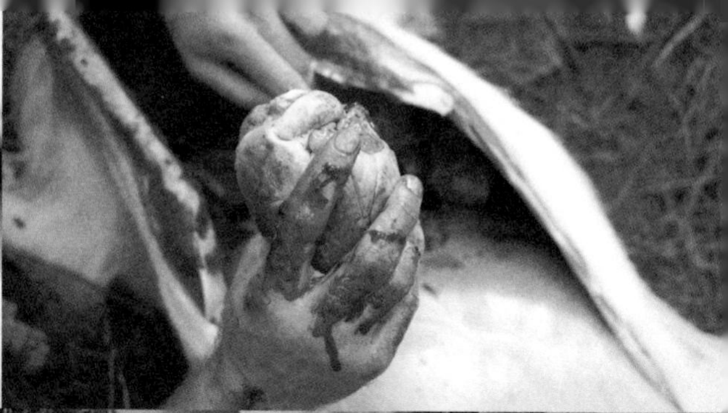

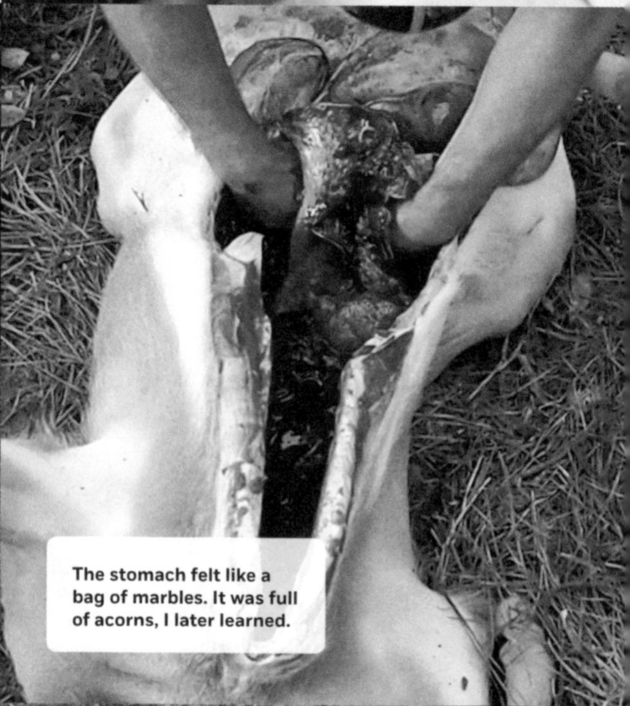

The stomach felt like a bag of marbles. It was full of acorns, I later learned.

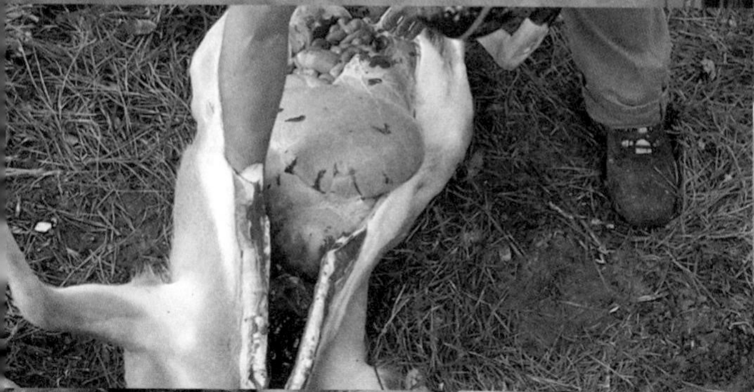

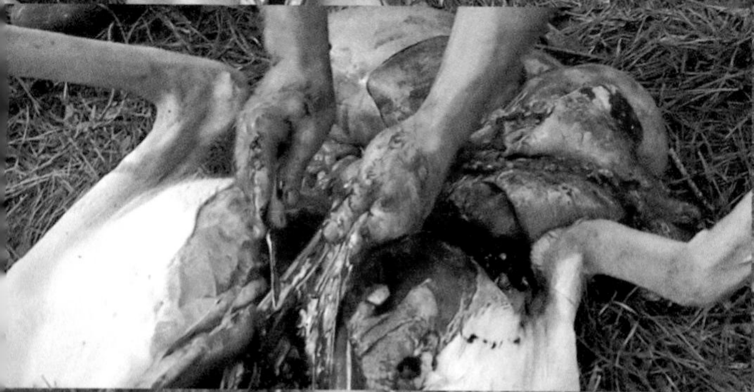

If you dislike the term *gutting*, you can use the Gaelic equivalent, which you'll hear in the U.K.: *gralloching*.

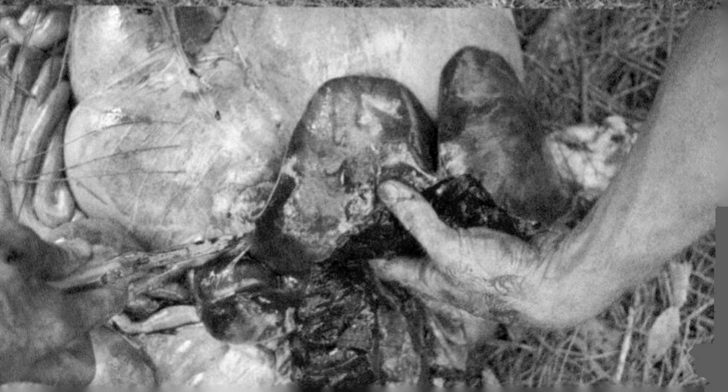

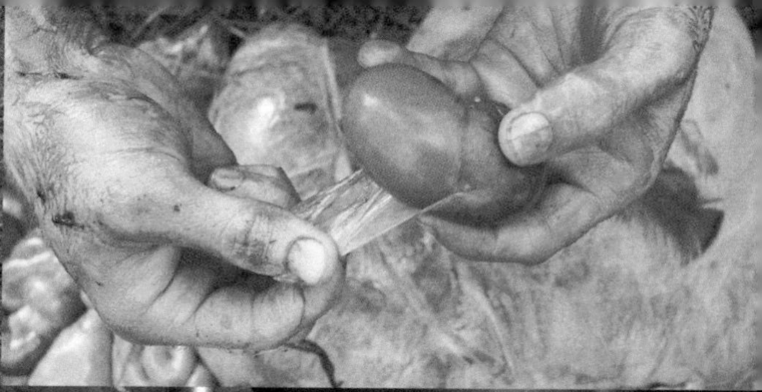

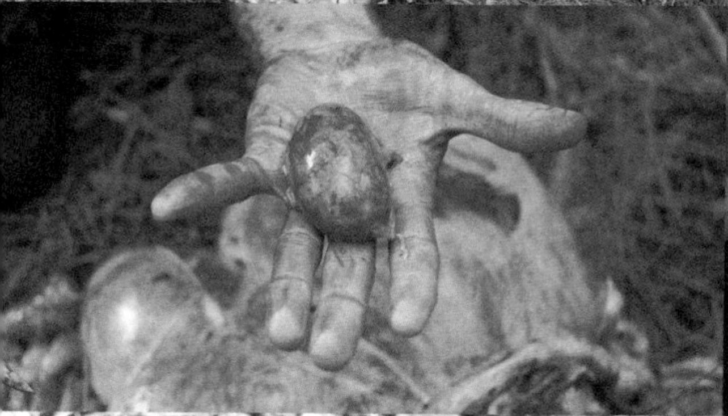

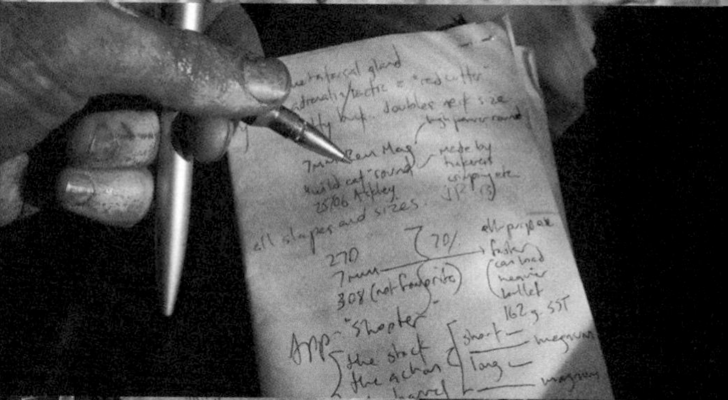
all shapes and sizes
270
7mm
308
"Shooter"
the stock
the action
162 g. SST

Break from dismembering to play with dog.

ICE
ICE

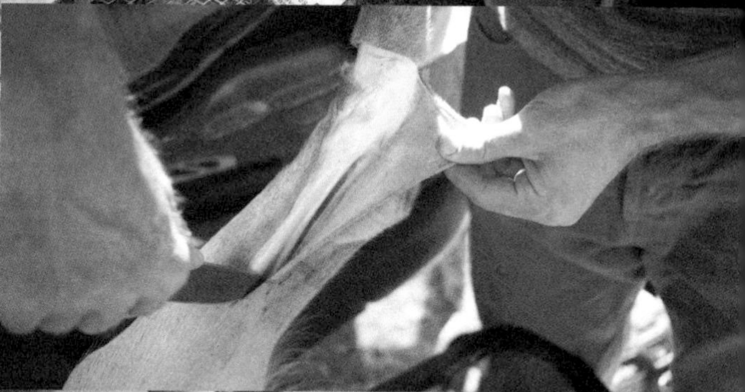

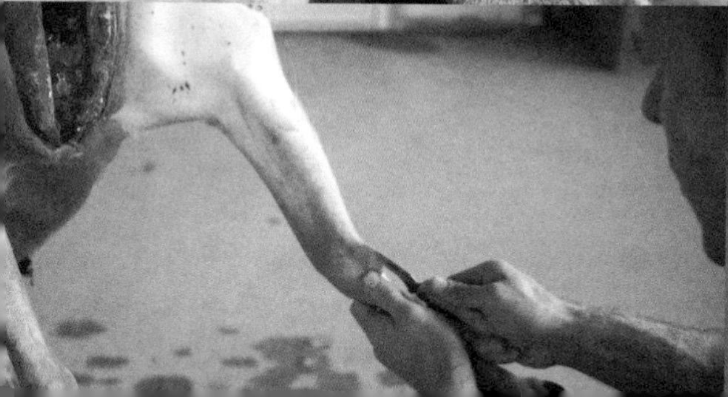

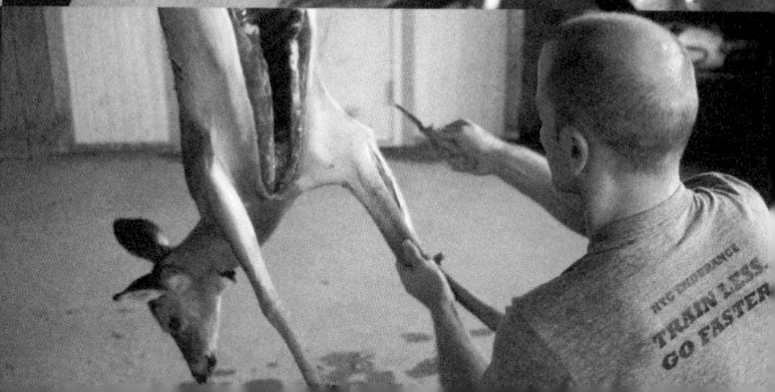
TRAIN LESS
GO FASTER

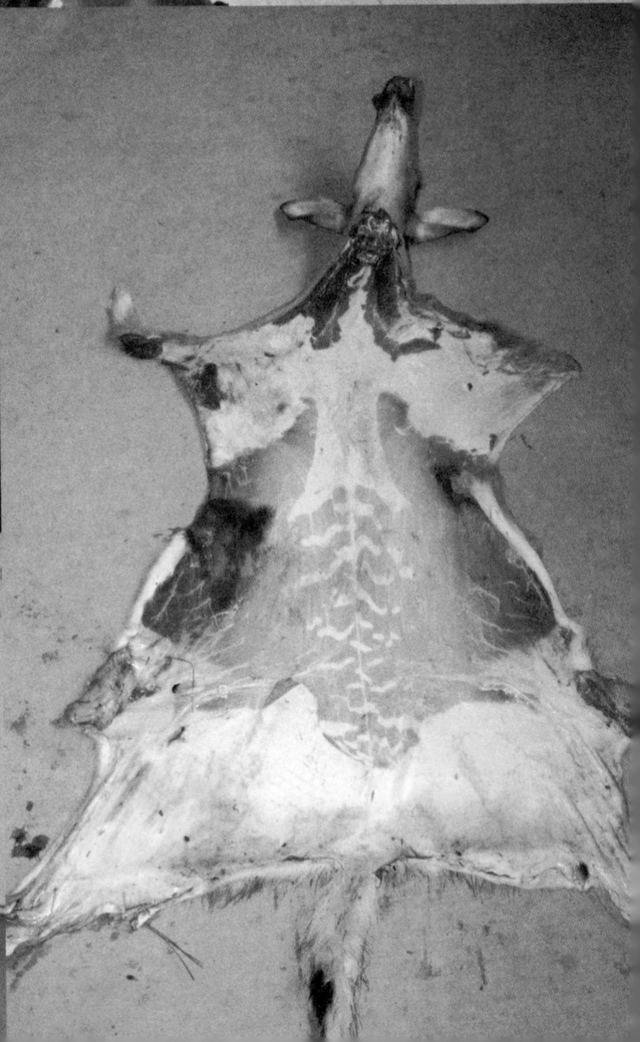

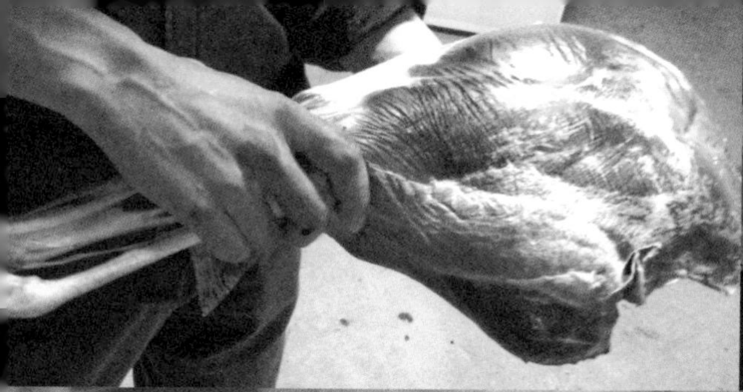

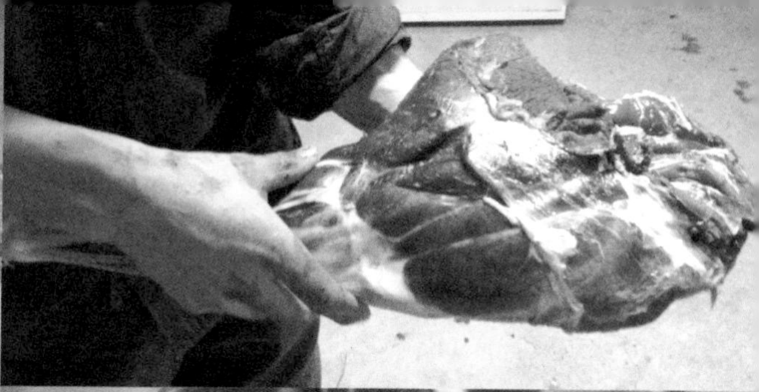

A healthy deer will yield roughly 40% of its weight in boneless meat.

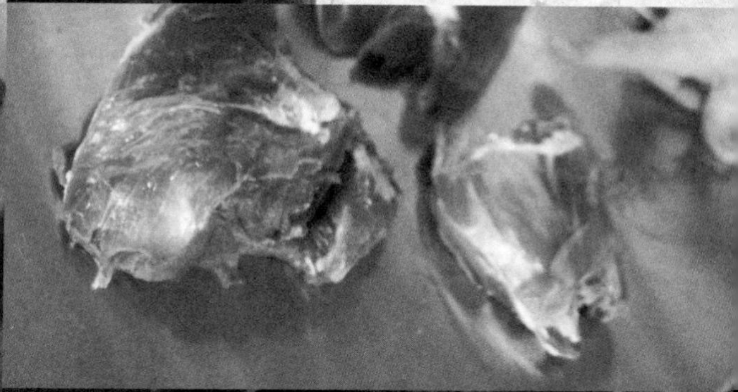

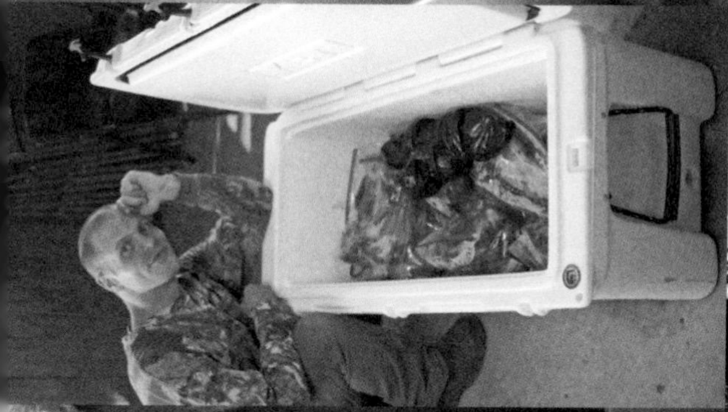

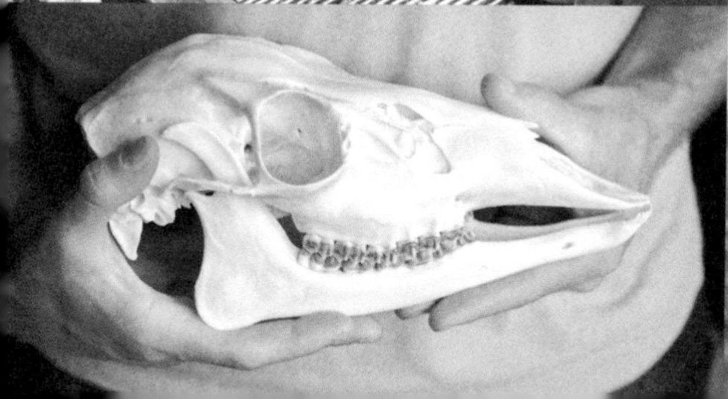

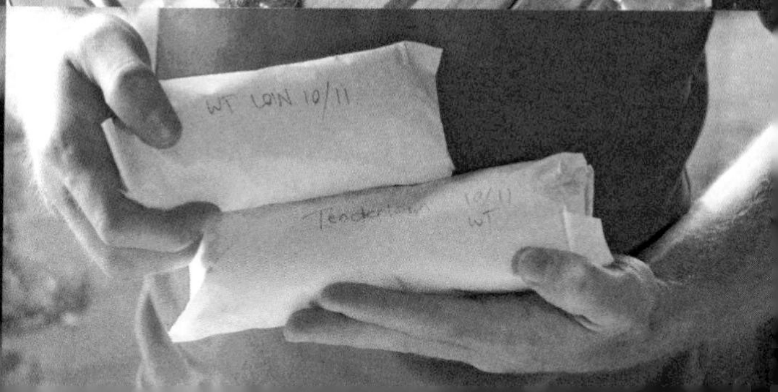
WT LOIN 10/11
Tenderloin 10/11 WT

THE GUN

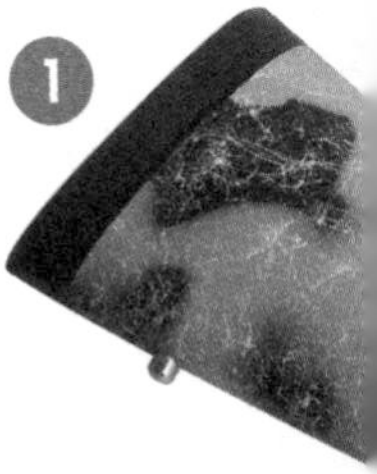
1

11

The 7mm Remington Magnum ("Rem Mag")

This is a custom rifle from David Amick of Carolina Custom Rifles (CCR). It is the right-handed version of Steve's gun.

I seldom splurge, but I did here. This fine-tuned machine is worth more than my VW Golf. To preface the sticker shock, I want to be clear: there are excellent, affordable, off-the-shelf options. Based on recommendations from full-time gun makers, below are three options for moderate weight (ultra-lightweight = ultra-hard kick), moderate cost, and high-accuracy rifles:[10]

Remington 700 (≈$900)

Remington Sendero (≈$879)

.280 Browning (≈$575)

Then you'd add $60–$70 for rings/bases (mounts) and a scope like the Vortex Viper PST 4-16x50 FFP, which Steve uses on his custom rifle, and which I therefore used for my first kill. Configured thus, you can easily hit a kill zone on a deer at 100 yards. Do *not* skimp on mounts. A great rifle and great scope with shitty mounts = a shitty gun. The smallest thing can turn a great gun into a useless gun, much like the O-ring on the Challenger. Since good mounts only cost $60–$70, get the best you can.

Preamble complete, here's my baby. Notice the engraved name (opposite close-up):

1.

HS-Precision Stock in Tan/Black Camo.

2.

Stiller *action*.[11]

3.

Spiral fluted bolt and tactical bolt knob.

4.

Hart match-grade barrel with helical fluting and 26" finish. The helical fluting reduces weight and improves heat dissipation. Plus, it looks amazing.

5.

Upgraded BDL bottom metal—this is what "marries" the action to the stock.

6.

Timney trigger adjusted to 2½ lbs pull to improve accuracy. Most factory triggers fall in the 4–5-lb range.

7.

Talley rings and bases.

8.

Scope lens cover.

9.

Black duracoat finish and personalized engraving.

Rifle total: $4,100

10.

Schmidt & Bender Precision Hunter 4-16x50 scope, favored by Marine snipers for their official-issue Rem 700s (i.e., M40): $2,500.

11.

RipSling survival sling (braiding made of 60+ ft of multipurpose 550 paracord): $120 (ripcordsurvival.com).

12.

50 rounds of custom ammo developed specifically for this gun: $100.

13.

A 7mm *round* (also called a *cartridge*): this refers to the combination of the casing, bullet, powder, and primer.

You put a round into a gun; the bullet is what comes out of the barrel.

14.

A used 7mm shell—this is the actual shell left after my deer shot.

15.

Plano hard-shell tactical gun guard (not pictured): $175.

Complete package: $6,995

Pushing the limits, this gun allows me to shoot at targets up to the max range of the scope: 600 yards (approximately ⅓ mile or 0.6 km).

Custom Ammo

How and why does David make custom ammo? "Every rifle has its own 'palette,'" he explains, "meaning it likes certain brands of powder, certain brands of bullets, and it likes them seated at a certain overall length. Finding the perfect recipe is sometimes a laborious task. But when you find it, your rifle will reward you with great groups at the range or dependable shots in the field."

In more detail: "Load development for every rifle starts at 100 yards. Once perfected (= ½" groupings), it is sighted in at the customer's preferred yardage, usually a 200-yard zero, like your rifle. On your rifle, the load was chronographed and run through a ballistic program to calculate the flight of your bullet out to 600 yards (which is the turret range capacity of your scope). This info, or the 'drop chart,' is put on the rifle, engraved into a custom turret, or carried by the shooter to the range or field so they can effectively practice and hunt out to those yardages."

---

10 Assuming you've sighted properly, of course.

11 The *action* is the physical mechanism that loads/manipulates the cartridge.

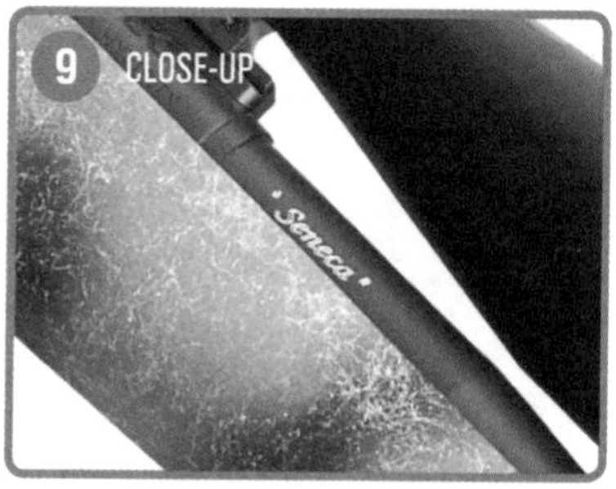
9 CLOSE-UP
Seneca

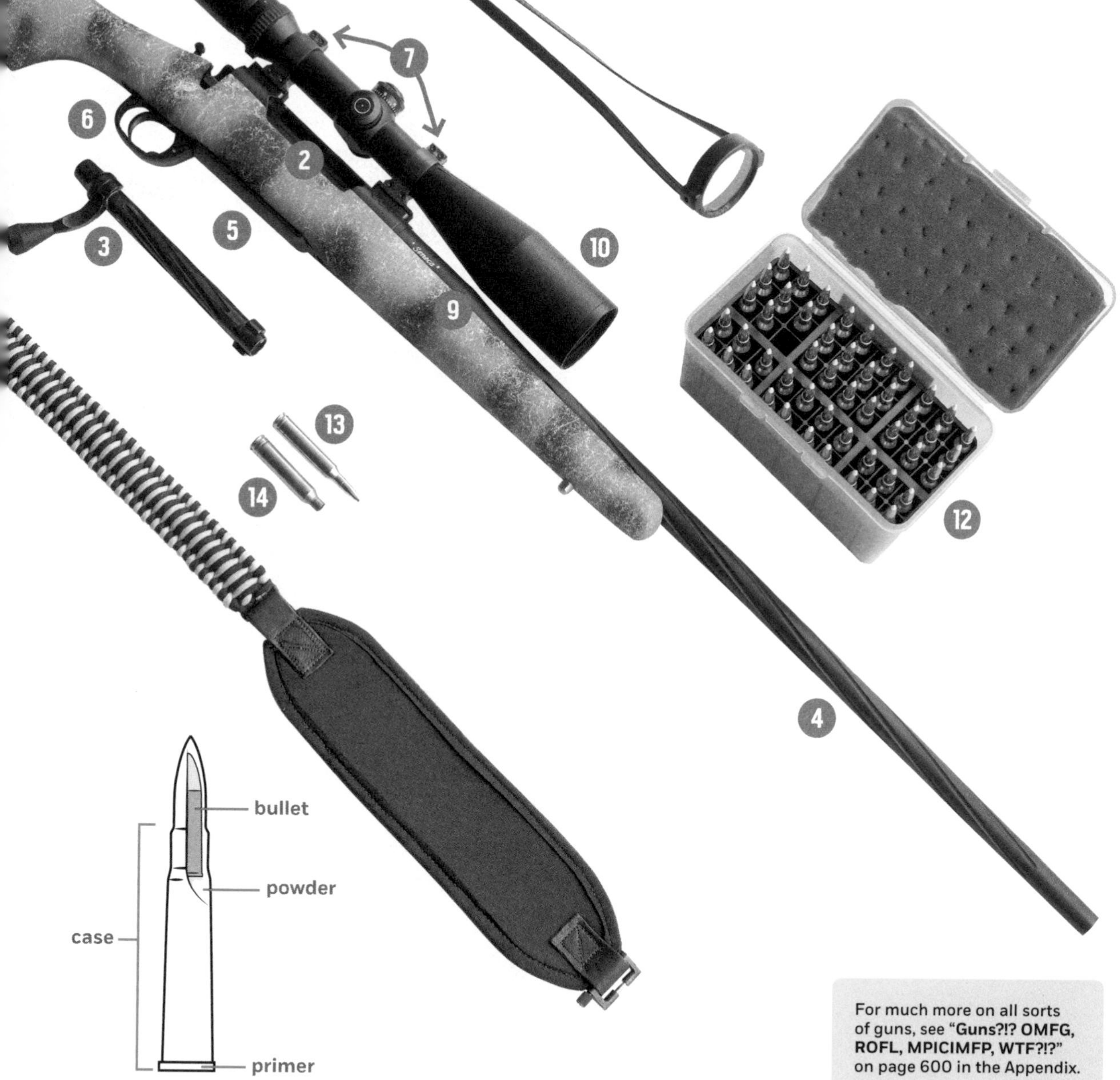
8
7
6
2
3
5
10
9
13
14
12
4
bullet
powder
case
primer

For much more on all sorts of guns, see **"Guns?!? OMFG, ROFL, MPICIMFP, WTF?!?"** on page 600 in the Appendix.

TOP 10 U.S. HUNTS ACCORDING TO STEVE RINELLA

What follows is meant to serve as a guide, but it's not comprehensive. Don't underestimate what's involved with hunts like these, regardless of difficulty level.

There are far too many rules and other considerations—property lines, the weather, how much hunter orange you're required to wear, etc.—to list everything here. In the field, ignorance is no excuse. Game laws change every year, and it's up to you to be informed. The best place to start is each state's hunting regulations, or "proclamation," invariably found on the respective state's game department website. There's also an extensive network of fish and game employees whose job it is to help you. Not only is it in your best interest to be prepared, it's in the best interest of the game we pursue.

Be respectful, be responsible, and be safe.

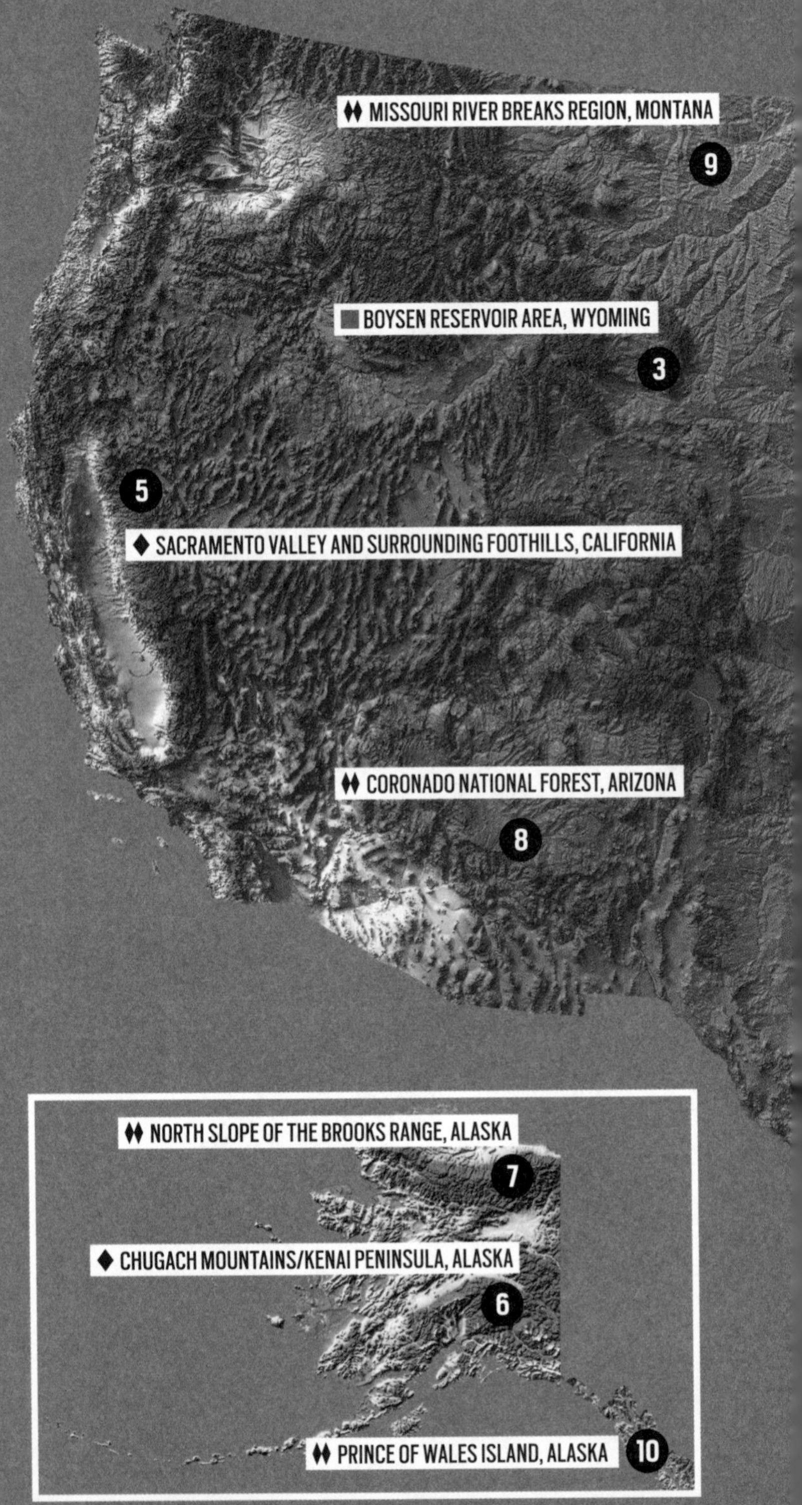

MISSOURI RIVER BREAKS REGION, MONTANA
9
BOYSEN RESERVOIR AREA, WYOMING
3
5
SACRAMENTO VALLEY AND SURROUNDING FOOTHILLS, CALIFORNIA
CORONADO NATIONAL FOREST, ARIZONA
8
NORTH SLOPE OF THE BROOKS RANGE, ALASKA
7
CHUGACH MOUNTAINS/KENAI PENINSULA, ALASKA
6
PRINCE OF WALES ISLAND, ALASKA
10

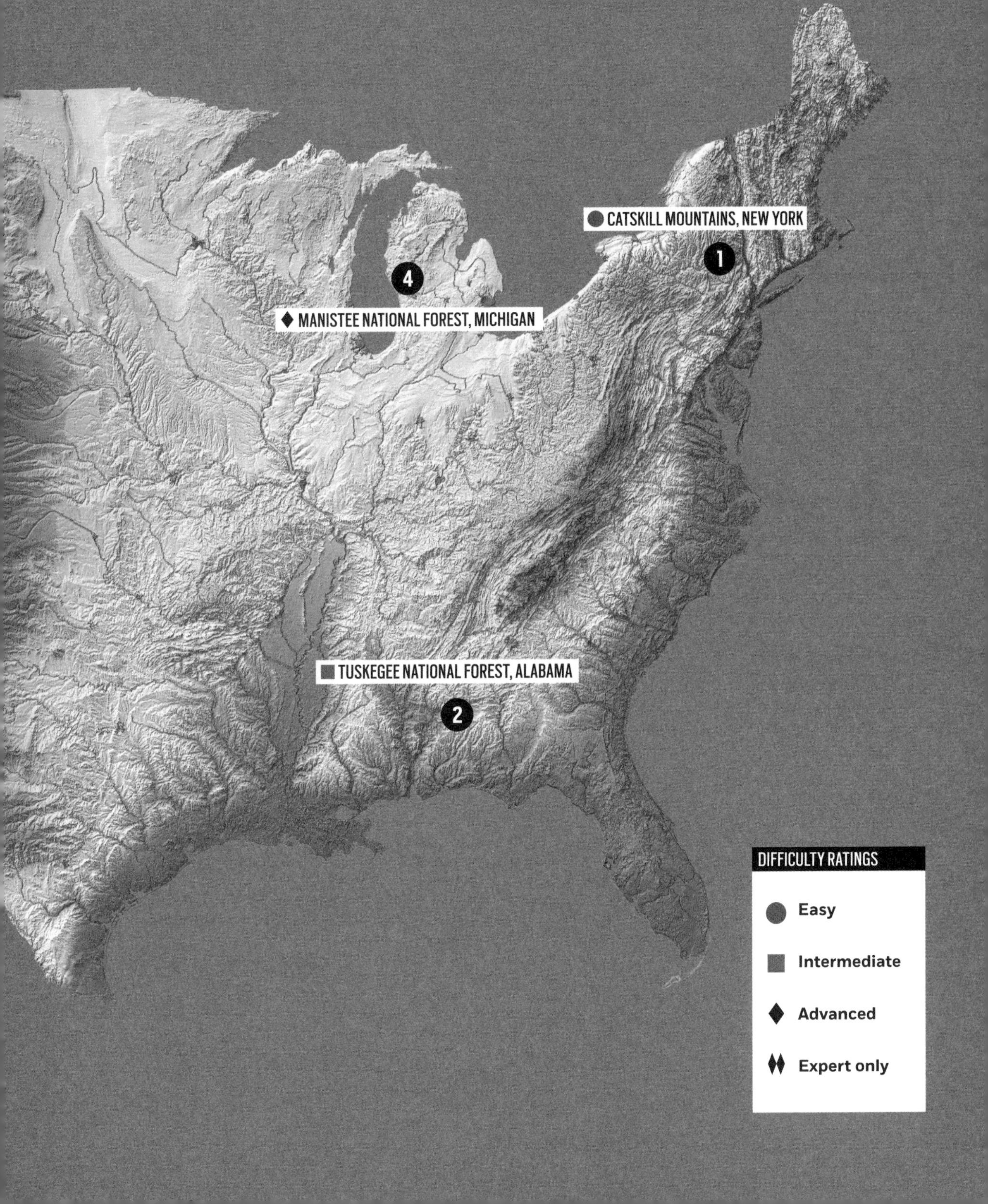
CATSKILL MOUNTAINS, NEW YORK
1
4
MANISTEE NATIONAL FOREST, MICHIGAN
TUSKEGEE NATIONAL FOREST, ALABAMA
2
DIFFICULTY RATINGS
Easy
Intermediate
Advanced
Expert only

1 ●

CATSKILL MOUNTAINS, NEW YORK

Squirrels

Difficulty: 1

Season: Sept. 1–Feb. 28, though I particularly like January and February.

Weapon of choice: .22 rifle or shotgun (any gauge) loaded with #6 shot.

Permits: Small game license.

Special equipment: A squirrel call can come in handy. The Primos Squirrel Buster and the Knight & Hale 4-in-1 Squirrel Call are both good bets and can be found at basspro.com.

2 ■

TUSKEGEE NATIONAL FOREST, ALABAMA

Whitetail Deer

Difficulty: 2

Season: Oct. 15–Jan. 31

Weapon of choice: Scoped rifle ranging in caliber from a .243 to a .300.

Permits: Hunting license.

Special equipment: A tree stand is a must. Visit Bass Pro Shops to find a stand that matches your budget. Many companies make great tree stands. API Outdoors Alumi-Tech Climbing Treestand is one of the best (basspro.com).

3 ■

BOYSEN RESERVOIR AREA, WYOMING

Cottontail Rabbits

Difficulty: 2

Season: Sept. 1–Mar. 1; I recommend going when there's snow, as being able to find fresh tracks aids tremendously in locating the animals' hangouts.

Weapon of choice: .22 caliber rifle, preferably with a scope.

Permits: Small game license (residents). Combination game bird and small game license (nonresidents).

Special equipment: My strategy here is to walk slowly through good areas while looking for rabbits that are out basking in the winter sun. Good binoculars are very helpful in spotting these well-concealed critters.

4 ◆

MANISTEE NATIONAL FOREST, MICHIGAN

Ruffed Grouse

Difficulty: 3

Season: Sept. 15–Nov. 14 and Dec. 1–Jan. 1.

Weapon of choice: 20-gauge or 12-gauge shotgun, loaded with #7½ shot.

Permits: Small game license.

Special equipment: A dog trained for flushing and retrieving "upland" birds is a great asset, though hardly mandatory.

5 ◆

SACRAMENTO VALLEY AND SURROUNDING FOOTHILLS, CALIFORNIA

Wild Hogs

Difficulty: 3, largely because of access issues.

Season: In California, there is no closed season on wild pigs; you can chase them all year.

Weapon of choice: Scoped rifle ranging in caliber from a .243 to a .300. Plan on shots from 10–300 yards.

Permits: California hunting license and wild pig tag (dfg.ca.gov).

Special equipment: When hunting in hot weather, you need a solid plan for keeping the meat cool and clean once you've made a kill. Bring along several large coolers filled with gallon-size jugs of frozen water.

6 ◆

CHUGACH MOUNTAINS/ KENAI PENINSULA, ALASKA

Black Bears

Difficulty: 4, due to environmental conditions.

Season: Though it's possible to hunt black bears year-round, it's best to pursue them in late summer when they're loaded with fat.

Weapon of choice: .270 and 7mm Rem Mag, on up to .300 Win Mag. Don't be afraid to aim for the front shoulder on bears. If you aim for the ribs, as is common, they don't leave a good blood trail (due to body fat, etc.), and you don't want to end up chasing a wounded bear. Aiming for the shoulder will increase the likelihood of hitting vitals like the heart (which are located further forward than in a deer), and it will also drop them where they stand.

Permits: Hunting license, bear tag, and a metal locking tag if you're a nonresident.

Special equipment: A comfortable frame pack capable of handling heavy loads of meat is a must. I prefer those with expandable pods to accommodate extra gear. The Optics Hunter, by Outdoorsmans (outdoorsmans.com), is a superb pack.

7 ◆◆

NORTH SLOPE OF THE BROOKS RANGE, ALASKA

Caribou

Difficulty: 5, due to many factors.

Season: Mid-September is ideal, as you might get lucky and hit that elusive sweet spot between mosquito season and winter.

Weapon of choice: A .270 is great, but don't go much smaller. Something in the .30-06 or 7mm Rem Mag category is ideal. A .300 Win Mag is not too much gun.

Permits: Hunting license, caribou tag, and a metal locking tag if you're a nonresident.

Special equipment: Good-fitting rubber knee boots are lifesavers on this trip, as day upon day of tundra-soaked boots can take a toll on your mental outlook. The 16" insulated neoprene boot by XTRATUF (xtratufboots.com) is a great piece of footwear.

8

CORONADO NATIONAL FOREST, ARIZONA

Coues Whitetail Deer

Difficulty: 5

Season: There are four Coues deer seasons around Coronado National Forest that occur in weeklong blocks starting in late October and ending in late December. The most coveted tags are in December, which tend to coincide with the deer's breeding season, or rut. But numbers are limited, and demand is high. For a surer bet, try for the early season tags. Visit the Arizona Game and Fish Department website (azgfd.gov) for information on applying for tags.

Weapon of choice: Something capable of flat shooting, and no smaller than a .243. I like the .270 and 7mm Rem Mag.

Permits: Hunting license and Coues deer tag.

Special equipment: Good optics are an absolute must, and they need to be mounted on a tripod for maximum performance. The best place to find everything you need is Outdoorsmans (outdoorsmans.com), an iconic Phoenix sporting goods store that handles region-specific equipment. Another great asset would be a professional guide. Jay Scott (jayscottoutdoors.blogspot.com) is a personal friend and one of the best.

9

MISSOURI RIVER BREAKS REGION, MONTANA

Mule Deer

Difficulty: 5

Season: Montana's general deer season runs from late October to late November. The best time to hunt mule deer is usually during the third week of November, but at this time of year, you risk having the river freeze. Stay tuned to local conditions before embarking on this trip.

Weapon of choice: Flat-shooting calibers from .270 up to .300 Win Mag. The 7mm falls within this range.

Permits: Montana residents need a general deer license. Nonresidents need a general deer combination license. Applications must be submitted by mid-March for a fall hunt. See the Montana Department of Fish, Wildlife, and Parks website (fwp.mt.gov) for details. Additional information on the Breaks can be found at blm.gov/mt.

Special equipment: A hunting partner and a good canoe capable of carrying two people, camping gear, and meat. I like canoes in the 17-ft class, particularly those made by Old Town (oldtowncanoe.com).

10

PRINCE OF WALES ISLAND, ALASKA

Black-tailed Deer

Difficulty: 5

Season: Aug. 16–Dec. 31.

Weapon of choice: Scoped rifle ranging in caliber from a .243 to a .300. Plan on shots from 10–300 yards.

Permits: Hunting license, deer harvest tickets, and tag (for nonresidents).

Special equipment: High-quality hunting boots built for mountainous terrain. I recommend the Granite, by Schnee's (schnees.com).

For 10+ pages of material on these hunts, visit FOURHOURCHEF.COM/HUNTING-MAPS

STEVE'S CALIBER CHART

SIZE OF GAME (LBS)	COMMON CALIBERS	SAMPLE SPECIES
0–50	.17 HMR, .22 LR, .223 Rem	Squirrel, cottontail rabbit, jackrabbit
50–100	.22-250 Rem, .223 Rem, .243 Win	Collared peccary (javelina)
100–150	.243 Win, 6mm, .243 Win, .257 Roberts, .270 Win, .30-30, .30-06	Wild boar, pronghorn antelope, smaller whitetail deer
150–250	.25-06 Rem, .270 Win, 7mm-08 Rem, 7mm Rem Mag, .300 Wby, .308 Win, .30/06	Larger whitetail deer, mule deer
250–500	.270 Win, 7mm, .308 Win, .30-06	Black bear, caribou
500–1,000	.270 Win. 7mm, .308 Win, .338 Win, .30-06, .300 Mag	Elk, moose
1,000–2,000	.300 Mag, .338 Win, .375 H&H, .45-70	Bison (buffalo)

"This chart represents typical caliber selections for common game animals in North America. These are merely suggestions. There are bound to be overlaps, exceptions, and plenty of contradictory opinions. The above are what I consider to be safe, comfortable choices, and I leave the finer points to ballistics manuals and deer-camp debates. HMR = Hornady Magnum Rimfire; LR = Long Rifle; Rem = Remington; Win = Winchester; Mag = Magnum; Wby = Weatherby; H&H = Holland & Holland"

LESSON 20

SKILLS

BLENDING CUISINES, SALVAGING MEAT

VIETNAMESE VENISON BURGERS AND BAGNA CAUDA

INSPIRED BY

Elisabeth Rozin, Chris Cosentino, and Marco Canora

SHORTHAND

Mix 1lb venison, 1T fish sauce, 1t lemongrass, 1 mashed garlic clove, 1 pinch chile into 4 patties; sear in 1T grapeseed oil 3min per side. Sauté 1c EVOO, 1 garlic clove, 4 smashed anchovies 15min, serve w raw veg.

HANDS-ON TIME

20 minutes

TOTAL TIME

20 minutes

GEAR

- Immersion blender with chopper attachment
- Nonstick skillet
- Silicone spatula
- Cast-iron skillet
- Peltex
- Dipping bowl

OPTIONAL MUSIC PAIRING

♪ "Final Home" by DJ Krush (featuring Esthero)

"Whoa, whoa, whoa! There's still plenty of meat on that bone. Now you take this home, throw it in a pot, add some broth, a potato . . . baby, you've got a stew going!"

—CARL WEATHERS, *ARRESTED DEVELOPMENT*

Now, to the cooking!

I once annihilated a piece of venison, overcooking it to the point of no return.

Unwilling to toss it, I looked for a means of resurrecting it. I polled my readers, put it in an immersion blender's chopper attachment, minced it into ground meat, and added it to eggs the following morning (the venison had already been seasoned with Montreal steak rub). It was *amazing*.

Using the same technique to mince raw venison (or beef) using your chopper attachment, you can enjoy the unnatural union of "Vietnamese" venison burgers and classic Italian *bagna cauda*.

Bagna cauda first blew me away at Chris Cosentino's Incanto, where it was served with the fractal-like Romanesco broccoli.

The combination of Vietnamese flavors, venison, and *bagna cauda* is as delicious as hamburger with almond butter, a strange combination that, like this one, just works.

You can serve the burger with no bun for a slow-carb meal, but on a cheat day, indulge in Martin's Potato Rolls, used by the legendary Shake Shack in New York City (toasted and buttered, of course).

Romanesco, technically a variant of cauliflower, has a nuttier and creamier flavor.

Grapeseed
Partanna
RED BOAT

INGREDIENTS	TO SERVE 4
FOR THE BURGERS	
Venison chunks (or beef—ideally an 80% lean/20% fat blend of sirloin and chuck, short rib, or brisket)	**1 lb (0.5 kg)**
Fish sauce, preferably a sugar-free brand such as Red Boat or Rufina (Vietnamese cuisine would traditionally call for nuoc mam, a mixed fish sauce, but it contains sugar)	**1 T**
Crumbled dried lemongrass (hard to find)**, or 1½ t fresh lemongrass**	**1 t**
Garlic	**1 large clove**
Hot red chile flakes	**3-finger pinch**
Grapeseed oil	**1 T**
FOR THE *BAGNA CAUDA*	
EVOO	**1 c (240 ml)**
Chopped garlic	**1 small clove**
Anchovy fillets (smashed; don't use paste)	**4**
S+P	**To taste**
Raw (or lightly cooked) **vegetables, such as broccoli and cauliflower florets, carrot sticks, fennel slices, or asparagus**	

PREP

00 Using chopper attachment, blend the 1 lb (0.5 kg) meat, 1 T fish sauce, 1 t lemongrass, 1 clove garlic, and a 3-finger pinch of chile flakes until thoroughly combined. Form into 4 (½"/1.25-cm-thick) patties.

PICKUP

00 To make the *bagna cauda*, combine the 1 c (240 ml) EVOO, 1 clove garlic, and 4 anchovies in a nonstick skillet. Cook over low heat for 15 minutes, stirring occasionally.

01 Meanwhile, cook the burgers. Heat the 1 T grapeseed oil in a cast-iron skillet over medium-high heat. When the oil shimmers, add the patties and cook without touching them for 3 minutes on one side, or until the bottom is nicely browned. Flip the patties and cook on the second side for about 3 minutes, until nicely browned and medium-rare inside.

02 Season the *bagna cauda* with S+P to taste. Pour into a communal bowl and provide vegetables for dipping.

A

B

C

D

LESSON 21

SKILL

FERMENTATION

SAUERKRAUT

INSPIRED BY

Jeffrey Zurofsky

SHORTHAND

Julienne 1 cabbage; masticate w 1T sea salt. Compact in bowl under 2nd weighted bowl. Store dry & cool 1 week, covering w brine if needed.

HANDS-ON TIME

5 minutes

TOTAL TIME

15 minutes, plus 1 week fermenting

GEAR

- Knife + cutting board
- 1 medium and 1 large stainless-steel or other nonreactive[12] bowl (glass, ceramic, and plastic are all fine)
- 1 weight, such as a heavy stone, brick, or large can of tomatoes
- Hand grater (optional)
- Meat mallet (optional)

OPTIONAL MUSIC PAIRING

"Sour Girl" by Stone Temple Pilots

> "Eating bacteria is one of life's great pleasures... Katz says. Beer, wine, cheese, bread, cured meats, coffee, chocolate: our best-loved foods are almost all fermented."
>
> —"NATURE'S SPOILS" BY BURKHARD BILGER, *THE NEW YORKER*

Let's keep that testosterone in check with a light appetizer à la Martha Stewart. All flesh and no play makes Jack an unhinged boy.

As you've no doubt noticed, things rot when exposed to air.

But if you protect food from air, making the environment *anaerobic*, quite a few goodies ferment instead and become delicious. Sauerkraut is the poster child for this (and also the reason Germans were called "Krauts" during WWII).

Unlike most store-bought sauerkraut, which is pasteurized and devoid of bacteria (unless the label says "raw" or "naturally fermented" and is found in the refrigerated section), our homemade version will be loaded with, for lack of a better term, "good" bacteria.[13] There are an estimated 10 times more bacterial cells in your body than human cells: 100 trillion of them to 10 trillion of you. These 100 trillion stowaways have been nicknamed the "microbiome." The two primary strains of bacteria so far identified that influence fat absorption are *Bacteroidetes* and *Firmicutes*. Lean people have more *Bacteroidetes* and fewer *Firmicutes*; obese people have more *Firmicutes* and fewer *Bacteroidetes*. As obese people lose weight, the ratio of bacteria in their guts shifts to favor *Bacteroidetes*.

Given that a strong cycle of antibiotics can leave your microbiome off-kilter for up to four years, I view sauerkraut as a smart investment in immune function and fat-burning capabilities.

Forthwith fermentation 101—how you create food by taking the path of least resistance. That is, doing nothing.[14]

Still worried about a recipe with bacteria? I wouldn't be. Fred Breidt, a microbiologist with the United States Department of Agriculture, has never found a single case of sickness from contaminated sauerkraut.[‡] It's the perfect gateway drug for an entire class of hands-off "cooking."

12 Metals like copper, cast-iron, and aluminum can interfere with fermentation.

13 To preserve them, don't heat your homemade sauerkraut.

14 As Sandor Katz, author of *Wild Fermentation*, describes it.

What Else Is Fermented?

These foods, when traditionally made and not pasteurized, are also loaded with good bacteria:

- **Miso** (fermented bean paste; contains the lactic acid bacteria *Pediococcus halophilus, Streptococcus faecalis, and Tetragenococcus halophilus*)
- **Nama shoyu** (unpasteurized soy sauce; contains the lactic acid bacteria *Tetragenococcus halophilus*)
- **Raw apple cider vinegar** (fermented by *Mycoderma aceti*; this is called a "mother"; the slight cloudiness that settles to the bottom of the bottle indicates the bacteria are alive)
- **Kefir** (cultured milk; the unpasteurized milk keeps the enzymes alive; contains *Lactobacillus Caucasus, Leuconostoc, Acetobacter*, and *Streptococcus* species)
- **Fish sauce** (fermented anchovies or sardines; contains *Tetragenococcus halophilus*)
- **Kombucha** (effervescent beverage made from tea, bacteria, and yeast; contains *Acetobacter, Lactobacillus, Pediococcus*, and *Gluconacetobacter kombuchae*)

Maldon
SEA SALT

INGREDIENTS	TO MAKE 3 CUPS
Large cabbage	**1**
Sea salt	**1 T**

PREP

00 Quarter the cabbage through the core (see pic B).

01 Cut the cabbage quarters finely (core and all) from the tip to the base. You can also grate the cabbage using the ¼" (0.5-cm) holes of a hand grater or the fine grater of a food processor or mandoline.

PICKUP

00 Place the cabbage in a large, nonreactive bowl.

01 Add 1 T salt; mix it in well. It's important for the salt to really get into the cabbage. Either squeeze the cabbage by the handful with the salt, using full force to masticate[15] it, or take a meat mallet and pound the hell out of it. If you're scaling[16] up the recipe, you can put the cabbage in a food-grade plastic bucket and pound it with the end of a baseball bat.

02 Place a second, smaller bowl on top of the cabbage.

03 Place a weight (e.g., a brick, a can of tomatoes) in the second bowl to press down on the cabbage.

04 A cloudy-looking brine (salty liquid) will begin to rise to the surface as a result of the salting and squeezing. Cover everything loosely with a clean dish towel.

05 Leave the cabbage in a cool, dark place for a week. Check daily to ensure that the cabbage is below the surface of the brine. This keeps fermentation anaerobic, and keeps you safe. If the cabbage has reabsorbed the liquid (the brine fails to cover it) at any point, dissolve ½ T sea salt in ½ c (120 ml) boiling filtered or spring water[17]; cool the water, and then add enough of it to cover the cabbage.

Scrape off any mold that forms on the surface of the brine. The cabbage is ready to eat when it has a tangy fermented flavor and the shreds turn translucent, usually around 1 week. For more sour palates, ferment it up to 10 days total.

15 Basically beat it to a pulp. Tenderize it.
16 Cookbook jargon for adjusting a recipe for larger or smaller serving sizes.
17 Chlorinated water inhibits the growth of microbes; we need microbes to help fermentation.

06 Remove the weight and discard any bubbly foam or discolored kraut from the surface of the bowl. Place the kraut in a jar and store in the refrigerator. It keeps for up to 6 months.

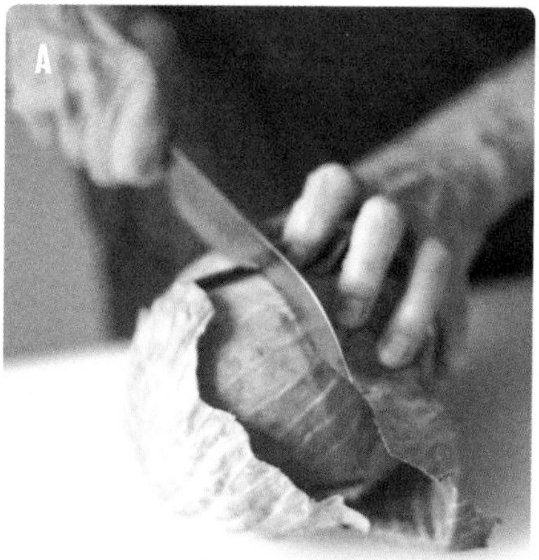
A

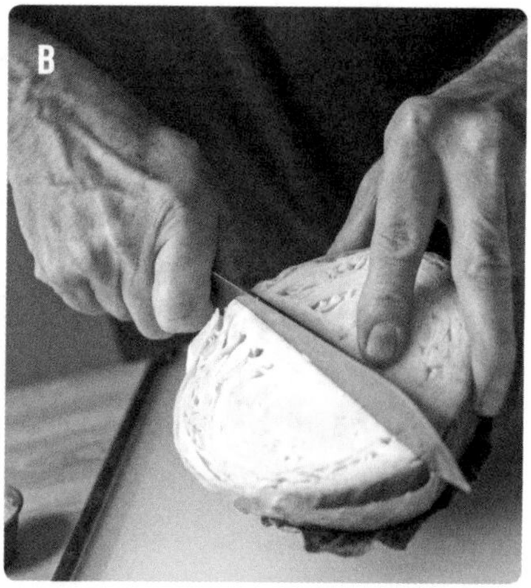
B

Kraut Variations

- To spice things up, add a dried chile or 1 t of grated ginger.
- For a boost of iodine, add sea vegetables, such as dulse or arame. (Iodine supports thyroid function.)
- To change the flavor, substitute some of the cabbage with shredded carrot, turnip, or daikon. Use beet for a ruby red kraut.
- For a traditional seasoning, add about 1 t caraway seeds. Dill seeds, juniper berries, peppercorns, and cumin seeds are also good choices.
- For a tangy salad dressing, save the kraut juice from the bottom of the jar and mix it with EVOO and pepper (no salt needed).

Lazybones Approach

Get a Perfect Pickler (perfectpickler.com) and do this all in 3–4 days.

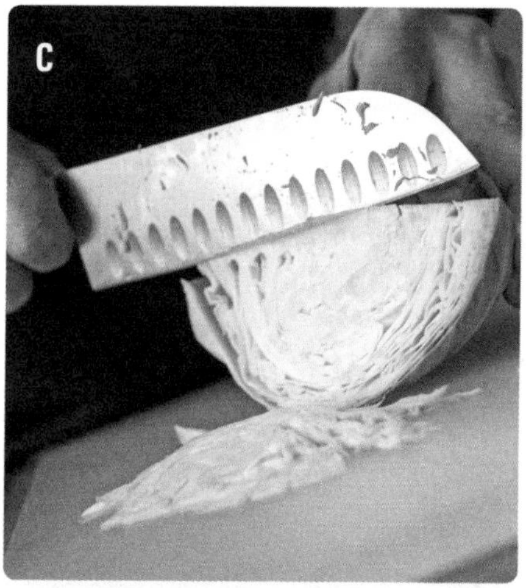
C

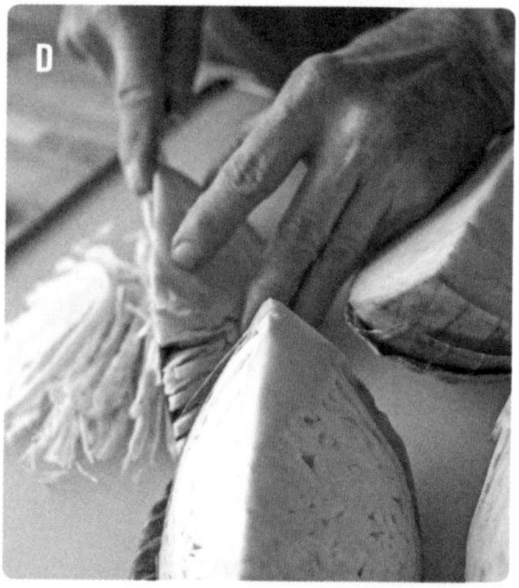
D

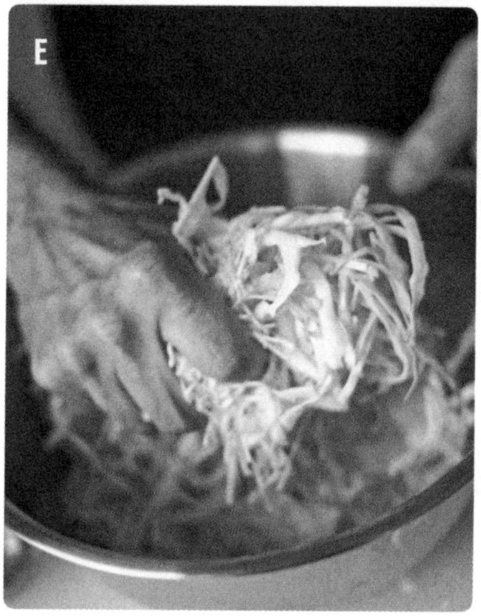
E

F
San Marzano

LESSON 22

SKILL

OFFAL CONSUMPTION

SAUTÉED BEEF HEART

SHORTHAND

Marinate 3lb sliced heart, 1 bunch thyme, 1 grated garlic clove, 1t salt, ½t pepper, juice of 1 lemon, ¼c EVOO 30min. Sauté ½ meat, 1T EVOO 3min. Add ⅛c white wine, cook till evaporated. Repeat for 2nd half.

HANDS-ON TIME

15 minutes

TOTAL TIME

20 minutes, plus at least 30 minutes marinating

GEAR

- Knife + cutting board
- Fork
- Large mixing bowl
- Mortar and pestle
- Microplane
- Cast-iron combi

OPTIONAL MUSIC PAIRING

♪ "You Give Love a Bad Name" by Bon Jovi

"Why is it worse, in the end, to see an animal's head cooked and prepared for our pleasure than a thigh or a tail or a rib? If we are going to live on other inhabitants of this world, we must not bind ourselves with illogical prejudices, but savor to the fullest the beasts we have killed."

—M.F.K. FISHER, *HOW TO COOK A WOLF*

Deer heart smells exactly like pastrami. It's also easy to cook and an inoffensive introduction to organ meat. It's pure muscle, and the fat (all exterior) can easily be removed.

To make it so good that guests fight over it, Steve uses a marinade borrowed from Jamie Oliver.

Deer heart might be sold out at Whole Foods, but you can easily order beef heart from any butcher shop worth its salt.

COPPOLA

INGREDIENTS	TO SERVE 6
Beef heart	**1 (3 lb/1.4 kg)**
Coarse salt	**1 t, plus more to taste**
Ground black pepper	**½ t**
Thyme ("stemmed"—stems removed)	**1 bunch**
Garlic clove, grated with a Microplane	**1**
EVOO	**¼ c (90 ml) plus 2 T**
Lemon juice	**1 lemon**
White wine	**¼ c (60 ml)**

PREP

00 First off, you'll be doing a lot of trimming, so make sure your chef's knife is sharp.

01 Lay the heart on a cutting board, fat side down. Separate the 4 chambers of the heart by cutting between them with a chef's knife. (See next page for pics.)

02 Cut away the silver skin,[18] fat, connective tissue, valves, membranes, veins, and tendons, until you're left with vibrant red heart meat. It's OK if a little fat remains here and there. It won't hurt you.

03 Cut the heart into ¼" (0.5-cm) slices.[19] Pierce each piece of meat with a fork a few times, and place them in a large mixing bowl.

04 Mash the 1 t coarse salt, ½ t ground pepper, 1 bunch fresh thyme, and 1 clove garlic with a mortar and pestle. Then add ¼ c (90 ml) EVOO and lemon juice and mix.

05 Add the marinade to the mixing bowl and stir to coat the heart. Set aside on the counter for at least 30 minutes, or cover and refrigerate overnight.

PICKUP

00 Heat 1 T of the remaining EVOO in the skillet (lid) of a cast-iron combi over medium-high heat. Add half of the heart slices and cook, flipping a couple of times, 2–3 minutes for medium-rare.

18 A layer of silver-tinted connective tissue (fascia) attached to various pieces of meat. It's too tough to eat.

19 Placing the heart in the freezer for 30 minutes beforehand makes it easier to slice.

A
B
C
D
E
F
G
H

I

J

01 Add ⅛ c of the wine and cook, stirring to remove any browned bits from the bottom of the pan, until most of the wine is evaporated, no more than 2 minutes. Now, remove the heart from the pan to a serving bowl.

02 Repeat with the remaining 1 T EVOO, heart, and ⅛ c wine. Once done, salt it all to taste, if needed, and serve immediately.

LESSON 23

SKILL
FORAGING
FERAL HUMANS AND THE GOLDEN GATE BUFFET

GEAR
- Eyes
- Hands

> "Nature never said to me: Do not be poor; still less did she say: Be rich; her cry to me was always: Be independent."
>
> —NICOLAS CHAMFORT

San Francisco is a strange city. Feel free to walk into a Starbucks naked and order a Grande Frappuccino, but—horrors of horrors—if you decide to eat a handful of grass, you are breaking the law. It is technically illegal to forage in the Bay Area.[20]

Pondering this, I found myself at a trail entrance to Golden Gate Park with Kevin "Feral Kevin" Feinstein. It was a pleasant Sunday morning, and a group had assembled for a wild food walk organized by foragesf.com. Kevin, our guide, started with the first rule of foraging: "Foraging is not a guessing game. It's not like eating blowfish at a Japanese restaurant for a rush. If you can't identify it 110%, don't eat it. Not sure? Don't eat it."

For instance, anything from the carrot or parsley family should be avoided in the wild.[21] The risk-benefit ratio just isn't worth it. Remember hemlock? It can blend in, and if it killed Socrates, it can certainly kill you.

Before we set foot in nature's produce aisle, Kevin gave us two more warnings:

- **Remember "Leaves of three, leave it be." This will help you avoid poison oak (West Coast) and poison ivy (East Coast).[22]**

- **It's best to avoid anything that grows out of the water in or next to a city. That watercress might look delicious, but, in the wrong place, it's also soaking up lead, arsenic, dioxin, and other toxins.**

GOING COSMOPOLITAN

Kevin next explained the importance of focusing on "cosmopolitan weeds" found nationwide, such as dandelion, instead of hyperlocalized fare. You can identify bay nuts from the Marin Headlands, you say? You know the three main spring edibles in Tahoe? That's fantastic, but this newfound knowledge does you little good even 50 miles away, let alone in a different state in a different season.[23]

Planning for the worst case, we'd also like to have a lexicon of edibles that will survive in the fall (the

20 In some states, it's even illegal to capture rainwater.

21 The only exception to this rule might be fennel, but why risk it?

22 Pro tip: if you go hiking or camping in a poison oak/ivy area, use a product called Tecnu in the shower when you get home as insurance. It washes off the urushiol oils from both plants.

23 I'd still suggest learning a few plentiful local varieties. Just as people are most likely to get in a car accident within 10 miles (16 km) of their homes, you are statistically most likely to get lost in a wilderness close to your home. This also makes nature walks with friends more fun.

least rain in SF and many places), not just April (the most abundant harvest).

Our first stop on the tour was stinging nettles, sitting 20 ft from the street. "I had this last night on pizza!" I exclaimed when Kevin pointed it out, excited to see my favorite topping sprouting out of the ground.

Why do I love nettles? Let me count the ways. First, they taste great. Second, in contrast to dinosaur kale, which is widely considered a "superfood" due to its 7% mineral content, nettles can reach 20% mineral content. This makes them one of the most nutritious greens ever studied. Third, if you're looking to increase your testosterone, it also has anti-aromatase effects, reducing testosterone's conversion to estrogen.

But nettles were just our starting point.

In our romp through Golden Gate Park, where we <ahem> didn't munch on a thing, we spotted an incredible bounty of food, all hidden in plain sight. The starred plants that follow are perennial weeds, which grow all over and all year round:

✱ **Nettles** To harvest nettles, wear rubber gloves and cut off the top 3–4" (8–10 cm) of the plant, aiming for younger growth, and you're in business. Blend into some pesto and enjoy. Just make sure that they are, in fact, stinging nettles. The stinging hair (formic acid) will sting you. Brush them with your arm or the side of your hand to confirm, as your fingertips are too thick and insensitive.

If you want to grow them indoors,[24] which is easy, cut off a section by severing near the center stalk and place the cut end in water. It will quickly grow roots, after which it's plantable. Keep it in the shade or in an area that receives spotted sun. Once the plant gets big enough, cut off the top 3–4" (8–10 cm) of leaves, and—like a chimera—it will sprout two new shafts. Repeat to multiply them like Gremlins. It's a weed, remember.

✱ **Broad-leaf plantain** Unrelated to the Central American banana look-alike. For medicinal purposes, it's common in salves, and you can chew it up and apply it as a paste on burns. The seeds are in husks and look like mini cattails. If you need something to keep you regular, they work just like psyllium husks.

• **Cattail** One of the most common plants in North America. It's everywhere and has high caloric value in the root. Cliff Hodges has been on survival trips where he subsisted on nothing but. Nearly the entire plant is edible and nutritious: the young shoots and "heart" are tasty boiled or stir-fried, and the immature flower heads taste remarkably like corn.

• **Nasturtium flowers** Almost every part of this plant is delicious. The flowers are light, the leaves are spicy, and the seeds clear your sinuses like wasabi. I first encountered the flower, unbeknownst to me, when I visited Chez Panisse in Berkeley with my girlfriend. There was a gorgeous flower bouquet just inside the entrance. As we passed by in our evening attire, my girlfriend snatched a few leaves and ate them, leaving me shocked (yes, even me). Had she dropped LSD before our date? "No, dum-dum," she chided me, "nasturtiums are edible." Still weird to eat decor, in my opinion, but the weirdness is probably what makes us compatible.

NETTLES

BROAD-LEAF PLANTAIN

CATTAIL

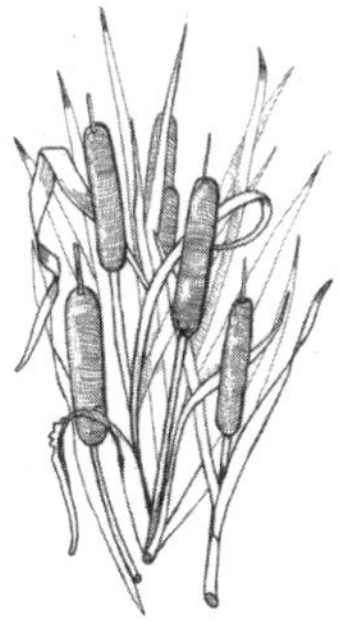

NASTURTIUM FLOWERS

24 From the park, the easiest to transplant and hardest to kill are nettles, New Zealand spinach, and chickweed.

NEW ZEALAND SPINACH

DANDELION

PINE TREE

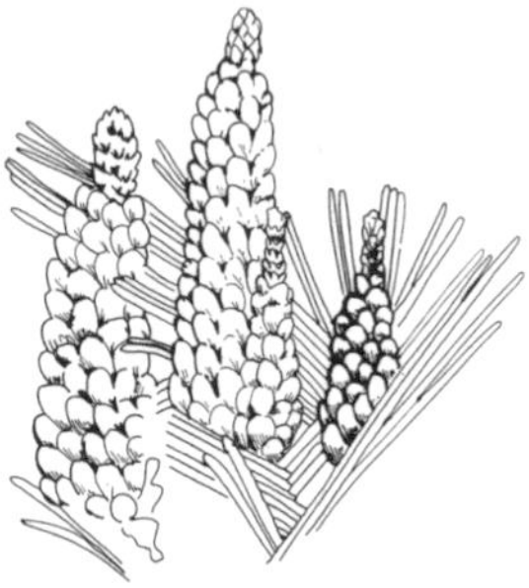

MALE PINE FLOWERS

• **New Zealand spinach** It has a delicious natural salty flavor, even if located far from the coast. I love this stuff.

✱ **Dandelion** All parts of the dandelion are edible. But if you see fuzzy or silvery leaves, skip it, as it's an imitator. Dandelion features what's called a "basal rosette": all the stems come out of a central roselike button in the ground. Unlike many household plants, it doesn't have small branches coming off bigger branches. Assuming you've confirmed your dandelion, the flowers can be fried and eaten. Or, in homage to Ray Bradbury, you could make delicious dandelion wine.

✱ **Pine tree** Edible parts include the inner bark flesh, pine needles (in tea), pine nuts inside pinecones, and pine pollen.

As discussed on page 186, pine pollen, produced by male flowers, doesn't just act as a precursor to testosterone—it *is* testosterone. Several species contain not just androstenedione but also DHEA and testosterone itself.[‡] Starting around February, the male flowers appear as small yellow cones in bundles and can be harvested for pollen. The female cones are the more familiar "pinecones" and are much larger.

Once you've removed a few male cones from, say, a Monterey pine between February and May, place them in a bowl and let them sit. They'll open naturally, neatly depositing the pollen at the bottom. This yellow gold can then be sprinkled on salad, in pesto, or on just about anything else you'd care to make disgusting. As mentioned in the good ol' days of DOM, take it as a shot in water to keep your food down.

✱ **Evening primrose** This is another plant that offers multitudes: its flowers are sweet, delicious, attractive additions to salads; its leaves can be eaten as greens (in salads or cooked), and its boiled young roots taste like a slightly peppery turnip.

• **Common mallow** Related to the marshmallow plant that long ago gave campfire marshmallows their gooey texture, common mallow has similar muciferous leaves. This means that, like okra, they can be used as a thickener for soups (dry the leaves and grind them first). The leaves can also serve as a pleasant, though mild, addition to salad greens.

✱ **Oxalis/sourgrass** As the name implies, this plant has a sour flavor thanks to high levels of oxalic acid. Its leaves and flowers can add bite to salads or be used as a garnish

EVENING PRIMROSE

How to Make Dandelion Wine

- **1 gal (4 L) dandelion blossoms (no stems; full, open flowers are best), rinsed if possible**
- **2–3 lb (0.5–1.5 kg) sugar (depending on how sweet you like it)**
- **2 lemons, chopped up**
- **2 oranges, chopped up**
- **1" (2.5 cm) ginger root**
- **5 t active dry yeast**

Pour 1 gal (4 L) of boiling water over the flowers in a 2-gal (8-L) crock or food-safe plastic bucket. Cover with cheesecloth and leave for 2–3 days, stirring occasionally.

Strain the liquid through the cheesecloth into a large pot and add the sugar, chopped lemons and oranges, and ginger. Bring to a boil, then let simmer for about half an hour.

Remove from heat. Combine the yeast with ¼ c (60 ml) warm water and add to the pot. Let cool for up to 1 day.

Strain back into the (clean) crock or bucket. Cover it with more cheesecloth and let stand for 2–3 weeks.

Strain into sterile bottles and cork; store the bottles in a cool, dark place for 3–6 months before drinking.

COMMON MALLOW

OXALIS/SOURGRASS

YARROW

SHEEP SORREL

SOW THISTLE

MUGWORT

for fish, and if you pour boiling water over them and let them steep for half an hour, you get a pungent tea.

✶ **Yarrow** If you're a home-brew beer fan, you can substitute yarrow for hops. It's stimulating and purportedly an aphrodisiac. Meow.

✶ **Sheep sorrel** Has a mild sour flavor and tastes great. One of my favorites, by far.

✶ **Sow thistle** Its leaves taste like a slightly bitter lettuce, and are accordingly tasty in salads. They're traditionally used as one of the ingredients in *preboggion,* a cooked-greens delicacy from the northwestern coastal region of Italy called Liguria.

✶ **Mugwort** Traditionally taken before bed for enhanced dreams.

✶ **Grass** (not pictured) Ever had a wheatgrass shot? It turns out that you can have an anything-grass shot. All grasses are drinkable, but the solids are not edible. Unless you have a rumen like a cow, you can chew them up, take in the nutrient-rich nectar, then spit it all out. Grass's monocot appearance (single blade) sets it apart from dicots (two blades) like basil. Just remember that the leaves should be fibrous, not soft.

So . . . chewing and spitting out grass doesn't seem like a great way to stay alive? It isn't. You can get almost all of your nutrition from plants, but you can't get all of the calories you need. Unless, that is, you win the acorn lottery, which brings us to our next recipe.

Bring Foraging into Your Home

I was totally allergic to owning plants until I found nearly bulletproof "woody" herbs that are multipurpose (food and tea). For your maiden plant voyage, if only to add some temporary green to your house, buy a potted rosemary or thyme plant. It's convenient and, if you're single, oddly soothing to care for something besides yourself.

To learn more about minimalist gardening, including tiny door-hanging hydroponic gardens (super-cool) and garden shares, I found these resources helpful:

WindowFarms (windowfarms.org): DIY building instructions, as well as mail-order kits.

Hyperlocavore (hyperlocavore.ning .com): online yard-sharing community.

American Community Gardening Association (acga.localharvest.org): searchable database of local communal gardens.

LESSON 24

SKILL

LEACHING & COOKING ON COAL

KEVIN'S "BEST PANCAKES OF MY LIFE" ACORN PANCAKES

+ CLIFF'S VARIATION

INSPIRED BY

- Kevin Feinstein's *The Bay Area Forager*
- Cliff Hodges

SHORTHAND

Mix 1½c acorn meal, ½c pastry flour, 1T baking powder, 1T butter, small spoon wildflower honey, 2 eggs. Cook on oiled skillet. Serve w maple syrup.

TOTAL TIME

Varies depending on acorn source and how hot your griddle is

GEAR

- 5 gal (19 L) bucket
- Nutcracker
- Mortar and pestle, food processor, or blade grinder
- Cast-iron skillet

OPTIONAL MUSIC PAIRING

♪ "Little Acorns" by the White Stripes

> "Genius unexerted is no more genius than a bushel of acorns is a forest of oaks."
>
> —HENRY WARD BEECHER, CLERGYMAN

Ah, acorns. Who knew they were so amazing? You can eat acorns even if they've fallen off an oak tree next to the airport. Fruits and nuts are effectively "filtered" by the plants or trees that bear them.

More good news: though thought of as nuts, acorns are better described as grains. They're primarily carbohydrate (42%) and fat (52%) rather than protein (6%), and proteins are responsible for nut allergies. This means that one of Kevin's forager friends, who is deathly allergic to nuts and travels with an EpiPen, also eats acorns with abandon. This makes them a "cheat" food, but a safe one. By some accounts, acorns were the primary food source for nearly 75% of native Californians. It's easy to see why:

- If the season is in full swing, you can gather enough acorns in one week to last you an entire year, squirrel-style.
- Once dried, acorns can be stored for years.
- If you're lucky, you'll also collect acorn grubs to fry and throw on your lentils.

Here are the proper steps, perfect to start on a Friday or Saturday for the subsequent cheat day.

INGREDIENTS	TO SERVE 4
Wet and leached acorn meal	1½ c (180 g)
Organic pastry flour/cattail starch/other flour that sticks	½ c (60 g)
Baking powder	1 T
Mostly melted butter	1 T
Wildflower honey	1 small spoonful
Fresh eggs	2

PREP

00 **Gather your acorns.** A full 5-gal (19-L) bucket from Home Depot will yield 4–5 c (500–600 g) of acorn flour in the end. If you'd like assistance with the gathering, a broomlike "nut gatherer" might be worth $15. Discard any acorns that feel soft, appear moldy, or have holes in them. The holes indicate insect inhabitants.

You can also order edible acorns at acorno.com. Get white oak or black oak if available, red oak if not, and skip to step 02: "deshell and grind." Otherwise...

01 **Dry.** Lay out your acorns and sun-dry them. If it's really hot, 1 day could suffice. Otherwise, budget 2–3 days. Bring them inside at sunset or, alternatively, place them on a tray next to a window that receives sun. If you're impatient like me, you can also dry them in an oven at 170°F (75°C) or so for 20–30 minutes, leaving the door slightly ajar. Using an oven will reduce flavor more than gradual sun-drying.

02 **Deshell and grind.** Remove the shells using your hands or a nutcracker, as needed. Next, pulverize the acorns into a flour using a mortar and pestle, a food processor, or a cheap blade grinder.

03 **Leach.** High levels of tannic acid in acorns can drop-kick your digestive tract and interfere with protein metabolism. To make them edible, the next step is leaching. There are two options: hot leaching and cold leaching. The sidebars on this page cover my preferred methods for both.

PICKUP

00 Mix up the ingredients listed above and cook on oiled (or buttered) skillet.

01 Serve with maple syrup and butter, or a wild berry jam.

Hot Leaching

Hot leaching is fast but removes flavor and nutritional properties. It's also best for lower-tannin acorns like the valley oak and white oak common around San Francisco.

Kevin's friend Kim Curiel uses a coffeemaker or French press (my choice) to brew ground acorns, then does the opposite of normal: she discards the liquid at least two or three times and retains the grounds. I steep each time for 30 minutes and can complete leaching in one evening. The grounds are ready when no longer overly bitter or astringent.

Cold Leaching

Regardless of acorn type, cold leaching produces better-tasting acorn meal and it's equally simple.

If you're stuck with a high-tannin variety of acorn (e.g., red oak), cold leaching should be your default. It's a 7–10-day process for low-tannin species and 10–14-day for high-tannin species. Here's the process, as described by Cliff Hodges:

"I keep it in a jar of water for about a week, sometimes a few days more. The acorn 'mush' falls to the bottom, and the water on top gets dark as it pulls out the tannic acid. Once a day, I pour out the water from the top [straining through a cheesecloth], add new water, shake it up, and set it back down. I just keep going until the water stays clear."

Change the water first thing in the morning (or before bed) and you could be ready for pancakes by the weekend.

VARIATION

CLIFF'S ACORN ASH CAKES

SHORTHAND

Burn campfire till white ash. Mix 4-5c flour (40% acorn, 40% almond, 20% coconut), 2 eggs; add H2O till it forms 'snowballs.' Cook on coals till congealed.

TOTAL TIME

2 hours, including fire-starting time

GEAR

- Small mixing bowl
- Your hands

If you want to go über-rustic, try Cliff Hodges's variation, based on techniques from *It Will Live Forever: Traditional Yosemite Indian Acorn Preparation.* These "ash cakes" are what we had for breakfast in the Santa Cruz mountains, and they rocked.

Since Cliff cooks without measuring cups, his recipe relies more on observation.

PICKUP

00 For taste, Cliff often uses a flour ratio of 40% acorn, 40% almond, and 20% coconut. You can use 100% acorn, but it is blander.

01 Mix a small bowl of flour (4–5 c/500–600 g) with 2 eggs and roughly ½ c (120 ml) water. Add the water little by little to make a soft dough: you'll need to form loose snowballs, which should barely hold together.

02 Cliff: "I start my campfire, let all the logs burn down to coals, rake them out once there are no more branches, and then wait a few minutes to let the coals turn white (instead of being fully red-hot). From first lighting the fire, this generally takes anywhere from 10–30 minutes, depending on how much wood was used and what kind of wood it is."

03 Carefully place your acorn snowballs directly on the coals (see pic D).

04 Cliff: "I know the ash cakes are done when they appear to have congealed together and won't fall apart when I pick them up. Usually a couple of small burn marks (but not totally charred all over) help to indicate that. Just as with a pancake, you'd prefer for them to cook slow and turn brown (probably cooked on the inside) than to cook quickly and turn entirely black on the outside."

05 Brush off any remaining ash and enjoy. I expected them to taste like charcoal, which wasn't the case at all. Two cakes later, I still wanted more.

Not a pancake aficionado? Take your pick of these alternate dishes:

- **Acorn "oatmeal"—add whatever you like to your acorn meal, mix it up, and chow down.**
- **Acorn coffee—OK, this is a cheat, as the prep is slightly different: roast the nuts for 15 minutes, crush, roast again for 15 minutes, then crush as fine as possible. Add hot water. Acorn coffee was consumed by both the Confederate army during the Civil War and the Germans during WWII.**

A
B
C
D
E
F

LESSON 25

SKILL

WINNING FEAR FACTOR

MUSCLE CRICKET™ PROTEIN BARS

+ CHAPULINES, SIMPLE "CHIRP" COOKIES, AND BEYOND

SHORTHAND

200F 1-2hr: roast ¼oz crickets till nutty & crispy; remove wings & legs. Mix crickets, 1½c whey protein, ½c oats, ½c coconut, ½c H2O, 2t vanilla, 1c almond butter. Refrigerate 30min.

HANDS-ON TIME

5 minutes

TOTAL TIME

10 minutes plus cricket prep

GEAR

- 1 carrot
- Cast-iron skillet
- Large mixing bowl
- 8" x 8" (20 x 20-cm) Pyrex baking dish

OPTIONAL MUSIC PAIRING

♪ "All My Friends Are Insects" by Weezer

> "C.F. Hodge (1911) calculated that a pair of houseflies beginning operations in April could produce enough flies, if all survived, to cover the earth 47 feet deep by August. . . . If one can reverse for a moment the usual focus on insects as enemies of man, Hodge's layer of flies represents an impressive pile of animal protein."
>
> —GENE DEFOLIART, FORMER CHAIR OF ENTOMOLOGY AT THE UNIVERSITY OF WISCONSIN

Do you like peanut butter? I do. And Reese's Peanut Butter Cups? Crack every Halloween. What a home-run combo.

But shrimp? I couldn't choke them down until my late 20s. I'm not alone. Oaxacan Mexicans in Santa María Atzompa, for instance, traditionally find them disgusting.

But what about cockchafers? Man, I love me some cockchafers. What? No, silly, it's not something you buy in the Castro next to Orphan Andy's.

They're bugs! Many cultures prize bugs, including the same Oaxacans who hate shrimp. They are famous for *chapulines*: grasshoppers with garlic, lime, and chile. In the U.S., bugs aren't thought of as delicious. Regardless, most Americans consume them at least once a week. In peanut butter, 30 insect parts per 3.5 oz (100 g) is permissible. In chocolate, it's 60 parts per 3.5 oz (100 g). So next time you eat a Reese's, think cockchafers.

This lesson will introduce new "meats" you can eat or impose on your in-laws. A few reasons to actually try this:

- Even James Beard Award–winning chefs, like José Andrés, are jumping on the insect bandwagon. It's what all the cool kids are doing.
- They're practically crispy Flintstones vitamins. Protein-rich grasshoppers, for instance, contain a third of the fat found in beef, and water bugs offer almost four times as much iron.
- You can exact quiet revenge upon dinner guests, who will never know the difference. Cricket salt, anyone?

Cockchafers, coming to a menu near you.

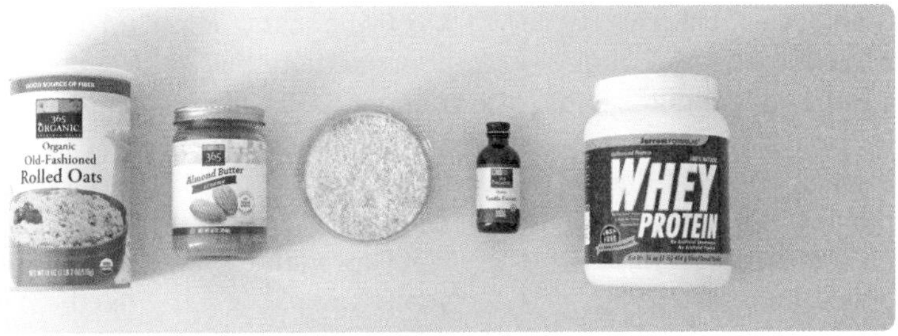
365 ORGANIC
Organic
Old-Fashioned
Rolled Oats
Almond Butter
WHEY
PROTEIN

INGREDIENTS	TO MAKE 8 BARS
Fluker Farms crickets	**¼ oz (6 g)**
Unflavored whey protein powder	**1½ c (135 g)**
Uncooked rolled oats, like unsweetened Quaker Oats	**½ c (50 g)**
Unsweetened shredded coconut	**½ c (45 g)**
Water	**½ c (120 ml)**
Vanilla extract	**2 t**
Unsweetened almond butter (peanut butter also works)	**1 c (250 g)**

To help with recipes, I reached out to Matt Krisiloff, University of Chicago student and CEO of Entom Foods, a start-up that aims to take insect cuisine mainstream. His short list of starter bugs included:

- San Diego wax worms
- Fluker Farms mealworms
- Grasshoppers
- Fluker Farms crickets

Personally, I thought worms (at least labeled as such) were a rough introduction. I crossed them off. Grasshoppers? The good hoppers are apparently the caviar of insects. Imported Thai grasshoppers cost a wing and a leg. Legit *chapulines* from Oaxaca by the kilo? Joe Raffa, head chef at Oyamel in Washington, D.C., can justify the costs, but we decided on a better substitute: crickets.

Crickets will get you similar nutrition and taste (nutty!) without breaking the bank. We'll start there.

MUSCLE CRICKET™ BARS

These bake-free specialties are taking the world by storm. Muscle Cricket bars are now mandatory in children's lunch boxes in southern Japan. See musclecricket.com if you think I'm kidding. To make them at home, just follow these directions:

PREP

00 Order live crickets, the larger the better, from flukerfarms.com.

01 When they arrive in their cardboard shipping tube, put the crickets in the fridge for 3 hours to sedate them, just like lobsters. This makes sense, as they're both arthropods.

Safety sidenote: if you're allergic to shellfish, you probably don't want to eat insects.

02 After 3 hours, open up your tube and remove any cardboard fragments. The crickets will appear dead, but they're not. Break a carrot into thirds and put 1–2 pieces in the cylinder. You might squish a few crickets, but, let's face it, you're going to kill all of them anyway.

Close the tube and leave it on your counter, where it can warm to room temperature. The crickets, revived after an hour or so, should be left alone to eat the carrots for 24 hours. This last meal is to cycle out the cardboard your hungry boys ate in transit.

03 After 24 hours, put the tube in the freezer to kill them.

I neglected to do this prior to my first roasting. Suffice it to say, merely sedated crickets make horrible noises if you roast them, and the visual is far, far worse. Do yourself a favor and freeze them. Related: this allows you to roast only what you need. As Matt told me, "I've had some in my freezer for about a year now, and they still taste fresh once they are roasted or fried. If you want to roast everything at once, though, and simply keep it in the refrigerator, crickets or mealworms should stay good for at least 4 or 5 days."

04 Preheat your oven to 200°F (95°C).

05 Place your dead crickets in your cast-iron skillet and roast them in the oven for 1–2 hours. Taste test them (see sidebar at the bottom of the opposite page) at 60 minutes and 90 minutes. You want them dried and crunchy but not burnt to a crisp. Aim for nuttiness, like hollow peanuts.

06 Once finished, if you like, roll off all wings and legs as you did in the taste test. I highly recommend this step if you're serving to insect virgins (including yourself).

07 **Optional:** If you prefer to ambush friends at this point, you can put the cricket torpedoes in a peppermill with some salt and pass it off as "Oaxacan nut salt."

PICKUP

00 Put the roasted crickets in a large Ziploc bag and roll a wine bottle over them until a coarse powder.

01 Add all ingredients to a large mixing bowl. I use an electronic scale to weigh each item as I add them one by one. To make things easier, microwave the almond butter for 20 seconds on medium-high beforehand.

02 Mix this cricket concrete together with your hands. It will be *very* sticky, so wet your hands first.

03 Wet your hands again (you'll lose some mix, which is expected) and press the mass into an 8" x 8" (20 x 20-cm) Pyrex baking dish or other baking pan. You'll lose another 10% of the mix on hands and the bowl. Don't sweat it.

04 Cover and refrigerate for 30 minutes or more, then cut into bars or squares. If hard to cut, let them sit at room temperature for 10 minutes first. You can wrap them individually in plastic for protein bars on the go. Snacks for coworkers! It's about time you did something nice for them.

Muscle Cricket™!

VARIATIONS

MAKE THAT BUG A FEATURE!

CHAPULINES (GRASSHOPPER/CRICKET) FAJITAS

1 T EVOO
2 scallions, cut in pieces
5 serrano chiles, sliced
5 garlic cloves, mashed
2-finger pinch salt
8 oz (225 g) grasshoppers or crickets, roasted
Corn tortillas, warmed
8 oz (225 g) chopped tomatoes
½ c (65 g) toasted pumpkin seeds
1 handful parsley, chopped

1. In a large skillet, heat the 1 T olive oil. Add the 2 scallions, 5 chiles, 5 garlic cloves, and 2-finger pinch of salt, and cook until softened, 2–3 minutes. Transfer to a bowl and set aside.

2. Add the 8 oz (225 g) roasted grasshoppers or crickets to the skillet and cook to heat through; add the vegetables back and stir together for 1 minute more. Remove from heat.

3. Place a portion of the mixture in the center of each tortilla, and top each with tomatoes, pumpkin seeds, and parsley.

SIMPLE "CHIRP" COOKIES

¼ oz (6 g) roasted crickets (crushed in a Ziploc)
1 package refrigerated cookie dough

1. Knead the dough until soft, then mix in cricket powder.

2. Roll dough into tube shape, and cut into ½" (1.3-cm) slices.

3. Bake at 350°F (180°C) for 10 minutes, cool, and enjoy.

MEALWORM FRIED RICE

1 egg, beaten
1 t olive oil
¾ c (180 ml) water
4 t soy sauce (or tamari)
⅛ t garlic powder
¼ c (40 g) minced red onion
1 c (195 g) brown rice, cooked
1 c (230 g) roasted mealworms

1. Stir egg in frying pan with 1 t oil until cooked, then add ¾ c (180 ml) water, 4 t soy sauce, ⅛ t garlic powder, and ¼ c (40 g) onion. Bring to a boil.

2. Stir in 1 c (195 g) rice and 1 c (230 g) mealworms. Remove from heat and allow to cool for 3 minutes.

Your First Cricket Tasting

After roasting, roll the crickets between your thumb and index finger to remove the wings and legs. Not required for eating, but recommended for first-timers.

BEFORE

AFTER

THE ODD APPEAL OF STREET QUAIL

"Hemingway developed an appetite for rock doves earlier in his career. When living as a poor writer in Paris, he had found them to be a unique and inexpensive source of protein for his young family. '[I] am also fond of the Jardin [du Luxembourg],' Hemingway wrote to Hotchner, 'because it kept us from starvation. On days when the dinner pot was absolutely devoid of content, I would put Mr. Bumby . . . into the baby carriage and wheel him over to the Jardin. Once my selection was made, it was a simple matter to entice my victim with the corn, snatch him, wring his neck, and flip his carcass under Mr. Bumby's blanket.'"

—*PIGEONS: THE FASCINATING SAGA OF THE WORLD'S MOST REVERED AND REVILED BIRD*

"Lunch."
"No."
"Lunch."
"No."
"Lunch."
"No. That's gross. Stop looking at pigeons. C'mon . . ."

I kept walking, pointing at birds, and getting chastised by my girlfriend. I'd become rather obsessed with rock doves (aka pigeons) as soon as I started to see them as food.

MONTHS EARLIER IN SOUTH CAROLINA

Like all good love stories, it started with a shotgun and a grain silo. The first rule was simple: if you aim for all of them, you'll hit none; but if you aim for one, you might hit two. Rule number two: shoot ahead of the bird in its predicted trajectory ("leading" it) so that the birdshot meets its mark. The key, it seemed, was sweeping the shotgun horizontally from behind the bird, tracing its path, and then shooting 2–3 bird lengths ahead of it without stopping. If you tried to stop and aim, you'd miss nine times out of 10.

Steven Rinella was once again my teacher, and within minutes, we had two handfuls of pigeons.

Back at the ranch (literally) in Batesburg, South Carolina, we began the thankless job of plucking. As Steve painstakingly worked, feather by feather, Dave Amick, our host and owner of Carolina Custom Rifles, stood next to us. He chuckled, picked up a pigeon, and, in a flurry of motion and two seconds, held up two perfectly clean pigeon breasts, ready for the grill.

"Let me see that again," Steve asked. He was impressed. I was dumbfounded.

The subsequent tutorial prompted Steve to reminisce about snatching pigeons by hand in NYC.

"But aren't you concerned about urban pigeons that eat garbage?" I asked.

"I don't think they eat garbage, actually. I've never seen a pigeon—and I pay attention to pigeons—eat dog shit."

"Don't the city pigeons taste funny compared to rural pigeons?"

"I wouldn't want to do a Pepsi Challenge."

And this, dear reader, is when I went off the deep end.

Curiosity piqued, I began to make phone calls to UC Berkeley, UC Davis, toxicologists, pest exterminators, and chemists. Given that nearly all cities have an endless supply of pigeons, I wanted to test things out firsthand. But I didn't want to poison myself. This meant I needed to answer the question:

"How likely am I to get sick from eating city pigeons?"

THE OFFICIAL CHANNELS

In a conversation with a wonderful team at UC Davis, I provided the context: I wanted to determine the toxic loads of pigeons that might be consumed by homeless people in San Francisco. This wasn't complete fiction. I'd taken daylong homeless tours of the Tenderloin through vayable.com, and though most homeless people know where to get food from shelters, pigeons weren't out of the question.

The call with the UC Davis team centered on potential study design:

- We could do a full necropsy (studying the entire bird for parasitology, bacterial load, and more) or simply analyze the livers. The latter would have higher concentrations of toxins than muscle tissue.

- It would be easy to run a pesticide, plant toxin, anticoagulant, and heavy metal report, which would cover more than 120 line items. We could then comb the SF county pesticide-use reports to add more contaminant suspects to the list.

- Once the pigeons had been analyzed, we could compute how many "average" pigeons a 70-kg (154-lb) male, for instance, could consume while staying under toxin limits such as the arsenic acceptable daily intake (AADI).

After an exciting 30-minute brainstorm, we hit the deal killer:

"How exactly are you planning on getting the pigeon liver samples? We just need to ensure you have the right authorizations."

Authorizations?

Perplexed, I told them I'd follow up. Later that night, El Google helped me resolve the confusion. On the one hand, the SF Department of Public Health categorizes pigeons as vectors:

> "Vectors include living organisms, such as mosquitoes, fleas, wasps, pigeons, raccoons, mice, and rats, that have the potential to spread filth and disease, to contaminate food and water, to destroy property, and/or to cause injury or severe annoyance." ‡

And yet, on the other hand:

> "In San Francisco it is not legal to poison, trap, or shoot pigeons."

Minchia. Granted, the Davis team kindly offered to introduce me to their California Public Health Office contact, who could help me navigate the official channels. But I knew that would be too slow. The results would never arrive before my book deadline.

What's an aspiring pigeon snatcher to do?

THE UNOFFICIAL CHANNELS

"I'm happy to use my obscure but sordid connections in Mexico to help."

I had broadened my horizons. The person now on the phone was a CEO with lab contacts outside of the U.S. Let's call him "Moreau."[25]

I had considered flash-freezing pigeons from a legal killing zone and shipping them to a Mexican forensics lab, but Moreau had a better idea:

"Why not test pigeons *from* Mexico City with a lab there?"

The more I thought about it, the more it made sense. Mexico City is one of the most polluted cities in the world. Thermal inversion puts smog at ground level, and if local pigeons ended up safe to eat (at a 1–2-pigeon-per-day survival volume), they'd almost certainly be safe to eat in SF.

After a week of back-and-forth e-mails, he called to explain the black-market process. The Mexico logistics required two teams: forensic scientists and local gangbangers' street lieutenants. The latter could gather pigeons from a cathedral, but they'd offered, as it was just as easy, to get human livers if more useful.

Yipes.

It was at this point that I threw in the towel. I'd spent a ludicrous amount of time OCD'ing on pigeons already, and being an accessory to murder wasn't high on my to-do list.

And, as one PhD toxicologist put it to me quite rightly, pointing out the relative size of pigeons, "I doubt that any contamination would cause an acute toxicity in a human. The pigeon would simply die before you found them . . . though that might make them easier to catch."

But you could rightly ask: why the hell did I get so obsessed with pigeons to start with?

Because they're ubiquitous and delicious, of course.

25 He and I both share a fascination with the exposome: in simple terms, the study of how genes can change due to environmental exposure to compounds, ranging from benzenes to endocrine-mimicking pesticides like atrazine, commonly found in Nor-Cal groundwater.

How to Pop a Pigeon

Assuming you are in a legal kill zone, all you need to debreast the dark, moist meat of the ubiquitous pigeon (or its smaller cousin, the dove) is your own two hands. No knife required. Here's how David Amick of Carolina Custom Rifles does it.

1. If necessary, kill the pigeon

Just grab the neck and push away as if opening an umbrella. The spine's like a candy necklace, and the head will likely pop off.

2. Snap off the wings

It's going to be messy. Stretch one wing out and, using your thumb, break the wing bone as close to the breast as possible. Work on one wing at a time. (Dave compares the breaking resistance to a short stack of popsicle sticks.)

3. Pluck the pigeon's breast (optional)

If you like skin on your roast, thoroughly clear the breast of its downy feathers. I didn't bother with this.

4. Pop the pigeon

The end of the breastbone that's closest to the pigeon's legs is called the sternum. Pierce the soft cavity beneath the sternum with your off-hand thumb. Slide your other thumb into the cavity and then, using all your might, alternate gradually between two motions: running the second thumb along the bird's spine and pulling outward with both thumbs. You're efficiently peeling the entire breast off the carcass. (If you skipped Step 2, the wings will make Step 4 considerably harder.)

5. Clean the breast

Remove the pigeon's innards (you can cook the heart and the liver if you like) and, if you skipped Step 3, its skin. Chances are there will be undigested grain in the pigeon's "craw," which is where many animals store food prior to digestion. Don't eat that.

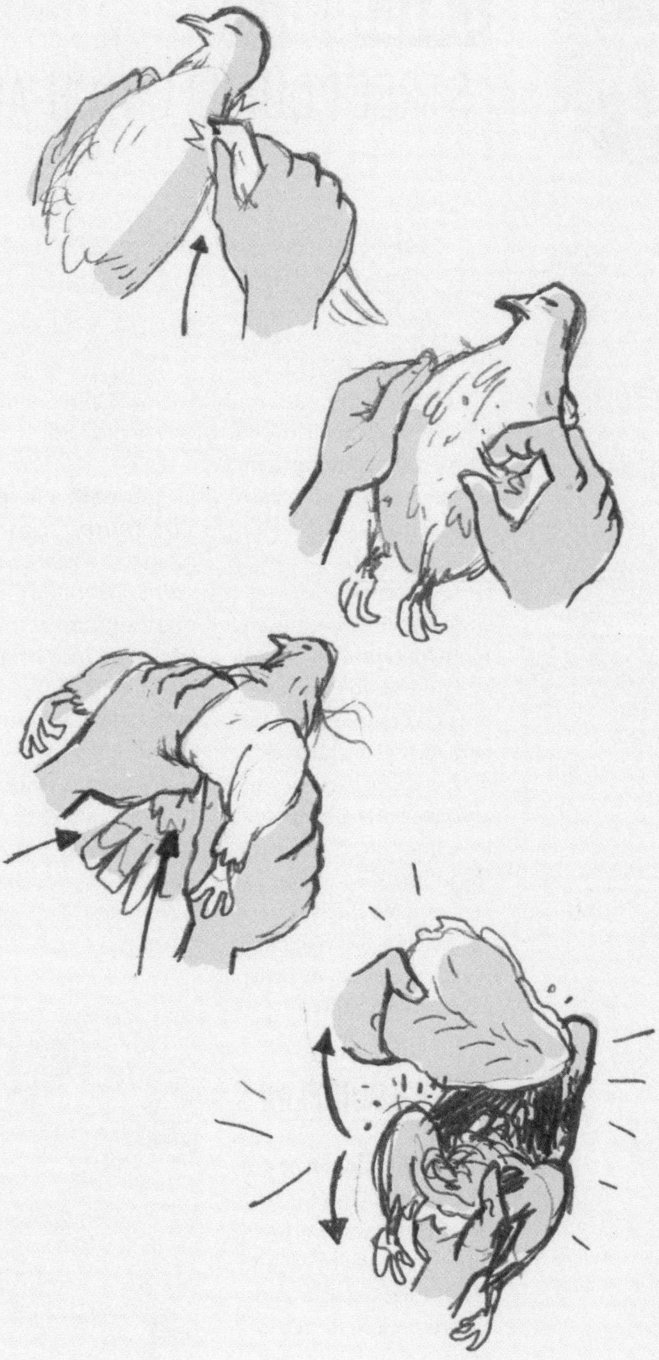

LESSON 26

SKILLS

CATCHING BY HAND

"STREET QUAIL" CATCH-AND-RELEASE

TOTAL TIME

Varies

GEAR

- Hands
- Jacket with a pocket
- Feed

> "I feel totally ridiculous. Like, why do I have to be in camouflage? So the big bad quail doesn't see me?"
>
> —JEREMY (VINCE VAUGHN), *WEDDING CRASHERS*

For hand-catching a pigeon, you'll be sitting on a bench and pinning them to the ground. Don't crush them. This is "you break (injure) it, you eat it," so wear winter gloves if you want some cushioning and room for error.

For feed, you can use bread crumbs or corn, but parakeet food or generic birdseed is better. Pet stores and grocery stores carry at least one type. If you want the ultimate, sauté the feed in some chicken fat or, seriously, pigeon (squab) fat if you can get it. The little cannibals go ballistic.

STEVE'S GUIDELINES

00 **Pick a park, if possible.** Don't go after hard-hitting underpass pigeons. They're wise to predators. Go to a park where people feed the buggers and lull them into semi-domestication. When in doubt, follow the old Chinese men or chess players.

01 **Create a feeding frenzy.** The pigeons have to be more concerned with fighting one another than with you. Steve recommends gathering at least 5 pigeons with generous food.

02 **Take a walkabout.** If they're too wary of you, leave some feed in front of your planned bench seat and go for a 10-minute walk. Come back, sit down, and put more food in the same place. They'll acclimate to the danger-free zone and at least a few will ignore you.

03 **Hold your "grabbing" hand at knee height.** Keep your elbows on your thighs. You'll be tempted to hang your hand as low as possible, but this will scare them off, even if you keep it still. Pros can break this rule; novices shouldn't.

The novice starting position.

04 Choose the sexiest pigeon. Even if this is catch-and-release, you want to develop good habits. Go for a shiny coat and intact, normal-looking feet. "Bumblefoot," a form of staph infection, can cause screwed-up feet, and viral avian pox can lead to wartlike growths. Aim for sexy feet.

05 When you go for it, pin them, don't grab them. The goal is to drop straight down and trap them between your hand and the ground. The fingers act as a cover, not a clamp.

06 Extra credit: the pocket papoose. Once you have the bird trapped, hold it with both hands on the sides, almost as if you're going to hike it like a football. Then, stick it headfirst into a big jacket pocket. I've never done this, but Steve swears: "They calm right down and barely move. It's odd." This "pocket papoose" is legal insurance. If a cop stops you and asks, "Is that a pigeon in your pocket, or are you just happy to see me?" you have some plausible deniability. "Oh, this guy? Just taking him for a relaxing walk!" Then you let him go. The last thing you need is a criminal record for something idiotic like killing a pigeon when A) you don't need to, and B) it's illegal where you happen to be.

07 Don't get frustrated. If you don't catch a pigeon, just remember two things. First, like anything, it takes practice. That's why we're practicing! Second, as a Sonoma hunter named Jake told me after our first unsuccessful 6 a.m.–6 p.m. hog hunt, "That's why they call it 'hunting' and not 'killing.'"

The more advanced pigeon grab, perfected by Steven Rinella.

LESSON 27

SKILL

IMPROVISED STOVES

HOBO-CAN "HOBOKEN" COOKING

SHORTHAND

High-heat hobo oven: grill whole squab, 2T oil, thigh side 3min, breast side 3min till internal temp 130F. Rest 6min.

HANDS-ON TIME

10 minutes

TOTAL TIME

40 minutes

GEAR

- Knife
- Tin can
- Fire-starting material
- Optional: License plate, aluminum foil, or flat rock
- Optional: Sticks to support your pot

OPTIONAL MUSIC PAIRING

"Ghettoblaster" by Cirrus

"I'm tired of taking. I want to make things. I want to add something to this world."

—REMY, *RATATOUILLE*

The hobo-can "Hoboken" stove is a portable, high-speed, and low-headache method of fire cooking, whether in the outback or in the parking lot of an Outback Steakhouse.

The following how-to is written by Tim Anderson, author of the "Heirloom Technology" column in *Make* magazine. Tim can build almost anything from scavenged materials, which he attributes in part to his "reverse Peace Corps": learning from poor people all over the world.

ENTER TIM ANDERSON

This is the tin can twig stove hoboes have used for cooking since time immemorial.

It's quick to make and easy to light, and does a lot of cooking with mere handfuls of twigs for fuel. It doesn't make much smoke or shine much light, in case you don't want to be found. It also doesn't leave fire scars or start forest fires very well. That's good for both fugitives and environmentalists.

My favorite container for a hobo stove is a 3-qt olive oil can with three "doors" at the bottom for air intakes. I've cooked salmon heads and giblets into soup on a driftwood pile in the rain in British Columbia with one. I consumed the olive oil during the weeks it took me to learn to catch salmon.

If that's not your thing, you can use the common beverage can. We're going to make the hobo stove seen in pic I on the opposite page.

A license plate is optional, but something like that, even a folded piece of aluminum foil or a flat rock, will be nice so you don't harm the surface under your stove. This stove is tall and narrow (hence, easy to tip over), so you'll want to pound three sticks around it to support your pot, or put the can between three rocks, or hang your pot over it using a tree branch.

Find the tallest can possible. You need height for convection, or airflow. The pictured coconut juice can is good. It's tall and the steel is pretty heavy for a drink can, so it'll last a while.

Food cans had lead solder in the joints until 1993, so don't use old cans. Pineapple cans have zinc plating inside, in case you think you need to breathe more zinc.[26]

26 Attention, Darwin Award winners: This is a joke. Don't inhale zinc.

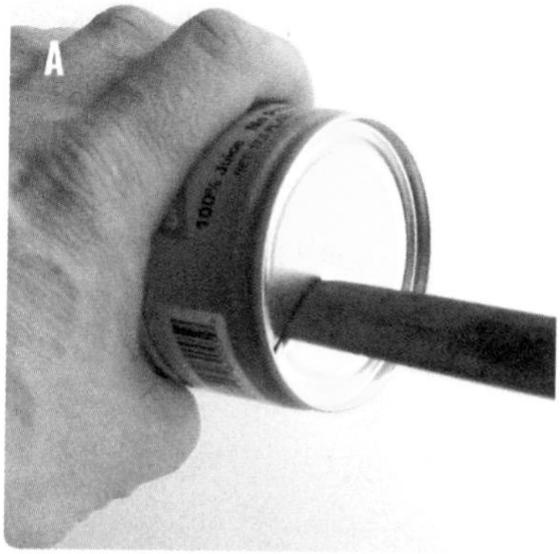
A

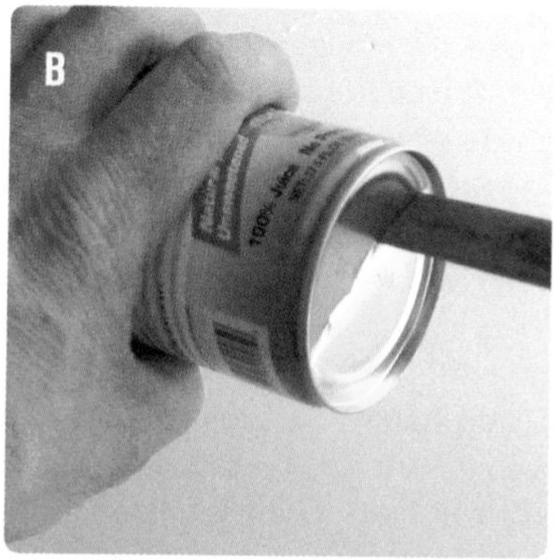
B

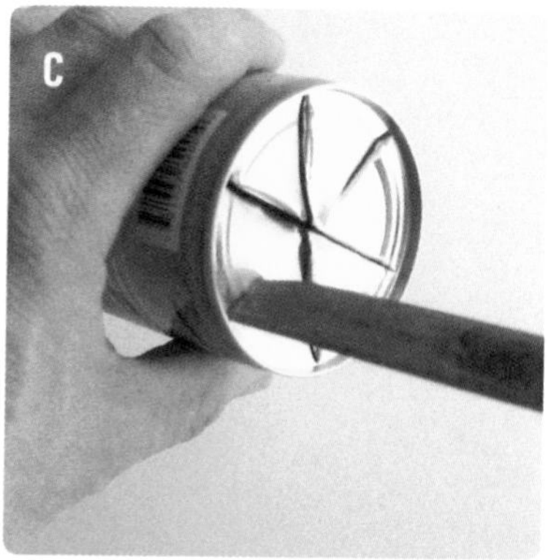
C

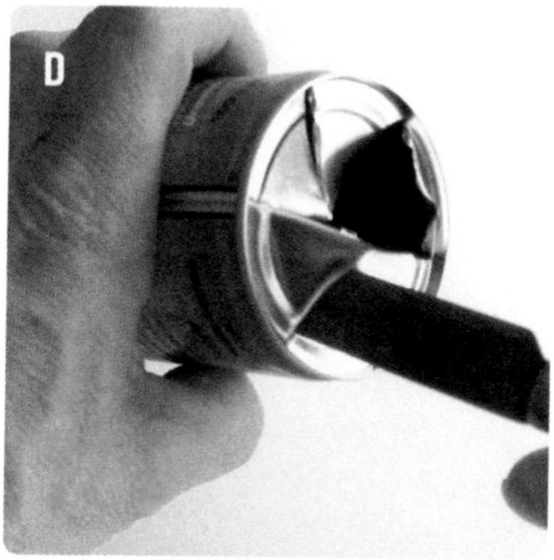
D

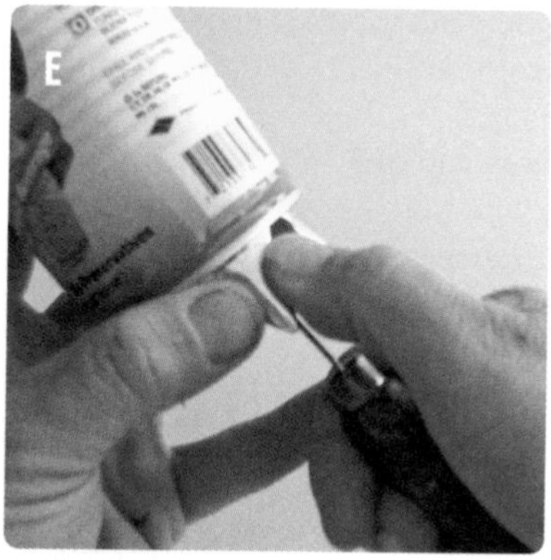
E

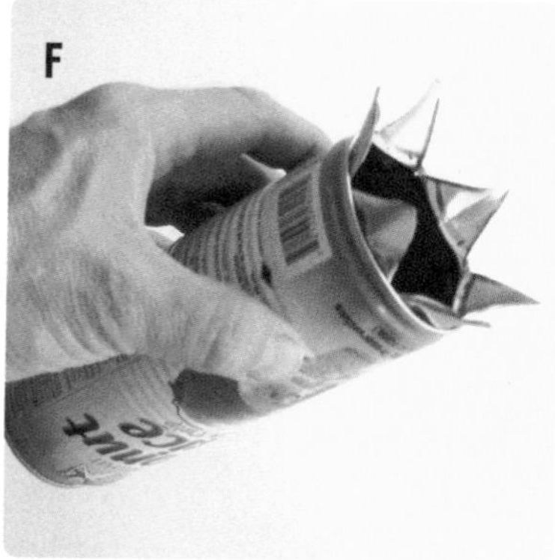
F

G

H

I

PREP

00 **Make the initial incision.** Cut an X or asterisk in one end of the can. These flaps are going to be the pot supports. The bottom on this can is heavier than the top, and the top has the pry-tab open, so we're using the bottom.

Warning from my grand-dad: "Don't cut toward yourself and you won't get cut."

01 **Pry up and crease the flaps.** Pry up the flaps. Don't cut yourself on the sharp corners. Crease each flap down the middle as seen in pic E. That makes them a lot stronger.

02 **Cut doors.** Cut some drawbridge-style doors—3 should do it—in the sides near the bottom (see pic H). Those are the air intakes and stoking doors.

03 **First use.** It's really easy to start a fire in one of these stoves. Start with wispy stuff or paper, if you're still that close to civilization. Then work up to pencil-size stuff. Thumb thickness is probably the most you'll want for cooking. Thicker than that tends to smoke, because you'll put in wet ones by accident.

The first time you use it, let the paint burn off before you start cooking. Stay back and don't breathe the fumes. Leave that for the youngsters who still enjoy the smell of burning plastic.

Before you put the pot on, you can simply toss the twigs in the top. Once cooking, poke them in under the pot. You can feed longer sticks in gradually through the doors in Seminole star-fire fashion. If you're worried your pot will topple the can, as mentioned earlier, you'll want to pound 3 sticks into the ground around your can as supports. If it's windy, you'll want to put a windscreen around your stove. Palm leaves or ferns can work well for this, as can palmetto leaves, which I used in the jungle on the Yucatán Peninsula.

It's so quick to start one of these can fires, sometimes I'll pull over and do my cooking at a rest stop or by the side of the road. I don't worry about hassles from authorities, because it's so easy to move the fire or put it out. But I've never been hassled. The rules about fires are usually about "open fires," and this isn't that.

04 **Optional step: Get cooking!** Sticking with our pigeon theme, you could procure a small whole squab (a diner-friendly term for pigeon), but chicken breast strips, other thin protein, or even sliced eggplant are all acceptable.

If you haven't already, go outside and get a small fire going in your can stove. Support your nonstick skillet (lighter than cast-iron) above it. Hold your hand an inch over the skillet every few minutes, and once you can't hold it there for more than 3 seconds, you're ready to cook.

For squab, per Josh Skenes's recommendation:

- Oil the pan.
- Place the squab down, thigh-side first, for 3 minutes.
- Turn to breast for another 3 minutes.
- Take off heat and let rest for 6 minutes.
- Eat. Unlike chicken, the juices will still run red when cooked to medium or medium-rare. Feel free to use your probe thermometer during resting (aiming for internal temp of 130°F/55°C) if you like.

Opening a Bottle When You're (Un) Screwed

One of the finest episodes of the old *Twilight Zone* starred a misanthropic bookworm who survives a nuclear apocalypse. He emerges from an underground shelter to find himself alone—at last!—with all the libraries of the world. But then, irony of ironies, he drops his glasses and steps on them.

Similarly, if you end up like Tom Hanks in *Cast Away,* it would be a shame to find a life-affirming bottle of fine wine, only to be helpless without a bottle opener. Praise Odin, drunks figured this puzzle out eons ago. You have three options for brute-forcing a bottle to unleash the nectar. The choices are *in, out,* or *off.*

In

Find a 2–3"-long stick of slightly smaller diameter than the cork. Remove the foil, put the stick on top of the cork, and carefully knock the cork in with a shoe or rock.

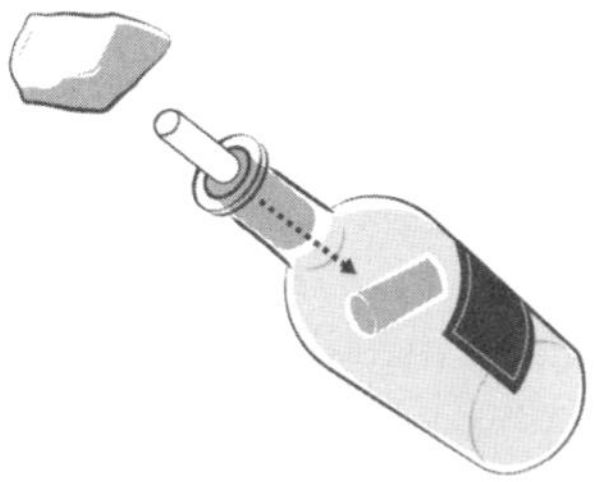

Out

I learned this one from a Polish wino. Remove the foil, put the base of the bottle in a shoe (ensure a decent heel), and smack the shoe-plus-bottle against a tree or wall until the agitated carbon dioxide forces the cork out far enough to remove. Don't hold the bottle too tightly, and prepare for a workout, as this could take 4–5 minutes.

Off

"Saber" the bottle with a heavy-ish knife. This is a traditional service with champagne, but it'll work on any bottle that has a decent lip on the rim. *Never* try after drinking, as you will cut your hand off. So, common sense intact and using the *blunt* edge of large chef's knife or utility/survival knife like the ESEE-5, the movement looks like the illustration. I suggest rehearsing with empty bottles before anything expensive.

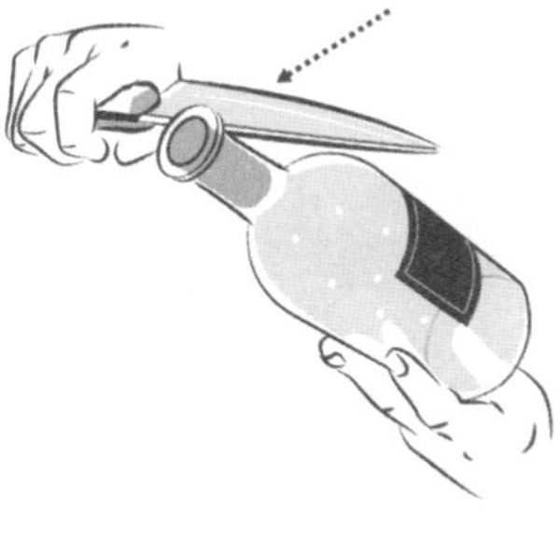

Be sure to angle the blade up at 45 degrees so you're less likely to hack yourself on the back windup, which should be done slowly.

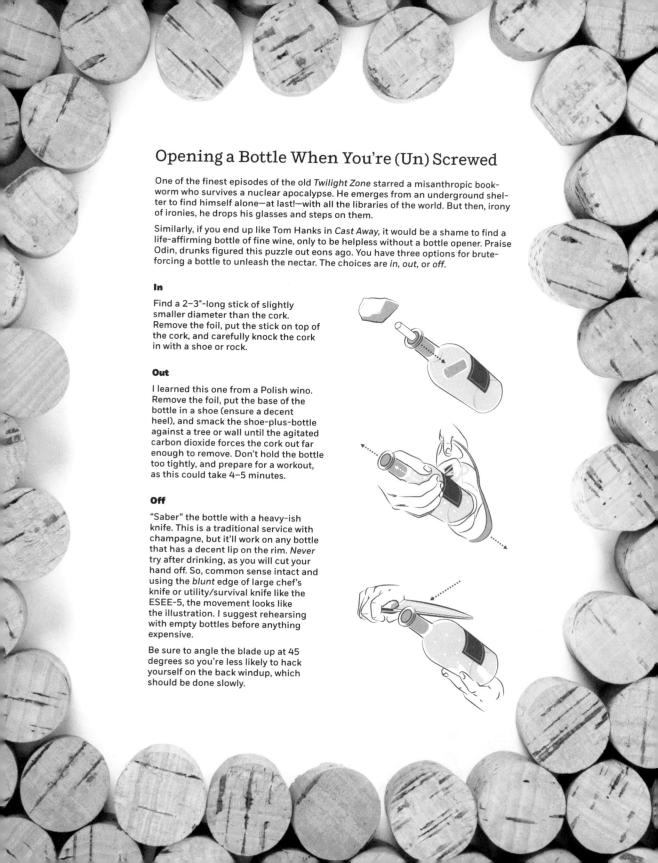

FISHING: FROM GILL NETS TO YO-YO TRAPS

Paul: "Couldn't you find him?"
Norman: "The hell with him."
Paul: "Well, I thought we were supposed to help him."
Norman: "How the hell do you help that son of a bitch?"
Paul: "By taking him fishing."

—*A RIVER RUNS THROUGH IT*

Corey Arnold caught his first fish at age three. He started commercially fishing salmon in Alaska at age 19. Since then, he has starred on *Deadliest Catch*, had his photography featured in galleries worldwide, appeared in everything from *Rolling Stone* to *Audubon* magazine, and served as official documentarian for Ocean2012, a coalition of fisheries and environmental groups that promote sustainable fishing practices and policy in the EU.

ADRIAN
CONSTRUCTION

Corey Arnold, age nine.

For moving meditation, fly-fishing is a wonderful art. For acquiring food when you're starving, the methods change dramatically. This Q&A with Corey explores a few lesser known approaches, and his recommendations require little or no fishing experience.

Links to all recommendations can be found at fourhourchef.com/fishing.

If you had to pick one easy-to-use tool for survival fishing, what would it be?

I think the gill net is the best possible option to have on hand, although they take up a bit more space than fishing line and a lure or hooks.

Gill nets rely on entanglement rather than enticement and can be effective in lakes, streams, even in the ocean. Trout can see the nets in the day, so they should be placed overnight and checked in the morning. If you are setting the net in a stream or small creek, place it entirely across a narrow portion, then sneak around upstream and run through the water toward the net, herding fish into it. They'll panic, swim downstream, and get snared. There is a reason why gill netting is illegal for noncommercial fishermen in U.S. streams—it's highly effective. A second option, for use in a small or shallow pond, would be to tie one end of the gill net to land (like a tree or stump) and then walk around the pond with the other end, whether on land or wading.

A compact 12 x 4–ft net can also be used for rabbits and small game. It's multipurpose, unlike most fishing gear.

What about hooks? Useless or useful?

Useful. There are some very compact all-in-one survival kits for hook-and-line fishing, and these come in a close second after the gill net. I'd bring both. The BestGlide ASE kit (fourhourchef.com/bestglide-ase) is one such option.

There is also a tiny, lightweight auto fishing reel called the Yo-Yo trap. It costs six bucks. This is a companion to the all-in-one kit, not a replacement, but it makes sense to have both.

You can hang the Yo-Yo off branches over a lake and return later, effectively making it a reel that fishes by itself while you're gathering other food. When a fish hits, the reel automatically hauls the fish in close so that the line can't go slack and the hook can't slip out. You will need to buy hooks and 4- or 6-lb test leader material, as the included line is thick (and could be used for setting up tents, etc., in a bind). Don't forget to study your knots.[27] Tying monofilament fishing line is a lot harder than tying your shoelaces.

Unlike with the gill net, you can often practice using the all-in-one kit and Yo-Yo trap without breaking the law. (To be safe, always check with your local department of fish and game.)

What about spearing fish? It shows up a hell of a lot on TV and in movies.

Spearing a fish with a homemade spear in the wilderness would be extremely difficult, unless you happened to crash-land near a salmon-spawning creek in late summer.

If you want to go mountain-man style with no lines or nets, I'd be more inclined to create a fish trap by pounding in a series of stakes to create a wall, which strategically funnels the fish into a small opening. If the entrance to the trap is pointed downstream, the fish will swim upstream inside the trap, and they will never see the exit behind them as they tread water. This concept can be applied

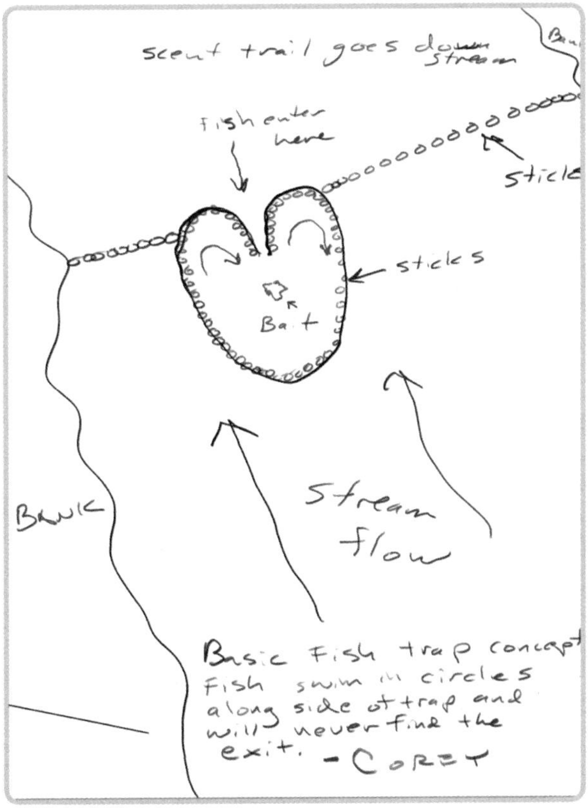
scent trail goes down stream
fish enter here
stick
sticks
Bait
Bank
Stream flow
Basic Fish trap concept
Fish swim in circles along side of trap and will never find the exit. -Corey

to fish traps large and small, and in a variety of environments, including the ocean.

I've witnessed excellent examples of primitive fish traps while working with the traditional mullet fisherman of the Messolonghi-Etoliko Lagoons in Greece. These are simple traps built on a huge scale, but the design of the trap is noteworthy and can be re-created on a much smaller scale. Similar fish traps have been used by native Alaskans and Pacific Northwest Native Americans.

27 See page 614 in the Appendix for the nine must-know knots.

LESSON 28

SKILL

COOKING WITH ACID

CEVICHE

INSPIRED BY

Fish Bar Chicago, Raymond Sokolov

SHORTHAND

Marinate 1lb wild shrimp, 1c lime juice 3hr till opaque. Mix in 2 cubed tomatillos & avocados, 2t red pepper, S+P to taste.

HANDS-ON TIME

15 minutes

TOTAL TIME

15 minutes, plus at least 3 hours marinating

GEAR

- Large stainless-steel mixing bowl or other nonreactive[28] bowl (glass, ceramic, and plastic are all fine)
- Knife + cutting board

OPTIONAL MUSIC PAIRING

"Sel" by Smadj

"Somebody just back of you while you are fishing is as bad as someone looking over your shoulder while you write a letter to your girl."

—ERNEST HEMINGWAY

Ceviche introduces us to a new form of cooking: chemical cooking. The highly acidic[29] lime juice kills bacteria while making the protein more palatable.

Instead of using fish for this recipe, which you certainly could, we're going to use shrimp, because you haven't used this versatile protein yet, and we have fish coming soon.

This is a low-labor dish and a rest break, as you'll need your wits about you for the next lesson, mussels.

28 Many acidic foods—like ceviche, since it contains lime juice—can react with untreated surfaces like cast-iron, unlined copper, and aluminum, giving the food a metallic taste. Plan accordingly.

29 Lime juice has a pH of 2.2–2.4 on a scale from 1–14, where 1 is most acidic.

INGREDIENTS	TO SERVE 4 TO 6
Small wild Gulf shrimp or wild Maine shrimp, peeled and deveined (ask your fishmonger to do this)	**1 lb** (450 g)
Freshly squeezed lime juice (8 limes or so)	**1 c** (240 ml)
Large tomatillos (or Roma tomatoes)	**2**
Large, ripe avocados	**2**
Red pepper flakes	**1–2 t**
S+P	**To taste**
OPTIONAL	
Basil leaves, torn into pieces	**8**
Fresh cilantro, chopped	**½ c** (10 g)

The Silo

For extra presentation points, cut a disposable cup in half. Place the top half on the serving plate (or bowl) like a silo, and pile the ceviche inside. Gently remove the cup and voilà—your food is stacked and high.

Making food tall, instead of flattened and nondescript, is so common in restaurants that they purchase circle cutters of various diameters exclusively for this purpose. Desserts, appetizers, tartare... it's all piled high. For flourish, consider adding a lime wedge as a garnish.

PREP

00 The night before serving time, or at least 3 hours before eating, peel and wash the sand veins (black lines) out of the shrimp, if your fishmonger didn't do this for you. Cut the shrimp in half if you like.

01 Toss the shrimp in the large nonreactive bowl, add the 1 c (240 ml) lime juice, cover, and marinate in the refrigerator for at least 3 hours. I just leave them overnight.

PICKUP

00 The shrimp are ready to eat when they look opaque.

01 Cut the 2 tomatillos and 2 avocados into roughly ¼" (0.6-cm) cubes, if you want to be precise. I don't worry about precision and rough-cut sizes that look appealing. For the avocado, use the technique on page 183.

02 Add the tomatillos, avocados, and 1–2 t pepper flakes to the bowl. Include the basil and/or cilantro, if using. Mix gently by hand and add S+P to taste.

03 Serve immediately or chilled. I prefer chilled with a cold glass of Rombauer chardonnay. Yes, I'm that guy.

LESSON 29

SKILLS

JŌYŌ KNIFE CUTS, GATHERING

MOULES MARINIÈRE WITH FENNEL

INSPIRED BY

Sarah Jay

SHORTHAND

Sauté 1 chopped onion, ½ sliced fennel bulb, 2 garlic cloves, 2T EVOO 5min till soft. + ¼t salt, ½c white wine; boil. Add 1lb mussels 3min covered till open. Serve w 5 basil leaves.

HANDS-ON TIME

10 minutes

TOTAL TIME

20 minutes

GEAR

- Knife + cutting board
- Vegetable scrubber
- Finished cast-iron Dutch oven, or raw cast-iron with PanSaver

OPTIONAL MUSIC PAIRING

"Skillz" by Gang Starr

> **"It's the little details that are vital. Little things make big things happen."**
>
> —JOHN WOODEN, HALL OF FAME NCAA BASKETBALL COACH (10 NCAA TITLES IN 12 YEARS)

Moules marinière ("mussels in the marine style") are mussels cooked in white wine. Hungover chefs worldwide love this dish. It's easy and fast, so it's a popular item at Saturday and Sunday brunches. Even if you limit the ingredients to just mussels, white wine, and garlic, you'll still have a delicious meal in less than 10 minutes.

This lesson is also the Jōyō Knife Cuts recipe, much like my *jōyō* (common usage) Japanese character poster on page 35.

This recipe tests for all the knife skills you're likely to need. It includes everything we've learned thus far, plus a few new skills, including the litmus test for all chefs: fine-dicing an onion.

COPPOLA
Maldon

INGREDIENTS	TO SERVE 2[30]
Small fennel bulb (about 5 oz/150 g)	½
Small yellow onion, ½ cut into radial slices, ½ fine-diced (see next page). If you're making this for the first time, get 2 onions—1 for the knife skills practice alone.	1
Garlic, finely diced	**2 cloves**
Mussels (ask your grocer to scrub and debeard, if possible)	**1 lb** (450 g)
Basil leaves	**5**
EVOO	**2 T**
Salt	**¼ t**
White wine	**½ c** (120 ml)

PREP

00 Cut the fennel in half lengthwise, cut off the green stalk and trim the top layer of any discolorations or tough areas. Lay the fennel half cut side down and thinly slice it (pic B). Don't worry about exact thickness.

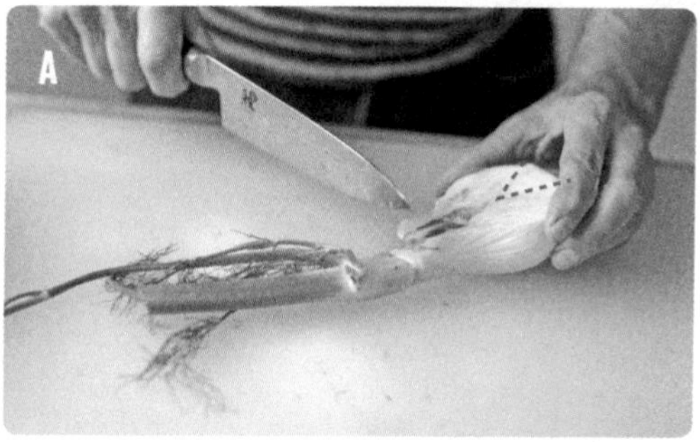
A

Don't forget to notch a V and cut out the core.

01 Cut the onions. For skill development, I want you to practice two new techniques the first time through the recipe. In the future, simply use your preferred method. Follow the next one-pager before continuing.

B

30 Serves two as an appetizer. Double the recipe to serve two as a main course, or four as an appetizer. You'll need a 6-qt stockpot if you double the size. Double all the ingredients and cook in your stockpot, increasing the cooking time for the mussels to 5 minutes.

NEW KNIFE SKILLS ONE-PAGER

Peel and halve an onion lengthwise (pole-to-pole). You'll first use radial cuts:

RADIAL CUTS

00 Take one of the halves and lay it on the cutting board, with the root end facing you. Slice the root off (see pic A).

01 Starting on one end of the onion half and following the onion's natural curve, make a series of evenly spaced cuts through the onion, angling your knife toward the core. You'll start with the knife nearly parallel to the cutting board; when you've reached the middle of the onion, your knife should be in a vertical position, perpendicular to the board.

02 When your knife is almost vertical and the onion is getting wobbly, tip the onion to the right side so it's flat again.

03 Repeat the cutting, again angling your knife toward the core, until the onion is too thin to continue.

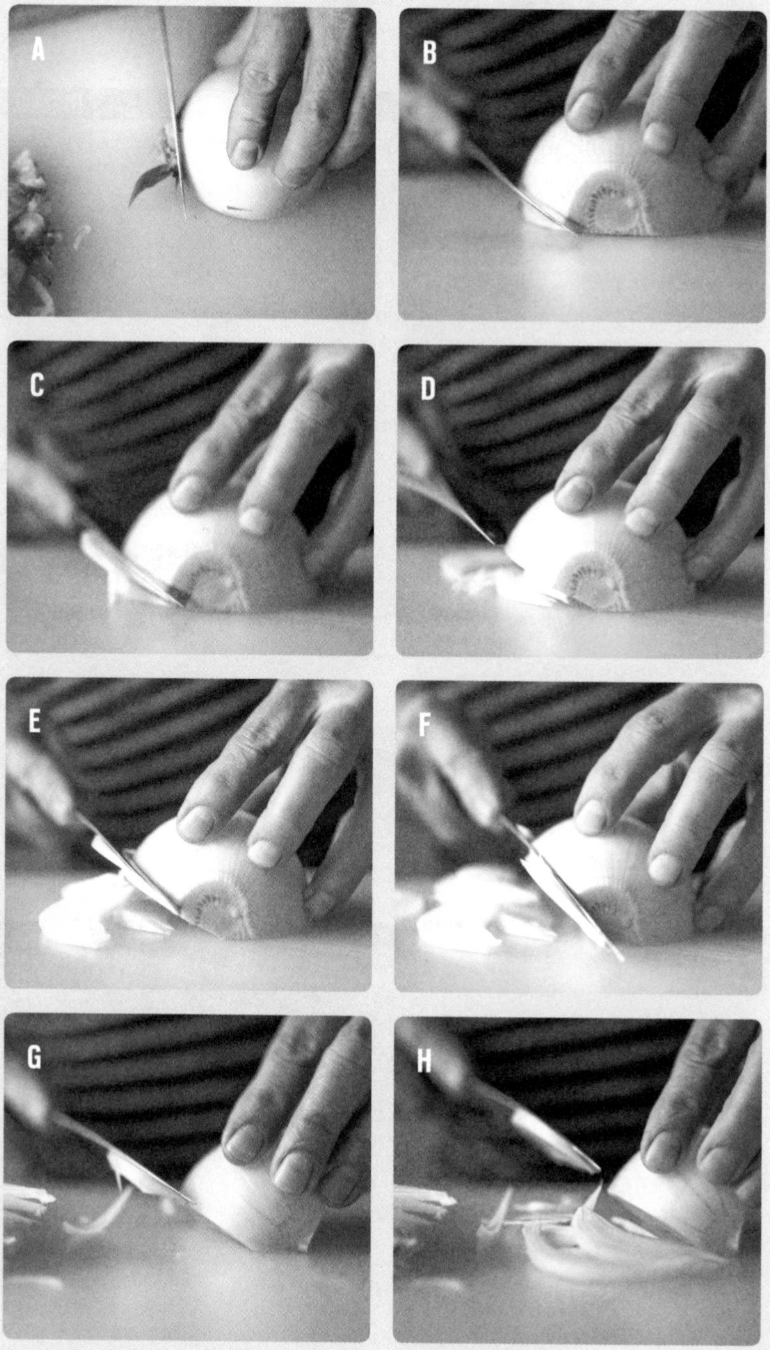
A
B
C
D
E
F
G
H

Next, you'll fine-dice the other half:

FINE-DICE

00 Take the second half of the onion. Don't cut off the root end (see pic A). The root holds everything together while you're cutting.

01 **First you'll make a series of horizontal cuts.** With your kung fu grip (like you're grabbing a dime), hold the top down. Cut near the edge of the cutting board, and clear your knife handle off the side.

02 Make a slight incision, then start slicing, *slow* and *steady*, toward the root end. *Don't* cut all the way through the onion—about ¾ through. If you think you might overshoot or cut yourself, you can tip the knife, still in the onion (sharp edge down), and tap the onion (and knife) on the cutting board to get where you need to be (see pic C).

03 Make 3–4 cuts total.

A

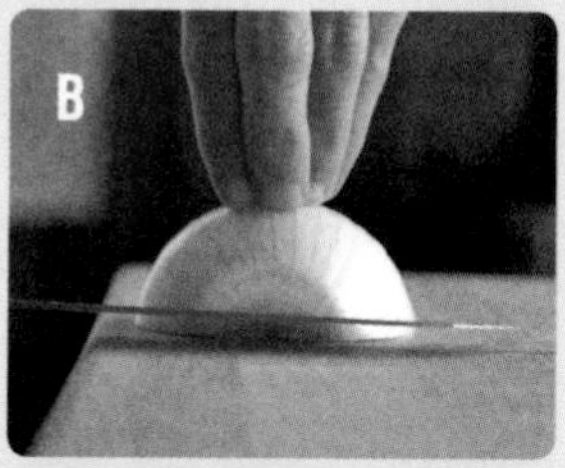
B

C

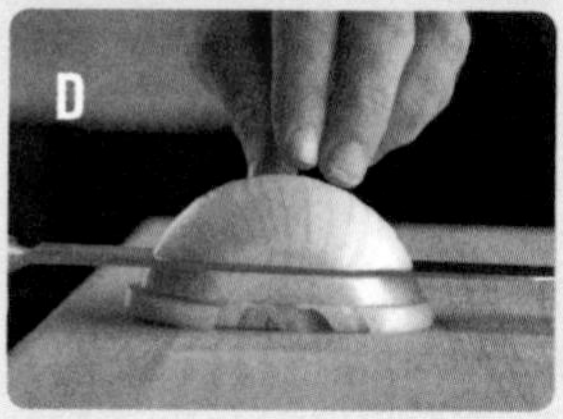
D

04 **Next you'll make vertical cuts.** Cut down, resting the blade on your fingernail, creating slices about the same size/width as your horizontal cuts. Do *not* cut the root end, circled at right. Little bits and pieces will always fall off at this point. Don't worry! Just do your best.

05 Turn the onion 90 degrees. Hold it together with your hand, gripping it like a tennis ball. Cut it again, into slices roughly the same width as your other cuts. *Don't worry* about getting every last bit of the onion—your fingers are more important. As always, the blade rests on the knuckle of your middle finger, with your fingers bent and pulled back from the blade so you don't cut them.

06 Congrats!

E

F

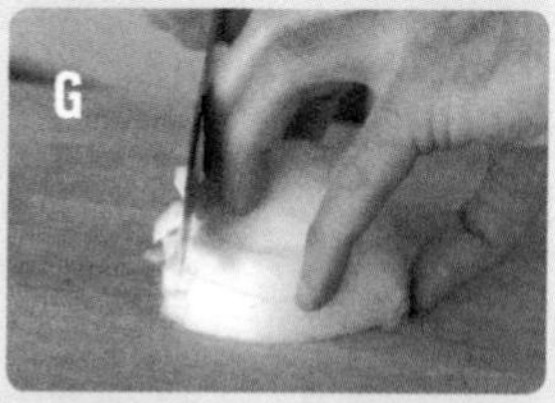
G

H

For practice:

Repeat both radial cuts and dicing on your second onion and set aside for another use.

For storage:

Put the diced onion in water and cover with plastic wrap; this temporarily keeps onions and all allium vegetables (shallots, leeks, garlic, etc.) from turning bitter.

For this time:

We'll use the two halves of radial cuts.

02 Dice the 2 garlic cloves. If you want to practice your cutting, you can dice the garlic exactly the same way you diced the onion, just on a miniature scale. Alternatively, you can fine slice or, my preference, use a garlic press. If you really want to add knife mileage, use a different technique on each clove.

03 If your grocer or fishmonger didn't do it (you should ask), scrub the 1 lb (450 g) mussels with a vegetable brush to clean and debeard them. If you look at where the 2 shells meet, you'll see what appear to be threads of brown seaweed. This is the mussel's "beard" (the byssus thread, which is what mussels use to attach themselves to rocks). Don't worry if you don't find it on every mussel. If your scrubbing doesn't remove the beards, just yank them out with your fingers.

04 Cut the 5 basil leaves into chiffonade (see page 213).

PICKUP

00 Heat the 2 T oil in a cast-iron Dutch oven over medium heat. Add the fennel, onion, and garlic and sauté, stirring occasionally, for about 5 minutes, until softened but not browned. Add the ¼ t salt, which is roughly four 3-finger pinches.

01 Add the ½ c (120 ml) white wine, increase the heat to high, and bring to a boil.

02 Add the mussels, cover, and cook until the mussels open, usually around 3 minutes. Shake the pot a couple of times during cooking to distribute the liquid and heat.

03 Spoon the mussels into 2 serving bowls, discarding any that remain closed. Spoon some of the vegetables and broth over each bowl.

04 Top with the basil and serve.

A

B

C

Foraging Mussels

Foraging wild mussels won't win you any points for sustainability. In fact, "farmed" mussels *are* new-and-improved wild mussels, generally grown on ropes at sea rather than in crowded areas like farmed fish. The mussels clean the water they are grown in, making them environmental darlings. They are a "best choice" on Monterey Bay Aquarium's Seafood Watch List. If you must forage, mussels are pretty easy to track down. Here are some pointers:

Beware of toxins: Mussels feed on plankton and other microscopic organisms, which means they can take in toxins, including pollution. (In California, there is an annual quarantine from May 1 to October 31.) Call the local health department to see if eating mussels in your area is safe. Take this seriously, as a sick mussel can kill you.

Where to look: Search for wild mussels in bays and estuary areas where they attach to rocks, wharves, and jetties.

When to go: At low tide, when the rocks are exposed.

What to look for: Identification is the most important part of foraging. There are more than 300 types of mussels in North America, so consult an identification chart for mussels native to your area; if you are in doubt about what you see, leave it.

What to bring: A heavy-bladed knife or pry bar to pry the mussels off the rocks, a bucket, rubber boots, and a fishing license (check your state's regulations before you go).

What to do before cooking: Wild mussels need a good cleaning to remove dirt and barnacles. Soak them in a bucket of seawater for about an hour, then dunk them in a fresh bucket of unsalted water. Immediately remove them from the water and scrape the shells with a scrub brush, then once again rinse to wash off the salt. Discard any mussels that are open. Debeard the mussels: hold a mussel in one hand, cover the other hand with a dry towel, and yank the beard off.

LESSON 30

SKILL

CREATING FIRE

FROM MODERN TO MALLMANN

Interviewer: "If your house were burning down and you could take one thing, what would it be?"

Jean Cocteau: "The fire."

"'Fire cooking' is actually a misnomer. You're cooking over the embers," said Joshua Skenes, chef-owner of Saison in San Francisco and one of *Food and Wine*'s Best New Chefs of 2011.

Sometimes, you don't even need the embers, as he demonstrated:

1. Use a broom to compress the embers in the corner, clearing just enough space for a small pot.

2. Use the cleared space, the hot bricks, as a "stovetop" for cooking.

Josh has become famous for his use of fire. He has classical training and loves his high-end Japanese Nenohi knives, but nothing captures his imagination quite like the open flame. The back of his business card sports three words, stark on ivory stock:

Play with fire.

"One of the first things that I cooked in a fire was a leek," Joshua recounts. "I gently turned it in the ash, and it got caramelized on the outside. I sliced it and put it on a plate with amazing olive oil, local sea salt from Monterey, and Meyer lemon juice.[31] I ate it and thought, *This is out of control.* The way fire pulls depth of flavor out is magical."‡

31 Meyer lemons have an intoxicating aroma and sweet taste, almost like a blend of lemon and orange.

Joshua, who's tried everything from fruit woods to fig woods, now uses almond wood from a farm in Northern California as his fuel of choice. He starts his fires with an Iwatani Torch Burner, and the flames are tended all day in the large brick oven outside of the Saison dining room. Much like the Olympic torch, it almost never goes out.

The Iwatani works beautifully, but let's look at how they do things in the world capital of grilling.

THE GAUCHO METHOD

I don't have a long history of wielding fire, but I am a seasoned consumer of *parrillada*, as grilled meat is known in Argentina. I've witnessed many all-day Sunday feasts—*asados*—in the provinces outside of Buenos Aires. These *asados* are a cultural mainstay and serious business. Roasting a whole lamb, as common in Patagonia as a stuffed turkey in the U.S., often starts at 6 a.m. and finishes near 2 p.m. Argies assume 4 lbs (2 kg) of meat will be eaten *per person* at such affairs. Bring your Pepto-Bismol.

Francis Mallmann is the Argentine figurehead of grilling, the capo, the Mickey Mantle of meat.

Raised in the Andes as the son of a preeminent nuclear physicist, Mallmann trained at the most famous French kitchens in the world, later becoming South America's most venerated Patagonian cook. But, in his own words, he was "tired of making fancy French food for wealthy customers in Buenos Aires" and so returned to his mother tongue: fire.

Patagonia is, as he describes it, still much like the Wild West was 100 years ago. Andean gauchos (cowboys) and the Indians before them used methods that he still recommends. For wood, he prefers, in descending order:

1. Oak
2. Maple
3. Birch or hickory

If you have to use charcoal instead of wood, use half the volume. For a serious, large-mammal meal, a minimum of 5 lbs (2.5 kg) of charcoal is needed.

All this in mind, Francis does the following:

LIGHTING A FIRE NEAR CIVILIZATION

00 Start with a crunched-up piece of newspaper or by making a small pile of wood chips.

01 Place a handful of small twigs over your newspaper or wood chips to create a cone.

02 Create a second layer around your cone using slightly larger wood pieces, such as kindling.

03 Gently place a few rolled sheets of newspaper through the gaps at the bottom of your cone; 5 should be sufficient.

04 Arrange a final layer around your cone using quartered logs no larger than 6" (15 cm) thick and 1½ ft (0.5 m) long.

05 Ignite the rolls of newspaper and let your fire steadily build until the quartered logs are burning efficiently.

06 Once your fire is burning well, add larger sections of logs or even whole logs up to 1½ ft (0.5 m) long and 10" (25 cm) in diameter.

To gauge the heat, hold your hand just above where the food will be placed. How long can you keep it there? To confuse people, you can count as they might in Argentina: *"uno matador, dos matador, tres matador, quatro matador"* and so on, just as Yanks say "one Mississippi, two Mississippi . . ."

A GENERAL GUIDE	
2 SEC	HIGH HEAT
3–4 SEC	MEDIUM-HIGH
5–6 SEC	MEDIUM
7–8 SEC	LOW HEAT

Seem complicated? Use Steve Rinella's rule of thumb: once you can hold your hand there for roughly 3 seconds but no more, you're ready to start cooking.

Speaking of Steve Rinella . . .

LESSON 31

SKILLS

GUTTING, SPIT COOKING

HOW TO GUT AND COOK TREE RAT (OR FISH)

SHORTHAND

Cook gutted, skewered squirrel 12-18" over a bed of coals, rotating every 2min. Remove when joints in back legs separate easily, about 20min.

TOTAL TIME

Approximately 35 minutes, plus time to start the fire and find your skewers

GEAR

- Kindling
- Optional: Coleman fire-starting paste
- Knife
- 1–2 sticks for skewering
- 2–4 forked sticks

OPTIONAL MUSIC PAIRING

♪ "Animal Rap Instrumental" by Jedi Mind Tricks

"Staying in the house breeds a sort of insanity always."

—HENRY DAVID THOREAU, AUTHOR

Perhaps you think that squirrels are cute, mute little creatures.

No so. They produce a chirp-squeal akin to a Jack Russell digging through a chalkboard. I know this because the little devils woke me throughout college from a branch outside my window at 6 a.m. or earlier. In Princeton, New Jersey, rumor has it, squirrels were once part of a breeding experiment at the university. The result? Thousands of racket-making rodents with odd coloration straight out of *Pimp My Squirrel*—dots, zebra patterns, racing stripes, and so on.

Just before Steve Rinella and I rendezvoused in South Carolina, where I could order a hunting license online instead of spending weeks on paperwork (in California), he sent me the itinerary via e-mail:

"OK, we'll shoot rifles on Friday. Saturday morning we'll go for deer. We'll hunt pigeons during the day with shotguns. Then we'll do deer again if we want that evening. Sunday we can hunt deer or squirrels in the morning or else concentrate on our meat packaging and preparations."

Reading this, I felt like Inigo Montoya in *The Princess Bride*. Did he say . . . squirrels?

INGREDIENTS	TO SERVE 1–2
Squirrels	**1–2**

COOKING SQUIRRELS

Steve once lived on a beach in Mexico (literally *on* the beach) for a month with his brother. The routine consisted of catch-and-release fishing for bonefish, and catch-and-kill fishing for barracuda and snapper, which they cooked on spits. They drank water from coconuts, and dried coconut husks served as fuel for the cooking fire.

Under more luxurious circumstances (i.e., having a decent backpack), he would have packed a multifuel stove like the Whisperlite or Optimus, sometimes referred to as "slut" stoves since they take anything: diesel, unleaded, propane, kitten farts, etc.

We'll explain spit cooking (*a la vara* in Spanish) with squirrel, which I used, but you'll practice on trout. Skip to page 336 if you'd like. Otherwise, the explanations under each step are Steve's.

PICKUP

00 **Get the fire started.** "I carry Coghlan's fire-starting paste. It's a great product for starting fires quickly in wet conditions. Good, dry kindling can be found beneath the canopy of pines and evergreens. Use the small, dry limbs, and start with match-size pieces. If it's very wet, use your knife to whittle toothpick-size pieces from the core of larger dry sticks. If the ground is soaked, you can also create a platform out of green branches, which you then build your fire upon." (As mentioned on page 244, the MacGyver replacement for fire paste is cotton balls rubbed in Vaseline and carried in a film canister.)

01 **In the meantime, get your sticks for the skewer.** "Make sure your skewers are green, taken from a live tree. The ideal size is 2 ft (60 cm) long, and 3/8"

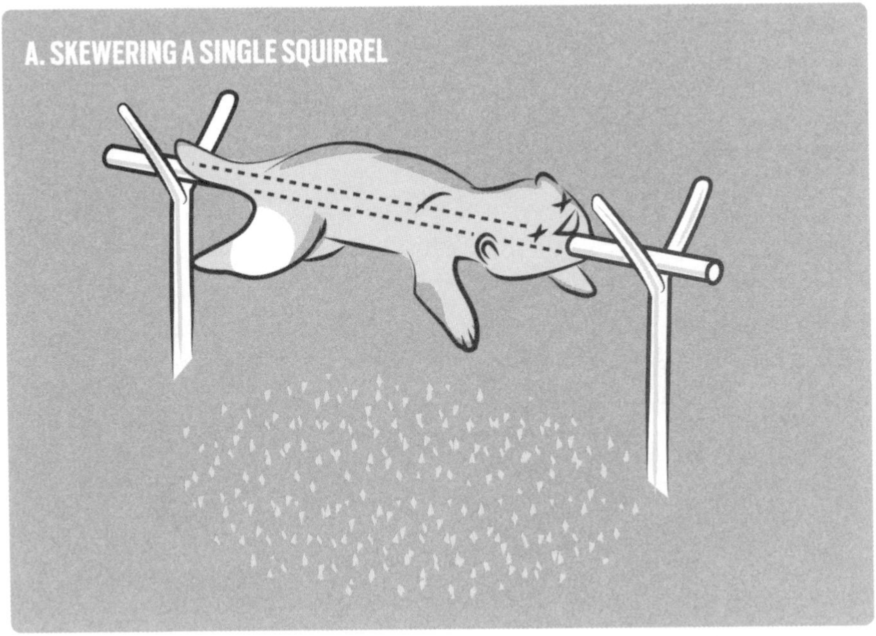
A. SKEWERING A SINGLE SQUIRREL

(9 mm) to ½" (13 mm) in diameter. Willow is a traditional skewer material, but almost any wood will work. Generally, hardwoods are better, as they are more durable and less prone to burning to nothing. We used maple."

02 **Optional: Cut off the feet and tail.** "I did this for aesthetic reasons, as a long, singed tail is a nasty sight and there isn't any meat there. Ditto with feet. However, this does not affect the process. It's a matter of personal preference."

03 **Once the fire is ready, burn off the hair.** "The fire is ready when you have a bed of coals the size of a dinner plate and a couple of inches deep. They should glow brightly. Now, toss the squirrel on the bed of coals, but where you can still reach the animal with a stick without getting burnt to hell. Keep it rolling and moving around, so that you burn off the hair without burning through the hide. Imagine toasting a marshmallow without catching it on fire. You wanna keep it moving."

04 **Slice open the belly and gut.** "It's important to save the gutting procedure until after burning the hair, as a gutting incision will allow the introduction of ash and debris. Start the incision at the squirrel's brisket, or sternum, and work toward the belly. Be careful to keep your knife just beneath the muscle and abdominal lining. Do not cut or nick any of the internal organs, especially the stomach. Run the incision all the way down to the pelvis bone, but do not split the pelvis in two. Next, grab the squirrel's heart and pull the whole package of innards downward. The lower intestine should pull out and disconnect from near the squirrel's anus. At this point, the squirrel is gutted."

B. SKEWERING MULTIPLE SQUIRRELS

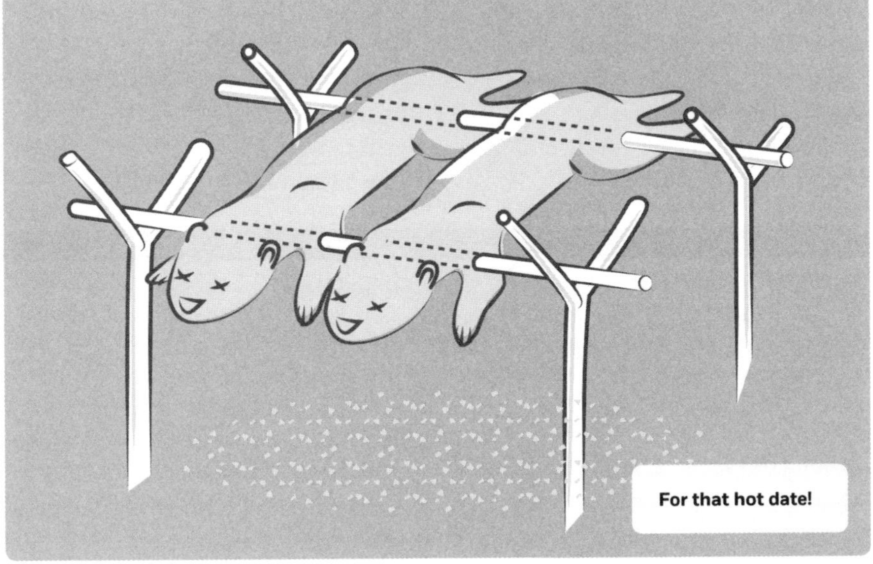
For that hot date!

05 **Skewer the squirrel and place it over embers.** "When doing a single squirrel (or rabbit), it's best to run a skewer through the pelvis bone, up the abdominal cavity, and then into the throat and out the mouth. It is very secure this way, and can be supported on just two forked sticks (see diagram A, opposite). When doing multiple animals, you can use two skewers (see diagram B). Run one through the rear legs and another through the front shoulders, so that the animals are positioned in a parallel fashion: two skewers require four forked sticks. "Position the squirrel over a bed of coals, *not* over the open flame. Cooking height depends on intensity of heat. Try to keep it where you can only hold your hand for a count of 2 or 3. Could be anywhere from 12–18" (30–46 cm), typically. Rotate frequently, every couple of minutes. The entire process could take upwards of 20 minutes. Remove when the meat is cooked so well that the ball joints of the rear legs begin to separate with a light twist, like how the leg of a well-cooked chicken can be removed with minimal effort."

06 **The payoff: eat your little morsel, which will taste like, you guessed it, chicken.** "Most of your meat is on the back hams, followed by the loins [along the spine]. Front legs are certainly worth the effort. In a pinch, cook and eat the heart, liver, and lungs."

Take It Slow

The key to fire cooking is to *not* speed-cook. Charring steak directly over a raging fire might seem manly, but it's also the route to burned on the outside and rare on the inside. This might be tasty (to some) as a blood-rare steak, but blood-rare tree rat won't win any Diners' Choice Awards.

NOW FOR YOU

TROUT ADAPTATION

WITH SOUTH INDIAN SPICES

INGREDIENTS	TO SERVE 2
Small whole trout (about 10 oz/280 g each), ungutted	**2**
Ginger-garlic paste (available bottled from any Indian grocer; or you can make your own—see next page)	**1½ T**
Rice vinegar	**1½ T**
Ground cayenne	**1½ t**
Ground turmeric	**½ t**
Salt	**1 t**
Lime juice	**½ lime**

SHORTHAND

Marinate 8hr: 2 trout, 1½T ginger-garlic paste, 1½T rice vinegar, 1½t cayenne, ½t turmeric, 1t salt. 400F 12–15min: bake trout, skewered. Serve w juice of ½ lime.

HANDS-ON TIME

20 minutes

TOTAL TIME

35 minutes, plus at least 8 hours marinating

GEAR

- Knife + cutting board
- Heavy-duty Ziploc bag
- 8 metal or wooden skewers (Make sure each skewer is a little longer than the length of the fish. If using wooden skewers, soak them in water for 30 minutes prior to using to avoid burning them in the oven.)
- 2 large baking pans

OPTIONAL MUSIC PAIRING

♪ "Fish Heads" by Barnes & Barnes

Roughly speaking, there are two types of fish: flat (flounder, sole, etc.) and fat (trout, salmon, snapper, etc.). We want something in the latter group. I've chosen trout because, quite frankly, it's easier. You skip scaling and move right on to cooking. To learn how to scale fish, see page 343.

PREP

00 Use a sharp fillet knife to cut the fish open at the abdomen, inserting the tip of the knife into the vent (just above where the tail starts) at the bottom of the fish and then slicing along the abdomen toward the head, until you reach the base of the lower jaw. Be sure not to cut inside too deep or you'll puncture the guts and your fish will end up tasting like excrement. Not delicious.

01 Reach into your incision at the base of the head and grab all the guts. They all connect, so on smaller fish, you can just reach in, pinch, and pull everything out at once. On larger fish, you'll likely need to use your knife to detach everything (1 cut where the organs attach to the head, another where they attach to the tail region should suffice) and pull it all out.

02 Look inside your incision. If needed, scrape out the liver, which will be attached to the backbone, and whatever is left of the whitish swim bladder. A good rule of thumb: anything that doesn't feel firm should go in the garbage.

03 Run your thumb along the backbone to dig out the bloodline, which looks like a thick vein.

04 Using your knife or a pair of kitchen shears, snip off the gills at their ends, where they attach to the inside of the fish, and remove them. If you leave them, the gills will impart a

A

B

Flying fish aliens.

bitter flavor and make the fish spoil faster.

05 If at home, rinse the fish in ice-cold water and put it on ice until ready to cook.

06 Make the ginger-garlic paste, if making your own.

To make homemade ginger-garlic paste: Combine equal amounts (by weight) chopped fresh ginger and garlic cloves in an immersion blender chopper attachment with a small amount of water. Process until smooth, scraping the sides a couple of times with a silicone spatula and adding more water as needed to make a paste.

07 Marinate the fish: combine the 1½ T ginger-garlic paste, 1½ T rice vinegar, 1½ t cayenne, ½ t turmeric, and 1 t salt in a small bowl. Place the fish in a heavy-duty Ziploc bag and add the marinade. Massage the marinade all over the fish, inside and out (put another plastic bag over your hand if you don't want it to reek of fish). Seal the bag and marinate in the refrigerator for 8 hours or overnight.

PICKUP

Follow the above pics.

00 Heat the oven to 400°F (200°C).

01 Remove the fish from the bag and prepare it for baking: place 1 fish on a cutting board or large plate and flatten it out so the flesh is facing up. Insert a skewer through the fish's mouth and rest it along the length of the fish past the tail. Balance 3 skewers along the width of a baking pan. Flip the fish over and rest it over the 3 skewers; rest the lengthwise skewer (holding the fish) over the edges of the pan. Repeat with the second fish.

02 Place the baking pans in the oven for 12–15 minutes, until the meat is opaque and flakes off easily with a fork.

03 Place the fish on the serving plates and squeeze lime over the top.

LESSON 32

SKILLS

EMBER COOKING, SALT BAKING

SWEET POTATO RESCOLDO

+ SALT-BAKED SWEET POTATOES VARIATION

INSPIRED BY
Francis Mallmann

SHORTHAND
Coal fire 1hr: place 2 foil-wrapped sweet potatoes & EVOO or ghee between burnt embers. Serve w more EVOO, S+P.

HANDS-ON TIME
40 minutes

TOTAL TIME
1 hour 40 minutes

GEAR
- Aluminum foil
- 5- or 6-qt galvanized steel pail
- About 4 handfuls of small dry twigs or kindling. You can buy kindling at a hardware store: half of a ⅓-cu-ft package will be plenty.
- Newspaper
- Matches
- Fire iron (the thing used to poke fires)
- About 1 lb (0.5 kg) untreated lump charcoal (my default is Lazzari mesquite lump charcoal)
- Flameproof barbecue mitts
- Large coffee can, old pot, or other flameproof vessel

OPTIONAL MUSIC PAIRING
"Ashes and Fire" by Ryan Adams

"My idea of heaven is a great big baked potato and someone to share it with."

—OPRAH WINFREY

Rescoldo means "embers" in Spanish but can refer to a cooking method: burying your food under coals. Argentines traditionally did this in outdoor fires, but we'll use a steel pail. For those who don't have outdoor access (though a driveway could work), we'll try salt baking, which is also popular in South America for cooking whole fish.[32]

32 It could be used for the trout we impaled on page 337. Just set a probe thermometer for 125°F (50°C).

Partanna

INGREDIENTS	TO SERVE 4
Medium sweet potatoes (about 11 oz/300 g each)	**2**
EVOO or ghee	**To taste**
S+P	**To taste**

PREP

00 Wrap the sweet potatoes in aluminum foil and bring them outside.

01 Place the steel pail on a flat, sturdy outdoor surface within spraying distance of your outdoor hose (or fire extinguisher) and away from fire hazards such as trees, grass, houses, piñatas, and origami.

02 Gather a few handfuls of small, dry twigs or kindling and place them on the bottom of the pail.

03 Make a few newspaper twists, nestle them into the sticks, and light them with a match. Use fire paste if needed. Tend the fire for 10 minutes, stoking it with the fire iron, then add a couple more handfuls of kindling. Let them burn, stoking a few times, for another 10 minutes.

04 Once you've got a good fire going, add coals until roughly halfway up the sides of the pail. Let sit for 10 minutes, poking and prodding a few times.

05 Add coals to almost the top of the pail, leaving enough room to add the sweet potatoes. Stoke for another 10 minutes or so, until the coals are ash white and there are no flames remaining.

06 Put on your flameproof barbecue mitts and pour ½ the coals into a large coffee can, old pot, or other flameproof vessel that you don't mind dirtying.

PICKUP

00 Place the sweet potatoes on top of the hot coals in the pail. Cover with the coals from the previous step.

01 Leave undisturbed for 1 hour (but don't leave the pail unattended!), then pour out half the coals into another vessel and remove the sweet potatoes. How to kill that hour? Watch the first half of the documentary *Bigger, Stronger, Faster*, which has an unbelievable 96% rating on rottentomatoes.com.

02 Carefully remove the foil from the sweet potatoes and cut them in half. Drizzle with EVOO or a pat of ghee, season with S+P, and serve.

VARIATION

SALT-BAKED SWEET POTATOES

Partanna

INGREDIENTS	TO SERVE 4
Inexpensive table salt	5 lb (2.5 kg)
Water	1 c (240 ml)
Medium sweet potatoes	2
EVOO or ghee	To taste
S+P	To taste

SHORTHAND

475F 45min: Bake 2 sweet potatoes covered w 5lb salt mixed w 1c H2O. Rest 15min; clean salt away from potatoes. Serve w EVOO, S+P.

HANDS-ON TIME

5 minutes

TOTAL TIME

1 hour

GEAR

- Large mixing bowl
- Cast-iron combi
- Potato scrubber
- A few sheets of newspaper or a couple of kitchen towels
- Hammer (or heavy knife)
- Large spoon
- Optional: oven mitts, pastry brush

PREP

00 Preheat the oven to 475°F (240°C).

01 Place the 5 lb (2.5 kg) salt in a large mixing bowl and add 1 c (240 ml) water. Using your hands, toss the salt with the water until the mixture has the consistency of wet snow.

02 Make a bed of about 1" (2.5 cm) of salt in the bottom of the cast-iron combi and pack it in nicely with your hands.

03 Scrub the 2 sweet potatoes under running water and place them on the bed of salt, spacing them so they don't touch each other or the sides of the combi.

04 Add the remaining moistened salt, patting it down well so the sweet potatoes are completely covered.

PICKUP

00 Place the uncovered combi in the oven and bake for 45 minutes. Line the counter next to the sink with a few sheets of newspaper or a couple of kitchen towels.

01 Remove the combi from the oven, place on the newspaper, and let the sweet potatoes rest for 15 minutes.

02 Using a hammer or the back (dull) edge of a heavy knife, sharply but shallowly crack the salt crust. When you've uncovered the top of the sweet potatoes, spoon out all the pieces of salt that you've cracked thus far. Crack, spoon, and brush off salt until you are able to gently lift out the sweet potatoes. They'll be soft.

03 Cut the sweet potatoes in half, drizzle each half with EVOO or a pat of ghee, season with S+P, and serve.

A
B
C
D
E
F
G
H

Uses for Leftover Salt

In my first salt-baking attempt, I cooked a ½-lb (225 g) trout in 3 lbs (1.4 kg) of pricey Diamond kosher salt. For some reason, I'd bought *much* more salt than needed and had 10–20 lbs (4.5–9 kg) left over.

Fortunately, salt can be used for all sorts of chores:

De-Grease Your Sink

To get rid of grease buildup in your kitchen sink, heat water and dissolve a generous amount of salt into it—approximately ½–1 c (70–140 g) of salt for 1 gal (4 L) of water. Pour the hot solution down the drain. Doing this regularly will also keep the sink odor-free.

Remove Rust from Iron Pans

For iron pans (even cast-iron), pour a little salt directly on the pan's surface and wipe with a dry paper towel. Rinse and dry the pan thoroughly before putting it away.

De-Stink Your Shoes . . .

Sprinkle some salt into your shoes. Rub the salt in using a paper towel, then let things sit for a few hours. Don't forget to pour out the salt before you put your shoes back on.

. . . And Your Hands

After handling onions, add white vinegar to salt, just enough to moisten it, then rub the resulting paste on your hands to get rid of the smell.

NOSE TO TAIL, A TO Z: LEARNING TO BUTCHER

"A human being should be able to change a diaper, plan an invasion, **butcher a hog,** conn [conduct or steer] a ship, design a building, write a sonnet, balance accounts, build a wall, set a bone, comfort the dying, take orders, give orders, cooperate, act alone, solve equations, analyze a new problem, pitch manure, program a computer, cook a tasty meal, fight efficiently, die gallantly."

—ROBERT HEINLEIN, AMERICAN SCIENCE-FICTION WRITER, AUTHOR OF *STRANGER IN A STRANGE LAND* (WHERE THE TERM *GROK* ORIGINATED)

Blake Avery *is a sous-chef and butcher at Commander's Palace in New Orleans, which has been recognized as one of the top 40 restaurants in the U.S.*‡

Who are your top three favorite butchers in the world?

Justo Thomas of Le Bernardin is the best fish butcher in the world. He is unreal. He is so efficient that it takes 2–3 sous-chefs to cover him when he is on vacation. He also butchers whole fish, and that is unheard of for a restaurant of that size. He only butchers a few pieces of meat, but his technique and thought process can be applied to any type of butchering.

Joshua and Jessica Applestone are a badass team in NYC. I'll count them as one. They are pioneers in bringing back the butcher shops of our parents and grandparents. They have slowly turned a little shop into an incredible place that handles whole sides of beef, carries farm-fresh eggs and milk, and makes their own sausage. They have shown that being a small shop in a Walmart-size America can be profitable. Their book, *The Butcher's Guide to Well-Raised Meat,* is the top one or two on the subject.

Fergus Henderson, chef of St. John in London, comes next. I've never had the food, but his book, *Nose to Tail,* is a must-read. It's more of a cookbook than a butcher's guide, but it teaches you how to use the whole pig in very inventive ways that are approachable for a home cook. He was about 10 years too early for the American *boucherie* (butchering) comeback.

I know I'm over three, but I can't leave out Brian Polcyn, author of *Charcuterie,* or Sean Brock, head chef of Husk restaurant in Charleston, South Carolina. Brian was ahead of his time, writing his book 10 years before anyone cared, and Sean is the present master of all things pig.

If you had to pick five animals to teach someone how to be a butcher, which ones would you choose and in what order?

The five animals I would choose are, in order:

1. **Chicken**
2. **Pig**
3. **Any fish similar to redfish** (trout, drum, red snapper)
4. **Any fish similar to grouper** (hake, triple tail, Chilean sea bass, salmon, etc.)
5. **Lamb**

In thinking about which animals to pick, I first looked at what not to pick. Cow or "red meat" usually jumps out at most people when in a butcher shop. It's hard to miss: rows of ground beef, fillets, rib eyes, T-bones, ribs.... What most people miss is how hard breaking down a whole cow actually is. The space requirement alone, even for primal cuts, will make this impossible for most home chefs. Other popular animals eliminated were veal (baby cow, although the racks are doable), tuna (very big and expensive for home), and duck (a bit different than a chicken but close enough to be doable at home).

Now, in the order I recommend:

CHICKEN. It's the most popular meat in America, it's cheap, it's easy to break down, and it can be broken down in several different ways for several different cooking methods. Just the thighs can be bone in or out, skin on or off, fried or braised, made into sausage or confited. Chicken can be broken down anywhere from 4–8 pieces, bone in or out for everything (except wings), and can also be boned out whole. Chicken can be super-easy (whole roasted) or kind of difficult (boned out whole and then grilled). But no matter what, chicken is approachable for just about anyone.

PIG. Every part of a pig can be used—from nose to tail—and a cook can learn so much from butchering just one whole pig. They are easy to get and can be had in sizes that are acceptable in a home kitchen. Unlike a cow, you can break down a pig with a knife, hammer, and chisel—no saw required. In breaking down pigs, you could learn how to cut chops, tenders, tenderloins, bone out a leg, make headcheese, make pork belly, make bacon, make sausage, and make stock. It is extremely cost-efficient because there is almost no waste. Pig also translates well into butchering other animals like lamb, some parts of veal or cow, and even rabbit. The only reason it isn't number one is because of space issues in home kitchens, and because butchering a whole, gutted pig with a head freaks some people out.

FISH. Butchering fish is an important skill that most people simply do not associate with being a butcher (due to the separation of the fish and other meats at grocery stores). In most restaurants I've encountered, the butcher does both fish and meat. The principles are the same, and fish will teach home cooks not to waste. Ten percent wasted on a trout is significant, whereas 10% on a pig might go unnoticed.

How to scale a fish. Holding the fish by the tail with a hand towel, scale it outside with the back of a knife. A utility knife is ideal, but the back of a chef's knife will work.

LAMB. Assuming you've successfully butchered the previous meats, lamb is your next step in the progression. It's similar to pig, it can be cooked almost as many ways, and because it's often more expensive, it will teach the cook to really care when cutting. It is slightly more complicated than a pig, but very accessible for the home kitchen in terms of size and cost. For instance, boning a leg out at home and then using the bones for stock and sauce will save the cook quite a bit of money and not take up very much space. Learning to break down a rack of lamb is easy, cost-effective, and impressive for parties.

What are the top mistakes novices make when trying to learn how to butcher?

1. **Starting too big.** There is no reason to try deboning a whole chicken if you haven't made boneless skinless thighs. Trying to cure prosciutto at home is probably not a good idea for a novice either. It's always better to start small with things like a bone-in pork tenderloin or whole chickens, rather than buying a side of veal and having everything turn out a complete disaster.

2. **Dull knives.** Most people don't have a knife that is near sharp enough. Your knives need to be razor-sharp. It's a safety issue: a sharp knife will go where you think it will go, a dull knife *will* slip on bones and hard fat and possibly find its way into your off hand. My favorite all-around knife is the 6" Shun SG0410 Elite Gokujo boning/fillet knife. I've used it for three years for 80% of my work, from lamb racks to whole pigs to flounder. It stays sharp and is easy to sharpen. There is also a very good, cheaper version of this knife, the classic gokujo[33] (fourhourchef.com/classic-gokujo), but it takes a bit longer to sharpen. The blade angle on both—the swoop—helps keep your knuckles off the board when cutting portions. If you're on a smaller budget, there is a $20 Victorinox knife that can handle most jobs (fourhourchef.com/victorinox).

3. **Poor sanitation practices.** One of the worst mistakes a butcher can make is not taking sanitation seriously enough, especially when making any type of charcuterie or dealing with different proteins in the same space. You can seriously fuck someone up with cross contamination of sausage that is above safe temperature. Cutting boards, knives, counters, and aprons (yes, aprons) need to be changed or sanitized whenever the protein is switched.

4. **Moving too fast.** Novices need to move slowly and thoughtfully, leaving themselves more than enough time to learn and absorb proper technique. There will be mistakes along the way, but there are two types: fixable and drastic. It's much easier to deal with a slightly deformed chicken breast than a slightly deformed left palm.

CLOSING TIP FROM TIM: THE MANUAL

Chris Cosentino, executive chef at Incanto in San Francisco, has a pig tattoo on his left bicep.

The ink traces anatomical lines, the primal cuts. He is a self-taught master butcher who has embraced offal (organs) and Italian peasant food as his calling. For six years, he went to no weddings, attended no funerals, enjoyed no concerts, and took no holidays from his craft. In 2012, he was nominated for the "Best Chef Pacific" James Beard Award. His constant companion all along has been a veterinary guide: *Spurgeon's Color Atlas of Large Animal Anatomy: The Essentials* by Thomas O. McCracken (fourhourchef.com/spurgeons).

If you want to learn how to disassemble animals, this is the book I'd suggest as your primary reference. Once you have the guide, it's a matter of deliberate practice. Be willing to push into discomfort. As Chris put it to me:

"When you are nervous, uncomfortable, that's when you're learning."

Truer words never spoken.

33 I use this one. —Tim

FOR FUN: WHAT THE HELL IS A PORTERHOUSE, ANYWAY?

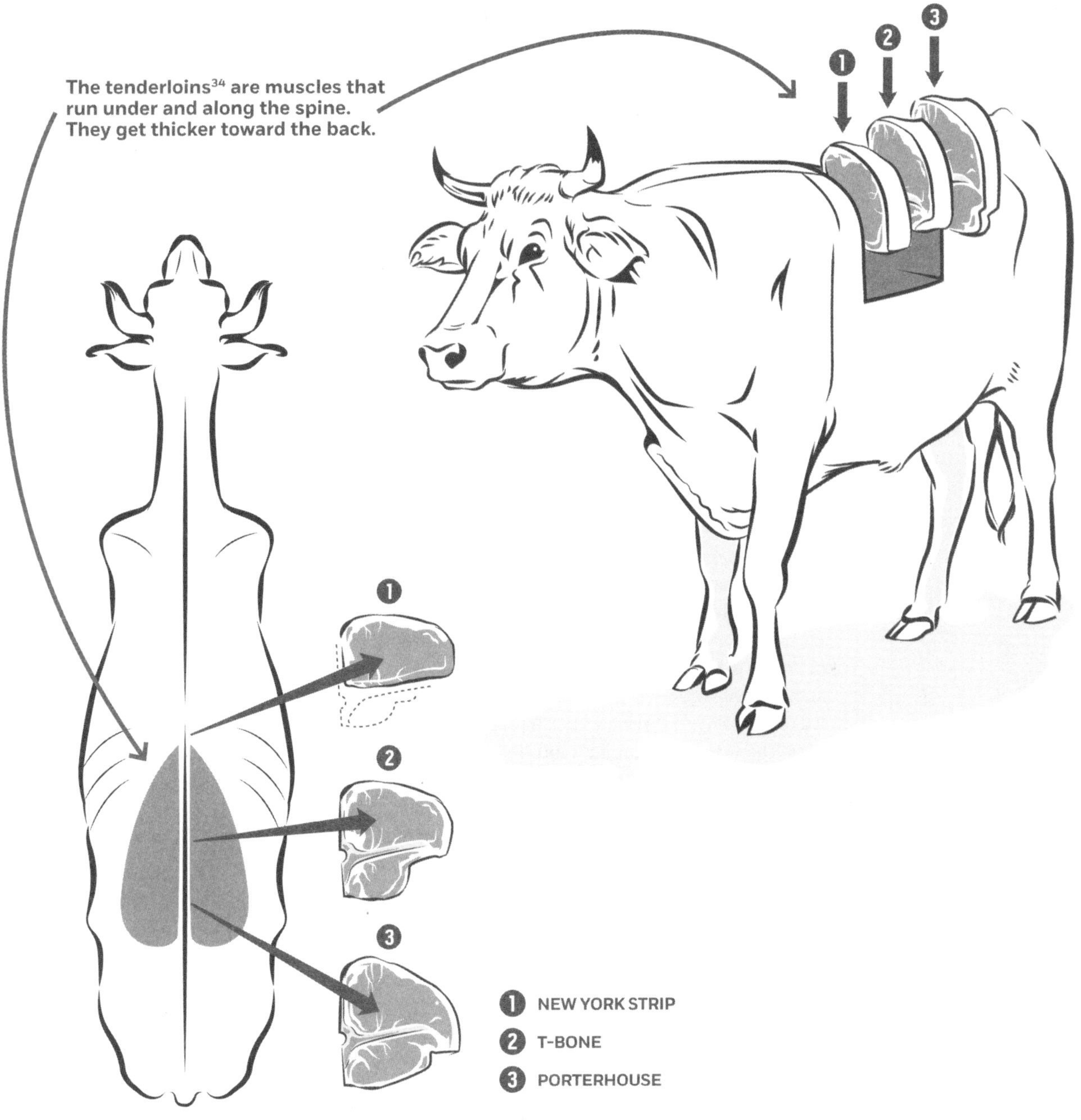
The tenderloins[34] are muscles that run under and along the spine. They get thicker toward the back.
1
2
3
1 NEW YORK STRIP
2 T-BONE
3 PORTERHOUSE

34 See the deer version on top right of page 278.

LESSON 33

SKILL

BASIC BUTCHERING

HOW TO BUTCHER A CHICKEN

TOTAL TIME

8–10 minutes

GEAR

- Boning knife (ideal) and/or chef's knife
- 1 whole chicken

OPTIONAL MUSIC PAIRING

"Genesis" by Justice

"If skill could be gained by watching, every dog would become a butcher."

—TURKISH PROVERB

Kingo (pronounced "KING-go") was a one-year-old Labradoodle with black-and-white patterning, including little white boots. He looked like a tiny cow.

He was frenetically jumping in front of me, begging for attention, so I put down my rum and Coke to play-fight. Steve Rinella was seated next to me on the couch, watching the Sportsman Channel and explaining how the Fu Manchu is the mullet of the 2010s. I gave Kingo another paw swipe, which led to wrestling, as it always does. Then I suddenly found myself giving the little 23-lb creature a deep-tissue massage. *Mmm . . . nice backstraps,* I thought.[35] Moving on, I noted that the flank wouldn't yield much, and that's when I creeped myself out. I turned to Steve: "Is it normal to start seeing backstraps in everything?"

"Oh, yeah. The same thing happens to me when I'm giving my wife a backrub."

Once you start butchering in any capacity, your selective attention will be weird for a while. I'd broken down my first deer that afternoon, and now all I saw was cuts—shank, flank, and so on—in everything that moved.

Chronologically, killing comes before butchering, but psychologically, butchering is better to learn first. It's a skill you can practice far more frequently.

With experience, butchering a chicken becomes an intuitive process. The bird's own anatomy guides you through the snaps and slices that reduce it to the familiar components. You need only your hands and a few low-finesse cuts with a chef's knife (a thin boning knife is helpful, but not necessary).

Here's how chef Marco Canora learned to carve his chickens into thighs, legs, wings, and breasts:

PICKUP

00 **Stretch skin.** Marco ensures good skin coverage by pulling on the legs and pinching the breast to spread the skin downward (see pic A, opposite). Later, if roasting the breast skin-side down, you'll be glad there is a good spread of skin to prevent the breasts from drying out.

01 **Break back.** Make slanted side cuts into the skin between thigh and breast on either side with a boning knife (see pic B), then use a chef's knife to cut down the center toward the spine at an angle until you hit the spine (see pic C). Finish the job by holding the breast and the thighs in either hand and then bending the chicken open so its back snaps at a vertebra

35 This is another name for the loin of the deer, which runs over and along the spine, above the tenderloin.

(see pic E). You now have 2 pieces of chicken: ⅔ with 2 thighs and 2 legs; ⅓ with double breast and 2 wings.

02 Remove thighs from back. Position the lower half of the bird with the thighs spread open and the legs toward you. Ride your boning knife into the crease at the hip and slice partway along and toward the backbone, trying to keep as much meat as possible (see pic F). Set aside the knife and use your hands to pop the hip toward you and expose the ball-and-socket joint. Slice the thigh away from the back completely, using the middle of the joint to guide you. Repeat on the other thigh.

03 Separate drumsticks from thighs. Find the knee—the joint between the thigh and drumstick (leg). You can detect this seam by running your finger along the joint and feeling the slight gap in the bone. Use the boning knife to separate each drumstick and thigh at the seam; there should be little resistance as you slice (see pics G and H).

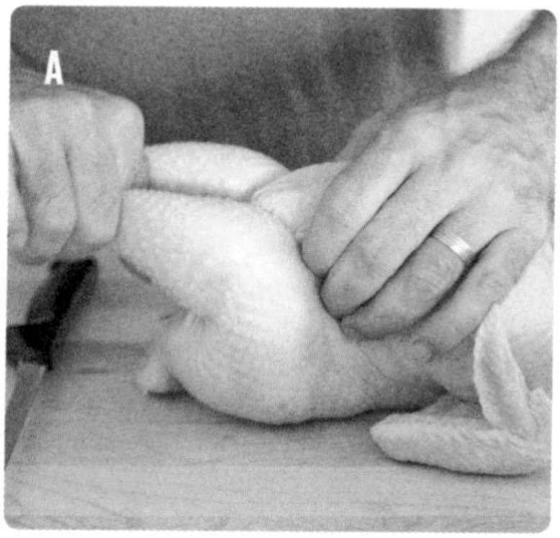
A

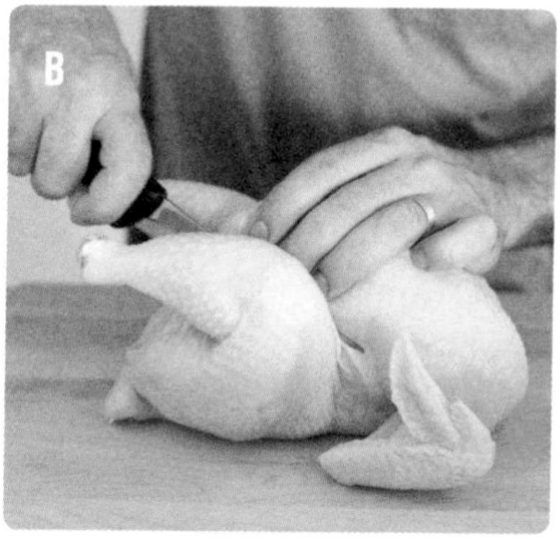
B

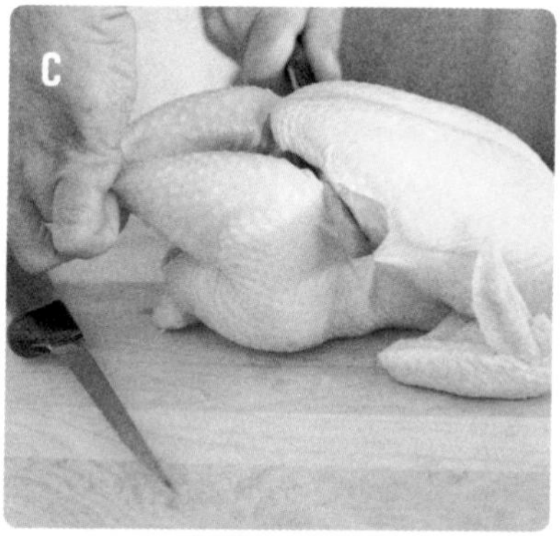
C

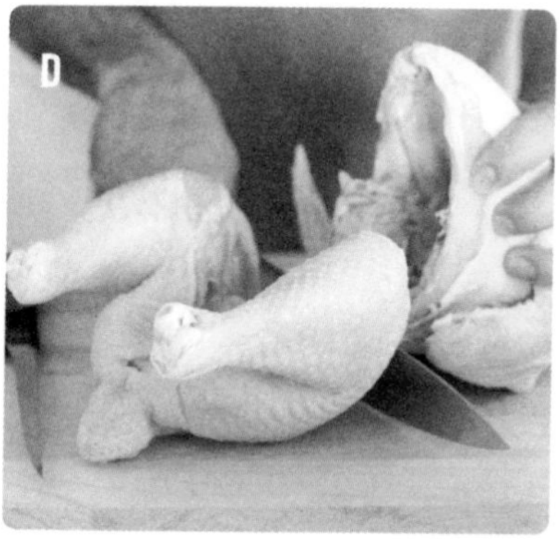
D

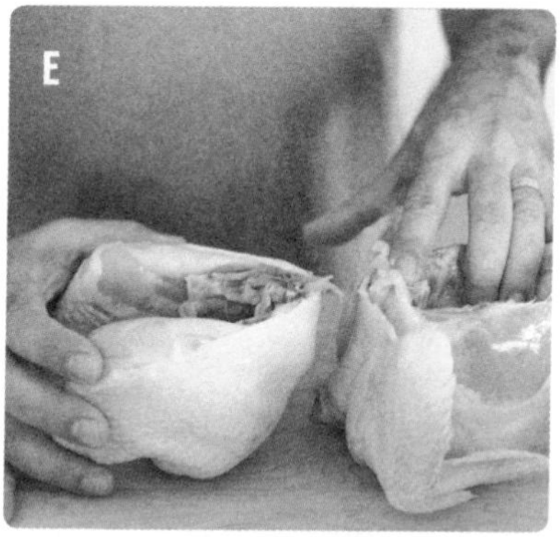
E

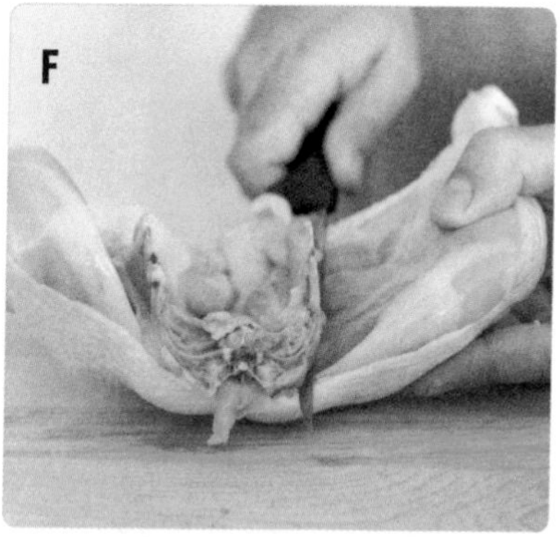
F

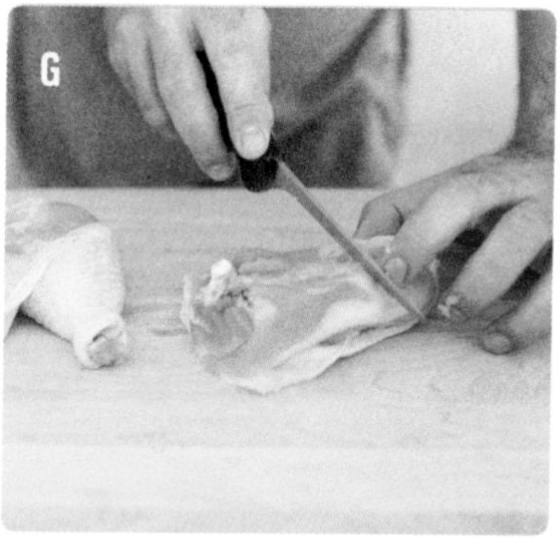
G

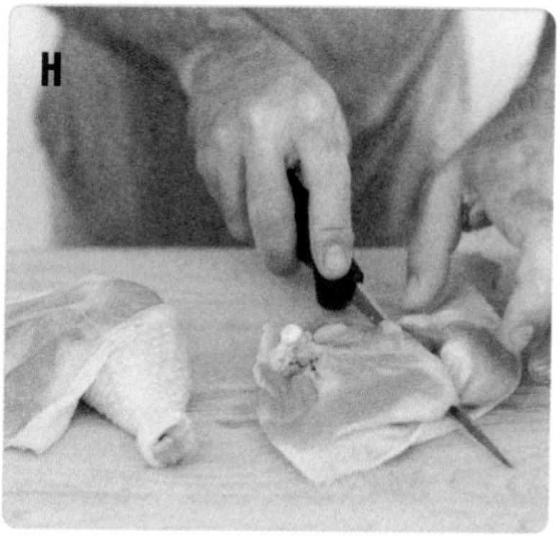
H

A

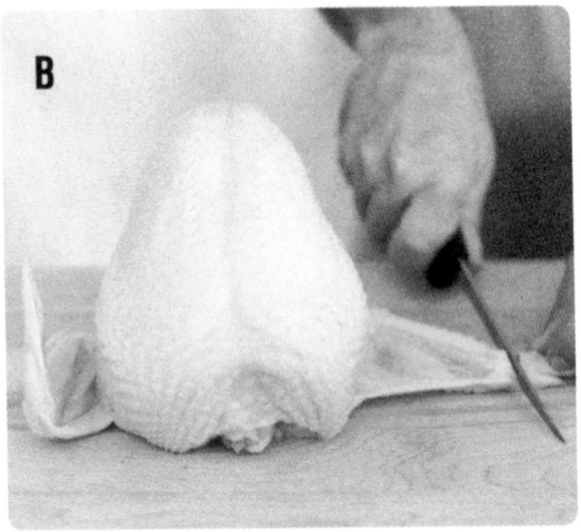
B

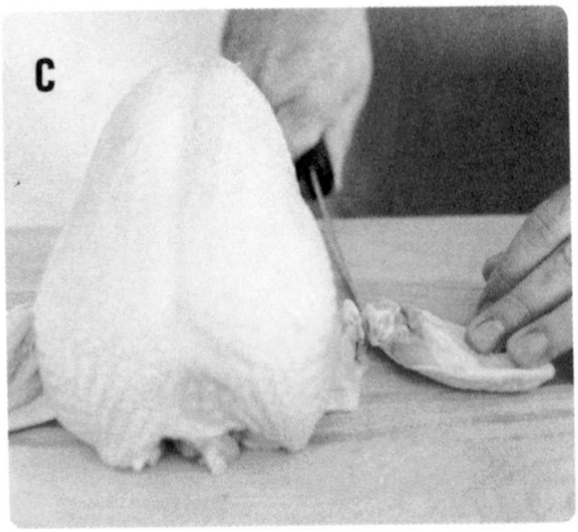
C

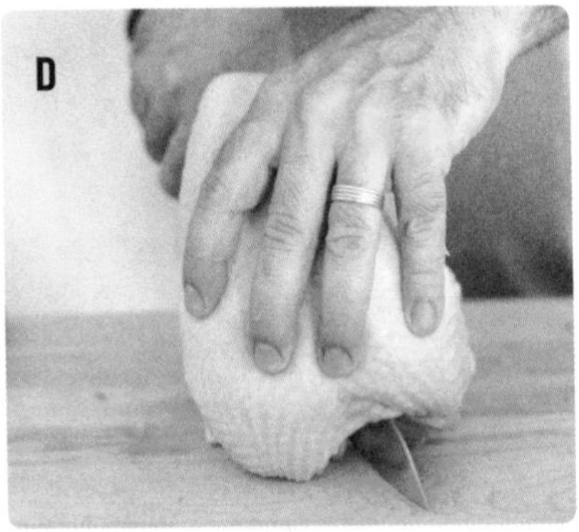
D

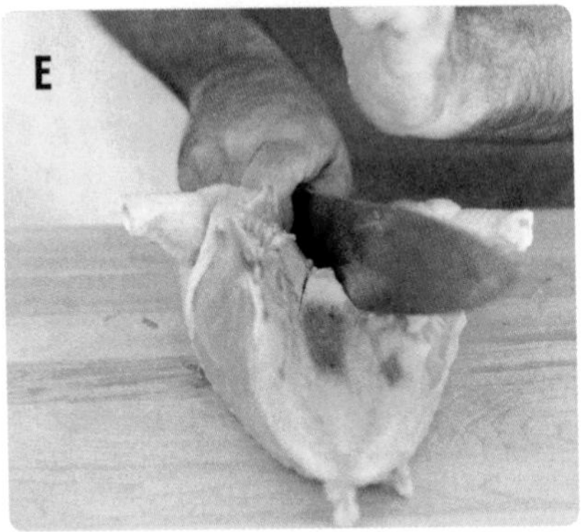
E

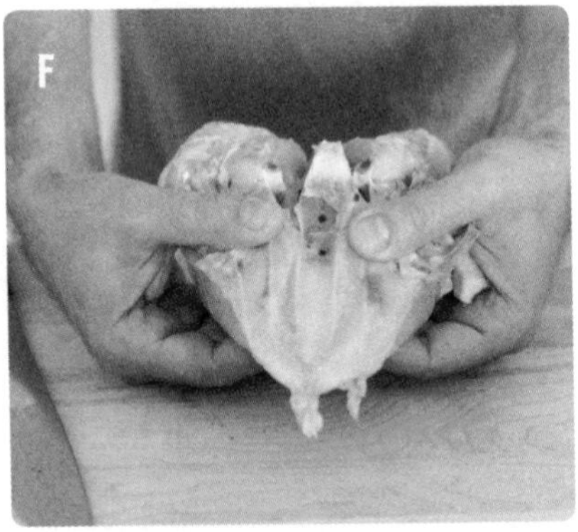
F

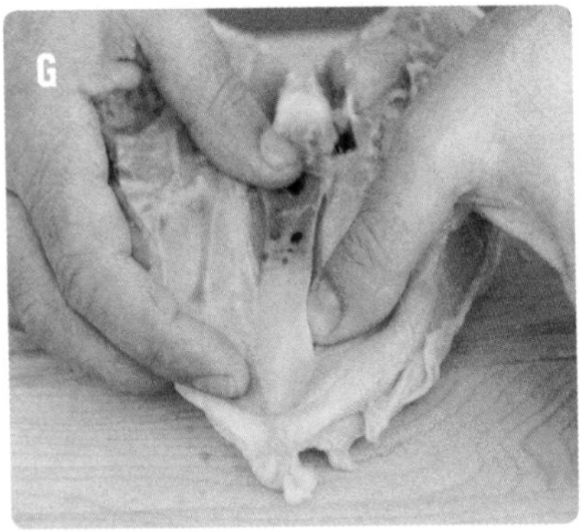
G

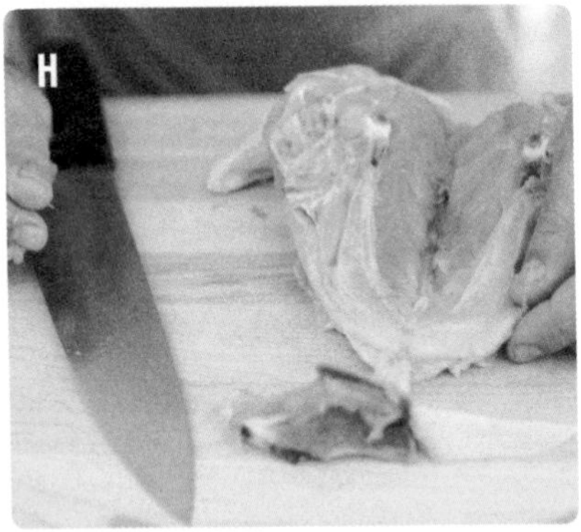
H

04 **Chop off knuckles and wing tips.** Marco suggests removing the nubby ends of the legs; as the drumsticks cook, the exposed bone enhances flavor. Position the heel of the chef's knife just above the knuckle and strike the spine of the blade with the palm of your hand (see pic A). Repeat. Similarly, Marco recommends slicing off the mostly meatless wing tips, which are better as stock. Slice off each wing tip at the wrist joint (see pic B).

05 **Cut off wings.** As with the knee, feel out the sliceable joint between the breast and wing of the bird (the elbow). Slice through the joint and repeat on the other side (see pic C).

06 **Separate double breast from back.** It's time to remove the rest of the backbone. Things get more difficult here. Position the double breast so that the neck is pointing away from you, chest side up. Fully insert the chef's knife into the chest cavity and point it directly into the cutting board with the bird draped over the knife's spine. You'll be making two diagonal, internal cuts to the left

and the right of the spine—Marco calls it "a leverage-snap-through-the-bone kind of scenario." Using your off hand to hold the chicken and knife point against the cutting board (you can use a kitchen towel for safety), crunch downward through the middle of the ribs on one side of the rib cage (see pic D). With the knife's point still in contact with the cutting board, repeat the same crunching, downward cut on the other side of the rib cage.[36]

07 **Dislodge the keel bone.** While you could split the breastbone in half at this point, you'd be skipping Marco's favorite step: pulling out the semisoft breastbone, or keel bone. Removing the keel bone makes it easier to serve the cooked breasts later. Turn the double breast around so that the wing nubs are nearest to you. Place the heel of your knife along one side of the keel bone and give the knife's spine a little pound—light enough to cut only the semisoft edge of the keel bone, not the breast itself (see pic E, opposite, and diagram at right). Make the same light cut on the other side of the keel bone. Splay the double breast open, pop the keel bone up (see pic F), then gradually run your thumbs under the ridge of the keel bone toward the tapered front, separating the keel bone from the breast until it can be pulled out completely (see pic G). Slice the double breast into two with a chef's knife by cutting through the recessed area where the keel bone was (see pic H).

Note: Directly under either side of the keel bone are the two tenderloins. In some cases, if the keel bone is removed with special care, the two tenderloins will be beautifully encased in a silver skin that keeps them attached to the breast for cooking.

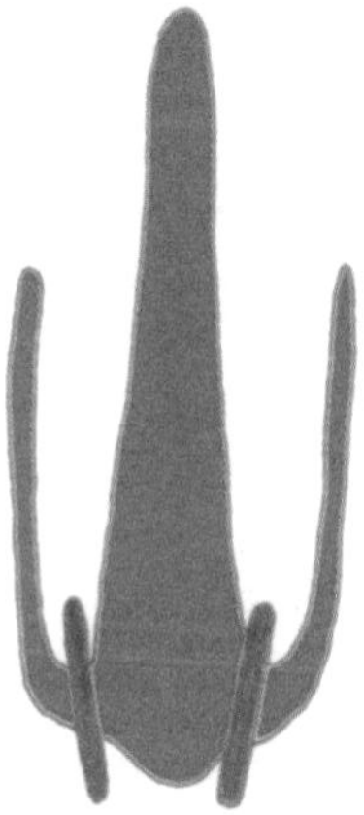

Cutting the keel. The keel/breast bone often looks something like a sword (red above). The cuts in pic E are therefore made where the gray lines indicate.

Recipe for Osso "Buko" 2.0

Not sure how to cook these pieces? Of course you are. Just substitute them for the lamb shanks in Osso "Buko" (page 134) and you're set for a meal and leftovers. If you wanted to braise this over a fire, you would place the cast-iron combi directly on the coals, cover, then shovel coals on top. The simple rule of thumb is to put ⅔ of the coals on the lid and ⅓ in a circle at the base.

If you'd like to get more precise, the table below spells out the specifics. It shows the total number of coals (coals on top/coals on bottom) required to cook at the specified temperature, depending on the size of your Dutch oven

	SIZE OF DUTCH OVEN				
	8" (2 QT)	10" (4 OR 5 QT)	12" (6 OR 8 QT)	14" (8 OR 10 QT)	16" (12 QT)
325°F/170°C	15 (10/5)	19 (13/6)	23 (16/7)	30 (20/10)	37 (25/12)
350°F/180°C	16 (11/5)	21 (14/7)	25 (17/8)	32 (21/11)	39 (26/13)
375°F/190°C	17 (11/6)	23 (16/7)	27 (18/9)	34 (22/12)	41 (27/14)
400°F/200°C	18 (12/6)	25 (17/8)	29 (19/10)	36 (24/12)	43 (28/15)
425°F/220°C	19 (13/6)	27 (18/9)	31 (21/10)	38 (25/13)	45 (29/16)
450°F/230°C	20 (14/6)	29 (19/10)	33 (22/11)	40 (26/14)	47 (30/17)

36 If the crunch doesn't cut through the ribs, drag back with a few hard slices afterward.

LESSON 34

SKILL

"HARVESTING," AKA KILLING

LOBSTERCIDE

SHORTHAND

Boil 2 lobsters, 2qt H2O, 2T salt according to weight. Tent in foil 5min. Halve. Serve w lemon, tarragon, S+P.

TOTAL TIME

Depends on the size of your lobster (see chart on opposite page)

GEAR

- 2 lobsters
- Stockpot
- Salt
- Tongs
- Aluminum foil
- Chef's knife

OPTIONAL MUSIC PAIRING

♪ "Eyes on Fire (Zed's Dead Remix)" by Blue Foundation

> "I must not fear. Fear is the mind-killer. Fear is the little-death that brings total obliteration. I will face my fear."
>
> —BENE GESSERIT "LITANY AGAINST FEAR"

This lesson and the next section, both on killing, will be the hardest in the book for many of you.

If you elect to "harvest" your first animal, I suggest the following progression:

1. **Boiling lobster**
2. **Bisecting lobster** ("Highlander")
3. **Killing chicken** ("Mexican towel snap")

Expect each to be emotionally and psychologically exhausting. That's the whole point. I'm not going to paint it as easy, because it shouldn't be.

Lobster is a triumph of marketing genius.

It's thought of as a fine delicacy for special occasions, but it wasn't always so. As David Foster Wallace wrote in "Consider the Lobster":

"Up until sometime in the 1800s, though, lobster was literally low-class food, eaten only by the poor and institutionalized. Even in the harsh penal environment of early America, some colonies had laws against feeding lobsters to inmates more than once a week because it was thought to be cruel and unusual, like making people eat rats."‡

On the positive side, lobsters are as fresh as any protein in modern urban life. Try and buy a dead lobster. You can't. It's the one food even white-collar folks have accepted you have to murder yourself.

I'll offer two options for dealing the death blow, in order of difficulty.

OPTION 1: BOILING

Boiling lobsters is what Mark Zuckerberg, founder of Facebook, started with in 2011. He then worked his way up the food chain, all the way to shooting bison. Mark has a thing for what he calls "personal challenges." In 2009, it was wearing a tie every day. In 2010, it was learning Chinese. He explained his 2011 challenge in an e-mail to *Fortune* magazine:

"This year, my personal challenge is around being thankful for the food I have to eat. I think many people forget that a living being has to die for you to eat meat, so my goal revolves around not letting myself forget that.... This year, I've basically become a vegetarian since the only meat I'm eating is from animals I've killed myself. So far, this has been a good experience. I'm eating a lot healthier foods, and I've learned a lot about sustainable farming and raising of animals.

"I started thinking about this last year when I had a pig roast at my house. A bunch of people told me that even though they loved eating pork, they really didn't want to think about the fact that the pig used to be alive. That just seemed irresponsible to me."‡

PREP

For simplicity, I'll assume you're cooking for 2 people. It's easy to adjust as needed.

00 Purchase 1 live hard-shell lobster per person and make a note of the weights. I like 1½-lb (0.5-kg) lobsters. Bring them home and put them in the fridge. Cooling zaps the creatures into a lethargic stupor, which helps prevent the backbend Jesus-crucifix pose when you pick them up. It also minimizes noise from the pot, more relevant later.

PICKUP

00 Fill a stockpot with roughly 2 qt (2 L) water per lobster, add 2 T salt per quart, and bring to a boil. It won't be necessary to drown the lobsters, as the steam kills them.

01 Pick up the first lobster from the back, just behind the "shoulder" joints, and place it headfirst in the pot. No need to remove the rubber bands on the claws. Do the same with the second. If you're using a small pot instead of a stockpot, hold the lid down for 60 seconds, after which you can go hands-free.

02 Cook for the following times, based on the size of your lobster:

SIZE	COOK TIME
1 LB / .5 KG	4-5 MINS
1¼ LB / .6 KG	6-7 MINS
1½ LB / .7 KG	7-9 MINS
2 LB / .9 KG	10-12 MINS
3 LB / 1.4 KG	12-13 MINS
5-6 LB / 2.3-2.7 KG	18-20 MINS

03 Remove lobsters from the pot with tongs, tent aluminum foil over them, and let rest for 5 minutes.

04 Use a chef's knife to split the tails down the middle (or the entire lobster, as I prefer), and serve with ghee and your favorite spices. I like to keep things simple: fresh lemon juice, tarragon, and S+P.

Bonus: Jail Break

For added excitement, Raymond Sokolov, former food editor of the *New York Times*, used to "liberate" six lobsters on the floor and ask his guests to catch their meals before boiling. A Kodak moment!

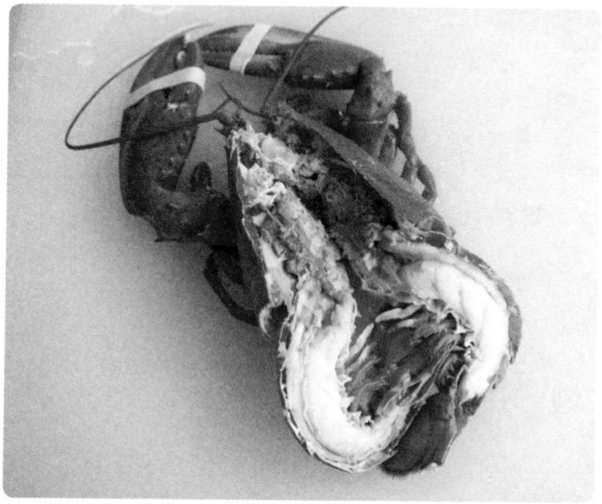

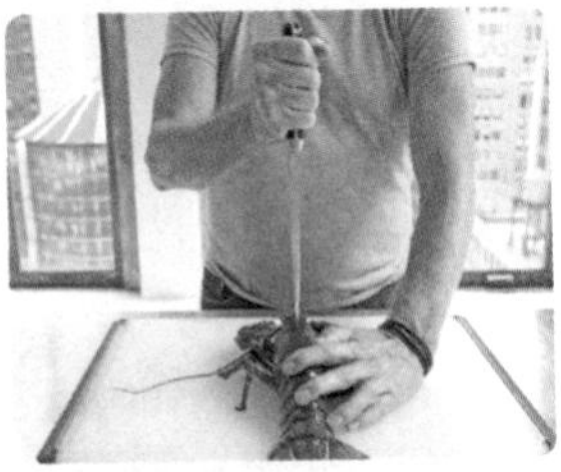

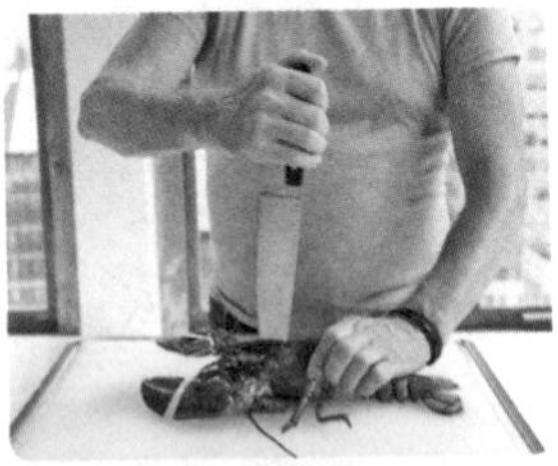

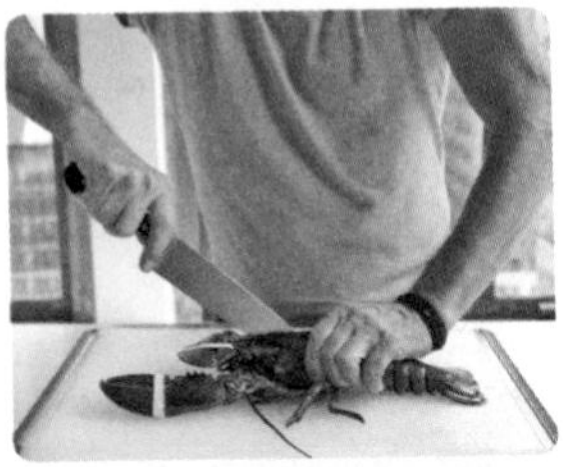

OPTION 2: "HIGHLANDER" TECHNIQUE

In his excellent book *Cook with Jamie*, Jamie Oliver recommends dispatching of lobsters with a knife through the middle of the head.

Compared to boiling, this seemed a more honorable method of slaughtering the crawlers. I wouldn't be hiding behind a shield, protecting myself from their silent death rattle.

My girlfriend videotaped my first Highlander lobstercide. I was anxious. Lobsters are effectively seaborne insects and not fun to look at, much less pin on a cutting board. Their legs claw the surface with Cookie Monster finger rhythm. It's creepy.

In the end, I said a little thank-you grace and went for the kill. Here's how:

- Holding the body in place with my left hand, I lined up the point of the knife at the "cross," where the head shell meets the body shell.

- Raising the knife vertically, I pushed it down through the head. Once the blade hit the cutting board, I sliced hard downward, bisecting the head.

Then . . . as many how-to instructionals write: instant death!

Well, no. It began doing the wiggly leg dance, and 30 seconds later, 60 seconds later, it was still moving. I took a deep breath and reflected on what I'd read:

"If the legs continue to wriggle afterward, don't worry; it's just a reflex reaction and will stop after a while."

Feeling terrible, I cut farther back, again to no effect. After five minutes, I cut the entire body in half. The Terminator lobster kept coming, like the Ghost of Christmas Past, pointing a shaking finger at me. It was horrible. "A while" was a hell of a long time.

Eventually, it stopped. My girlfriend kindly offered to rinse the halves while I put another lobster in a boiling pot of water. I had just opened the fridge when I heard her scream bloody murder.

As soon as the cold water hit the lobster half, it began flapping its tail like a bird trying to take off. She dropped it, of course, and all I could think was: cheese and rice, thank God that wasn't me.

Later on, I realized why the "instant death" accounts are totally right . . . but misleading. Lobsters lack a centralized brain-spine complex and have a distributed nervous system. If you cut the head in half, other nerve ganglions still control disparate parts of the body. While they might somehow technically *be* dead, they sure as hell don't *behave* dead.

If you choose this method, I suggest cutting the head in half, quickly followed by the rest of the body.

One vegetarian friend who has watched this repeated a mantra to herself. Perhaps you'll find it helpful: "It's just a bug. . . . It's just a big bug. . . ."

VARIATION

PAN-ROASTING LOBSTER

INGREDIENTS	TO SERVE 2
S+P	To taste
EVOO	To taste
Lobster, halved	1
Garlic powder	To taste
Red chile flakes	To taste
Lime juice	To taste

SHORTHAND

Grill split lobster flesh-side down, EVOO 5min covered. Flip, season w red pepper & garlic. Cook flesh side 5min, shell side 5min. Serve w lime.

HANDS-ON TIME

20 minutes

TOTAL TIME

20 minutes

GEAR

- Cast-iron Dutch oven
- Tongs

OPTIONAL MUSIC PAIRING

"Highlander Theme" by Michael Kamen

If you pull off the Highlander, pan-roasting (or grilling) is the way to go. This produces a less rubbery texture than boiling.

00 Heat cast-iron Dutch oven on medium-high.

01 Add S+P and EVOO to exposed flesh on both lobster halves.

02 Cook flesh-side down for 5 minutes (cover with lid).

03 Flip over to season flesh side with garlic (I suggest powder) and red chile flakes.

04 Cook seasoned flesh-side down for another 5 minutes (covered).

05 Flip and cook on shell side for 5 minutes (covered).

06 Remove, drizzle with lime juice, and serve.

Be sure to eat all the meat, lest you incur the wrath of lobster spirits. Use your teeth to shimmy out all the goodness. Bite down on the telson (part of the tail fan) and each leg 1–2" (2–4 cm) from an open end. Tease the meat into your mouth as you pull the appendage away from you. This is something like squeegy-ing toothpaste out of an almost-empty tooth-paste tube.

Remember "The Importance of Rabbits," and do not waste.

Ripert's Dip

If feeling more ambitious, try this vinaigrette dip by Eric Ripert:

2 T sherry wine vinegar

1 t Dijon mustard

6 T (90 ml) EVOO

1 T dried tarragon or finely chopped fresh tarragon

S+P (use Maldon)

THE KOLKATA (CALCUTTA) MARKET INCIDENT

*"Todo bicho que camina
Va a parar al asador."*

**"Every creature that walks
Ends up roasting on the iron cross."**

—ARGENTINE PROVERB

"For the Holi festival, we kill our own chickens," said Pawan.

"Ah . . ." I nodded understandingly, "for sacrifice."

"No, no . . . it's cheaper. The prices skyrocket afterward."

This conversation, in the lobby of the Tollygunge Club in Kolkata, India, reminded me of a video I'd seen of Chef Martin Yan butchering a whole chicken in 18 seconds. As he threw off each piece, he said, "This . . . $4.50. This . . . $4.50." It's a lot cheaper to buy chickens whole and butcher them ("break them down," in industry parlance) than to buy plastic-wrapped portions.

All that said, I never planned on killing my first chicken in India.

In fact, for the first 34 years of my life, I never planned on killing any chickens ever. But the morning following Pawan's pep talk, I found myself plunged headlong into a chaotic market for Gujarati vegetarians and Punjabi Sikhs. The mission: to kill a chicken.

Seeds for this idea were planted six months earlier, when I asked myself: if I had to, could I personally kill all the animals I consume? The vague plan formulated was to "master" one domestic animal (my pick: chicken) and one wild animal (my pick: deer). "Master" entailed raising or hunting, killing, processing (cleaning and butchering), and cooking each animal. Start to finish, I had to know it all.

Now the moment was at hand.

Passing through vegetable stalls at the entrance, my local host stopped to share a few gems ("Nothing called 'curry powder' is actually sold in Indian markets") and buy fenugreek for her cat. Fenugreek, it turns out, is also good for boners, as another tourist informed me, totally unprompted.

Just as I was forced to contemplate his strange greeting and cat boners, I noticed the local furry FDA inspector keeping a close (very close) eye on the product:

We forged ahead through noise and unfamiliar smells, to the avian quarters.

My host had arranged for me to kill my own hen, but she wouldn't watch. Before running off, she explained the two options for slaughter:

1. The Muslim method, which requires two and a half cuts to the neck and bleeding the chicken to death in a tub "after much struggle."

2. The Hindu method, which entails lopping the head off. Not much struggle.

I settled on the latter. The men at the stall, we learned through pantomime, were vegetarian but worked at the market for income. It quickly morphed into a surreal, confusing experience, as I was handed a knife and the chicken was held out to me by the legs. I asked about technique, but none of the Indians spoke English. Should I chop like an ax or saw like a hacksaw? A small crowd was gathering, and the conversation was over. With a bread knife in one hand, I grabbed the chicken by the head with my other hand, covering its entire head and beak, and sawed through the neck in less than a second.

The killing was over, but the dying was not. That would take another 20–30 seconds. As the man held the wings together and bled the chicken into a drain in the concrete, I could feel the chicken's head pulsing in my hand, which continued for several minutes. The chicken was long dead, but the nervous twitches went on for what seemed like an eternity, hence the expression "running around like a chicken with its head cut off."[37]

The body was immediately butchered using a *boti,* which looks like a harp with a razor-sharp blade instead of strings. The "player" in this case is the butcher, who sits cross-legged behind the *boti* and pushes the chicken through the blade. Never before or since have I seen such fast and clean butchering.

We wasted nothing—even the flesh on the head was removed and bagged. Arriving back at our hotel, I implored the restaurant manager to let me prepare the chicken in the kitchen. No dice. I reluctantly handed my bag off to the staff and explained repeatedly: very little seasoning, lots of vegetables, and no sauce. Two hours later, the package was delivered to my room in a foil box with paper lid. My heart sank as I saw white sauce seeping out of the edges: chicken Alfredo with pasta.

I was furious. This animal was my responsibility, and now I felt it had been desecrated. The chicken pieces had been chopped into tiny slivers and mixed into a horrible faux-Italian sauce, complete with sugar and cheap cream. It was like bad Russian dressing. Vegetables? None to speak of.

Thirty minutes later, I had fished out every last speck of chicken flesh and dutifully eaten it all, forkful by sickening forkful.

I felt ill from the sauce, but I felt good about the act. It marked a departure point for me, and I would never look at chicken quite the same way again.

37 One thigh, from an earlier butchered chicken, was twitching on a platter when we arrived, and was still twitching 10 minutes later.

STAFF RECOMMENDS

SKILL

KILLING A CHICKEN

THE MEXICAN TOWEL SNAP

Cutting off a live chicken's head is, I later learned, not the most elegant approach.

In the movie *Traffic,* I was introduced to a less macabre (in fact, bloodless) option, which appears in a Mexican birthday scene. My ex-farmer uncle then confirmed that this "Mexican towel snap" method is the most humane chicken-killing technique.

Here's how it works:

1 Grab the chicken by the head.

SQUAK!

2 Swing it by your side violently for 10–20 seconds, as if winding up a towel to snap someone in the ass (hence the name) or racing to get a car up on jacks.

3

The chicken is now dead. Alas, as noted earlier, dead doesn't mean still. It will likely flap around for a few minutes. If you wish to hasten the end, you can sever the head by pinning the chicken to a board and using a machete or heavy cleaver to decapitate the poor bird. This will cut the main nervous circuits.

4

Wearing rubber gloves, hold your chicken by its feet and dunk it into scalding (140°F/60°C) water. Dunk it all the way in—far enough that even the little feathers on the bottom of the legs are submerged. Hold it still in the water for 30–75 seconds, then vigorously agitate it up and down for a minute or so. Remove the chicken and try to pull out a large wing and tail feather. If they come out easily, you're ready to pluck. If not, dunk it again for another 10 seconds or so, then try the wing/tail feather again. Keep this up until both come out without resistance. Dunk the chicken quickly in cold water. (This will help prevent the skin from tearing as you pluck.) Start plucking right away. If you've done your scald well, the feathers will come right out. Most farmers seem to start with the legs (since they're holding the chicken by the feet), dragging feathers off in a downward motion, then go along the sides and under the wings, to the belly and breast, then back up to the thighs and around the back.

5 Butcher and cook as you like. Avoid chicken Alfredo.

LESSON 35

SKILLS

PIT COOKING, WEEKEND DEBAUCHERY

CLAMBAKE IN A GARBAGE CAN

SHORTHAND

Soak overnight: 20lb seaweed in H2O & 8 ears corn in salted H2O. Layer in seaweed: 8 foil-wrapped sweet potatoes & 16 onions, 8 foil-wrapped trout, corn, 8lb clams, 8 lobsters. Cook 2hr till lobster is bright red; serve w butter & lemon.

HANDS-ON TIME

About 2 hours to gather your equipment and make the clambake basket

TOTAL TIME

About 6 hours

GEAR

- 2 buckets or large pots
- Clean 30-gal (120-qt) galvanized garbage can
- About 7 ft (2 m) steel galvanized chicken wire (18"/45 cm wide) (you'll find chicken wire at the hardware store)
- Permanent marker (like a Sharpie)
- Leather gloves
- Wire cutter
- Galvanized steel wire (for steamer basket)
- Drill with a large bit or a large nail and hammer (neighbors love these)

CONTINUED OPPOSITE!

> **"Civilized life has altogether grown too tame, and, if it is to be stable, it must provide harmless outlets for the impulses which our remote ancestors satisfied in hunting."**
>
> —BERTRAND RUSSELL, PHILOSOPHER

This massive undertaking, should you accept it, is your graduation ceremony for the entire WILD section.

Pit cooking—cooking food on smoldering coals or hot rocks underground—holds a sacred place for just about every culture.

There's the Hawaiian luau and similar methods throughout the Pacific, where pigs are wrapped in banana leaves and steamed underground. Then you have the Central Asian tandoor oven, a cross between a pit oven and brick oven, where dishes like chicken tandoori and naan flatbread are cooked. In North Africa, you find the tandir earth oven, similar to the luau but used for cooking whole lamb. It goes on and on.

In New England, we have the clambake, a tradition that, as legend has it, the Pilgrims picked up from the Native Americans, who were cooking underground long before the *Mayflower* landed. To begin, a long shallow pit is dug on the beach and a fire is started in the depression. Large stones are placed on the fire, which is then burned down to a smolder. Buckets of seaweed are thrown in to cover the hot rocks, then large quantities of seafood, potatoes, corn, etc. are layered in and covered with more seaweed. The whole pit is covered with a tarp (weighed down with rocks), and it's all left to cook by the heat of the rocks. Fortunately for us, a similar but smaller-scale clambake can be replicated in your backyard.

The garbage-can clambake is for the urban pyromaniac in all of us. That is <ahem> if your local fire department approves it, of course.

You'll need to designate a clambake master before you get started. The clambake master is part Smokey Bear and part platoon leader. He or she will be in charge of directing the show and keeping people safe, which includes having a water supply or hose (or fire extinguisher) nearby, keeping kids from eating coal or lighting themselves on fire, etc.

Things are easier if you order the seafood and seaweed in advance. Time it so someone picks up the order (bring a cooler to the fish store and have them pack it with ice) while the fire is building, and bring the food directly to your garbage can. Stuffing a fridge with eight lobsters is for amateurs.

Traditional clambake

INGREDIENTS	TO SERVE 8
Big bucket of seaweed, preferably rockweed[38]	About 20 lb (9 kg)
Corn[39]	8 ears
Large sweet potatoes, scrubbed	8
Small trout (about 250 g/10 oz) or other fish, gutted and scaled as needed[40]	4
S+P	To taste
Softshell clams, scrubbed[41]	8 lb (3.5 kg)
Small onions/baby onions, unpeeled	16/32
Chicken lobsters,[42] live (1 lb/450 kg)	8
Salted butter, melted	2 sticks (225 g)
Lemons, cut into wedges	8

PREP

00 The night before the clambake, soak the seaweed overnight in a bucket or large pot with enough water to cover the seaweed. If the seaweed is muddy, wash it with fresh water before soaking.

01 In a separate bucket or large pot, soak the corn for at least 1 hour or overnight in enough salted water to cover the corn.

02 Designate a clambake master (see opposite page).

. . . AND MORE GEAR

- Outdoor hose or fire extinguisher
- Stones about 4" (10 cm) in diameter. If you don't have access to stones, try the garden department at your local home improvement store, or check the Farm/ Garden section of Craigslist.
- 10-lb (4.5-kg) bag untreated charcoal. No chemicals on your charcoal to poison your food; no lighter fluid, either.
- A couple of buckets of kindling (applewood, maple, or ash are good choices)
- Newspaper
- Matches
- Fire iron
- 1 roll aluminum foil
- Cheesecloth
- Kitchen twine
- 1 large stone or 2–4 bricks
- Extra-long flameproof barbecue mitts (for reaching down into the can while cooking)
- Extra-long metal tongs
- Nut or lobster crackers

OPTIONAL MUSIC PAIRING

"Clambake" by Elvis Presley

38 Rockweed has little bubbles in it that hold seawater; when it cooks, the bubbles pop and add a burst of salty steam to the mix. For a fanciful (nonedible) garnish, boil a few handfuls of seaweed for a few seconds and watch it turn bright green.

39 No need to husk it or remove the silk; the silk will come right off after it's cooked.

40 See the recipe for Trout Adaptation with South Indian Spices on page 336 for instructions on how to gut fish, or ask your fishmonger to clean it for you.

41 Clams live in sand and mud and contain a lot of grit. To clean them, fill a large bowl with water and a good amount of salt. Add the clams and gently swish them every few minutes for 30–60 minutes, no longer, then remove. Or ask your fishmonger to clean them for you.

42 A chicken lobster is a young, small lobster.

Make a Garbage Can Steamer Basket

1. Roll the chicken wire out on the ground so it's flat. (Have a second person hold the far end down.) Flip the garbage can over onto the chicken wire, the rim at the edge closest to you.

2. With a permanent marker, trace the outline of the garbage-can rim on the chicken wire. Wearing leather gloves and using a wire cutter, cut out this circle of chicken wire. This will be your basket's bottom.

3. Put this circle inside the garbage can, about 1 ft (30 cm) from the bottom to leave room for your stones and coals. Fit it snugly by bending the edges up around the circumference. If it's hard to bend the edges, or to fit in at all, use a piece of your kindling to knock it into place.

4. Next, trim the remaining chicken wire so it's once again rectangular. This will be wrapped to form the sides of the basket, so measure the shorter side of the rectangle against the height of the can (minus 1 ft/30 cm for the rocks) to make sure it will fit. Trim as needed. Roll it and place inside the garbage can. If, when rolled, the edges overlap (like cigarette papers), that's fine.

5. Remove all the chicken wire from the garbage can. Stitch the seam of the basket sides with steel wire to secure it; then stitch the base to the sides.

6. Use more wire to make and attach handles at the sides of the top of your basket, as shown. It's okay if they protrude a little, as they can be bent before you place the lid on the can. If you have spare metal bucket handles, even sturdier, you can attach them with the wire.

1.

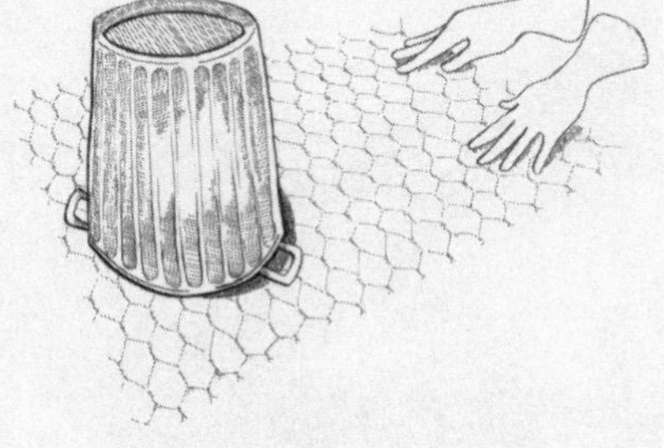

2.

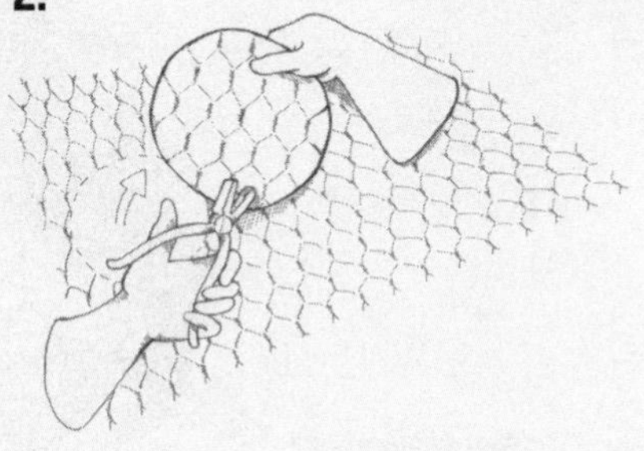

3.

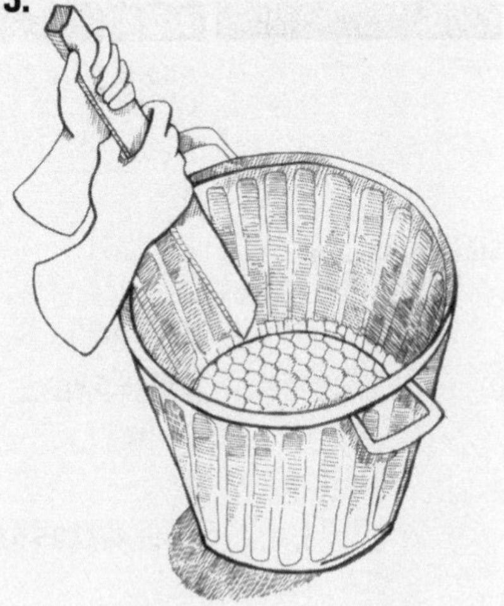

4.

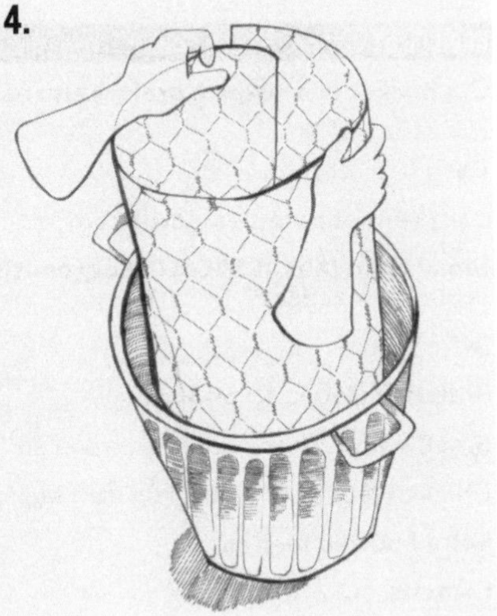

5.

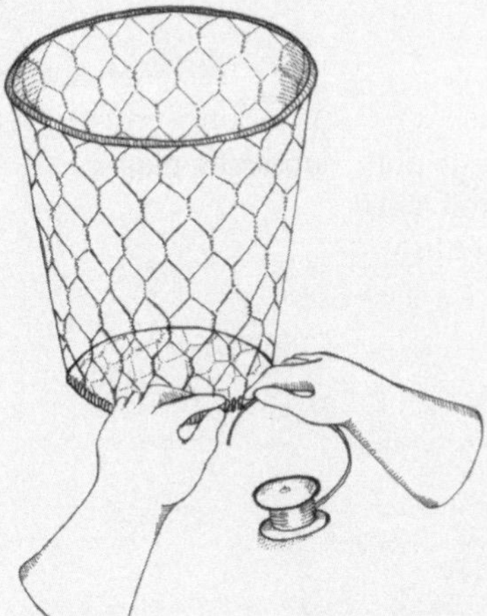

6.

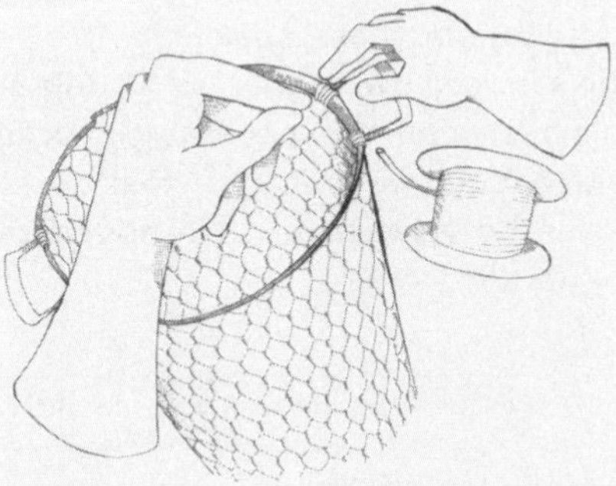

03 Make a garbage can steamer basket (see opposite page).

04 About 4" (10 cm) from the bottom of the can, drill or punch holes spaced 4" (10 cm) apart all around the can. Make another line of holes about 2" (5 cm) above the first line, with the holes alternating with the first line of holes. Make a third line of holes another 2" (5 cm) up; space these holes to line up with the first line of holes[43] (see finished pic C).

05 Place the garbage can on a flat, sturdy surface outdoors, downwind from your dining table(s) and away from any fire hazards: trees, grass, houses, dynamite, Labradors, etc.

06 Prep the ingredients.

07 Wrap the sweet potatoes individually in foil.

08 Season each fish with salt and pepper and wrap them individually in foil.

09 Loosely wrap the clams in one cheesecloth bundle (so the clams will have room to spread out in one layer in the steamer basket) and tie it with kitchen twine.

PICKUP

00 Line the bottom of the garbage can with a double layer of the medium-size (4"/10-cm diameter) stones.

01 **Build a fire on the stones:** Empty the charcoal over the stones and throw in a bucket of kindling. Make a few newspaper twists and nestle them into the kindling. If you have fire paste, you can play with it here. Light the newspaper with a match to start the fire. Stoke the fire as it burns.[44] Add the rest of the kindling as the fire burns down. When you see a red-orange glow from the center of the fire and coals appear ash white—about 2 hours—use your iron to spread the coals out evenly and get ready to build your clambake. You'll want to have all your ingredients prepped and ready to go as soon as the fire is ready.

A

B

C

D

43 You could also use a garden incinerator, which is like a metal garbage can with the holes already drilled in it.
44 This is a good time to toast marshmallows.

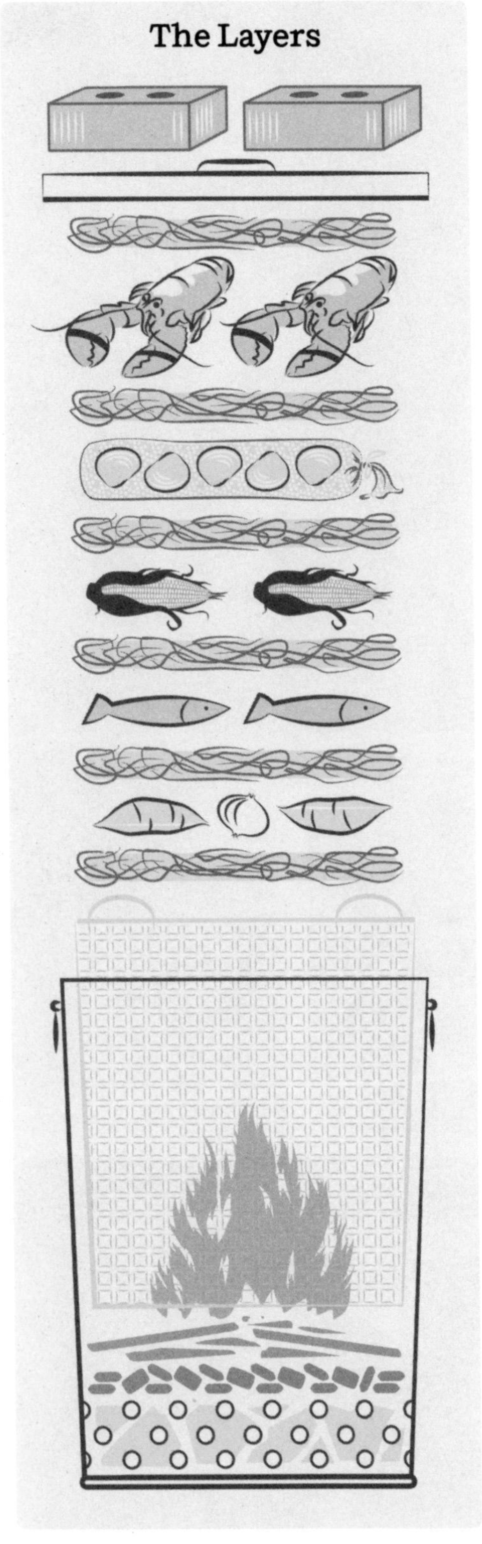
The Layers

E

F

G

02 When you're ready to load the garbage can with food, lay the chicken wire basket on a flat surface and add a 4" (10-cm) layer of seaweed. Start adding your ingredients in single layers (no overlapping). Follow the illustration at far left. Here goes . . .

03 Make your first layer of food with the sweet potatoes and onions. Add a layer (about 3"/8 cm) of seaweed to cover the sweet potatoes and onions.

04 Make your second layer of food with the fish. Add a layer of seaweed to cover the fish.

05 Make your third layer of food with the corn. Add a layer of seaweed to cover the corn.

06 Make your fourth layer of food with the clams. Add a layer of seaweed to cover the clams.

07 Make your fifth and final layer of food with the lobsters, keeping the rubber bands around their claws. Top with a final layer of seaweed.

08 Pick up the steamer basket with the handles and carefully lower it into the garbage can (you'll need two people for this). Bend the handles inward if they extend over the top, until you are able to close the lid.

09 Cover the garbage can with the lid, place a large stone or 2–4 bricks on top to secure it, and cook for 2 hours. Lift the lid and check the lobster: If they are bright red, you're done. To be absolutely sure, break open a leg and check the meat; it should be firm, white, and opaque.

10 Remove the lobster from the basket and place on serving dishes.

11 Wearing extra-long flameproof barbecue mitts, have two people carefully lift the steamer basket out of the garbage can. Do a quick check to see that each element is ready: the clams are opened (discard any that aren't open), the corn is tender, the fish is cooked through, and the onions and sweet potatoes are soft. If any element doesn't seem cooked through,[45] remove the ingredients that are ready and return the steamer basket with under-cooked ingredients to the garbage can to finish, layering seaweed in between as before.

12 Arrange everything on serving plates and serve: Each person gets 1 lobster, 1 ear of corn, 1 lb (0.5 kg) of clams, ½ a fish, 1 sweet potato, and 4 onions. Pass around small ramekins of melted butter, lemon wedges, S+P, and plenty of napkins. Have lots of bowls on hand for the empty shells. Relax and enjoy your bounty.

Whether thousands of years ago, at a Hawaiian luau, or at a Labor Day feast, humans haven't changed much. Sometimes, we should embrace our simplicity.

45 I don't need to remind you about the dangers of consuming undercooked seafood, but I will. When in doubt, cook it longer or toss it.

SCI

THE SCIENTIST

SCI is where we'll explore the questions "What if?" and "Why not?"

Making ice cream in 30 seconds? Hitting 26 restaurants in 24 hours? Eating 15,000 calories in 20 minutes? It's all nuts, but as the Cheshire Cat said to Alice, "Oh, you can't help that. Most everyone's mad here." The following pages double as a decadent cheat day smorgasbord, where slow-carb becomes "go-carb." I do love my chocolate croissants on Saturdays.

In the process of learning about the science of food (without really trying), you'll also learn tricks for next-generation fat loss. For instance, how can you consume 600% of your normal daily calories without getting fat . . . or while *losing* fat? Biochemical sleight of hand, of course. My specialty.

Above all, let's resurrect your childlike curiosity. Embrace the absurd, from forgotten ingredients to spectacular new techniques, and consider it a Choose-Your-Own-Adventure buffet: skip around, pick your favorites, and ignore the rest. Nothing here is mandatory (but I do suggest reading all the recipe headnotes).

Go nuts!

MODERNIST CUISINE
Salt and Vinegar Chips
potato starch, spray dried vinegar
Bread and Butter
pea butter on walnut toast, ham butter on pullman,
hominy
Elote
freeze dried corn
ultrasonic bath
sseline, demi-glace gelée
Snow Ball
apple sorbet, fresh wasabi fluid gel snow
Liquid Caprese
constructed cream, tomato seed juice
Oysters Cocktail
cryo shucked, oyster cream, lemon gelée
Ankimo
sous vide monkfish liver torchon, fresh walnuts, yuzu
Spaghetti alle Vongole
geoduck, bagna cauda, sea beans, dried miso
France in a Bowl
foie gras custard, snails, frog's legs, ramp green broth, chanterelles
Spring in Autumn
Taki's turnips, mint, centrifuged pea broth

SODIU
ALGINA
CALCIUM
GLUCONAT
BACARDI
SUPERIOR

Everything a growing boy needs.

A TRIP TO SEATTLE

"Don't worry about people stealing your ideas. If your ideas are any good, you'll have to ram them down people's throats."
—HOWARD AIKEN, AMERICAN COMPUTER ENGINEER AND MATHEMATICIAN

THE HOST

"I bought a T-Rex, put it in my living room, and then . . . I found my own in Montana! It's a bit like having someone else's deer head on your wall." Most people don't have a T-Rex to greet them in the morning. Then again, most people aren't like Nathan Myhrvold, former CTO of Microsoft and founder of Microsoft Research. He seems to have a hand in everything.

To start, his expedition team found not just one T-Rex, but 30% of all T-Rexes ever found (they tend to be in Montana, South Dakota, and Canada). He's created laser systems to zap mosquitoes out of the air. Not long ago, he designed high-tech thermoses that keep vaccines for 10,000 people cool for up to six months . . . without power. It's hard to keep track, since Nathan has filed more than 500 patents and acquired well over 30,000 more through his latest company, Intellectual Ventures.

Somewhere along the line, Nathan developed a small obsession with food.

First, he became a master chef in France. Then, he became fascinated with the micro-regional cuisine of the American south: BBQ. Naturally, he competed in the 1991 World Championship of Barbecue in Memphis, Tennessee, where his team finished first place in multiple categories, including pasta.[1]

But then what? If you had worked on quantum theories of gravity under Stephen Hawking, were an award-winning photographer (yep, he did that, too), had earned a few hundred million dollars, and loved cooking, how might you spend your time?

Nathan's answer, a book titled *Modernist Cuisine: The Art and Science of Cooking*, is what brought me to Seattle to experience a 32-course (!) dinner at his food lab. I had earlier met his son, Conor, then an undergrad at Princeton, who'd helped me finagle the invite.

Calling *Modernist Cuisine* (MC) a book is a bit like calling an aircraft carrier a boat:

- 2,438 pages, bound in five volumes, housed in a Plexiglas case
- 4 lbs of ink
- 1,522 recipes
- 5,000+ photographs, carefully selected from 147,000+ taken

For three years, his team of five full-time scientists and 10 world-class chefs (39 total staff) tested all the old wives' tales and measured everything imaginable. The results were fascinating.

For instance, did you know that bacon and olive oil have near identical amounts of oleic

1 Yes, BBQ pasta. Who knew?

acid, which is commonly touted as olive oil's healthy differentiator?

That cucumber has a higher water content (95%) than whole milk (88%)?

That you can inject your chickens with brine and hang them in the oven for a perfectly crisp exterior and succulent interior?

This isn't your grandma's kitchen. As Tim Zagat of *Zagat Survey* put it, "[This is] the most important book in the culinary arts since Escoffier."‡

THE DINNER

Our evening in Seattle began around a conference table, where a cadre of luminaries had gathered from around the world. Nathan provided a science overview via flat screen as champagne was handed out. I wasted no time in embarrassing myself.

"Are you a chef?" I asked one iconic chef across from me. The person seated next to him cringed. Thankfully, the maestro found it amusing. I politely asked for more champagne.

A sympathetic server, witnessing my tomfoolery, pointed out the legends and rising stars:

- Chef Johnny Iuzzini, then head pastry chef at Jean Georges
- Jeffrey Steingarten, writer for *Vogue*
- Chef Andoni Aduriz from Mugaritz restaurant in Spain
- Chef Oswaldo Oliva, Andoni's development chef
- Chef Pierre Hermé, pastry chef from Paris
- Charles Znaty, Pierre's business partner
- Claire Robinson, Food Network TV host
- Fred Carl, Jr., CEO of Viking Range
- Sara Dickerman, freelance food writer
- Katrina Heron, editor-at-large for *Newsweek* and *The Daily Beast*
- Joe Hagan, writer for *Men's Journal, New York,* and *Rolling Stone*
- Chef Scott Boswell of Restaurant Stella! in New Orleans

We migrated to our assigned seats for dinner, and as my small table relaxed, the friendly banter poured forth.

Scott immediately put me at ease. Cuisine was his third career, and he *staged* (apprenticed) at Jean Georges at the age of 42. Johnny pointed out the subtleties of the Japanese citrus *yuzu*, which looks like a miniature lime but tastes markedly different. Everyone debated pressure cookers. The most experienced chefs pointed out that saving time wasn't the main advantage; you should use pressure primarily for enhancing flavor, as flavors don't evaporate off. The pressure cooker is best suited to stocks, for instance, and anything you'd like to caramelize to otherworldly levels, like carrots.

Around 20 dishes (and six wine pairings) later, I became infatuated with a centerpiece on our table: Buddha's hand, a fruit that looks like a mutant chicken foot with lemon skin. It smelled better than any fruit I'd ever encountered.

Then someone loudly recommended a restaurant called Red Medicine. I apparently had to visit L.A. to witness the most amazing "tweezer cuisine" on the planet. It's where Jordan Kahn ("Spelled like *Revenge of Khan*?" I asked, not entirely sober[2]) assembles plates like miniature MoMA pieces. He was a pastry chef who'd made the jump "from sweet to savory" and was reaping the rewards of transplanting technique.

2 The *Star Trek* sequel is actually *The Wrath of Khan.*

After this anecdote, I grabbed my notebook and messily jotted down "Culinary cross-training?"

REVISITING NATURE, NOT REINVENTING IT

The powder-heavy cooking we ate that night is often referred to as *molecular gastronomy*, which is sometimes derogatory.[3] Even smart people rail against the use of so-called "industrial" ingredients.

In reality, the majority of these ingredients, made famous by behemoths like Kraft and therefore hated by the granola crowd, have been used for hundreds or even thousands of years. Agar-agar for thickening? Derived from red algae, it's been used for millennia in Japan for making jellies. Bromelain? That comes from pineapples, which have been used by cultures around the world to tenderize pork and other meats.

Beyond "nothing artificial added," my favorite modernist cuisine actually focuses on *removing* things, not adding them. One of Nathan's favorite tools is the centrifuge. Using it, he can separate flavor from filler, just as one might distill fine whiskey.

So why is all of this thought of as new? Easy: technology and interest have reached a point where it's finally cost-effective for the amateur to play with one-off dishes. Making everything from Nutella Powder to Bacon-Infused Bourbon is surprisingly simple. Beet Foam or Olive Oil Gummy Bears? Far easier than much of WILD, certainly.

All it takes is a little experimentation, which brings us to your next step: outfitting the mini-laboratory.

3 Hence substitutes like "modernist cuisine."

THE GNC GOURMET: THE FUN OF MULTIPURPOSE INGREDIENTS

Don't let unfamiliar terms bring back fears of high school chemistry. Note two things:

First, you don't have to kill yourself hunting all these down. **The simplest solution is to buy a preassembled kit from Molecule-R (fourhourchef.com/molecular). Done and done.**

Second, most of these ingredients are multipurpose.

I was confused when I spotted GNC-bought jars of whey protein and D-ribose on shelves in Nathan's food lab. Was his team doping for the Tour de France? Nope. There's just incredible overlap between performance-enhancing supplements and flavor-enhancing compounds.

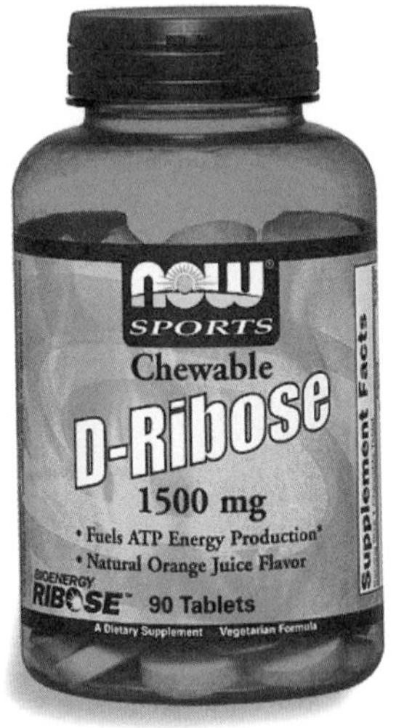
NOW
SPORTS
Chewable
D-Ribose
1500 mg
• Fuels ATP Energy Production*
• Natural Orange Juice Flavor
BIOENERGY RIBOSE
90 Tablets
A Dietary Supplement
Vegetarian Formula
Supplement Facts

For meatheads, meat eaters, and everyone in between.

We'll therefore start our journey with a roll call of ingredients that both chefs and athletes love.

Special thanks to Chris Young for help with this entire section. Chris first hit the limelight by launching the Fat Duck Experimental Kitchen for chef Heston Blumenthal. During Chris's five-year tenure, the Fat Duck was voted the best restaurant in the world. Chris then coauthored *Modernist Cuisine*. These days, Chris, Grant Crilly, and Ryan Matthew Smith run Delve Kitchen (delvekitchen.com), which is focused on inventing the future of cooking and how people learn to cook.

The following tables are comprised of three columns: ingredient, cooking use, and sports/health use. In the last column, most notes are mine; any claims in quotations come directly from manufacturers and don't represent our endorsements. If you don't know a given term, skip it and we'll cover it all later.

And now, to a list fit for Louis Pasteur or Lou Ferrigno. Use it for cooking or performance/physique enhancement.[4] **All items can be found at fourhourchef.com/molecular.**

4 There are four ingredients with no known sports uses, which have "not applicable" in that column.

SKIP THIS TABLE IF IT STRESSES YOU OUT, M'KAY?

NutriBiotic
Pharmaceutical Grade
Ascorbic Acid
with Antioxidant Bioflavonoids
Crystalline Powder
NET WT. 8 OZ. (227 g)
NOW
NAC
CRITICAL ANTIOXIDANT
600 mg
250 Vcaps
Supplement Facts
ALGIN
100 CAPSULES

	INGREDIENT	COOKING USE	SPORTS/HEALTH USE
ANTIOXIDANTS (SLOW DOWN OXIDATION REACTIONS)	**Ascorbic Acid** (aka vitamin C)	**Prevents browning** of fruits and vegetables. Can also be used as a seasoning to add mouthwatering acidity, particularly to fruit-based dishes.	For injury and sickness recovery, I've dosed up to 20 g/day orally with effervescent vitamin C. I've tested 50+ g via IV, but this must be done under close medical supervision, as you can become hypoglycemic if blood sugar isn't monitored. Megadosing is not recommended. "Antioxidant; helps protect against free radical damage; essential for healthy bones, teeth, blood vessels, and collagen; may help support the immune system."
ENZYMES (INCREASE THE RATE OF CHEMICAL REACTIONS)	**Bromelain** (derived from pineapples)	**Meat tenderizer.** A little goes a long way. When overused, you'll turn delicious steak into mush. When used perfectly, you get something like the rare beef consommé in *Modernist Cuisine*.	I don't use this for digesting protein (humans are pretty good at that), but I depend on it for accelerating bruise healing. I use 250 mg 3x/day orally between meals, per the Royal Pharmaceutical Society of Great Britain. "Aids in the digestion of proteins; prevents swelling and muscle soreness."
	Trans-glutaminase	**So-called "meat glue"** (even sold as "Moo Gloo") forms bonds between proteins. In nature, it is an enzyme and clotting agent that heals wounds. In cooking, we might use it to turn chunks of stew meat into filet mignon. Wear rubber gloves unless you want webbed hands: • Mix the meat with the powder. • Wrap it tightly in cling wrap. • Refrigerate for 12 hours. • *Voilà!* That $5 meat has become $50 meat. Well . . . maybe. Some media claim they're indistinguishable, but chef-scientist Chris Young would certainly disagree.	Not applicable. More on this later.

POLYMERS (LONG, CHAIN-LIKE MOLECULES)

INGREDIENT	COOKING USE	SPORTS/HEALTH USE
Gelatin	**Gelification.** One of the most versatile gelling ingredients known to man. Nothing melts in your mouth the way gelatin does.	"Improves bone/joint/tendon health; natural anti-inflammatory; shortens recovery time after exercise and sports-related injury."
Xanthan Gum	**Emulsification,[5] stabilization,[6] and thickening.** This is the closest thing the culinary world has to a gluten replacement. If you want to thicken something, whether making water like soup or soup like cement, xanthan gum can do the job. Useful for gazpacho (0.25% of total weight).	"Good source of fiber; lowers blood sugar and cholesterol in diabetics."
Sodium Alginate (A component of the cell walls of colder-water brown seaweeds. It gives seaweed some of its flexibility to move with the motion of the ocean.)	**Spherification[7]** (when combined with calcium lactate), **stabilization, and thickening.** First used in the late 1940s, this ingredient became popular when chefs like Ferran Adrià used it to create faux caviar, faux egg yolks, etc. The pimentos in most olives are made this way. A pimento puree is made with alginate in it and then pumped into the center of a pitted olive, the calcium in the olive causes the alginate in the puree to set, and then you have a pimento-stuffed olive.	Used by some as a chelator to remove heavy metals from the bloodstream. Highly controversial. I'd consider MD-supervised DMPS (2,3-dimercaptopropane-1-sulfonic acid) first.
Maltodextrin	**Stabilization and thickening.** Maltodextrin falls somewhere between a simple sugar and a starch. It's also a bulking agent used to create a syrup-like consistency (e.g., red-pepper puree) without unpleasant sweetness or masking of flavor. Plain maltodextrin shouldn't be confused with tapioca maltodextrin. The product that can turn oils into powders is derived from tapioca maltodextrin (N-Zorbit, made by National Starch), but it is very different from plain maltodextrin, which won't work for that purpose.	"Helps sustain energy levels during endurance-oriented workouts and/or athletic events; supports weight gain."
Agar-Agar (from red algae)	**Gelification**	Not applicable.
Carrageenan (from red seaweed)	**Gelification, suspension, and thickening.** The Irish have used this for hundreds of years to create panna cotta–like desserts that won't melt when warm, unlike with gelatin.	Not applicable.
Isomalt	**Sugar replacement** in some confections; it is more resistant to humidity and crystallization, and it spikes insulin levels less than sucrose.	Not applicable.

5 Here *emulsify* means smoothly mixing fats and nonfats. Simply put, mixing two things that usually don't mix.

6 A *stabilizer* is an additive that maintains the texture of food, like the firmness of a gel or the smoothness of mayonnaise.

7 Imagine a mojito trapped in a caviar-like bubble. That's *spherification*.

AMINO ACIDS (SAVORY FLAVOR)

INGREDIENT	COOKING USE	SPORTS/HEALTH USE
Glutamine	Can be combined with other sugars in a meat marinade to **help produce greater Maillard reactions** (see page 435), contributing to the deliciousness of roasted chicken skin, toasted bread, or seared steak.	Replaces glutamine lost in the body during high-intensity exercise. I routinely take 8–10 g post-workout. Used at high doses to help repair leaky gut syndrome (50–80 g/day in divided doses of 10 g), it can eliminate muscle soreness, even after high-rep squat workouts.
L-Cysteine	**Reducing agent.** Gluten gives dough its elasticity, and it also produces dome-like bread. So how do you get flat sides on hamburger or hot dog buns? Just add L-cysteine, an amino acid that interacts with sulfur bonds and also extends shelf life.	L-cysteine is used to improve skin, hair, and skin conditions. It aids in the formation of structural proteins, such as collagen and keratin. Personally, I find N-acetyl cysteine (NAC) more interesting for its effects on glutathione and taurine, particularly during multi-bout sports with 60+ minutes between sessions.
D-Ribose	D-ribose is the backbone of many molecules and **caramelizes at low temperatures** (<93.3°C/<200°F). Dust it on meat before grilling for unparalleled "meaty" flavor. It's a modern secret ingredient in BBQ dry rubs, which typically contain paprika, brown sugar, allspice, etc. On the sweet side, it can be used in water to make fudgy caramel candies.	Popular with power athletes (including me) for regenerating ATP. Has a synergistic effect with creatine supplementation, though I prefer to combine beta-alanine with creatine. "Enhances cardiac energy levels and supports cardiovascular metabolism; plays a role in supporting energy recovery during/after exercise; may strengthen and support the body's antioxidant defenses."
Whey Protein Isolate (WPI)	Whey protein *isolate* (not "concentrate," which spoils too easily) **has an enormous number of uses.** Found in Old Mother Hubbard's "eating her curds [think cottage cheese] and whey," whey is a fraction of milk. It can be used as a thickener, a gelling agent, a foaming agent, or to emulsify everything from vinaigrette to mayo. For mayo, you can even sub it for the egg yolk, starting with 0.5% by weight and adjusting as needed. It can be used to create gels; just combine your favorite liquid, 10% WPI by weight, and some calcium lactate (or nigiri salts used for tofu) to trigger the gelling. Perhaps my favorite use is chocolate wine. It's existed for hundreds of years, but here's the modern method: • Melt and mix dark chocolate (it's good for you) into a red dessert wine like Banyuls (around 50°C/122°F). • Blend well with an immersion blender and then let settle for a few hours (off heat) until the cocoa butter rises to the top. Skim off the fat and save the chocolate-flavored wine underneath. • Add 0.5% WPI (by weight) to the chocolate wine, warm to a nice drinking temperature (I like 55°C/ 131°F), and use an Aerolatte or similar foaming wand, or the hand blender, to froth it into a velvety texture.	I routinely use unflavored WPI to satisfy the "30 grams within 30 minutes" fat-loss rule. I also consume either 1 T coconut oil or almond butter to slow the uptake of amino acids, as WPI can act like the simple sugar of proteins: rapid rise and rapid fall into catabolism. Given the many sports and culinary uses, I buy WPI in ridiculously sized jars.  NOW SPORTS Whey Protein Isolate 100% Pure *R* is for *ridiculous.* "May preserve muscle glycogen stores and help reduce the amount of protein breakdown during exercise."

INGREDIENT	COOKING USE	SPORTS/HEALTH USE
Calcium Lactate	**Spherification** (used to trigger gelling of alginate and other calcium-sensitive gelling compounds). Calcium lactate tastes better than calcium chloride, but you need to use three times as much.	"Supports bone health."
Sodium Citrate	**Spherification,** but also an emulsifying salt. This salt of citric acid is often used to soften "hard" water to aid spherification; if your water or liquid has too much calcium in it, you won't be able to get things to successfully spherify. It's also the secret to a great fondue, in which you want cheese that melts smoothly and not into lumps. The mark of a ruined fondue is separation: curd that burns on the bottom of your pot and a slick of oil floating on top. Traditionally, this was fixed in Switzerland by using low-quality, overly tart wine (high citric acid) that loosened up casein proteins, helping to keep the fondue emulsified and smooth. Luckily, it's hard to find wine sufficiently bad anymore. Now the solution is what built the Kraft empire: sodium citrate. James Kraft used citrate as a melting salt to make it easy to cast cheese into cans and then sterilize the cans so that the cheese could be shipped unrefrigerated. Emulsifying salts are why Velveeta melts as smoothly as it does. But you can make your own Velveeta using real cheese. It's easy: • Shred your favorite hard cheese. If you're using a really mature cheese like a hard Parmesan, you should blend it with a softer, mild cheese for the best results. • Add a small amount of water or wine to a pot, add about 0.5% the weight of the cheese in sodium citrate to the liquid, and heat to dissolve. • Add the cheese a little at a time and stir until it all melts. • When the cheese is melted, you can adjust the consistency by adding more liquid to make it thinner, or you can pour the molten cheese into a mold, wait for it to harden, and then slice it into your own singles.	Ingested by some athletes 90 minutes prior to race time for events 2–15 minutes in duration. Orally dosed sodium citrate (often at 0.5 g per kg body weight) quickly degrades into sodium bicarbonate—baking soda—which has been demonstrated to improve performance in events 1–7 minutes in length. Empirically, I can say that there are high responders who see great endurance gains and nonresponders who see nothing at all. For anyone who tries it, use it near a bathroom the first time. It can cause rapid "evacuation," if you catch my drift. Sodium citrate is hard to find at GNC, but the Internet provideth.

	INGREDIENT	COOKING USE	SPORTS/HEALTH USE
SURFACTANTS (GO TO THE SURFACES BETWEEN OIL AND WATER)	**Soy Lecithin**	**Emulsification and thickening.** Oil-based soy lecithin is used to make smooth chocolate and can be used to make a really smooth mayonnaise or salad dressing that won't separate into oil and water over time. The "de-oiled" powder, on the other hand, can be used to make dish suds-like foam. el Bulli restaurant brought this to the forefront with a mignonette sauce (shallots, pepper, vinegar) "cloud" served on oysters in the half shell.	"Helps the body emulsify fat; supports a healthy cardiovascular system, nervous system function, and liver function; supports normal choline levels during exercise."
ACIDS (SOUR/TART FLAVOR)	**Malic Acid** (often derived from cherries or apples)	**Gives food a tart/sour flavor.** Good food triggers a saliva response, which malic acid does in spades. Chris uses it to season many things (cherry puree, lentil salad) at the end of prep, just like you'd use a pinch of salt. It makes everything taste fresher.	"Prolongs the body's ability to produce energy during physical activity and reduces the onset of fatigue."

ACHTUNG!

The next 10 pages are excerpted from *The 4-Hour Body*. I couldn't *not* include them. They answer an important question before we dig in: How do you minimize fat gain when eating carbs like a little piglet?

Used with permission from Crown Publishers.

DAMAGE CONTROL

Preventing Fat Gain When You Binge

"Life itself is the proper binge."

—Julia Child

"Doughnuts are a normal part of a healthy, balanced diet."

—Brooke Smith, Krispy Kreme spokeswoman

I was on a first date at Samovar Tea House in San Francisco.

The incense, subdued global music, and meticulous track lighting made us feel like we were somewhere between a Buddhist-inspired Last Dragon and a Dutch coffee shop. Then, as if on cue, both of us ordered Schizandra berry tea. The description?

> *2000 years ago Shen Nong first identified this potent elixir as an "adaptogenic tonic" (i.e., it gives you whatever you need: energy, relaxation, beauty, sexual prowess).*

Things were off to a good start.

After some flirting and playful verbal sparring, I made my move.

"Don't let this weird you out."

I took an electronic food scale out of my man-purse,[6] which I use to carry odd items, and

6. Strange enough to begin with.

began separating all of my food so I could weigh the individual pieces. This was, of course, the beginning of the end.

Ah, l'amor. . . . It is fickle and not fond of serial-killer-like behavior.

But love could wait. I had other things on my mind.

It was just the beginning of a 12-hour quest for fatness, and it was my second attempt. The first attempt, done with more than 10 lbs of fatty cuts of grass-fed beef, had failed. That is, I could consume only 6 lbs without vomiting, and I didn't gain one gram of fat.

Why the hell do a quest for fatness at all, you ask?

Because I wanted to prove, once and for all, that the calories-in-calories-out model was plain wrong, or at least incomplete. The easiest way I could do this was by consuming a disgusting number of calories in a short period of time and documenting the aftereffects.

This time, I had a different approach.

At 11:43 p.m. that evening, with two minutes remaining, I struggled to choke down a final package of Nutter Butters. I had polled my Twitter followers the previous night for their favorite calorically dense foods, and I had committed to consuming as many as possible. Everything I ate or drank would be photographed and either measured or weighed.

Here's how it added up, with noneating but important events indicated with an asterisk:

11:45 a.m. start

- 1 c steamed spinach (30 kcal)
- 3 T almond butter on one large celery stalk (540 kcal)
- 2 heaping T Athletic Greens in water (86 kcal)
- Chicken curry salad, 195 g (6.87 oz) (approximately 350 kcal)

  Total = 1,006 kcal

12:45 p.m.

- Grapefruit juice (90 kcal)
- Large coffee with 1 t cinnamon (5 kcal)
- 2% milk, 315 ml (11 oz) (190 kcal)
- 2 large chocolate croissants, 168 g (5.92 oz) (638.4 kcal)

  Total = 923.4 kcal

2:00 p.m.

- Citrus kombucha, 16 oz (473 ml) (60 kcal)

*2:15 p.m.

- Poo
- AGG (see sidebar, right)
- Butter fat and fermented cod liver

*3:00–3:20 p.m.

- 15 repetitions x 3 sets each:
  1. Bent row
  2. Incline bench press
  3. Leg press

3:30 p.m.

- 1 L (1 qt) Straus cream-top organic whole milk (600 kcal)

*4:00 p.m.

- Probiotics
- 20-minute ice bath

4:45 p.m.

- Quinoa, 230 g (7.86 oz) (859 kcal)

5:55 p.m.

- Zzang candy bar (216 kcal)
- Yerba mate (30 kcal)

  Total = 246 kcal

*6:20 p.m.

- Poo

*6:45 p.m.

- 40 air squats and 30 wall tricep extensions

6:58 p.m.

- Assorted cheeses, 33 g (1.16 oz) (116 kcal)
- Honey, 30 g (1 oz) (90 kcal)
- Medium apple (71 kcal)
- Crackers, 8 g (0.3 oz) (30 kcal)
- Chai tea with soy milk (not my choice), 340 g (12 oz) (175 kcal)

  Total = 482 kcal

*9:30 p.m.

- 40 air squats in men's room

9:36 p.m.

- Pizza (nettles, red onion, provolone, mushroom, pancetta, and olive oil with one whole egg), 8 pieces (64 g/2.25 oz each) (1,249 kcal)

What the Hell Is PAGG™?

PAGG is a fat-loss stack that I developed for personal use. It's unique because it contains no stimulants. In 2004, after suffering multiple side-effects (e.g., sinusitis, chronic fatigue, etc.) from ephedrine-based products and pre-workout stimulants, I began experimenting with new compounds and split-testing dosages. Six years later, the end result was PAGG:

P = Policosanol: 20–25 mg

A = Alpha-lipoic acid (ALA): 100–300 mg (Start low.)

G = Green tea flavanols/extract (decaffeinated, with at least 325 mg EGCG): 325 mg

G = Garlic extract (aged): 200 mg

Recommendations:

- **Consult with a medical doctor prior to using any supplement or drug. If you are pregnant or breast-feeding, don't use PAGG. Fat loss ain't for babies.**
- **Take AGG 15–30 minutes before meals.**
- **Take PAGG before bed. If decaffeinated green tea keeps you up, it can be omitted.**
- **Take one day off per week. I take Fridays off to sensitize for PAGG on Saturday, my cheat day.**
- **Take one entire week off (as I recommend with all supplements) every eight weeks to avoid tolerance development.**
- **Take a daily B-complex vitamin while using PAGG or, at least, 300 mcg of biotin (B7) daily. Some believe ALA can affect B-vitamin metabolism, and it's cheap insurance.**

For more details, resources, and suppliers, please visit pagg.com.

- 1 small glass red wine, Nero d'Avola, 5 oz (124 kcal)
- Bi-Rite vanilla ice cream, 59 g (2 oz) (140 kcal)
- Double espresso (0 kcal)

  Total = 1,513 kcal

10:37 p.m.

- 2 heaping T Athletic Greens in water (86 kcal)

*10:40 p.m.

- PAGG (see sidebar, opposite)
- 60 standing band pulls

*11:10 p.m.

- Poo

11:37 p.m.

- Peanut cookie, 40 g (1.41 oz) (189 kcal)
- Nutter Butter package, small (250 kcal)

  Total = 439 kcal

2:15 a.m.

- Bedtime/face-plant

For a grand total of . . . drumroll, please . . . 6,214.4 calories in 12 hours.

Based on basal metabolic rate (BMR) calculations that took into account my lean mass vs. fat mass at the time, my BMR for 24 hours was approximately 1,764.87 calories, which would make my 12-hour BMR 882.4 calories.

There are two things we need to add to this: the 20-minute moderate-intensity weight lifting session (80 calories maximum, which we'll use here) and walking.

I walked approximately 16 flat blocks and one mild uphill block during that period of time, which adds no more than 110 calories in this case, given the 1.4-mile distance at two miles per hour speed and 168 lbs body weight. I otherwise avoided movement and standing whenever possible, with the exception of the brief air squats. Twenty minutes of lifting + walking = 190 calories. Let's call it 200.

Using this math, **I still consumed 6.8 times my resting metabolic rate in my 12-hour quest for fatness.**

So what happened? Let's look at my body fat and weight measurements, which were taken using the BodyMetrix ultrasound device, and the average of three separate weighings:

Saturday, August 29, 2009 (the morning of the binge): 9.9% body fat at 169 lbs
Monday, August 31, 2009 (48 hours later): 9.6% body fat at 165 lbs

WTF?
Now let's look at how I did it.

The Lost Art of Bingeing

Sitting down for Thanksgiving dinner or butter cookies at Christmas?

Sounds like a binge. That, in and of itself, doesn't need to mean horrible guilt and extra fat rolls afterward. If you plan ahead of time and understand a little science, it's possible to minimize the damage. I eat whatever I want every Saturday, and I follow specific steps to minimize fat gain during this overfeeding.

In basic terms, our goal is simple: to have as much of the crap ingested either go into muscle tissue or out of the body unabsorbed.

I do this by focusing on three principles:

PRINCIPLE #1: MINIMIZE THE RELEASE OF INSULIN, A STORAGE HORMONE.

Insulin release is minimized by blunting sharp jumps in blood sugar:

1. Ensure that your first meal of the day is not a binge meal. Make it high in protein (at least 30 g) and insoluble fiber (legumes will handle this). The protein will decrease your appetite for the remainder of the binge and prevent total self-destruction. The fiber will be important later to prevent diarrhea. In total, this can be a smallish meal of 300–500 calories.
2. Consume a small quantity of fructose (fruit sugar) in grapefruit juice before the second meal, which is the first crap meal. Even small fructose dosing has an impressive near-flat-lining effect on blood glucose. I could consume this at the first meal, but I prefer to combine the naringin in grapefruit juice with coffee, as it extends the effects of caffeine.
3. Use supplements that increase insulin sensitivity: AGG and PAGG.

The example intake in this chapter is quite mild, so I dosed only twice. If I'm going whole hog, I will have another PAGG dose upon waking. This reduces the amount of insulin the pancreas releases in spite of mild or severe glucose surges. Think of it as insurance.

4. Consume citric juices, whether lime juice squeezed into water, lemon juice on food, or a beverage like the citrus kombucha I had.

PRINCIPLE #2: INCREASE THE SPEED OF GASTRIC EMPTYING, OR HOW QUICKLY FOOD EXITS THE STOMACH.

Bingeing is a rare circumstance where I want the food (or some of it) to pass through my gastrointestinal tract so quickly that its constituent parts aren't absorbed well.

I accomplish this primarily through caffeine and yerba mate tea, which includes the additional stimulants theobromine (found in dark chocolate) and theophylline (found in green tea). I consume 100–200 mg (0.0035 oz) of caffeine, or 453 g (16 oz) of cooled yerba mate, at the most crap-laden meals. My favorite greens supplement, "Athletic Greens" (mentioned in the schedule), doesn't contain caffeine but will also help.

Does this really work? Taking the goodies from taste buds to toilet without much storage in between?[8]

More than a few people have told me it's pure science fiction.

Too much information (TMI) warning: I disagree, and for good reason. Rather than debate meta-studies, I simply weighed my poo. Identical volumes of food on and off the protocol. On protocol = much more poo mass (same consistency, hence the importance of fiber) = less absorption = fewer chocolate croissants that take up residence on my abs. Simple but effective? Perhaps. Good to leave out of first-date conversation? Definitely.

On to one of the cooler aspects of this whole craziness: GLUT-4.

PRINCIPLE #3: ENGAGE IN BRIEF MUSCULAR CONTRACTION THROUGHOUT THE BINGE.

For muscular contractions, my default options are air squats, wall presses (tricep extensions against a wall), and chest pulls with an elastic band, as all three are portable and can be done without causing muscle trauma that screws up training. The latter two can be performed by anyone, even those who have difficulty walking.

8. It's true that increasing the speed of gastric emptying can increase the glycemic index of meals; that makes it all the more important to blunt that response with a small dose of fructose.

But why the hell would you want to do 60–90 seconds of funny exercises a few minutes before you eat and, ideally, again about 90 minutes afterward?

Short answer: because it brings glucose transporter type 4 (GLUT-4) to the surface of muscle cells, opening more gates for the calories to flow into. The more muscular gates we have open before insulin triggers the same GLUT-4 on the surface of fat cells, the more we can put in muscle instead of fat.

Longer answer:

GA

"Geek's Advantage" (GA) is only for nerds. You can skip.

GLUT-4 has been studied most intensely for the last 15 years or so, as it became clear around 1995 that exercise and insulin appear to activate (translocate) GLUT-4 through different but overlapping signaling pathways. This was exciting to me, as it meant it might be possible to use exercise to beat meal-induced insulin release to the punch—to preemptively flip the switch on the biological train tracks so that food (glucose) is preferentially siphoned to muscle tissue.

But how much contraction is enough? It turns out, at least with animals, that much less is needed than was once thought. In one fascinating Japanese study with rats, high-intensity intermittent exercise (HIT: High-Intensity Training) (20-second sprints × 14 sets, with 10 seconds of rest between sets) was compared to low-intensity prolonged exercise (LIT: Low-Intensity Training) (six hours of extended exercise) over eight days.

The surprising result? Bolding is mine:

> *In conclusion, the present investigation demonstrated that eight days of* ***HIT lasting only 280 seconds*** *elevated both GLUT-4 content and maximal glucose transport activity in rat skeletal muscle to a level* ***similar to that attained after LIT ["Low-Intensity Training" of six hours a session],*** *which has been considered a tool to increase GLUT-4 content maximally.*

Compared to a control, GLUT-4 content in the muscle was increased 83% with 280 seconds of HIT vs. 91% with six hours of LIT.

Now, of course, animal models don't always have a direct transfer to humans. But I wondered: what if 280 seconds was all it took? This thought produced even more questions:

Do we have to get the 280 seconds all at once, or can they be spread out?

Is 280 seconds really the magic number, or could even fewer seconds trigger the same effect?

Is it even plausible that 60–90 seconds of moderate contractions could have a meaningful impact?

To attempt to answer these questions, I contacted researcher after researcher on three continents, including GLUT-4 specialists at the Muscle Biology Laboratory at the University of Michigan at Ann Arbor.

The short answer was: it did appear plausible.

The most important research insight came from Dr. Gregory D. Cartee and Katsuhiko Funai:

> *The insulin-independent effect of exercise begins to reverse minutes after exercise cessation with most or all of the increase lost within 1–4 hours. A much more persistent effect is improved insulin sensitivity that is often found approximately 2–4 hours and as long as 1–2 days after acute exercise.*

I started with 60–120 seconds total of air squats and wall tricep extensions immediately prior to eating main courses. For additional effect, I later tested doing another 60–90 seconds approximately one and a half hours after finishing the main courses, when I expected blood glucose to be highest based on experiments with glucometers.

Exercises are best done in a restroom stall and not at the table. If you can't leave the table, get good at isometric (without moving) contraction of your legs. Try to look casual instead of constipated.

It takes some practice.

In China, I was taught a rhyming proverb: *Fàn hòu bǎi bù zǒu, néng huó dào jiǔ shí jiǔ* [飯後百步走，能活到九十九]. If you take 100 steps after each meal, you can live to be 99 years old.

Could it be that the Chinese identified the effect of GLUT-4 translocation hundreds, even thousands, of years before scientists formalized the mechanism? It's possible. More likely: they just liked rhyming.

In all cases, if you do 60–90 seconds of contraction after each meal (and a bit before, ideally), you might live to see your abs.

Don't forget the air squats.

STALLING MANEUVERS: AIR SQUATS, WALL PRESSES, AND CHEST PULLS

I aim for 30–50 repetitions of each of the following:

Air Squats

Awww... Timmy with hair

Not sure what's happening here

Wall Presses

Chest Pulls

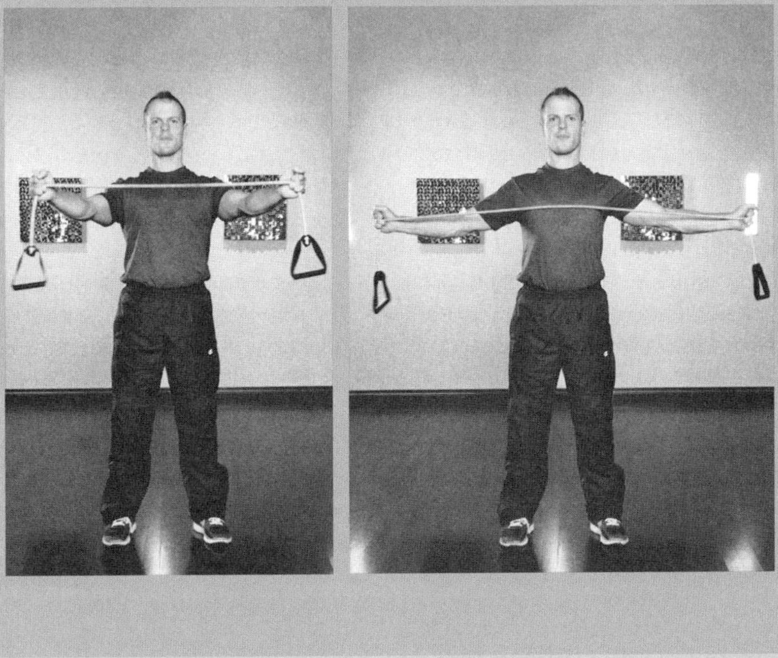

For everything imaginable related to physical performance and appearance enhancement, please consult *The 4-Hour Body*.

Now, back to our regular *4-Hour Chef* programming!

THE BASICS: ELEMENTARY, MY DEAR WATSON . . .

"As to methods, there may be a million and then some, but principles are few. The man who grasps principles can successfully select his own methods."

—RALPH WALDO EMERSON

It's helpful to think of cooking in two categories: **texture changes** (which typically happen below the boiling point of water) and **chemical changes** (which typically happen above the boiling point of water). It's the chemical changes above 100°C (212°F) that change flavor. To get the benefits of both, you might cook a steak sous-vide, then sear it on a blistering hot grill, for instance.

Texture changes are exactly what they sound like. Chemical reactions, however, are the transformation of matter from one form to another.

Most of the "cooking" you know, and that we'll discuss, involves **irreversible** phase transition thanks to chemical reactions. Cooking an egg is irreversible, since the white doesn't become a clear liquid when it cools back to room temperature. Freezing an egg in liquid nitrogen will turn it solid, but that isn't considered "cooking," since it will melt back to a normal-looking egg. To take it a step further, even though no heat is involved, making stable mayonnaise (irreversible) could be considered cooking, whereas stirring together oil and water (reversible) is not.

To grasp even one chemical reaction is to begin to truly understand food. Understanding 14 of them will put you ahead of many seasoned chefs.[8] With this very achievable goal in mind, we'll take a romp through 14 beauties:

For a more in-depth look at all of these, I wholeheartedly recommend *Cooking for Geeks* by Jeff Potter, *Modernist Cuisine*, and the granddaddy, *On Food and Cooking*.

8 A disclaimer for the professional chemists: The explanations in this section are intended to be accurate. They are, however, also simplified for a lay audience. It's a balancing act, of course.

MAILLARD
REACTION
CHOC
GELS
FOAM
POWDER
PERIODIC TABLE OF ELEMENTS
ID NITROGEN
SOUS VIDE 2000

LeVon: This is a box of puddin', Barry.

Barry: What does it say?

LeVon: It says, "Cook . . . and chill."

Barry: Awww, yeah.

LeVon: And, baby, that's what I do every night. I cook, and then I chill.

Barry: (bumping and grinding) Awww, yeah.

—FROM *THE STATE*

THE SCIENCE OF

GELS

A colloid is a way of organizing matter and, by extension, a hydrocolloid is a way of organizing water.[9] Think Jell-O—liquid particles trapped in a solid matrix. Hydrocolloids also occur in nature. Lettuce is nothing more than a crunchy water bottle, comprised of more than 98% water! Man-made hydrocolloids include jams and jellies (gels), vinaigrette (an emulsion), and whipped cream (a foam).

Gels are simply water made solid. They're the type of hydrocolloid we'll look at first. Imagine a mesh of intertwined molecules that keep water from sloshing around. Though many ingredients help create gels, there are broadly two classes: carbohydrates that gel and proteins that gel. Cornstarch is the best-known carb gelling agent. Agar-agar is another. Gelatin is the best-known protein gelling agent. Casein, the protein in milk that makes cheese possible, is another. Then there's myosin, a protein that helps muscles contract. And when that muscle (meat) is cooked, myosin denatures and gels.... Yes, cooked or cured meats are also gels!

9 For the geeks: *hydrocolloid* is a culinary term for long-chain molecules that are attracted to water, technically known as "hydrophilic polymers." *Gesundheit!*

CRUNCHY BLOODY MARY

SHORTHAND

Boil 120ml tomato juice, 1t Worcestershire, ½t celery salt, 1t agar-agar, 1t hot sauce. Stir in 60ml vodka. Pour mix into 1 bunch celery ribs. Chill 30min.

HANDS-ON TIME

10 minutes

TOTAL TIME

10 minutes, plus 30 minutes chilling

GEAR

- Aluminum foil
- Baking sheet, large plate, or small tray
- Nonstick skillet
- Spouted measuring cup
- Knife and cutting board

INGREDIENTS	TO MAKE 60 PIECES
Celery, separated into ribs (see pic E), tops cut off	1 bunch
Tomato juice	120 ml (½ c)
Worcestershire sauce	1 t
Celery salt	½ t
Agar-agar powder (key ingredient)	2 g (1 scant t)[10]
Vodka	60 ml (¼ c)
OPTIONAL	
Sriracha or other hot sauce (I like Cholula)	½–1 t
Grated fresh or prepared (jarred) horseradish	To taste

Nearly any vodka will work for this recipe, but Josh Volz (previously bartender at Marvin in D.C.), a walking encyclopedia of cocktail knowledge, recommends Hangar One Roasted Chipotle Vodka when making a Bloody Mary.

PREP

00 Fold a long sheet of aluminum foil into pleats (ridged like a tin roof) and put it on a baking sheet. Nestle the celery ribs between the pleats, open side up. This will help keep them from tipping and spilling the tomato juice mixture. You can also try simply leaning the celery ribs against one another.

PICKUP

00 In a nonstick skillet, combine the 120 ml (½ c) tomato juice, 1 t Worcestershire sauce, ½ t celery salt, 2 g (1 scant t) agar-agar, and ½–1 t hot sauce, if using. Bring to a boil, then stir in the 60ml (¼ c) vodka.

01 Using a spouted cup, carefully pour the Bloody Mary mixture into the celery stalks. It's OK if it drips onto or over the sides—you can wipe the excess off later. The mixture will start to thicken and firm up as you fill the celery. Go back and top off the celery ribs as needed so they're as full as possible.

02 Put in the refrigerator to chill for at least 30 minutes. The Bloody Mary mixture will firm up almost immediately, but it's best consumed very cold.

03 Cut into bite-size (2.5-cm/1") pieces. If you like, top each piece with a tiny bit of horseradish. Delish.

10 In cookbooks, *scant* means "just barely."

A

B

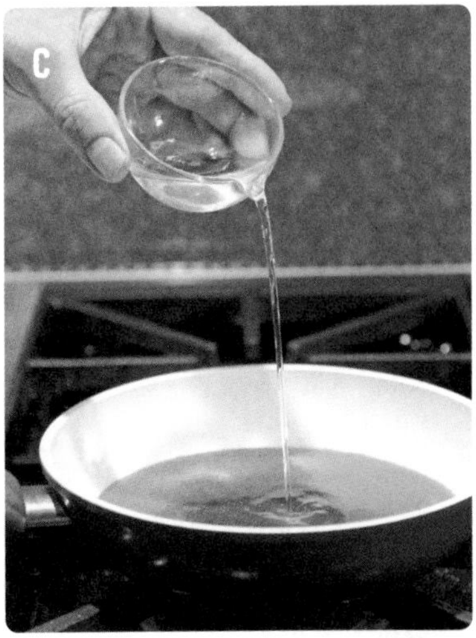
C

D

E

No one will know you're drunk at that board meeting!

THE SCIENCE OF
GELS

ARUGULA SPAGHETTI

SHORTHAND

Fill bowl w ice H2O. Puree 15g arugula, 180ml veg broth. Boil puree & 2g agar-agar. Syringe into tubes; chill. Extract directly onto plate.

HANDS-ON TIME

45 minutes

TOTAL TIME

45 minutes

GEAR

- Large mixing bowl
- Immersion blender with chopping attachment, or blender
- Nonstick skillet
- Syringe—available at molecule-r.com or modernistpantry.com.
- Flexible silicone tubing that fits over the syringe tip, preferably several long spaghetti-length pieces; often comes with aforementioned syringe.

INGREDIENTS	TO SERVE 6–8[11]
Arugula, chopped	**115 g (2 c, packed)**
Vegetable broth	**180 ml (¾ c)**
Agar-agar powder	**2 g (1 scant t)**

Serve this unusual spaghetti with any creative topping you'd like! Season with salt and pepper and pile a mound of olive oil powder (prepared like Nutella Powder, page 416) on top, or drizzle with a warmed tomato or cream sauce and scatter fresh herbs over it. For a variation and more flavor, feel free to blend in fresh herbs like basil or parsley in place of some of the arugula. This is the perfect project for getting rid of leftovers.

Don't try to toss it or twirl it around a fork. It looks like regular spaghetti, but it's as fragile as Stuart Smalley's ego. Chop it up and eat it.

PREP

00 Fill a large bowl with ice water.

PICKUP

00 Using an immersion blender with the chopping attachment, puree the 115 g (about 2 packed cups) arugula with the 180 ml (¾ c) broth. If you don't have the chopping attachment, use a knife, as in "How to Coarsely Chop" (page 165).

01 In a nonstick skillet, combine the arugula puree and 2 g (1 scant t) agar-agar and bring to a boil.

02 Fill a syringe with the mixture. Secure a piece of silicone tubing on the syringe and fill the tube with the arugula mixture. Repeat with the remaining tubes. Put the filled tubes in the bowl of ice water for 3 minutes.

03 If the syringe still has arugula mixture in it, empty it back into the skillet.

04 Fill the syringe with air and fit it over one of the filled tubes. Press to extract the arugula spaghetti directly onto a serving plate. Repeat with the remaining tubes. If it begins to solidify before all the spaghetti is made, rewarm the tubes in the saucepan briefly (not too high a heat!).

11 As an appetizer.

A

B

C

D

E

F

G

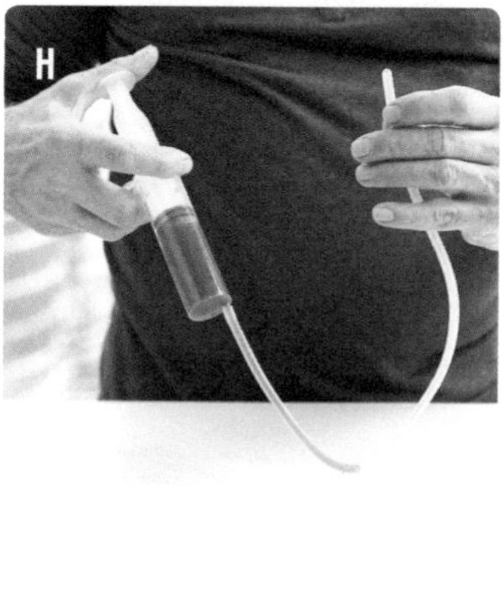
H

THE SCIENCE OF
GELS

BALSAMIC VINAIGRETTE PEARLS

SHORTHAND

Freeze 240ml EVOO 45min-1hr. Boil 120ml balsamic, 2g agar-agar. Draw into syringe; dribble into cold EVOO. Sieve out pearls; gently rinse.

HANDS-ON TIME

15 minutes

TOTAL TIME

15 minutes, plus 45 minutes–1 hour chilling

GEAR

- Tall drinking glass or other container
- Small saucepan
- Syringe—available at molecule-r.com or modernistpantry.com.
- Small sieve (see pic B, opposite) or pierced spoon (a slotted spoon with small holes)

INGREDIENTS	TO MAKE 118 ml (½ c)
EVOO	240 ml (1 c)
Balsamic vinegar	120 ml (½ cup)
Agar-agar powder	2 g (1 scant t)

This recipe takes traditional balsamic vinaigrette and turns it into something that will wow friends and lesser deities . . . with minimal effort. By mixing agar-agar with balsamic and adding it to EVOO that you've chilled, you end up with cool jet-black pearls you can use like any salad dressing. Pretty slick, eh, Spy Hunter?

A

PREP

00 Put the 240 ml (1 c) EVOO in a tall drinking glass or beaker and put it in the freezer for 45 minutes–1 hour. It should be very cold and just starting to turn opaque and thicken slightly when you begin the Pickup section below.

PICKUP

00 In a small saucepan, combine the 120 ml (½ cup) balsamic vinegar and 2 g (1 scant t) agar-agar and bring to a boil.

01 Remove the oil from the freezer.

02 Slightly tip the saucepan and fill a syringe with the vinegar mixture (the mixture will be very hot, but this won't melt the syringe).

03 Holding the syringe horizontally (parallel to the work surface), dribble the vinegar mixture a drop at a time into the cold oil in the drinking glass (or beaker). I recommend doing this over the kitchen sink, since the vinegar can ejaculate out. It should form small spheres that slowly sink to the bottom. When you've made as many as you'd like, pour the oil and spheres through a sieve set over a bowl or drinking glass (to collect the oil for another use), drain well, then rinse gently under cold running water. Alternatively, scoop out the spheres a few at a time with a slotted or pierced spoon and rinse gently in a bowl of cold water, then drain.

04 Serve or store in a container in the fridge until ready to use.

Serving Suggestions

Try serving these in the well of an avocado half and season with coarse salt (my fave), or sprinkled over the Arugula, Avocado, and Roma Salad on page 180. There's no need to rinse the pearls first, since the oil clinging to them is a nice addition in both applications.

Or simply slice a super-ripe tomato, fan the slices out on a beautiful plate, season with S+P, and scatter the pearls over the whole thing (see pic, opposite).

OLIVE OIL GUMMY BEARS

WITH THYME AND VANILLA

INSPIRED BY

Nathan Myhrvold

SHORTHAND

Let 40g H2O & 12g gelatin stand 5min. Low-heat 1min. Boil 110g H2O & 100g isomalt, 55g honey, 25g glucose syrup, 20g gum arabic; whisk w gelatin mix. +75g EVOO, 1 vanilla bean, 1 drop thyme oil. Pour in coated mold, chill 4hr.

HANDS-ON TIME

10 minutes

TOTAL TIME

10 minutes, plus 5 minutes standing and 4 hours chilling

GEAR

- Plastic bear-shaped molds about 3.8 cm (1½") tall or silicone denture molds[12]
- Digital scale
- 2 small saucepans
- Silicone spatula
- Whisk or immersion blender
- Spouted measuring cup
- Bamboo skewer or toothpick

INGREDIENTS	TO MAKE ABOUT 20 (3.8-cm/1½") BEARS
Olive oil or olive oil spray	Enough to coat molds
Water	10 T
Powdered unflavored gelatin	12 g (1 T)
Isomalt	100 g (7 T)
Clear honey	55 g (2½ T)
Glucose syrup	25 g (1 T)
Gum arabic[13]	20 g (3 T)
EVOO	75 g (5½ T)
Vanilla bean, split and scraped[14]	1
Thyme oil	1 drop

We've all downed handfuls of gummy bears at one time or another. These are little guys you'll want to savor, as the combo of olive oil, vanilla, and thyme is out of this world.

You can easily find gummy bear molds online. Or try fishing-lure molds, denture molds, ice-cube trays—whatever! If you don't have anything on hand, you can jury-rig your own molds like my friend Maneesh Sethi did:

- Pour cornstarch in a layer onto a flat surface so that it's about 6 mm (¼") thick.
- Take a gummy bear that you've bought, stick a toothpick in it, press it into the cornstarch dozens of times, and . . . *voilà!* Instant mold.
- Pour your gummy bear mixture inside and let it set, then pull out your finished bears with another toothpick. (You may need to wash off the thin layer of cornstarch that sticks to the bears once they're done.)

PREP

00 Spray molds with olive oil spray (or other neutral nonstick spray), or lightly oil the molds with a paper towel.

12 Available at fourhourchef.com/puffybear.

13 A natural gum made of sap from the acacia tree. Commonly used in candy and postage stamps.

14 To split and scrape a vanilla bean: cut it in half lengthwise; then, one half at a time, use a knife to scrape all the tiny beans inside into a bowl. Discard the shell. Whole vanilla beans can be purchased in the spice aisle of most supermarkets.

PICKUP

00 Put 40 g (3 T) water in a small saucepan and sprinkle the 12 g (1 T) gelatin over it evenly. Let stand for 5 minutes, then stir and place over low heat, stirring until just dissolved but not boiling, about 1 minute. Remove from heat.

01 In a separate small saucepan, combine 110 g (7 T) water, 100 g (7 T) Isomalt, 55 g (2½ T) honey, 25 g (1 T) glucose syrup, and 20 g (3 T) gum arabic and bring to a boil.

02 Whisk this Isomalt mixture into the hot gelatin you dissolved in pickup step 00.

03 Whisk in the 75 g (5½ T) EVOO and whisk further (or use an immersion blender) to emulsify. Whisk in the vanilla and 1 drop thyme oil.

04 Transfer the mixture to a spouted measuring cup (for easier pouring) and fill the prepared molds; let cool, then transfer to the refrigerator to chill and set for at least 4 hours.

05 Carefully remove from the molds, using a bamboo skewer or toothpick. Serve, or cover and refrigerate for up to 1 week.

A

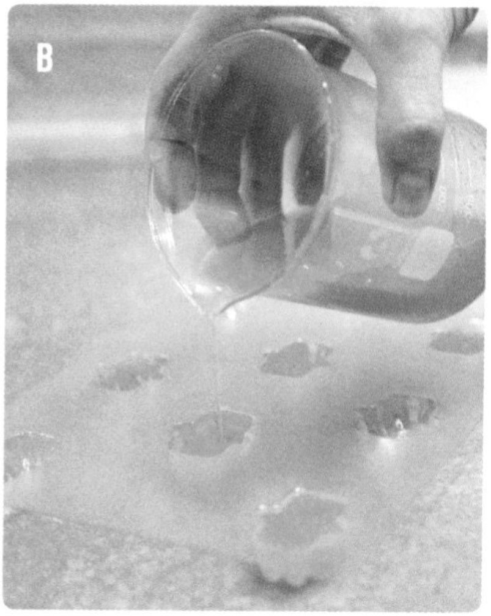
B

"Hacking is much bigger . . . than clever bits of code in a computer—it's how we create the future."

—PAUL BUCHHEIT, CREATOR OF GMAIL

THE SCIENCE OF SPHERIFICATION

Spherification is a cool-looking subset of the gelling process. Certain carbohydrate-based gelling compounds, such as alginate, will only gel in the presence of mineral salts like calcium chloride. This allows you to work magic in the kitchen. First, prepare a flavorful liquid (melon juice mixed in with alginate, for example) that contains the gelling compound. Next, add this drop by drop into a water bath containing the dissolved mineral salts. As soon as the juice hits the water, it will quickly gel, but only at the surface. Surface tension ensures that the drops tighten into spheres—hence "spherification." After letting the spheres soak briefly, they are strained from the water, rinsed to remove excess mineral salt (it tastes bitter), and served immediately. This technique was made popular among modernist chefs by Ferran Adrià in 2003, but the original patent on the process was filed in the U.K. in 1942. The technique has been used by industrial food manufacturers to prepare everything from pimento-stuffed olives to fake blueberries and cherries for muffins and pies.

THE SCIENCE OF

SPHERIFICATION

MOJITO BUBBLES

SHORTHAND

Muddle 0.8g calcium lactate, 1t sugar, 3 lime wedges, 12 mint leaves. Stir in 3T rum, 60ml soda, ⅛t lime juice. Strain in 8 molds w mint leaves; freeze till solid. Blend 2g sodium alginate & 470ml H2O. Unmold bubble into alginate. Stand 3min; rinse.

HANDS-ON TIME

10 minutes

TOTAL TIME

10 minutes, plus 1 hour freezing

GEAR

- Cocktail mixing glass or sturdy drinking glass
- Cocktail muddler or wooden spoon
- 4-cm (1½") silicone half-sphere molds (available at amazon.com or modernistpantry.com)
- Sieve or cocktail strainer
- 2 medium (4–6-c) mixing bowls
- Immersion blender or eggbeater
- Slotted or pierced spoon

INGREDIENTS	TO SERVE 8
Calcium lactate (key)	0.8 g (¼ t)
Sugar	1 t
Lime wedges	3
Fresh mint leaves	12, plus 8 small
White rum	3 T
Club soda	60 ml (¼ c)
Freshly squeezed lime juice	⅛ t
Sodium alginate (key)	2 g (1 scant t)
Water	470 ml (2 c)

PICKUP

00 In a mixing glass, add the 0.8 g (¼ t) calcium lactate, 1 t sugar, 3 lime wedges, and 12 mint leaves. Mix and crush using a muddler or the end of a wooden spoon handle.

01 Add the 3 T rum, 60 ml (¼ c) club soda, and ⅛ t lime juice, and stir to combine.

02 Put 1 small mint leaf in each of 8 silicone half-sphere molds. Strain the lime mixture into a glass, then pour into the molds. Freeze until solid, at least 1 hour.

03 In a medium bowl, combine the 2 g (1 scant t) sodium alginate and 470 ml (2 c) water, blending with an immersion blender or eggbeater. Set aside for 15 minutes.

04 Unmold the frozen half spheres and gently drop into the sodium alginate mixture. Let stand for 3 minutes.

05 Using a slotted or pierced spoon, transfer the spheres to a second bowl of plain cold water to rinse gently.

06 Put each sphere in a tasting spoon and serve immediately.

A

B

C

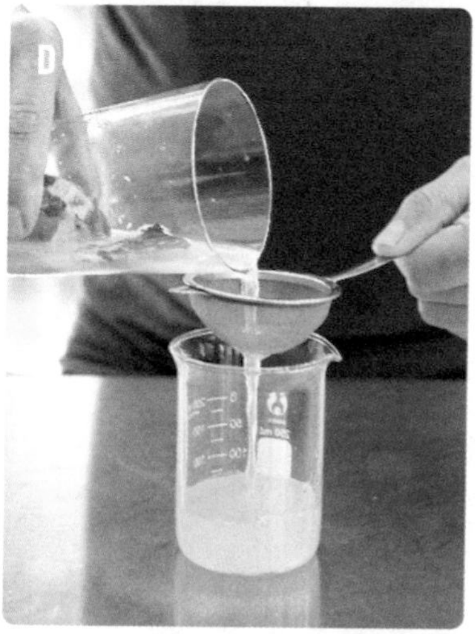
D

E

"Everything is a miracle. It is a miracle that one does not dissolve in one's bath like a lump of sugar."

—PABLO PICASSO

THE SCIENCE OF EMULSIFICATION

OIL
VINEGAR

Just like solids can hold liquid particles in hydrocolloids, liquids can hold particles in different states. When your food is a liquid holding on to solid particles, it's a suspension (e.g., oregano floating in a salad dressing). When it's a liquid mixed well with another liquid, it's an emulsion (e.g., vinaigrette dressings). And when it's a liquid holding on to air, it's a foam (whipped cream), coming next.

Emulsions are tricky bastards. How do you get oil and water (or vinegar) to mix and stay mixed? Chemically, they hate each other. This is because oil is insoluble in water.[15] The solution is to use an "emulsifier," which is a third ingredient that helps the other molecules get along. Mustard is a good one for salad dressing: one area of the mustard particle attracts a water/vinegar molecule, another area attracts an oil molecule, so the macro result is a well-blended vinaigrette.

15 *Insoluble* means something cannot be dissolved. This is why insoluble fiber (vs. soluble) passes right through you and is used to improve, ahem, regularity.

THE SCIENCE OF

EMULSIFICATION

CHAMPAGNE VINAIGRETTE

SHORTHAND

Rub bowl w halved garlic. Whisk 1 yolk, ½t salt, ¼t pepper, 1t mustard, 60ml champagne vinegar till combined. Add 120ml EVOO, whisking to emulsify.

HANDS-ON TIME

5 minutes

TOTAL TIME

5 minutes

GEAR

- Medium mixing bowl
- Whisk

INGREDIENTS	TO MAKE 240ml (1 c)
Garlic clove, halved	**1**
Egg yolk, large	**1**
Salt	**½ t, or more to taste**
Freshly ground black pepper	**¼ t / 10 turns**
Dijon mustard	**1 t**
Champagne vinegar	**60 ml (¼ c), or more to taste**
EVOO (or half EVOO and half mild oil like grapeseed oil)	**120 ml (½ c)**

Here, both the lecithin in the egg yolk and other chemicals in the mustard help the emulsification of the oil and vinegar. More accurately, they help keep the emulsion from separating over time. You can leave out the egg or the mustard, but you may have to rewhisk, and who wants that?

PREP

00 Rub the inside of a medium mixing bowl with the cut sides of the garlic; reserve[16] the clove for another use if you like.

PICKUP

00 In the mixing bowl, whisk together the egg yolk, ½ t salt, ¼ t pepper, 1 t mustard, and 60 ml (¼ c) vinegar until well combined and salt has dissolved. **Pro tip:** to stabilize your bowl, take a hand towel and form it into a circle with a hole in the middle. Set your bowl on top and *voilà*—rock solid.

01 Slowly drizzle in the 120 ml (½ c) EVOO in a thin stream, whisking constantly to emulsify. If you want to tempt the Fates, say a Hail Mary and use an immersion blender. Taste and add more salt, pepper, or vinegar if necessary.

Use the vinaigrette right away on a salad or on veggies. Try it to dress a simple white bean salad or as a marinade for chicken.

Pour extra into a clean glass or plastic container, cover with tight-fitting lid, and refrigerate for up to one week. Shake well before serving or, if necessary, whisk again.

C'est la vie!

16 In cookbook parlance, to *reserve* something is to set it aside or store it for later use.

"I've got poetry in my fingertips. Most of the time—and this includes naps—I'm an F-18, bro. And I will destroy you in the air. I will deploy my ordnance to the ground."

—CHARLIE SHEEN, WINNER

THE SCIENCE OF
FOAMS

POP

As mentioned, foams are emulsions where air bubbles, rather than droplets of oil, are dispersed through a liquid. A surprising number of foods are foams: whipped cream and steamed milk on your latte are obvious examples, but bread and popcorn are also foams (technically solid foams). To make a foam, you must always have an ingredient that helps form a skin on the air bubbles so that they don't burst too quickly. Most emulsifiers are good at doing this, and egg whites are one well-known example. You also need something that thickens the liquid. The sugar you dissolve in whipped cream, for example, helps to thicken the water in the cream so that the foam isn't too delicate.

THE SCIENCE OF
FOAMS

BEET FOAM
AKA "THE PANTY MELTER"

INSPIRED BY
Ryan Baker

SHORTHAND
Pour 60ml beet juice into each of 6 small glasses. Blend 110ml beet juice & 2g soy lecithin till foamy. Dollop atop juice.

HANDS-ON TIME
5 minutes

TOTAL TIME
5 minutes

GEAR
- 6 small glasses
- Small mixing bowl or 500 ml (or larger) beaker
- Immersion blender

INGREDIENTS	TO SERVE 6
Beet juice or pomegranate juice (beet is far more beautiful)	**470 ml (2 c) raw**
Soy lecithin powder	**2 g (1 scant t)**

Soy lecithin can be thought of as the egg white of soy. Just as egg whites can be beaten to a froth, so can lecithin. Granulated versions (like those found at GNC) sometimes work, but I suggest getting a *powdered* food lecithin at Whole Foods or online through Molecule-R. Refrigerate it at home.

If beet juice is too strong by itself, you can add a dash of pomegranate juice.

This drink is so gorgeous, especially when put into small sherry glasses, that chef Ryan Baker told me it's nicknamed "The Panty Melter."

PICKUP

00 Pour 60 ml (¼ c) beet juice into each of 6 small glasses.

01 Combine the remaining 110 ml (½ c) beet juice with the 2 g (1 scant t) soy lecithin in a small bowl or beaker and blend using an immersion blender. To foam more effectively, tilt the bowl so that a small portion of the blender is above the liquid (just an edge). Blend until you have a beautiful, ethereal foam. Dollop this on top of the beet juice in each cup and you're ready for action.

Bonus: Sprinkle a few grains of fennel pollen on top of the foam. The green contrasts beautifully with the red, and the licorice (anise)-like flavor pairs well with the beet.

To give it a little more kick, feel free to add a splash of vodka (or dollop the foam on top of champagne separately).

Warning: Beet juice might make you pee red in the morning. It doesn't mean you're dying.

Chemist Humor:

Q: If both a bear in Yosemite and one in Alaska fall into the water, which one dissolves faster?

A: The one in Alaska because it's Polar!

THE SCIENCE OF
SOLVENTS

VODKA

If you've ever made Kool-Aid, you've experienced the power of a solvent—in this case, water. You start with red powder, but you end with a drink that isn't powdery or grainy in the slightest, because the powder has dissolved.

A solvent is a substance capable of dissolving another substance. Solids, liquids, and gases are all capable of being solvents. In the kitchen, however, the most common solvents are water, alcohol, and oils. Cooks typically use solvents to extract flavor. Stocks, infused oils, tinctures, and bitters are all examples of flavor being extracted with solvents.

Alcohol works wonders. Add it to a sauce or stew and it releases the molecules locked up in the other ingredients and makes them available to your nose and taste buds. A marinara sauce with a bit of red wine will taste and smell richer than one without. Alcohol helps strip the flavor out of one food—say, a vanilla bean—and transfer it to another (vanilla extract). It even works with the all-powerful vegan seducer: bacon.

THE SCIENCE OF

SOLVENTS

BACON-INFUSED BOURBON

CONTRIBUTED BY

Jeff Potter

SHORTHAND

Infuse 2t bacon fat, 240ml bourbon overnight. Freeze till fat solid. Remove fat; sieve bourbon.

HANDS-ON TIME

2 minutes

TOTAL TIME

2 minutes, plus 12+ hours infusing

GEAR

- 2 small glasses or freezer-proof jars with tight-fitting lids (a 240 ml [1 c] Ball canning jar works well)
- Immersion blender + container (optional)
- Fine-mesh sieve
- Coffee filter or good-quality paper towel

INGREDIENTS	TO MAKE 240 ml (1 c)
Melted bacon fat (from cooking a few slices of bacon)	**2 t**
Bourbon (I like Bulleit, which is high in rye content)	**240 ml (1 c)**

Fat washing is traditionally used to refine alcohol. Put a neutral-tasting fat like lard into vodka, for instance, and you can remove the off-tasting impurities it binds to. But what if you put in a *flavored* fat? Ahhh . . . the alcohol (a solvent, after all) keeps some of the flavor!

Here you'll create an infusion of 3–5% fat and 95–97% alcohol. Bourbon + bacon = winning. 'Nuff said.

PICKUP

00 Pour the 2 t melted bacon fat into a small glass jar and add the 240 ml (1 c) bourbon. Stir well, or put the lid on and shake it.

You can speed up the infusion process with an immersion blender: mix the ingredients in a deep container, hit them with a blender for a few seconds, then put in the glass jar.

01 Set aside at room temperature for at least 12 hours. Longer times and warmer air temperatures will yield a stronger infusion. I typically leave overnight, infusing from Friday evening to Saturday evening, for instance.

02 After your infusion, place the jar in the freezer until the fat has solidified, about 1 hour, then remove the fat from the treasure elixir. You can save the fat for future cooking.

03 Pour the bourbon into a second jar or a glass, through a fine-mesh sieve lined with a coffee filter, cheesecloth, or paper towel. Discard the fat bits you catch. Put in a clean container and store at room temperature, tightly covered, until it's bourbon hour. Or is that always?

Faking It: "Aging" Bourbon in Two Minutes

Take a sip of a nice aged bourbon, say a 12-year-old W.L. Weller. Smooth, right? Next, grab a cheap 750-ml bottle of new bourbon (the same size as a bottle of wine) for $15. Anything will do. Then add the following:

- **¾ t of vanilla extract**
- **⅛ t of liquid smoke**
- **1 T of dry sherry**

Give this weird concoction a sip. If you're anything like people blind taste tested by *Cook's Illustrated* magazine, you might think you're drinking more aged bourbon! It's not alchemy, and it won't fool experts, but it's a cool illusion.

Serving Suggestions

Try pairing this cocktail with a plate of blue cheese, nut butters, or other fatty treats.

A

B

C

D

E

I like the taste to be a surprise to guests, but you can also give them a bacon strip "mixer."

“I bought some powdered water, but I don’t know what to add to it.”

—STEPHEN WRIGHT

THE SCIENCE OF POWDERS

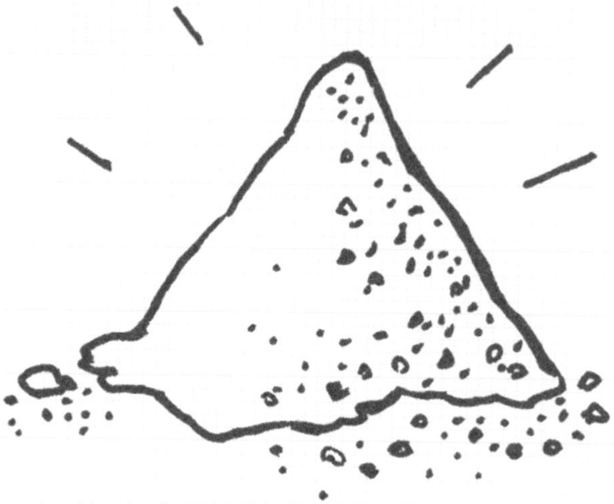

This reaction is more of a principle, which we'll illustrate with one decadent recipe: Nutella Powder.

Nutella Powder isn't listed under "dehydration," which comes later. This is because most people think of dehydration as drying. To create a dry texture, you don't always need to remove liquid. The maltodextrin technique we'll use works for pure oils, no water whatsoever. Tapioca maltodextrin is a really long molecule, with many side chains that can bind to oil, so the combination becomes a snowy powder. The maltodextrin is also soluble in water, so it dissolves in the saliva in your mouth.

Yep—it melts in your mouth and not in your hand. Prepare your taste buds for a chocolaty erotic massage.

NUTELLA POWDER

+ HOMEMADE NUTELLA

INSPIRED BY

Will Goldfarb

SHORTHAND

Blend 60g Nutella, 40g tapioca maltodextrin till powdered.

HANDS-ON TIME

5 minutes

TOTAL TIME

5 minutes

GEAR

- Digital scale
- Large mixing bowl
- Immersion blender
- Airtight container

INGREDIENTS	TO MAKE 590 ml (2½ c)
Nutella (use store-bought Nutella or see sidebar)	**60 g (2.1 oz, ≈4 T)**
Tapioca maltodextrin powder (such as N-Zorbit)	**40 g (1.4 oz)**

This recipe uses tapioca maltodextrin, a powdery starch derivative that binds to oil. Whisk enough maltodextrin into a bowl of olive oil or browned butter and—Optimus Prime!—faster than a North Korean election, you have flavored "snow."

This Nutella Powder makes an amazing dessert garnish. You can sprinkle it on ice cream, dust it on pastries, or dip slices of fruit in it (strawberries, pineapple, and tart apples are especially good). If you prefer to mainline it, lick your thumb and go to town.

PICKUP

00 Weigh your mixing bowl, hit tare, and add 60 g (2.1 oz) Nutella. Next, add the 40 g (1.4 oz) tapioca maltodextrin. Note: Maltodextrin is *very* light, so it will take a lot to reach 40 g.

01 Using an immersion blender, beat it all together until a light, granular soil forms. If you'd prefer a finer powder, you can pass it through a fine-mesh sieve. Serve, or store in an airtight container in the refrigerator until ready to use (up to 1 week).

How to Make Your Own Nutella

Put 200 g (7 oz) canned hazelnut-praline paste (available at specialty food stores and online) and 100 g (3.5 oz) softened unsalted butter in a deep container and blend with an immersion blender until smooth.

Add 75 g (2.6 oz) melted chocolate (ideally 64% cacao bittersweet) and beat again until smooth.

The paste can be stored in an airtight container in a dark, dry place at cool room temperature for up to 3 months. This recipe makes 370 g (13 oz), enough to kill a small monkey, so storage is key.

"It has been my experience that folks who have no vices have very few virtues."

—ABRAHAM LINCOLN

THE SCIENCE OF

FERMENTATION

When bacteria and yeast[17] digest the carbohydrates in food, like the flour in bread dough or the lactose in milk, they convert them to alcohols and carbon dioxide. This is the process of fermentation.

The CO_2 is great, because it gives food lift, which creates airy breads, fluffy baked goods, or fizzy kombucha. The alcohol acts as a preservative, so fermented foods and drinks are often stable far longer than their original ingredients would be. This is one reason wine was so popular in the Roman Empire. And a by-product of this process is acid, which makes fermented foods taste sour—think plain yogurt, vinegar, or sourdough bread.

17 Yeast is a microorganism, often airborne. *Yeast* comes from the Old English *gyst,* meaning foam or bubble. Those old-timers liked their beer.

THE SCIENCE OF

FERMENTATION

GO-CARB YEAST WAFFLES (OR PANCAKES)

CONTRIBUTED BY

Jeff Potter

SHORTHAND

Whisk 300g flour, 15g yeast, 410ml milk, 113g butter, 2t sugar, 1t salt & 2 eggs. Set aside covered 2hr or overnight. Cook in waffle iron.

HANDS-ON TIME

20 minutes

TOTAL TIME

20 minutes, plus 2 hours, or overnight, rising

GEAR

- Large mixing bowl
- Whisk
- Waffle iron (or bootleg)

INGREDIENTS	TO SERVE 5
All-purpose flour (can sub whole-wheat or oat flour for 50%)	**300 g (2½ c)**
Instant yeast (*not* active dry yeast)	**15 g (1 T)**
Milk (preferably whole milk—it'll taste better)	**410 ml (1¾ c)**
Unsalted butter, melted	**113 g (½ c)**
Sugar, honey, or maple syrup	**2 t**
Salt	**1 t**
Eggs, large	**2**

Bakers use yeast that contains a number of enzymes. One of them, zymase, converts simple sugars (dextrose and fructose) into carbon dioxide and alcohol. It's this enzyme that gives yeast its rising capabilities. Zymase doesn't break down lactose (milk sugar), though, so doughs and batters made with milk will end up sweeter.

If your waffles don't come out as crisp as you'd like, toss them in an oven preheated to 130°C (250°F), which is hot enough to quickly evaporate out water but cold enough to avoid caramelization and Maillard reactions (coming later). Remove after 5–10 minutes.

PREP

00 At least 2 hours in advance, but preferably the night before, in a large mixing bowl, whisk together the 300 g (2½ c) flour, 15 g (1 T) yeast, 410 ml (1¾ c) milk, 113 g (½ c) butter, 2 t sugar, 1 t salt, and 2 eggs. Cover and set aside at room temperature. Make sure to use a large bowl or container that will allow the batter to double in volume.

PICKUP

00 Briefly stir the batter, then bake in a waffle iron according to the manufacturer's instructions. Sprinkle with Nutella Powder (page 416).

No Waffle Iron?

If you don't have a waffle iron but have a George Foreman Grill, try this bootleg version, inspired by bloggingforburgers.com.

To make the Foreman level, prop up the lower side with an upside-down measuring cup, or whatever else you have around the kitchen.

Roll up pieces of aluminum foil and place on opposite sides of the grill surface to keep the two plates from touching each other when closed.

Coat the grill with cooking spray, pour the batter onto the grill, cook for a few minutes, and... shazam! Oddly shaped but delicious waffles.

“Water is the driving force of all nature.”

—LEONARDO DA VINCI

THE SCIENCE OF DEHYDRATION

Dehydration is all about removing water from food. Doing this helps to preserve the food (bacteria need water) and concentrate flavor. It's a common misconception that you need heat to dehydrate food. But low humidity, not heat, is the driving force behind dehydration. Warming the air surrounding the food helps keep it dry, but if the air doesn't move, the food will stay wet. So when dehydrating food in the kitchen, make certain that air can freely circulate around it.

Sidenote: You can achieve the same preservation of dehydration by leaving the water in food but making it unavailable to bacteria. Just add substances like sugar and salt, which bind to water molecules and lock them away. Lox (salt-cured salmon) and salted butter are safe to keep at room temperature for this reason—but unsalted butter is not!

THE BEST JERKY IN THE WORLD

INSPIRED BY

Neil Strauss

SHORTHAND

Thin slice 2kg brisket. Whisk 470ml soy, Worcestershire & teriyaki sauce, 240ml liquid smoke, 120ml dark corn syrup. Stir in 3T garlic powder, onion powder, sesame seeds & brown sugar, 1t cayenne. Chill marinade and meat 24hr. Dry 70C for 3hr w door open, turn, dry for 3 more hr.

HANDS-ON TIME

15 minutes

TOTAL TIME

15 minutes, plus 24 hours for marinating and up to 24 hours for drying and cooling

GEAR

- Knife
- Large container with lid
- Aluminum foil
- Wooden or plastic serving spoon

INGREDIENTS	TO MAKE 2.3 kg (5 lb)
Lean brisket	**2 kg (5 lb)**
Kikkoman soy sauce	**470 ml (2 c)**
Worcestershire sauce (Neil likes Lea & Perrins)	**470 ml (2 c)**
Thick, flavorful teriyaki sauce (Kikkoman Takumi Garlic & Green Onion or, surprisingly great, Soy Vay Veri Veri Teriyaki)	**470 ml (2 c)**
Liquid smoke (it's not always easy to find, so any brand will do)	**240 ml (1 c)**
Karo dark corn syrup (you can also try blackstrap molasses)	**120 ml (½ c)**
Garlic powder	**3 T**
Onion powder	**3 T**
Sesame seeds	**3 T**
Brown sugar	**3 T**
Cayenne pepper	**1 t**

Sometimes a survival skill isn't just about preparing for hard times. Six-time *New York Times* best-selling author Neil Strauss learned this while writing about apocalypse-proofing your life in his book *Emergency*. Yes, learning to preserve meat was useful. But learning to flavor meat was an *art*.

In search of the perfect marinade, he polled everyone: hard-core survivalists, friends' grandfathers, chefs, and beyond. Then he split-tested the best and simplest recipes that didn't require a smoker or a food dehydrator. He submerged near-identical meat slices into 2–5 containers of marinade at a time. Sometimes he tested a different brand or amount of teriyaki sauce, and other times he added a random ingredient like truffle oil or mustard. It became something of an obsession.

The following recipe is what won all the taste tests.

This recipe is intended for home cooking, not for the wilderness, but it can be adapted for the wild.

PREP

00 Put the meat in the freezer for an hour to make slicing easier. Slice meat *with* the grain as thin as possible (less than 0.6 cm or ¼"). If you're lazy or not great with the knife, call the butcher ahead of time and ask him to slice 2 kg (5 lb) of lean brisket at this thickness. The leaner the meat, the better and longer-lasting the jerky.

A

B

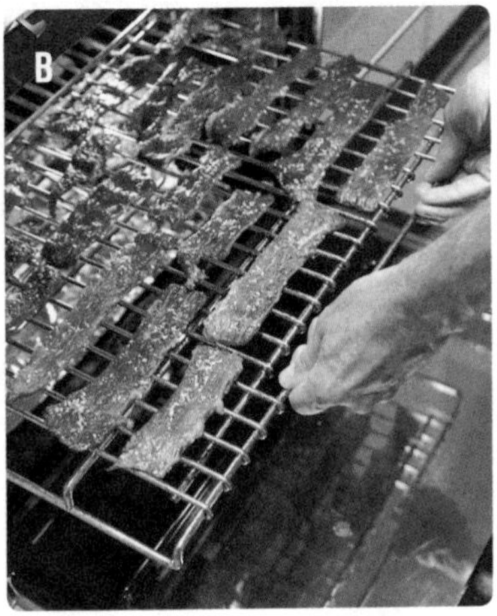

C

500 ml
APPROX
400
300
200
100

PICKUP

00 In a large container, mix the 470 ml (2 c) soy sauce, 470 ml (2 c) Worcestershire sauce, 470 ml (2 c) teriyaki sauce, 240 ml (1 c) liquid smoke, and 120 ml (½ c) dark corn syrup.

01 Add the 3 T garlic powder, 3 T onion powder, 3 T sesame seeds, and 3 T brown sugar. Throw in 1 t of cayenne pepper. Add more if you like it spicy, but a little goes a long way. Note: cayenne pepper is also great for putting on a cut to stop bleeding, and it doesn't sting.

02 Stir well, then drop your meat into the marinade. Your meat should be fully submerged.

03 **OPTIONAL:** Sometimes I'll take a smaller container and play with a slightly different marinade, adding in different oils, spices, and notes (even soda, wine, or beer) to the same base marinade. I'll add in a little of the sliced meat for a batch of experimental jerky.

04 Close or cover the container(s), then leave in the refrigerator for at least 24 hours.

05 Once the meat is well marinated, it's time to dry it: Cover the bottom of your oven with aluminum foil. Things will get messy.

06 Place the meat on the racks of your oven, one next to the other (see pic B). The higher the racks are placed in the oven, the better.

If you like, you can put the meat on aluminum foil or hardware cloth.

07 Set your oven temperature to 70°C (160°F), or 80°C (180°F) if you're in a rush. Crack open the oven door by sticking a wooden or plastic serving spoon in the top of the door. Steve Rinella uses a crunched beer can. The goal is to dry the meat but avoid cooking it.

08 Let it dry for 3 hours, then turn over the jerky. After another 3 hours, it should be done. The total time, however, is dependent on the thickness of the meat and the temperature of the oven. The jerky is done when it's dry enough that you can rip off a piece easily, but before it snaps when you bend it.

09 Leave meat out in the air to cool. It is now ready to eat. The longer you leave it out to cool, the drier it will get. After no longer than 24 hours, store it in sealed Ziploc bags. Without refrigeration, it will be good for 4–6 months.

Jack: Pinot noir? Then how come it's white?

Miles: Oh, Jesus. Don't ask questions like that up in wine country. They'll think you're some kind of dumbshit, OK?

—FROM *SIDEWAYS*

THE SCIENCE OF

OXIDATION

Rust is probably the most visible example of oxidation, which is literally the burning of iron with oxygen. The rusty scales are the ash of this slow-motion blaze, but oxidation is occurring everywhere you look. Our bodies, for example, rely on oxidation to burn glucose and create the ATP that fuels us. In the kitchen, oxidation is often a problem. Rancid-smelling food or browned fruit, for example, are often telltale signs of oxidation at work. You may not realize it, but when you open a package of, say, cereal, the "air" inside is really nitrogen or some other mostly inert gas. If it were regular air, the oxygen would ruin your Chocolate Frosted Sugar Bombs.

But oxidation isn't always bad. When skillfully managed, oxidation imbues dry-aged meat with its characteristic nutty aroma. The flavor of cured meats like country ham wouldn't be the same without oxidation, and cheese just wouldn't be cheese.

HOW TO CHOP WINE: HYPERDECANTING IN 20 SECONDS

"Your French is correct, sir—that item is a sneaker filled with gasoline."

—*NEW YORKER* CARTOON

Wine tends to attract snobs who use bad French to ruin things. Therefore, I take great pleasure in sharing a brutal technique for making wine more delicious.

Done at the dinner table, hyperdecanting will appall that Muppet with the popped collar on his polo shirt. It will also make you a hero to everyone who wants to slap his smug little face.

On a practical level, you can outgun most faux-sommeliers (see what I did there?) with a little brute force. But first . . .

WHEN IN ROME—AERATION?

Letting wine "breathe" or *aerate* means increasing the surface area of the wine exposed to air for a set period of time.

In wine-speak, this "opens the bouquet" (releases aroma compounds) and "softens" the flavor. In simple terms, it usually makes it taste better. Though the mechanism is debated, it appears to reduce the cotton-mouth effects of tannins, which makes aeration great for "big" red wines like cabernet sauvignon and Bordeaux. Aeration may also minimize wine defects like mercaptans, not to be confused with midichlorians.

So how do you do it?

We'll look at four methods: swirling and swishing, decanting, using a Vinturi wine aerator, and beating the shit out of it.

METHOD 1: SWIRLING AND SWISHING

This is the standard tabletop move. To avoid making an ass of yourself: Hold the glass by the stem, keeping the base on the table, and move it in fast but small circles. Take a small sip, hold the wine in your mouth, tilt your head forward, and suck in a thin stream of air, almost as if you're gargling upside down. Swallow and make a *mmm* sound to indicate deep thought.

Punch yourself if you do this while drinking Coronas.

METHOD 2: DECANTING

Decanting is, strictly speaking, transferring liquid from one container to another. The Romans pioneered the use of glass decanters, which they used to remove sediment, leaving the gunk in the original storage vessel.

Decanters with wide bases are now used to expose wine to air, often for 1–3 hours or more.

METHOD 3: THE VINTURI

The Vinturi wine aerator is a handheld plastic device that capitalizes on Bernoulli's Principle. Mr. B's rule dictates that as you increase the speed of a fluid's movement, you decrease its pressure. Decrease the pressure of wine and you infuse more air in less time.

If you pour wine from the bottle, through the Vinturi, and directly into a friend's wineglass, you will hear the accelerated siphoning of air into the stream, which puts decanting on fast-forward.

The difference is subtle, but less waiting and less cleanup make it a win. Sure, it's less classy, but who needs that? Speaking of which...

METHOD 4: BEATING THE SHIT OUT OF IT

This method isn't subtle.

If aeration is exposing more liquid surface area to air, how can we take this to its logical extreme?

Blend it, of course, a technique I learned from Nathan Myhrvold. He has done this with vintage wine gifted to him by Spanish royalty, but I'd suggest a practice run on something from Trader Joe's. Here's how I do it:

- Pour 1–2 glasses of the wine into a large mixing bowl or (my favorite) a 500-ml or larger Bomex beaker. If the latter, leave plenty of room at the top. I fill to around 400 ml (14 oz). Take a sip for a good sense of "before" taste.

- Lower an immersion blender into the glass, tilt the glass, and blend for 20–30 seconds. If you have a standing blender like a Vitamix, feel free to use.

- The wine should now have a heady froth like a Guinness. Pour into a serving cup and enjoy. I favor a 250-ml Bomex, which is exactly one-third of a standard bottle of wine.

And that, ladies and gents, is how you achieve 3 hours of decanting, sans fancy descriptors, in 20–30 seconds. It should taste markedly different. Wink at your most offended guest and ask them if they want to arm wrestle.

"Chemistry can be a good and bad thing. Chemistry is good when you make love with it. Chemistry is bad when you make crack with it."

—ADAM SANDLER

THE SCIENCE OF
TRANSGLUTAMINASE

GLUE

In cooking, we often want to encourage molecular bonds that prevent our food from falling apart. Simple glues include things like egg whites. Mix a white into your ground beef before making hamburger patties and they'll never crumble on the grill again. (Might be a little chewy, though.)

Chefs sometimes use a compound called transglutaminase. Derived from mushrooms (and all sorts of meats and vegetables), this molecule sews proteins together. Transglutaminase is why some store-bought sausages don't crumble if you cut them up or remove the casing. There are tons of uses, but don't inhale it—you're made out of proteins, too. And in case you were wondering, it's best not to inhale any powders, South American or otherwise.

THE SCIENCE OF

TRANSGLUTAMINASE

TUNA AND YELLOWTAIL CHECKERBOARD

INSPIRED BY

Nathan Myhrvold

SHORTHAND

Whisk 3T H2O, 10g Activa to form slurry. Brush on 200g yellowtail & tuna in 2cm strips. Stack into 3x3 rectangle; vacuum seal, chill 4hr. Slice, garnish w 15g diced jicama, 12 cilantro leaves, 4t passion fruit seeds, sesame oil.

HANDS-ON TIME

15 minutes

TOTAL TIME

15 minutes, plus 4 hours chilling

GEAR

- Latex gloves
- Knife + cutting board
- Plastic wrap
- Small mixing bowl

Optional:

- Pastry brush
- Vacuum sealer and bag

INGREDIENTS	TO SERVE 6
Sushi-grade yellowtail[18] (Japanese amberjack)	**200 g (7 oz)**
Sushi-grade tuna (yellowfin or albacore)	**200 g (7 oz)**
Water	**3 T**
Activa RM (transglutaminase)	**10 g (4 t)**
OPTIONAL GARNISH	
Jicama, small dice	**15 g (¼ c)**
Cilantro leaves	**12**
Passion fruit seeds	**4 t**
Sesame oil	**A drizzle**

In this recipe, you're using transglutaminase (don't worry, it's tasteless) to adhere two kinds of fish—tuna and yellowtail—to create a sushi "checkerboard."

PREP

00 Put on latex gloves.

01 Cut the fish into long strips 2 cm x 2 cm (¾" x ¾") thick (see pics A and B, opposite). Think square-sided cigars.

02 Lay a large piece of plastic wrap across the table or cutting board.

PICKUP

00 In the mixing bowl, combine 3 T water and 10 g (4 t) Activa RM to form a *slurry* (thin paste). Rub or brush the slurry evenly all over the fish strips.

01 Quickly align and stack alternating red and white strips of fish to form a 3-strip-wide, 3-strip-high checkerboard rectangular prism on the plastic wrap. Wrap the checkerboard tightly in plastic wrap and put in a vacuum-sealer bag. Vacuum seal to press strips firmly together. Alternatively, wrap very tightly in several layers of plastic wrap.

02 Refrigerate the fish for at least 4 hours to ensure bonding.

03 After slicing into pretty squares (see pic C, opposite), garnish with the 15 g (¼ cup) diced jicama, 12 cilantro leaves, and 4 t passion fruit seeds, then drizzle with sesame oil and serve.

18 Nathan uses escolar, sometimes referred to as butterfish, oil fish, or white tuna. It is a rich, delicious fish. Unfortunately, it is also known to cause gastrointestinal distress in some people, and therefore it should never be consumed in quantities greater than 170 g (6 oz). If you'd prefer not to take the risk, yellowtail is a simple substitution.

A

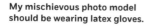

My mischievous photo model should be wearing latex gloves.

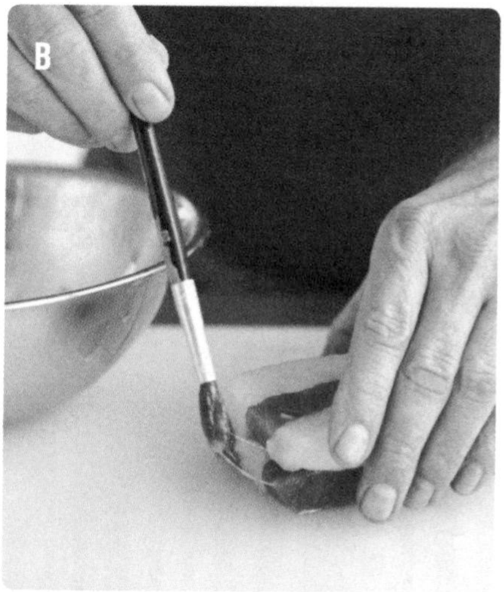
B

C

Don't Believe the Hype!

Activa RM is the most popular transglutaminase used by chefs. It can be purchased online (fourhourchef.com/activarm). It's not as dangerous as many in the media claim. From chef-scientist Chris Young:

"There is a very bad Australian documentary that claimed some nonsense about this ingredient, but it is extensively studied and permitted by both Japan and Germany (two of the strictest countries as far as food regulation goes).

"Indeed, the Activa product is mostly composed of maltodextrin and sodium caseinate, which are used as bulking agents and bond enhancers for the enzyme, respectively. If you eat the powder, your body will treat the maltodextrin as a starch, and the caseinate will happily be digested as a protein. The enzyme will also be quickly denatured and digested by your gut.

"There are only two potential health issues: 1) if you are dairy intolerant or have a dairy allergy, you will want to use one of the variants of Activa that does not include the sodium caseinate, and 2) when transglutaminase is added to products containing gluten (often done to strengthen noodles), it can enhance the reaction a person with celiac disease will have to the gluten."

That's it. Pretty innocuous stuff.

"Sometimes me think, 'What is love?' And then me think, 'Love is what last chocolate cookie is for.' Me give up the last chocolate cookie for you."

—COOKIE MONSTER

THE SCIENCE OF
THE MAILLARD REACTION

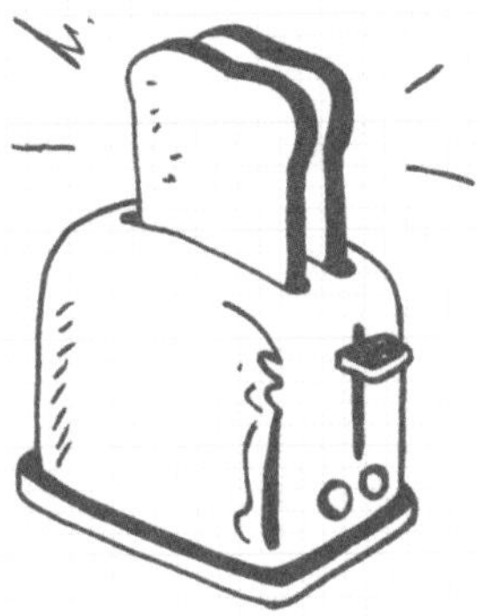

The Maillard reaction is arguably the most important flavor-producing transformation in cooking. It is named after the French physician Louis Camille Maillard, who discovered the reaction between amino acids (from proteins) and simple sugars in 1912. Its importance in the kitchen wasn't appreciated until after World War II, when Army food scientists noticed that skim-milk powder in C-rations went brown during storage and developed a distinct smell, especially at higher temperatures. Since there was very little water and the material was sterile, they couldn't figure it out—until someone rediscovered Maillard's research and realized that lactose sugar was reacting with the milk proteins to generate the brown pigments, as well as the toffee-like aroma.

Anytime a recipe includes proteins and sugars and applies plenty of heat without too much water, the reaction will start. This is why we got our Sexy-Time Steak surface so dry (page 186) before searing. This is why toast looks brown and smells the way it does. You can amplify the aroma by making things more alkaline (e.g., cooking vegetables with a small pinch of baking soda), or by adding a bit more simple sugar and protein (try dusting chicken wings with skim-milk powder before frying or seasoning steak with a little ribose sugar and whey-protein isolate).

The Maillard reaction is often confused with caramelization (think crème brûlée). If there is no protein mixed in with the sugar, you won't get a Maillard reaction. Another key: caramelization reactions all smell about the same, but the effect of the Maillard reaction smells far more potent and can vary a lot (baking bread smells different than roasting meat or chicken skin, for example).

ROSEMARY PISTACHIO COOKIES
WITH WHITE CHOCOLATE CHIPS

SHORTHAND
190C 14min: Beat 224g butter, 330g brown sugar till smooth; +2 eggs. Mix in 290g flour, 1t baking powder, 60g pistachios, 170g white choc chips, 1t rosemary till incorporated. Bake 12 1T-size lumps (¼ of batch) till brown.

HANDS-ON TIME
20 minutes

TOTAL TIME
35 minutes

GEAR
- Baking sheets
- Parchment paper or reusable Silpat
- Hand or stand mixer
- Mixing bowl
- Rubber spatula
- Spoon or fork
- Airtight container

Optional:
- Wooden spoon

INGREDIENTS	TO MAKE 48 COOKIES
Unsalted butter or ghee at room temperature	**224 g (1 c)**
Light brown sugar	**330 g (1½ c) packed**
Eggs, large	**2**
Self-rising flour, if you can find it (or my preference: 440 g (3½ c) gluten-free all-purpose flour)	**290 g (2⅓ c)**
Pistachios, shelled	**60 g (½ c)**
White chocolate chips	**170 g (1 c)**
Fresh rosemary, minced	**1 t**
Baking powder (use only with gluten-free flour)	**1 t**

This recipe is a pain in the ass.

But . . . sometimes pain is totally worth it. I courted my girlfriend for almost a year before I won the war of attrition and entered the Promised Land. These odd little cookies are the culinary equivalent. Like most good things, they have a story.

On a rare trip to La-La Land (L.A.), I walked into the Apple Store in Hollywood after seeing Mario Lopez inexplicably dancing to "Livin' La Vida Loca" outside the Barnes & Noble next door. Inside at the Genius Bar, I was paired with Delvyn, who started to run diagnostics on my crippled Mac Air.

Five minutes in, for no particular reason, I asked him, "By chance, do you like to cook?"

He didn't cook much, it turned out, but his wife—known as "Tinywino" online—certainly did. In fact, she'd pitted her skills against thousands of other home cooks in epicurious.com's

15th-anniversary recipe contest. She dominated and was flown to NYC to demonstrate her masterpiece (Rosemary Pistachio White Chocolate Chip Cookies) to a panel of famous chefs. She won, and the universe conspired to get her recipe to me.

The following recipe is my slight variation.

As you're baking these, you'll notice an incredible smell coming from your oven. This is the Maillard reaction at work. As every real estate agent hosting an open house knows, this is nasal catnip.

The unusual addition of rosemary is fragrant icing on the cake.

PREP

00 Preheat the oven to 190°C (375°F).

01 If you want to cook 24 cookies, set racks in the middle and bottom third of the oven. Line two baking sheets with parchment paper. If you want to cook fewer than 12 cookies, set one rack in the middle and line one baking sheet.

PICKUP

00 **Option A** (less work): Using a hand mixer or stand mixer fitted with paddle attachment, beat the 224 g (1 c) butter and 330 g (1½ c) light brown sugar on high speed until smooth, lighter in color, and a little fluffy. Add the 2 eggs, one at a time, beating well after each addition. Scrape down the sides of the bowl with a rubber spatula as needed.

Option B (what I did and only half-recommend): Beat the dough by hand with a wooden spoon or a rubber spatula. Be sure to mix the butter and brown sugar vigorously until the mixture lightens in color and the sugar has started to dissolve. This will be a serious workout, especially if you're going to use gluten-free flour. I'm serious.

01 Add the 290 g (2⅓ c) flour, 1 t baking powder (if using), 60 g (½ c) pistachios, 170 g (1 c) white chocolate chips, and 1 t rosemary, and mix on medium speed (whether using tools or manual labor) until thoroughly incorporated.

02 Using a spoon or—as I prefer—a fork, drop tablespoon-size (2.5-cm/1") blobs of dough at least 5 cm (2") apart onto the baking sheet(s). Don't forge bigger, palm-size cookies, which end up tasting mediocre. Smaller always tastes better. Use no more than ¼ of the dough (for a maximum of 12 cookies) on each baking sheet.

03 Bake until lightly browned at the edges and spread flat, about 14 minutes. Let cool on the pans.

04 Store leftovers in an airtight container at room temperature for up to 2 days.

FOR THE NON-BINGERS

Prepare the remaining dough for freezing. Line a tray or plates with waxed paper and drop blobs of dough onto the paper, as close together as possible without touching. Place it all in the freezer. Once the blobs have frozen, transfer them to a freezer bag or other airtight container and label the bag, including the following instructions: Thaw, then bake 5 cm (2") apart at 180°C (350°F) for 14 minutes.

I love giving frozen bags of these to friends as gifts.

Mastering the Art of Baking Cookies

Here are some tips to make sure your cookies always turn out perfectly:

- **If the recipe calls for butter at room temperature, leave the butter out on the counter for 2 hours before starting. Don't microwave it—you'll end up with a partially melted, partially cold mess that puts butter icebergs in your cookies. Not delicious.**
- **If you must use measuring cups, stir the flour in the bag with a large spoon, then spoon it into the cup until it piles up and slightly overflows. Don't tamp it down; use a knife to scrape the excess flour off the top.**
- **Make sure the baking sheet is at room temperature when you put dough on it. If it's hot out of the oven, the cookies will start to spread before they reach the oven, and you'll end up with one thin sheet of cookie.**

“There is no such thing as talent. There is pressure.”

—ALFRED ADLER, AUSTRIAN PSYCHOTHERAPIST

THE SCIENCE OF

PRESSURE COOKING

PRESSURE

We've talked a lot about time and temperature in cooking. Now we introduce another variable: pressure. If you cook at lower pressure (like when mile high in Denver), you have to cook longer or hotter to see the same results.

Conversely, pressure cookers accelerate cooking. They also keep food moist by raising the boiling point of water, avoiding evaporation. At maximum pressure in a pressure cooker (about 1 bar/15 psi above surrounding atmospheric pressure), the temperature of water and food inside can be as high as 120°C (250°F) without boiling, instead of the usual 100°C (212°F) at sea level. Cooked at this temperature, melting tender carnitas or making risotto takes only 20–40 minutes.

CARAMELIZED CARROT SOUP

INSPIRED BY

Nathan Myhrvold

SHORTHAND

Pressure cooker 20min: 500g chopped carrots, 80g butter, 1t salt, ½t baking soda. Puree & sieve. Simmer puree w 590ml carrot juice till separate, + H2O for consistency; + 60g carotene butter. Garnish w 1t ginger & tarragon, ¼t ajowan seeds.

HANDS-ON TIME

30 minutes, plus 1 hour 45 minutes if making carotene butter

TOTAL TIME

50 minutes, plus chilling overnight if making carotene butter

GEAR

- Star Peeler
- Knife + cutting board
- Pressure cooker (I like Kuhn Rikon)
- Immersion blender
- Fine-mesh sieve
- Mixing bowl
- Soup bowls

INGREDIENTS	TO SERVE 4
Carrots	**500 g (1 lb)**
Unsalted butter	**80 g (⅓ c)**
Salt	**1 t**
Baking soda	**½ t**
Carrot juice, brought to a simmer and centrifuged	**590 ml (2½ c)**
Carotene butter (see sidebar; or use plain unsalted butter)	**60 g (⅓ c)**
OPTIONAL GARNISH	
Fresh ginger, minced	**1 t**
Fresh tarragon, minced	**1 t**
Ajowan seeds,[19] lightly crushed	**¼ t**

In this recipe, we'll enhance the Maillard reaction by adding baking soda, which raises the pH slightly, making it more alkaline. Acidity is the fourth variable in cooking, and it has to be on the low side for pressure-induced Maillard reactions to shine.

PREP

00 Peel and quarter the 500 g (1 lb) of carrots lengthwise. To remove the slightly bitter core, swipe it with the peeler. Cut into 1.5-cm (⅝") pieces. No need to be exact.

PICKUP

00 Melt the 80 g (⅓ c) butter in the pressure cooker with the top off. Add the carrots, 1 t salt, and ½ t baking soda. Stir well to coat the carrots with the melted butter. Cover and cook under high pressure (15 psi) for 20 minutes to caramelize. When the time is up, release the pressure according to the manufacturer's instructions.

01 With an immersion blender, blend the carrot mixture to a smooth puree and press it through a fine-mesh sieve into a bowl. This velvety liquid is your carrot puree.

02 In the pressure cooker pot, combine the 590 ml (2½ c) carrot juice and carrot puree and bring to a simmer; simmer just until it separates and a lighter orange liquid

19 Look for ajowan seeds at Indian grocery stores or online spice sellers. Make sure to buy the ajowan seeds used for cooking, not those used for tea.

comes to the top. This is all now "the soup."

03 Blend just enough water into the soup to achieve the desired consistency.

04 Blend in the 60 g (⅓ c) carotene butter (see sidebar) or unsalted butter. Remove from the heat and season with more salt, if needed. If you'd like, push the soup through the sieve again for a silky-smooth texture.

05 Pour into bowls, garnish with the 1 t ginger, 1 t tarragon, and ¼ t ajowan seeds, and serve.

How to Make Carotene Butter

To make carotene butter, bring about 2.2 L (9⅓ c) carrot juice to a simmer in a large pot or Dutch oven and blend in 1.4 kg (3 lb) unsalted butter with an immersion blender. Simmer for 1½ hours. Let cool to room temperature, then cover and refrigerate overnight so that the butterfat solidifies. Pour through a fine-mesh sieve set over a large container to strain out the congealed butterfat, reserving the carrot juice for another use. Warm the butterfat, and pour through the sieve, this time lined with a good-quality paper towel, to remove all particulates. Refrigerate to set.

"*Nouvelle cuisine*, roughly translated, means: I can't believe I paid ninety-six dollars and I'm still hungry."

—MIKE KALIN

THE SCIENCE OF DENATURATION

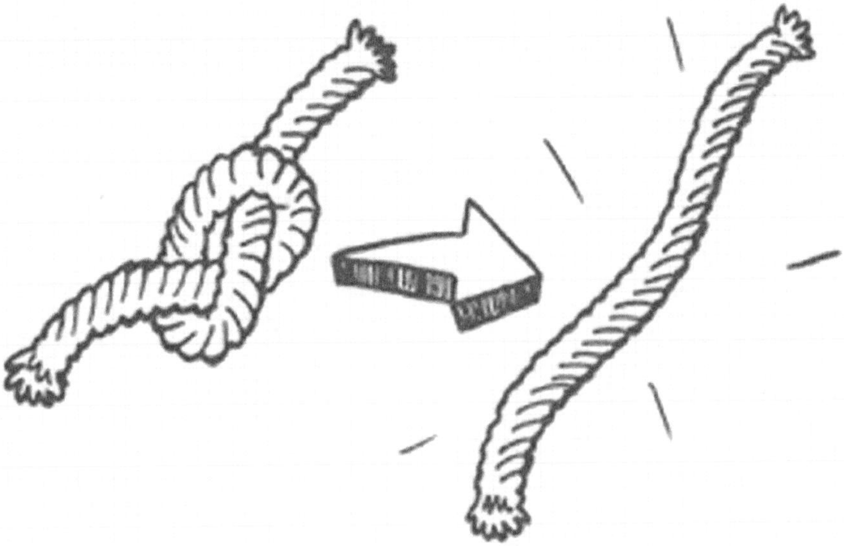

Proteins are one of the basic ingredients of life, which makes them one of the basic ingredients of cooking. Although all proteins are built from the same collection of amino acids, each one has a specific shape that determines its function. Think of a protein like rope tied into a knot: There are many kinds of knots, each with a specific shape that makes it useful for a particular task. Loosen or untie the knot and its function is lost. The same is true for proteins. Distort or unfold a protein by changing its environment—make it too hot, too acidic, too salty, or too boozy, for example—and the function of the protein changes. Denaturing a protein is often exactly what we want to accomplish when cooking. This is how cooking can transform meat from raw to cooked. Denaturing is also how artisans make cheese and bakers bake bread.

THE SCIENCE OF

DENATURATION

PERFECT POACHED EGGS

CONTRIBUTED BY

Jeff Potter

SHORTHAND

Heat 1L H2O, 1T salt, 1T vinegar 82–93C, steam, no bubbles. Add eggs one at a time, cook 4-5min.

HANDS-ON TIME

10 minutes

TOTAL TIME

15 minutes

GEAR

- Mixing bowls
- Nonstick skillet
- Probe thermometer
- Peltex

INGREDIENTS	TO SERVE 4
Eggs, large	**4**
Water	**1 L (1 qt)**
Salt	**1 T**
White vinegar	**1 T**
S+P	**To taste**

To get a firm egg white and a yolk that's only partially set, the hallmark of a perfectly poached egg, there's a very, *very* narrow temperature band you need to hit. This is because whites and yolks begin to denature at different temperatures: 62–65°C (144–149°F) for the whites and 65–70°C (149–158°F) for the yolks.

Gentle heat is the key, but acids (like vinegar) and salt increase the rate of denaturing and assist. Adding those to the water will help set the outer portion of the egg white. The other trick is to keep the water as still as possible. Make sure that your water is steaming hot but not bubbling, and use room-temperature eggs.

PREP

00 Place the eggs (still in shells) in a mixing bowl and cover with your hottest tap water for 5–10 minutes to bring them to room temperature.

PICKUP

00 In a nonstick skillet or saucepan big enough to hold all 4 eggs when cracked, combine 1 L (1 qt) water, 1 T salt, and 1 T vinegar and heat to between 82–93°C (180–200°F). Use your probe thermometer to check the temperature. You don't want to see any bubbles moving around (other than the initial layer of bubbles you'll see as the water heats). The pan should look like a hot bath: a light amount of steam coming off the top.

MY RECOMMENDATION: Get the water to 93°C (200°F) and and then turn off the heat entirely. This minimizes turbulence.

01 One at a time, crack the eggs into a small bowl and, holding the bowl close to the surface of the water (pic B, opposite), gently pour them into the water, keeping them apart.

Alternatively, crack the eggs just above the surface of the water, skipping the bowl.

Cook for 4–5 minutes. Use the Peltex to remove, and serve with S+P to taste.

Make-Ahead Brunch Tip

The eggs can be poached up to 1 day in advance. Put them in an airtight container and cover with ice water. To reheat, immerse them in just-below-simmering water for 1 minute.

Hawk's Tavern Tip

Once you're a little more seasoned (wokka wokka wokka!), try this combo from Hawk's Tavern in Mill Valley: sautéed wild mushrooms, arugula, poached egg, and salsa verde (see page 213).

A
Polder

B

C

Toxic Avenger Variation: Poach an Egg in Plastic Wrap

This variation guarantees that your egg white won't break apart. You'll have a perfectly round poached egg every time. One caveat, though: plastic can leach into food when heated to high temperatures, so don't make this your daily habit!

1. **Bring 4 eggs to room temperature.**
2. **Take a piece of microwavable plastic wrap (a 30-cm/12" square should do it) and push it down into a cup to line it.**
3. **Break an egg into the plastic wrap, then gather the plastic wrap at the top and knot it, or tie it with a piece of kitchen twine or a twist tie, to make a little egg package. Repeat with the remaining eggs.**
4. **Add 1 L (1 qt) water to a nonstick skillet or pot and heat to between 82–93°C (180–200°F).**
5. **Drop your egg packages into the water and cook for 4–5 minutes.**
6. **Remove eggs from the water with a Peltex, remove from plastic wrap, and season with S+P to taste.**

THE SCIENCE OF
DENATURATION

PERFECT BEEF SHORT RIBS

INSPIRED BY
Doug McAfee

SHORTHAND
Sous-vide 56–62C 72hr: 1kg vacuum-sealed, S+P-seasoned short ribs.

HANDS-ON TIME
5 minutes

TOTAL TIME
72 hours

GEAR
- Vacuum sealer and plastic bags
- SousVide Supreme or other immersion circulator

INGREDIENTS	TO SERVE 4
Boneless beef short ribs	**1 kg (2 lb)**
S+P	**To taste**

"Hi, Heston. I know this is probably a novice question, but I'd like to ask you about beans. . . ."

That was how I, as a culinary idiot, proceeded to geek out with Heston Blumenthal for almost 20 minutes about cooking beans. He was giving a sous-vide demonstration in 2009, the first I'd seen, at a press junket for the SousVide Supreme machine, designed by my friends Drs. Michael and Mary Dan Eades.

The SousVide Supreme allows you to do things that are impossible or impractical with the stockpot approach we used in DOMESTIC (page 218). One of the mantras in BBQ is cooking "low and slow." Well, what if we went, as Nathan Myhrvold put it, "lower and slower"?

Doug McAfee encouraged me to try beef short ribs cooked for 72 *hours*. They not only tasted phenomenal, they also served as an immediate conversation piece for the dinner I threw. Best of all, the process required zero management. Nathan suggests something similar for brisket: 63°C (146°F) for 72 hours.

For this recipe, in addition to the immersion circulator, you'll need a vacuum sealer, whether it be the SousVide Supreme brand or the FoodSaver (fourhourchef.com/foodsaver).

PICKUP

00 Season the short ribs with nothing more than S+P. Yes, that's it.

01 Vacuum seal in plastic bags. Doug puts 7 ribs in each 3.8 L (1 gal) bag.

02 Cook sous-vide for 72 hours at 56–62°C (133–144°F). Mary Dan Eades prefers the lower range; I cooked mine at 60°C (140°F).

Flank Steak Variation

Season with S+P and rosemary, or Montreal steak rub. Cook sous-vide for 48 hours at 54°C (130°F), followed by a 1-minute sear to finish. Oh, Maillard!

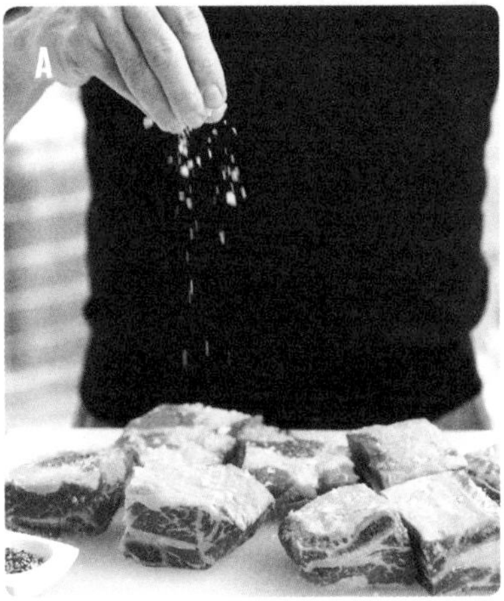
A

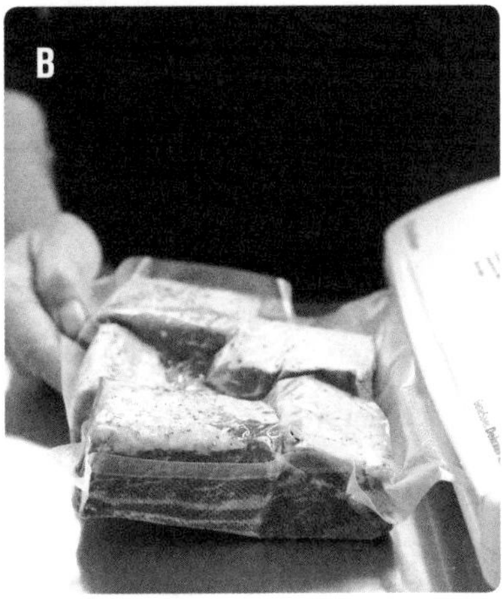
B

C
SousVide
62.1

"Ice cream is exquisite—what a pity it isn't illegal."

—VOLTAIRE, FRENCH ENLIGHTENMENT PHILOSOPHER

THE SCIENCE OF LIQUID NITROGEN

Although it seems like an exotic ingredient, nitrogen makes up more than 78% of the air we breathe (as a gas). Cool it down enough and you get liquid nitrogen. At -196ºC (-321ºF), few things are colder than liquid nitrogen, which makes it useful for quickly freezing just about anything. Try whisking up some fresh ice cream with this stuff the next time you go on a picnic. Or try freezing last night's leftover steak and microplaning it over your breakfast eggs for a modernist take on steak and eggs. It's easy to get this stuff, too; you'll need to buy or rent a Dewar flask as a storage container (try eBay), but with this in hand, most welding supply stores will sell you as much as you want.

THE SCIENCE OF

LIQUID NITROGEN

30-SECOND COCOA-GOLDSCHLÄGER ICE CREAM

CONTRIBUTED BY

Jeff Potter

SHORTHAND

Whisk 240ml milk & heavy cream, 177ml Goldschläger, 75ml choc syrup, 80ml melted bittersweet choc, 2T sugar, ½t salt & cinnamon. In mixer, slowly add liquid nitrogen to mixture in a 1:1 ratio.

HANDS-ON TIME

5 minutes

TOTAL TIME

5 minutes, 30 seconds

GEAR

- Stand mixer with metal mixing bowl
- Wooden cutting board
- Wooden spoon or whisk
- Safety gloves and goggles
- IR laser thermometer (for gauging the temperature before serving)
- Dewar flask

INGREDIENTS	TO SERVE 2–4
Milk	240 ml (1 c)
Heavy cream	240 ml (1 c)
Goldschläger (cinnamon liqueur)	177 ml (¾ c)
Chocolate syrup	75 ml (¼ c)
Bittersweet chocolate, melted	80 ml (2.8 oz)
Sugar	2 T
Salt	½ t
Cinnamon	½ t
Liquid nitrogen	≈710 ml (3 c)[20]

Ice cream is actually one of the most complicated foodstuffs out there. It's an emulsion, part liquid and part solid. The weird freezing properties of sugar water make it prone to horrible grittiness if any variable goes wrong.

So how do you make the perfect pint of ice cream? Typically, this is done with an ice cream maker, which churns the batter as it freezes to prevent large ice crystals from forming. But there are other ways. For instance, if you can freeze it *fast* enough, ice crystals won't have time to aggregate into chunks.

Cue the liquid nitrogen.

"Cooking" with liquid nitrogen (LN_2) can be a lot of fun, but let's go over the risks. First, and most obviously, it's extremely *cold.* Liquid nitrogen boils at -196°C (-321°F), so thermal shock and container breakage are real possibilities. Splashes can be dangerous, so wear close-toed shoes, eye protection, and gloves whenever you're handling it.

Another thing: liquid nitrogen is *not oxygen,* which means that you can asphyxiate if breathing it in an enclosed space. Make sure you're in a well-ventilated area, like a big kitchen or other room with the windows open. Ideally, handle it outside.

Finally, liquid nitrogen is *boiling,* which means it likes to expand. *Never* store liquid nitrogen in a completely sealed container, as it will have nowhere to go and become a ticking time bomb.

So, ready to tempt the Fates? You'll first need a Dewar flask, an insulated container designed to handle extremely cold temperatures. Try eBay, local chemical or welding supply shops, or le-sanctuaire.com. Depending on the supplier, you may be able to rent one.

20 The amount of nitrogen depends on the size of your Dewar and the size of your ice cream mixture. It should be a 1:1 ratio.

You'll want to get a *non-pressurized* Dewar, which is like a large Thermos and doesn't require a hazmat license when properly secured and transported in a car. (You should still check the regulations for transporting hazardous materials in your area, of course.)

When working with liquid nitrogen in this recipe, place it in a metal mixing bowl on top of a wooden cutting board so you don't crack your countertop—remember, it's *really* cold!

And finally, check the temperature of your ice cream using an IR thermometer (infrared laser) before trying it or serving it to guests. You want to make sure it's not too cold. As a guideline, a standard freezer runs at around -23°C (-9°F), and ice cream is easiest to serve at around -13°C (9°F), so make that your target.

PICKUP

00 In the metal bowl of the stand mixer, place all of the ingredients except the liquid nitrogen. Mix with a wooden spoon or a whisk until blended. Taste the mixture and adjust to your liking. Once frozen, the mixture will not taste as strong, so you want the flavors to be a little overpowering at this point.

01 Turn on the stand mixer and slowly and carefully (with gloves and goggles on!) pour in the liquid nitrogen. It takes about a 1:1 ratio of ice cream mixture to liquid nitrogen to set things. If you don't have a stand mixer, you can use your wooden spoon or whisk to mix it.

Bam! Thirty-second ice cream!

KitchenAid

A Few Words for the *Schnäppchen Jäger*[21]

Building a world-class lab doesn't require a Learjet budget. Even billionaires like to be frugal, and Nathan gave a few examples at dinner:

"See that hood over there? $100."

He then pointed to the other side of the room: "That freeze-dryer sells for $250,000. We got it for $5,000."

Jaws dropped at the dinner table. But . . . how?!?

Sometimes it's as easy as looking for the product in a different vertical (industry). For instance, contacting florist suppliers for a freeze-dryer instead of the industrial food titans,[22] or buying a jeweler's scale instead of a high-end lab scale. But the real steals are found at biotech company bankruptcy auctions. Nathan outfitted nearly his entire food lab by scouting them. Find local auctions via auctionzip .com, Craigslist, and the tiny-print classifieds in local papers. Boston's a biotech hotbed, as is Santa Clara, California.

Lastly, there's no need to go expensive when cheaper stuff will do the job. I picked up one gorgeous red serving dish in Nathan's multimillion-dollar facility, and it was reassuring to see a familiar name on the bottom: Pier 1 Imports.

21 German for "bargain hunter." You might recognize *jäger* from Jägermeister—"hunter master."

22 Nathan blast-freezes most food items and stores them at -60°C (-76°F) to avoid ice crystals, freezer burn, and other problems.

A SKINNY MAN HASN'T A CHANCE. I WISH I COULD GAIN FLESH
NEW EASY WAY ADDS 5 to 15 LBS.—QUICK!
Results guaranteed
Special FREE offer!
"I'LL TELL YOU HOW TO GAIN POUNDS QUICK!"
Skinny GIRLS ARE NOT GLAMOUR GIRLS
HOW TO ADD Glamorous Curves TO YOUR FIGURE
If you are a normal healthy, underweight person and are ashamed of your skinny, scrawny figure, NUMAL may help you add pounds and pounds of firm, attractive flesh to your figure. For NUMAL, a doctor-approved formula, contains essential minerals and vitamins that may aid your appetite. Then you eat more and enjoy what you eat. But that isn't all. NUMAL contains a food element which is also a great help in putting on weight. So don't let them snicker at your skinny, scrawny figure. A skinny, scarecrow figure is neither fashionable nor glamorous. Remember, the girls with the glamorous curves get the dates.
So start NUMAL today. SEND NO MONEY. Just name and address. When postman delivers NUMAL in plain wrapper, pay him only $2 plus postage and C.O.D. fees, or send $2 with order and save postal charges.
MONEY BACK GUARANTEE
If you aren't pleased after using one bottle of NUMAL, you get your money back. Order now.
U. S. NATURE PRODUCTS CORPORA...
3560 B'way...
...eak, Rundown, Nervous, Skinny!
HERE'S PROOF THAT IN 1 WEEK YOU CAN BUILD UP HUSKY, NEW RED-BLOODED STRENGTH, NEW ENERGY AND AT LEAST 5 EXTRA POUNDS OR NO COST!
Accept This Startling No Risk Offer!
Your Money Back If Kelpamalt Does Not
1. Improve Appetite.
2. Add at least 5 lbs. of Good Solid Flesh.
3. Strengthen Nerves.
4. Banish Ordinary Stomach Trouble.
5. Make You Sleep Sounder.
6. Give you New Strength, Energy and Endurance.
7. Clear up Skin...
SPECIAL FREE
GROVE
MAKES CHILDREN AS FAT AS PIGS
TASTELESS CHILL TONIC
IS JUST AS GOOD FOR ADULTS.
WARRANTED. PRICE 50 cts.
GIRLS DESPISED HIS SKINNY, PIMPLY LOOKS
but now he's gained 21 POUNDS
new health and popularity
Roy Rigby
SKINNY? Thousands Gain 10 to 25 Lbs. With New IRONIZED YEAST Tablets
Why it builds up quick
Make money-back tes...
Special FREE offe...
MEN WOULDN'T LOOK AT ME WHEN I WAS SKINNY
but...
Since I Gained 10 Pound...
This New, Easy Way
I Have All the Dates I Wan...
Concentrated 7 times
Results guaranteed
Special FREE offer!

THE TRIPLE CROWN OF CHEAT DAY: FOR THE PIGGIES (IN MORE WAYS THAN ONE)

The Triple Crown is for those readers who want to push the limits of cheat day.

The three challenges are:

1. The Vermonster

2. The Turbacon Epic

3. The NYC Food Marathon

Brute force isn't enough. As you now know, it takes finesse to eat like a fatty without getting fat. Can you thread the needle? Can you hit the sweet spot of decadence? We'll find out.

As my favorite stoic has said:

> "*Aliquando et insanire iucundum est.*"
> "Sometimes it's enjoyable to be insane."‡
> —SENECA

Tim's Disclaimer

Don't do anything stupid like eat yourself to death. It would make both of us very unhappy.

#1 WELCOME TO THE JUNGLE: THE VERMONSTER

"If you got the money, honey, we got your disease
In the jungle, welcome to the jungle
Watch it bring you to your . . . kn-kn-kn-kn-kn-kn-knees, knees. . . ."
—GUNS N' ROSES, "WELCOME TO THE JUNGLE"

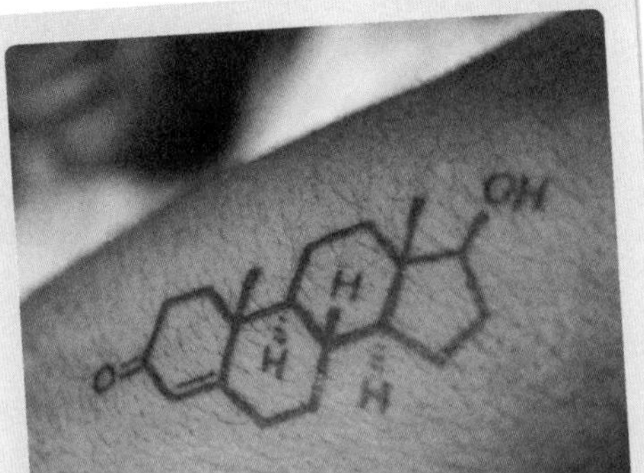
OH
H
H
H
ROMAN'S FOREARM, FEATURING ONE OF THE REASONS WE DO DUMB THINGS: TESTOSTERONE.

"Why did you want to do this again?" Roman asked.

"Because I wanted to see what would happen," I replied.

John "Roman" Romaniello looked across the room at the six people who'd assembled for the spectacle. "By the way, that's Tim's answer to almost any question. Really."

The latest misguided project, T-minus 20 minutes, had started with an e-mail to my New York–based book production team:

Subject: Roman eat-off in NYC
Sent: Thu, 15 Dec 2011, 10:37am

Hi Holly and All,

For the book, I'd like to show an example of horrifying indulgence on cheat day. Roman and I will be having a competition with the Vermonster:

The Vermonster is a large ice cream sundae found in Ben & Jerry's "scoop shops," which is served in a "Vermonster Bucket" and consists of 20 scoops of ice cream, a fudge brownie, four bananas, three cookies, 10 scoops of walnuts, four toppings, four ladles of hot fudge, and whipped cream. It contains 14,000 calories and 500 grams of fat.

Each Vermonster is intended to be shared by four or more people. Roman and I will consume one each.

Can you please contact him and coordinate best location(s), etc? He's expecting to hear from you.

Thanks! Oh, and bring at least two buckets, just in case . . . you know.

Tim

TRAINING FOR THE ABSURD

Surprisingly, none of the world's fastest eaters is fat.

Sonya Thomas holds 29 world titles and weighs 98 lbs soaking wet. She's nicknamed "The Black Widow" because she routinely demolishes men 4–5 times her size. On Sunday, September 4, 2010, she ate 181 chicken wings in 12 minutes. When pro football player Randy Thomas challenged her to a shrimp-eating contest, he fought through 1.5 lbs in 10 minutes. Sonya? 6.5 lbs.

She doesn't carry the visceral fat (internal organ fat) of fatties, so her stomach can, counterintuitively, expand further.

But what about technique? Some competitive eaters eat heads of lettuce to stretch their stomachs; others use water. The day prior to tournaments, some fast and others overfeed with protein shakes. Kevin Lipsitz, former American pickle-eating champion, prepared at one point by having eating races with his dogs,[23] but animal rights advocates intervened to stop him.

After surveying the landscape, I hunted down Patrick Bertoletti, the Mr. Miyagi of ice cream force-feeding. The #2-ranked competitive eater in the world behind Joey Chestnut, Patrick is 6'2" and an athletic 190 lbs. He sports a flawless mohawk and once crushed the Vermonster in an ungodly *three minutes*.[24]

The horrifying realities of this consumption (you'll see) are both gut-wrenching and awe-inspiring. I organized as many of his tips, routines, and rituals as possible in my notebook and tried to emulate everything. The oddest piece of the puzzle was his go-to music. He apparently listened to Jesse and the Rippers, John Stamos's crooner band, during competition. When I asked him about it, he responded with: "Oh, yeah. My girlfriend thought it'd be funny to change my Wikipedia page." Phew.

For performance-enhancing gear, I settled on a few tactical items:

- Propane torch: for melting the ice cream, making it easier to consume.

- Metal spoon: to avoid breakage of standard-issue Ben & Jerry's plastic. I was told to put the spoon in my mouth ice cream–side down, to minimize brain freeze.

- Anbesol: topical painkiller for numbing my gums and lips.

- Anti-diarrheal pills, Pepto-Bismol, Tums, and Lactaid: to minimize the likelihood of violence at either end of my body, at least until crossing the finish line. Vomiting during competition disqualifies you.

DOING AS THE ROMAN DOES

Roman stands 5'8" and has been 191 lbs at 4.6% body fat. He can deadlift 660 lbs for three repetitions. As a celebrity personal trainer, his meteoric rise has come from testing and refining promising fringe science on himself.

Like me, he's also fond of testing dumber things. Most relevant, he'd tackled the Vermonster twice before. He failed both times, but being a smart meathead, he'd learned lessons and taken notes. To level the playing field, he shared them with me.

In an e-mail to the interns, Roman stressed explicit no-no's and instructions for buying the Vermonsters. The next page features a few actionable excerpts from his hysterically long novella.

23 Not with pickles, of course.

24 His other records will blow your brains: deepdisheats.com.

Dear Interns,

On Flavor Selection:

- Avoid anything too uniquely flavored (banana base, mint base, sorbet, etc.). Cherry Garcia, while great on its own, is bad when it's at the bottom of the barrel and it commingles with five other flavors. As they say in French, "*No bueno.*"[25]
- Avoid rich flavors with a chocolate base.
- Choose six flavors, MAX.
- Flavors will ideally be complementary and vanilla-based.

For OUR Vermonster Challenge, I submit the following flavors:

- Imagine Whirled Peace
- Late Night Snack
- Sweet Cream & Cookies
- Milk & Cookies
- Americone Dream
- Chocolate Chip Cookie Dough
- Half Baked
- Chubby Hubby
- S'mores
- Everything But The...

NOTE: These are 10 flavors, but I do not recommend that you select all of them; I'm giving you options because I do not know what is available at the scoop shop. Simply select four of the above, and get 4–5 scoops of each. Fill out the remainder with 1–2 random scoops to keep things interesting.

Next, Pay Attention to Geology:

With the Vermonster, I failed to take into account the order of ingredients as they were added to the bucket. You see, left to their own devices, the kids at the scoop shop will simply add ingredients as you rattle them off. This is a mistake. Instead, you must stratify your Vermonster.

You see, in addition to 20 scoops of ice cream, the Vermonster is also comprised of one fudge brownie, three chocolate chip cookies, and four bananas.

These are normally added at the end, meaning they'll be thrown on top of the ice cream pile. The obvious result is that you'll have to eat through one brownie, three cookies, and four bananas (not to mention a mound of whipped cream) before you get to the ice cream.

Do you know how much room you'll have left for ice cream after plowing through one brownie, three cookies, and four bananas? The answer is, "not much." It will fill you up too quickly.

So, we must avoid this. Instead, we want exposure to these pieces slowly, over the course of the Vermonster.

What I NEED you to do is be an active participant in the construction of your Vermonster. It should be constructed in layers, very much like a lasagna. Only instead of alternating layers of pasta with layers of meat and cheese, you're alternating layers of ice cream with layers of cookies and brownies.

THIS IS OF PARAMOUNT IMPORTANCE.

When you tell the Ice Cream Elves that you're ordering Vermonsters, have them set aside the brownie, cookies, and bananas. Then, have them break these up into pieces. At the smallest, they should be quartered, but in the case of the bananas, sliced into eighths.

From there, construction can begin. Again, think lasagna.

To help, and wanting to leave nothing to chance, I have taken the liberty of drawing you a handy-dandy diagram. This is built from the bottom up:

^^^^^
^^^^^^^ ⟵ Whipped cream, hot fudge, and toppings

======= ⟵ Top layer of broken-up brownie, bananas, and cookies (one-fifth of total). Sprinkle as evenly as possible.

oooooo ⟵ Top ice cream layer (3–5 scoops). The least mix-ins. Imagine Whirled Peace is good here.

======= ⟵ Layer of broken-up brownie, bananas, and cookies (two-fifths of total)

oooooo ⟵ Ice cream layer (4–6 scoops)

======= ⟵ Layer of broken-up brownie, bananas, and cookies (two-fifths of total)

oooooo ⟵ Foundation layer of ice cream (6–8 scoops) should be made of flavors containing crunchy things to break texture monotony. Good examples are Half Baked, Everything But The..., and Chubby Hubby.

Yes, I said toppings. In addition to everything, the Vermonster also allows you four toppings. Keep these light: sprinkles and cookie crunches are good choices.

That's it.

Now, as you can imagine, and as stated above, this is serious business. You, interns, hold the fate of us all in your hands.

Roman

25 This is a joke. He is fond of acting the meathead role.

FRIDAY—3 DAYS PREGAME

Erik "The Red" Denmark was another advisor to my training camp. His claims to fame include records for Native American fry bread, and he offered the following benchmark to my team: "If Tim can down a gallon [of Gatorade] in under five minutes, then he should be able to do the challenge."

This ounces-per-minute metric made a lot of sense, but I also needed to increase my enzymatic ability to handle lactose (milk sugar) and milk fat, so I used milk instead of Gatorade.

Dinner:

- **900 ml (4 c) Straus Creamery raw milk, then**
- **5 portions salmon**
- **5 portions pork**
- **2 bottles wine, split among 3 people**

SATURDAY'S SCHEDULE—2 DAYS PREGAME

1:30 p.m.	**900 ml (4 c) raw whole milk, 2 caps acidophilus, followed by wall presses, air squats (20 reps each)**
1:45 p.m.	**900 ml (4 c) raw whole milk (+ cissus quadrangularus,[26] 300 mg ALA)**
2:15 p.m.	**Wall presses, air squats (20 reps each)**
6 p.m.	**2 caps acidophilus + 30 g whey isolate + water to maximum capacity/discomfort**
10 p.m.	**• Osso "Buko" (see page 134)**
	• Roasted Garlic (see page 208)
	• Steamed kale
	+ DESSERT: Pint of ice cream and 1,800 g (½ gal) of whole milk (pasteurized but not homogenized)

The last half gallon slaughtered me. I ended up in the fetal position on the floor while my friend and dinner companion shrugged his shoulders and checked his e-mail.

The pasteurization appeared to be a merciless gut killer. Though widely disputed, raw milk advocates believe that the process kills many of the beneficial bacteria that can aid in milk digestion in humans.

This didn't bode well.

MONDAY, DECEMBER 19TH—GAME DAY

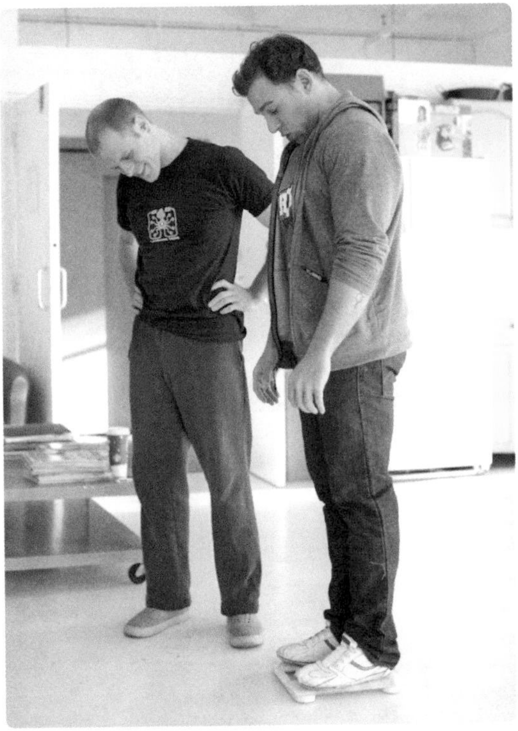

Before the fight, weigh-ins: Roman at 195.2 lbs. I topped out at 166.4 lbs. I measured my body-fat percentage using a BodyMetrix handheld ultrasound wand, popular with teams like the New York Yankees and AC Milan. After connecting it to my Mac Air with a USB cable, the numbers showed a puffy post-Thanksgiving bloat: 16.5%.

26 For anti-obesity effects. Refer to *The 4-Hour Body* for details.

LAUGHING SQUID

The propane torch fails and amateur hour begins.

LAUGHING SQUID

I used my own bowl in place of the flimsy B&J bucket. I thought I was very clever.

Several masters of the esophagus had recommended I sprint from the whistle. The goal is to sucker punch your stomach before it can send an SOS to your brain. "Start fast," they advised. "It should take 10–12 minutes to finish, so eat as much as possible in the first 10 minutes. You'll feel like you've hit a wall, but push through it."

I couldn't push through the wall. Eating the Vermonster, it turned out, was like running a marathon. For amateurs, at least, a marathon really starts at mile 20. Anyone can look at the sunshine, speed walk, and enjoy the first 75%. The last 6.2 miles are what separate the boys from the men, the dainty girls from the Black Widow, and the smart people from the Darwin Award winners.

At 20 minutes, our 20-mile point, Roman said what we were both thinking: "There's nothing fun about this anymore." He looked straight down at the table and then picked up the Vermonster bucket to drink melted sugar, food coloring, and milk. I took a bite of a syrupy, soggy cookie, and my diaphragm jumped like a frightened cat.

At this point, the photographer, Bonnie, almost puked just from watching us.

Pepto
BISMOL
5 SYMPTOM RELIEF
Lactaid
Fast Act
WORTHINGTON
PRO GRADE
PROPANE
DANGER

BEN&JERRY'S

Notice the improv: using a hot cup of tea to melt the ice cream.

The beginning of the end.

Who's laughing now, tough guy?

I tapped out at 23:28. One more nibble would've sent me to the garbage can.

Roman tapped shortly thereafter at 25:51.

Neither of us had finished, but neither of us wanted a tie. So we weighed the remains on an electronic scale. And . . . I'd been beaten fair and square: Roman had a mere 220 g (8 oz) left, whereas I had an embarrassing 590 g (21 oz) staring me in the face. A plate of disgrace.

Soaking up defeat, I lay on the couch in our photo studio, curled into a ball. Roman didn't look like a million bucks, but he sat upright, looking like I Am Sam after a bottle of Grey Goose. After five minutes, I was able to open my eyes; 10 minutes later, I was able to stand. As the crew packed up, I put on my jacket, picked up my backpack, and slung my camera around my neck. It was time for the walk of shame back to my hotel.

Roman was already waiting at the elevators, and I skipped, Mary Poppins–style, to catch up. I don't know why.

In that moment, the universe rightly decided to kick me in the nuts. My camera *should* have been draped diagonally across my chest, but I'd hung it around my neck like Peter Parker. As I skipped, it bounced three times on my stomach, ever so lightly, like a 90-year-old Japanese woman pawing me on the solar plexus.

My eyes started to water. Then my mouth filled with saliva. "I . . . I . . . I gotta go," I stammered to Roman, as I shed my jacket and backpack onto the floor on the way to the bathroom. Shoulder-checking the door open, I promptly unloaded a disgusting miasma of brown Vermonster sludge.

After washing my face, I marched past a stunned Roman, back into the photo studio.

"Is the scale still here?" I asked.

"Uh . . . sure," one of the crew said.

"Roman, could you come in here, please?" I half-whispered out the door.

Roman is one tough mofo, but he looked a little too good (comparatively speaking) after such an ordeal. So I had us clock in our "after" weights, a step I'd forgotten.

Roman's "before" weight was 195.2 lbs. After: 199.5 lbs, for a repulsive 4.3-lb gain.

I had weighed in at 166.4 lbs "before." Now, I shot up to 172 lbs, for a 5.6-lb gain *after* vomiting! That meant the Vermonsters weren't the same size! I had eaten more!!!

I spent the next four hours strolling through NYC with Roman, walking the High Line, discussing life, and working off calories.

The very next morning, I girded my loins for a food marathon (#3 in our trifecta), and the day after that, I measured my body fat percentage with ultrasound. It was 12.7%, a full 3.8 points *less* than my pre-Vermonster 16.5%.

If you play your cards as described in "Damage Control" (page 376), cheat day doesn't have to be guilt day.

VERMONSTER
A sad day for the Ferriss clan.

LAUGHING SQUID
But...

#2 THE TURBACON: SIN AGAINST NATURE OR MEAT-GLUE MASTERPIECE?

"I have a great diet. You're allowed to eat whatever you want, but you must eat every meal with naked fat people."

—ED BLUESTONE, STAND-UP COMEDIAN

"What's the big deal? It doesn't hurt anybody. Fuck, fuckity, fuck-fuck-fuck!"

—ERIC CARTMAN, *SOUTH PARK: BIGGER, LONGER, AND UNCUT*

In early 2010, Harley Morenstein was a 25-year-old substitute teacher in Montreal.

One fateful evening, a friend filmed him eating a six-patty Wendy's hamburger covered with 18 bacon slices. The footage was overlayed with the *Terminator* theme song and uploaded to YouTube. Epic Meal Time, nicknamed "Jackass in the Kitchen," had been born.

Two short years later, "EMT" has become a force of nature. More than 2.5 million people subscribe to Harley's videos (epicmealtime.com), and each weekly video routinely gets upwards of 5 million views. He is represented by Hollywood agencies: writing books, creating apps, and producing his own line of sauces and bacon salts.

EMT's tipping point, the video that started the stampede, was Turbacon Epic. The Turbacon is a Turducken on steroids: a quail inside a Cornish hen inside a chicken inside a duck inside a turkey inside a pig.

The most-upvoted comment on this YouTube phenomenon reads:

> "Sooooo . . . why am I fatter than them for eating normal food?"
>
> —KudFTW

The answer: Harley follows the Slow-Carb Diet® in between juggernaut meals! Now you can join him.

The following recipe, which totals 79,046 calories, was written by Harley himself. May it disgust and inspire you.

TURBACON EPIC by Harley Morenstein

SHORTHAND

190C 45min; cook 2kg bacon till crisp. Drain most grease; + 339g butter & 12 chopped croissants. Layer—in order—deboned & butterflied turkey, duck, chicken, Cornish hen & quail w sausage meat glue & bacon stuffing between; cover w bacon strips & thread w twine. Bake. Sew into dry-rubbed pig. Smoke 12hr, basting every 45min with 2L Dr Pepper, 240ml butter sauce. Halfway through cooking, cover w bacon.

HANDS-ON TIME

4–6 hours

TOTAL TIME

12–16 hours

Even if you're a big eater, you'd better invite the whole family over for this badass culinary fucker of mothers!

GEAR

- Mixing bowls
- Large nonstick skillet or frying pan (for the bacon)
- Cooking twine and needle
- Metal baking pan
- Large pot
- BBQ smoker (or use the powers of the Internet to look up how to turn a regular BBQ into a smoker)

INGREDIENTS	TO SERVE 8–10
Medium-size pig, preferably dead	**1 (≈9 kg/20 lb)**
Dry rub	**≈1 c**
Sausage meat (if you can't find meat, cut open some sausage links; we used veal-pork sausage). This is important, as it's your meat glue.	**2 kg (5 lb)**
Bacon (10 lb!! Getting pumped yet?!?)	**5 kg (10 lb)**
Butter	**339 g (1½ c)**
Butter croissants, chopped (don't fuck around with pronunciation!)	**12**
Medium-size turkey, deboned and butterflied	**1 (≈4 kg / 8 lb)**
Duck, deboned and butterflied	**1 (≈3 kg / 6 lb)**
Chicken, deboned and butterflied	**1 (≈2 kg / 4 lb)**
Cornish hen, deboned and butterflied	**1 (≈1 kg / 1½ lb)**
Quail, deboned and butterflied	**1 (≈142 g / 5 oz)**
Brown sugar	**2 kg (5 lb)**
Dr Pepper (we used Dr Pepper, but you can use whatever the fuck soda you want!)	**2 L (68 oz ≈1 bottle)**
OPTIONAL GARNISH	
Wendy's Baconators—garnish it with Baconators! We did 'cause we were fuckin' stoned!	**6**

PREP

00 Preheat the oven to 190°C (375°F).

01 Cover the pig inside and out with your favorite dry rub. Any flavor will do (we used bacon salt). Set aside.

PICKUP

MAKE THE MEAT GLUE

00 Place the sausage meat in a mixing bowl. With your hands, mix and knead the sausage until it has a sticky consistency.

MAKE THE BACON CROISSANT STUFFING

00 Chop up 2 kg (5 lb) of the bacon and throw it in a skillet over medium heat.

01 When the bacon becomes somewhat crisp, drain 90% of the bacon grease and add

A
Layering the duck on top of the turkey.

B
Layering on the bacon.

C
Getting ready to fold up all of the assembled bird layers.

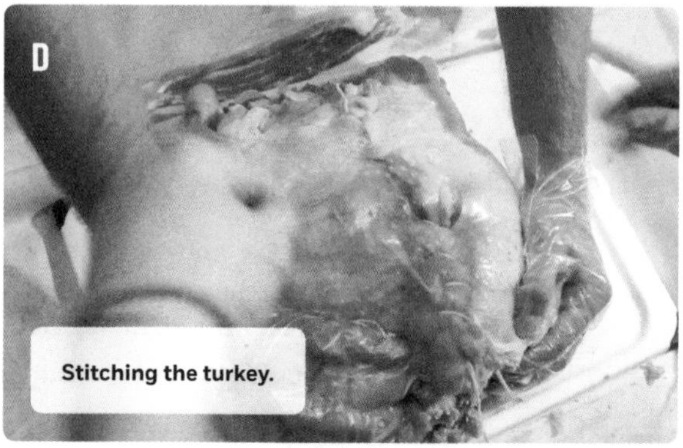
D
Stitching the turkey.

E
Stuffing the cooked, bacon-wrapped birds in the pig.

F
Smoking the pig.

G
The finished Turbacon Epic, complete with Baconator garnish.

H
Check out the cross-section!

113 g (½ c/1 stick) butter and half the chopped croissants.

02 Mix well and add the remaining croissants.

03 When the stuffing is all mixed together, transfer it from the skillet to a mixing bowl.

ASSEMBLE AND COOK THE BIRDS

00 Lay out the turkey with the skin down.

01 Apply the meat glue on top of the turkey.

02 Add some stuffing.

03 On top of the stuffing, add the duck and then some more meat glue.

04 Lay ⅓ of the remaining bacon strips over the entire duck. Add more meat glue.

05 Lay out the chicken, then apply more meat glue.

06 Lay out the Cornish hen, then apply more meat glue.

07 Lay out the quail, then (yep) more meat glue.

08 Fold the bird pile in half (be careful that the insides don't fall out). Use the outside turkey to hold all the birds together.

09 Use cooking twine and a needle to thread the turkey. Start at the top of the turkey and work your way down the entire structure until all the birds are together. You don't have to thread through all the birds; threading through the turkey will work fine. You might need some assistance to hold the whole thing together.

10 Place the birds in a metal baking pan and lay ½ of the remaining bacon strips over the top.

11 Sprinkle with brown sugar for some intense flavor.

12 Place the birds in the oven for 45 minutes at the preheated 190°C (375°F). When the 45 minutes are up, take the birds out and let sit for 30 minutes.

STUFF THE PIG

00 Stuff your cooked birds into your pig and sew it shut. You'll probably need a thicker twine for this, as pigskin is tougher than bird skin. You will also probably need an extra set of hands to hold the pig shut while you sew. Use the remaining bacon-croissant stuffing to fill the gaps of the pig cavity.

MAKE THE DR PEPPER BUTTER BASTING SAUCE

00 Empty the Dr Pepper into a large pot.

01 Add 226 g (1 c/2 sticks) butter and heat until combined.

COOK THE PIG

00 Throw the pig on the smoker and cook according to its size and weight. For the ≈9 kg (≈20 lb) recommended, that's usually about 12 hours.

01 Baste with Dr Pepper sauce every 45 minutes. If you run out, make more.

02 Halfway through, cover the pig with the remaining bacon strips to make a coat of bacon "armor."

Now, serve it to your family or a whole bunch of bacon-horny sluts!

#3 THE NYC FOOD MARATHON: 26.2 DISHES IN 26 LOCATIONS IN 24 HOURS

"The body's not a temple. It's an amusement park."
—ANTHONY BOURDAIN

In my favorite food memoir, *Heat,* I highlighted close to 100 passages. Most were related to topics for further exploration, questions I needed answers to.

Six months later, only two passages remained mysteries. Both related to professional chefs who had gone on "food tours," eating at 15–30 restaurants in single days. One had done it for pleasure while in Italy, the other for research prior to opening his own joint in NYC.

I couldn't figure out the logistics. How is it possible to hit that many places? How could anyone eat that much food? Was it remotely plausible, or a literary exaggeration? I asked JZ to help me test-drive it.

I proposed an "NYC Food Marathon": 26.2 dishes, all at different places, in 24 hours. It was a nod to the 26.2 miles in a normal marathon, and we would walk the whole thing.

But which 26.2 dishes? To narrow it down, JZ asked more than 40 NYC chefs and foodie friends: "If it were your last day to live, what would you eat in NYC?" That created the starter list, which JZ honed down to items unique to (or iconic in) NYC. Needless to say, all of them had to be *amazing*. The locations also had to be close enough together that we could hit them by foot in a single day. For this reason, we focused on Manhattan.

On December 20, 2011, less than 24 hours after I'd tackled the 14,000+ calorie Vermonster, we did it. Like all first-time marathons, it was *brutal.*

Without a doubt, it was also totally worthwhile. We ended up eating 20+ *New York Times* stars from 9 a.m. to 3:23 a.m. In a footrace, that'd be slower than the bag lady pushing the broken grocery cart, but in a food marathon, 18 hours is an MVP hustle. The morning we started, JZ's partner and chef-owner at Riverpark, Sisha Ortuzar, texted: "I want reports every hour." He expected us to lose our lunch before lunch.

We didn't.

A meticulous plan, a minute-by-minute blueprint, was our savior. It's included in the next spread, with adjustments and notes in parentheses.

Seem like a lot of food? It wasn't. It was a freaking Godzilla-killing buttload of food.

To replicate our NYC Food Marathon (or a food marathon in your own city), which I totally encourage you to try, a few guidelines are mission critical. It's all worth saving up for. Think of the stories for the grandkids! Now the golden rules:

- Do this with a friend. It's 100 times more fun.

- Split everything (food quantities and cost). Our marathon cost about $550 total, but your mileage may vary.

- If you don't want to finish something, don't force yourself. This is supposed to be fun. Challenging? Of course. Nausea-inducing for days? No. JZ and I left quite a few bits unfinished, even though we tried to polish off anything that wasn't a complete gluten bomb. Pierogies were tough.

- Have backup plans in case of rain, which could be as simple as umbrellas, a tighter cluster of restaurants, or the budget for cab fare between 26 places.

- In all seriousness: Do not expect to get anything productive done in the subsequent 24 hours. It ain't gonna happen. Remember Lance Armstrong (freakin' Lance Armstrong) walking sideways downstairs after his first marathon? That's how your brain will feel.

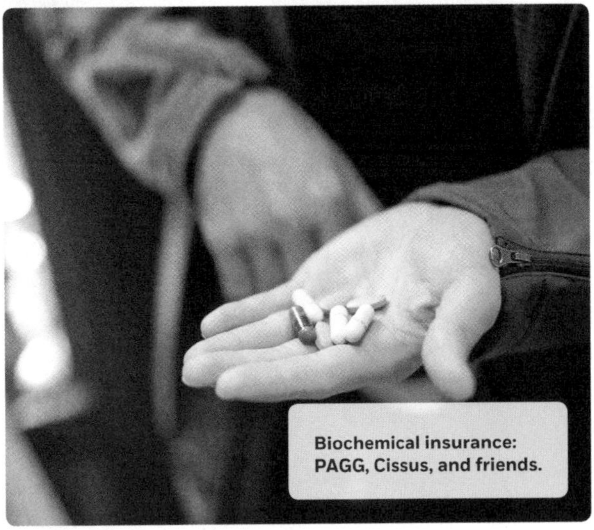

Biochemical insurance: PAGG, Cissus, and friends.

E 32ND ST
E 30TH ST
W 29TH ST
9TH AVE
8TH AVE
7TH AVE
6TH AVE
4TH AVE
5TH AVE
MADISON AVE
PARK AVE
LEXINGTON AVE
3RD AVE
2ND AVE
1ST AVE
19
W 25TH ST
20
W 24TH ST
W 23RD ST
E 23RD ST
W 22TH ST
W 21ST ST
FDR DR
12
21
W 20TH ST
W 19TH ST
13
11
W 18TH ST
W 17TH ST
W 16TH ST
W 15TH ST
W 14TH ST
E 14TH ST
W 13TH ST
HUDSON ST
16
24
W 12TH ST
E 12TH ST
7
3
9
W 10TH ST
E 10TH ST
10
WAVERLY ST
15
25
2
E 9T
W 8TH ST
ST MARK'S PL
6
17
14
E 7T
18
1
26
E 10TH ST
E 5T
BROADWAY
BOWERY
25B
E 3R
WEST ST
5
W HOUSTON ST
ALLEN ST
ESSEX ST
SULLIVAN ST
23
WILLIAMSBURG
8
DELANCEY ST
BROOME ST
4
GRAND ST
CANAL ST
CHURCH ST
MANHATTAN BRIDGE
WORTH ST
22

NYC FOOD MARATHON

ARRIVAL	EAT	DEPART	RESTAURANT	DISH
9:00 AM	9:05	9:15	1. ABRAÇO 86 East 7th Street	**Cortado and egg sandwich with pickled beets, and olive cookies** They were out of egg sandwiches, so we had cortado and bought olive cookies to save for our last 0.2 meal of the 26.2.
9:17 AM	9:27	9:42	2. CAFÉ MOGADOR 101 Saint Marks Place	**Haloumi and shakshuka**
9:45 AM	9:53	9:59	3. TARALLUCCI E VINO 163 1st Avenue	**Almond croissant**
10:20 AM	10:25	10:30	4. DOUGHNUT PLANT 379 Grand Street	**Coconut cream and carrot cake doughnuts**
10:45 AM	10:53	11:04	5. RUSS & DAUGHTERS 179 East Houston Street	**Belly lox on an everything bagel with capers, tomatoes, and onions** The bagel with lox truly saved us. We couldn't have done another sweet dish, and the salty wonder of the cream cheese with salmon offered the taste-bud contrast we needed to continue.
11:14 AM	11:24	11:34	6. 'WICHCRAFT 60 East 8th Street	**Beer-braised beef brisket with pickled vegetables and cheddar on ciabatta** We took the top slice of bread off of our sandwiches to treat them like tartines, open-faced French sandwiches. I wanted to minimize gluten-loading too early in the game.
11:44 AM	11:49	11:54	7. LIQUITERIA 170 2nd Avenue	**All Greens smoothie** This provided both ginger for digestion/force-feeding and a small amount of fructose to help prevent enormous blood sugar swings. I drank half and saved the rest for later.
12:09 PM	12:14	12:29	8. COCORON 61 Delancey Street	**Pork kimchi soba and green tea**
12:44 PM	12:49	1:04	9. MOMOFUKU 171 1st Avenue	**Pork buns** This is where I said to JZ, "I think I burned my mouth at the last soba place," to which he rightly responded, "That's like getting a hangnail at mile four." He was right. Taking stock of the rest of my body, I noticed another problem: "Uh-oh. I dropped two of my pills." I had brought nine capsules of anti-obesity cissus quadrangularis (CQ) and 6 g L-lysine (an immune system hedge), all to be taken in three divided doses during our race.
1:11 PM	1:16	1:26	10. TAIM 222 Waverly Place	**Sabich sandwich**
1:46 PM	1:56	2:06	11. ABC KITCHEN 35 East 18th Street	**Kabocha squash toast, chicken liver toast, cheeseburger with fries, and roasted Jerusalem artichokes** One of the biggest challenges of doing a food marathon with JZ was that most of the chefs and managers know him, so free dishes came out. This happened at ABC, one of my favorite spots (chef Dan Kluger trained JZ in his first job). I felt a second wind and sprinted through two bread dishes—"Ah, feeling light!" I said, smirking at JZ—and then I dove headfirst into the shallow end. This was my first sensation of "bonking." In real marathons, this hitting the wall is associated with running out of stored glycogen, a carbohydrate. In food marathons, "bonking" is the opposite, something like insulin intoxication: stuffing too many carbohydrates in your maw.
2:26 PM	2:36	3:01	12. CRAFTBAR 900 Broadway	**Veal ricotta meatballs and two glasses of wine** A Dolcetto d'Alba 2009 and an Elena Walch Lagrein 2009.
3:04 PM	3:09	3:14	13. CITY BAKERY 3 West 18th Street	**Pretzel croissant** Right on the tail of the Vermonster, there was no way I could even taste chocolate and peanut butter ice cream without puking, so we scratched our original plan to get ice cream at Sundaes & Cones. Then we took a 20-minute nap at JZ's apartment and did GLUT-4 exercises. Sadly, 10 minutes after entering comatose bliss, a dog walker came banging through the door and started yelling, "Abbey, sit! Abbey, sit! Abbey, sit!" at JZ's pit bull/dachshund mix. The dog defiantly freaked out instead, and nap time was concluded. With a sigh, I finished our brief time-out with 40 airsquats and 40 wall presses, both designed to increase recruitment of GLUT-4 receptors in muscle tissue.

NYC FOOD MARATHON (CONTINUED)

ARRIVAL	EAT	DEPART	RESTAURANT	DISH
3:29 PM	3:39	3:49	14. **PORCHETTA** 110 East 7th Street	**Porchetta plate with white beans and sautéed kale**
3:56 PM	4:06	4:21	15. **GRAFFITI** 224 East 10th Street	**Hummus-and-zucchini pizza**
4:26 PM	4:36	4:51	16. **HEARTH** 403 East 12th Street	**Ribollita, autumn vegetable salad with whipped ricotta, cotechino with lentils, braised rabbit with olives, and a glass of Colli Orientali del Friuli** Marco, a good friend of JZ's whom I love to death, decided to pull a Tanya Harding here. He's a mischievous one. "Oh, so you want a tasting?" Out came four dishes for each of us. "And you can't leave without trying.... Just a little bit. Hold on...." It was incredible, and he knew we'd eat it all. This little side-gorge was like stopping in the middle of a real marathon to do 100-meter sprints for 10 minutes before continuing.
5:16 PM	5:21	5:36	17. **STAGE** 128 Second Avenue	**Fried pierogis with sautéed onions**
5:43 PM	5:48	6:09	18. **PODUNK** 231 East 5th Street	**Cupcake and a chocolate-chip cookie** At this point, JZ did not feel well and couldn't finish his cookie. I'm proud to report that I ate all of the cookies.
6:18 PM	6:28	6:48	19. **RIVERPARK** 450 East 29th Street	**Avocado-and-hamachi salad and Chilean bitters (for digestion)** I finished off the second half of the Liquiteria ginger greens at this point.
7:08 PM	7:23	7:53	20. **ELEVEN MADISON PARK** 11 Madison Avenue	**Chemex coffee, venison loin with brussels sprouts, and a glass of Saint-Emilion Grand Cru**
7:58 PM	8:08	9:08	21. **CRAFT** 43 East 19th Street	**Braised short ribs, butternut squash puree, and a glass of Domaine Vincent Paris Cornas Granit 60** All delicious, in part because of the decadent sauces. I nicknamed the butternut squash "butter, not squash."
9:25 PM	9:35	9:55	22. **BRUSHSTROKE** 30 Hudson Street	**Your choice cocktail, sencha, and chawan-mushi (steamed egg custard)** Brushstroke treated me to the best chawan-mushi I've ever had. The book-lined walls of the far-right bar are incredible, and the food and drink are even better. The sencha, a strong green tea, was consumed first for inhibition of fat-storage and better recruitment of GLUT-4 receptors in muscle cells. Then, we went for the house-made ginger ale with shochu.
10:15 PM	10:30	10:50	23. **BLUE RIBBON** 97 Sullivan Street	**Bone marrow with oxtail ragout, half-dozen oysters, and a Brooklyn lager** Anything tastes amazing if you're drunk and hungry. It's quite another thing if you've had 24 meals sober and something tastes incredible. That was this dish. Truth be told, JZ and I expected it to be the final nail in the coffin.
11:00 PM	11:10	12:00 AM	24. **TERROIR** 413 East 12th Street	**Pork blade steak with arugula salad and a glass of 2009 Solane Santi Valpolicella**
12:30 AM	12:35	12:45	25. **SOUTH BROOKLYN PIZZA** 122 1st Avenue	**Slice of pepperoni pizza (alternate location 25B: Joe's Pizza)**
1:00 AM	1:15	3:20	26. **EMPLOYEES ONLY** 510 Hudson Street and	**Cocktails, including two Ginger Smashes** With one of the coolest logos and bartenders I'd ever met (Bratislav from Serbia), this was the perfect place to cross the finish line.
			26.2.	**Leftover olive cookie from Abraço**

DOUGHNUT PLANT
NEW YORK CITY
HOURS
DOUGHNUT PLANT
NEW YORK CITY

Crossing the finish line and polishing off the last 0.2 miles.

Pro

The Professional

Hearth and Alinea restaurants provided two of the best meals of my life, bar none.

But which should the ambitious emulate? Well, which is better: a tuxedo or a summer linen suit? It depends on what type of evening you have planned, of course. The same is true with food.

Alinea offers a near-transcendental experience. It was one of the most surreal evenings imaginable. Everyone should go there at least once, budget allowing, and it will blow your mind. But would I go there five days a week? No. It would defeat the magic, make me immune to the wonder. In NYC, however, I could easily have dinner at Hearth three or four nights a week for the rest of my life.

Alinea does not aspire to be Hearth, and Hearth does not aspire to be Alinea. So forget about either/or. Forget about Michelin stars and the like. The real question is: what makes someone a true "professional" in any field? In other words, what do the best have in common? To answer this, **PRO is split into three sections:**

"Classics"—First, we'll cover timeless dishes that embody near-universal principles. These are the must-haves you're missing. It's also time for the training wheels to come off. There is no more separation of prep and pickup, as you will need to learn to read (and mentally reformat) "standard" recipes after you graduate from this book.

"Avant-Garde"—Second, we'll push the envelope on everything. I mean EVERYTHING. This is a creative rite of passage.

"DragonForce Chaconne"—Last, we have the grand finale . . . a near-impossible recipe. Don't miss it. It's a monster.

EXIT

A TALE OF TWO CITIES: NEW YORK

> "Bite your teeth into the ass of life."
> —PASCAL, *BIG NIGHT*

"It's really assy, right?"

"Grassy?" I asked.

"No . . . *assy*," Marco repeated loudly, over the bustle of the bar.

It was true. The red wine that Paul Grieco, Marco's partner and master sommelier, had handed me smelled just like a barn. The hints of wet horse ass were unmistakable. This excited me for three reasons: the Chinon (Bernard Baudry, 2010, Loire Valley) was the best cabernet franc I'd ever had; I'd finally found a wine descriptor I could understand; and I'm very fond of ass in general.

Marco Canora is co-owner and executive chef of the James Beard Award–nominated Hearth, where we now stood, just inside the entrance. He's also executive chef and partner of Terroir Wine Bar. Prior to striking out on his own, he held various positions at Gramercy Tavern and the famed Cibreo in Florence, Italy. He was Tom Colicchio's right-hand man as original chef of Craft restaurant, which won a James Beard Award for Best New Restaurant during his tenure.

By the end of the evening, I concluded what many others had: Hearth is the most underrated restaurant in all of New York City.[1]

THE MANTRA

"Cooking is not hard. Cooking is *not* hard."

Marco repeated this five times during our evening together. "I feel like I've pulled the wool over everyone's eyes as a 'successful chef in New York City.' Anyone could do this."

"C'mon," I said as I pointed to my vegetable salad, which was ethereal and juicy (not an adjective I use for salads), easily one of the best salads of my life.

He laughed and waved a hand dismissively. "People say, 'Oh, my God! This is amazing!' Just dress it while the vegetables are warm—it all soaks in. Pour the oil on after the red wine vinegar, and add salt and pepper. Anyone could do this."

1 This is saying a lot in a city with 24,000 restaurants.

Oil *after* the vinegar? Why?

Marco explained, "If you put the oil on first, it deflects the vinegar into the bottom of the dish, where it pools."

JAPANESE TUSCANS: WHEN SIMPLICITY WORKS

Two hours into my meal (I ordered everything on the menu), I asked to see Marco's knife collection. I'd heard about it through the grapevine.

Nearly all of his blades are Japanese, which led us to a discussion of Korin Trading Co. (his favorite knife shop) and Japanese cuisine.

"The Tuscans and the Japanese are dead similar: seasonality, a 'less is more' mentality, simplicity, letting ingredients speak for themselves, and, of course, they're both umami focused. The Tuscans use tomato paste, anchovies, Parmesan; the Japanese use soy and dashi."

Marco studied both together as a result. "You should try nepitella, a type of mint with hints of oregano flavor. But for beef cheeks, you should visit the NoHo Japanese butcher."

In mid-sentence, he heard something through the chaos—perhaps the crackling of duck skin getting overcooked or the crunch of a dull knife on vegetables—and disappeared around the pass to tune the orchestra. Not unlike fine music, fine dining needs to be unerringly consistent. "Yes, Chef!" yelled a member of his brigade, responding to orders. "Yes, sir!" shouted another as flames licked at her sleeves. One of the line cooks confirmed that the olive oil poach, a tub of olive oil inside a larger heated tub of water, was still at exactly 140°F. Black steel pans clanged everywhere.

Marco calmly plated another perfect dish, and his tiny team proceeded to serve 160 people in the next 90 minutes.

As things wound down around 2 a.m., I polished off my never-ending glass of wine. Over what Marco later referred to as "The 4-Hour Dinner," we had demolished a small bodega full of bottles. The entire affair had started at 8:30 p.m., so it was technically the 5½-hour dinner.

I spent all of that time marveling at Marco's attention to detail.

Making perfect roast chicken might *seem* simple. Simple like a diagram of a Michael Jordan free throw. But easy? Hitting 100 out of 100 foul shots in competition? Making 50 perfect chickens in a night? That's another story. Marco saw me furrowing my brow and repeated yet again, "It's not hard, and it's delicious, and you'll trick all of your friends into thinking you're an amazing chef."

Hearth

CSI Marco preparing his whole roasted red snapper.

THE CLASSICS

> "I had to spend countless hours, above and beyond the basic time, to try and perfect the fundamentals."
>
> —JULIUS "DR. J" ERVING, 11-TIME NBA ALL-STAR

In modern break dancing, feats of strength called "power moves" are all the rage. Sadly, aspiring pros sometimes let Olympic gymnastics *replace* rhythm. It ceases to be dancing, and their careers are a flash in the pan. In contrast, the best of the best, those who win competitions like Red Bull BC One, master the fundamentals—footwork matched to music—and *complement* rhythm with jaw-dropping acrobatics.

In the world of cooking, Marco is in the latter category.

Before going avant-garde, we need to get your fundamentals up to snuff. If you can make Vietnamese venison burgers, for God's sake, you can't be left slack-jawed when someone asks you about roasted chicken. Moreover, if you're a hydrocolloid one-trick pony, your cooking will have no soul.

There are certain dishes and techniques no self-respecting cook should be without. In defining these "classics," I deferred to a cadre of incredible chefs, starting with Marco. Our goal is not to be exhaustive (for that, refer to books like *La Varenne Pratique*), but rather to fill *a few* important gaps in your repertoire.

To that end, we'll start where thousands of dishes start: *soffritto*

Hearth

First Course

SUMMER LETTUCES AND VEGETABLES
Celery, Radish, String Beans, Cherry Tomatoes, Cucumber
Red Wine Vinaigrette 12.

WARM VEGETABLE SALAD
Beans, Summer Squash, Red Onion, Cauliflower, Potato 12.

ARUGULA AND FENNEL SALAD
White Anchovies, Bread Crumbs, Pickled Cipollini Onion 13.

BEET SALAD
Greek Yogurt, Sunflower Sprouts and Seeds, Herbs 13.

SUMMER TOMATO SALAD
Sicilian Tuna, Beans, Celery 13.

PHILADELPHIA BURRATA
Marinated Market Vegetables 15.

CHILLED ZUCCHINI SOUP
Basil, Parmesan, Pine Nuts 12.

GRILLED OCTOPUS
Fresh Cannellini Beans, Soffrito Crudo, Radicchio, Basil 16.

GRILLED QUAIL
Farro, Cucumber, Red Onion, Quail Egg, Tomato 15.

Put Yourself in Our Hands

Seven Course Tour of the Menu 76.

We kindly request the participation of the entire table for the tasting menu.

Dishes to Share

HOUSE-MADE CHARCUTERIE
Cured Duck Breast, Lardo, Mortadella, Lonza,
Chicken Liver Paté, Duck Rillette, Coppa, Rabbit Ballotine
Finocchietti, Pickled Vegetables, Beer Mustard 40.

~~~

WHOLE ROASTED FISH OF THE DAY
Roasted Potatoes, Fennel, Red Onion 56.

~~~

ROASTED FLATTENED ORGANIC CHICKEN
Braised Romano Beans 58.

~~~

20oz DRY-AGED SIRLOIN
Creamed Swiss Chard 86.

Main Course

Fish

ROASTED SCOTTISH SALMON
Freekeh, String Beans, Pickled Garlic Scape,
Trout Roe, Mint 29.

ROASTED WILD TILEFISH AND PRAWNS
Corn, Zucchini, Tomatoes, Tarragon 30.

OLIVE-OIL POACHED EAST COAST SWORDFISH
Smoked Clams, Fennel, Artichokes, Parsley 34.

Meat

ROASTED HAMPSHIRE PORK CHOP
Swiss Chard Gnudi, House-Smoked Bacon, Spring Onion 32.

WASHUGYU BEEF CHEEKS
Grilled Radicchio, Dandelion Greens, Turnips, Radishes 29.

VEAL AND RICOTTA MEATBALLS
House-Made Spaghetti 28.

Pasta

PAPPARDELLE
Roast Pork, Tuscan Kale 28.

CANESTRI ALLA NORMA
San Marzano Tomato, Eggplant, Ricotta Salata 28.

Sides

Anson Mills Polenta 7.
Gnocchi 10.
Hen Of The Woods 12.
Sautéed Greens 10.
Braised Romano Beans 11.
Creamed Swiss Chard 9.

Supporting local farmers and knowing where our food comes from has always been important at Hearth.

If you would like to learn more about where we get our ingredients, turn the page and have a look.

Summer of Riesling Menu September 2nd, 2011

Chef Marco Canora
Chef de Cuisine George Kaden
Sous Chef Brian Moxey

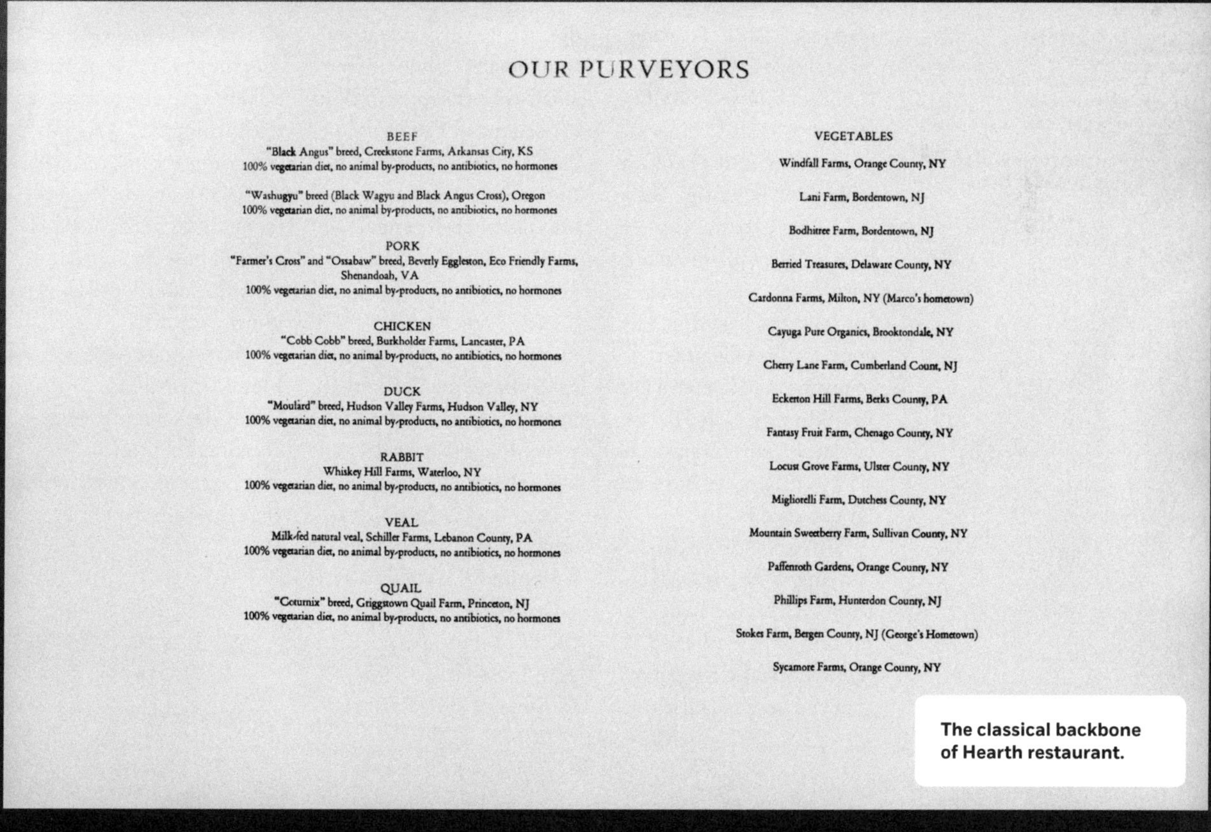

OUR PURVEYORS

BEEF
"Black Angus" breed, Creekstone Farms, Arkansas City, KS
100% vegetarian diet, no animal by-products, no antibiotics, no hormones

"Washugyu" breed (Black Wagyu and Black Angus Cross), Oregon
100% vegetarian diet, no animal by-products, no antibiotics, no hormones

PORK
"Farmer's Cross" and "Ossabaw" breed, Beverly Eggleston, Eco Friendly Farms, Shenandoah, VA
100% vegetarian diet, no animal by-products, no antibiotics, no hormones

CHICKEN
"Cobb Cobb" breed, Burkholder Farms, Lancaster, PA
100% vegetarian diet, no animal by-products, no antibiotics, no hormones

DUCK
"Moulard" breed, Hudson Valley Farms, Hudson Valley, NY
100% vegetarian diet, no animal by-products, no antibiotics, no hormones

RABBIT
Whiskey Hill Farms, Waterloo, NY
100% vegetarian diet, no animal by-products, no antibiotics, no hormones

VEAL
Milk-fed natural veal, Schiller Farms, Lebanon County, PA
100% vegetarian diet, no animal by-products, no antibiotics, no hormones

QUAIL
"Coturnix" breed, Griggstown Quail Farm, Princeton, NJ
100% vegetarian diet, no animal by-products, no antibiotics, no hormones

VEGETABLES

Windfall Farms, Orange County, NY

Lani Farm, Bordentown, NJ

Bodhitree Farm, Bordentown, NJ

Berried Treasures, Delaware County, NY

Cardonna Farms, Milton, NY (Marco's hometown)

Cayuga Pure Organics, Brooktondale, NY

Cherry Lane Farm, Cumberland Count, NJ

Eckerton Hill Farms, Berks County, PA

Fantasy Fruit Farm, Chenago County, NY

Locust Grove Farms, Ulster County, NY

Migliorelli Farm, Dutchess County, NY

Mountain Sweetberry Farm, Sullivan County, NY

Paffenroth Gardens, Orange County, NY

Phillips Farm, Hunterdon County, NJ

Stokes Farm, Bergen County, NJ (George's Hometown)

Sycamore Farms, Orange County, NY

The classical backbone of Hearth restaurant.
~~~

The Classics

LESSON

BUILDING FLAVOR

SOFFRITTO

INSPIRED BY

Marco Canora

SHORTHAND

Heat 4T oil till shimmering. Sauté 2c diced onion, 1c diced celery & carrot 8-10min till light brown. Refrigerate up to 1 week.

HANDS-ON TIME

20 minutes

TOTAL TIME

20 minutes

GEAR

- Knife and cutting board
- Optional: Food processor or immersion blender with chopper attachment
- Finished or raw cast-iron skillet or Dutch oven
- Silicone spatula

"*Soffritto* is something you need to understand. It's the key to making things taste delicious."

—CHEF MARCO CANORA

INGREDIENTS	TO MAKE 1½ CUPS
Red onion, diced	2 c (320 g), ≈1 onion
Carrots, diced	1 c (130 g), ≈3 carrots
Celery, diced	1 c (100 g), ≈2 large ribs
Olive oil	4 T
Kosher salt	1 pinch

I first met Walter Isaacson on a terrace at the Aspen Institute, where he is CEO. He is also a famed biographer of Einstein, Franklin, and—most recently—Steve Jobs. Just two months before Jobs's unfortunate passing, we were discussing food and learning. The conversation meandered to my fascination with Ben Franklin, which led to the subject of experimentation. Walter, originally from New Orleans, said:

"In New Orleans, there's a saying, 'First, you make a roux.'" This has two meanings, he explained. Metaphorically, it means that you need to learn by doing. Literally, it means that most of Creole cuisine starts with the roux, or flour cooked in fat. The standard addition, he added, is the "holy trinity": celery, onions, and bell peppers.

Hearing this was déjà vu all over again.

The French have *mirepoix* (onions, carrots, celery), and the Italians have *soffritto*, which is 50% red onion, 25% carrots, and 25% celery. (The 2:1:1 ratio is key.) Why is the onions-and-celery combination so common? As Marco observed: "If you look at the most typical dishes in popular cuisines—Thai, Chinese, Middle Eastern, and beyond—you realize that they're fundamentally all the same: flavoring fats with aromatics." Aromatics, including onions, carrots, and celery, are vegetables (sometimes herbs) used as a flavor base for something else. They add depth to almost any dish.

Here, we'll create a blond *soffritto* base. *Soffritto* can be darkened by longer cooking, but blond is the starting point and therefore the most important.

00 Finely mince the 2 c (320 g) onion, 1 c (130 g) carrots, and 1 c (100 g) celery. The smaller the vegetable cuts, the better the *soffritto* will taste. Marco uses a food processor for the carrots and celery but cuts the onions by hand. Unless your processor's blades are very sharp, it'll make a juicy mess of onions.

01 In a heavy skillet or Dutch oven, heat the 4 T oil over medium-high heat until it shimmers. Add the onion, carrots, and celery, and a pinch of salt.

02 Cook, stirring frequently with a silicone spatula, until lightly and evenly browned, 8–10 minutes. If the mixture starts to brown too quickly (it should gradually turn golden, not take on specks of black), lower the heat a bit and keep stirring. The vegetables in *soffritto* should sizzle as they lightly fry, hence the name *soffritto*. Add more oil if necessary.

03 Scrape the *soffritto* into a clean container, let cool, and refrigerate, covered, for up to 1 week. If you want to keep it on hand in the fridge for up to 2 weeks, cover it with oil.

Blond
Amber
Dark

The three shades of *soffritto*. Blond *soffrittos* are great for summer dishes, like fish stews; amber-colored are for fall and early spring dishes, such as braised lamb shanks (Osso "Buko"!); and dark are for cold winter days, when only a meat ragu will do.

LESSON

DOING THINGS "WELL"

HELICOPTER-BLADE PEA SOUP

SHORTHAND

Boil 1lb frozen peas in 3c H_2O 1min (fresh 3-4min). Blend w 1½c cooking water & ½t salt 10min. Sieve into saucepan. Reheat or chill 4hr to serve cold.

HANDS-ON TIME

30 minutes

TOTAL TIME

30 minutes

GEAR

- Saucepan
- Very-fine-mesh sieve, or colander and cheesecloth or chinois
- Bowl
- Heavy-duty blender, like a Vitamix (see page 124)
- Silicone spatula

Nigel: "What we do is, if we need that extra push over the cliff, you know what we do?"
Marty: "Put it up to 11."
Nigel: "Eleven. Exactly. One louder."

—*THIS IS SPIÑAL TAP*

INGREDIENTS	TO SERVE 2 OR 3, OR MORE AS AN HORS D'OEUVRE
Good-quality frozen baby peas or *very* fresh English peas, shelled	**1 lb (455 g)**
Salt	**½ t salt, plus more to taste**
OPTIONAL	
Prosciutto, very thinly sliced	**2 slices**

If you open the French Laundry or Alinea cookbooks, you will see soup recipes with phrases like the following:

"Blend well and pass through a chinois."

If you try the recipe, it probably won't work. But I assure you that the book isn't wrong, and you aren't a knuckle-dragger. The problem lies in how you define *well*. To lay folks, blending "well" means using a Waring bar blender with 12 buttons for things like "blend," "crush," and so on, blitzing the food for 30 seconds on high. This leaves the puree resembling sand instead of pudding.

In recipe form, here's how to fix things.

00 In a saucepan, bring 3 c (710 ml) water to a boil. Add the 1 lb (455 g) peas, cover, and bring back to a boil. Boil frozen peas for 1 minute. Boil fresh peas 3–4 minutes, until tender but still bright green. Drain in a sieve set over a bowl; reserve the cooking liquid.

01 Put the peas and ½ t salt in a heavy-duty blender with 1½ c (355 ml) of the cooking water. Then *blend*. The rule of thumb at Alinea is, "If you think you've blended enough, blend it for another 5 minutes." That's right: 5–10 minutes of blending with an outboard motor of a machine. This is the crucial detail that will make your guests ask you, "Did you use cream or chicken stock in this?" Your answer: "Nope, I just went ape-shit at 10,000 rpm for 10 minutes." People won't believe you.

02 But you're not done. At this point, you will have soft baby food. You need to refine it by straining: using a silicone spatula, push the puree back into the saucepan through a very-fine-mesh sieve, or a colander lined with cheesecloth or a chinois. Left behind, you'll have a grainy mass of pea solids that has about the consistency of cookie dough,[2] and the soup in the saucepan will be perfectly smooth and silky. Reheat over low heat, season with more salt if necessary, and serve. Alternatively, refrigerate for at least 4 hours and serve chilled.

Optional: This soup benefits from (but by no means needs) a crisp garnish of fried prosciutto. Cut 2 slices crosswise in half. Heat about ¼" (0.6 cm) grapeseed oil in a heavy saucepan or skillet over medium-high heat until faint signs of smoking. Add the prosciutto and cook, turning with tongs, until lightly browned, 1–2 minutes; the prosciutto will shrink and wrinkle in the oil. Remove to paper towels to drain, then set (or crumble) a piece atop each serving of soup.

The moral of the story: Making better food often requires exaggerating a step, not adding more ingredients. The fancier the restaurant, the more specialized the restaurant, the more you can assume they're doing something *well*.

2 You can use the solids as ravioli filling or combine them with goat cheese for the ultimate crostini topping.

The Classics

LESSON

FRYING

BEAR FAT (OR NOT) FRIES

SHORTHAND

Soak overnight: 4 sliced potatoes, 1T vinegar, 3-finger pinch salt. Pat dry; fry as desired. Serve w sea salt.

HANDS-ON TIME

30 minutes

TOTAL TIME

30 minutes, plus 30 minutes or overnight soaking

GEAR

- Star Peeler
- Knife and cutting board
- Large mixing bowl
- Folded paper bag (ideal) or paper towels for draining
- Cast-iron Dutch oven
- Probe or candy thermometer (good enough) or IR (infrared) thermometer (ideal)
- Peltex, slotted spoon, or mini sieve, such as the OXO 3" or a Chinese-style "spider" (wide-wire strainer)

"I like children—fried."

—W.C. FIELDS, ACTOR AND COMEDIAN

INGREDIENTS	TO SERVE 4
Russet potatoes or sweet potatoes, my fave	**4**
Salt	**3-finger pinch**
Vinegar	**1 T**
Bear fat, duck fat[3], beef tallow, or other (see recipe)	**Enough to cover potatoes**
Maldon sea salt	**To taste**

BEAR OIL

Durian is a fruit so horribly smelly that it is illegal in Singapore to eat it on subways. Its odor can be described as rotten onions plus gym socks. But it *is* delicious. Bear fat is similar. It's horrible to the nose and absolutely amazing in the right foods, such as fries.

If you don't have a Bear-Mart near your home, you can use another "cheat" from the pros: duck fat.

Or how about beef tallow? It's what McDonald's used until 1990. (A subsequent lawsuit brought to light that their fries still contain "natural beef flavor.")

If you'd like to avoid animal fats altogether, go for coconut oil or traditional canola oil. Not all fats are safe at frying temperatures, so don't roll the dice.

Here we'll be frying the potatoes twice, first at a

3 Rendered (melted, strained, and cooled) duck fat is available from good butchers or in cans in specialty food shops. Ditto on beef tallow.

lower temperature to cook the inside, then at a higher temperature to create a crisp, golden exterior.

00 Peel the 4 potatoes and cut into long ¼" (0.6-cm) sticks. Cover with cold water in a large bowl and stir in the 3-finger pinch of kosher salt and 1 T vinegar. Soak for at least 30 minutes. I soak overnight.

01 Drain, then dry the potatoes as thoroughly as possible. Set out a folded paper bag or several layers of paper towels near the stove top.

02 In the cast-iron Dutch oven, bring the fat or oil to 320°F (160°C) using a probe or candy thermometer. Carefully add the potatoes and stir gently with the Peltex to separate them. (If you're using bear fat, don't worry: it will taste much better than it smells.)

Note: If you're using a stove top, you will very likely overshoot temperature targets. It can be hard to fine-tune with oil. Two suggestions: (1) Use a ring of aluminum foil to elevate your pot above the burner, which will make your "low" setting lower and give you better control. (2) For the second frying, put a few popcorn kernels in the oil; they pop at around 360°F (182°C) and offer a good cue.

Things can get splatter-ific if you haven't dried the food properly. If this happens, minimize oil shrapnel by flipping a colander upside-down over the pot as a make-shift splatter guard.

03 Remove the fries when they're half-cooked, still pale, and a little floppy, 7–10 minutes. I typically use my Peltex to remove fried goodies, but you can also use a handheld mini-strainer (like the OXO 3"), or a Chinese "spider." Spread the fries out on the paper bag or towels to drain.

04 Next, heat the oil up to 360°F (182°C). Return the fries to the oil and cook until golden brown, 3–4 minutes. Remove again to the paper bag or towels.

05 Sprinkle with Maldon sea salt and let cool to an edible temperature.

06 Slather the bounty all over your hands and face.

Variations:

Cold Fusion Fries

To avoid splattering and draining altogether, you can use the "cold fat"method, which Joël Robuchon popularized. This involves gradual heating and allows you to use less fat and reuse it afterward. The lower temperatures don't damage fatty-acid chains as higher temps do. The only downside is that it takes far longer, more than an hour.

1. Put the potatoes in the Dutch oven and pour in enough oil to cover them.

2. Place over medium-low heat and cook until the potatoes are very tender, about 45 minutes. (You'll see bubbles after about 15 minutes, but not the splattering kind.) Raise the heat to medium and cook, stirring gently with the Peltex if you'd like, until the fries are nicely browned, another 15–30 minutes. Remove from the oil, letting as much of the oil drain back into the pot as possible, then spread out on the paper bag to drain.

3. Season while hot with salt, and serve immediately, alone or with condiments (below).

Unfried Fries

If frying in animal fat ain't your thang, baked fries are your friend. Here's a recipe I like. I always use sweet potatoes:

1. Preheat the oven to 400°F (200°C). Cut the potatoes into thin wedges.

2. Coat all slices with olive oil (or other oil) and spread out on a baking sheet. Since I'm a piggy who eats a lot of wedges, I save time by putting olive oil in a spray bottle: Lay out wedges, spray all, flip them, spray again. My model is the Orka oil mister, but the more common Misto will also work nicely.

3. Thirty minutes in the oven and you're done.

4. Dip in coconut oil or coat with truffle oil, sprinkle on salt, and eat.

For even more flavor: Create a mixture of 2–3 T EVOO, 2 t cumin (this is the key), 2 t cayenne pepper, 1 t cinnamon (just remember the "3 Cs"), and/or garlic powder. Dunk each wedge before putting on the baking sheet, or—my preference—put them on the baking sheet and paint this mixture on all of them.

Condiments

In addition to Maldon, I suggest trying the following sauces:

- Truffle oil
- Warm coconut oil for dipping (just microwave a small container)
- Garlic aioli (page 212)

The Classics

LESSON

THE LITMUS TEST

THE "HAREILLER" ROAST CHICKEN

INSPIRED BY

Marcella Hazan, Ruth Reichl, and Thomas Keller

SHORTHAND

450F 60min: Roast chicken stuffed w 5 sprigs thyme, 2 pierced lemons, 1T butter under breast skin till internal temp 165F. Remove from cast-iron, baste w juices. Rest 10-15min.

HANDS-ON TIME

20 minutes

TOTAL TIME

1 hour 30 minutes

GEAR

- Fork or paring knife
- Paper towels
- Cast-iron skillet
- Probe thermometer

"Once you understand the foundations of cooking—whatever kind you like, whether it's French or Italian or Japanese—you really don't need a cookbook anymore."

—CHEF THOMAS KELLER

INGREDIENTS	TO SERVE 4
Whole chicken	**3 lb (1.4 kg)**
Lemons, small	**2**
Ghee/butter or chicken fat (from inside the bird)	**2 T**
S+P	**To taste**
Thyme	**7 sprigs**
Garlic, peeled	**3 cloves**
OPTIONAL	
EVOO	**1 T**

Chefs' opinions about roast chicken are like mouth holes—everyone has one.

When the dust settled, I favored Marcella **HA**zan's method. It makes everything juicier than Serena Williams's buttocks. And yet, I wanted more, so I added influence from Ruth **REI**chl and Thomas Ke**LLER**. Thus was born the awkwardly named Hareiller Roast Chicken. As always, read the whole recipe before beginning.

00 Preheat your oven to 450°F (230°C). Leave the chicken on the counter for 30–60 minutes to temper.

01 Roll 2 lemons on the counter, and poke at least 20 holes in each using a fork or paring knife.

02 Dry the chicken completely with paper towels. If it steams in the oven, results will suffer.

Note: Josh Skenes of Saison suggests keeping your chicken in the fridge for 1 week before cooking, as almost all poultry is wet-packed and doesn't roast properly. Straight from the store, the chicken simply has too much moisture in the skin to make it super crispy.

03 If using ghee or butter, get out 2 T and put it on a paper towel. If using chicken fat, remove extra fat from inside the chicken and put to the side. Using chicken fat means one less ingredient for you to fuss with.

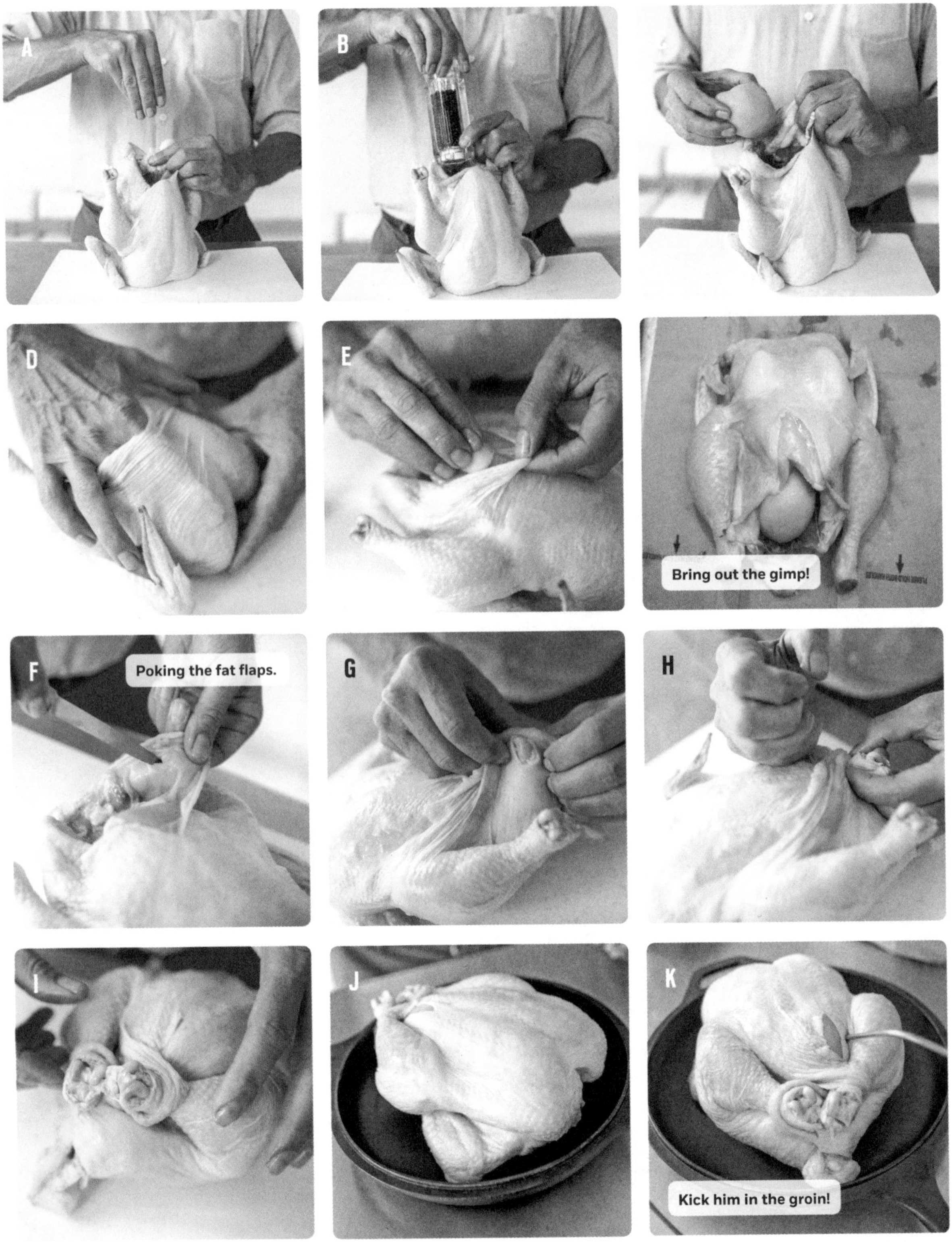
A
B
D
E
Bring out the gimp!
F
Poking the fat flaps.
G
H
I
J
K
Kick him in the groin!

04 Season the inside with S+P. Don't worry about getting chicken Ebola on the peppermill. Just clean it later.

05 Stuff the cavity: first add 1 lemon, then 5 sprigs of thyme, then 3 garlic cloves. The other lemon is last.[4]

06 Put 1T of ghee (or chicken fat) under the skin over each breast. If you're ambitious, you can mix chopped herbs into the ghee/fat. The mechanics: loosen the skin at the top of the cavity, then work your index and middle fingers underneath, after which you spread them. Tuck the pats under these pockets. The bird will now look something like the gimp from *Pulp Fiction.*

Did you know that *chikan* is Japanese for pervert? Well, now you do.

07 Next: truss the chicken.

Just kidding. That's too much work for me. Do what French butchers do instead: cut or poke little holes in the back fat flaps, then stick the legs through, crossing them.

08 Now put the chicken in the cast-iron skillet breast side up, tucking the wings under the body as best you can. Rain salt down on it like snow, which will help ensure a crisp skin. Use more than you think you should, and coat the entire bird. Keller likes the grains of salt to be visible on the skin when it's served. Give it a few (or many) twists of pepper; whatever you think is pretty.

Optional: Pour a little EVOO over the top.

09 Stick the probe in the groin and throw the chicken in the oven. Leave it alone for approximately 60 minutes (calculate for 20 minutes per 1 lb), until the probe hits 165°F (74°C). But "in the groin"? I always found that "probe in the leg" wording in cookbooks confusing, and it caused a lot of screw-ups. It should really read "in the groin": at the top of the crease made by the drumstick (see pic K).

10 Remove the chicken from the oven and move it to another platter (the cast-iron would continue to cook it).

11 Put the remaining 2 sprigs of thyme in the pan juices in the cast-iron. Take the lemons out of the cavity and squeeze the juice into this mixture. Stir. This is your sauce.

12 Let the chicken rest for 10–15 minutes uncovered.

13 **Optional:** Remove the breastbone. This will allow you to easily cut your chicken in half (and serve to 2 people) without hacking it into a machete'd mess. Personally, I just hack away.

14 Devour your Hareiller and develop strong opinions.

4 Some chefs think you could stuff a few socks in and get the job done. Why? Their argument: stuffing the cavity is not for flavor; it's to prevent the oven air from cooking the meat from the inside, which would lead to the muscle being cooked before the fat properly *renders*. My two cents: view this step as optional, but try it this time. Thomas Keller does not stuff his chicken. That said, using the lemons for sauce is enough reason to include them.

The Classics

LESSON

BROWN BUTTER

BROWN BUTTER PLANTAINS

SHORTHAND

Simmer 2 plantains (1" pieces), salted H2O 25-30min. Drain water, remove skins. Brown butter. Pour over plantains. Mash or stir.

HANDS-ON TIME

10 minutes

TOTAL TIME

40 minutes

GEAR

- Knife and cutting board
- Small saucepan
- Cast-iron Dutch oven
- Fork
- Colander
- Whisk (optional)

"Butter, butter, butter! Give me butter! Always butter!"

—CHEF FERNAND POINT

INGREDIENTS	TO SERVE 4
Large, ripe plantains	2 (about 1½ lb/680 g)
Unsalted butter, cut into tablespoon slices	4 T
Salt	To taste

Making brown butter, or *beurre noisette* (hazelnut butter), is an easy-to-execute technique for Frenchifying your food. It also allows you to indulge in perhaps the world's greatest "luxury fat." By cooking butter a little past the melting point, the milk solids separate out, fall to the bottom of the pan, brown, and give off a wonderfully nutty aroma and flavor.

My friend Gabe Luna introduced me to brown butter and claims it changed his life. It can be *that* good.

As a delivery vehicle, I've chosen the banana look-alikes I came to love in Panama: plantains. Go, go, gadget fast carbs!

00 Wash the plantains, cut off the ends, peel, and slice them 1" (2.5 cm) thick. To remove the peel, cut a slit down the length of the skin and peel it off. (Imagine cutting a roll of quarters down the side.)

01 Place the butter slices in a small saucepan on the stove top. Your white Aeternum is ideal. Leave the heat off for now.

02 Fill a separate cast-iron Dutch oven with water, add a couple pinches of salt, and bring to a boil over high heat. Add the sliced plantains, return to a boil, then reduce to a simmer for 25 to 30 minutes, until the plantains are softened. Check by piercing a piece with a fork. It should glide in easily.

03 Drain in the colander and return the plantains to the now empty pot to keep warm. Season with salt.

04 Make the brown butter in your saucepan: Turn the burner below the pan to medium. Do not move from this spot until your butter is ready. Stir or whisk the butter until it melts, foams up, the foam subsides, and *lightly* browned specks appear at the bottom of the pan, 2–3 minutes. This will give off a nutty aroma.

Note: Butter can go from browned to burned in a heartbeat. As soon as the *lightly* (critical word) browned specks show up, yank it off the heat.

If you burn your butter, you'll need to trash the batch and start over. To stage an intervention, a little splash of lemon juice will stop the cooking and save your precious liquid gold.

05 Remove from the heat and pour over the plantains. Mash together or stir it in. Serve immediately.

Variation: If you have an enameled cast-iron Dutch oven with a light interior (for spotting brown specks), you can use one pot for all of this.

LESSON

BASTING

BISTRO-STYLE BAVETTE STEAK

INSPIRED BY

Thomas Keller

SHORTHAND

Season/sear 10oz steak, 2t oil 2 min. Flip, top w ¼–½ stick butter, baste 5min. Flip, cook 2min, remove. + 1c sliced shallot 2min, + 1t minced thyme 3min. Serve over steak.

HANDS-ON TIME

30 minutes

TOTAL TIME

30 minutes, plus 1 hour for steak tempering

GEAR

- Knife and cutting board
- Cast-iron skillet

"One thing you can't do with babies . . . you can't give them steak."

—FLAVOR FLAV

BUTTER

INGREDIENTS	TO SERVE 2
Shallots, thinly sliced	1 c (160 g)
Minced thyme	1 t
Bavette (outside skirt) steak	10 oz (284 g)
S+P	To taste
Canola oil	A drizzle
Butter	¼–½ stick

Thomas Keller, founder of three-Michelin-star restaurants the French Laundry and Per Se, likes to start amateur chefs with the "outside skirt" (*bavette*) cut. Here is my shortened interpretation of his recipe, excluding the more involved *jus* (sauce, often from a base of pan drippings).

00 Thinly slice 1 c (160 g) shallots and mince[5] 1 t thyme, separately, and set aside.

01 Leave the steak at room temperature for at least 30 minutes—ideally an hour or more—to temper.

02 Season the steak with S+P all over.

03 Put a cast-iron skillet on high heat with a drizzle of canola oil. When the oil barely starts to smoke, toss on the meat.

5 Remember the visuals on page 165? The windshield wiper will work for this.

04 After 2 minutes or so, flip the steak over and put $\frac{1}{4}$–$\frac{1}{2}$ stick of butter on top. As the butter melts, baste the steak. (See sidebar, right.)

05 After 5 minutes on that side, flip to the first side for 2 minutes, then take it off heat and "rest" the meat on a cutting board or other surface.

06 As the steak is resting (for a total of 10 minutes), add the sliced shallots to the skillet and cook for 2 minutes. Turn the heat down to medium, add the thyme, and mix everything together (steak juices, butter, shallots, thyme). Cook for 3 minutes more.

07 Keep the sauce warm until the steak's 10 minutes are up, then spoon it all on top and serve, being sure to cut the steak *across* the grain.

HOW TO DO IT: Look at the top of your steak. The direction of the muscle fibers is called the "grain." Think of these fibers as a bundle of straws. To make the meat as chewable (and delicious) as possible, cut *across* the straws. If you cut *with* the straws, you and your guests need to gnaw, gnaw, and gnaw some more. The grain is easier to see on certain cuts, like *bavette*. Seeing the grain on rib eye is like divining with turtle shells, so don't sweat it.

HOW TO PAN-BASTE

Once the butter (or other fat) has melted but stopped bubbling, tilt the far side of the pan up.

Next, using a metal spoon, quickly flick the butter on top of the steak in small circles. Repeat for about a minute at a rapid pace, similar to the tempo of rapping your knuckles on a door to be let in. If you move too slowly, the butter won't stay hot enough to cook the meat from the top down.

This technique can be used with any protein. Here it is, demonstrated by chef Mark Garcia with fish:

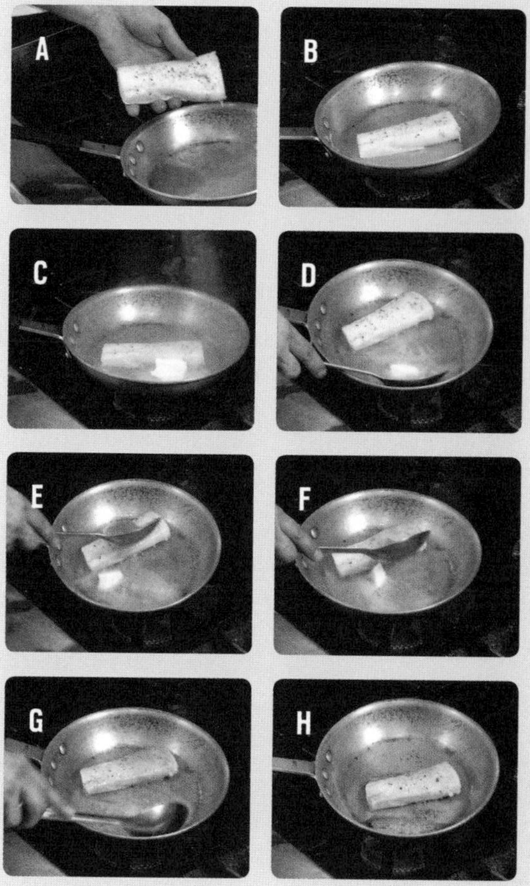
A
B
C
D
E
F
G
H

The Classics

LESSON

FRAGILE FOOD AT HIGH HEAT

FRENCH OMELET

SHORTHAND

Heat 1T EVOO med-high heat. Add 2 beaten eggs, stir rapidly till they pull together. Remove from heat, fold to one side, roll onto plate; S+P to taste.

HANDS-ON TIME

5 minutes

TOTAL TIME

5 minutes

GEAR

- Nonstick skillet
- Mixing bowl
- Fork
- Silicone spatula

A word to the wise: Don't use a fork on a nonstick pan; you'll ruin it. JZ destroyed my best nonstick this way. Stick with spatulas. And don't put egg in your cast-iron—eggs on cast-iron are like eggs on your carpet: a pain in the arse to clean.

"Be content to remember that those who can make omelets properly can do nothing else."

—HILAIRE BELLOC, WRITER AND HISTORIAN

INGREDIENTS	TO SERVE 1
Eggs	2 large
S+P	To taste
EVOO	1 T
OPTIONAL	
Chives, finely chopped	To taste

The French omelet is how many chefs measure other chefs. Can you cook eggs perfectly over real heat? Can you make something delicate while taming the inferno?

I made my first French omelet during cram school (page 78). Lady Luck was with me, and it turned out far better than I deserved. I begged JZ to e-mail a picture of it to my technical hero, Jacques Pépin, who'd taught JZ at the French Culinary Institute in NYC.

Now, to head off any chive grumbling. . .

The food elite might look down on me for elevating the lowly chive. But as overused as it was by '80s restaurants, it's underused by home cooks. Vibrantly green and simple to cut, it's beautiful on top of anything pale, such as eggs or a white fish.

OK, campaigning complete, here's *ze* French Omelet:

00 Heat a nonstick skillet over medium-high heat.

01 Beat the 2 eggs in a bowl with a fork until fully incorporated. No egg whites should be visible as strands.

02 When the skillet is hot, season the eggs with S+P. Done any sooner, the salt will break down the egg.

03 Drizzle 1 T EVOO in the skillet and coat it. Butter also works.

04 Pour the eggs into the skillet and keep them moving. Move the skillet back and forth by the handle (as if quickly sawing wood), and simultaneously stir rapidly with the spatula. The goal is to avoid large clumps (curds) of egg and prevent anything from browning. Keep it spread wide. Use the whole surface.

05 After the eggs cook for 2 minutes, keep the pan still for 10 seconds. Then remove from heat and delicately

A

B

C

D

E

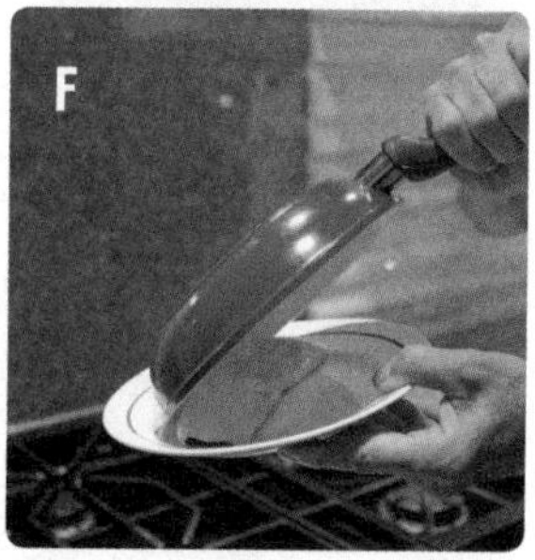
F

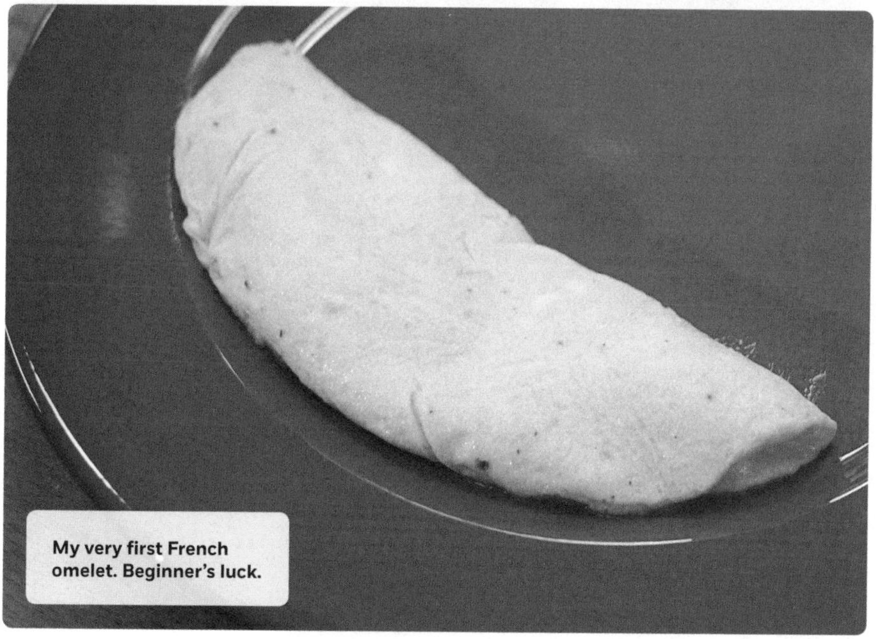

My very first French omelet. Beginner's luck.

Tamago Nori-Style Omelet

For a Japanese twist on the French omelet, try this simplified version of tamago nori rolls (sweet omelet rolled with nori seaweed). Peel and shred half of a thin burdock root and half of a medium carrot. In your nonstick skillet, heat 2 t EVOO over medium heat. Add the burdock, carrot, and 1 minced garlic clove and sauté until softened, about 3 minutes. (Think of this as Japanese *soffritto.*)

Season with a 1-finger pinch of salt and squeeze in a little lemon juice; stir and remove from the pan; wipe the pan out with a paper towel and set aside for the omelet. Beat the eggs for the omelet and add 1 t sugar, 1 t tamari, and 1 t white wine. Follow the instructions for making the French omelet; when it is partially cooked but still wet and just coming together, place a sheet of nori (cut into a circle to fit in the pan) on top. Top with a slice of lox if you like. Lay the burdock mixture over the half of the roll closest to you, roll as directed, but a bit tighter, onto a cutting board. Cut the omelet into 4 "rolls," plate with eggs on the outside, and serve.

run the spatula around the edges, to lift. It'll still be creamy on top.

06 Now fold it in half until it looks like a taco (see pic D).

07 Grab the pan handle from underneath with your palm facing up. Gently knock the edge of the skillet on your counter to get the omelet to the edge.

08 Place the plate just under the pan and flip the omelet onto the plate.

09 Garnish with finely chopped chives.

10 Bow 10 times and light a candle for the demi-glace demigod, Jacques Pépin.

A TALE OF TWO CITIES: CHICAGO

"Know the rules well, so you can break them effectively."

—DALAI LAMA XIV

THE JUSTIN TIMBERLAKE TEST

Teenage girls are relentless.

One evening, a mob of them were chasing Justin Timberlake through the streets of Chicago. To save himself, he pulled a sharp 90-degree turn and sprinted through an unmarked doorway.

His refuge was a red-lit hallway and complete silence: the entrance to Alinea restaurant. No more than 10 seconds behind him, the fever pitch of screaming girls hit the same entrance, and a female maître d' pushed Justin into the coat closet, shutting the door.

"Stop!" She straight-armed the first girl, bringing the wolf pack to a screeching halt.

As staff members busied themselves ushering craziness out of the normally serene restaurant, chef Grant Achatz (pronounced "Ackets") came running out of the kitchen, thinking a fire had broken out:

"What the hell is going on?!"

"Sorry, Chef. It was Justin Timberlake." Girls gone, Justin emerged from the closet next to Grant.

"Who the hell is Justin Timberlake?!"

At this, Justin introduced himself and apologized for the commotion.

"Why are teenage girls chasing you?" Grant asked, puzzled. Justin looked down at his feet sheepishly: "I ask myself that every day."

SO YOU WANT TO BE A PROFESSIONAL CHEF . . .

For the first three years after Alinea opened, Grant had one futon in his apartment and no other furniture.

"What are Grant's interests outside of cooking?" I asked Nick Kokonas, Grant's genius business partner and co-owner of Alinea, hoping I could find a foothold for rapport. I didn't want to waste Achatz's time, and I didn't want to ask the same questions he'd heard a thousand times.

"He has no outside hobbies. All he does is cook."

And that is why Grant Achatz, who started cooking at age five, is Grant Achatz. That is why Alinea is the #1-ranked restaurant in the U.S. and #6 worldwide, according to the 2011 San Pellegrino Top-50 rankings.[6] That is why famed chef Jean-Georges Vongerichten, when asked who he feared of his colleagues, responded, "Grant Achatz . . . he does things I cannot do. I have no idea how he puts those dishes together."[‡]

Grant started cooking in his family's diner in Michigan, attended culinary school at the CIA,[7] worked under Thomas Keller at the French Laundry, did a stint at el Bulli in Barcelona with Ferran Adrià, then arrived at Trio in Chicago. That is where he met Nick Kokonas, who was then a derivatives trader.

6 At the time of this writing.

7 The Culinary Institute of America. Believe it or not, they also have the FBI: Food and Beverage Institute.

"It was like meeting Miles Davis when he was 28," Nick said of their first meeting. Everyone wanted to open a restaurant with Grant after tasting his food, and Nick was no different.

"What type of restaurant do you want to open?" Grant asked him. Nick replied, "I don't know. I build businesses. I don't know the first thing about restaurants."

And *that* is what made Nick different. He was the only suitor in years to get a call back, precisely because he said, "I don't know."

- A year to the day after that meeting, Alinea opened.

- Eighteen months later, *Gourmet* magazine called Alinea, with its 29 chefs for a maximum of 82 guests per night, the #1 restaurant in the U.S.

- Twelve months later, Grant was diagnosed with stage 4B tongue cancer. There is no stage 4C, nor stage 5; 4B is the worst-case scenario.

Grant was told he might lose 70% of his tongue, and he informed Nick that he would rather die. Because his ability to taste was compromised, there was a time when Grant cooked entirely from memory, not unlike Beethoven, who composed his final full symphony, Symphony No. 9 in D minor, Op. 125, completely deaf.[8] The food never faltered.

Grant's comeback from the brink of death[9] was worthy of a dedicated book, which it got, titled *Life, on the Line*. He returned to cooking with a vengeance. Nothing went unquestioned or untested, even the obvious. In fact, *especially* the obvious:

Obvious: Menus are handed out before the meal.
Alinea: Menus are provided after the meal.

Obvious: Big dining rooms.
Alinea: Residential-scale dining rooms.

Obvious: Receptionist behind a counter or podium.
Alinea: No one inside the main door. Motion sensors open a second door at the end of the first hall, after which staff greet you by name.

Obvious: Diners go to the bathroom at will.
Alinea: Diners ask for permission to go to the bathroom. This isn't to be pompous. If a guest goes to the bathroom, a message goes to the kitchen, such as "Table 29—up," at which point the chefs scrap your dish and start again. Each dish is timed to be perfect when it arrives at your table, not five minutes later.

Obvious: Straight, short staircases.
Alinea: Deliberately long, winding staircases.

Obvious: Flowers on tables.
Alinea: No flowers on tables. The centerpieces are all interactive, often edible.

Some of these innovations preceded the cancer, but the dogma busting was amplified with Grant's new lease on life. From ingredients to service, menus to business model, *all* sacred cows were put on the chopping block.

FLAVOR IS THE STARTING POINT

I explored every nook and cranny at Alinea, hoping to find the secret sauce. Spherical ice, molded in copper and imported from Japan? Check. A kitchen cleaner than any hospital I've seen? Double check. Enough liquid nitrogen tanks to blow up a small city? Roger that—right next to where employees smoke outside.

Alinea's tiny business office was our final stop. Scanning the walls, eying the coveted awards unceremoniously shoved in one

8 Critics widely think it to be his best work, perhaps the best piece of music ever written.
9 He kept his tongue and miraculously recovered.

corner or another, I landed on a proudly framed napkin. It was embroidered in stitching, like something grandma might make. It read:

FLAVOR
IS FOR
PUSSIES.

"Uh, Nick?" I asked. "What the hell is that?"

And so the story began:

Once upon a time, there was a young chef at Alinea, roughly 22 years old. He was at the canapé station, making single-bite hors d'oeuvres and other small items. Chef Achatz saw him sending out their now-famous "hot potato, cold potato" soup to a guest.

Grant stopped the dish and touched the potato. Then he dipped his finger in the soup.

"What's wrong with this?" Grant asked. The young chef, confused, tasted both.

"Chef, I think the taste is spot on."

<Cue deafening silence>

"Are you fucking kidding me?!" Grant yelled. "Flavor is for fucking pussies!!!" Pointing at the dish, he continued, "This is *warm* potato, *warm* potato."

The soup should have been precisely 40°F. The "hot" potato should have been similarly precise. It was the well-tested contrast that made the entire dish.

When the young chef left Alinea four years later, he gave the embroidered napkin to Achatz as a thank-you for the lesson. As Grant elaborated to me,"To cook delicious food is not good enough. It's good enough if you're eating at home, but we're trying to create nostalgia, emotional triggers, etc. Anyone can make a delicious potato truffle soup. What people can't do is honor the execution of doing something elevated."

For chefs at the best restaurants in the world, great flavor is the starting point, the price of admission. That is like Roger Federer knowing how to serve properly. Then come the nuances that separate the best from the rest. To create a meal that people talk about for years, you have to consider a full sensory experience, including texture, presentation, service, and more.

But why bother if you're not working in a restaurant?

Well, I'll tell you. When you think about food creatively, you begin to think about *everything* more creatively.

The 4-Hour
CHEF
The Simple Path

In the middle of my meal at Alinea, I overcame weeks of design deadlock with this cover sketch. It popped to mind immediately after scrutinizing the restaurant's unusual Black Truffle Explosion.

AVANT-GARDE

Léon: "You need some time to grow up a little."
Mathilda: "I finished growing up, Léon. I just get older."
Léon: "For me it's the opposite. I'm old enough. I need time to grow up."

—*THE PROFESSIONAL*

So let's push your limits and attempt the avant-garde, a term originally used to describe the foremost part of an army advancing into battle (also called the *vanguard* or "advance guard," literally). In my mind, the avant-garde has nothing to do with abstract art or fashion. It has everything to do with being "professional" as I've embraced it.

Travis Haley, the CEO of Haley Strategic Partners, is an elite tactical firearms instructor. One of his credos is: "The amateur trains until he gets it right; the professional trains until he gets it wrong." In other words, the amateur plays within his or her sphere of comfort, where nothing can go wrong. Amateurs never see their true potential. In contrast, the professional constantly pushes the envelope, until something *inevitably* goes wrong. This is how they uncover weaknesses and become the best in the world. It's also how they get an awesome high through their craft.

Making restaurant-quality dishes for a few friends isn't complicated. By this point, you already have the skills. In "Avant-Garde," we'll raise the bar in a few areas: creativity, complexity, volume, timing, and consistency.

We'll start with creativity, because it's fun and an *Alice in Wonderland*—like trip. It's also a lens through which you can view everything else. As Albert Szent-Györgyi, the Nobel Prize—winning discoverer of vitamin C, famously said: "Discovery consists of seeing what everybody has seen and thinking what nobody has thought."

Scott Adams, creator of *Dilbert*, put it another way: "Creativity is allowing yourself to make mistakes. Art is knowing which ones to keep."

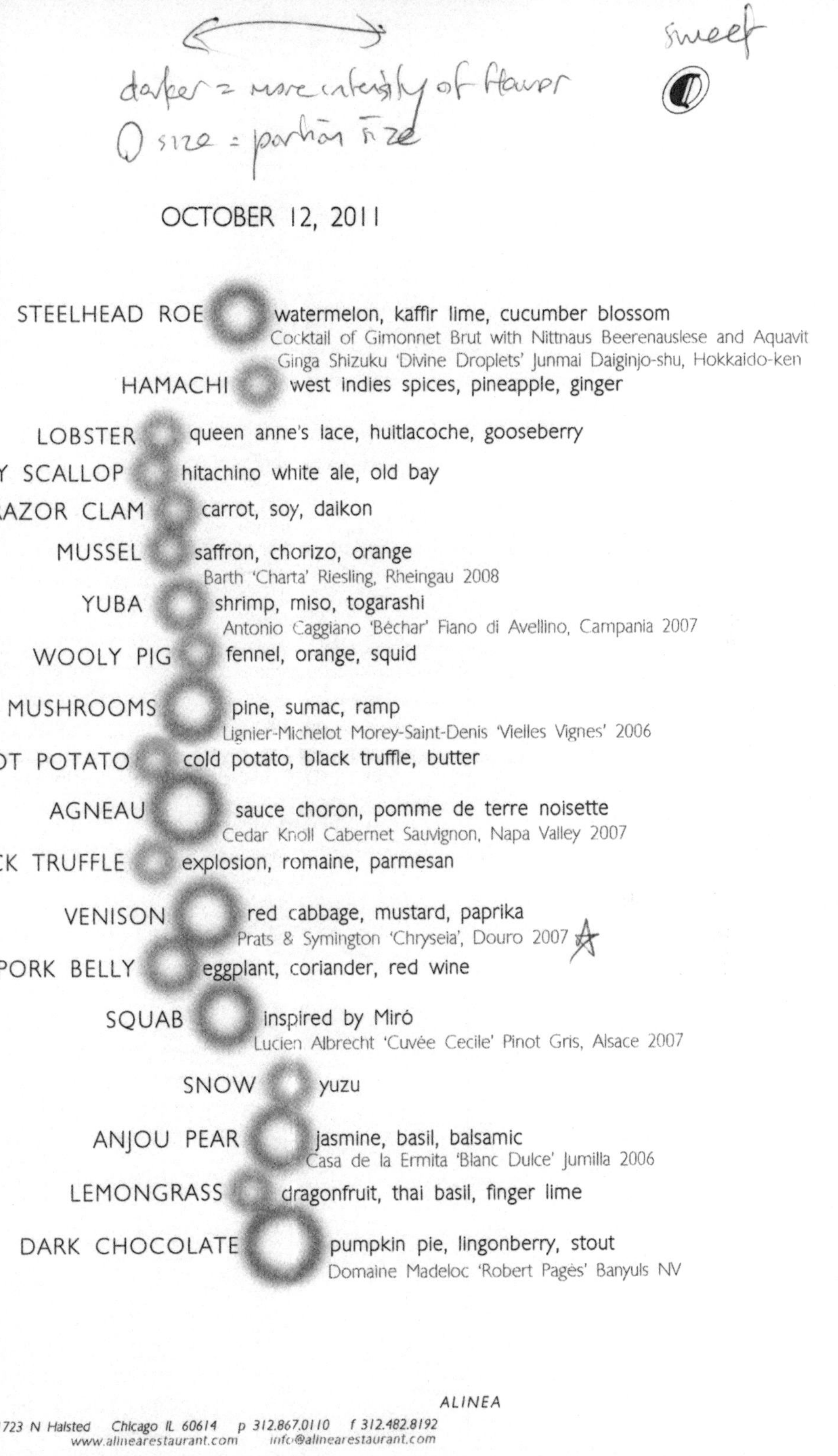

sweet
darker = more intensity of flavor
○ size = portion size
OCTOBER 12, 2011
STEELHEAD ROE watermelon, kaffir lime, cucumber blossom
Cocktail of Gimonnet Brut with Nittnaus Beerenauslese and Aquavit
Ginga Shizuku 'Divine Droplets' Junmai Daiginjo-shu, Hokkaido-ken
HAMACHI west indies spices, pineapple, ginger
LOBSTER queen anne's lace, huitlacoche, gooseberry
TAYLOR BAY SCALLOP hitachino white ale, old bay
RAZOR CLAM carrot, soy, daikon
MUSSEL saffron, chorizo, orange
Barth 'Charta' Riesling, Rheingau 2008
YUBA shrimp, miso, togarashi
Antonio Caggiano 'Bèchar' Fiano di Avellino, Campania 2007
WOOLY PIG fennel, orange, squid
WILD MUSHROOMS pine, sumac, ramp
Lignier-Michelot Morey-Saint-Denis 'Vielles Vignes' 2006
HOT POTATO cold potato, black truffle, butter
AGNEAU sauce choron, pomme de terre noisette
Cedar Knoll Cabernet Sauvignon, Napa Valley 2007
BLACK TRUFFLE explosion, romaine, parmesan
VENISON red cabbage, mustard, paprika
Prats & Symington 'Chryseia', Douro 2007
PORK BELLY eggplant, coriander, red wine
SQUAB inspired by Miró
Lucien Albrecht 'Cuvée Cecile' Pinot Gris, Alsace 2007
SNOW yuzu
ANJOU PEAR jasmine, basil, balsamic
Casa de la Ermita 'Blanc Dulce' Jumilla 2006
LEMONGRASS dragonfruit, thai basil, finger lime
DARK CHOCOLATE pumpkin pie, lingonberry, stout
Domaine Madeloc 'Robert Pagès' Banyuls NV
ALINEA
1723 N Halsted Chicago IL 60614 p 312.867.0110 f 312.482.8192
www.alinearestaurant.com info@alinearestaurant.com

My 19-course tasting meal at Alinea.

The size of the circles represents portion size (bigger circle = bigger size). The farther right the circle is, the sweeter the dish; the farther left, the more savory. The lighter font lists the wines, which are paired to groups (or pairs) of dishes with similar flavor profiles.

HOW GRANT CREATES: 10 PRINCIPLES

> "Anyone can look for fashion in a boutique or history in a museum. The creative explorer looks for history in a hardware store and fashion in an airport."
>
> —ROBERT WIEDER, JOURNALIST

Grant comes up with novel dishes all the time. Does the spirit just move him, or is it a God-given talent?

I'm sure it's both, but fortunately for us mortals, there are thought exercises you can borrow from Grant and use to great effect. I've adapted the below list of 10 from the inimitable Alinea cookbook. I've also taken liberties to help cooks lacking six-figure food budgets, so all mistakes (or bastardizations) are mine.

We'll stretch your creativity one principle at a time. Feel free to skip around until something strikes your fancy.

THE 10 PRINCIPLES

- **Serviceware**
- **Reversal**
- **Technology**
- **"Bouncing" Flavors**
- **Rare Ingredients**
- **Form Mimicking**
- **Texture Manipulation**
- **Profile Replication**
- **Themes**
- **Aroma**

SERVICEWARE

As Grant puts it: "The service pieces are a unique defining element of the Alinea experience." Circa 2002, Grant reached out to Martin Kastner to create custom serviceware for Trio. Martin has since created more than 30 pieces for Alinea, many of which can be bought on crucialdetail.com (when not sold out).

"Serviceware" refers to all the plates, dishes, silverware, etc., that food is served on or with. It can range from a piece of bark from your backyard to art suitable for MoMA.

To experiment, ask yourself: "If I couldn't use any of the plates or cups in my house, what would I serve food on? What would I serve drinks in?" Get creative. It might feel ridiculous, which is why you tell guests that you're playing with odd serving pieces for fun. Give yourself permission to mess around. All work and no play makes Jack a dull boy, indeed.

REVERSAL

Imagine a cheese plate with goat cheese, pistachios, roasted red peppers, and fresh raspberries. That's not so unusual. But how about a dessert (last course instead of first) of raspberry goat's milk, red pepper taffy (peppers

Serviceware: A snapshot from one of the best meals of my life, courtesy of Saison in San Francisco. Here, a piece of Kindai bluefin tuna ham, smoked and aged for 28 days. That shimmering surface, beautifully suspending the food in midair, is cling wrap. Simple, cheap, and wonderful.

cooked down to a taffy-like consistency), and pistachios? We already know the flavors will work, but the presentation is entirely new.

To experiment, ask yourself: "What dishes can I flip? Which ingredient textures can I swap? Is there a 'dessert' I can serve as a first course, or vice versa?" And so on.

TECHNOLOGY

Everyone knows that smoked salmon and sour cream go together . . . like PB&J or Mork and Mindy. The unique "anti-griddle," created by Philip Preston at PolyScience, however, allows us to reinvent this everyday duo. It has a surface that can be lowered to 45°F. Using it, we can freeze the bottom of a dollop of crème fraîche to give it a brittle texture, then powder salmon and pink pepper on top using a Microplane. The salmon becomes almost an aroma.

But . . . anti-griddles are freakin' expensive! $1,000+ to start.

This is why we should define "technology" broadly: a tool for achieving a specific outcome. No need to break the bank, no need for buttons or LEDs. Have you seen those chimps on the Discovery Channel using sticks to fish ants out of anthills? That's technology, baby.

Chefs get to use "roto-vaps" (rotary evaporators), volcano vaporizers, and anti-griddles to create consistency for 100 dishes a night. The home chef can improvise and still get great results. The original Alinea menu was tested in Nick's home kitchen. The anti-griddle didn't exist then, so he used a baking sheet (sometimes the back of a spatula) placed on dry ice. You can, too.

To experiment, ask yourself: "What tools in my house might I repurpose for food? Are there any safe off-label uses for the objects around me? What gadgets on the PolyScience website (cuisinetechnology.com) will I buy when I win the lottery?"

"BOUNCING" FLAVORS

For help with "bouncing" (free-associating) flavors, I strongly recommend the Belgian wonder of foodpairing.be, as well as *Culinary Artistry,* which Grant named his "most-used cookbook" a month after Alinea was picked as the #1 restaurant in the U.S. by *Gourmet* magazine.‡

Here's how it works. First, pick an ingredient you'd like to experiment with: say, peanuts. Next, use the above resources to choose a peanut-friendly ingredient, like bacon. Repeat the search, now finding a bacon-friendly ingredient to add to your "recipe," such as ginger. Continue this "bouncing" until you have your desired number of ingredients for the dish. Now you just need to make it look and taste good (and don't forget texture).

You can use Google to speed up cooking. Search the entire list of ingredients, adding "recipe" at the end (e.g., "peanut bacon recipe") to see what pops up. This shortcut also works for making meals out of leftovers in your refrigerator.

To experiment, ask yourself: "What is a vegetable I love but have never cooked with?" Or choose a random letter—say, G—search for "foods that start with the letter G," and begin there.

RARE INGREDIENTS

Ever had small-batch trout roe? How about *ayu,* also known as "watermelon fish"? Its flesh smells like—you guessed it—watermelon. Rare ingredients like these can be expensive, but you can fake it. Remember: they just need to be new to *your* guests.

To experiment, ask yourself: "What have my guests never had . . . at least at a home dinner party?" The fastest way to find something, even a variation on a common item, is to visit an ethnic grocery store, whether it's Mexican, Chinese, or another nationality. There's always something quirky. "Black chicken"[10] with black meat and white feathers? Geoduck ("gooey" duck)? As you already know, using an uncommon ingredient is a great cheat for appearing better than you are. If you roast a chicken, everyone's an expert and an armchair quarterback. But who the hell is going to say, "Well, not exactly the best geoduck I've ever had . . . " and roll their eyes? If you stay away from trotter-eating hipsters on 10-speeds, no one.

FORM MIMICKING

Grant once saw a fallen tree while walking with his boys in the woods. Captivated by the visual, he replicated it in the kitchen using salsify, which resembled the gnarled roots.

To experiment, ask yourself: "What do I find beautiful and why?" Look at your artwork, favorite colors, clothing, etc.—are there any patterns? Can you implement those characteristics on your dinner table or on plates? In serviceware?

TEXTURE MANIPULATION

How many ways can you present one ingredient? How about "seven-textured" rhubarb—seven dishes, seven pairings, and seven textures? The variations: liquid (juiced), crispy (dehydrated), crunchy (compressed under vacuum), spongy (injected with whipped air), soft mouthfeel (traditionally slow cooked), creamy (sorbet), and gelatinous (hydrocolloid).

To experiment, ask yourself: "If I had to create an entire meal from [one food/ingredient in your fridge], how might I do it? What would the appetizer, entrée, and dessert be? Can I, as with eggs, separate out different elements (yolk and white, skin and meat, etc.)?"

PROFILE REPLICATION

Take something nostalgic and beloved (e.g., A&W Root Beer), determine what ingredients were used in the handmade original, then recombine them with a dish or main protein. For example: Beef with "A&W" (fennel, burdock root, prunes, etc.), inspired by Grant's love of burgers and root beer floats. I like to call these "shape-shifters."

10 It requires slightly more cooking than standard chicken.

To experiment, ask yourself: "What favorite childhood foods could I deconstruct and even make healthy? Doritos? Peanut butter and jelly (including the bread)? KFC seasoning? Others?"

THEMES

I added this one to the list. Grant no doubt thinks in themes as second nature, but I find it helpful to consider a list and build dishes around one of the ideas. Here are two I use often:

- **Ethnic/national themes:** Perhaps too obvious to mention, but cooking dishes from a specific cuisine.
- **Ingredient themes:** Related to "texture manipulation," you make multiple dishes with different appearances of the same ingredient.

Or! Get crazy creative like Mission Street Food's Anthony Myint, who likes themes like Fancy McDonald's, Stoner Food, and Egg Dinner.

AROMA

As we discovered in "Learning to 'Taste'" (page 50), taste is actually a small part of flavor. Human smell, with more than 10,000 perceptible scents, offers the best palette of options for changing flavor.

Alinea servers sometimes place a plated dish on a pillow of scented air, which is gradually released by weight and gravity. You probably don't have the means for that, but how about an aromatic utensil? Could you use a cinnamon stick or vanilla bean to serve food, or give them to diners like forks? Alinea has used smoldering oak leaves to accompany pheasant, and you could do the same. Ratcheting it back one level, you could easily experiment with:

- **Vapor:** Place a hyacinth in a bowl and douse it with hot water at the table.
- **Heat activation:** For a goose accompaniment, put orange zest, sage, sweet spices, and goose fat in a ramekin and place a hot river stone on top.
- **Veil:** Cover the dish (e.g., lamb) with a lid (e.g., eucalyptus leaves), which, when removed, provides a sudden release of aroma to the diner.
- **Fragrant film:** Need something more challenging? All right, whippersnapper. Put on your latex gloves and make a few dissolvable films with modified starches (think non-disgusting Listerine strips). Flavors can be as simple as cinnamon or other brown spices. Ask your guests to put one film on the *tops* of their mouths, so the "flavor" (mostly olfactory) lasts for the duration of the subsequent dish.

Phew . . . got all 10 principles memorized? Don't worry; you don't have to.

We'll explore one or two examples of each in turn. Skip liberally and make only your favorites.

So let us begin with . . .

Grant's Principles #1

SERVICEWARE

PARAFFIN WAX BOWLS

HANDS-ON TIME
45 minutes

TOTAL TIME
45 minutes

GEAR

- Double boiler (or bootleg version)
- Piece of paper or cookie sheet

INGREDIENTS	TO MAKE 4 BOWLS
Paraffin candle wax	1 lb (454 g)
Good-quality balloons	4 (or more, in case of breakage)

This one is too much fun to postpone. Remember the "hot potato, cold potato" story? At Alinea, that dish is served in single-use paraffin wax bowls. To re-create these beauties at home, you just have to bootleg a little brilliance. For that, I rely on designer and illustrator gone rogue Martin Lindsay.[11] His technique is borrowed from candlemakers, who use this approach to create "luminaries" (lanterns), in which votive candles are placed.

00 Put your wax in the top of your double boiler and fill the bottom portion with an inch or so of water. If you don't have a double boiler, bootleg one by placing a mixing bowl or metal pitcher inside a large saucepan.

01 Bring the water to a simmer, then turn it down to medium-low (you don't want it to boil).

02 Fill your balloons with water, one for each desired bowl.

03 Once the paraffin has melted, start dipping your balloons into the wax. Dip them deep enough to create your desired bowl shape. After about 8 dips or so (for thickness), take each balloon out and hold it while the wax hardens, about 1–2 minutes.

04 Then place each on a piece of paper or a cookie sheet, pushing down a bit. This creates a flat bottom for the bowl.

05 Repeat steps 03 and 04 three times for each balloon for a total of 24 dips.

06 Let all balloons cool completely.

07 Hold your balloons over the sink (see pic C, opposite) and pop them to release the water. Peel off the balloon bits and discard.

08 Let the paraffin bowls dry off, and then trim off any thin, straggly tendrils of wax.

09 For smooth edges, heat a small skillet and place each bowl upside down on the hot surface—any uneven or rough edges will melt away. Done!

Note: The melting point for paraffin wax is 125–165°F (52–74°C), so be careful not to serve anything like scorching-hot soup in these bad boys.

11 Creator of alineaphile.com.

A

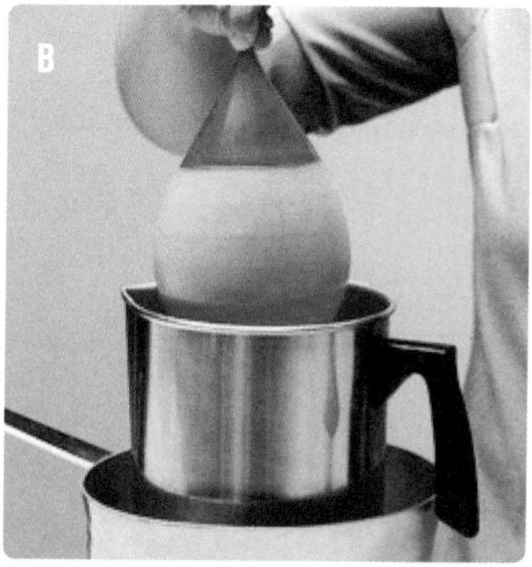
B

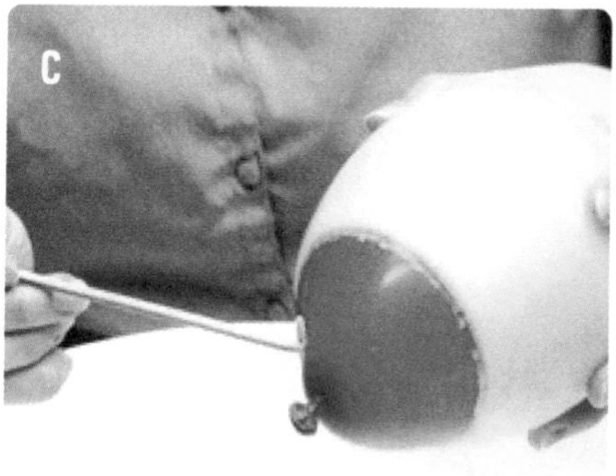
C

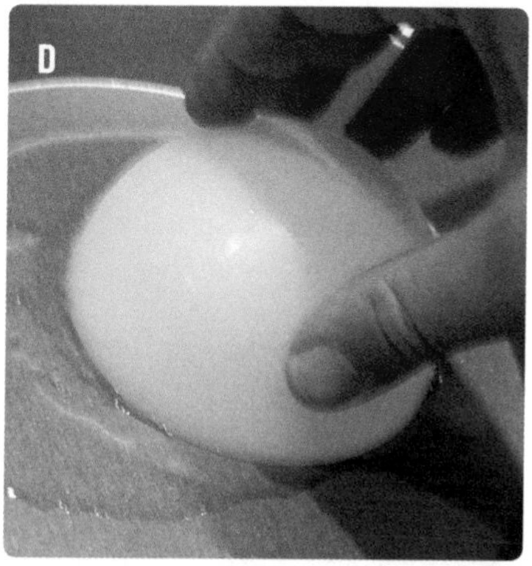
D

Turn the bowls upright after you finish melting the rough edges.

Spending Money Instead of Time

Not ready to go custom-made? I asked Martin Kastner of Crucial Detail for his off-the-shelf recommendations for nonprofessionals. Here's the rundown.

On a Budget

- Corelle at Target
- CB2
- Wasara Disposables
- Heath Ceramics (my fave)
- Eva Zeisel
- Normann

On a Bigger Budget

- Herlig Berlin
- Aldo Bakker
- Ole Jensen
- Faces, Ferran Adrià

On a Richie Rich Budget

For the Traditionalist:

- Bernardaud Chenonceaux Cobalt-Incrustation ($2,580 for a dinner plate!)

For the Modernist:

- Puiforcat Cercle d'Or et Cercle d'Argent ($1,650 a plate, thanks to the gold and silver)

For the Hybrid:

- Lalique

All of these items can be found at fourhourchef .com/serviceware

Grant's Principles #1

SERVICEWARE

ALMOND ZA'ATAR CRACKERS WITH TUNA

SHORTHAND

325F 15min: bake 1c almond meal, 1T ground flaxseed, 1 egg white formed into dough, flattened to ⅛" between parchment, seasoned w ¾t salt, 1½t za'atar.

HANDS-ON TIME

15 minutes

TOTAL TIME

30 minutes

GEAR

- Medium mixing bowl
- Parchment paper
- Rolling pin or wine bottle
- Baking sheet
- Pizza or pastry cutter (ideal) or knife
- Plastic wrap

"I know people that could serve me canned tuna and saltine crackers and have me feel more at home at their table than some people who can cook circles around me."

—ALTON BROWN

INGREDIENTS	TO SERVE 6–8 AS AN APP (MAKES ≈ 32)
Almond meal (almond flour will work)	**1 c (95 g)**
Flaxseed, ground with a spice mill or mortar and pestle	**1 T**
Egg white	**1**
Salt	**2-finger pinch**
Za'atar	**3-finger pinch**
Good-quality tuna packed in olive oil (with salt added), drained	**1 can (5 oz/140 g)**
Fresh flat-leaf parsley leaves	**To taste**

Yes, plastic wrap on glass is a stunning—and stunningly easy—way to serve your food, but there's more serviceware at hand here: the crackers.

We'll top these crispy slow-carb delights with za'atar, a Middle Eastern mixture of dried herbs (usually oregano, thyme, marjoram, savory, and parsley) and sesame seeds. Then we'll add a few flakes of oil-packed tuna and fresh parsley. This combo makes an impressive appetizer to go with cocktails. Very easy. Very civilized.

00 Preheat the oven to 325°F (190°C).

01 In a medium bowl, combine the 1 c (95 g) almond meal, 1 T ground flaxseed, and 1 egg white to make a dough; shape the dough into 2 roughly equal balls.

02 Put one ball in the center of a large piece of parchment paper and flatten slightly with your hands.

03 Cover the dough with a second piece of parchment and use a rolling pin or a wine bottle to roll it out to about ⅛" (0.3 cm) thick and roughly square (see pic B, opposite). To smooth out the wrinkles that form as you roll, gently lift the top piece of parchment after every few rolls and pat it back down.

04 Once it's flat, flip the whole thing over. Lift the new top piece of parchment. Pat it back down and continue to roll, repeating the flattening/smoothing process.

05 Put the sandwiched sheet of dough on a baking sheet and remove the top piece of parchment.

06 Sprinkle evenly with the 2-finger pinch of salt and 3-finger pinch of za'atar. Gently press the seasonings into the dough with your palm.

07 Use a pizza or pastry cutter to cut the dough into roughly 1½" (4-cm) squares directly on the parchment. Don't cut through the paper.

08 Trim off the rough edges, if you'd like. Now you have your very own slow-carb "Wheat" Thins.

09 Repeat steps 02–08 with your second dough ball.

10 Bake all until nicely browned, about 15 minutes, then let cool. Arrange on a platter or glasses (see pic, right) and top each with a bit of tuna and a parsley leaf. Serve immediately.

A
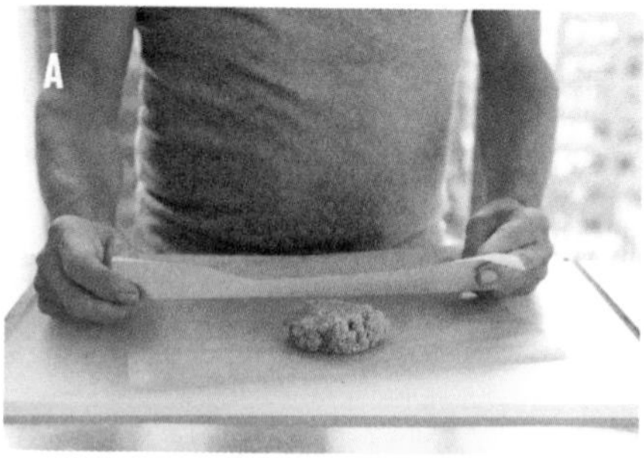

B

C

D

Wham, bam, thank you, Van Damme!

Grant's Principles #2

REVERSAL

CAULIFLOWER CRÈME BRÛLÉE

DESSERT AS APPETIZER

CONTRIBUTED BY

Matthew Dolan and Chad Bourdon

SHORTHAND

Cook low heat: 2 heads chopped cauliflower, 2T oil, salt 5min till soft. + 1 diced shallot till transparent. + ½c white wine, med heat til dry. + 4c milk 20min. Puree w S+P, 1 lemon's juice. Sieve, cool. 275F 1hr: bake in ramekin till firm but jiggly. Top w sugar, torch.

HANDS-ON TIME

1 hour or longer

TOTAL TIME

1 hour or longer, plus cooling

GEAR

- Knife + cutting board
- Large pot
- Hand blender
- Sieve
- 6–8 ramekins or ovenproof serving dishes
- Baking sheet
- Brûlée torch

"Desserts are like mistresses. They are bad for you. So if you're having one, you might as well have two."

—CHEF ALAIN DUCASSE

INGREDIENTS	TO SERVE 6–8
Cauliflower, roughly chopped	2 medium heads
Grapeseed or canola oil	2 T
Salt	To taste
Shallot, small dice	1
White wine	½ c (120 ml)
Whole milk	4 c (1 L)
White pepper	To taste
Lemon juice	1 lemon
Egg yolks	10
Coarse sugar, such as turbinado	See Step 10

Crème brûlée is done to death at restaurants. Everywhere is the same—the same but different. That's why I fell in love with this odd take from 25 Lusk in SF: a savory crème brûlée! It has just enough subtle sweetness to make the cauliflower pop, and it's their most famous appetizer. Make a few and you'll understand why.

This is a great recipe to make while watching a movie (see page 90) on your iPad.

00 Begin by cooking the chopped cauliflower in a large pot over low heat in 2 T grapeseed or canola oil. Season lightly with salt.

01 Add the diced shallot when the cauliflower begins to soften, after about 5 minutes. Continue this gentle cooking method until the shallots are translucent, about 3 minutes.

02 Add the ½ c (120 ml) white wine and increase the heat to medium. Cook until the pan is almost dry, about 5 more minutes.

03 Add the 4 c (1 L) milk and cook for another 20 minutes.

04 Puree the mix with a hand blender and season with salt, white pepper, and lemon juice.

05 Blend in the 10 egg yolks, one by one. Taste and add more salt or pepper if necessary.

06 Strain this all through a sieve and cool. The velvety liquid/pudding is your base. Discard any roughage left behind.

07 Set the ramekins or oven-safe serving dishes on a baking sheet and pour the base into them.

08 Preheat the oven to 275°F (140°C). Bake until the custard is set in the center but still a little jiggly; this could take up to 1 hour, depending on the depth of the ramekins. At 20 minutes, start checking every 5 minutes.

09 Once the brûlées have set (gently shake them to ensure the base with which you began is no longer liquid), remove and cool.

10 Sprinkle coarse sugar evenly atop the cooled brûlées.

11 Using a camping torch or brûlée torch (25 Lusk uses a BernzOmatic), burn the sugar until it's dark brown. Serve.

Suggested Garnishes

- Sweet tomatoes and arugula
- Sautéed mushrooms
- Truffles/truffle oil (as always)

Grant's Principles #3

TECHNOLOGY

"ANTI-GRIDDLE" PEPPERMINT CHOCOLATE POPS

SHORTHAND

Mix ½c simmered cream, 4oz chopped dark chocolate, pinch salt, ½t peppermint extract till melted ganache. Cool 30min. Chill baking sheet over dry ice. Freeze 1T ganache 1-2min, flip 30sec.

HANDS-ON TIME

20 minutes

TOTAL TIME

20 minutes, plus about 1 hour cooling

GEAR

- Knife + cutting board
- Medium mixing bowl
- Small saucepan
- Silicone spatula
- Kitchen towel
- Large block of dry ice
- Heavy single-thickness baking sheet, sheet pan, or large metal cake pan
- About 12 popsicle sticks
- Peltex

"I just invent, then wait until man comes around to needing what I've invented."

—R. BUCKMINSTER FULLER, ARCHITECT AND INVENTOR

INGREDIENTS	TO MAKE ABOUT 12
High-quality bittersweet chocolate (at least 60% cacao)[12]	4 oz (110 g)
Heavy cream	½ c (120 ml)
Salt	A pinch
Peppermint extract	½ t
Dry ice[13]	1–2 lb (0.5–1 kg)
Cooking spray	See Step 04

These simple pops are a classic dark chocolate ganache,[14] flash-frozen using dry ice. Imagine an elegant version of Girl Scout Thin Mint cookies, the crack cocaine of sweets.

00 Finely chop the 4 oz (110 g) chocolate and put it in a heatproof medium mixing bowl.

01 In a small saucepan, bring the ½ c (120 ml) cream barely to a simmer over medium heat (don't let it boil), then pour it over the chocolate. Let stand for a few minutes, then add a pinch of salt and the ½ t peppermint extract and stir with a silicone spatula until the chocolate is melted and completely smooth. Set this ganache aside in the refrigerator to cool and thicken to the consistency of melted ice cream, which should take about 30 minutes.

02 Meanwhile, prepare the "anti-griddle": Fold a towel and place it on a work surface or cutting board. Using oven mitts, a folded towel, or tongs, move the dry ice on top of the towel, and be careful not to touch it with bare hands. (You can leave it in the plastic bag so it's easier to move around.)

03 Set a heavy metal baking sheet, sheet pan, large cake pan, or roasting pan on top

---

12 I used Trader Joe's Pound Plus 72% Belgian chocolate: inexpensive yet surprisingly good.

13 Available at many grocery stores and specialty ice dealers.

14 Ganache is chocolate that's been melted by hot cream and stirred until smooth. Depending on the amount of chocolate used, it can cool to be thick like a truffle or runny like a glaze on a cake.

of the dry ice so that as much surface is in contact with the ice as possible. Let chill until frost appears on top of the metal.

04 When the ganache is ready, lightly spray the surface of the baking sheet with nonstick cooking spray (such as Pam), then scoop *scant* tablespoonfuls (that is, a little less than 1 T) of ganache onto the frosty part of the baking sheet to form pools roughly 2" (5 cm) across. Make no more than 6 at a time. Lay a popsicle stick in each pool.

05 Let freeze for 1–2 minutes. Most of the top of the ganache should now be solid and matte instead of shiny. Using a Peltex, turn the pops over and chill the second side for about 30 seconds, then serve immediately. Repeat with the remaining ganache and popsicle sticks.

A

B

C

D

E

F

G

H

Don't Have Extract?

No problem. When bringing the cream to a simmer, just drop in some peppermint or mint. The latter is easier to find. Remove before you pour it onto the chocolate.

Grant's Principles #4

"BOUNCING" FLAVORS

OYSTER + KIWI

INSPIRED BY

L'Air du Temps

SHORTHAND

Mix ½c coconut puree, 1t lemon juice, ¾T tara gum, sieve. Mix ¼c sepia ink, ⅛t methylcellulose. Refrigerate both. Peel & cut 2 kiwis, mix w 1t wasabi powder. Arrange 4 oysters on kiwi, garnish with sauces.

HANDS-ON TIME

15 minutes

TOTAL TIME

15 minutes

GEAR

- 3 small mixing bowls
- Sieve
- Star Peeler
- Knife + cutting board
- Oyster utensils: towel and oyster knife

"Kia kaha!"

—NATIVE NEW ZEALAND MĀORI PHRASE MEANING "STAY STRONG"

INGREDIENTS	TO SERVE 4
Coconut puree	½ c (120 ml)
Lemon juice	1 t
Tara gum powder (or guar gum)	¾ t (1.5 g)
Kiwis	2
Wasabi powder	1 t
Oysters	4
OPTIONAL	
Fresh squid ink (or sepia ink)	¼ c (60 ml)
Methylcellulose powder	⅛ t (0.25 g)

L'Air du Temps is a Michelin-starred restaurant located in Noville sur Mehaigne, Belgium. In 2007, chef Sang Hoon Degeimbre used one of his neighbor's tools—foodpairing.be—to create an unusual (and unusually tasty) dish called the "Kiwître." Primary ingredients: oysters and kiwifruit.

Replicating this dish requires the full ingredients list. However, you can experience the flavor combination by bringing a store-bought kiwi to a restaurant that serves oysters. Prepare for odd stares and dig in.

00 Mix together the ½ c (120 ml) coconut puree, 1 t lemon juice, and ¾ t (1.5 g) tara gum in a bowl. Run the mixture through a sieve, then set aside the filtered liquid in the refrigerator.

01 **Optional:** In a separate bowl, mix together the ¼ c (60 ml) squid ink and the ⅛ t (.25 g) methylcellulose. Set aside in the refrigerator.

02 Peel the 2 kiwis and cut them into small pieces, about ¼" square (0.6 cm) each, discarding the white parts. Mix the 1 t wasabi powder with the kiwi pieces.

03 Open the 4 oysters.

04 Put a spoon of kiwi pieces on each of 4 plates. Put an oyster on top of each, then garnish each with a drop of the squid ink (optional) and a spoonful of the coconut puree.

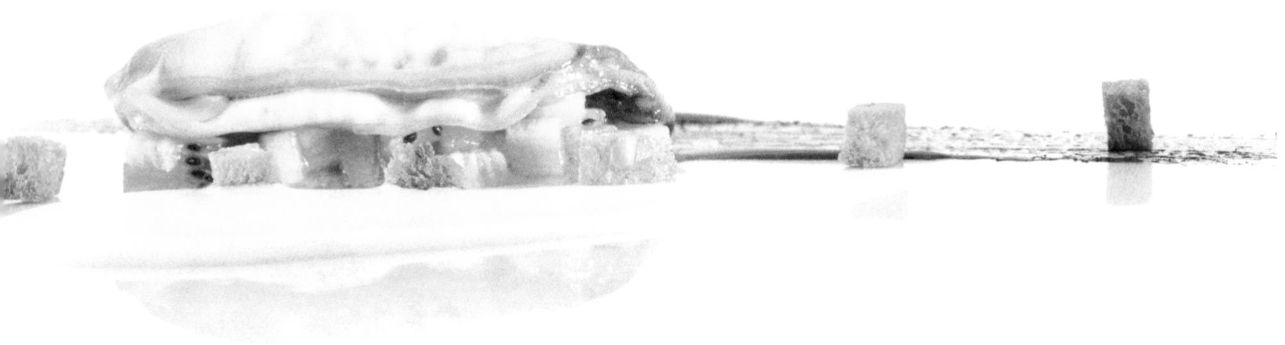

Grant's Principles #5

RARE INGREDIENTS

TAKASHI INOUE'S "TONGUE EXPERIENCE"

INSPIRED BY

Takashi, New York

SHORTHAND

Marinate 1 thin-sliced tongue, 2T sesame oil, 1T grated garlic, S+P 10min. Grill high heat 5sec per side. Serve w 4T soy, 2T lemon juice, 1T honey, 2T chili powder, 2T sesame seeds.

HANDS-ON TIME

10 minutes

TOTAL TIME

10 minutes, plus 10 minutes marinating

GEAR

- Knife + cutting board
- Mixing bowl
- Heavy skillet
- Tongs

"The inarticulate speak longest."

—JAPANESE PROVERB

INGREDIENTS	TO SERVE 2
Beef tongue meat, removed from its outer membrane (instructions opposite, or ask your butcher)	**¼–½ lb (113–227 g)**
Sesame oil	**2 T**
Grated garlic	**1 T**
S+P	**To taste**
Soy sauce (or tamari)	**4 T**
Lemon juice	**2 T**
Honey	**1 T**
Red chile powder	**2 T**
Crushed sesame seeds	**2 T**

A visit to Takashi, a small yakiniku-style restaurant in Manhattan's West Village, is a journey in meat eating. The restaurant serves nothing but beef, raw or flash-cooked on grills embedded in the dining tables. If it seems too limited, you clearly haven't had chef Takashi Inoue's diced raw beef liver, ultra fresh and seasoned with just salt and sesame oil. Nor have you had his meticulously sourced skirt steak and sweetbreads, grilled at the table and dragged through dipping sauce. Nor, of course, have you had his "Tongue Experience."

Tongue is one of those cuts that doesn't let you forget where meat comes from—but with a little peeling and trimming, and a quick sear in a hot skillet (the best way to replicate Takashi's grills at home), it becomes wonderfully delicate.

Cooked similarly in Mexican cuisine, it's perhaps my favorite taco filling.

00 Cut the tongue meat into thin, bite-size pieces: it's important that the tongue is sliced very thinly for fast grilling.

If you want to make this recipe 10 times easier, just buy sliced tongue at an ethnic grocery store (e.g., Mexican). Otherwise, stick the tongue in the freezer for 30 minutes to make it easier to slice.

01 Mix the 2 T sesame oil and 1 T grated garlic, adding some S+P to taste. Marinate the tongue pieces in this mixture for 10 minutes, turning occasionally. If you like, lightly massage the meat for a stronger marinade infusion.

02 Combine the remaining ingredients in a separate bowl to make the spicy lemon soy sauce.

03 In a heavy skillet over medium-high heat, grill the tongue pieces quickly, about 5 seconds on each side. You should see the juices appear on the ungrilled side of the meat, which is an indication to turn the meat over. Overcooking will make it chewy.

04 Dip the grilled tongue in the lemon sauce and enjoy!

Extra Credit: How to Skin a Beef Tongue

The outer layer (or skin) of a beef tongue is tough and somewhat awkward to eat (sandpapery taste buds and whatnot), so it needs to be removed before you slice. You can have your butcher do it for you, but if you're the DIY type, here's how to get at that gloriously deep-red meat.

1. Put the tongue on a clean cutting board. Knead and pull firmly all along the length of the tongue—this will make the outer skin easier to remove.

2. Trim off the light-colored sides of the thick end of the tongue with a sharp knife, then lay the tongue out so that the connective muscle (the part that was attached to the cow) is on top. Cut horizontally to remove the lumpy part so you're left with a long, roughly cylindrical piece.

3. Knead and pull on the tongue some more, then lay it flat on the cutting board, right side up (imagine the cow looking straight ahead). Make a shallow horizontal slit in the tip of the tongue, then grab the top layer of skin above the slit and lift it from the meat, using the knife to carefully scrape the meat from the skin as you pull the skin back toward the base of the tongue. Flip and repeat the process to remove the skin from the bottom of the tongue, then the sides, taking care that you remove as little meat as possible. Trim off any bits of skin that remain. You should have a beautiful piece of meat that resembles a tenderloin.

4. The back and front ends of the tongue are usually used as two separate cuts of meat due to their varying densities. To separate them, lay the skinned tongue flat on the cutting board. With your fingers, feel around the meat, about a third of the way from the back (attached-to-the-cow) end. Where you feel the density of the meat change, make a clean cut down through the entire tongue. Thinly slice both sections crosswise (again, much like a tenderloin), keeping slices from front and back separate so you can cook them depending on your guests' preferences.

Grant's Principles #6

FORM MIMICKING

BACON ROSES

CONTRIBUTED BY

Instructables.com

SHORTHAND

375F 30-40min: Bake tightly rolled 1 pack thin-, 1 pack thick-cut bacon in drilled muffin sheet atop broiler pan till done. Secure to fake rose stems.

HANDS-ON TIME

20 minutes

TOTAL TIME

1 hour

GEAR

- 12 fake rose stems
- Glass vase
- Drill with bit (≈1/8"/0.3 cm)
- Mini-muffin pan
- Baking sheet
- Optional: Tongs
- Optional: Gravel or marbles for vase

"Is there anything more beautiful than a beautiful, beautiful flamingo, flying across in front of a beautiful sunset? And he's carrying a beautiful rose in his beak, and also he's carrying a very beautiful painting with his feet. And also, you're drunk."

—JACK HANDEY

INGREDIENTS	TO MAKE 24 ROSES
Bacon, regular	1 pack (≈16 slices)
Bacon, thick cut	1 pack (≈12 slices)
Also see GEAR, left	

Romance can be confusing. This recipe bridges the gender gap. What do women love? Roses. What do men love? Bacon. Sooo . . . we create bacon roses. She gets the Valentine's Day she always wanted, you get a snack, and it's win-win! For bonus points, scatter real rose petals on the floor to lead her to this treasure.

PREPARE THE ROSE STEMS

00 Separate each piece of the fake roses. Pull the fake roses off of the stems, then pull the green backing off (see pic A, opposite). Discard the center red piece and the petals, or save the latter for scattering.

01 Reassemble the remaining green parts (stem, leaves, green backing). Push the green backing down so that roughly 1" (2.5 cm) of the stem protrudes (see pic B).

02 Tape the stems together like a bouquet. Place them in the vase and, if needed, fill it with gravel or marbles to hold the stems in place.

PREPARE THE BACON ROSES

00 Preheat the oven to 375°F (190°C).

01 Drill holes in the bottom of the muffin pan to allow the grease to drain (see pic C). Place the muffin pan on top of the baking sheet.

02 Tightly roll the bacon strips (see pic D), starting with the widest end of the bacon. I recommend using a combination of thick and thin bacon for a variety of rose shapes. 'Tis the spice of life, you know.

03 Place all of the bacon roses in the muffin pans, pushing down on each slightly so the bottoms flare out a bit (see pic E).

04 Place the muffin tin and baking sheet in the oven. Bake for 30–40 minutes. Check on them occasionally—you may have to lightly lift the roses with tongs to let all the grease drain out.

05 When the roses are done, remove everything from the oven. Take out the bacon roses and place them on a paper towel to cool (see pic F). Choose the best-looking roses to slide onto the protruding stems (see pic G).

06 Sexy time! Consider combining with Sexy-Time Steak on page 186.

For more fun with bacon, Google "redneck turtle burgers." You're very welcome.

A

B

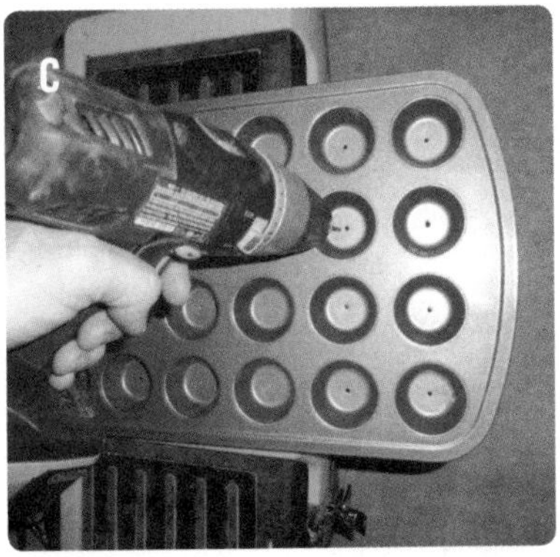
C

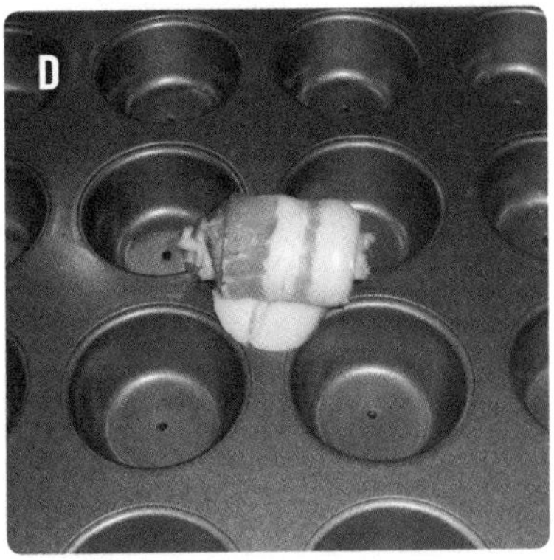
D

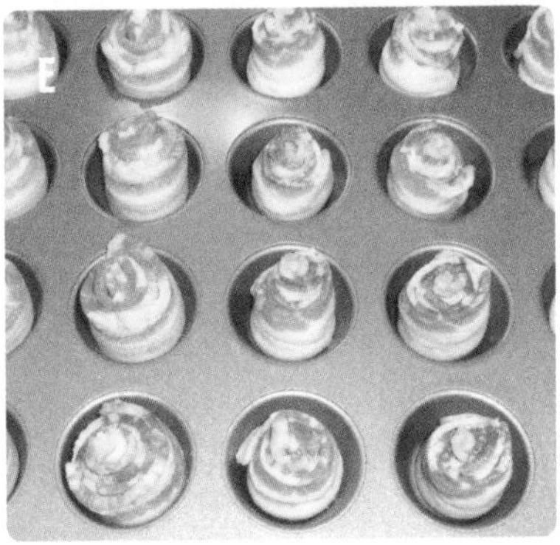
E

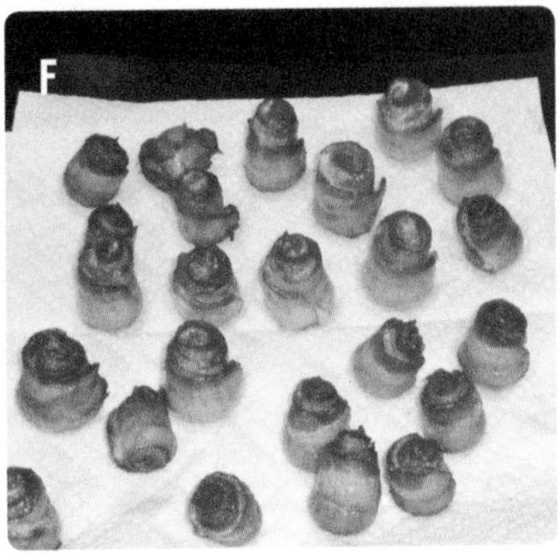
F

G

Grant's Principles #6

FORM MIMICKING

EDIBLE DIRT CENTERPIECE

INSPIRED BY

René Redzepi and Wylie Dufresne

SHORTHAND

Soak overnight: 2c almonds, 6c H2O; blend, strain. Boil 1hr: ½c black rice, 1c almond milk, ¾c coffee, 5c H2O, 2T cocoa powder, ¼c raisins, 1t tamarind, 2-finger pinch salt. 350F 1½–2hr: Process mixture of ¾c black olives, 2T black sesame seeds, 2T tamari, 2T white wine vinegar, 1T red miso till smooth; + almond pulp, bake till dry. Garnish w edible flower.

HANDS-ON TIME

20 minutes

TOTAL TIME

3½ hours

GEAR

- Blender
- Fine-mesh strainer
- Cheesecloth
- Large mixing bowl
- Jar
- Medium saucepan
- Coffeemaker
- Baking sheet
- Waxed paper or a silicone mat

"In the spring, at the end of the day, you should smell like dirt."

—MARGARET ATWOOD, AUTHOR

INGREDIENTS	TO MAKE ≈2 C (450 ML)
ALMOND MILK	
Almonds (raw and unsalted)	2 c (280 g)
Water	6 c (1.5 L)
DIRT	
Leftover almond pulp from making almond milk	—
Black rice (uncooked)	½ c (100 g)
Brewed coffee	¾ c (170 ml)
Almond milk	1 c (220 ml)
Water	5 c (1.2 L)
Cocoa powder	2 T
Raisins	¼ c (35 g)
Tamarind concentrate	1 t
Salt	2-finger pinch
Pitted black olives	¾ c (90 g)
Black sesame seeds	2 T
Tamari	2 T
White wine vinegar	2 T
Red miso	1 T
GARNISH	
Edible flowers of your choice, such as arugula blossoms, yellow mustard blossoms, and pansies	—

In the quest to satisfy that earthy fifth taste known as *umami*, some hunt exotic mushrooms, others look to aged meats or cheeses, and still others search out pu-erh tea from the mountains of China. Here's another suggestion: eat dirt.

If you've ever made almond milk (also

explained in this recipe), you may have wondered if there's something you can do with those dregs besides compost them. Well, the dregs look like dirt, only lighter in color. With the addition of several black foods—black coffee, black rice, black olives, etc.—you can make your very own hyper-umami edible dirt.

If you're making the almond milk specifically for the dirt, you'll be left with extra that beats the pants off the processed, overly sweet garbage found on supermarket shelves.

Now, let's talk dirty.

00 **Make the almond milk:** Combine the 2 c (280 g) almonds and 6 c (1.5 L) water in a blender and soak overnight.

01 The next day, turn on the blender and blend the almonds and water for about 3 minutes, until the almonds are pulverized and almond milk is formed.

02 Line a fine-mesh strainer with cheesecloth and place it over a mixing bowl. Pour the almond milk through the cheesecloth and squeeze to extract all the milk. You'll have about 1 qt (1 L) of almond milk. (You'll be using 1 c/220 ml and saving the rest.) Transfer the almond milk to a jar and refrigerate until ready to use.

03 **Make the dirt:** Place the almond pulp in the mixing bowl and set aside.

In a medium saucepan, combine the ½ c (100 g) black rice (uncooked), ¾ c (170 ml) coffee, 1 c (220 ml) almond milk, 5 c (1.2 L) water, 2 T cocoa powder, ¼ c (35 g) raisins, 1 t tamarind, and 2-finger pinch of salt. Bring to a boil, then reduce to a high simmer for about 1 hour, until the rice is very soft.

Add a little water if the rice starts to dry out—you want it to be fairly moist, rather than completely dry, as it would be if you were serving it with dinner.

04 While waiting, preheat the oven to 300°F (150°C) and line a baking sheet with waxed paper or a reusable silicone mat (e.g., Silpat).

05 When the rice sludge is done on the stove top, transfer the mixture to a blender or food processor. Add the ¾ c (90 g) olives, 2 T sesame seeds, 2 T tamari, 2 T vinegar, and 1 T miso, and blend until mostly smooth with a few small pieces remaining for texture.

06 Add this mixture to the lonely almond pulp and stir well to incorporate. This will color the pulp dirt-black.

07 Spread the new mixture over the prepared baking sheet, place in the oven, and bake for 1½–2 hours, stirring occasionally, until the dirt is dry, with just a bit of moistness remaining, like potting soil.

08 Cool on the baking sheet, then transfer to a large vase or a few small vases, and garnish with edible flowers. (The dirt can be stored in a jar in the refrigerator for up to 1 week.)

To serve, put in the middle of the dining table. Drink a few glasses of wine with your guests, then ask, "Sooo... what are you all waiting for?" Hand them spoons and invite them to "dig" in.

Take that act on the road, you filthy-minded illusionists!

Grant's Principles #7

TEXTURE MANIPULATION

ONE INGREDIENT, MANY USES

COCONUT MEAL (APERITIF[15])

DANDELION "COFFEE" WITH COCONUT MILK

SHORTHAND

Brew 1-2T ground dandelion root, 10oz H2O. + coconut milk to taste; + pinch cardamom if desired.

HANDS-ON TIME

2 minutes

TOTAL TIME

5 minutes

GEAR

- Coffee grinder
- Teapot or small saucepan
- Coffee filter

"Simplicity is the ultimate sophistication."

—LEONARDO DA VINCI

INGREDIENTS	TO SERVE 1
Ground dandelion root	1–2 T
Water	1¼ c (300 ml)
Coconut milk[16]	To taste
OPTIONAL	
Ground cardamom	A pinch

Dandelion makes a surprisingly good coffee substitute. It's a great way to start a meal and stimulates digestion.

If you opt for store-bought dandelion coffee like Dandy Blend, the root comes dried, chopped, roasted, and ground into coarse granules. You take those granules, grind them further in the coffee grinder, and steep them just like coffee. Be prepared for bitterness. I like it, but it's an acquired taste.[17] Sweet and creamy coconut milk counters some of that bitterness, as does a pinch of aromatic cardamom.

Dandelion root is also routinely used by competitive wrestlers for its potassium-sparing diuretic effects. In plain Timglish: if you want to reduce caffeine addiction and excess water-bloat simultaneously, this is your new fix.

If you'd prefer pre-ground 100% dandelion root instead of a blend that includes grains, check your local health food store or visit Starwest Botanicals (starwest-botanicals.com).

00 Grind 1–2 T dandelion root in a coffee grinder. The finer you make it, the more pronounced the flavor.

01 Bring the 1¼ c (300 ml) water to a boil in a teapot or small saucepan.

02 Place the 1–2 T ground dandelion in a coffee filter on a cup and pour the water over it, just as you would for regular coffee.

03 Stir in coconut milk to taste, top with cardamom, if using, and drink.

15 A beverage to stimulate the appetite. The liquid equivalent of an appetizer.

16 Almond milk is also a good option; see the recipe on page 522.

17 You may want to start with a small amount of dandelion coffee and work your way up. Or start with half regular coffee, half dandelion root, and progress up to 100% dandelion in stages.

Dandelion "Coffee" with Coconut Milk.

Crisp-Baked Sesame-Coconut Chicken.

Coconut Paleo Pops.

Grant's Principles #7

TEXTURE MANIPULATION

ONE INGREDIENT, MANY USES

COCONUT MEAL (ENTRÉE)

CRISP-BAKED SESAME-COCONUT CHICKEN

SHORTHAND

450F 20–22min: coat 1½lb chicken breast in ½c mayo, 1 yolk, 1t sesame oil, ¾t mustard powder, ½t salt, pinch pepper; dredge in 6T sesame seeds, 4T coconut flakes; bake till cooked through.

HANDS-ON TIME

10 minutes

TOTAL TIME

30 minutes

GEAR

- Parchment paper
- Baking sheet
- Mixing bowl
- Plate

INGREDIENTS	TO SERVE 4
Mayonnaise or garlic aioli (ideally homemade, page 212)	**½ c (120 g)**
Egg yolk	**1**
Toasted sesame oil	**1 t**
Dry mustard powder	**2-finger pinch**
Salt	**2-finger pinch**
Freshly ground black pepper	**3-finger pinch**
Boneless, skinless chicken breasts, cut into 1" (2.5-cm) chunks	**1½ lb (680 g)**
Sesame seeds	**6 T (55 g)**
Unsweetened dried coconut flakes	**4 T**

This is comfort food: satisfying, unchallenging, and quick. The coconut flakes have a natural sweetness, and the sesame seeds provide a crunchy but light crust. If you're feeling experimental, try adding some Cajun spice mix, ground cayenne, or hot red chile flakes to the mayonnaise.

00 Preheat the oven to 450°F (230°C).

01 Line a baking sheet with parchment paper.

02 In a medium bowl, whisk together the ½ c (120 g) mayonnaise, 1 egg yolk, 1 t sesame oil, 2-finger pinch of mustard powder, 2-finger pinch of salt, and 3-finger pinch of pepper. Add the 1½ lb (680 g) of 1" chicken chunks and toss to coat.

03 Spread the 6 T (55 g) sesame seeds and 4 T coconut flakes on a plate and combine with your fingers. With one hand, lift each piece of the chicken from the mayonnaise mixture and set it on top of the sesame-coconut mixture. With the other (clean, dry) hand, sprinkle some of the sesame-coconut on top.

04 Transfer the chicken to the prepared baking sheet as you do so. The pieces don't have to be completely coated with sesame-coconut to end up heavenly.

05 Bake until golden brown and cooked through, 20–22 minutes. Let cool for 1–2 minutes (to allow the crust to firm up a bit), then serve.

If you *really* want to go overboard, now's the time to bring out the chilled coconut water.

COCONUT MEAL (DESSERT)

COCONUT PALEO POPS

SHORTHAND

Whisk 2½c coconut milk, ½c yacón syrup, 3T Lucuma powder, ¼t salt; pour in pop mold. Freeze 6hr.

HANDS-ON TIME

5 minutes

TOTAL TIME

At least 6 hours, or overnight for freezing

GEAR

- Mixing bowl
- Whisk
- Six 4-oz (120 ml) ice pop molds

INGREDIENTS	TO MAKE 6 POPS
Coconut milk	**2½ c (600 ml)**
Yacón syrup	**½ c (120 ml), plus 1 T for topping**
Lúcuma powder	**3 T**
Salt	**Small 2-finger pinch, plus more for topping**

These creamy, dairy-free pops are possible thanks to coconut and two secret ingredients from South America: yacón syrup and lúcuma powder.

Yacón syrup comes from a root plant (the yacón plant) found in the Andes and is similar to blackstrap molasses. Its sweetness mostly comes from FOS, or fructooligo-saccharides, which pass through the body largely unmetabolized, leaving little caloric trace and negligible effects on blood sugar. In fact, in South America, yacón is used to regulate blood sugar in diabetics. It's also considered a "prebiotic" that assists in production of beneficial gut bacteria.

Yacón's partner, lúcuma, is a fruit with notes of butterscotch and caramel. It also hails from the Andes, where it makes its way into many recipes, including lúcuma ice cream. In Peru, it's more popular than chocolate or vanilla. The dried powder is available in some health food stores, as is yacón syrup, often in the raw foods aisle.[18]

00 In a large bowl, whisk together all the ingredients.

01 Drizzle a little yacón syrup in the bottom of six 4-oz (120-ml) ice pop molds and sprinkle in a few grains of salt.

02 Divide the mixture among the molds and freeze until solid, at least 6 hours, or overnight. To loosen and remove, dip them in a bowl of warm water. If they refuse to come out, wedge a butter knife between the sides of the molds and jimmy them free.

Variations

A) Fill ice cube trays with the mixture, freeze for an hour, then stick toothpicks in the middle of each cube and freeze another couple of hours until solid.

B) Make the pops in tiny paper cups, stick an ice pop stick in each, and freeze. Rip off the paper before eating.

18 If not, sunfood.com is a good source.

Grant's Principles #8

PROFILE REPLICATION

PEKING DUCK WRAPS

INSPIRED BY

Anthony Myint and Karen Leibowitz

SHORTHAND

Refrigerate 10 salted duck-leg quarters overnight. 300F 3hr: cook duck in fat till tender. Discard bones. 300F 45min: crisp 1lb salted skin between 2 parchments & baking sheets. Whisk ⅔c tamari, 1½T rice vinegar, 1T sesame oil, 2t chile-garlic, 5T peanut butter, 2 minced garlic, ½t pepper. Blend w 5–10 thai chiles. Wrap duck meat, skin w lettuce. Serve w ½c cucumber/cilantro/scallion/sauce.

HANDS-ON TIME

20 minutes

TOTAL TIME

4 hours

GEAR

- 2 baking sheets/trays
- Parchment paper
- Aluminum foil
- Blender
- Mixing bowl
- Silicone spatula

"Donald Duck never wore pants. But whenever he's getting out of the shower, he always puts a towel around his waist. I mean, what is that about?"

—CHANDLER BING, *FRIENDS*

INGREDIENTS	TO SERVE 6
Raw duck skins or chicken skins	**1 lb (454 g)**
Duck or chicken leg quarters	**10**
Salt	**Enough to generously season duck legs**
Rendered duck or chicken fat	**2 qt (2 L)**
Hoisin sauce (buy sweetened or see below)	**2 c (470 ml)**
Thai chiles	**5–10**
Butter or romaine lettuce leaves	**12**
Cucumber, scallion, and cilantro for garnish	**½ c (50–100 g each)**
SLOW-CARB HOISIN SAUCE (whisk the following together):	
Tamari	**⅔ c (160 ml)**
Seasoned rice vinegar	**1½ T**
Toasted sesame oil	**1 T**
Chinese chile-garlic sauce	**2 t, or to taste**
Smooth peanut butter (no sugar added)	**5 T (80 g)**
Garlic, finely minced	**2 cloves**
Freshly ground black pepper	**½ t**

It's the hoisin, crispy skin, and cucumber that make Peking duck so incredible, so why not separate the trio, perfect 'em, and recombine it all? Here's how.

THE NIGHT BEFORE:

00 **Make the skins:** Salt the 1 lb (454 g) duck or chicken skins and lay them on a baking sheet in a single layer between pieces of parchment paper.

01 Cover with another baking sheet to keep the skins flat.

A

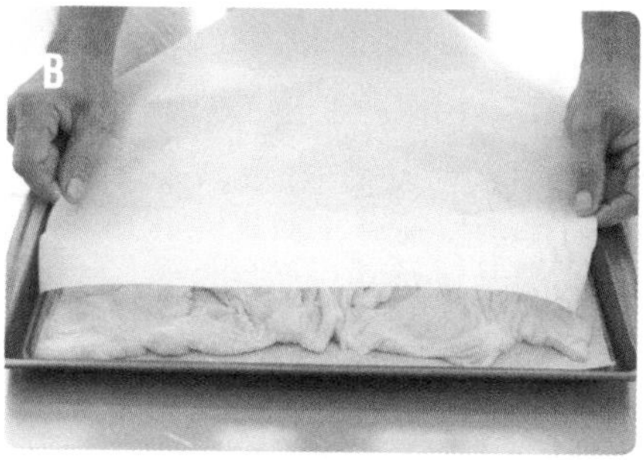
B

C

02 Bake for 45 minutes at 300°F (150°C) or until there are no soft, fatty parts.

03 The skins will crisp up once they cool down. Once they've cooled, break them into bite-size pieces.

04 **Make the duck or chicken legs:** Salt the 10 duck or chicken leg quarters generously, put in a baking pan, and refrigerate overnight.

THE DAY OF:

05 Cover the duck or chicken leg quarters with fat, then cover (baking pan and all) with parchment paper and 2 layers of foil. Cook in a 300°F (150°C) oven for 3 hours. The meat should be very tender. Cool before you continue, in order to keep the meat moist.

06 Separate the quarters into skin, meat, and bones. Discard bones.

07 Blend the 5–10 chiles with 1 c of the hoisin sauce, then fold[19] the hoisin-chile puree into the rest of the hoisin sauce.

08 To serve, place some bird meat and crispy skins in each of the lettuce leaves; add some cucumber, scallion, and cilantro for garnish; and top with a small dollop of the hoisin sauce—or put out a communal bowl and let everyone claw at each other.

19 In cooking, to fold something means to mix it into another substance by turning it gently with a spoon or spatula.

Grant's Principles #9

NATIONAL THEMES

BRAZILIAN MEAL

HEARTS OF PALM SALAD + CAIPIROSKA COCKTAIL + FEIJOADA

"Patience, n. A minor form of despair, disguised as a virtue."

—AMBROSE BIERCE, *THE DEVIL'S DICTIONARY*, 1911

Some words are hard to translate into English. One such word is *saudade* (pronounced "saw-daw-ji") from Portuguese. It roughly means "nostalgic longing or remembering."

I feel *saudade*[20] when I think back to 2007. My girlfriend had dropped the most recent Victoria's Secret catalog in my lap and asked for shopping suggestions. Following orders, I flipped through. Then I did it again. Each time, I was stopped in my tracks by one picture, the first I'd seen of Alessandra Ambrosio. It was a profile shot of her in women's slacks, and I thought she was the most beautiful woman I'd ever seen.

Alessandra "Ale" Ambrosio

(COURTESY OF RUSSELL JAMES FOR VICTORIA'S SECRET)

Just for the hell of it, five years later, I reached out to "Ale" to include her favorite slow-carb Brazilian foods in this meal (thanks, Ale and Aline!). I also added a *caipiroska*, a sugar-free twist on the Brazilian national drink *caipirinha* (pronounced "caipir-inya").[21] These recipes are as close to a date as I'll ever get, since she is happily married with two kids.

Congratulations, Ale <sniff>. You <sniff> deserve nothing but the <sniff> best!

Here's the sequence:

- **HEARTS OF PALM SALAD**, served with
- **CAIPIROSKA COCKTAIL**, followed by the entrée,
- **FEIJOADA**

20 Similar to the Japanese *natsukashii*.

21 Just as *piranha* is pronounced "piranya."

Hearts of Palm Salad and Feijoada.

Grant's Principles #9

NATIONAL THEMES

BRAZILIAN MEAL (APPETIZER)

HEARTS OF PALM SALAD

SHORTHAND

Rub bowl w halved garlic. Whisk in 6T red wine vinegar, 1t salt, ¼t pepper till salt dissolves. + 8T EVOO gradually. + 2 cans sliced hearts of palm, 2 chopped tomatoes, 2 diced avocados; toss.

HANDS-ON TIME

10 minutes

TOTAL TIME

10 minutes

GEAR

- Knife + cutting board
- Salad bowl
- Whisk

INGREDIENTS	TO SERVE 6–8
Garlic	1 clove, halved
Red wine vinegar	6 T (90 ml)
Salt	1 t, or more to taste
Freshly ground black pepper	10 turns, or more to taste
Sliced hearts of palm, drained and rinsed	2 cans (14 oz/397 g)
Large, ripe tomatoes, cut into bite-size chunks	2
Ripe Hass avocados, halved, pitted, peeled, and diced	2
EVOO	8 T (120 ml)

Brazil is a major producer of canned hearts of palm, which are harvested from the young buds of palm trees. It's best to serve them simply, as the Brazilians do, in salads with light vinaigrettes, or with olive oil and lemon juice. Don't convolute their delicate flavor with other ingredients.

00 Rub the cut sides of the garlic clove all over the inside bottom of a large salad bowl; discard the garlic or save for another use.

01 In the bowl, whisk together the 6 T (90 ml) vinegar, 1 t salt, and 10 turns of black pepper until the salt is dissolved.

02 Add the 2 cans hearts of palm, 2 chopped tomatoes, and 2 diced avocados. Drizzle the 8 T (120 ml) EVOO around the sides of the bowl and toss to combine. Taste and season with more salt and pepper if needed. Serve.

The salad can be made up to 1 hour before serving; keep at room temperature.

BRAZILIAN MEAL (DRINK)

CAIPIROSKA COCKTAIL

SHORTHAND

Stir 2oz vodka, juice of ½ lime. + crushed ice.

HANDS-ON TIME

5 minutes

TOTAL TIME

5 minutes

GEAR

- Knife + cutting board

INGREDIENTS	TO SERVE 1
Lime, cut into wedges	**½–1**
Vodka (Joshua Volz, former bartender at Washington, D.C.'s Marvin, recommends Hangar One)	**2 oz (60 ml)**
Crushed ice	**1 c or to taste**

This variant of the national drink of Brazil features clean-tasting vodka in place of cachaça, a rum-like liquor made from fermented sugarcane juice. Usually a generous quantity of sugar is muddled with the lime wedge, but who needs it? (Do Russians add sugar to their vodka? Then neither should you.)

Take care not to muddle the rind of the lime much, or the essential oils can make the drink bitter.

00 Squeeze the juice from the lime wedges into an old-fashioned or highball glass.

01 Place 1 of the lime wedges into the glass. Pour in the 2 oz (60 ml) vodka and stir well.

02 Add crushed ice and stir to melt some of the ice. Garnish with a lime slice or wedge.

BRAZILIAN MEAL (ENTRÉE)

FEIJOADA

SHORTHAND

Soak overnight: 1lb dried black beans, H2O. 350F 1½–2hr: Brown all sides 1½lb beef short ribs, 1T grapeseed oil, S+P 3min; remove. + 1lb sausage 3min till brown. + 1 diced garlic, 1t coriander 30sec. + ribs, 2 bay leaves, drained beans, 12oz smoked pork chops, H2O to cover. Boil; bake in oven till beans tender.

HANDS-ON TIME

20 minutes

TOTAL TIME

1 hour 50 minutes to 2 hours 20 minutes

GEAR

- Knife + cutting board
- Cast-iron Dutch oven
- Tongs

INGREDIENTS	TO SERVE 6–8
Dried black beans, rinsed, soaked, and drained	**1 lb (455 g)**
Grapeseed oil	**1 T**
Beef short ribs	**1½ lb (680 g)**
S+P	**To taste**
Chouriço or other spicy smoked pork sausage (see Notes), **sliced ½" (1 cm) thick**	**1 lb (455 g)**
Garlic, finely chopped	**1 clove**
Ground coriander	**½ t**
Smoked pork chops	**12 oz (340 g) (2 or 3 chops)**
Bay leaves	**2**
OPTIONAL	
Onion, diced (see Notes)	**1**
Almond meal or flour, toasted (see Notes)	**6 T (40 g)**

Feijoada is, of course, the national dish of Brazil, a hearty, long-cooked stew featuring black beans and as many different meats, fresh and smoked, as possible.

00 If you haven't, soak the 1 lb (455 g) of beans!

There are two ways to soak dried beans, depending on how much time you have: 1) Cover them with cold water by at least 1" (2.5 cm) and let stand for 8 hours or overnight. **OR** 2) Put in a saucepan, cover with cold water by 1" (2.5 cm), bring to a boil over high heat, then remove from the heat, put a lid on, and let sit for 1 hour. Drain well.

01 Preheat the oven to 350°F (180°C).

02 In a large Dutch oven, heat the 1 T oil over medium-high heat. Season the 1½ lb (680 g) short ribs with S+P and add them to the pot, meaty side down. Cook undisturbed for 3 minutes, then turn and continue to cook until nicely browned on all sides, about 6 minutes total. Remove to a plate.

03 Add the 1 lb (455 g) sausage to the Dutch oven and cook over medium-high heat, stirring frequently, until all of the pieces are browned on at least one side, about 3 minutes. If any bits of beef that are stuck to the bottom start to burn, lower the heat to medium.

04 If using onion, add it to the pot and cook, stirring, until just softened, about 3 minutes.

05 Add the 1 garlic clove and ½ t coriander and stir for 30 seconds.

06 Return the browned short ribs to the pot and add the drained beans, the 12 oz (340 g) pork chops, 2 bay leaves, and enough water to cover the beans (about 4 c/1 L). Bring to a low boil, then carefully transfer the pot to the oven. Bake, uncovered, for 1½–2 hours, until the beans are very tender and beginning to break down. The short rib meat should have pulled back from the ends of the bones significantly. Add more water if necessary to keep the beans covered.

07 Fish out and discard the bay leaves. If you like, remove and discard the bones. Up to you. I don't bother.

Season with salt to taste. Spoon the meats and beans into shallow serving bowls and (optional) serve with the toasted almond flour for sprinkling.

NOTES

- Chouriço is a Portuguese-style smoked pork sausage lightly spiced with paprika. It can be found in the refrigerated section of good supermarkets near the smoked pork chops and ham hocks. Substitute another smoked pork sausage such as andouille or kielbasa if you can't find it.

- If not using onion, use a good low-sodium beef or chicken stock instead of water so the broth is plenty flavorful.

- Toasted almond flour appears above as a substitute for toasted manioc/cassava/yucca flour, which is called *farofa* and is always sprinkled liberally on feijoada. To toast almond flour, heat a dry sauté pan over medium-high heat and add the flour. Cook, stirring frequently with a heatproof silicone spatula, until it becomes a couple of shades darker and slightly fragrant. Immediately remove to a plate to cool.

The Top 10 Cuisine-Specific Cookbooks

At 163 West 10th Street in Manhattan, more than 3,000 books are kept straight... in Bonnie Slotnick's head. She has handpicked every out-of-print and antiquarian book in her store, Bonnie Slotnick Cookbooks. Beyond the issues of *Gourmet* magazine dating back to the 1940s, the shelves contain the best of the best, all sorted by cuisine.

Since she's the cookbook Oracle of Delphi, I naturally asked Bonnie to help create an all-time Top 10 list, one per culture. Here it is:

1. James Beard: ***American* Cookery**
2. Penelope Casas: **The Foods and Wines of *Spain***
3. Julia Child: **Mastering the Art of *French* Cooking**
4. Marcella Hazan: **The Classic *Italian* Cookbook**
5. Madhur Jaffrey: **An Invitation to *Indian* Cooking**
6. Diana Kennedy: **The Cuisines of *Mexico***
7. Claudia Roden: **A Book of *Middle Eastern* Food**
8. David Thompson: ***Thai* Food**
9. Barbara Tropp: **The Modern Art of *Chinese* Cooking**
10. Shizuo Tsuji: ***Japanese* Cooking: A Simple Art**

And one bonus that Bonnie couldn't leave out:

Alan Davidson, ed.: **The Oxford Companion to Food.** A fascinating reference work to dip into for the rest of your life.

- To make a simple true *farofa* with manioc flour (available at some Latin American grocery stores and markets), perhaps as a cheat day extravagance, heat 3 T ghee or pure butter in a medium sauté pan over medium heat. When it's hot, add 1 c (120 g) coarse-ground manioc flour and a pinch of salt, and stir to moisten it evenly. Cook, stirring constantly, until the mixture is a shade darker and becomes fragrant and toasty, 2–4 minutes.

- Scrape into a bowl and serve alongside the feijoada as a condiment.

Grant's Principles #9

INGREDIENT THEMES

SAGE & PAPRIKA MEAL

KOKKARI PRAWNS + THE MEDICINE MAN + SAGE GELATO

"Finding a really good spice is a major accomplishment. There's my Paprika!"

—DR. KŌSAKU TOKITA, *PAPRIKA*

"This is very typical of me. I finish cooking and there's nothing extra for me to clean. I can make eight different dishes in little dishes, each served in what they're cooked in. One pot is nice, but it's boring."

Erik Cosselmon was explaining why he's fond of using small Staub serviceware at his San Francisco–based Greek restaurant, Kokkari. The first time I came across one, it was in the spot's Palo Alto–based sister restaurant, Evvia. Face-to-face with this serviceware for the first time, I did what I always do: I sized everything for later research (see below).

The following meal is intended to demonstrate ingredient-themed dishes. Here, sage and paprika will be the stars. We'll also use small oven-to-table gear. It's a light meal with a sweet ending.

The order:

- **KOKKARI PRAWNS,** served with
- **THE MEDICINE MAN,** finished with
- **SAGE GELATO**

Using my pen to size the Staub. In the upper left, Greek cuisine notes I took during appetizers.

KOKKARI
ESTIATORIO
Erik A. Cosselmon

Erik Cosselmon in the Kokkari kitchen.

Grant's Principles #9

INGREDIENT THEMES

KOKKARI PRAWNS (ENTRÉE)

GARIDES TOU FOURNO

CONTRIBUTED BY

Erik Cosselmon

SHORTHAND

Simmer 16 H2O-covered prawn shells, 1 onion slice 10min. Sieve for stock. Simmer 1c tomato sauce, ⅓c stock; remove from heat. + 2oz feta, ¼c dill, ¼c scallions, ¼c EVOO, ½t paprika. Spoon over prawns in baking dish. Sprinkle w 2oz feta, 2T EVOO. Broil 5–7min till pink.

TOTAL TIME

30 minutes, plus 20 minutes if making sauce

GEAR

- Knife + cutting board
- Small saucepan
- Small skillet
- Baking dish

INGREDIENTS	TO SERVE 4
Large prawns in the shell	**1 lb (455 g) (about 16)**
Off-the-shelf tomato sauce, or Kokkari Tomato Sauce (see sidebar)	**1 c (240 ml)**
Crumbled Greek feta cheese	**¾ c (115 g)**
Fresh dill, coarsely chopped	**¼ c (15 g)**
Scallions, thinly sliced, including green parts	**¼ c (25 g)**
EVOO	**¼ c (60 ml), plus 2 T**
Spanish smoked sweet paprika	**½ t**
S+P	**To taste**
OPTIONAL	
Yellow onion	**1 thick slice**

"We bake these prawns in our wood-burning oven, which imparts a smoky scent; although not traditional, smoked paprika can help you achieve similar results at home," Erik says.

You will not use all the prawn stock you make, so freeze the extra for soup.

00 Peel the 1 lb (455 g) prawns, reserving the shells and leaving the tail attached if desired. Slit the back of each prawn and remove the black vein. Put the shells in a small saucepan and add just enough cold water to cover. Add a slice of onion if you have it. Simmer gently for 10 minutes over medium heat. Strain through a sieve set over a bowl, pressing on the shells to extract their flavor.

01 Preheat the broiler and set a rack 6–8" (15–20 cm) from the heating element.

02 In a small skillet, combine the 1 c (240 ml) tomato sauce and ⅓ c (80 ml) of the prawn stock and bring barely to a simmer over medium heat. Remove from the heat and add ½ of the feta, crumbling it into the hot sauce. Stir in the ¼ c (15 g) dill, ¼ c (25 g) scallions, ¼ c (60 ml) of the EVOO, and ½ t paprika. Stir well. The mixture will be slightly soupy, like a thin tomato sauce. The feta will not melt completely.

03 Season the prawns with S+P and place them in an oven-to-table baking dish, such as a Staub cocotte or a terracotta dish (page 130), just large enough to hold them in one layer.

04 Spoon the sauce over the prawns. Sprinkle with the remaining feta and 2 T olive oil.

05 Broil until a nice crust develops on top and the prawns are pink and firm, 5–7 minutes. Because the prawns are cloaked in sauce, you will need to scrape away a little sauce to confirm doneness. Serve sizzling hot.

Kokkari Prawns and the Medicine Man.

Kokkari Tomato Sauce

Makes about 2½ cups:

- Puree 1 can (28 oz/ 800 g) San Marzano tomatoes in food processor.
- Heat ¼ c EVOO in saucepan at medium heat.
- Add 2 peeled and crushed garlic cloves. Discard cloves when browned.
- Add tomatoes, keep at a simmer, and stir for approximately 15 minutes until they've lost their raw taste.
- Add ½ t crumbled dried oregano; simmer 5 minutes.
- Add 1 sprig fresh basil, remove from heat. Salt to taste.

Keeps for 3 days refrigerated.

Grant's Principles #9

INGREDIENT THEMES

THE MEDICINE MAN (DIGESTIF[22])

CONTRIBUTED BY

Ian Scalzo

SHORTHAND

Shake 2oz rum, ¾oz lemon juice, ½oz maple syrup, ½t paprika, 2 dashes orange bitters w ¾-full ice shaker 20 sec. Garnish w spanked sage.

HANDS-ON TIME

2 minutes

TOTAL TIME

2 minutes

GEAR

- Cobbler shaker (you could also use a Boston shaker with Hawthorn strainer, but the Cobbler is all-in-one: fourhourchef.com/shaker)
- Large cocktail glass

INGREDIENTS	TO SERVE 1
White rum[23]	2 oz (60 ml)
Lemon juice	¾ oz (20 ml)
Maple syrup[24]	½ oz (15 ml)
Smoked paprika	4 dashes (½ t)
Orange bitters[25]	2 dashes
Sage	4 leaves (3 for mixing, 1 for garnish)

"Should I dress up?" my friend asked me.

I nodded: "Sure. Just be sure to wear shoes you can run in."

We were headed to my favorite cocktail bar, Bourbon & Branch. B&B operated from 1923 to 1935 as JJ Russell's Cigar Shop, an illegal speakeasy working hand-in-hand with Vancouver's most famous bootleggers. Still at the same address but now nestled among crackheads in San Francisco's Tenderloin district, it has no signage. To enter through an unmarked door, you need a password.

Once inside, you enter another epoch. Up a small flight of stairs resides the Library, a real Sherlock Holmes–like library that's been converted into a gorgeous standing-only bar. It was here, under stained glass, that I discovered one of the most sublime drinks in the world: the Medicine Man.

Developed by bartender Ian Scalzo, it uses our now familiar seasonings, paprika and sage. I love that something so delicious, and seemingly fancy, can be made from ingredients commonly left over after cooking.

00 Fill up ¾ of a shaker with ice cubes.

01 Put in everything except 1 sage leaf (save it for garnish).

02 Shake (depends on the ice, but 20 seconds should do it) and strain. Serve up, which means no ice.

03 To use the fresh sage leaf for garnish, first "spank" it (put it on one open palm and slap it with the other hand a few times) to release the essential oils. Place it on top of the drink.

22 In this context, a drink to aid digestion. Usually code for "an excuse for more alcohol."

23 The slight body and sweet molasses notes of white rum pair well with the sage/paprika/maple flavor profile. Though a far second choice, Scotch also turns out well.

24 Grade A Medium Amber is ideal; I like Ledgenear Farm brand.

25 Bitters bottles usually have a dasher top built in, but if not, one dash equals 3–5 drops. I use Angostura bitters. Fee Bros. is another type of bitters.

Bourbon & Branch.

Grant's Principles #9

INGREDIENT THEMES

SAGE GELATO (DESSERT)

SHORTHAND

Heat to simmer: 3c coconut milk, ¾t salt, 1 tied bunch sage; steep 1hr. Remove sage; reheat to 170F. Whisk 4 yolks, ½c sugar; + coconut mix slowly; reheat til 185F, + ½c honey. Strain & cool; refrigerate 4h. Pour into food processor, freeze 1hr, process 3–5 seconds, return to freezer. Repeat every 30min till soft gelato; freeze overnight to firm.

HANDS-ON TIME

20 minutes

TOTAL TIME

About 6 hours, plus at least 4 hours chilling the custard and 4 hours firming the gelato in the freezer

GEAR

- Kitchen string
- Medium saucepan
- Whisk
- Probe or candy thermometer
- 2 medium heatproof bowls (metal or silicone)
- Fine-mesh strainer
- Food processor or 8" (20 cm) baking dish
- Immersion blender (optional)
- Wooden spoon
- Firm spatula

INGREDIENTS	TO MAKE JUST OVER 1 PINT
Sage	1 bunch (⅔ oz/19 g)
Egg yolks[26]	4 large
Coconut milk	3 c (700 ml)
Salt	¼ t
Sugar	½ c (100 g)
Light honey (I like orange blossom honey)	½ c (120 ml)

There's no reason to invest in a dedicated electric ice cream machine. It's easy enough to make your own with a work-around.

An ice cream machine breaks up ice crystals to make your gelato smooth and creamy, so we'll do the same using a food processor or whisk. Fat also keeps ice crystals from forming, hence plenty of egg yolks and fatty coconut milk for our recipe. And forgoing the machine means less air is introduced into the gelato, making it super-dense. As an added bonus for the lactose-intolerant, this gelato is dairy-free.

Fragrant sage and honey make for an ethereal fusion

26 Save the egg whites for another recipe, such as Harissa Crab Cakes (page 172) or Almond Za'atar Crackers with Tuna (page 510). You can freeze them for longer storage: pop each white into individual ice cube tray compartments and freeze until firm, then pop out and store in a freezer bag.

that must be tasted to be believed. Sage gelato may be new to Americans, but it's no stranger to Italians. Savory flavors such as rosemary and Gorgonzola can be found on typical Italian dessert menus in the gelato section.

00 Separate the eggs and tie up the bunch of sage in kitchen string.

01 In a medium saucepan, combine the 3 c (700 ml) coconut milk and ¼ t salt; whisk to dissolve the salt. Add the sage. Heat the coconut milk mixture over medium-low heat until bubbles start to form around the edges (do not bring to a boil). Stir occasionally so a skin doesn't form.

Once bubbles appear, remove from heat and cover. Let stand for 1 hour to infuse the coconut milk with the sage.

02 Remove the sage bundle from the coconut milk and squeeze any liquid from the sage back into the saucepan. Reheat over medium-low heat to a temperature of 170°F (75°C) as measured by candy or probe thermometer.

03 Once near 170°F (75°C), in a medium heatproof bowl, whisk the 4 egg yolks with the ½ c (100 g) sugar until a custard forms, then slowly add the warm coconut milk mixture, whisking constantly. Scrape this custard back into the saucepan and cook, stirring, over medium-low heat until the mixture thickens enough to coat the back of a wooden spoon and reaches a temperature of 185°F (85°C). Do not boil.

04 Stir or whisk the ½ c (120 ml) honey into the custard until it's dissolved.

05 Pour the entire custard through a fine-mesh strainer into a clean heatproof bowl; this will remove any egg solids that might have formed.

06 Cool the custard to room temperature, stirring every 5 minutes or so for about 30 minutes. To get it cool in just 10 minutes, make an ice bath by filling the bottom of a large bowl with ice and water; place the bowl with the custard in it and stir until cooled.

07 Cover and refrigerate the custard until very cold, at least 4 hours, preferably overnight. You can do this 2 days ahead of time.

08 To make the ice cream, choose one of two methods: food processor or baking pan. For either method, you'll need to clear some space in your freezer.

09A **For the food processor method:** Pour the cold custard into a food processor, detach container from unit, place in the freezer, and freeze for 1 hour. Take it out and scrape the mixture from the sides of the bowl,[27] then run the machine for a few seconds. Scrape the sides again and run the machine for a few more seconds. Return the food processor container to the freezer. Now freeze for 30 minutes at a time, processing and scraping, until a very soft gelato forms, 3–4 hours total (it will firm up more later). Transfer the gelato to a freezer-safe container and freeze at least 4 hours.

09B **For the baking pan method:** Pour the cold custard into an 8" (20-cm) baking dish, place in the freezer, and freeze for 1 hour. Take it out, scrape the mixture from the sides of the pan, and mix it all vigorously with a whisk or immersion blender. Freeze again. Repeat the drill every 30 minutes until a very soft gelato forms, 3–4 hours total (it will firm up more later). Transfer to a freezer-safe container and freeze at least 4 hours or overnight.

27 Remember the hard plastic spatula that came with your food processor that you tossed into a drawer, bewildered by its inability to properly scrape the sides of the processor bowl? Go find it, because it finally found its purpose as a gelato scraper: its inflexibility is just what is needed to detach the semifrozen gelato from the sides of the bowl; a regular flexible silicone spatula is what you need for scraping nonfrozen food from your processor, but it doesn't have the strength to do this job.

Grant's Principles #10

AROMA

CIGAR-INFUSED TEQUILA HOT CHOCOLATE

INSPIRED BY
Craig Schoettler

SHORTHAND
Smoke 4c milk, ¼c sugar, ¼t salt mixed w lit cigar 30min; set aside. Stir 2c simmered milk, ¼c sugar, pinch salt w 3½oz chocolate till melted. Mix 6T tequila, 2t Fernet Branca. Combine 7oz hot chocolate, w ½ alcohol; top w foamed cigar milk.

HANDS-ON TIME
20 minutes

TOTAL TIME
1 hour 30 minutes, max (1 hour of passive smoking)

GEAR
- A largish cereal or soup bowl
- A large stockpot
- Aluminum foil
- A candle lighter or butane lighter/torch
- Saucepan or skillet (or both, if you want to melt the chocolate separately)
- Immersion blender

"What this country needs is a really good five-cent cigar."

—THOMAS R. MARSHALL, FORMER U.S. VICE PRESIDENT

INGREDIENTS	TO SERVE 2 (PLUS EXTRA CIGAR MILK)
CIGAR MILK	
Whole milk	4 c (945 ml)
Sugar	¼ c (40 g)
Salt	1 big pinch
Cigar (something inexpensive is fine)	1
HOT CHOCOLATE	
Whole milk	2 c (470 ml)
Sugar	¼ c (40 g)
Salt	1 pinch
Bittersweet chocolate, chopped (e.g., Alpaco 66%)	3½ oz (100 g)
FOR THE BOOZE	
Tequila (Craig prefers Fortaleza Blanco)	6 T (90 ml)
Fernet Branca	2 t

This spectacular drink was taught to me by Craig Schoettler, the executive chef at the Aviary in Chicago, without a doubt the most awe-inspiring "bar-less cocktail kitchen" in the world.

To set the scene: customers are prevented from harassing the bartenders by a cage barricade. The drinks come out like restaurant dishes. Perhaps you'd like an old-fashioned served in an ice dinosaur egg? The liquid is injected with a syringe, and you drink it after shattering the bourbon-filled casing with a slingshot attached to the rim of the glass. Or how about a botanical-infused whiskey that changes colors like a chameleon over 30 minutes? They have that, too. Bartending through the lens of world-class chefs is a trip.

This recipe has been modified to fit a few standard measurements. These tweaks take it from super-insanely awesome (the Aviary) to merely very insanely awesome.

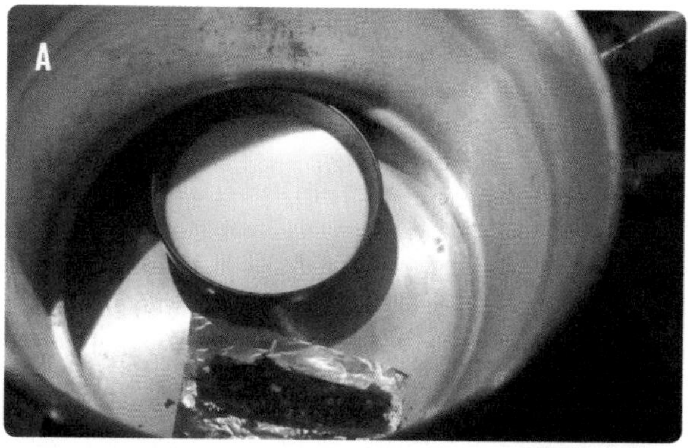
A

B

C

D

E
STREET
FOOD

F

G

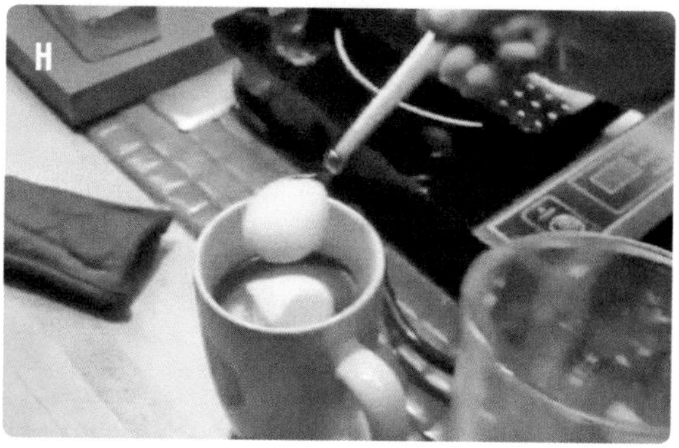
H

MAKE CIGAR MILK:

Though regular folks might use two baking or roasting pans of different sizes, I have a more ghetto-fabulous approach.

00 Mix the milk, sugar, and salt in a largish cereal or soup bowl.

01 Put this bowl inside a stockpot. I prefer a cheap ($25) large stockpot that I use mostly for cooking sous-vide and lobsters.

02 Split the cigar in half lengthwise and place it on a piece of aluminum foil at the bottom of the stockpot.

03 Light the cigar with a candle lighter or a butane lighter/torch, cover the pot, and let smoke for 30–45 minutes (30 minutes is plenty, in my experience).

Note: Later, to de-stench your stockpot, just clean it out and put a bowl of white wine vinegar mixed with peppermint oil inside, cover the pot, and leave for 1–2 hours.

MAKE HOT CHOCOLATE:

00 In a saucepan or skillet, combine the 2 c (470 ml) milk, ¼ c (40 g) sugar, and 1 pinch salt and bring to a simmer.

01 Remove from the heat and slowly add the 3½ oz (100 g) chopped chocolate. I like to put the chocolate in a separate skillet and slide it in. Do NOT add the chocolate by hand; scalding milk can splash upward and burn your hands. Stir until chocolate is melted, then cover and set aside.

FOAM THE MILK:

00 Pour the smoked milk into a saucepan and heat it to a light simmer. Use an immersion blender—ideally one fitted with the cream-whipping attachment or a milk frother—to blend until foamy. No attachment? Tilt everything, blend for 45 seconds, then wait 2–3 minutes for the bubbles to surface. Or just put it in a French press and rapidly move the plunger up and down.

01 Combine 6 T (90 ml) tequila and 2 t Fernet Branca into one of your serving cups, then pour ½ of it into the other. You can use a scale, but I eyeball. Into each cup, pour about 7 oz (210 ml) of the hot chocolate base and top with some of the cigar milk foam. Serve warm and love life.

If you don't finish the cigar milk, freeze it in ice trays to surprise future guests with high-octane iced coffee.

Or Keep It Simple: Herb Bowl

Here's an idea for an aromatic centerpiece that isn't meant to be eaten. Gather a small bunch of your favorite herbs—I like basil, mint, and thyme—and place them in a nice bowl on the table. Once guests are seated, pour steaming-hot water over the herbs to release a fragrant vapor. Ahhhh, calms the spirit *and* clears the sinuses.

DRAGONFORCE CHACONNE

> "Nine out of 10 English chefs have their names on their chests. Who do they think they are? They're dreamers. . . . Just ask yourself how many chefs in this country have Michelin stars and how many have their names on their jackets. We all wear blue aprons in my kitchen because we're all *commis* [apprentices]. We're all still learning."
>
> —MARCO PIERRE WHITE, *WHITE HEAT*

"Chaconne," from Johann Sebastian Bach's *Partita No. 2 in D Minor,* is a beast. Violin virtuoso Joshua Bell calls it "not just one of the greatest pieces of music ever written, but one of the greatest achievements of any man in history."

Bach's "Chaconne" is also considered one of the most difficult violin pieces to master. Many try; few succeed. It's exhaustingly long—14 minutes—and consists of a single, succinct musical progression, repeated in dozens of variations, to create a cathedral-like architecture of sound. Composed around 1720, on the eve of the European Enlightenment, it is said to be a celebration of the breadth of human possibility.‡

But imagine . . . what if you nailed it? Tackled something of that complexity and got a standing ovation?

If Bach is too highbrow, let us consider DragonForce's "Through the Fire and Flames." It is the "Chaconne" of *Guitar Hero 3.* Many try, and again, few succeed.

So, what is the equivalent of Chaconne or DragonForce in the cooking universe? To find out, I asked chefs, hired researchers, and interviewed recipe testers—people who find, test, and refine recipes as a full-time job. The top 10 spirit-breaking dishes that came up

The Top 10

1) **Baked Alaska:** Ice cream surrounded by cake and baked. Since there's an intrinsic contradiction between ovens and ice cream, the key is to make sure your ice cream is *very* frozen before you start.
2) **Beef Wellington:** Beef fillet and foie gras baked in puff pastry—decadent and challenging.
3) **Coq au Vin:** Braised "rooster in wine," although chicken is now generally used. It's more time-consuming than difficult, unless you go super-traditional and use real rooster and add blood at the end to thicken the sauce.
4) **Croissants:** When made from scratch, these buttery pastries require a Buddha's worth of patience.
5) **Mole:** A traditional Mexican sauce that can take at least three days to make, often containing upward of 20 ingredients.
6) **Napoleon:** A dessert made with alternating layers of puff pastry and custard cream.
7) **Paella:** The renowned Valencian rice-and-whatever-you-have-on-hand dish. The biggest challenge is getting the proper crust, or *socarrat*, on the bottom layer.
8) **Rabbit Roulade:** Rabbit loin pounded thin, then rolled around a vegetable-and-starch stuffing. Just to get started, you must debone an entire rabbit, keeping it whole.
9) **Savory soufflés:** For these famously difficult and puffy baked-egg recipes, the trick is beating enough air into your egg whites to prevent them from collapsing.
10) **Timpano:** A tableful of food—pasta, meat, sauce, eggs, cheese—baked in a crust. This is what they make as the grand finale at the end of *Big Night*.

In the end, while certainly hard, the above list didn't seem next-to-impossible. I wanted still odder ingredients, insanely intricate manual precision, and more headache and heartache across the board. But, being a kind soul, I wanted to avoid recipes that require large teams or industrial equipment (e.g., Alinea's green-apple edible balloons).

What follows is one grand recipe that fits the bill.

It is included as a foolish dare for those of you who believe too much is never enough. After all, as I was once told, "Don't refuse to go on an occasional wild goose chase—that's what wild geese are for." View the cost of ingredients as entertainment budget, regardless of outcome. Or, if it helps, view this as your final exam.

This recipe will also underscore how much you still *don't* know. The true masters are a breed apart, and we wouldn't want your head to get too big, aye?

Enjoy, my sick little puppies, enjoy.

DRAGONFORCE CHACONNE

CARP À L'ANCIENNE

INSPIRED BY

Auguste Escoffier, author of *Le Guide Culinaire*

HANDS-ON TIME

10–20 hours, depending on multitasking skills

TOTAL TIME

1 long weekend, or 2 epic days

GEAR

- Knife + cutting board
- Silicone spatula
- Mixing bowls
- Nonstick skillet
- Food processor
- Airtight containers
- Stockpot
- Strainer
- Medium and large saucepans
- Whisk
- Cookie sheet
- Sieve
- Tablespoons
- Paring knife
- Mandolin
- Melon baller
- Plastic wrap
- Parchment paper
- Roasting pan
- For serving: fish platter or other large serving platter

"In all professions without doubt, but certainly in cooking, one is a student all his life."

—AUGUSTE ESCOFFIER

When Grant Achatz launched Next, his highly anticipated second restaurant, he did so with a "Paris 1906" menu. It was an homage to the man hailed as the father of French cuisine: Auguste Escoffier. Next's sold-out table reservations were scalped for $3,000 on Craigslist.

Escoffier ran the kitchen at the Paris Ritz Hotel in 1906. He also *created* kitchens as we know them (e.g., he popularized the *brigade de cuisine* organization), menus as we know them (e.g., the first à la carte menu), and haute cuisine as we know it. His landmark cookbook, *Le Guide Culinaire,* was published in 1903 and is still feared by culinary school students. Now you'll know why.

The following Carp à l'Ancienne recipe "borders on the realms of fantasy," as Escoffier himself admitted. In simple terms, fish forcemeat (ground fish) is molded into the shape of a carp and topped with black truffle "scales." This can get expensive. To lessen the sting, I've included a recipe for faux truffles using potatoes soaked in squid ink, courtesy of Martin Lindsay.

This recipe is a showstopper. It's also a back- and will-breaker. May the Force be with you.

INGREDIENTS	TO SERVE 8–10
FISH	
Whole carp	1 (4–5 lb)
Water (enough to cover roe sacs)	4¼ c (1 L)
Kosher salt	2 T
BREAD PANADA[28]	
Stale white bread, cubed	2½ c (270 g)
Whole milk	1¼ c (300 ml)
CARP FORCEMEAT[29]	
Onion, chopped	⅓ c (50 g)
Leek, chopped	¼ c plus 1 T (25 g)
White button mushrooms, diced	1 c (85 g)
Unsalted butter	2½ T
Reserved carp fillets (see above) cut into 1" pieces	2¼ lb (1 kg)
Bread Panada (see above)	1 lb (454 g)
Parsley	2 T plus 2 t
Egg	1
Egg yolks	3
Unsalted butter, cubed	1 c (228 g)
Truffle oil	½ t
Kosher salt	To taste
Freshly ground pepper	To taste
FUMÉT DE POISSON (FISH STOCK)	
Reserved carp bones and scraps (see above)	
Canola oil	Enough to cover bottom of roasting pan
Onion, chopped	⅔ c (100 g)
Leeks, chopped	1 c (100 g)
White button mushrooms, chopped	1½ c (128 g)
Unsalted butter	1 T
White wine	¾ c (180 ml)
Water (to completely cover fish bones)	1½ gal (5.5 L)
Fresh parsley, chopped	⅓ c (20 g)
Black peppercorns	12
Fresh thyme sprigs	1½ T
Lemon juice	¼ c

28 A *panada* is a mixture of bread and milk used as a base to thicken forcemeats.
29 *Forcemeat* is just an old-fashioned term for ground-up meat or fish emulsified with fat. Placed in casings, it's sausages. In a loaf, it's meatloaf. In a Pyrex bowl and baked, it's salmon loaf or the like.

INGREDIENTS (CONTINUED)	
ROUX BLANC (WHITE ROUX)	
Clarified butter	1 c (240 ml)
All-purpose flour, sifted	2¼ c (275 g)
ROUX BLOND (BLOND ROUX)	
Clarified butter	1 c (240 ml)
All-purpose flour, sifted	2¼ c (275 g)
ROUX BRUN (BROWN ROUX)	
Clarified butter	1 c (240 ml)
All-purpose flour, sifted	2¼ c (275 g)
SAUCE ESPAGNOLE MAIGRE (FISH ESPAGNOLE SAUCE)	
Carrots, diced	½ c (65 g)
Onion, diced	¼ c (40 g)
Button or brown mushrooms, roughly diced	¾ c (65 g)
Unsalted butter	2½ T
Tomato paste	2 T
White wine	½ c (120 ml)
Fumét de Poisson (see page 551)	4 c (1 L)
Fresh thyme sprigs	2
Bay leaf	1
Roux Brun (see above)	1 c (125 g)
VELOUTÉ DE POISSON (FISH VELOUTÉ)	
Fumét de Poisson (see page 551)	4 c (1 L)
Roux Blond (see above)	1¼ c (155 g)
MUSSEL STOCK[30]	
Onion, diced	⅔ c (100 g)
Celery, chopped	⅔ c (100 g)
Dried fennel seed	2 t
Unsalted butter	2½ T
Dry vermouth (I like Dolin)	1 small bottle (13 oz/375 ml)
Absinthe (I like La Fée Absinthe Parisienne)	1 oz (30 ml)
Bay leaf	1
Black peppercorns	12
Fresh or frozen mussels (any type)	2 lb (1 kg)

30 This recipe is adapted from the cookbook *Alinea*.

INGREDIENTS (CONTINUED)	
MUSHROOM STOCK[31]	
Mushrooms,[32] chopped	8 c (700 g)
Carrots, chopped	1 c (125 g)
Onion, chopped	½ c plus 1 T (87 g)
Leeks, chopped	1 c (87 g)
Fresh parsley, chopped	⅓ c (20 g)
Unsalted butter	2½ T
Thyme sprigs	1½ T
Sweet curry powder	⅓ t
Water	½ gal (2 L)
SAUCE NORMANDE (NORMANDY SAUCE)	
Velouté de Poisson (see left)	2¾ c (660 g)
Mushroom Stock (see above)	½ c (120 ml)
Mussel Stock (see left)	½ c (120 ml)
Fumét de Poisson (see page 551)	⅔ c (160 ml)
Lemon juice	½ t
Egg yolks	5
Heavy cream	1¼ c (300 ml)
Unsalted butter	½ c (114 g)
SAUCE GENEVOISE (GENEVA SAUCE)	
Carrots, chopped	¾ c (100 g)
Onion, chopped	½ c (80 g)
Fresh parsley, chopped	⅓ c (20 g)
Unsalted butter	2½ T
Thyme sprigs	4
Bay leaf	1
Black peppercorns	16
Salmon heads, split in half and cleaned	2 lb (1 kg/≈3)
Red wine	1 bottle (750 ml)
Sauce Espagnole Maigre (see left)	2 c (470 ml)
Red wine	2 c (470 ml)
Fumét de Poisson (see page 551)	2 c (470 ml)
Unsalted butter	⅔ c (150 g)
Anchovy paste or fish sauce	½ t, or to taste

31 This recipe is adapted from the Next restaurant Escoffier cookbook.

32 Regular white button mushrooms work perfectly. Or you can use half white button mushrooms and half black Asian mushrooms for a more savory taste.

INGREDIENTS (CONTINUED)	
BEURRE D'ECREVISSE (CRAYFISH BUTTER)	
Carrots, finely chopped	½ c (64 g)
Onions, finely chopped	⅓ c (58 g)
Leeks, finely chopped	⅔ c (50 g)
Unsalted butter	2½ T, plus 2 lb (908 g)
Tomato paste	3 T
Whole cooked crayfish bodies	2 lb (1 kg)
Thyme sprigs	2 t
Bay leaves	4
Old Bay seasoning	1 T
Sweet paprika	2 t
Ground cayenne pepper	½ t
WHITING FORCEMEAT[33]	
Boneless sole or whitefish fillets	1 lb (454 g)
Egg whites	2 T
Beurre d'Ecrevisse	⅓ c plus 1 t (85 g)
Kosher salt	2 t
Heavy cream	2⅛ c (500 ml)
Water or fish stock (for poaching the quenelles)	4½ c (1 L)
Sauce Normande (see page 553)	2¾ c (650 ml)
Chopped chives and microgreens (for garnish)	To taste
OYSTERS WITH MIGNONETTE[34] SAUCE	
Shallots, minced	½ c plus 2T (100 g)
Red wine vinegar	⅔ c (160 g)
Coarsely ground black pepper	1½ t
Oysters, shucked	12
Radish, finely chopped (for garnish)	To taste
Chives, chopped (for garnish)	To taste
Sea salt	To taste
FLUTED MUSHROOMS	
White button mushrooms (the whitest you can find!)	10
Lemon juice	2 t
Water	1 c (240 ml)

33 This recipe was adapted from recipes by both Escoffier and Julia Child.

34 A traditional accompaniment to oysters, *mignonette* comes in many variations, depending on the whim and creativity of the chef. This is a simple but classic recipe that goes well with any type of oyster.

INGREDIENTS (CONTINUED)	
FLUTED MUSHROOMS (CONTINUED)	
Clarified butter	2 T plus 2 t
Mushroom Stock (see page 553)	¼ c (60 ml)
Cooked crayfish tail meat	⅓ c (85 g)
Carp Forcemeat (see page 551)	⅓ c (85 g)
Beurre d'Ecrevisse (see left)	⅓ c (85 g)
Capers	20
Canola oil	Enough to cover capers
BLACK TRUFFLE SLICES	
Whole black truffles	3 or 4 (about 60 g)
Olive oil	Enough to cover truffles
Truffle oil	1 t
FAUX TRUFFLE SLICES[35]	
Yukon Gold potatoes, peeled and diced	2 c (300 g)
Dried black trumpet mushrooms	3 oz (82 g)
Dried black Asian mushrooms	1½ oz (40 g)
Reserved black truffle trimmings (see above)	
Truffle oil	1 T
Salt Farm black truffle salt	1½ t
Egg yolk	1
Flour	1¾ c (219 g)
Canola oil	Enough to cover potatoes
Quaker instant grits	2 packets
Squid ink	2 (0.14 oz/4 g) packets
Water	¼ c (60 ml)
BREADED CARP ROE	
Carp or other fish roe (see page 551)	1 lb (500 g)
Panko breadcrumbs	¼ c (17 g)
Eggs	2
All-purpose flour	2 c (50 g)
Eggs, beaten	2
Panko bread crumbs	2 c (50 g)
Canola oil	See recipe steps

35 Even in Escoffier's day, truffles were a delicacy. But they were much more plentiful, less expensive, and easier to get. It has been estimated that today's truffle production is one-tenth of what it was then. Needless to say, serving whole fresh truffles as a side dish isn't realistic for most. So here we're making faux truffles—effectively truffle-based gnocchi, fried as fritters for a crunchy skin and then dyed black using squid ink. This recipe is inspired by Mario Batali.

CLEAN THE FISH

00 Fillet the fish, reserving the head and tail.

01 Remove the roe sacs (skeins) and place them in a bath of 4¼ c (1 L) water and 2 T salt to cure. Save the bones and scraps for Fumet de Poisson.

MAKE THE BREAD PANADA

00 Remove the crust from the 2½ c (270 g) bread and cube it.

01 Soak the bread cubes in 1¼ c (300 ml) boiled milk. Mix to form a smooth paste.

MAKE THE CARP FORCEMEAT

00 Sauté the ⅓ c (50 g) onion, ¼ c plus 1 T (25 g) leeks, and 1 c (85 g) white mushrooms in 2½ T butter. Cool.

01 Place the fish, 1 lb (454 g) panada, onion, leeks, mushrooms, 2 T plus 2 t parsley, 1 egg, and 3 egg yolks in a food processor. Blend until smooth, adding 1 c (228 g) cubed butter as needed.

02 Add ½ t truffle oil and S+P to taste at end. Transfer to a container and chill in the fridge.

MAKE THE FUMÉT DE POISSON

00 Roast the fish bones and scraps in a little canola oil in a 400°F (200°C) oven until browned.

01 In a stockpot over low heat, sauté the ⅔ c (100 g) onion, 1 c (100 g) leeks, and 1½ c (128 g) mushrooms in 1 T butter until translucent.

02 Add the fish scraps and cook for about 5 minutes more.

03 Deglaze the pan with ¾ c (180 ml) white wine and reduce until almost dry.

04 Add the 1½ gallons (5.5 L) water, ⅓ c (20 g) chopped parsley, 12 peppercorns, 5 t thyme, and ¼ c lemon juice. Simmer for about 1 hour, skimming any foam off the surface.

05 Let cool, then strain into a container. This may be refrigerated for several days, or frozen and used later.

Note: Do *not* cover and refrigerate hot stocks or sauces, as they can sour quickly in the fridge—always let them cool before you refrigerate!

MAKE THE ROUX BLANC

00 To clarify the 1 c (240 ml) butter, melt it over low heat and strain. You'll notice that it renders into three distinct layers. There is a white foam on the top, which is salt and casein. Skim this off. Next is the actual butterfat. This is what you want to use. And on the bottom is a layer of water and whey—you can discard that, too.

01 Mix the clarified butter and 2¼ c (275 g) flour together in a heavy pan and cook on low heat, whisking until the flour smells a little nutty and takes on a sheen. You want to cook it just enough to cook out the real floury taste.

MAKE THE ROUX BLOND

00 Mix the 1 c (240 ml) clarified butter and 2¼ c (275 g) flour together in a heavy pan and cook on low heat, whisking until the flour smells nutty and takes on a sheen. Keep cooking until it turns a golden yellow.

MAKE THE ROUX BRUN

00 Mix the 1 c (225 g) clarified butter and 2¼ (275 g) flour together in a heavy pan and cook on low heat, whisking until the flour turns a medium brown.

Note: When mixing roux into a sauce, be careful to either A) mix cold roux into a hot sauce, or B) mix hot roux into a cold sauce. This activates the starch so it thickens the sauce.

MAKE THE SAUCE ESPAGNOLE MAIGRE

00 In a large stockpot, sauté the ½ c (65 g) carrots, ¼ c (40 g) onion, and ¾ c (65 g) mushrooms in the 2½ T (40 g) butter until translucent.

01 Add the 2 T tomato paste and let the vegetables brown.

02 Deglaze the pot with the ½ c (120 ml) white wine and reduce until almost dry.

03 Add the 4 c (1 L) Fumét de Poisson, 2 thyme sprigs, and 1 bay leaf. Gently simmer, skimming off any foam from the surface, for about 5 hours.

04 Strain and add the 1 c (125 g) Roux Brun to the reduced stock. Simmer gently for another hour, stirring so it does not stick.

05 Taste the sauce. If it has a floury flavor, simmer some more. Remove from heat, strain, and stir occasionally until the sauce is completely cold.

MAKE THE VELOUTÉ DE POISSON

00 Heat the 4 c (1 L) Fumét de Poisson in a medium saucepan, and gradually stir in the 1¼ c (155 g) cold (or room temperature) white roux.

01 Simmer for 90 minutes, stirring occasionally to avoid a skin forming on the surface.

MAKE THE MUSSEL STOCK

00 In a large saucepan, sauté the ⅔ c (100 g) onion, ⅔ c (100 g) celery, and 2 t fennel seed in 2½ T butter until translucent.

01 Add the small bottle (375 ml) vermouth, 1 oz (30 ml) absinthe (or any licorice-y spirit), 1 bay leaf, 12 peppercorns, and 2 lb (1 kg) mussels. Cover, bring to a gentle simmer, and let steam for 30 minutes.

02 Remove from heat and reserve the broth. (And don't forget to eat the mussels—you deserve them!)

MAKE THE MUSHROOM STOCK

00 Process the 8 c (700 g) mushrooms, 1 c (125 g) carrots, ½ c plus 1 T (87 g) onion, 1 c (87 g) leeks, and ⅓ c (20 g) parsley in a food processor until they are finely chopped.

01 Add the 5 t thyme and ⅓ t curry powder, and sauté everything together in ⅓ t butter in the bottom of a stockpot.

02 Cover with ½ gal (2 L) water and simmer for at least 1 hour. (Longer is better!)

03 Strain into a saucepan, simmer, and reduce by half.

MAKE THE SAUCE NORMANDE

00 In a large stockpot, whisk together the 2¾ c (660 g) Velouté de Poisson, ½ c (120 ml) mushroom stock, ½ c (120 ml) mussel stock, and ⅔ c (160 ml) Fumét de Poisson. Bring to a simmer.

01 In a bowl, whisk together the ½ t lemon juice, 5 egg yolks, and ¾ c (180 ml) of the heavy cream.

02 Whisk this "sour milk" into the sauce, and reduce it by a third.

03 Strain and finish with the remaining ½ c (120 g) heavy cream and ½ c (114 g) butter.

MAKE THE SAUCE GENEVOISE

00 In a large saucepan, sauté the ¾ c (100 g) carrots, ½ c (80 g) onion, and ⅓ c (20 g) parsley in 2½ T butter until tender.

01 Add the 4 thyme sprigs, 1 bay leaf, 16 peppercorns, and 2 lb (1 kg) salmon heads. Cover and let steam for 20 minutes.

02 Uncover, drain off the butter, and add the bottle (750 ml) of red wine. Simmer and reduce by half.

03 Stir in 2 c (470 ml) Sauce Espagnole Maigre and gently simmer for an hour.

04 Strain into a clean saucepan, add 2 c (470 ml) red wine and 2 c (470 ml) Fumét de Poisson, and reduce some more.

05 Finish the sauce with ⅔ c (150 g) butter and ½ t anchovy paste or fish sauce to taste.

GARNISH RÉGENCE (REGENCY GARNISH)

This "garnish" is actually composed of multiple items. From Escoffier: "20 quenelles prepared from a forcemeat of whiting and crayfish butter molded with spoons; 10 poached and bearded oysters; 10 very white button mushrooms; 10 truffles trimmed olive-shape; 10 thick slices of poached soft roe. Sauce Normande finished with truffle essence."

MAKE THE BEURRE D'ECREVISSE

00 Sauté the ½ c (64 g) carrots, ⅓ c (58 g) onion, and ⅔ c (50 g) leeks in 2½ T butter for about 10 minutes.

01 Add the 3 T tomato paste, 2 lb (1 kg) crayfish, 2 t thyme, 4 bay leaves, 1 T Old Bay seasoning, 2 t paprika, and ½ t cayenne, and cook covered for 30 minutes on low heat to infuse the flavors. Turn out onto a cookie sheet to cool.

02 Place in a food processor with 2 lb (1 kg) butter and blend until smooth. The shells will give the butter a reddish color.

03 Take your time and press the mixture through a tamis or sieve, and refrigerate. (The longer you process, the easier this part will be.) This can be frozen for future use.

MAKE THE WHITING FORCEMEAT

00 Cut the 1 lb (454 g) fish into 1" pieces and place in a food processor with the 2 T egg whites, ⅓ c plus 1 t (85 g) Beurre d'Ecrevisse, and 2 t salt. Process until smooth, slowly adding in the 2⅛ c (500 ml) cream.

01 Refrigerate until very cold.

02 Heat up a pan of 4½ c (1 L) water or fish stock to almost a boil (if you boil it, the quenelles will disintegrate!). Using 2 tablespoons, form some of the cold whiting forcemeat into football-shaped "quenelles," then poach in the water for 15–20 minutes. You know they're done when they have doubled in size.

03 Remove each quenelle very carefully—they will be very delicate.

04 Dress each with some Sauce Normande and serve topped with chopped chives and microgreens.

MAKE THE OYSTERS WITH MIGNONETTE SAUCE

00 Place the ½ c + 2 T (100g) minced shallots in a bowl with the ⅔ c (160 ml) red wine vinegar and 2½ T coarsely ground black pepper.

01 Shuck your 12 oysters, loosen up the meat so it will slide out, and top with a spoonful of the mignonette. Sprinkle with some radish, chives, and a touch of sea salt to taste.

MAKE THE FLUTED MUSHROOMS

00 Flute the 10 mushrooms with a paring knife. (See a tutorial here: fourhourchef.com/flute.) Remove the stems and reserve for another use.

01 Soak the fluted mushroom caps in 2 t lemon juice and 1 c (240 ml) water to prevent them from turning brown.

02 Sauté the mushroom caps in the 2 T + 2 t clarified butter and ¼ c (60 ml) mushroom stock for a few minutes, then drain on paper towels.

03 In a food processor, process the ⅓ c (85 g) crayfish meat and ⅓ c (85 g) whiting forcemeat with ⅓ c (85 g) Beurre d'Ecrevisse until smooth. Use this to stuff each mushroom cap.

04 Bake all of the stuffed mushroom caps in an oven at 400°F (200°C) for about 20 minutes.

05 Meanwhile, make the fried capers. Let the 20 capers drain on some paper towels. Heat the canola oil to 375°F (190°C), then fry the capers until crispy. (Be careful! The wetter they are, the more the oil will sputter and pop.) Drain on paper towels.

06 Remove the mushrooms from the oven and top each with 2 fried capers.

MAKE THE TRUFFLE SLICES

00 Using a mandoline, slice the truffles as thinly as you can. If your truffles are a bit on the dry side, soak the slices in olive oil mixed with 1 t truffle oil.

01 Use a melon baller to cut out circle and crescent shapes from the slices.

02 Reserve slices in the truffle oil mixture. Save the scraps for the Faux Truffles (see below).

MAKE THE FAUX TRUFFLE SLICES

00 Boil the 2 c (300 g) diced potatoes in salted water until tender, then drain and cool.

01 Reconstitute the dried mushrooms by soaking them in water for at least 30 minutes. Drain and pat dry with paper towels.

02 Place the potatoes, mushrooms, truffle trimmings, 1 T truffle oil, and 1½ t truffle salt in a food processor and process until smooth.

03 Turn the mixture out onto a floured surface, and make a depression in the center of the mound. Add the egg yolk and 1¾ c (219 g) flour and mix to make a dough.

04 Knead dough for 15–20 minutes, set in a covered pan, and refrigerate until chilled.

05 To cook, heat a pan of canola oil to 375°F (190°C).

06 Make truffle-size blobs of the dough and roll in the 2 packets instant grits.

07 Fry until crispy brown on the outside. Check one to make sure the interior is cooked and not too doughy. If so, adjust the heat of the oil.

08 Cool on paper towels until you can pick them up with your fingers. Then quickly dip each in a bath of 2 (0.14 oz/4 g) packets squid ink and ¼ c (60 ml) water.

MAKE THE BREADED CARP ROE

00 Remove the reserved skeins of roe from their brine. Drain on paper towels, and remove the roe from the sacs.

01 Place 1 lb (454 g) of roe in a food processor with ¼ c bread crumbs and 2 eggs and process until smooth.

02 Flatten a sheet of plastic wrap on your counter, spoon some roe out in a line, and roll it up tightly into a log shape. Tie off the ends of each of the roe logs and freeze.

03 When frozen, remove the roe from the freezer. Then remove the plastic wrap.

04 Heat a pot of canola oil to 375°F (191°C) for frying the roe.

05 Cut the frozen roe into bite-size pieces and dust each with flour, dip into the egg wash, and then coat with bread crumbs.

06 Fry in the oil until golden brown, and drain on paper towels. Serve while hot.

TO ASSEMBLE AND SERVE THE FINISHED DISH

00 Reassemble the carp on buttered parchment paper in a roasting pan.

01 Make a base from a large slice of bread, cut into the shape of the fish body. Pour some clarified butter over this. Then place the head and tail on each end.

02 Mold the carp forcemeat into the shape of the fish's body. Then decorate it all over with disks of black truffle cut into graduated sizes so as to represent the scales of the fish.

03 Cover the eye with an olive slice. Drizzle with clarified butter, then cover the entire fish with strips of salted pork.

04 Cover with parchment paper, and bake in a 375°F (190°C) oven for 90 minutes.

05 When ready, carefully lift the fish out of the roasting pan using the parchment as a sling, and place on an oval fish platter.

06 Decorate with Garnish Régence: 20 whiting quenelles dressed with Sauce Normande, 10 oysters with mignonette sauce, 10 stuffed white button mushrooms, 10 faux truffles, and 10 pieces of fried roe.

07 Serve at the table with boats or dishes of Sauces Normande and Genevoise.

08 Have a drink, faceplant, and sleep for 2 days.

Chef Marco Pierre White (right).

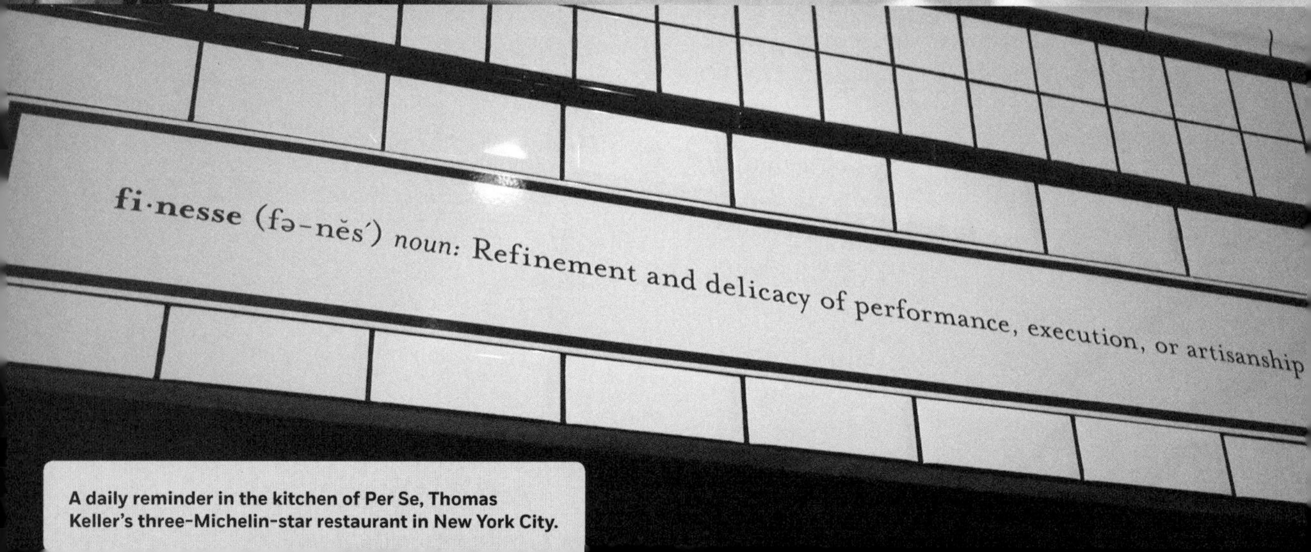
fi·nesse (fə-nĕs′) noun: Refinement and delicacy of performance, execution, or artisanship

A daily reminder in the kitchen of Per Se, Thomas Keller's three-Michelin-star restaurant in New York City.

Sense of Urgency

Once again, the kitchen of the inimitable Thomas Keller.

CLOSING THOUGHTS— ON MORE PERFECT DAYS

"One reason I make sculpture is that I have stared long enough at the glowing flat rectangles of computer screens. . . . Let us give more time for doing physical things in the real world and less time for staring at (and touching) the glowing flat rectangle. Plant a plant, walk the dogs, read a real book, go to the opera. Or hammer glowing hot metal in a blacksmith shop. . . . "

—EDWARD R. TUFTE, WORLD-RENOWNED STATISTICIAN[†]

"If, while washing dishes, we think only of the cup of tea [as reward] that awaits us, thus hurrying to get the dishes out of the way as if they were a nuisance . . . we are not alive during the time we are washing the dishes. In fact, we are completely incapable of realizing the miracle of life while standing at the sink. If we can't wash the dishes, chances are we won't be able to drink our tea either. While drinking the cup of tea, we will be thinking of other things, barely aware of the cup in our hands. Thus, we are sucked away into the future—and we are incapable of actually living one minute of life."

—THICH NHAT HANH, VIETNAMESE BUDDHIST MONK, NOMINATED FOR THE NOBEL PEACE PRIZE BY DR. MARTIN LUTHER KING, JR.[‡]

THE ALCHEMY OF AUGUST 11

My friend Dan Doty spent four years "rebuilding" troubled teens through extended wilderness experiences. The trips ranged from 21 to 120 days in duration. In the outdoors, these kids, raised as digital natives, learned "to be more human," as he put it. Pulled outside of their fixed (often self-destructive) mindsets long enough to reengage with the world around them, they learned self-awareness that transferred to everything else. Dan underscored the point that people miss: it's not about being outdoors; it's what you learn outdoors.

Similarly, this book isn't about cooking, as I mentioned long ago. It's about what you learn *through* cooking. To quote writer Anne Lamott, ". . . while you thought you needed the tea ceremony for the caffeine, what you really needed was the tea ceremony."

It's not about sitting on the banks of a remote Alaskan lake, eating harvested caribou meat and foraged blueberries. It's not about sitting in a rarified four-star restaurant, eating 12-syllable entrées with fine red wine. "Rebuilding" your humanness doesn't require the exotic or expensive.

Saturday, August 11, 2012, was neither.

I'd surprised my parents by landing in Amagansett, Long Island, the night before. I awoke around 10:30 a.m. with no alarm clock and sauntered into the kitchen in my boxers, pulling leftovers out of the fridge as I steeped green tea. After a small breakfast, I put on shorts and walked across the yard to the pool, where my little brother, now a lawyer, was clearing the perimeter. He had been hacking at underbrush and overgrown trees all morning. Sweaty and covered with dirt, sporting swollen red calluses on his hands, he couldn't have looked happier.

I helped him move the debris over a fence and into the back of my dad's pickup truck. After a quick dip in the pool, I headed to my parents' porch to write for a few hours.

At afternoon siesta time, I grabbed my bathing suit and goggles. I'd driven or biked to the bay hundreds of times, but that day I decided to walk the route, something I hadn't done in 20 years. After completing my new summer ritual—swimming a long arc around my family's favorite sandy point—I began the stroll back. I turned off my cell phone, took in deep breaths of the warm salty air, and walked slowly. Luxuriating in the light breeze, I looked ahead to the bends in the road as I went. Eastern red cedar canopies arched over the road, creating a ceiling of green, punctured by pockets of bright blue sky.

There was a fork in the road a mile in, and I decided to stay left, taking a path I'd never traveled by foot, despite living practically around the corner my entire childhood. I first noticed beautiful little homes tucked into the woods. Then a brown rabbit, camouflaged until it fled into a thicket. I slowed further. The slower I walked, the clearer things became. Behind a cottage, I saw something I'd never seen before: a family of five wild turkeys, gobbling quietly 200 feet from the roadside, perfectly blended into the brown underbrush.

I slowed yet again. A quarter mile later, I caught a glimpse of nearly a dozen deer grazing on the front yard of a Manhattanite's summer home. It was beautifully manicured but clearly empty this weekend. Too much work, I supposed. The deer were thrilled to help with landscaping and didn't notice me until I had stalked within 15 feet of a sheen-coated, healthy doe. She raised her head and we looked at each other for several long minutes until a bellowing "Hello!!!" came from right behind my head. I jumped like a spastic cat, the deer scattered, and a little boy in a yellow helmet waved back at me from his BMX bike. "Son of a bitch. . . ," I laughed to myself, my heart pounding in my ears. So that's what I was like as a kid. . . .

I walked the last 30 minutes back to my driveway, where I took off my flip-flops and walked through the long grass up to the house, feeling the cool blades pass between my toes. For a city dweller, it was like getting reacquainted with an old friend.

Around 7:30, the sun began to fade. Dusk was coming, and while the crickets chirped, dinner prep began. My parents worked on Fasolia Gigantes Plaki (a Greek giant-white-bean dish), my brother and his girlfriend made a salad of corn, red onion, and beets, and I prepped the grill for seared ahi tuna and barbecued chicken strips. Naturally, I also grabbed a bottle of 2011 Felino Viña Cobos, a fruity Malbec. The tiny kitchen was crowded, and bodies bumped into the table and each other. Laughter echoed through the house and out onto the porch, where we set out the silverware and simple plates I'd used since I was a toddler.

When the last timer went off, all the food was shuttled out onto a lazy Susan, and we feasted. We grabbed a cheap cabernet sauvignon after finishing the Malbec, and the aromas of garlic, tomatoes, oregano, and thyme filled the air. For dessert, I brought out a surprise: a new batch of chocolate chip cookies from my friend Umber, who is planning to open a bakery in the West Village. We devoured them in minutes. Slouching back in the old wooden chairs, satisfied, we leisurely enjoyed the second bottle of wine.

Conversations drifted into the night, and people headed off, one or two at a time, to bed. I received a surprise call from a college friend I hadn't seen in more than a decade, so I went for a late-night walk around the property, looking up at the stars as we reminisced about old times and caught up.

When all was said and done, I went upstairs and fell asleep in the room where I grew up.

It was the perfect day.

MEMENTO MORI

How many perfect days have you had in the past six months? Much more important, how many will you have in the *next* six months?

The Latin *memento mori* is often translated as "Remember you will die." If you look at my picture on the inside back flap of this book, you will notice a small skull in the bottom right-hand corner. This imagery has been used by artists for centuries to remind them of their own mortality, that they, too, will die. For me, it's a call to action and a benevolent warning not to squander time.

I'm often asked how I define "success." It's an overused term, but I fundamentally view this elusive beast as a combination of two things—achievement and appreciation. One isn't enough:

Achievement without appreciation makes you ambitious but miserable.

Appreciation without achievement makes you unambitious but happy.

I've always been hardwired for achievement at all costs. Protestant work ethic, college-job-retirement, and all that. Forward motion, keeping up with the Joneses, and competing, competing, competing. It's culturally written into my DNA, and I enjoy the fight. But to avoid making myself and my loved ones miserable, I need tools for that missing ingredient: appreciation.

Perhaps the most valuable tool I've found is cooking. Done as I recommend it, it teaches you to become fully conscious and aware of the incredible things that you *already* have. My perfect day cost next to nothing. It wasn't about the material sum of its parts. Despite common belief, having a nicer car or even a private jet won't fix your problems.

The good news is that slow meals, twice a week with friends and family, just might.

I hope to see you on the journey.

—Tim

SIMPLIFY

"As long as you live, keep learning how to live." —***Lucius Annaeus Seneca***

the End?

APX

THE APPENDIX

In the spirit of ABL (Always Be Learning), I bring you the APX (Appendix). Just like the body part, it *might* not be essential to life. But, oftentimes, the most enjoyable things in life aren't exactly essential, are they?

In **(More) Cooking Like a Pro,** you'll get a complete tour of the world's cuisines, a who's-who guide to master chefs, and a full program for becoming a "pro" without culinary school.

In **(More) Learning Anything,** you'll learn to outshoot LeBron, get an education in fine weaponry, memorize a deck of cards, out-knot MacGyver, and make fire without matches.

And in **(More) Living the Good Life,** we return to creature comforts: how to become a VIP in the food world, the 100 best restaurants in the US, and culinary maps of my favorite cities.

MORE COOKING LIKE A PRO

THE BITE-SIZE WORLD: 193 RECIPES, 193 COUNTRIES

Why not unleash your cookery on the entire world? In this collection of deliciousness, inspired by *@cookbook* and thanks to Blake Royer, you can try every country the U.N. recognizes!

193 nations, slow-carb whenever possible, each in 140 characters or less.

In other words: 193 countries 193recipes 140char <10ingred <20minpreptime; # = lb; ~ = until; garlic is minced and onion diced.

#eatyourheartout!

COUNTRY	DISH	RECIPE
AFGHANISTAN	WINTER SQUASH	Saute 1 onion/1T oil ~translucent. + .5t cumin&coriander&cardamom/.25t grnd cloves. + 1 cubed butternut squash, cook ~ tender.
ALBANIA	LAMB STEW WITH OKRA (Lahm Lhalou)	Grill or roast 1# lamb chunks. Saute 1# okra/2T oil 5m. + 1c diced grn pepper&celery/4garlc/s&p, cook 10m. + .5c h2o/lamb chunks. Simmr 30m.
ALGERIA	LAMB & PRUNES WITH ALMONDS	Brwn 2# lamb/2T butter. + 1c h2o, 1 cinn stick, 1c slivered almonds, .75# prunes. Simmer ~ lamb is tender.
ANDORRA	SPINACH WITH RAISINS & PINE NUTS	Saute .25c pine nuts/2T oil. + .25c raisins/2c fresh spinach/.25c h2o. Boil off h2o, s&p.
ANGOLA	LEMON SALAD	Whisk 2T lemon juice/4T olv oil/s&p. Toss with 2 thinly sliced fennel bulbs.
ANTIGUA & BARBUDA	BLACK BEAN CAKES	Blend 32oz draind blck beans/.5 onion/.25t cumin/1 chopd jalapeno ~smooth. Form 2T cakes. Fry in 2T oil. Top w/salsa.
ARGENTINA	LOCRO DE CHOCIO DESGRANADO (Thick Corn Stew)	Simmr c diced pumpkin&h2o/2c corn kernels/1# beef chunks ~tender. Saute 1 onion&chopd green pepper/2 chopd toms 15m. Combine all + s&p.
ARMENIA	GANANACH FAOULYA (Lamb Stew)	Brwn .5# lamb chunks/1 onion/1T oil, +1c h20, 16oz cannd tom/1t mint/1t cayen/s&p. Simmr 45m, +16oz grn beans/2T lemjuice. Cook ~tender.
AUSTRALIA	MACADAMIA NUT & ASPARAGUS SALAD	Roast 1 bnch asparagus/2T oil 375F 15m. Mix .25 c olv oil/.5 lemjuice/2 garlc/2T chopd basil/.25c macadamia nuts/6 chopd toms/s&p. Toss all.
AUSTRIA	AUSTRIAN LAMB CHOPS	Brwn 6 lamb chop/3T oil, rmv. Simmr 2 onion/16oz chopd tom/1 grn pep/1t rosemry/s&p 30m. Pour over lamb.
AZERBAIJAN	BADIMJAN CHIGIRTMASI (Aubergine Omelet)	Salt 2 peeld&slcd eggplants, sit 2h. Saute 1 slcd onion/eggplant/2t oil. Beat 4 egg, s&p, pour over eggplant on low heat. + parsley.
BAHAMAS	BLACK-EYED PEA BAKE	Boil 1c black-eyed peas/1.5c h2o ~ tender. Drain half liq. Brwn .25# bf w half chopd onion, + to peas/.5c bbq/1T mustard. Bake 200F 1.5h.
BAHRAIN	MASALA WHOLE GRILLED FISH	Rub 1T fish masala powder/s&p into 1 whole grouper. Stuff w 1garlic/1 minced green chile. Drizzle w oil, grill or broil.
BANGLADESH	MAKHER TAUKARI (Fish Curry)	Saute 1 onion/1 garlc/4T oil ~soft, +.5t chili powdr/1t tumeric 5m, +1# fish filet/3 chopd grn chile/1 chopd tom/h2o to cvr. Simmr ~done
BARBADOS	COU-COU (Okra & Corn)	Boil 4 okras/4c h2o 10m. Mix in 2c cornmeal/1t salt to thicken. Simmr until stiff.
BELARUS	BITKI (Meatballs)	Mix 2# grnd beef/1 onion/2 egg/s&p. Form meatballs. Fry in 1T oil. Saute mushrooms in same pan.
BELGIUM	FLEMISH-STYLE COD	Saute 1 onion/4T oil ~soft. Combine w 2T parsly/1T chives/4 cod filet/1.5T lemjuice/.75c wt wine/s&p, bake 350F 20m.
BELIZE	BELIZEAN STEAK & ONION	Marinate 2# steak/2 garlc/1t adobo seasoning/.25t oreg/.25c vinegr/s&p 1h. Saute 2 onion ~soft. Brwn steak high heat. Top w/onion
BENIN	BENINESE BEEF STEW	Brwn 2# beef chunks/2T oil, rmv, brwn 1 onion/2garlc. +1T curry powder/.25c pnut butter/1t cayenne. + 1.5c cocnt milk/.75c h20. Simmr 2h.
BHUTAN	TSHOEM (Beef & Mushrooms)	Simmr 1# cubd beef/2 onion/.5c h2o/1t salt/2T oil 2h. +3 chopd grn peppers/1c oyst mushroom/1 garlc/2T chopd ginger, cook ~tender. + cilantro.
BOLIVIA	STUFFED AVOCADOS	Halve, pit 6 avocados. Mash avocado flesh/.25# cookd grnd meat/1c shreddd lettuce/1c mayo/s&p. Spoon into skins, garnish w slicd boild egg.

COUNTRY	DISH	RECIPE
BOSNIA & HERZEGOVINA	CHEVAP (Beef Stir-Fry)	Saute 2# grnd beef/2 onion/2 chopd carrot/2t parsly/3T oil ~brwn. + .5c h2o/2 chopd toms, cook ~evap. s&p.
BOTSWANA	CHICKEN GROUNDNUT STEW	Saute 1 onion/1T oil, + 2 chopd chix breast. + .5t cayenne/1t gratd ginger/.5c pnut butter/.25c tompaste/1.5c h2o. Simmr 1h.
BRAZIL	SQUASH SOUP	Boil 3c beef broth/1.5c h2o/1c tom/2# cubd squash/.5 onion/1/8t cayene, simmer 20m ~soft.
BRUNEI	DAGING GOREN LADA HITAM (Black Pepper & Ginger Beef)	Brwn .5# cubd steak/3T oil. +2 slicd onion/3 garlc/3T mincd gingr/2T lemjuice/1t black pepper, cook ~onion soft.
BULGARIA	KAVARMA (Pork & Leek Stew)	Brwn 1# pork stewing meat &3T oil; remove pork. Brwn 4 sliced leeks,+1T tom paste til darkened. + 1/2c h2o, 1/3c wt wine. Simmr till evap.
BURKINA FASO	CHICKEN WITH GOMBO SAUCE	Saute 1.5 onion/2T oil ~ soft. + .25c pnut butter&h2o/20 chopd okra/s&p. Simmer 10m. Grill 1# chicken pieces w oil/s&p. Serve w sauce.
BURUNDI	BURUNDIAN BEEF & GREENS IN PEANUT SAUCE	Boil 1# mixd greens ~tender. Drain, save 1.5c h2o, mix w .5# pnut butter. Brwn 1# stewbeef/2T oil, +pnut, +greens. Simmr 1h, +paprka/s&p
CAMBODIA	HOT & SOUR BEEF SALAD	Grill 1# steak, slice. Save juice. Mix 4T fishsauce/4T limejuice/2 chopd shallot&rdchili/steak juice. Toss all w 4c lettuce.
CAMEROON	ZOM (Meat & Spinach)	Saute 1 onion/1T oil, + 2# beef chunks/2c h20/2 chopd toms/2T pnut butter. Simmr ~tender. + 2# spinach, simmer 20m.
CANADA	SALMON WITH LEMON & DILL	Bake 1# salmon/5T lemjuice/.25c olv oil/1T dill/1 garlc/s&p 350F 25m.
CAPE VERDE	XEREM (Tuna Stew)	Season .5# cubd tuna w salt&red chile. Saute 1 onion/2t oil ~ soft, +tuna/3.5c coconut milk, simmr 15m. +.5# cornmeal, stir, simmr 15m.
CENTRAL AFRICA REPUBLIC	SQUASH WITH PEANUT	Saute 2# cubd squash/2T oil 10m. +3c crsh pnuts, simmr 5m. s&p. Mash squash, serv hot.
CHAD	DARABA (Vegetarian Stew)	Simmer 20 okra/3 chopd toms/.25# mixd grns/1 peeld chopd eggplant/1c h2o 30m. + .5c pnut butter, simmr ~thick. s&p.
CHILE	CHILEAN WHITEFISH	Arrange 2 sliced onions/1T oil in baking dish. s&p 4 fish filets, place atop onions. Cover w 2T lemon juice. Bake 15m 400F.
CHINA	SUNG CHOY BAO (Pork Lettuce Wraps)	Stirfry 2T chopd ginger&garlic, add 1# ground pork. When no longer pink, add .25c hoisin sauce, simmr 5m. Serve in lettuce wraps.
COLOMBIA	SOBREBARRIGA (Rolled Flank Steak)	Brwn 2# flank stk/s&p/3T oil, rmv. + 1 onion/1 dicd celery/1 garlc/1T cumin ~soft. Roll stk, cvr w veg/.5c h2o. Bake 250F 2h, 425F 15m.
COMOROS	AVOCADO & SMOKED FISH SALAD	Mix 1 mashed avocado/.25c shredded smoked fish/1 hrd boiled egg/2T limejuice.
CONGO, D.R.	CHICKEN MOAB (Chicken Stew)	Simmr 3# chix thighs/3c h2o 1h. Saute 1 onion/.25t cayen/1t ntmg/16oz tom/1T oil ~soft, + .25c pnut butr. Combine all, bake 350F 30m.
COSTA RICA	SOPA NEGRA (Black Bean Soup)	Simmr 2c blck beans/2c h2o/1 bnch cilan/.5t oreg ~soft. Mash. Saute 1 garl/1 onion ~soft, + beans/salt/1c h2o. Top w/ chopd celery.
COTE D'IVOIRE	CHILLED AVOCADO SOUP	Blend 2 avocado/4c chix stock/2T limejuice/1T yogurt/1t Tabasco/s&p ~smooth. Refrigerate 1h.
CROATIA	FORSKA GREGODA (Whitefish Stew)	Saute 1 onion/.5c oil ~soft, +3# whitefish/5 garlc/.5 bnch parsley, saute 3m.+ 5c h2o/2t oreg/1t thym/1c white wine/s&p, simmr 10m.
CUBA	PORK CON MOJO (Grilled Pork Chops with Mojo Sauce)	Marinate 2 pork chops/.75c sour OJ (or .5 OJ/limejuice)/1t oreg/.5t cumin/5 garlc/s&p 30m. Grill.
CYPRUS	SOUVLA	Marinate 2# pork chunks/1t oregano/2T red wine&olv oil/s&p 2h. Thread on skewers, grill directly over coals 3m, move away to slow-cook 10m.
CZECH REPUBLIC	STEAK IN CAPER SAUCE	Saute .25# bacon/onion ~soft. + 1# steak cubd ~ brwn, rmv. + 2T mustrd/2T caper/1c h2o, reduce ~thick. Reheat steak in sauce.
DENMARK	BONELESS BIRDS (Stewed Beef or Lamb)	Mix 1t grnd gingr/s&p/.25t grnd clv. Slice 2# flank stk/12 pc, roll 1T chopd bacon/1T chopd onion/.25t mix. Brwn/3T oil. Simmr/4c bfbroth 2h
DJIBOUTI	DJIBOUTI LENTILS	Saute 2 mincd grn chile/2 onion/berbere spice mix/2T oil ~soft. +2c lentils/3.5c h2o/1t mincd gingr/2 garlc/s&p, simmr 40m.
DOMINICA	DOMINICA CRAB	Saute 4 chopd scalion/1 garlc/1 rd chile/5T oil ~soft. + 1t currypowdr/1# crab/2t cilantro/2t parsly/1c h2o/s&p, simmr 20m.
DOMINICAN REPUBLIC	REPOLLO GUISADO (Cabbage Stew)	Brwn 1c choppd onion/1garlc/1 sliced red pep/.33c olv oil. + 3c shredded cabbage/1c tom sauce/.33c wt wine vinegar&h2o. Simmr ~tender, s&p.
EAST TIMOR	GRILLED TUNA STEAK	Marinate 2 tuna stk/3 garlc/4T oil/salt 1h. Grill tuna 3m per side to rare.
ECUADOR	CEVICHE DE CAMARÓN (Shrimp Ceviche)	Boil 2# shrimp/saltd h2o 1m. Mix shrimp/1c OJ&limejuice/1onion/1 mincd rd chile/1 chopd tom/s&p. Refrigerate 1h.
EGYPT	FUL MEDAMES (Breakfast Beans)	Simmr 1.5c fava (or kidney) beans/2T olv oil/1 garlc/1 onion/1 chopd tom/2T lemjuice/.25c fresh parsley ~ soft. s&p. Top w fried egg.
EL SALVADOR	PICADILLO O SALPICÓN (Beef Salad)	Simmr 1# stewing beef/3c h2o 20m. Rmv, cool, chop, mix w 1 onion/3 chopd radish/2T lime juice/5T chopd mint. s&p.
EQUATORIAL GUINEA	SPINACH SAUCE	Saute 1 onion/2T oil ~soft.+ .25c pnut buttr/3c h2o/3c spinch/.5# cooked fish/1 mincd chile, simmr 25m.
ERITREA	ALITCHA BIRSTEN (Lentil Stew)	Saute 6 garlc/5T oil ~brown. +2 peeld&slicd tom, simmr 5m. +1c lentils/1T mincd gingr/s&p simmr 2m. +2 mincd chiles/4c h2o. Cvr, simmr 1h.

COUNTRY	DISH	RECIPE
ESTONIA	MULGIKAPSAD (Cabbage Stew)	Brwn .25# bacon/2garlc/1T oil 10m. +2# saukraut/1# pork chunks/3c h20/s&p, simmr 2h. Garnish fresh dill.
ETHIOPIA	MISIR WOT (Stewed Red Lentils)	Simmr 1.5c red lentils/2c h2o 30m. Saute 1 onion/2 garlc/2T olv oil ~ soft, + 2T Berbere (or garam masala+turmeric). + lentils, simmr 30m.
FIJI	KOKODA (Fijian Coconut Ceviche)	Cube 1# fish filet, +4T lime juice/salt. Marinate 30m. + 1c coconut cream/1 onion/1 minced red chile/2 chopped toms. Stir well.
FINLAND	SIENISSALAATI (Mushroom Salad)	Simmr 1T lemjuice/.75c h2o/3c mushrooms ~soft. Drain&cool, +.25c cream/.25c h2o/2T chives/s&p. Serv w lettuce.
FRANCE	SIMPLIFIED CASSOULET	Bake 1# cookd white bns/3 garlc/3T fresh sage/1 lamb shank/h2o to cvr bns 250F 2h. Rmv bone, shred meat. s&p.
GABON	POISSONS EN SAUCE AUX ARACHIDES (Fish in Groundnut Sauce)	Brwn 1.5# fish stks/3t oil, rmv. + 2c h20/3 onion/4 chopd toms, simmr 20m. Stir in .25c pnut butter/1c liquid whisked. +fish, simmr ~done.
GAMBIA, THE	PEPPER SOUP	Simmr 2# chix thighs/8c h2o 15m. + 4 garlc/.5 onion/4 chiles/3 chix bouillon pureed, simmr 1h. +2oz tompaste, simmr ~thick.
GEORGIA	KIDNEY BEAN SALAD	Mix 2c kidney beans/.5c chopd scallion/3T oil/2T cidr vinegr/.5c chopd walnt/.5t cayenne/s&p in bowl. Garnish w/mint.
GERMANY	ROULADEN (Rolled Steak)	Roll .25c chopd bacon/.5 onion/3 chopd pickle in 4 steaks rubbd w 3T mustard; tie w string. Brwn rolls,+ 1c h2o/.5c rd wine, simmr 1.5h.
GHANA	PEANUT SOUP	Brwn 4 garlic/14oz choppd toms/1T minced ginger/2T oil. + 1 whl chicken/1qt h2o/1c peanut butter/s&p; simmr 60m. remove, shred chicken.
GRENADA	CALLALOO (Meat & Spinach Stew)	Simmer .5# salt pork/1# chopd spinach/1 onion/.5t thyme/1c chix broth 20m. +8oz crab/s&p, simmr 15m. Garnish w 1 mincd grn pep.
GREECE	STIFATHO (Beef & Onion Stew)	Brwn 3# beef chunks/.75c oil, +6 whole onion/6T rd wine vinegr/10 whole garlc/2T tom paste/s&p/2 bay. Simmr 4h.
GUATEMALA	CURTIDO DE REPOLLO (Cabbage Salad)	Shred 1 cabbage/1 onion/2 carrot. Mix w/.5c h20/1c cidr vinegr/1T salt/2T oil/1.5t oreg/1t cayenne/1t cumin. Cool, serve w/fish.
GUINEA	POULET YASSA (Chicken with Lemon and Onion)	Marinate 3# chix breast/6 sliced lemons/2 garlc/6 onion/3t oil 12h. Rmv chix. Saute all ~soft, +1 bay/.5t cayen/s&p/chix. Stew ~ tender.
GUINEA-BISSAU	BOLINHOS DE MANCARRA COM PEIXE (Peanut Fish Balls)	Marinate 4 tilap filet/3T lemjuice/s&p 30m. Brwn filets/2t oil, rmv, form w 1 onion/.25c pnut/.5c h2o into balls, saute in pan.
GUYANA	FRIED OKRA WITH SHRIMP	Brwn .25# shrimp/3T oil. +1# crosscut okra/1 chopd tom/1 onion/1 mincd chili/s&p, cook ~tender.
HAITI	GRIOTS (Glazed & Braised Pork)	Brwn 2# pork loin/.25c oil, + 1onion/1c OJ/.25c limejuice/.25c h2o/.25t thym/s&p. Simmr 30m covrd, uncvr, cook high 10m to glaze.
HONDURAS	GROUNDNUT SOUP	Simmr 1c pnut butter/5c chix stock/2t hot sauce/s&p 20m. Stir in 2 egg yolk/1t angosture bitters, simmr ~thick.
HUNGARY	HALÁSZLÉ (Fisherman's Soup)	Brwn 1 onion/2T oil ~ caramelized. + 2T Hungarian paprika, saute 2m. + 8c fish stock/1c tom juice/s&p. Boil, + 1.5# whitefish, simmr 10m.
ICELAND	SALTKJÖT OG BAUNIR (Split Pea Soup with Lamb)	Simmr 1# splitpea/8c h2o/1 onion/2# lamb shank 2h. + .5# carrot&rutabaga in last .5h.
INDIA	TOMATO DAL (Stew)	Saute 1 onion/1T oil ~soft. +2t garam masal/1t cumin/1c rd lentil/14oz cannd tom/3c chix stock. Simmr 20m. Garnish 2t chopd cilantro.
INDONESIA	REMPAH (Meatballs)	Combine 1# ground pork/.75c shredded cocnt/1T cilantro/.25t cum/1 egg. Form into balls, fry in 3T oil ~brwn.
IRAN	LAMB WITH EGGPLANT	Saute 3 cubed eggplants/3t oil, rmv. Saute 1 onion/1# lamb chunks ~brown. Covr w/ h2o/s&p, simmr ~tender. +eggplant/2 chopd tom, simmr ~thick.
IRAQ	BAKED KUFTA (Baked Meatballs)	Mix 1c chopd parsly/1 onion/4 garlc/3# grnd beef/1T allspic/s&p. Bake covrd w/1 slcd tom 425F 45m.
IRELAND	CABBAGE & SMOKED PORK	Simmer 2# smoked pork ribs/3c h2o/1 cabbag/2 onion 2h ~tender. Rmv ribs, broil ~caramelized, serve w/draind cabbage.
ISRAEL	ISRAELI COUSCOUS	Brwn 1c couscous/2T oil, + 2c h2o. Simmr 5m. In wok cook .5t cumin seed/1T oil, +2 chopd chili. +couscous/.5c pnuts/1T lemjuice/s&p.
ITALY	FLORENTINE STEAK	Marinate 2 thick tbone stk/2 garlc/.5c old oil/salt 1h. Grill high heat ~md rare. Slice .5" thick. Serve on argula w/oil&balsmic.
JAMAICA	JERK LAMB CHOPS	Marinate 4 lambchop/1T jerk sauce/1 garlc/1 thyme/3T oil/s&p 1h. Grill or broil ~med rare.
JAPAN	IKA-GESO-AGE (Squid Tentacles)	Marinate 1# chopd squid/1T soya/1T sake/.5t mincd gingr 1h. Coat in cornstarch. Fry in 3T oil 2m.
JORDAN	MENSAF (Lamb Stew)	Brwn 2# lamb chunks/2T oil. +4c h2o, simmer ~tender. Whisk 2c buttermilk/1 egg/1c broth, return to pot. Garnish toasted pinenuts.
KAZAKHSTAN	SHALGAM (Pepper Salad)	Salt 1# peeld&sliced radsh & 2 chopd carrot. + 1.5 onion/1 garlic/2 dicd banana pepper. Toss w oil/vinegr, + cayenne, s&p.
KENYA	MBAAZI (Mung-Bean Soup)	Boil 1.5c kidney beans/2c h2o ~tendr, +1c cocnt milk/1 onion/1t currypowdr/1t tumerc/salt, boil ~dry. .25c cocnt cream, boil ~dry
KIRIBATI	CRAB STARTER	Marinate .5# cookd crab/3T lemjuice/2 chopd celery ribs/2T mayo/3 onion 1h. Serve w/2 boild egg/lettuce/lem wedges.

COUNTRY	DISH	RECIPE
KOREA, N.	GRILLED PORK CHOPS	Marinate 6 pork chop/.25c soya/3T sesoil/.5t mincd gingr/2 onion/2 garlc 1h or overnight. Grill 6m per side.
KOREA, S.	GALBI (Barbecued Short Ribs)	Marinate 3# flanked short ribs .75c soya/.75 rice wine/4 garlic/4 scallion/1 kiwi pureed 3h. Grill.
KUWAIT	LEMON CHICKEN	Marinate 4# chx breasts/.5c olvoil/.75c lemjuice/2T thyme/2 garlc 1h. Grill or broil ~brown.
KYRGYZSTAN	PALOO (Lamb Stew)	Brwn 2# lamb/4T oil, +2 onion/2 chopd grn pep/5 chopd carrot, saute ~soft. Simmer w/5c h2o/5 garlic/2c couscous 30m.
LAOS	LAOTIAN SAUSAGE	Mix together 1# pork/.25c tom yum paste/1 chopd shallot. Form into patties, fry in 2T oil. Garnish with 2T chopped cilantro.
LATVIA	LATVIAN LIVER PÂTÉ	Saute 1 onion/1 garlic/2T oil ~soft. +1# chx liver, simmr 45m. Cool, process into thick paste. Thin w h2o ~spreadable.
LEBANON	LEBANESE CHICKEN	Saute 1 onion/1 garlic ~soft, rmv. Saute 4 chx breasts ~brwn, +2t orange zest/.5c OJ/.75t cinn&allspc/1t honey/s&p. Simmr 20m.
LESOTHO	LESOTHAN CHAKALAKA (Vegetarian Stew)	Fry 1 dicd carrot/1 onion/1 dicd rd pepper/2 mincd rd chiles/2T oil 5m, +2 chopd tom, cook ~soft. s&p.
LIBERIA	MONROVIAN COLLARDS & CABBAGE	Simmer 1 bnch collard grns/.5# bacon chopd/1 onion/1T s&p/rd pep/1q h2o 30m. +2 cabbage/1T oil simmr ~tender. Drain h2O.
LIBYA	ALMOND CHICKEN	Grill 2# chx breast/1T oil. Simmr 2c chx stock/1# peas/1T sherry/.5c sliverd almonds/1c diced celery 10m. + 2T cornstarch/h2O. + chx.
LICHTENSTEIN	LAMMSCHULTER MIT EI (Lamb with Egg)	Brwn 1.5# lamb chunks, + 1onion/1garlc/3T oil~soft. +1c rd wine, reduce by .5. Whisk in 3 eggs/2t parsly/.25t nutmeg/.5 lemon; simmr 5m.
LITHUANIA	PORK MEATBALLS	Mix 2# grnd pork/2 onion/.5t allspice/2 egg/s&p. Shape into meatballs, brwn 2T oil.
LUXEMBOURG	BOUNESCHLUPP (Green-Bean Soup)	Saute .5c chopd bacon ~crisp, rmv. + large chopd shallot&carrot, saute 5m + 2 garlc/1# green beans. Cvr w h2o, simmer 40m. s&p +.5c sr crm
MACEDONIA	ZELKA MANDZA (Sauerkraut Stew)	Saute 2 onion/2T oil 10m, + 2T smoked paprika/2c sauerkraut/.5# sliced smoked sausage/h2o to cvr. Simmr 1h, s&p.
MADAGASCAR	LASOPY (Vegetable Soup)	Simmr 6c veal stock/3 carrots/1 chopd turnip/6 scallion/1c strng beans/2 chopd toms 1h. Puree.
MALAWI	NDIWO (Vegetable Relish)	Saute 1 onion/2T mincd ginger&oil ~soft, +2t curry powder/2T h2o, +.5 shredded cabbage/.25c h2o. Simmr covrd ~tender.
MALAYSIA	STICKY PORK CHOPS	Brwn 4 pork chops, rmv. +.33c sherry/1T soya/1T mincd gingr/2T mincd chile/2T honey. reduce ~ syrupy. +pork, cook 2m per side ~ done.
MALDIVES	MASHUNI (Tuna-Coconut Salad)	Mix 1c smoked canned tuna/1c grated coconut/1 minced chile/.5 onion/.5c lemon juice/salt to taste.
MALI	MALIAN FISH STEW	Simmr 2# salt fish/3c h2o/20 crushd okra 25m. Saute 3 onion/3 mincd rd chile ~soft, +4 dicd tom, saute ~soft, + to stew pot.
MALTA	ALJOTTA (Fish Soup)	Saute 1 onion/2 garlc/2T olvoil ~ soft. + 1 chopd tom/2 sprigs mint/2 bay leaves/s&p. + 1.5# whitefish, simmr 2 m. Garnish lemon.
MARSHALL ISLANDS	BARBECUED LIMAS	Saute 1 onion/1 garlc/1T oil ~soft. +1# crumbld sausage, brwn. +28oz can toms/1t spcy mustard. Bake w 45 oz canned lima beans 350F 45m.
MAURITANIA	CARI JACQUES (Jackfruit Curry)	Brwn 1# pork/2T oil, +1garlc&onion/1t chopd gingr/1T thyme~soft. +14oz crushd toms/1c h2o/2# cubd jackfruit/4T curry powder, simmr ~ soft.
MAURITIUS	BABY BOK CHOY WITH CASHEWS	Boil 5 baby bokchoy/2c h2o 3m, rmw. Saute 4 garlc/2T sesame oil. +1 cup corn kernels&cashews, simmr 5m. Pour over bokchoy.
MEXICO	CARNE ASADA (Grilled Beef)	Marinate 2# flank stk/4 garlc/1 chopd serrano/1t cumin/1 bnch cilan/4T lim/.5c oil/s&p 4h. Grill med heat 4m per side.
MICRONESIA	MICRONESIAN CHICKEN	Marinate 4 chix breast/.5c lemjuice/2T soya/12oz beer/1 garlc/1 onion overnight. Grill med heat ~ cooked.
MOLDOVA	NARKEL SHORSHER CHINGRI (Shrimp in Coconut-Mustard Sauce)	Marinate 1# shrimp/1T mustard seeds/2T mustard/2 chopd red chiles/.25t turmeric. Brown shrimp in 2T oil, +.25c coconut milk/s&p.
MONACO	MONEGASQUE MUSHROOMS	Saute 1.5# quartd mushrooms/5T oil 5m, +8 mincd anchovy fillets/.5t mint/.33c lemjuicem cook ~evap. Garnish 3t parsley.
MONGOLIA	KHORKHO (Lamb Stew with Cabbage, Carrots & Caraway Seeds)	Simmr 2# lamb chunks/2c h2o/2 chopd carrots/1/2 shredded white cabbage/3T caraway seeds 2-3hrs ~ tender.
MONTENEGRO	CEVAPCICI (Meat Cylinders)	Mix 1# grnd beef/.5# grnd pork&grnd lamb/4 garlc/1t paprika/1t bkgsoda/s&p, shape into 2in cylinders. Broil 8m per side.
MOROCCO	STEWED LENTILS	Simmr 2c lentil/3 chopd toms/1 onion/3 garlc/4T cilantro/2.5t cumin&paprka/1.5t mincd gingr/s&p/.33c oil/2q h2o 1.5h.
MOZAMBIQUE	MATATA (Clam & Peanut Stew)	Saute 1 onion/2T oil ~soft, + 4c canned clams/1c pnuts/2 chopd toms/s&p/1t cayenne. + .5c h2o, simmr 30m. + 8oz spinach. Cook covrd ~wiltd.
MYANMAR	PYI-GYI NGA KAZUN YWET (Squid & Dandelion)	Stirfry 1 garlc/2T oil, + 1# squid rings cook 2m; + 1t cayenne/1T lem juice/2t soya/5c Dandelion leaves. Cook 2m more.
NAMIBIA	MAGIC LAMB	Puncture 1 leg lamb, fill w/.25c grn pepcorns&pomegran seeds/3 garlc/8 sprigs rosemary/8 anchovy. Wrap in foil, bake 350F 2.5h.
NAURU	COCONUT FISH	Season whitefish fillets s&p, dip in 1 whisked egg, .5c breadcrumbs&shredded coconut. Sear in 2T oil ~golden, sprinkle with lime juice.

COUNTRY	DISH	RECIPE
NEPAL	WO (Lentil Pancake)	Mash 1.5c cooked lentils w enough h2o to make a paste. + 1T ground gringer/1t cumin/1 garlc. Form into patties. Fry in 2T oil.
NETHERLANDS	ORANGE SOUP	Roast 1 peeled, chopped pumpkin&buttrnut squash/2 carrot 475F 30m. Simmr w 6c veg stock/1 pinch saffron 20m. Puree.
NEW ZEALAND	COLONIAL GOOSE	Melt 4T honey&butter, + 1c dried apricots. Stuff into 2# boneless leg lamb, tie. Marinate w 1c red wine 12h, cook in 300F oven uncvrd 2h.
NICARAGUA	BISTEC ENCEBOLLADO (Steak)	Brwn 2 steak/s&p/3T oil, rmv. Saute 3 onion/4 garlc ~soft, +.5c white wine/1 bay leaf, reduce by .5, pour over steak.
NIGER	CECENA (Black-Eyed Peas)	Blend 1# cookd blackeyd peas/1 onion/1 rd chile/s&p. Beat in 1 egg. Fry in 2T oil ~brown.
NIGERIA	OBE EJE TUTU (Fish-Pepper Soup)	Marinate .25# cubd whitefish/2T lem 5m. Saute 1 rd pep/1grn pep/4 dicd tom ~soft, +2c fish stock, boil 10m. +fish, simmr 7m
NORWAY	SPINACH SOUP	Saute 1 onion/1T oil 5m, + 3.5c chix broth. Boil, + 1# spinach/.25t nutmeg. Simmr 10m, garnish w sliced hard-boiled egg.
OMAN	SHAKSHOUKA (Egg Dish)	Saute 1 onion/2T oil, +3 dicd tom/.5t cayen/3T coriander, simmr 20m. +7 egg/s&p, cook 5m
PAKISTAN	CHICKEN TIKKA	Marinate 2 chix breasts/.25c lemjuice/.25c yogurt/2t chili powdr/2t salt/1t mincd gingr/1 garlc/1T cumin 2h. Broil or grill on skewers.
PALAU	DEMOK LEAF SOUP (Crab & Spinach Soup)	Simmr 1# spinch/5c h2o 30m. +.1# chopd crab/salt, simmr 30m. + 1c cocnt milk, simmr 5m.
PANAMA	CEVICHE	Marinate 2 can flaked tuna/1 onion/1.5c lem juice/2 minced chiles/s&p 2h or overnight. Serve with fresh salad.
PAPUA NEW GUINEA	CURRIED FISH	Saute 2T mincd gingr/1 onion/2 garlc/1.5t chili powdr ~soft. +5oz cocnt milk/2t currypowdr, simmr 10m. + 1# cubd whitefish, simmr ~done.
PARAGUAY	SO'O-YOSOPY (Beef Soup)	Saute 1 onion/1.5 chopd grn pepper/2T oil ~softened. + 2 chopd toms, cook ~ thick. + 2# grnd beef/5c h2o/s&p. Simmr 30m, garnish w parm.
PERU	LOMO SALTADO (Stir-Fried Beef & Potatoes)	Stirfry 1# cubed beef in oil, + 3 chopped chili, 2t red vinegr, 3t soya. Cook ~ evap.
PHILIPPINES	ADOBON PUSIT (Squid Adobo)	Saute 4 garlc/2T oil ~soft, +1 chopd tom/.25c soya&wt vinegar&h2o/2# squid. Simmr ~tender, rmv squid, reduce sauce to glaze squid.
POLAND	SPLIT-PEA & SAUSAGE SOUP	Puree .25# kielbasa/7oz beef broth. + 1.5c beef broth/1 onion/1 bay/.75# kielbasa/s&p 30m, +2 chopd carrot/1# split pea, simmr ~soft.
PORTUGAL	ROJOES A CAMINHO (Pork Stew with Cumin, Lemon & Cilantro)	Brwn 2# cubed pork/2T oil, + .5c wt wine/1.5t cumin/1 garlc/s&p. Simmr 25m. + .25c wt wine/1 sliced lemon. Simmr ~ thick, garnish cilantro.
QATAR	EGGPLANT SPREAD	Roast 3 halved eggplants w 2T oil 350F 40m; cool,peel. Blend w .33c tahini/2garlc/1 chopd grn pepper. Season w 4T lemon juice, s&p.
ROMANIA	CIORBA TERANEASCA (Bacon & Cabbage)	Saute .5c minced bacon/2 onions ~soft, +1 shredded cabbage/1T dill//6c h2o/s&p, simmr ~tender. Whisk in 2 egg/1T vinegr ~egg cooked.
RUSSIA	BASTURMA (Marinated Beef)	Marinate 2# cubd bf filet/1 onion/2t basil/1t pep/.25c red wine vinegr 5h. Broil on skewr turning 12m.
RWANDA	IBIHARAGE (Fried Beans)	Saute 3 onion/2 garlc/2T oil ~soft, +4c white bns/s&p/1t cayenne. Simmr 10m.
SAINT KITTS & NEVIS	RIKKITA BEEF	Marinate 1# steak w/5 garlc/2 mincd chiles/1c white wine 2h. Simmr all w 1t currypowder ~ tender.
SAINT LUCIA	BAKED WHITE FISH	Bake 3 tuna stk/1t onion pwdr/2.5 chopd tom/.5t thym/2T oil/s&p 350F 20m. Broil 1m or ~brown.
SAINT VINCENT & GRENADINES	FRIED JACK FISH	Marinate 1# jackfish fillets/.25c lemjuice 15m. Rinse, dry, rub w 2T dried onion&garlc&thyme. Dredge in flour, fry in .5c oil 5m ~golden.
SAN MARINO	SAN MARINO STEAK	Bake 4 beef stk/s&p/4oz crsh tom/1 chopd onion/2 chopd celery ribs/2T Italian seasoning/1 bay/1T hot sauce 250F 2h or ~ tender.
SAMOA	OKA I'A (Raw-Fish Stew)	Brine 1# cubd fish/2T salt/2c h2o 45m. Drain, + 1 chopd tom/.5 onion/.5 diced cuke/1c coconut milk/1T cilantro/.5c lime juice. Chill.
SAO TOMÉ & PRINCIPE	BOILED PORK	Simmr 2# cubd pork/2c h2o ~tender, drain. Saute 2 onion/1 garlc/1 bay/3 tom/s&p/3T palm oil ~soft, +pork/1 pkg spinach. Simmr 20m.
SAUDI ARABIA	ACORN SQUASH PASTE	Roast 3 peeled, chopd acorn squash/2T oil 325F 1.5h. Mix flesh/3T lem juice/2 garlc/2T tahini/1t oil/s&p. Garnish parsley.
SENEGAL	MAFÉ (Meat in Peanut Sauce)	Brwn 2# beef chunks/2T oil, rmv. Saute 1 onion/4 garlc, + meat/1T tom paste. Cook ~drkened, +1.5c h2o, .25c peanut butter. Simmr 40m.
SERBIA	GOULASH	Simmr 2c h2o/.25# smoked salami/.5# beef chunks/28oz canned chopd tom/.5 onion/1t paprka/1t chile powdr ~ pork is tender.
SEYCHELLES	TUNA WITH COCONUT	Brwn 1# tuna/2T oil, rmv. Saute 1 onion/3 garlc/3 mincd chile/1t mincd gingr/1T tumeric ~soft. +1 can cocon milkt/tuna, cook ~thick.
SIERRA LEONE	MEAT STEW	Boil 1# meat/4c h2o ~tender, +3 choppd eggplant/1 onion/5 tom/3T tom paste, cook ~soft. Rmv meat, puree veg, return meat. Simmr 10m.
SINGAPORE	HATI AYAM GOREN KICAP (Chicken Liver in Soy Sauce)	Season .5# chx livr/1t salt&tumerc&coriandr. Saute 1 onion/2T oil ~soft. + liver/3 mincd rd chiles, cook 3m. + 2T soya, cook ~done.
SLOVAKIA	SEGEDIN GOULASH	Saute 1 onion ~soft, +1.5# cubd pork/1t paprka/.5t caraway seed/s&p ~brwn. + 1# sauerkraut/4c h2o, simmr 1h.

COUNTRY	DISH	RECIPE
SLOVENIA	LECINA JUHA (Lentil Soup)	Brwn 1 sliced onion/2T oil. + 4c h2o/2c lentils/1c cooked wt beans/2 smoked ham hocks/s&p. Simmr 2h, rmv bones, add meat back in.
SOLOMON ISLANDS	CORNED BEEF WITH VEGETABLES	Saute 2 garlc/1 onion/1T oil ~soft, +3 rd chiles/1t gingr/1# corned beef. Simmr 10m.
SOMALIA	CHICKEN SUQAAR	Saute 1 onion/1T oil ~soft. + 1# cubed chx/1t cum&chile powdr/s&p, brwn. + 1 zucchini/1T lem juice/1t vinegr, cook ~zucchini soft.
SOUTH AFRICA	LAMB BRAAI	Marinate 2# bonless lamb leg/3T honey/3T lem/1T oil/2T mustard/1T rosemry/s&p 24h. Slow-grill ovr wood burnd to embers 40m.
SPAIN	CHULETAS DE CERDO A LA MADRILENA (Madrid Pork Chops)	Marinate 4 pork chop/2 garlc/2t parsly/1 onion/1t paprka/2T oil 1h. Roast 425F 12m. Turn, pour over marinade, 425F 12m.
SRI LANKA	FISH CURRY	Coat 1# cubed tuna or other fish/2T vinegr/1t salt. Saute 1 garlc/4T chile powdr/2T curry powd 3m. + tuna, saute 3m. + h2o to loosen.
SUDAN	KHOODRA MAFROOKA (Meat Dish)	Saute 1 onion/2T oil ~soft, +1# beef, brwn, +2c h2o, simmr ~tender. Saute 8oz spinach/5 garlc/s&p, simmr ~thick. Pour over meat.
SURINAME	MATJERI MASALA (Fish Curry)	Sear 2# whitefish fillets/2T oil/s&p, rmv. Saute 1 onion/3 garlc ~ soft. + 2T masala curry powder, + 2T ketchup. + fish + 1c h2o; simmr 10m.
SWAZILAND	SWAZI AVOCADO SLAW	Marinate 2 dicd avocado/2T lem juice/1t mincd ging&salt 10m. Mix in 1c pnuts.
SWEDEN	SWEDISH-STYLE STEAK	Simmr 2.5# cubd beef round/1c beef stock/1 onion/2T dill/s&p ~tender.
SWITZERLAND	PUMPKIN STIR-FRY	Stir fry 2c pumpkin cubd/1 chopd tom/1# corn/.5c h2o ~soft. +1t paprika, simmr 5m. Drizzle with olv oil.
SYRIA	SHURBAT ADDES (Red Lentil Soup)	Saute 6 garlic/1t coriander&cumin/2T oil, +2c rd lentil/2q h2o, simmr 30m. Stir in 1t lemon juice, simmr 10m.
TAJIKISTAN	MUNG-BEAN SOUP	Saute 1 onion/3 garlc ~soft, +6 slicd carrot/1t cumin/1t dried basil/s&p, saute ~soft, +6c h2o/.5c mung bean, simmr 40m
TANZANIA	DUCKLING DAR ES SALAAM (Curry-Braised Duck)	Saute 1 onion/4T oil ~soft, +2 chopd tom/1t currypowdr/1t chili powdr/salt, saute ~soft. +4# duck legs/2q h2o, simmr covrd 30m.
THAILAND	GARLIC SHRIMP STIR-FRY	Marinate 15 shrimp/2T oyster sauce/1T soya/1T fish sauce/2T limjuice/1 chopd rd chile 1h. Stir fry 3m.
TOGO	PEANUT CHICKEN	Simmr .5# chix breast/3c h2o 15m. Drain, shred. Saute 1 onion/1 garlc/2T oil ~soft, +chix/16oz stewd tom/3T pnut buttr, simmr 5m.
TONGA	KAPISI PULU (Corned Beef in Coconut)	Cook 1 cabbage/16oz corned beef/1 onion/1 slicd tom/10oz coconut cream cvrd 350F 1.5h.
TRINIDAD & TOBAGO	GARLIC PORK	Blend 8 garlc/2t thym/2 onion/.5 habanero/2T lime/2c wt vingr/salt ~smooth. Marinate 4# cubd pork 2d. Saute ~brwn, +marinade, reduce 2 glaz.
TUNISIA	TOMATO SAUCE WITH EGGS	Saute 3 jalapenos/1 onion/5 garlc/1t cumin/4T oil ~ soft. + 28oz cannd toms, simmr 15m. + 4 eggs to sauce, simmer ~ wt is set. Garnish feta.
TURKMENISTAN	LAMB SHORBA	Brwn 1# lamb chunks/.25c oil. +2 chopd tom/1 onion/1 cubd pumpkin/salt, saute ~caramelizd. + 4c h2o/1T paprka, simmr ~ lamb tender.
TUVALU	LAULU (Spinach-Fish Stew)	Bake 4 fish fillets/2T oil/2t sesame oil 20m. Saute 2 garlc ~brwn, +1c cocont milk/3T lem/14oz spinach/fish, simmr ~spinach wiltd.
TURKEY	SARIMSAKLI KUSKONMAZ (Garlic Asparagus)	Boil 1# asparagus in salted water ~tender; drain. Saute 2garlic/1T olv oil, + 1t paprika/s&p. Cook 5m low heat.
UGANDA	CHICKENNAT (Chicken Stew)	Saute 2# chix breast/s&p/.25c oil ~brwn, +1c chix stock. Stir in .75c pnut buttr/2 egg yolk, whisk ~smooth. Simmr ~chix is cookd.
UNITED ARAB EMIRATES	CHENNAD (Kingfish)	Season 2# kingfish fillets/1t garam masala/1t tumeric/1t cum/1t salt 30m. Fry 4c oil 5m per side.
UKRAINE	BORSCHT	Julienne 1# peeld beets/2 med onion/2 med carrots/.75# cabbage. Saute in 2T olvoil&s+p. Cvr w 5C h2o,smr>25m; season w lemon.
UNITED KINGDOM	FISH & CHIPS	Mix 1c flour/1c cornstarch/12oz beer/1 egg, refrigerate 20m. + 4 cod filet, fry in 6c pnut oil 375F 5m per fillet. Serve w chips.
UNITED STATES	GRIDDLED BURGER	Sear .25# ball grnd beef/2t oil in v hot skillet 1m. Flip, smash flat, cook 1m. Flip, cook 1 m more. Serve on potato roll w condiments.
URUGUAY	BEEF TUCO	Saute 1 onion/1 gratd carrot/1 chop rd chile/2T oil ~soft. + .5# grnd beef, brwn. +16oz crushd tom/1T oreg/1T h2o, simmr 15m.
UZBEKISTAN	TUVOK PLOV (Chicken & Carrots)	Brwn 1# cubd chix breast/.25c oil, +3 onion/6 chopd carrot, sauté ~soft. +2c h2o, simmr 10m.
VANUATU	WHOLE FISH WITH CITRUS & COCONUT	Cvr 1 whole fish w 1 sliced lemon&orange/.5c coconut milk/s&p. Cvr, bake 350F 40m.
VENEZUELA	CONEJO EN COCO (Rabbit in Coconut)	Blend 1c gratd cocont/1c h2o/1c cocont milk ~smooth. Boil ~thick. Combine w 32oz crushd tom/1 onion/3# cubd rabbt/s&p, bake 350F 1h.
VIETNAM	MAHO (Chicken with Mandarin Orange)	Saute 2 garlc/3T oil ~brwn, +2 chix breast, saute 5m. Stir in 2T soya/.5 pnut butter, simmr ~ cooked. Serve w lettuce, mandarin orange.
YEMEN	ROAST CHICKEN WITH CUMIN	Mix 1T ground cumin&turmeric/s&p/2T oil; rub into 1 whl chicken. Roast 400F >45m until juices are clear.
ZAMBIA	AMARANTHUS SOUP (Vegetable Soup)	Simmr 1 onion/2 chopd carrot/3c h2o ~soft, +14oz spinach/2T paprka/.5 chopd cuke ~h2o evap. Stir in .5c milk, simmr 15m.
ZIMBABWE	HUKU YECHIBOYI (Zimbabwean Chicken)	Simmr 2# cubed chix thighs/s&p/2c h2o 1h. Saute 1 onion/3T oil, +1 chopd tom/chix/liquid. Simmr 30m.

THE CHEF GENEALOGICAL CHARTS: AN UNOFFICIAL WHO'S WHO (AND WHO TAUGHT WHOM)

THE CHEZ PANISSE GENEALOGICAL CHART (PAGE 578)

Founded in 1971 by Alice Waters and Paul Aratow, Chez Panisse spearheaded the "slow-food" movement, as it later became known. Since Chez Panisse opened its doors, its mantra has been an ever-changing menu based on seasonal produce and locally sourced, organic foods.

Executive chef Waters passed her philosophy on to many now **influential chefs who served in her kitchen (shown in black, connected by yellow).** These individuals went on to found their own establishments and impart Alice's ideology to **new generations of chefs and restaurateurs (shown in white). The green dotted lines show how chefs are indirectly connected to Panisse by working with Panisse-trained chefs** at various restaurants (e.g., Marsha McBride worked at Zuni Café under Panisse-trained Judy Rodgers).

Four decades ago, Chez Panisse started as a small group of idealists in Berkeley, California. Now it represents a philosophy of sustainable cooking and eating that has spread into cuisines and places no one could have imagined.

THE NYC GENEALOGICAL CHART (PAGE 580)

Behold . . . the tangled, incestuous web that is the New York City culinary scene! Traveling chronologically from left to right, past to present, you can see most of **New York's top restaurants (circled in dotted yellow)** and their **connections to the chefs who made them what they are (circled in black).** And what do you get when the who's who of NYC haute cuisine share restaurants like third-graders share baseball cards? An infectious style of cooking that sets the bar for the rest of the nation.

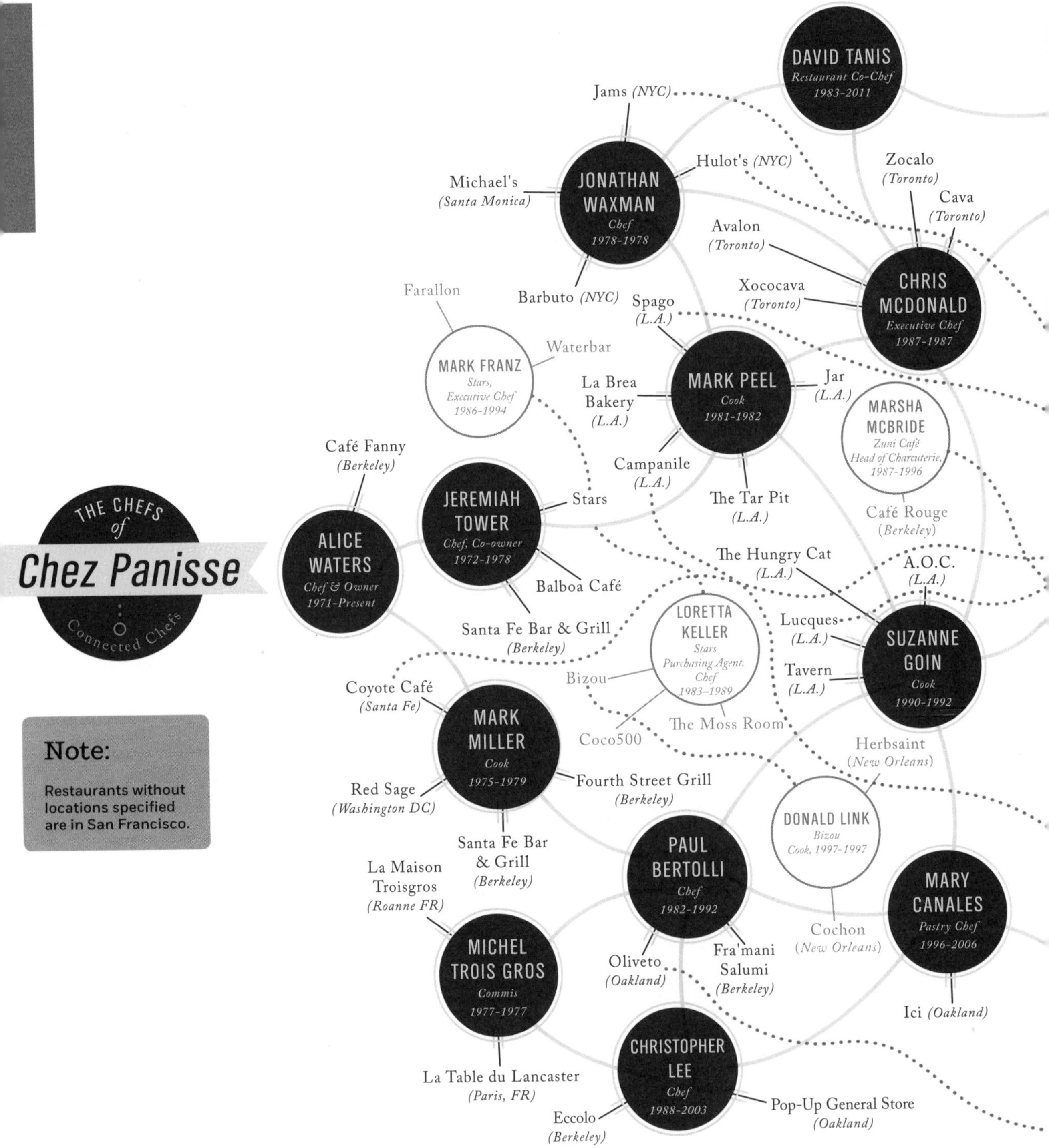
THE CHEFS of
Chez Panisse
Connected Chefs
Note:
Restaurants without locations specified are in San Francisco.
DAVID TANIS
Restaurant Co-Chef
1983-2011
Jams (NYC)
JONATHAN WAXMAN
Chef
1978-1978
Michael's (Santa Monica)
Hulot's (NYC)
Barbuto (NYC)
Zocalo (Toronto)
Cava (Toronto)
Avalon (Toronto)
Xococava (Toronto)
CHRIS MCDONALD
Executive Chef
1987-1987
Farallon
MARK FRANZ
Stars,
Executive Chef
1986-1994
Waterbar
Spago (L.A.)
MARK PEEL
Cook
1981-1982
La Brea Bakery (L.A.)
Jar (L.A.)
Campanile (L.A.)
The Tar Pit (L.A.)
MARSHA MCBRIDE
Zuni Café
Head of Charcuterie,
1987-1996
Café Rouge (Berkeley)
Café Fanny (Berkeley)
ALICE WATERS
Chef & Owner
1971-Present
JEREMIAH TOWER
Chef, Co-owner
1972-1978
Stars
Balboa Café
Santa Fe Bar & Grill (Berkeley)
The Hungry Cat (L.A.)
A.O.C. (L.A.)
LORETTA KELLER
Stars
Purchasing Agent,
Chef
1983-1989
Bizou
Coco500
The Moss Room
Lucques (L.A.)
Tavern (L.A.)
SUZANNE GOIN
Cook
1990-1992
Coyote Café (Santa Fe)
MARK MILLER
Cook
1975-1979
Red Sage (Washington DC)
Fourth Street Grill (Berkeley)
Santa Fe Bar & Grill (Berkeley)
Herbsaint (New Orleans)
DONALD LINK
Bizou
Cook, 1997-1997
Cochon (New Orleans)
PAUL BERTOLLI
Chef
1982-1992
Oliveto (Oakland)
Fra'mani Salumi (Berkeley)
MARY CANALES
Pastry Chef
1996-2006
Ici (Oakland)
La Maison Troisgros (Roanne FR)
MICHEL TROIS GROS
Commis
1977-1977
La Table du Lancaster (Paris, FR)
CHRISTOPHER LEE
Chef
1988-2003
Eccolo (Berkeley)
Pop-Up General Store (Oakland)

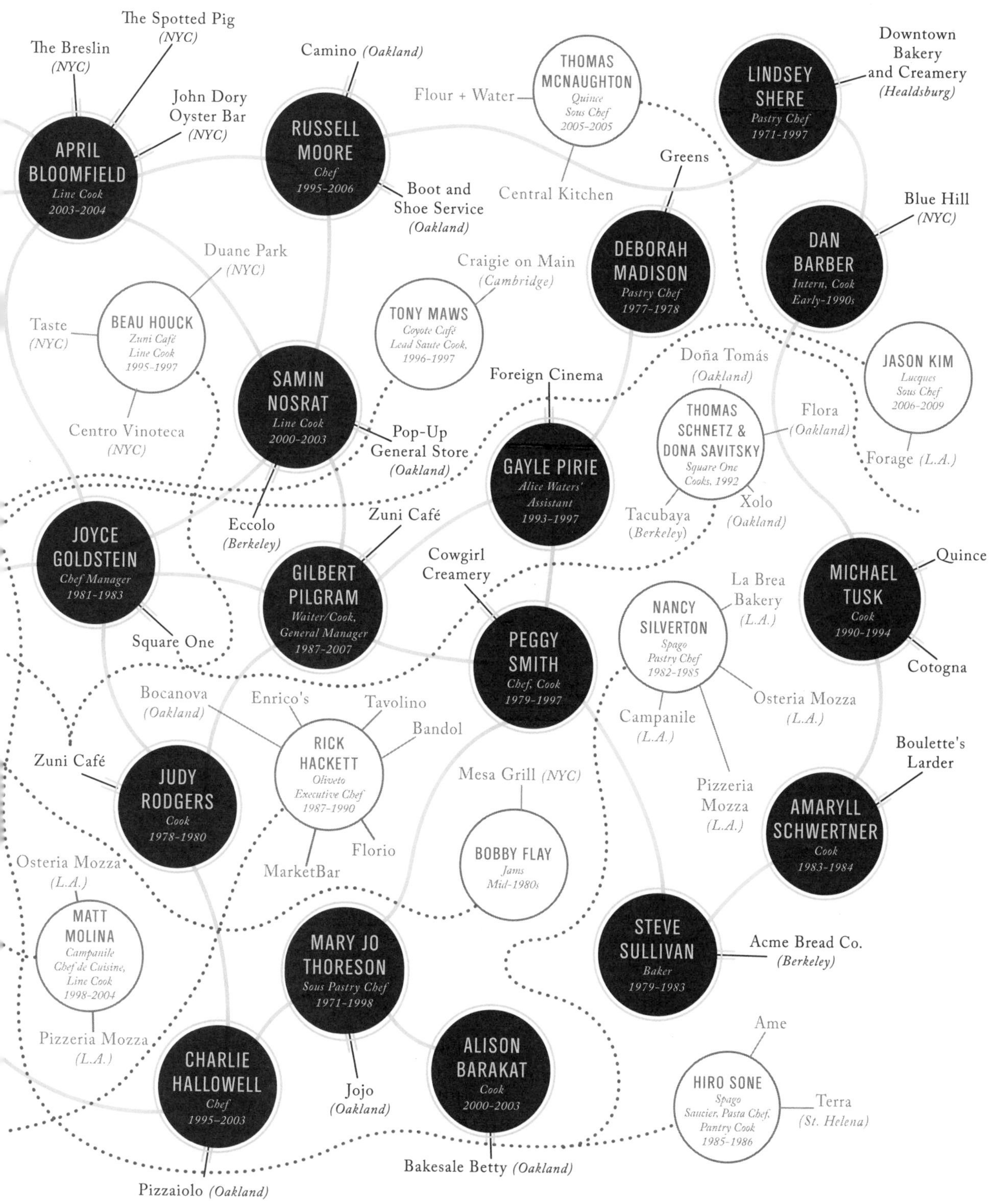
The Breslin (NYC)
The Spotted Pig (NYC)
John Dory Oyster Bar (NYC)
APRIL BLOOMFIELD
Line Cook
2003-2004
Camino (Oakland)
RUSSELL MOORE
Chef
1995-2006
Boot and Shoe Service (Oakland)
Flour + Water
THOMAS MCNAUGHTON
Quince
Sous Chef
2005-2005
Central Kitchen
LINDSEY SHERE
Pastry Chef
1971-1997
Downtown Bakery and Creamery (Healdsburg)
Greens
DEBORAH MADISON
Pastry Chef
1977-1978
Blue Hill (NYC)
DAN BARBER
Intern, Cook
Early-1990s
Duane Park (NYC)
Taste (NYC)
BEAU HOUCK
Zuni Café
Line Cook
1995-1997
Centro Vinoteca (NYC)
Craigie on Main (Cambridge)
TONY MAWS
Coyote Café
Lead Saute Cook,
1996-1997
SAMIN NOSRAT
Line Cook
2000-2003
Pop-Up General Store (Oakland)
Eccolo (Berkeley)
Foreign Cinema
GAYLE PIRIE
Alice Waters' Assistant
1993-1997
Doña Tomás (Oakland)
THOMAS SCHNETZ & DONA SAVITSKY
Square One
Cooks, 1992
Flora (Oakland)
Tacubaya (Berkeley)
Xolo (Oakland)
JASON KIM
Lucques
Sous Chef
2006-2009
Forage (L.A.)
JOYCE GOLDSTEIN
Chef Manager
1981-1983
Square One
Zuni Café
GILBERT PILGRAM
Waiter/Cook, General Manager
1987-2007
Cowgirl Creamery
PEGGY SMITH
Chef, Cook
1979-1997
La Brea Bakery (L.A.)
NANCY SILVERTON
Spago
Pastry Chef
1982-1985
Campanile (L.A.)
Osteria Mozza (L.A.)
Pizzeria Mozza (L.A.)
Quince
MICHAEL TUSK
Cook
1990-1994
Cotogna
Bocanova (Oakland)
Enrico's
Tavolino
Bandol
RICK HACKETT
Oliveto
Executive Chef
1987-1990
MarketBar
Florio
Zuni Café
JUDY RODGERS
Cook
1978-1980
Mesa Grill (NYC)
BOBBY FLAY
Jams
Mid-1980s
Boulette's Larder
AMARYLL SCHWERTNER
Cook
1983-1984
Osteria Mozza (L.A.)
MATT MOLINA
Campanile
Chef de Cuisine,
Line Cook
1998-2004
Pizzeria Mozza (L.A.)
MARY JO THORESON
Sous Pastry Chef
1971-1998
STEVE SULLIVAN
Baker
1979-1983
Acme Bread Co. (Berkeley)
CHARLIE HALLOWELL
Chef
1995-2003
Jojo (Oakland)
ALISON BARAKAT
Cook
2000-2003
Ame
HIRO SONE
Spago
Saucier, Pasta Chef,
Pantry Cook
1985-1986
Terra (St. Helena)
Bakesale Betty (Oakland)
Pizzaiolo (Oakland)

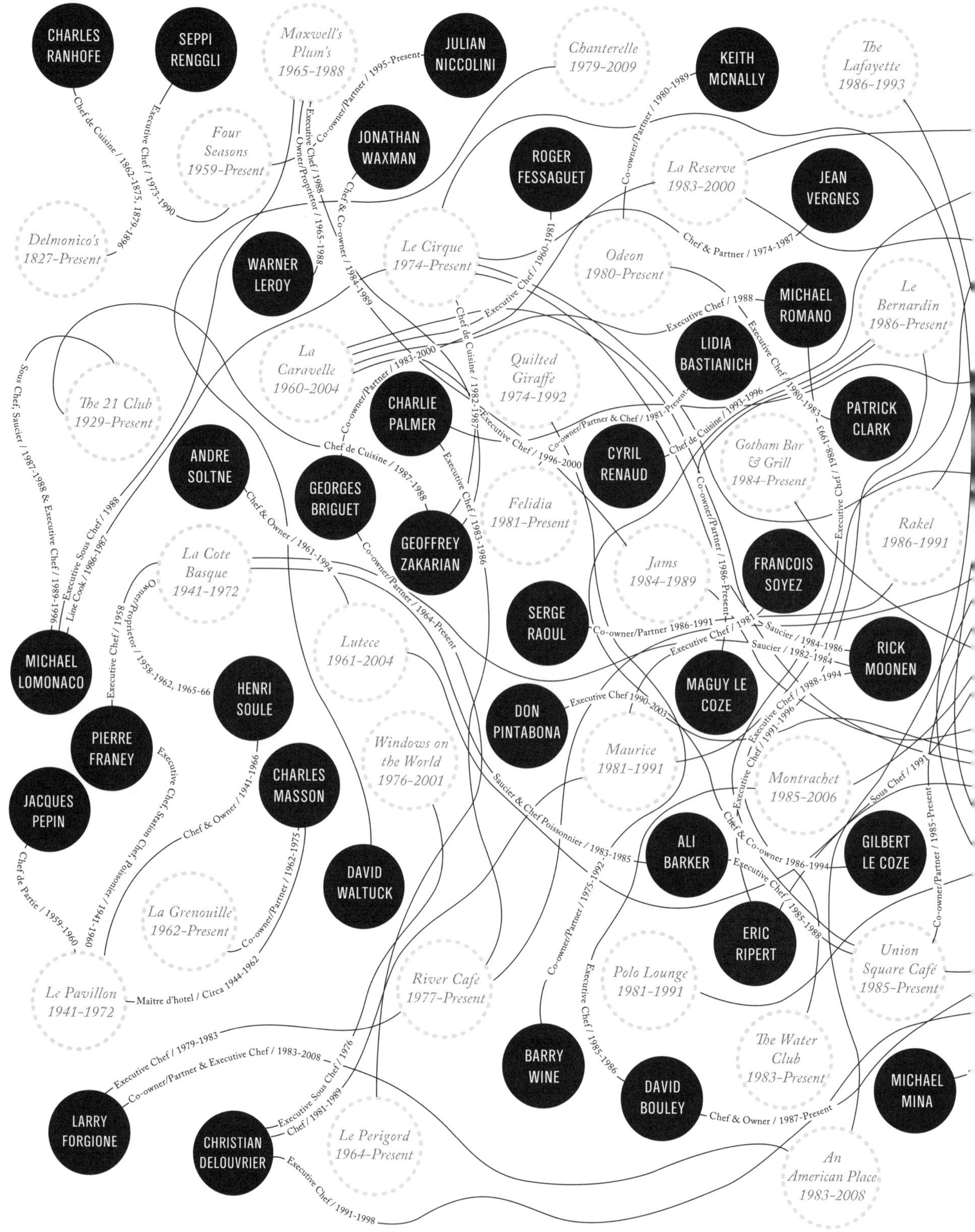
CHARLES RANHOFE
SEPPI RENGGLI
Maxwell's Plum's 1965-1988
JULIAN NICCOLINI
Chanterelle 1979-2009
KEITH MCNALLY
The Lafayette 1986-1993
Four Seasons 1959-Present
JONATHAN WAXMAN
ROGER FESSAGUET
La Reserve 1983-2000
JEAN VERGNES
Delmonico's 1827-Present
WARNER LEROY
Le Cirque 1974-Present
Odeon 1980-Present
MICHAEL ROMANO
Le Bernardin 1986-Present
La Caravelle 1960-2004
Quilted Giraffe 1974-1992
LIDIA BASTIANICH
The 21 Club 1929-Present
CHARLIE PALMER
PATRICK CLARK
ANDRE SOLTNE
CYRIL RENAUD
Gotham Bar & Grill 1984-Present
GEORGES BRIGUET
Felidia 1981-Present
GEOFFREY ZAKARIAN
Rakel 1986-1991
La Cote Basque 1941-1972
Jams 1984-1989
FRANCOIS SOYEZ
SERGE RAOUL
Lutece 1961-2004
RICK MOONEN
MICHAEL LOMONACO
MAGUY LE COZE
HENRI SOULE
DON PINTABONA
PIERRE FRANEY
Windows on the World 1976-2001
Maurice 1981-1991
Montrachet 1985-2006
CHARLES MASSON
JACQUES PEPIN
ALI BARKER
GILBERT LE COZE
DAVID WALTUCK
La Grenouille 1962-Present
ERIC RIPERT
Le Pavillon 1941-1972
River Cafe 1977-Present
Polo Lounge 1981-1991
Union Square Café 1985-Present
The Water Club 1983-Present
BARRY WINE
DAVID BOULEY
MICHAEL MINA
LARRY FORGIONE
CHRISTIAN DELOUVRIER
Le Perigord 1964-Present
An American Place 1983-2008
Chef de Cuisine / 1862-1875, 1879-1896
Executive Chef / 1973-1990
Co-owner/Partner / 1995-Present
Executive Chef / 1988
Owner/Proprietor / 1965-1988
Chef & Co-owner / 1984-1989
Co-owner/Partner / 1980-1989
Chef & Partner / 1974-1987
Executive Chef / 1960-1981
Executive Chef / 1988
Executive Chef / 1980-1983
Chef de Cuisine / 1982-1987
Co-owner/Partner / 1983-2000
Sous Chef, Saucier / 1987-1988 & Executive Chef / 1989-1996
Executive Sous Chef / 1988
Line Cook / 1986-1987
Co-owner/Partner & Chef / 1981-Present
Executive Chef / 1996-2000
Chef de Cuisine / 1993-1996
Executive Chef / 1988-1993
Chef de Cuisine / 1987-1988
Executive Chef / 1983-1986
Chef & Owner / 1961-1994
Co-owner/Partner / 1964-Present
Co-owner/Partner / 1986-Present
Owner/Proprietor / 1958-1962, 1965-66
Executive Chef / 1958
Co-owner/Partner 1986-1991
Executive Chef / 1981
Saucier / 1984-1986
Saucier / 1982-1984
Executive Chef / 1988-1994
Executive Chef 1990-2003
Executive Chef / 1991-1996
Sous Chef / 1991
Co-owner/Partner / 1985-Present
Executive Chef, Station Chef, Poissonier / 1941-1960
Chef & Owner / 1941-1966
Co-owner/Partner / 1962-1975
Saucier & Chef Poissonnier / 1983-1985
Chef & Co-owner 1986-1994
Executive Chef / 1985-1988
Chef de Partie / 1959-1960
Maître d'hotel / Circa 1944-1962
Co-owner/Partner / 1975-1992
Executive Chef / 1985-1986
Executive Chef / 1979-1983
Co-owner/Partner & Executive Chef / 1983-2008
Executive Sous Chef / 1976
Chef / 1981-1989
Chef & Owner / 1987-Present
Executive Chef / 1991-1998

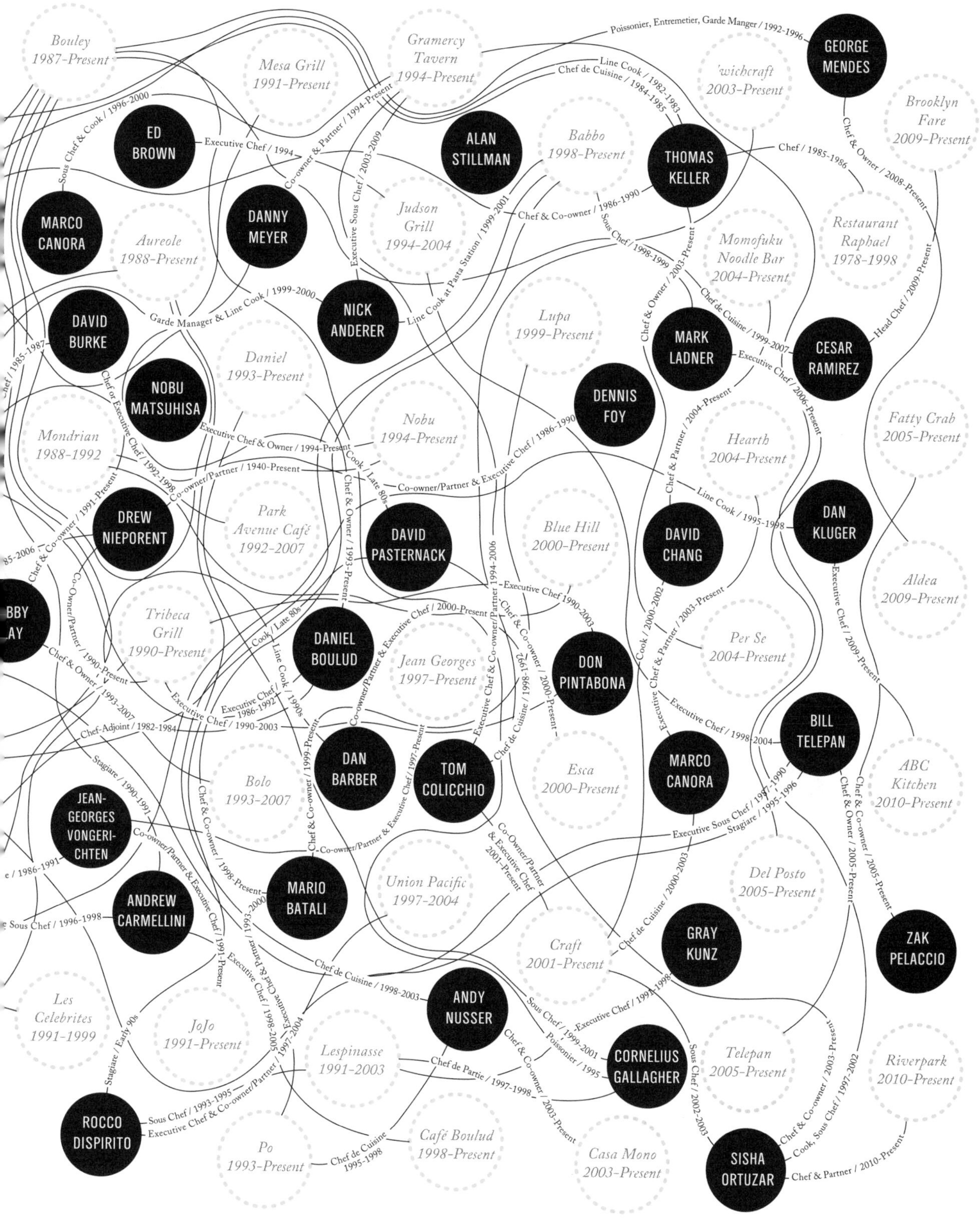
Bouley 1987-Present
Mesa Grill 1991-Present
Gramercy Tavern 1994-Present
'wichcraft 2003-Present
GEORGE MENDES
Brooklyn Fare 2009-Present
ED BROWN
ALAN STILLMAN
Babbo 1998-Present
THOMAS KELLER
MARCO CANORA
Aureole 1988-Present
DANNY MEYER
Judson Grill 1994-2004
Momofuku Noodle Bar 2004-Present
Restaurant Raphael 1978-1998
DAVID BURKE
NICK ANDERER
Lupa 1999-Present
MARK LADNER
CESAR RAMIREZ
NOBU MATSUHISA
Daniel 1993-Present
DENNIS FOY
Mondrian 1988-1992
Nobu 1994-Present
Hearth 2004-Present
Fatty Crab 2005-Present
DREW NIEPORENT
Park Avenue Café 1992-2007
DAVID PASTERNACK
Blue Hill 2000-Present
DAVID CHANG
DAN KLUGER
Aldea 2009-Present
BBY
AY
Tribeca Grill 1990-Present
DANIEL BOULUD
Jean Georges 1997-Present
DON PINTABONA
Per Se 2004-Present
BILL TELEPAN
ABC Kitchen 2010-Present
DAN BARBER
TOM COLICCHIO
Esca 2000-Present
MARCO CANORA
Bolo 1993-2007
JEAN-GEORGES VONGERICHTEN
MARIO BATALI
Union Pacific 1997-2004
Del Posto 2005-Present
ANDREW CARMELLINI
Craft 2001-Present
GRAY KUNZ
ZAK PELACCIO
Les Celebrites 1991-1999
JoJo 1991-Present
Lespinasse 1991-2003
ANDY NUSSER
CORNELIUS GALLAGHER
Telepan 2005-Present
Riverpark 2010-Present
ROCCO DISPIRITO
Po 1993-Present
Café Boulud 1998-Present
Casa Mono 2003-Present
SISHA ORTUZAR
Poissonier, Entremetier, Garde Manger / 1992-1996
Line Cook / 1982-1983
Chef de Cuisine / 1984-1985
Chef & Owner / 2008-Present
Chef / 1985-1986
Sous Chef & Cook / 1996-2000
Executive Chef / 1994
Co-owner & Partner / 1994-Present
Executive Sous Chef / 2003-2009
Line Cook at Pasta Station / 1999-2001
Chef & Co-owner / 1986-1990
Sous Chef / 1998-1999
Chef & Owner / 2003-Present
Chef de Cuisine / 1999-2007
Head Chef / 2009-Present
Garde Manger & Line Cook / 1999-2000
Executive Chef / 2006-Present
Chef / 1985-1987
Chef or Executive Chef / 1992-1998
Executive Chef & Owner / 1994-Present
Cook / Late 80s
Co-owner/Partner & Executive Chef / 1986-1990
Chef & Partner / 2004-Present
Co-owner/Partner / 1940-Present
Chef & Co-owner / 1991-Present
Line Cook / 1995-1998
Chef & Owner / 1993-Present
Executive Chef / 2009-Present
Co-Owner/Partner / 1990-Present
Executive Chef 1990-2003
Co-owner/Partner & Executive Chef / 1994-2006
Co-owner/Partner & Executive Chef / 2000-Present
Chef & Co-owner / 2000-Present
Chef de Cuisine / 1988-1992
Cook / 2000-2002
Executive Chef & Partner / 2003-Present
Cook / Late 80s
Line Cook / 1990s
Chef & Owner / 1990-Present
Chef & Owner / 1993-2007
Executive Chef / 1986-1992
Executive Chef / 1990-2003
Executive Chef / 1998-2004
Chef-Adjoint / 1982-1984
Stagiare / 1990-1991
Chef & Co-owner / 1999-Present
Co-owner/Partner & Executive Chef / 1997-Present
Executive Sous Chef / 1987-1990
Stagiare / 1995-1996
Chef & Co-owner / 2005-Present
Chef & Owner / 2005-Present
Co-owner/Partner & Executive Chef / 1991-Present
Chef & Co-owner / 1998-Present
Co-owner/Partner / 1993-2000
Co-Owner/Partner & Executive Chef 2001-Present
Executive Chef / 2000-2003
Chef de Cuisine / 2000-2003
Chef / 1986-1991
Sous Chef / 1996-1998
Executive Chef / 1991-Present
Executive Chef & Partner / 1997-2004
Chef de Cuisine / 1998-2003
Executive Chef / 1991-1998
Sous Chef / 1999-2001
Poissonier / 1995
Stagiare / Early 90s
Chef de Partie / 1997-1998
Chef & Co-owner / 2003-Present
Sous Chef / 2002-2003
Chef & Co-owner / 2003-Present
Cook, Sous Chef / 1997-2002
Sous Chef / 1993-1995
Executive Chef & Co-owner/Partner / 1997-2004
Chef de Cuisine 1995-1998
Chef & Partner / 2010-Present
85-2006

TURNING PRO WITHOUT CULINARY SCHOOL—THE FULL TRAINING PROGRAM

"'It's true,' Mario [Batali] said [after a guest complained the broccoli had fewer florets than during his last visit]. 'We've had larger florets, but nature isn't making big florets at the moment.' A new pasta was prepared, and Mario handed it to one of the runners. 'When you give this to him, please pistol-whip him with your penis.'"

—BILL BUFORD, *HEAT*

"The only way of finding the limits of the possible is by going beyond them into the impossible."

—ARTHUR C. CLARKE, SCI-FI AUTHOR

For the masochistic, let's look at the path to becoming a literal "professional."

You can travel the tried-and-true path through culinary school. This can be fun, almost like an MBA program: a semi-vacation that looks good on a résumé. Or you can create your own boot camp. That is what this chapter will teach you. I asked my chef consigliere, JZ, for his recommendations for going from Mickey Mouse to Terminator without formal schooling, one foolproof baby step at a time. He should know, as he's advised culinary schools on curriculum design.

OTTO

The world-famous Mario Batali, who left culinary school to focus on the faster-paced learning in professional kitchens.

Roll up your sleeves and prepare to get your ass kicked. That's the whole point. As little Coraline Jones of Neil Gaiman's *Coraline* wisely said, "I don't want whatever I want. Nobody does. Not really. What kind of fun would it be if I just got everything I ever wanted just like that, and it didn't mean anything? What then?"

Time to sweat and lay exhausted on the battlefield, enjoying every little victory you earn.

Chef Leoni warming up staff at Hotel Commodore, 1920.

THE TRIFECTA

The difference between cooking at home and cooking in a professional kitchen is akin to the difference between putting at miniature golf and driving in a Masters golf tournament. Organization and intense practice are key.

First and foremost, professional chefs have excellent time management. Keeping your cool (and fingertips) during a dinner rush requires mastery of **taste, technique,** and **volume.** Taste was handled on page 50. In the following pages, JZ and I will break down methods for mastering both technique and volume (including speed).

SYLLABUS

1.
REFINE TECHNIQUE

2.
PRACTICE VOLUME/SPEED

3.
HITCH YOUR WAGON TO A PRO

REFINE TECHNIQUE

Before peeling a whole case of potatoes, for instance, it is important to perfectly peel one potato as quickly as possible. There are many ways to peel the humble potato, but there are only a few ways to peel it efficiently. To learn professional technique, you should, in order:

REVIEW VIDEOS

These are your warm-ups. You don't want to pull those hammies:

- ☐ Great Chefs series—greatchefs.com/downloads
- ☐ Jacques Pépin—anything by Jacques is worth watching. *The Essential Pépin* DVD set is outstanding,[1] and YouTube has 100+ videos. Check out "Pépin Debone Chicken Galantine Ballotine."

DISSECT BOOKS

Only a few books address the techniques of cooking well. Here's a powerful trio of manual brilliance:

- ☐ *Mastering the Art of French Cooking,* Julia Child
- ☐ *La Technique,* Jacques Pépin
- ☐ *The Making of a Cook,* Madeleine Kamman

PRACTICE AT HOME

Every meal you cook should be an exercise in practicing great technique.

Incorporate steps that are normally reserved for restaurant-quality food:

- ☐ Practice knife work. Shape your vegetables to standard size (*taillage*) even if you are putting them into soup.
- ☐ Cut carrots into ½" dice.
- ☐ Chiffonade heads of lettuce (iceberg is fine), a few leaves at a time.
- ☐ Dice onions.
- ☐ Chop garlic to puree.
- ☐ Learn to fine-control temperature in your cooking.
- ☐ Learn to braise meat and keep the braise at a simmer. Controlling a simmer for an extended period of time is key to good temperature control.
- ☐ Make omelets quickly at high temperature. Learn to not be afraid of high temperatures while moving the pan over heat.
- ☐ Practice working cleanly:
  - Wear an apron or chef coat. Practice keeping it pristinely white until you have finished preparing entire meals. Don't wipe your hands on it; don't lean against the cutting board. The biggest "shoemakers"[2] in the kitchen have the dirtiest aprons.
  - Practice working with a clean cutting board. Clean as you go. Never leave trimmings on your cutting board.
  - Leave no mess on the floor.

1 If you have an Amazon Prime account, you can stream this entire series for free, choosing to watch only the dishes you want to learn.

2 Derogatory kitchen slang for someone who lacks the skills to be a chef.

PRACTICE VOLUME/SPEED

Once you start feeling consistent with your accuracy, it's time to ramp up speed. To see how the masters bolt their way through these tasks, visit fourhourchef.com/speed. Once you get to the target time for any task, add more repetitions or volume.

- ☐ Time yourself on every technique.
- ☐ Keep a log and track your performance.

Measure the time it takes to do the following:

- ☐ Peel 10 potatoes
  Target time: less than 15 seconds per potato or 2½ minutes per 10 potatoes.
- ☐ Dice 5 large peeled carrots
  Target time: under 30 seconds to dice each.
- ☐ Butcher a chicken (see page 346)
  Target time: under a minute.

NEXT, WORK FOR A CATERER

Working for a caterer will put real mileage on your résumé in terms of preparing large quantities of food in short periods of time.

- Call a high-quality caterer and ask if you can work (even volunteer) in production.
- You will be asked to peel tons of potatoes, etc., under real-time pressure. Fortunately, you've already trained against the clock.
- Moreover, you will be surrounded by people who are so fast and effective at managing large volumes of food on deadline that learning by osmosis will take over. In other words, unspoken peer pressure will force you to become the average of the 4–5 people you work with most.

HITCH YOUR WAGON TO A PRO

Ready to take your studies to the next level? Work with the people who do this day in, day out. Make a shortlist of the best restaurants nearby and . . .

BECOME A *STAGIERE*

Go to a restaurant and ask to *stage* (pronounced like *mirage*). The traditional *stagiere* was a 6–12-month live/work arrangement at a classic French restaurant. Imagine a combination of indentured servitude and frat-house haze week. Be prepared to work for free. Consider it a rare bonus if you get paid anything at all.

Remember: they're doing *you* a favor, since you're more of a liability than a help at this point.

Your *stage*[3] could be two weeks of working five or six days from noon until midnight, or it may be 3–6 months of one or two days per week, or six months of six days a week.

How to make the approach:

1. Visit your favorite restaurant, or the best restaurant you know.
2. Eat at the bar. The bartender will talk to you more than a server running from table to table will. Have him/her introduce you to the GM. Have the GM introduce you to the chef.

3 This is different from a "trail," which is an audition for a full-time job and typically entails 1–2 nights of working a single station or dish.

3. Explain to the chef why you want to work in the kitchen and ask to *stage* (get the pronunciation right). Potential reasons include:

- You want to learn deeper respect for the work of a professional cook/chef.
- You want to understand the techniques of preparing restaurant-quality food.
- You want to improve the quality of your cooking technique.
- You want to improve your speed of prep work, volume production, etc.
- You want to refine your palate.

4. Have your uniform ready (including shoes, kitchen pants, chef coat). For gear, you can typically make it by with the minimum of the following:

- ☐ 8" chef's knife
- ☐ Paring knife
- ☐ Knife roll (fourhourchef.com/kniferoll or, if you want the men to harass the shit out of you, fourhourchef.com/girlykniferoll)
- ☐ Swiss peeler (Star Peeler)
- ☐ Dough scraper for cleaning your cutting board
- ☐ Tasting spoon (1 or 2 oz; I use the Gray Kunz 2 oz spoon, bought at jbprince.com)
- ☐ Small spiral notepad and a clickable pen (pen caps will find their way into food)

5. Ask for feedback and stay out of the way.

6. Focus on technique and aim to make everything perfect. Speed will continue to build over time. As Larry Vickers (retired special operations soldier) of Vickers Tactical would say, "Speed is fine. Accuracy is final."

BECOME AN APPRENTICE

An apprenticeship is a bit more formal than a *stage*. It is longer term and more structured, and the expectations of you are much higher. Use the following checklist as a curriculum and politely ask the chef to work you through each skill.

- Ask to work in prep, if possible.

- Learn alongside people who have peeled cases of fava beans in an afternoon. This will teach you how to embrace repetition like a machine.

- Remember that no task is too menial. Once again, they're doing you a favor, not the other way around. Stay humble and don't be a jackass.

APPRENTICE CHECKLIST

WORK COLD PREP

- ☐ Peel potatoes
- ☐ Peel carrots
- ☐ Dice onions
- ☐ Wash lettuce
- ☐ Slice leeks
- ☐ Chop garlic
- ☐ Chiffonade basil or other leafy herbs
- ☐ Prep artichokes
- ☐ Make pasta[4]

WORK HOT PREP

- ☐ Make stock
- ☐ Make soup
- ☐ Make sauce
- ☐ Braise vegetables

BUTCHERING

- ☐ Butcher chickens
- ☐ Butcher fish
- ☐ Butcher beef
- ☐ Butcher pork

WORK *GARDE MANGER*

This is the person in charge of cold dishes and other foods stored under refrigeration. This is an entry point for working on the line.

- ☐ Assemble salads and cold plates
- ☐ Shuck oysters and clams
- ☐ Make vinaigrette
- ☐ Make aioli

WORK ON THE HOT APP STATION

This is perhaps the best place to quickly learn a lot of portable skills.

- ☐ "Pick up" hot apps
- ☐ Work the fryer
- ☐ Work the pasta station

WORK SAUTÉ

- ☐ Cook greens and vegetables to order
- ☐ Pan-roast fish and meats

WORK GRILL

This is considered well up the food chain, though not as high as a *saucier* ("sauce maker") in a French kitchen.

- ☐ Line items vary by restaurant—expect to lose eyebrows

WORK AT A RESTAURANT ON THE LINE

When you are mentally and technically prepared, it's time for the real deal: work full-time at a restaurant for six months in a line position. This will refine all you've learned, give you some battle scars, and teach you to be adaptable.

- ☐ Learn how to be ready for service (*mise en place*).
- ☐ Learn how to cook *à la minute* (on demand, as needed).
- ☐ Learn knife work under much more pressure. Expect a lot of yelling.
- ☐ Create automatic habits that keep things in order and in place.
- ☐ Learn to apply real-time skills as needed, often interrupting whatever else you might be doing: sautéing, searing, roasting, braising, frying, etc.

4 This is sometimes reserved for specialists and not considered basic prep.

ACE YOUR FINAL

With all that under your belt, let's see how you handle pressure on your own turf.

THE COCKTAIL PARTY PRACTICE EXAM

Throwing a cocktail party will help you learn the art of preparing miniature versions of larger dishes. The components should all require rigorous technique. Create a written timeline, working backward from the time of serving to learn when to begin each dish (see example, page 592). This party will be lower pressure than working in a restaurant, as your "customers" are your more forgiving friends. It's also less expensive to throw a cocktail party than a large dinner party, and you can supply it out of most home kitchens and refrigerators. I suggest starting with a menu of finger foods, dips, and other food that can be served at room temperature.

Prepare at least six types of hors d'oeuvres (think crostini) that would normally be passed around.

Hors d'oeuvres should be made in a "rolling" fashion. In other words, put some out and then replenish with more when the beasts have eaten.

Once you've done that, graduate to the five-course challenge.

SAMPLE MENU

HORS D'OEUVRES

FRESH MOZZARELLA,
MARINATED TOMATOES, AND
PESTO ON TOASTED COUNTRY BREAD

ROASTED BUTTERNUT SQUASH
WITH SPICED PECANS
ON TOASTED COUNTRY BREAD

HAMACHI TARTARE WITH LEMON,
THYME, AND CHOPPED
NIÇOISE OLIVES ON FRIED POTATO

SLOW-ROASTED PORK SHOULDER
WITH PICKLED RED ONIONS
ON TORTILLA CHIPS

CHOPPED EGG SALAD ON RADISHES

MARINATED GOAT CHEESE,
CURED OLIVES ON CUCUMBER

Prepare at least three dips or platters that take time to prepare. In other words, store-bought sour cream dip does not count, but these might:

ARTICHOKE PARMESAN SPREAD

HOMEMADE HUMMUS

A HOMEMADE ANTIPASTO
PLATTER OF PICKLED VEGETABLES
AND SLICED, CURED MEATS

DESSERTS

Prepare at least two types of desserts. Like the passed hors d'oeuvres, these should be items you can "pick up" at the moment (à la minute).

CHOCOLATE POT DE CRÈME

MINI S'MORES

THE FIVE-COURSE CHALLENGE: AN 8-PERSON, 5-COURSE DINNER PARTY

Now you will learn to prep everything in a small home kitchen on a tight schedule. You will learn to budget your space and think four-dimensionally (time is the fourth dimension). And you will learn to plate eight dishes at once. I offer up the right-hand menu for those ready to take the challenge. The unfamiliar recipes, by far the least important aspect of the training program, can be found at fourhourchef.com/5course.

HOW TO ACE YOUR FINAL

1\.
MAXIMIZE YOUR *MISE*

2\.
SET UP TRAFFIC CONTROL

3\.
PLATE LIKE A PRO

SAMPLE MENU

Dinner

FIRST COURSE

TRIO OF DIPS
(CHICKPEA, PEAS AND
MINT, HERBED GOAT CHEESE)
AND VEGETABLES

SECOND COURSE

CAULIFLOWER SOUP WITH CHIVE OIL

THIRD COURSE

SEARED TUNA WITH LENTIL SALAD
AND DIJON VINAIGRETTE

FOURTH COURSE

ROASTED CHICKEN WITH
SAUTÉED ZUCCHINI, ARUGULA SALAD,
AND AIOLI

FIFTH COURSE

HONEY-ALMOND TART WITH
CHERRY-VANILLA ICE CREAM

MAXIMIZE YOUR *MISE*

JZ produced the previous page's five-course meal in a small kitchen to make it as replicable for readers as possible. He used three areas: his grocery holding counter (which served as a plating area at the end), his stove-top *mise*, and his cutting-board *mise*.

The only grocery item that required refrigeration was the tuna. This prevented constant trips to and from the fridge. Minimizing movement will minimize stress.

His primary workspace was his cutting board, which he kept clear unless he was working on it. Each dish was prepped with its own *mise en place* (see pics, opposite page).

Guidelines:

1. Choose one part of your counter to hold your groceries. That's where you'll place your lemons, your package of chives, etc.

2. Make your ingredients easily "gettable." Transfer your needed amounts to containers for easy grabbing, or try this alternative: rather than using a dozen different containers, layer your prepped veggies in one large mixing bowl. Just put sheets of cling wrap between them, and insert them in reverse order from last needed (bottom) to first needed (top).

SMALL KITCHEN *MISE* (JZ'S ACTUAL SETUP)

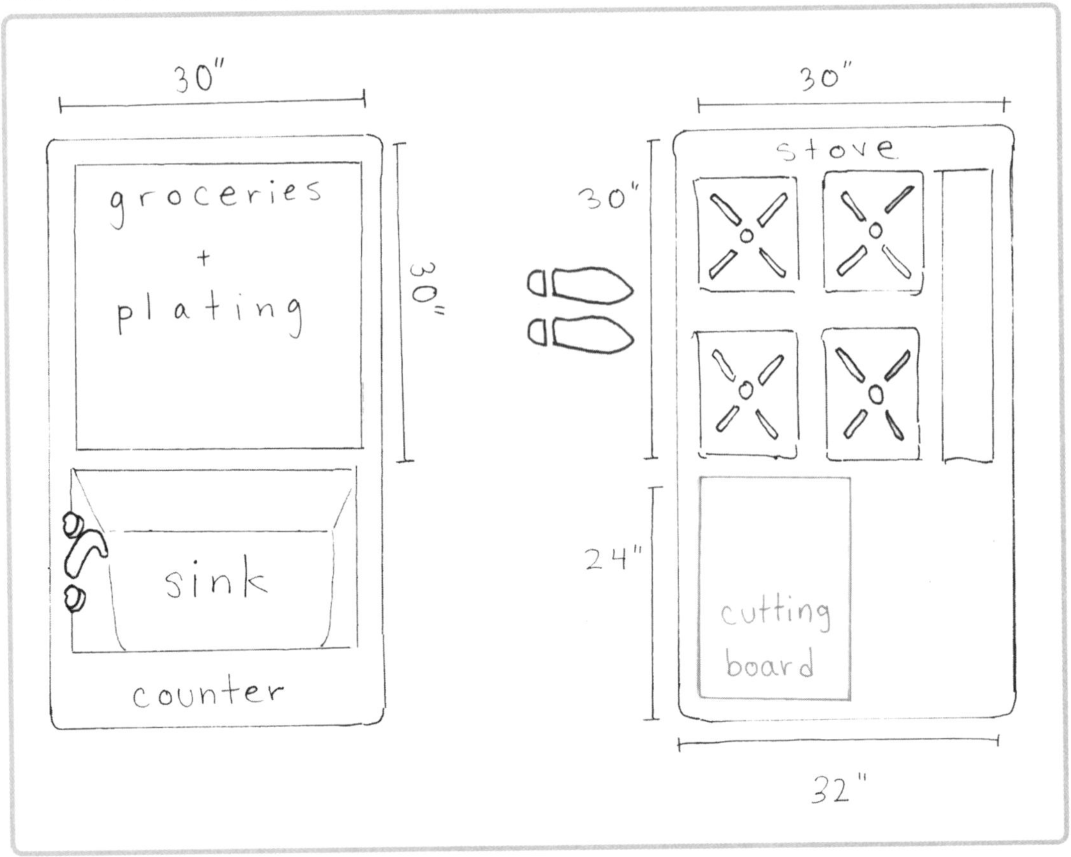
30"
groceries
+
plating
30"
sink
counter
30"
stove
30"
24"
cutting board
32"

3. Place a metal or ceramic container (not glass; try a cocktail shaker if you have one) in the center of your stove top so you can easily rinse or hold utensils. Fill it half full with water.

4. Set up an individual-dish *mise* right before you cook each dish. Your primary workspace will be your cutting board, which should be kept clear unless you're working.

WORKSPACE *MISE*

GROCERY-HOLDING COUNTER
(LATER USED TO PLATE)
GOYA

STOVE-TOP MISE

Note the center container full of hot water, used to rinse/hold utensils. A cocktail shaker will work.

INDIVIDUAL-DISH *MISE*

TART DOUGH *MISE*

TART FILLING *MISE*

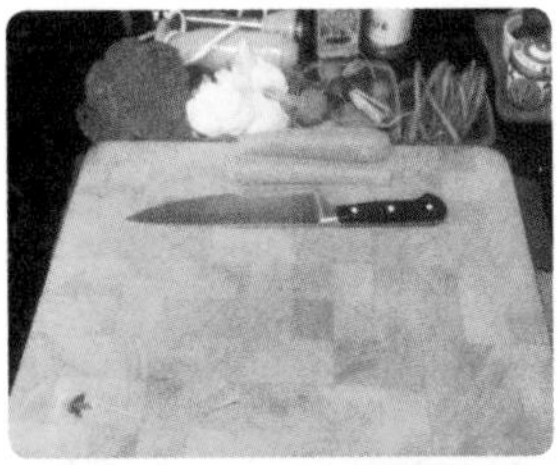

PICKLED VEG *MISE*

CHICKPEA *MISE*

PEA MINT *MISE*

GOAT CHEESE *MISE*

SOUP *MISE*

CHICKEN *MISE*

LENTIL *MISE*

LENTIL SALAD *MISE*

SET UP TRAFFIC CONTROL

Below is the schedule that JZ used for his dinner prep. As he worked through the schedule, he marked down his actual times (see last column), and I suggest you do the same.

JZ explains the value: "The Time Plan is sorted by what to do first and how long each step should take you. This is key to understanding the critical-path nature of how a great chef thinks about prep and priorities. With this list, you have the entire day mapped out. You can finish tasks well ahead of time or just as needed."

If you'll be cooking a few courses at home, you may not need a written blueprint, but this methodical approach is worth practicing at least once. It's a great dress rehearsal for a future dinner that's even more ambitious.

COURSE	ITEM	ACTIVE	PASSIVE	PLATING TIME	PRIORITY #	BEGIN TIME	READY TIME	JZ
5th	Make tart dough	45			1	12:30 PM	01:15 PM	30
5th	Rest tart dough		30		2	01:15 PM	01:45 PM	
5th	Chop almonds	10	0		2	01:15 PM	01:25 PM	10
5th	Chop cherries	10	0		3	01:25 PM	01:35 PM	5
5th	Mix tart filling	10	0		4	01:35 PM	01:45 PM	10
5th	Fill tart	5	0		5	01:45 PM	01:50 PM	5
5th	Bake tart	0	45		6	01:50 PM	02:35 PM	
1st	Prep vegetables	30	0		6	01:50 PM	02:20 PM	15
1st	Pickle vegetables	5			7	02:20 PM	02:25 PM	5
1st	Chickpea puree	15	0		8	02:25 PM	02:40 PM	10
1st	Peas & mint puree	15	0		9	02:40 PM	02:55 PM	10
1st	Herbed goat cheese	15	0		10	02:55 PM	03:10 PM	10
1st	Crostini	5	5		11	03:10 PM	03:20 PM	5
4th	Aioli	15	0		12	03:20 PM	03:35 PM	10
4th	Grate Parmesan	5	0		13	03:35 PM	03:40 PM	5
2nd	Cut *mise en place* for soup	15	0		14	03:40 PM	03:55 PM	5
2nd	Cook soup	5	0		15	03:55 PM	04:00 PM	5
2nd	Simmer soup		30		15	04:00 PM	04:30 PM	
4th	Prep chicken	30	0		16	04:00 PM	04:30 PM	10
4th	Roast chicken	0	90		17	04:30 PM	06:00 PM	
3rd	Cook lentils	0	25		18	04:30 PM	04:55 PM	
2nd	Puree soup	10	0		19	04:30 PM	04:40 PM	5
3rd	Cut garnish for lentil salad	15	0		20	04:40 PM	04:55 PM	5
3rd	Mix lentil salad	5	0		21	04:55 PM	05:00 PM	5
2nd	Chive oil	5	5		22	05:00 PM	05:10 PM	5
3rd	Portion tuna	10	0		23	05:10 PM	05:20 PM	5
3rd	Clean lettuces	10	0		24	05:20 PM	05:30 PM	5
3rd	Lemon vinaigrette	5	0		25	05:30 PM	05:35 PM	5
3rd	Dijon vinaigrette	5	0		26	05:35 PM	05:40 PM	5
4th	Cut zucchini	15	0		27	05:40 PM	05:55 PM	5
4th	Salt zucchini	5	0		28	05:55 PM	06:00 PM	5
4th	Drain zucchini		60		28	05:55 PM	06:55 PM	
4th	Rest chicken	0	15		29	06:00 PM	06:15 PM	
4th	Portion chicken	15	0		30	06:15 PM	06:30 PM	10
1st	Plate 1st course			10	31	06:50 PM	07:00 PM	10
2nd	Plate 2nd course			5	32	07:25 PM	07:30 PM	5
3rd	Sear tuna	10	0		33	07:30 PM	07:40 PM	10
3rd	Plate 3rd course			10	34	07:40 PM	07:50 PM	10
4th	Reheat chicken		10		35	08:00 PM	08:10 PM	
4th	Sauté zucchini	10	0		36	07:50 PM	08:00 PM	5
4th	Dress arugula salad	10	0		37	08:00 PM	08:10 PM	2
4th	Plate 4th course			10	38	08:10 PM	08:20 PM	15
5th	Plate 5th course			5	39	08:55 PM	09:00 PM	5

PLATE LIKE A PRO

To plate, you need a dedicated space. Don't scatter them around the kitchen haphazardly or precariously. The last thing you want is to knock something over and spill your day's work on the floor.

To set up a proper plating station, you have two options: unstacking one at a time, then plating; or plating all at once (if you have the space). In the latter, you should work from top to bottom, then left to right, to prevent dripping over food you have already plated.

TIPS

- If serving a hot dish, ensure the plates or bowls have been kept warm in the oven (hot plate = hot food). 200°F for 15 minutes is fine.
- Keep a clean, moist towel on hand to wipe the edges of plates before you serve them. Trace a line around the circumference of each plate.
- Before cooking, it's often helpful to sketch out what the finished plate will look like. Below is a professional example from Yoshi's Japanese restaurant in San Francisco. Have fun!

PLATING

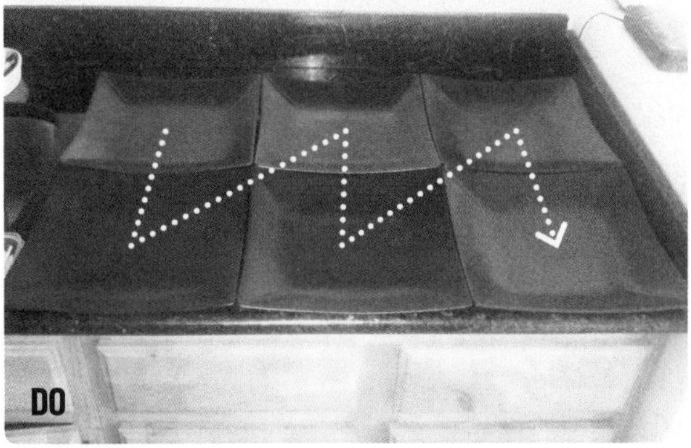
DO

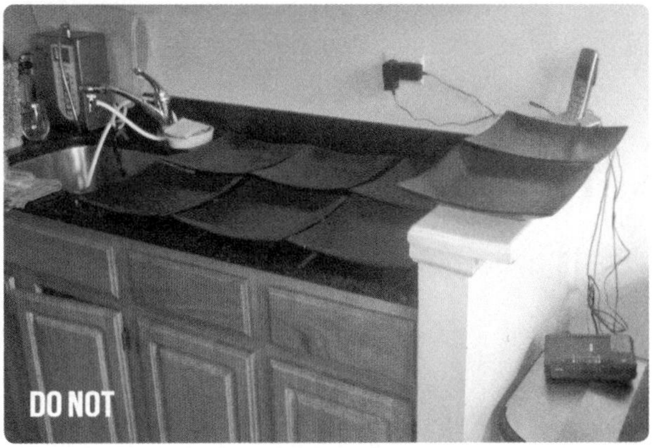
DO NOT

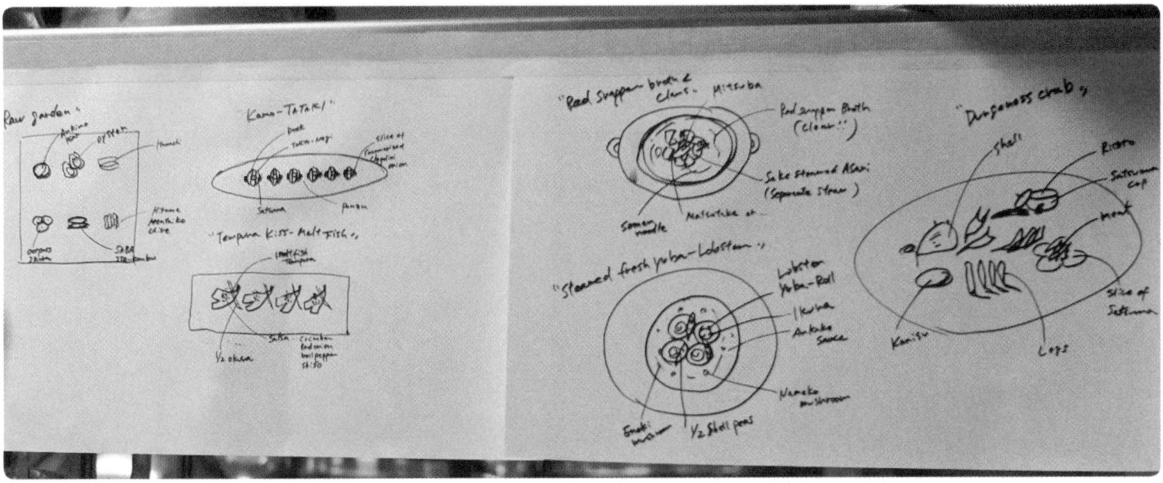

MORE LEARNING ANYTHING

HOW TO SHOOT A 3-POINTER WITHIN 48 HOURS

> "Me shooting 40% at the foul line is just God's way to say nobody's perfect."
>
> —SHAQUILLE O'NEAL

Below are the rules, pulled from Rick Torbett's e-mail (see page 42) that made the biggest difference for me. I've grouped them into Technique and Practice. I've included the entire how-to for two reasons: 1) It's really fun to hit shots for the first time; 2) It shows you what I chose to focus on, which was perhaps 10% of what Rick shared with me. Follow the illustrations below and opposite.

TECHNIQUE

ELBOWS AND WRIST AT 90 DEGREES

The right angle is your friend. The shot starts with the ball in the set position (1, below), about 12–18 inches in front of the belly button, with your shooting elbow and wrist bent as close to 90 degrees as possible. The ball then travels up the shot line and ends up in the fire position (2), where the angles remain 90 degrees. Then you extend and shoot (3 and 4).

SHOT LINE (AND EYE DOMINANCE)

This is the crux principle on which everything else depends. The ball will be set on your shot line and shot from your shot line, and you will finish your follow-through on your shot line. See the illustration on the opposite page.

So, how do you determine where *your* shot line is?

Erroneously, most basketball coaches have right-handed players line up on their right shoulders and lefties on their left

1 2 3 4

Using 90 degrees: In step 4, notice how the shooting hand is full stroked downward to achieve backspin. For most people, the ball should feel as though it's rolling off either a) the index and middle finger, or b) the index, middle, and ring fingers. Backspin increases the probability of a basket after the ball hits the backboard.

shoulders. This is why I personally never made baskets in the past. Rick starts with an eye-dominance test.

"Everyone has a dominant eye—the eye that you aim with. To find your dominant eye, create a circle with your hands extended and sight a target 50 feet away with both eyes open. Close your left eye. If the target is still in your 'circle sight,' then you are right-eye dominant. If the target jumps, then you are left-eye dominant. (Vice versa: if you sight the target, close your right eye, and the target does not move, then you are left-eye dominant.)"

If you "match"—e.g., right-handed with right-eye dominance—then just line your vertical shot line up with your dominant eye. Simple enough.

But many right-handed players are left-eye dominant, as I was (or vice versa for lefties), and they've been taught to line up the ball with the inside of their right feet, or their right shoulders, or (most commonly) their right eyes. When they shoot, their head will move in an attempt to line up their left eyes. And they can't understand why their accuracy suffers!

I never knew I was cross-eye dominant, which astonished me, given how much archery and marksmanship I've done. How the hell did I not know this?!?

Fortunately, things are easily adjusted in basketball. If you are right-handed but left-eye dominant, then move your shot line closer to the center of your body. It doesn't have to be exactly on the left eye, since no one is 100% one-eye dominant—we use both eyes to triangulate distance. This adjustment to the shot line is imperceptible to the casual observer. But when you move the shot line 2–4 inches for opposite-eyed shooters, they experience an instant increase in accuracy—as if you've given them a magic pill.

This one adjustment, using eye dominance properly, doubled my shooting percentage. I suggest aiming at the front of the rim, ideally on a net loop that is dead center on your shot line.

When you are setting up and shooting, the middle of the ball (I focus on my middle finger) should never leave your shot line. In games, keep the ball as close to your shot line as possible at all times, which allows you to pull the trigger at any moment. If you want to increase accuracy, eliminate excess motion. This is true whether you're shooting a basketball, firing a gun, swinging a baseball bat, or swinging a golf club.

LEGS FOR DISTANCE, ARMS FOR AIM

Do not "throw" the ball to the hoop. Rick can train young kids to shoot effortlessly from the 3-point line, and that's because he drills a rule into them: the legs are for distance, the arms are for aiming.

The force generated by straightening the arm and "breaking" the wrist should account for only 3–4 feet of distance. If the balls falls

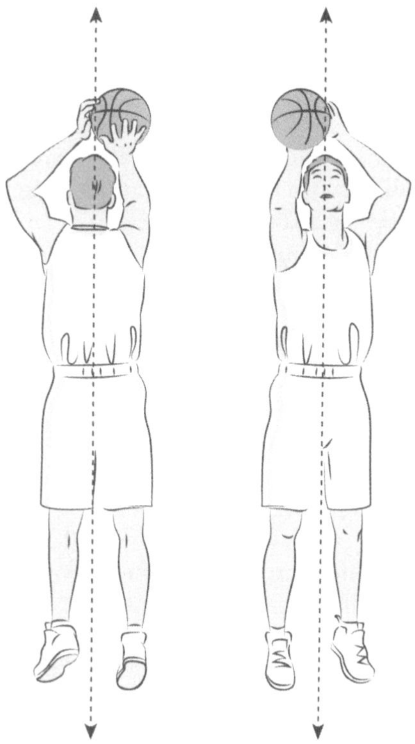

Shot line example: Notice that the "guide hand" (here, the left hand) offers no propulsion. It simply stabilizes from the side and finishes pointing at the ceiling in a karate-chop-like position.

Using legs, stepping into the shot.

short or is too long, don't try to fix it with your arms. Rick explains:

"Time the breaking of your shooting wrist (the release of the shot) with your feet coming off the ground. The ball will ride the power wave that's generated by your legs, and this power will exit your hands with the ball. Done properly, the shot will seem almost effortless. This allows your arms and hands to be free to do what they do best: control the flight of the ball—not generate it."

Practice all shots, even if from 5 feet away, with a small jump. Even a 1" clearance is enough. Develop the habit of channeling all your distance from your legs. The goal of our jump shots isn't to shoot *over* people by jumping higher; it's to use your legs to launch the ball.

There are two more techniques that can increase distance without sacrificing form:

1. **Speed up your hands** from the point of setting the ball in your shot pocket (see illustration 1, page 596) to the point of release. Everything else will speed up as well, assuming you have your feet and hands coordinated, and you'll find your range increasing by a couple of feet.

2. **Step into your shot.** This isn't always possible, but when it is, you'll get a few more feet of distance. Here's what I mean: Get ready to shoot with both feet square under your shoulders. If you're right-handed, step back with your right foot. Now step back up with your right foot and fire. This motion will load your legs. It's possible to catch most of your passes on the 3-point line with one of your legs already back. At the point of the catch, simply step up and shoot—almost one motion! This footwork can also be used off the dribble.

Last but not least, avoid one mistake common among pros: **negative motion.** This refers to hinging the forearm back toward the head just before the shot, which turns your arm into a lever and eliminates all power transferred from the legs.

Negative motion.

FOLLOW-THROUGH AND FRAMING THE GOAL

Even pros don't hold follow-through long enough.

After each shot, freeze your arms and spot-check your form. Are your toes pointing toward the goal? They should be, or your body twists, throwing the ball off your shot line. Your hands should end up **framing the goal,** as in the illustration at right.

The last piece of the puzzle is the much-neglected but critical guide hand:

"The guide hand should frame the side of the goal, so don't drop your guide arm. If you drop your guide arm/hand, it will allow your body to torque. Keeping the guide hand up is critical to straight shooting. If you're shooting to the left or right, the culprit can usually be traced to your guide arm and guide hand."

Framing the goal: Guide hand is left. Shooting fingers should finish pointing *down* your shot line into the goal. The fintertips can end up high, often near the top of the backboard. Personally, my best shots correlate to my shooting arm being at about a 70° angle from the ground at extension.

PRACTICE

- Take your first 25 shots from almost below the rim. Then move to 5 feet away and shoot another 25. Focus on your shot line and the breaking of the wrist. Many players have been ruined by the allure of the 3-point line. J. J. Redick of the Orlando Magic, famous for his 3-point and free-throw shooting, is the all-time leading scorer at Duke University, which retired his jersey in 2007. He takes his first 50 shots of every practice from 5–7 feet from the hoop. Good enough for J. J. means goods enough for you.

- If you have a partner, stand about 20 feet apart on a line. Each of you should straddle the line, lining it up with your shot line. Then shoot to each other, using a good shot at a phantom 10-foot basket, aiming to have the ball hit the line about 5 feet in front of your partner. This is to practice shooting in a straight line without chasing balls or obsessing over making shots. If you're solo, you can also aim for a line on a wall. In the beginning, make your goal to keep the ball straight for 20 out of 25 shots. If your shots are short or long, count it as a "make." Only misses that are left or right count as "misses."

If you can control the flight of the ball to the point where you don't miss left or right, it's only a matter of time before misses that are short or long correct themselves. Short or long misses are easy to correct. Misses left and right mean that something is wrong with your shot form.

Redefining success in this manner will keep you coming back day after day, because everyone likes being successful. Once you can keep 80% of your shots straight, then you can move to made shots as a test for success. Once made shots stop being a challenge, success is changed to mean only those shots that go in without touching the rim. Nothing but net.

A great shot is always under construction.

GUNS?!? OMFG, ROFL, MPICIMFP, WTF?!?

"The real cycle you're working on is a cycle called yourself."

—ROBERT M. PIRSIG, *ZEN AND THE ART OF MOTORCYCLE MAINTENANCE*

People go nuts worshipping and condemning guns. I simply enjoy exploring the most fascinating skills associated with them.

It started with the deer hunt, rifle sighting, and bullet drift. Then my curiosity expanded to shotguns for bird hunting, which led to examining *tactical* (military and law enforcement) modifications of the same firearm for rapid reloading, etc.

This led to the evergreen debate about shotguns versus handguns in home defense. The arguments were meticulously technical. To gather firsthand data, I tested dozens of handguns for groupings, malfunctions, and so on, and then experimented with shotguns and handguns used in combination.

I hope never to use a firearm in an emergency, but it's great fun learning the basic art and science required to do so. For those interested, the next few pages share some of my discoveries, gear, and conclusions, however novice.

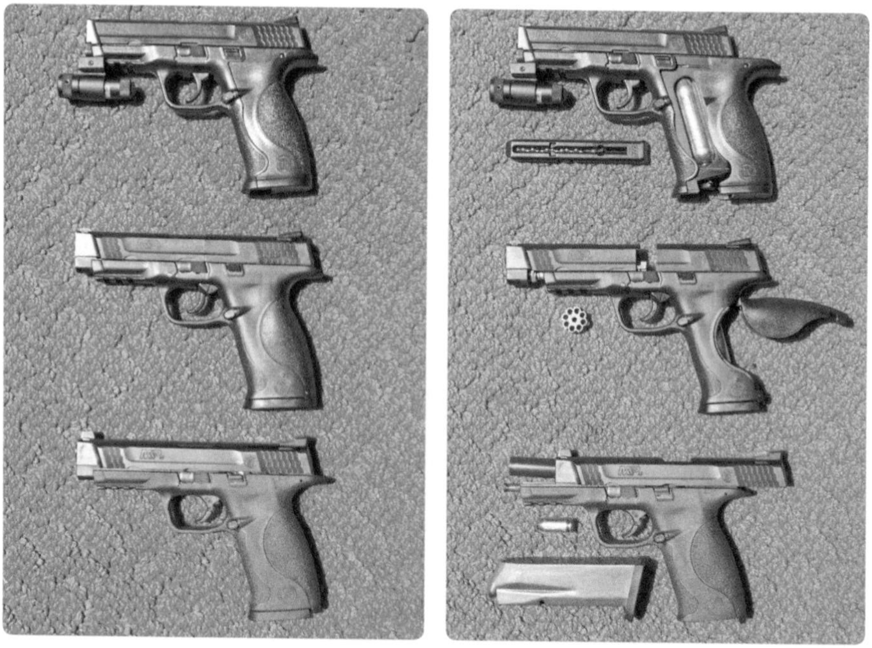

Low-stakes substitution accelerates learning. Near-identical BB, pellet, and real versions of the M&P .45.

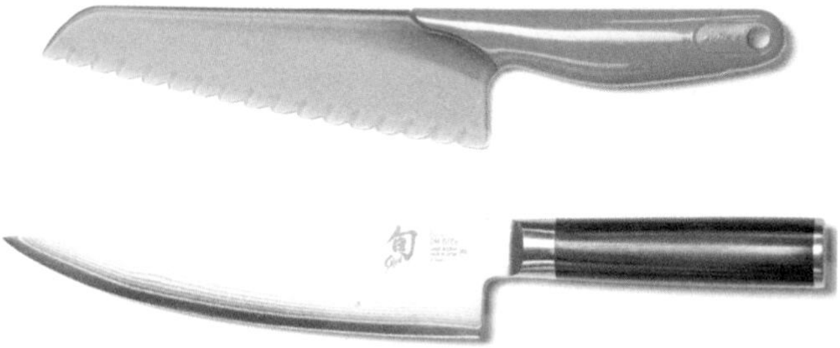

The same principle applied to knife practice. Notice the near-identical rise on the lettuce knife.

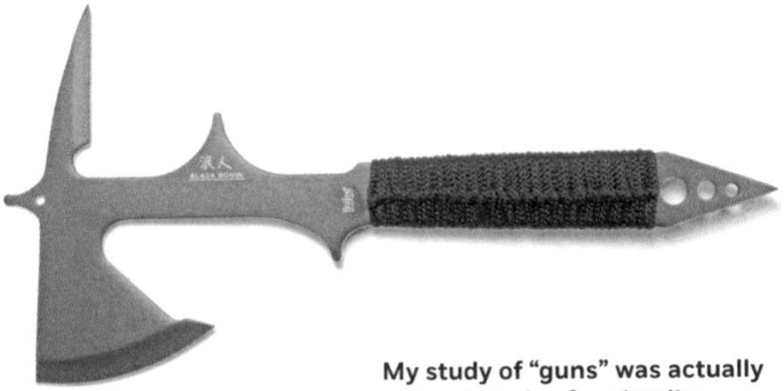

My study of "guns" was actually a broad study of projectiles. Here, a throwing axe.

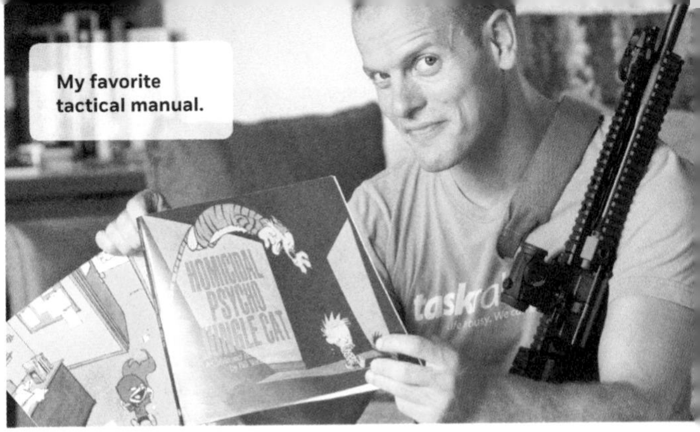
HOMICIDAL
PSYCHO

My favorite tactical manual.

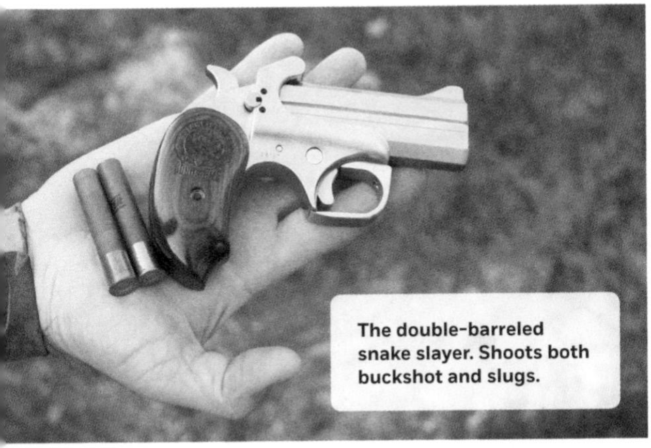

The double-barreled snake slayer. Shoots both buckshot and slugs.

PWS MK116 rifle, 5.56mm, with Aimpoint Micro T-1 Red Dot Sight.

Glock 17 9mm handgun (holstered) and MK 107 "Diablo" (improved M4 carbine).

REMINGTON 870 12-GAUGE SHOTGUN

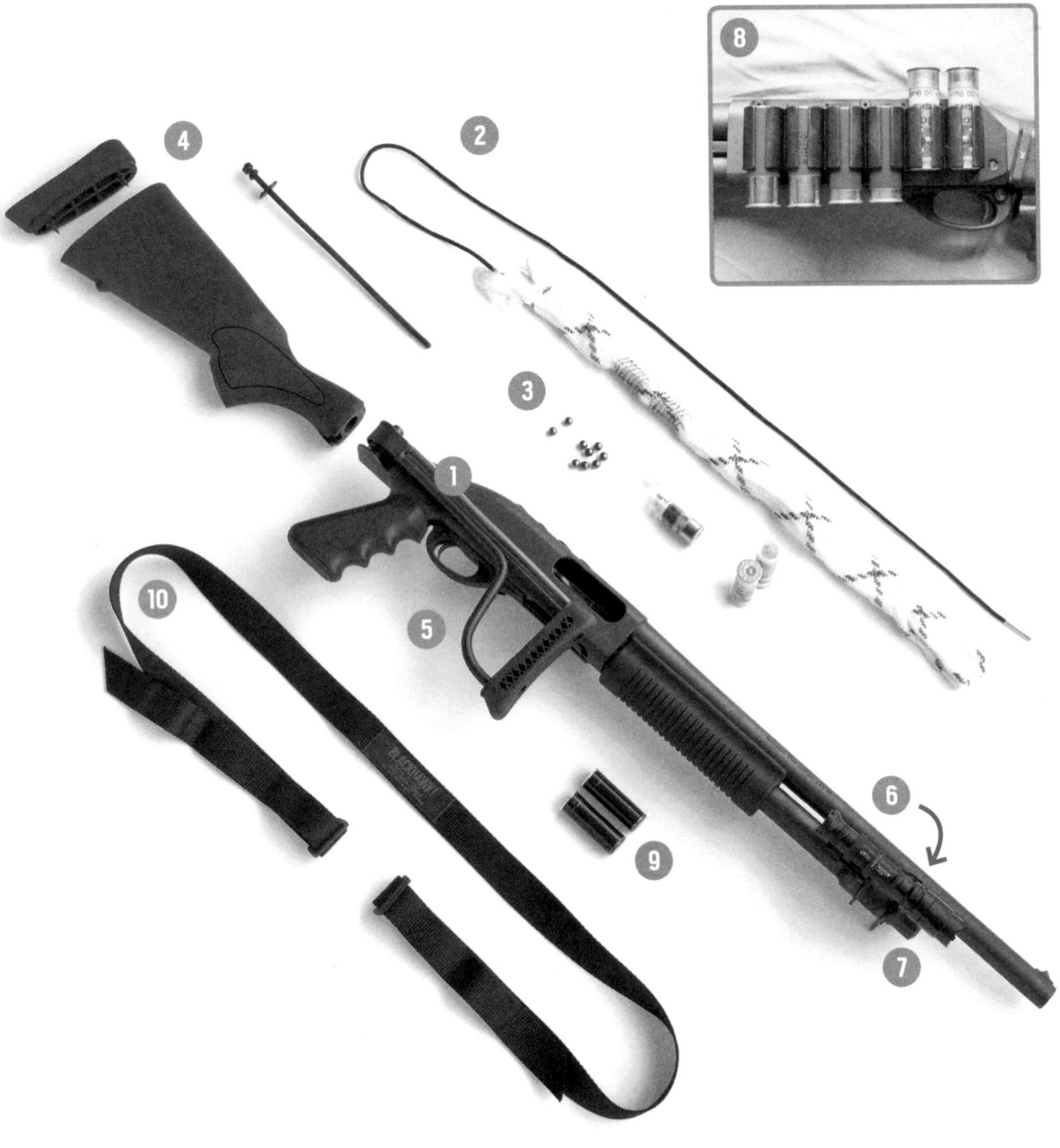
8
4
2
3
1
10
5
6
9
7
BLACKHAWK!

1.

Remington 870 Pump-Action 12-Gauge Shotgun

$400 base model

If you're going to buy one gun for everything, whether hunting or defending against zombies, this is it. The 870 is the most-sold gun in history: more than 10 million over 50+ years. It's pump-action rather than automatic, and mechanically resilient. Dropped in the mud, dragged through the snow, and covered in sand, it will still work. For the tinkerers, the 870 is also ideal for learning the basics of gun function. Considering I pay almost $500 per month for health insurance, a one-time $400 cost for marksmanship fun (skeet shooting, anyone?) and worst-case scenario insurance didn't seem outlandish.

There are a million and one ways to modify the 870, but I only made a few (see 5, 6, 7, 8).

2.

Hoppe's BoreSnake Shotgun Bore Cleaner

$15

Cleaning your gun is akin to cleaning up after cooking: the least fun part of the process. To minimize the tedium, a BoreSnake is a must. I own one for my Remington 12-gauge shotgun and others for my handguns. It doesn't replace the more thorough field stripping and cleaning, which requires disassembly, but it allows you to go far longer between sessions.

3.

00 Buck ("Double-Aught" Buckshot) Ammo

$10 (pack of five rounds)

Multiuse ammo and the 12-gauge standard.

4.

Factory Stock

This comes with the 870.

5.

Butler Creek FS-RB Side-Folding Stock

$80

This folding stock, which is low-tech and durable, was recommended as a space-saving measure by a former executive protection team leader who'd operated in Mexico City. It can be a pain to assemble, so have staff at your local gun shop help you the first time. If you prefer a top-folding stock, one readily available substitute is the ATI top-folding tactical stock.

6.

SureFire Lighting System for Nighttime Shooting

$230 total

Rather than a dedicated SureFire foregrip, which costs $400, I prefer a multipurpose combo that totals around $230.

The following A, B, and C constitute my "system":

A.

SureFire E2D LED Defender Flashlight

$170

Gifted to me by a hedge-fund manager, this flashlight is designed as a self-defense tool: you can temporarily blind an assailant with the LED (200 lumens).

AND

B.

VLTOR Adapter

$35

This attaches to the flashlight and connects to the below mount (C). It can be hand tightened or removed within seconds, making it easy to use the flashlight independently.

AND

C.

Streamlight 69906 870 Flashlight Mount

$21

This becomes a semi-permanent mount on the gun for the above VLTOR.

7.

Vang Comp Systems Magazine Extension

$75

This allows me to load an extra round in the gun. Unlike the Remington-brand mag extension, which can't be tightened or loosened without a screwdriver, the Vang Comp can be manipulated by hand in the field. There are also reports of shells jamming when newer 870s are fitted with the Remington factory extension.

8.

6-Shot TacStar Side Saddle

$34

The six-shot side saddle is for quick-access extra ammo. It's loaded in the inset picture with two rounds of buckshot and four rifled hollow-point slugs. For home defense, I would suggest smaller birdshot, which is less likely to penetrate walls. Slugs, on the other hand, are similar to solid lead chalk pieces and are a last resort for anything that withstands buckshot, like Mad Max marauders (joke). As one Navy SEAL put it, "Slugs are great for shooting bad guys *through* cars." Depending on your loading hand, different schools of thought exist for side-saddle setup. I've inserted the slugs primer side down in the front and the buckshot primer side up behind them, so that I can 1) load the slugs fastest, and 2) quickly distinguish between them, even in zero-light conditions.

9.

A-Zoom 12-Gauge Snap Caps

$10

These are gunpowder-free dummy rounds perfect for dry-firing exercises—anything where you pull the trigger without real ammo. This is how you practice speed reloading and tactical exercises without blowing a hole in your wall or cat. If you want to rack up training hours off the range, don't use real projectiles, silly goose.

10.

Blackhawk Universal Tactical 1¼" (3.17 cm) 2-Point Sling

$11

For carrying all this crap around you need a sling. Also fun for practicing shotgunning and handgunning at the range simultaneously.

SMITH & WESSON M&P .45 ACP

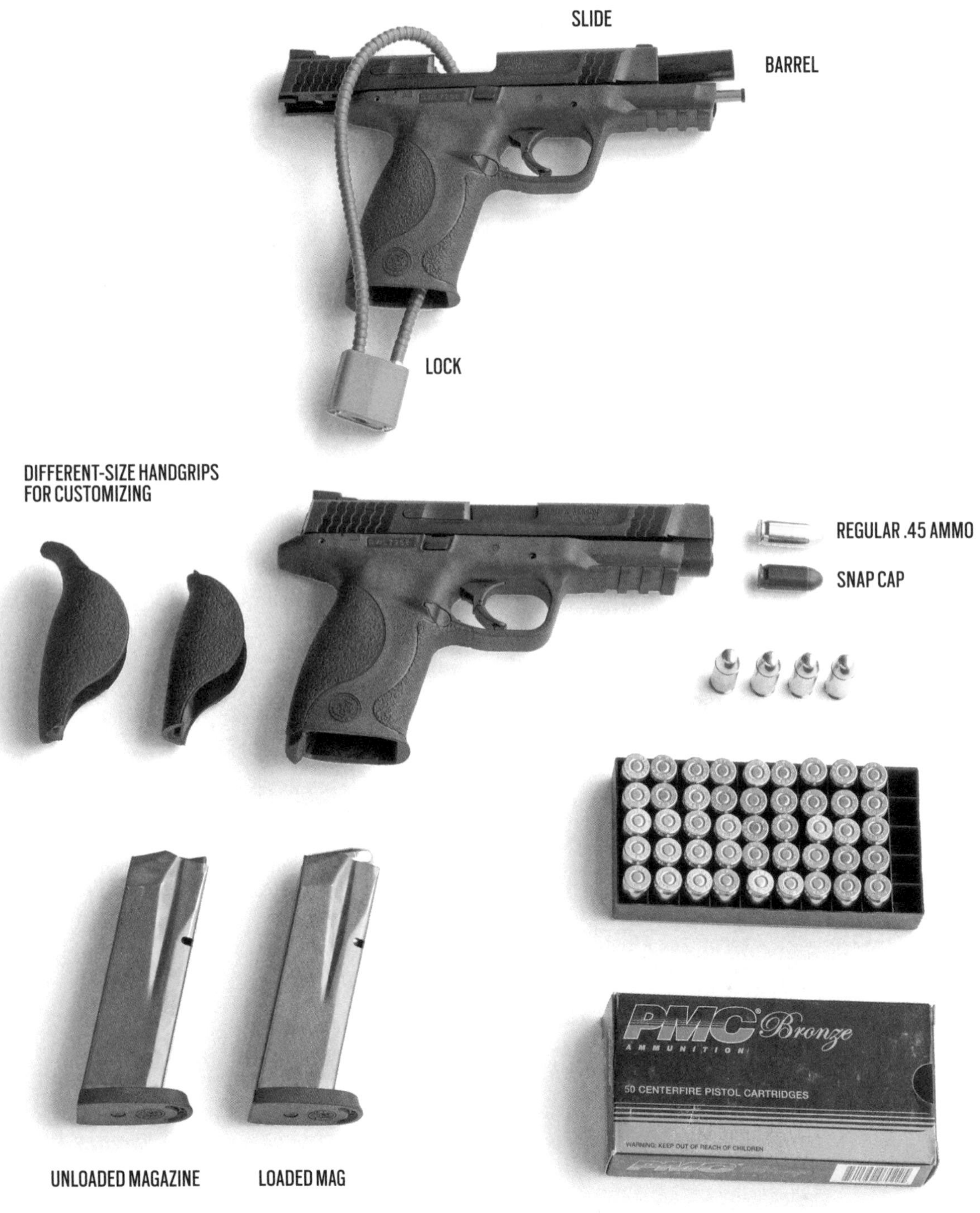
SLIDE
BARREL
LOCK
DIFFERENT-SIZE HANDGRIPS FOR CUSTOMIZING
REGULAR .45 AMMO
SNAP CAP
PMC Bronze
AMMUNITION
50 CENTERFIRE PISTOL CARTRIDGES
WARNING: KEEP OUT OF REACH OF CHILDREN
UNLOADED MAGAZINE
LOADED MAG

Smith & Wesson M&P .45 ACP, plus Trijicon HD Night Sights

ACP approx. $600/
Night Sights $150

The term *.45* refers to the diameter of the bullet: .45 inches. Things get confusing because you also see ballistics in metric. Here are a few common calibers, listed from smallest to largest and bolded as they typically appear:

.22 inches = 5.59mm

.354 inches = **9mm**

.45 inches = 11.5mm

I chose the M&P .45 after many comparisons and weeks of research. It felt better in my hand than the Glock .45, and I knew from good sources that A) it could be dropped from a Blackhawk helicopter at 180 mph and still work perfectly, and B) the DOD (Department of Defense) has plans to purchase the M&P .45 in 2014 as an option for SOCOM (Special Operations Command) members, which broadly refers to elite teams with discretionary selection of their weapons.

Does that mean you should choose a .45 for greater stopping power, as I did?

Not necessarily. Beyond the impractical "I'll make a headshot" argument, a much more compelling case for the smaller 9mm can be made if you agree with any of the following statements:

A) "My hands are small, and I'm much more comfortable holding a 9mm gun." I personally found the .45 Glock unwieldy and much like holding a brick.

B) "If I need to use it in an emergency, it won't be a single shot. I'll empty the entire magazine."

C) "9mm ammo costs a hell of a lot less [.45 ammo can cost 50 cents a shot at the range]."

D) "It's easier to shoot accurately with less kick. Bigger caliber means nothing if you miss."

I bought a 9mm Glock 34 after the M&P and love it.

But prior to buying anything, I suggest starting at a range with a .22 handgun. Once you have consistent 2–3" (5–8 cm) groupings at 7 yards (6.4 m), move to a 9mm. Once 2–3" (5–8 cm) groupings are again the norm, then graduate to the .45. For most people, the slim-profiled 1911 .45 will be the most comfortable of the .45 options.

In the case of handguns, I again use Snap Caps, but not for reloading practice. Instead, I'll mix up 10 rounds at the range and load the Snap Cap randomly among them. This helps diagnose flinching or subtle jerking before the shot. Second, it offers a chance to practice clearing malfunctions. If you want to get really fancy (or just have fun at home), buy a looks-like, feels-like M&P 40 BB gun,[5] which some law enforcement officers use for low-cost, high-volume training.

Keep in mind that guns are worse than useless if you don't know how to use them under pressure. To that end, I highly recommend Magpul's *Art of the Dynamic Handgun* DVD. The instruction is world-class. Chris Costa and Travis Haley show precisely how to deconstruct a complex skill for rapid recall. Frankly, I expected redneck VHS footage from the '80s and instead got HD multi-angle footage that I've watched again and again. For a taste of what I mean, see the trailer for their shotgun follow-up here: fourhourchef.com/trailer.

Last note on handguns: loading magazines while target shooting can be a pain, both figuratively and literally. Get a universal handgun loader to save your thumbs. This is the one accessory even accessory-hating shooters buy. I chose the Butler Creek LULA model.

Did You Know?

Modern guns owe much of their accuracy to *rifling*, a technology allegedly discovered by accident. Smooth bore muskets were prone to clogging with black powder, so riflemen began etching grooves inside the barrel to collect it and prevent misfires. It was found, through trial-and-error, that spiral etching collected the most powder. It also sent accuracy through the roof, because the etching spun the bullet much like a quarterback spirals a football.

Leave That Left Buttock Alone!

While in Chicago at a bar, I met a local ER physician. Several drinks in, I asked him about the most common gun wounds, since his hospital received a ton of them. His response: the left buttock. Huh? Well, as it turns out, right-handed people like to tuck their handguns in the backs of their belts and—POW!—a bullet in the left butt cheek. That'll sting. So, among the many other warnings I could offer: if you buy a handgun, don't tuck it in your belt. Getting shot in the ass is only one of several possible horrific outcomes, savvy?

5 I tried the pellet-firing M&P .45 replica, but the trigger pull was too heavy for useful simulation.

BICYCLESHOP AND THE $10,000 CHALLENGE: MEMORIZING A DECK OF CARDS IN 43 SECONDS

Iris: So, what are you doing in Las Vegas?
Ray: We're counting cards.
Iris: You're counting cards?
Ray: We're counting cards.
Iris: That's interesting.
Ray: We're counting cards.
Iris: I know you're counting cards. What else are you doing?
Ray: Are you taking any prescription medication?

—*RAINMAN*

To become a Grand Master of Memory—fewer than 100 in the world can claim that title—you need to satisfy each of the following in competitions approved by the World Memory Sport Council:

- Memorize the order of 10 decks of cards in 60 minutes.
- Memorize 1,000 random digits in 60 minutes.
- Memorize the order of one deck of cards in less than two minutes.

Ed Cooke first hit this trifecta when he was 23. He later came to international attention when he coached journalist Joshua Foer from ground zero to U.S. Memory Champion in one year, a feat chronicled by Foer in the best-seller *Moonwalking with Einstein*.[6] To win that championship, Foer had to memorize 120 random digits in five minutes, successfully commit to memory the first and last names of 156 strangers within 15 minutes, and (last but not least) memorize a shuffled deck of cards in less than two minutes.

My route to Ed was circuitous. Following a lecture in high-tech entrepreneurship at Princeton, which I give twice a year, a student named Greg Detre approached me to discuss angel investing. His new start-up, Memrise, focused on accelerating the acquisition of foreign languages. Detre was completing his PhD in computational neuroscience and aimed to crack the learning code by combining optimal spaced repetition with crowd-sourced (and crowd-vetted) images, among other things. As an aside, he'd also performed DARPA-sponsored research on using fMRI scans to read minds.

His partner for Memrise was an unassuming and affable Brit named Ed Cooke. Google helped me figure out the rest.

Ed has memorized a shuffled deck of cards in competition in 43 seconds. Of all memory feats, none is a more compressed act of mental athleticism.

6 An allusion to our now familiar friend: absurd imagery.

I asked him if he'd open the kimono and explain his method, and he very graciously agreed.

But before I unleash the algorithm, a warning: You are about to download the Photoshop of card memorizing. If you're going to edit a picture now and again with simple cropping, Microsoft Paint will do. It's a Swiss Army knife of an editing program, a mere 427 kb in size, and it takes two minutes to figure out. That's because it's designed as a flexible but mediocre tool for novices.

Adobe Photoshop CS6, in contrast, requires a whopping 2GB of hard-drive space to install. It takes at least 100x longer to download, and to become comfortable with the most common actions, it probably requires 100x longer than Paint.

It takes around four hours to get comfortable with Ed's best-of-breed system.

Since we put together a template matrix for you (see page 610), it'll probably take two to three hours. With a little practice, you'll be a third of your way to becoming a Grand Master.

(Im)practically speaking, it's just freaking amazingly cool. Few people in the world can pull it off, and that's reason enough to take a weekend or slow evening to try. Instead of watching another bad movie, you can become one of the memory illuminati.

ENTER THE BICYCLESHOP

I've taken to calling Ed's approach the Bicycleshop, a combination of the brand of playing cards and Photoshop.

We will learn the basics of Bicycleshop with a simple version; let's call it Bicycleshop Lite. Then we'll upgrade to Bicycleshop Pro. Learn to use them in that order.

BICYCLESHOP LITE

Bicycleshop Lite helps you do two things: memorize the cards and memorize the *order* of the cards.

Step One: Learning the Cards

First, you convert 52 cards into 52 celebrities.

The mind ignores the mundane and remembers the unusual, whether people (e.g., Lady Gaga) or a sudden motion in the underbrush. The more unusual, the more the brain forms a bookmark for recall.

To make recalling 52 celebrities easier, each suit corresponds to a personality type and each card (jack, 10, ace, etc.) corresponds to a profession (or category). This means that when you look at a given card, you'll have two cues to help you remember the celebrity.

The Suits (think: personalities):

Diamonds—rich people
Hearts—people you love
Clubs—tough or crazy people
Spades—amusing or absurd people

The Cards (think: professions):

All even numbers are female and all odd numbers are male, and they're paired up. You can just remember that, for instance, 9s are powerful men, and the 10s are therefore powerful women. The 5s are controversial males, so 6s are controversial females, etc.

Mnemonic suggestions are included below each "profession" to facilitate the association, but you can create your own. Skim this list once, read Ed's notes following the list, and then read them over again.

King—Male half of celeb couple
Queen—Female half of celeb couple
Celeb couples are the royalty of the present. Each suit will have its own celeb couple. Contrasting celeb couples—John and Yoko, David Bowie and Iman—can help the pairs stick.

Jack—Religious figures
Jacks are bachelors; religious figures were bachelors.

10 Famously powerful women
9 Famously powerful men
Highest numbers, highest-powered people

8 Famous female physiques
7 Famous male physiques[7]
Hourglass or busty or hunky or ripped—the bodies of your dreams.

6 Controversial females
5 Controversial males
Think of "five" and "effing"; "six" sounds like "sex."

4 Female movie stars
3 Male movie stars
Think of all those trilogies out there.

2 Sportswomen
Ace Sportsmen
Ace is a term associated with excellence in sports; think of "two" as "deuce" in tennis.

Ed explains how this is all put together:

"Having chosen 13 professions/categories and four personalities—just 17 things to learn—you can use your existent knowledge and opinions to fill out a 52-card matrix. The ace of diamonds, on my scheme, is a sportsman (ace) who got rich (diamonds)—OK, Michael Jordan. The jack of spades on my scheme would be a religious figure who's amusing—the Dalai Lama has a good sense of humor. The six of spades, a humorously controversial woman—Lady Gaga, no question.

"Using this method, it should take less than an hour to fill the matrix out and come to be able to slowly recall the people who now correspond to the 52 cards. Once you have your cast of card-people, go through shuffled decks and practice translating the cards to their images until it's automatic. This might take another hour to begin to master."

To save you time, I asked Ed to provide his actual matrix. Ignore the "actions" and "objects" for now, but you can take a peek at page 610 for the celebrities he uses. After "Ed Cooke's Card Matrix," you'll find "Your Own Card Matrix," where you can replace some or all of Ed's choices with your own celebrities.

Up to you. Either way, your cards are now memorable.

The next step is to put them in order.

Step Two: Memorizing the Order of a Shuffled Deck

This is where we revisit our old friend, the *loci* method, and use spatial memory.

Just as we memorized pi to 20 decimal places, you will now peg 52 cards to locations along a familiar route. It could be a path through your house, the journey from your front door to a favorite pub—whatever you like. Some memory competitors use their childhood homes: Scott Hagwood, who won the U.S. Memory Championship from 2001–2004, uses rooms from luxury homes he finds in *Architectural Digest*, 10 locations per room. If you choose that approach, you can mentally position yourself at the entrance to each room and move as follows: at your feet, closest left corner, then clockwise to left wall, then far left corner, opposite wall, far right corner, right wall, closest right corner, then two spots on the ceiling.

Choosing 52 locations should take no more than 30 minutes, and then you can start placing your celebrities (cards) at each point. Keep it simple for now, using a longer path if multiple points per room cause overload. Ed starts at his bed:

"For me, a pack beginning with the jack of spades would mean the Dalai Lama standing at the first point on my route—my bed. At the second point, my wardrobe, I'd deposit the image corresponding to the second card, perhaps it will be Michael Jordan—the ace of diamonds.

"Continue all the way through the pack, taking your time and lots of care to imagine

7 Ed uses physicists here, but I'm a meathead and find Arnie easier than Isaac Newton.

each person vividly in their position. Once you get to the end of the route, retrace it in your imagination and you will hopefully encounter all the people in the sequence that you imagined them. You will probably need to go through two or three times the first time you attempt it."

And just like that, bingo: you've memorized your first deck of cards!

BICYCLESHOP PRO

Now we upgrade you.

Bicycleshop Lite, while perfectly effective, is a little slow. Fifty-two separate goddamn images! Well, what did you expect for trial software? But it's the right place to start. Biting off all the features of Bicycleshop at once will just give you indigestion. Now that you've taken a ride with training wheels, it's time for phase two.

Bicycleshop Pro, the next step for power users, has a much more efficient *compression* algorithm. It builds on top of what you already know, but instead of 52 images, we'll reduce to 17 or 18 images. This makes it three times as fast. Here's how it works, in Ed's words:

"The next step is combining several cards into single images, which we achieve by assigning each card (celebrity) an action and an object. Jordan, the ace of diamonds, might have for an action a slam dunk, and his object a basketball. The Dalai Lama's action might be praying, his object a Buddha. Lady Gaga's action might be posing in a meat dress (memory, after all, loves to be disgusted), her object a load of paparazzi photographers (also disgusting)."

By adding this syntactic structure, combinations of three cards now form mini-sentences: the celeb from the first card, the action from the second, and the object from the third.

"For example, in my matrix, ace of diamonds–jack of spades–six of spades becomes Michael Jordan praying to the paparazzi; jack of spades–six of spades–ace of diamonds, on the other hand, translates into the Dalai Lama wearing a meat dress while holding a basketball. The two images, utterly distinct and deeply memorable, could never be confused."

And that, ladies and gentlemen, is Bicycleshop Pro. Elegant and, with practice, as fast as world champions.

For the type-A, obsessive sorts: once you get reasonably fluid and want to take racing the clock more seriously, I suggest getting a metronome. This will be your plateau breaker. If you stall and seem unable to memorize any faster, set the metronome for 10%–20% faster than you can currently handle. Force yourself to turn cards at this rate until you stop making errors. For instance, if you're stuck at 10 cards per minute (1 per 6 seconds) after a few weeks, set the metronome to 20% less time, so 4.8 seconds per metronome click. If a particular card causes hiccups, make a note of it (or draw a pen marking on it) and analyze the reasons later.

Just remember: this is fun, so keep it fun.

The grid on the next page is a suggested set of images, a starting point, but not gospel. Be sure to replace anyone whom you don't know, or in whom you have no interest. Feel free to add friends and family—the crazy narratives are always improved with a few familiar faces.

Perhaps a little friendly competition would help? Outstanding. I'll give you $10,000 if you're the first person to memorize a deck within the next 12 weeks,[8] in under one minute, with 100% accuracy. This is a real offer. Please read the full rules at fourhourchef.com/cards.

Enjoy the mind games.

8 Starting from this book's official publication date, November 20, 2012. This means no later than February 12, 2013.

ED COOKE'S CARD MATRIX

	♦ DIAMONDS: PERSON (EXPENSIVE, STYLISH, BLING)	♦ DIAMONDS: VERB	♦ DIAMONDS: OBJECT	♣ CLUBS: PERSON (TOUGH, SERIOUS, CRAZY, OR BAD)	♣ CLUBS: VERB	♣ CLUBS: OBJECT
KING CELEB COUPLE	PRINCE WILLIAM, THE RESCUE PILOT . . .	. . . AIRLIFTING SOMEONE OFF . . .	. . . THE SEA.	JAY-Z . . .	. . . RAPPING INTO . . .	. . . A GIANT MICROPHONE.
QUEEN CELEB COUPLE	PRINCESS KATE . . .	. . . WEARING A BEAUTIFUL DRESS IN . . .	. . . A CHURCH.	BEYONCÉ . . .	. . . POWER-DANCING ON . . .	. . . A BEACH.
JACK RELIGIOUS FIGURES	ZEUS . . .	. . . DISGUISING HIMSELF AS . . .	. . . A SWAN.	POPE JOHN PAUL II . . .	. . . TEARFULLY FORGIVING . . .	. . . THE MAN WHO JUST SHOT HIM.
10 FAMOUSLY POWERFUL WOMEN	OPRAH WINFREY . . .	. . . INTERVIEWING ON . . .	. . . A COUCH.	HILLARY CLINTON . . .	. . . SLAPPING . . .	. . . MONICA LEWINSK
9 FAMOUSLY POWERFUL MEN	BILL GATES . . .	. . . CACKLING MADLY AT . . .	. . . A CRASHING PC.	MARK ZUCKERBERG . . .	. . . UNFRIENDING . . .	. . . HIS BEST FRIEND.
8 FAMOUS FEMALE PHYSIQUES	MARILYN MONROE . . .	. . . 'S DRESS BALLOONING UP OVER . . .	. . . A SUBWAY VENT.	MEDUSA . . .	. . . TURNING TO STONE WITH AN ICY GLARE . . .	. . . A STATUE.
7 FAMOUS MALE PHYSICISTS	ISAAC NEWTON . . .	. . . GETTING HIT ON THE HEAD BY . . .	. . . AN APPLE.	GALILEO . . .	. . . LOOKING THROUGH A TELESCOPE AT . . .	. . . THE MOON.
6 CONTROVERSIAL FEMALES	MADONNA . . .	. . . STRIKING YOGA POSES IN FRONT OF . . .	. . . AN '80S BOOM BOX.	RIHANNA . . .	. . . HOLDING AN UMBRELLA IN . . .	. . . A RAIN STORM.
5 CONTROVERSIAL MALES	STALIN . . .	. . . TELLING AN AMUSING JOKE TO . . .	. . . A DANCING BEAR.	HITLER . . .	. . . GOOSE-STEPPING INTO . . .	. . . A BUNKER.
4 FEMALE MOVIE STARS	JULIA ROBERTS . . .	. . . FRENCH-KISSING . . .	. . . RICHARD GERE.	ANGELINA JOLIE AS LARA CROFT . . .	. . . KARATE KICKING . . .	. . . AN ANCIENT TOM
3 MALE MOVIE STARS	GEORGE CLOONEY . . .	. . . SMOKING . . .	. . . A CIGARETTE.	JOHNNY DEPP AS JACK SPARROW . . .	. . . MAKING PIRATICAL NOISES WITH . . .	. . . A PIRATE SHIP.
2 SPORTSWOMEN	ANNA KOURNIKOVA . . .	. . . SUNBATHING ON TOP OF . . .	. . . ENRIQUE IGLESIAS.	THE WILLIAMS SISTERS . . .	. . . LIFTING INTO THE AIR . . .	. . . THE WIMBLEDO TROPHY.
ACE SPORTSMEN	MICHAEL JORDAN . . .	. . . SLAM-DUNKING . . .	. . . A BASKETBALL.	MUHAMMAD ALI . . .	. . . PUNCHING . . .	. . . A BUTTERFLY.

♥ HEARTS: PERSON (VABLE, BEAUTIFUL, GOOD)	♥ HEARTS: VERB	♥ HEARTS: OBJECT	♠ SPADES: PERSON (HUMOROUS OR ABSURD)	♠ SPADES: VERB	♠ SPADES: OBJECT
ARACK OBAMA . . .	. . . FLY-SWATTING . . .	. . . A BUZZING FLY.	DAVID BECKHAM . . .	. . . KICKING . . .	. . . A SOCCER BALL.
ICHELLE BAMA . . .	. . . DOING JUMPING JACKS ON . . .	. . . THE WHITE HOUSE LAWN.	VICTORIA BECKHAM . . .	. . . APPLYING LIPSTICK IN FRONT OF . . .	. . . A MIRROR.
ESUS CHRIST . . .	. . . WALKING ON . . .	. . . A LAKE.	THE DALAI LAMA . . .	. . . PRAYING TO . . .	. . . A BUDDHA.
.K. ROWLING . . .	. . . WRITING A STORY ABOUT . . .	. . . HARRY POTTER.	SARAH PALIN . . .	. . . RIFLE SHOOTING . . .	. . . A MOOSE.
STEVE JOBS . . .	. . . TAKING LSD AND INVENTING . . .	. . . THE IPAD.	KEVIN ROSE . . .	. . . DRINKING . . .	. . . TEA.
PAMELA ANDERSON . . .	. . . SAVING . . .	. . . A DROWNING CHILD.	NAOMI CAMPBELL . . .	. . . SMACKING A MAID WITH . . .	. . . A HANDBAG.
EINSTEIN . . .	. . . TRAVELING AT LIGHT SPEED ALONGSIDE . . .	. . . A BEAM OF LIGHT.	STEPHEN HAWKING . . .	. . . SPEAKING WITH ROBOT VOICE FROM . . .	. . . A WHEELCHAIR.
TAYLOR SWIFT . . .	. . . BEING VICIOUSLY INSULTED BY . . .	. . . KANYE WEST.	LADY GAGA . . .	. . . WEARING A MEAT DRESS FOR . . .	. . . THE PAPARAZZI.
JULIAN ASSANGE . . .	. . . VANISHING IN . . .	. . . A PUFF OF SMOKE.	OSAMA BIN LADEN . . .	. . . RECORDING A GHETTO VIDEO WITH . . .	. . . A SUICIDE BOMBER.
SCARLETT JOHANSSON . . .	. . . GETTING DRUNK WITH . . .	. . . BILL MURRAY.	REESE WITHERSPOON AS JUNE CARTER . . .	. . . PLAYING GUITAR WITH . . .	. . . JOHNNY CASH.
TOM HANKS . . .	. . . RUNNING LIKE FORREST GUMP THROUGH . . .	. . . THE WOODS.	BEN STILLER . . .	. . . GETTING A LIE-DETECTOR TEST FROM . . .	. . . ROBERT DE NIRO.
FLO-JO . . .	. . . RECEIVING A GOLD MEDAL WHILE SINGING ALONG TO . . .	. . . "THE STAR-SPANGLED BANNER."	ANNIKA SÖRENSTAM . . .	. . . DRIVING . . .	. . . A GOLF BALL.
ROGER FEDERER . . .	. . . SERVING . . .	A TENNIS BALL.	USAIN BOLT . . .	. . . RUNNING RIDICULOUSLY FAST AFTER . . .	. . . A CHEETAH.

NOTES

- Odd numbers are male, even numbers are female.
- It's good to have occasional crazy ones.
- Read these as sentences.
- If you prefer, you can replace any or all of these with people you actually know.

YOUR OWN CARD MATRIX

	♦ DIAMONDS: PERSON (EXPENSIVE, STYLISH, BLING)	♦ DIAMONDS: VERB	♦ DIAMONDS: OBJECT	♣ CLUBS: PERSON (TOUGH, SERIOUS, CRAZY, OR BAD)	♣ CLUBS: VERB	♣ CLUBS: OBJECT
KING CELEB COUPLE						
QUEEN CELEB COUPLE						
JACK RELIGIOUS FIGURES						
10 FAMOUSLY POWERFUL WOMEN						
9 FAMOUSLY POWERFUL MEN						
8 FAMOUS FEMALE PHYSIQUES						
7 FAMOUS MALE PHYSIQUES						
6 CONTROVERSIAL FEMALES						
5 CONTROVERSIAL MALES						
4 FEMALE MOVIE STARS						
3 MALE MOVIE STARS						
2 SPORTSWOMEN						
ACE SPORTSMEN						

HEARTS: PERSON VABLE, BEAUTIFUL, GOOD)	HEARTS: VERB	HEARTS: OBJECT	SPADES: PERSON (HUMOROUS OR ABSURD)	SPADES: VERB	SPADES: OBJECT

NINE MUST-KNOW KNOTS

> "Twenty years from now you will be more disappointed by the things that you didn't do than by the ones you did do. So throw off the bowlines. Sail away from the safe harbor. Catch the trade winds in your sails. Explore. Dream. Discover."
>
> —MARK TWAIN

Knots are the lifeblood of the fisherman, outdoorsman, sailor, and survivalist. Whether you want to create shelter, raise a sail, boil water over a fire, or use bedsheets to climb out of a burning building, you need a basic vocabulary. Good knots are simple, strong (the rope reaches its breaking point before the knot comes undone), and easy to untie. Any fool can create a Gordian knot, but it takes technique to form a reusable tool.

I found it most effective, and fun, to learn a handful of 80/20 knots using unique associations for each: a different purpose or orientation.

FIRST:

Get some rope, ideally a 15-ft and a 5-ft length of ½" nylon rope, which is easily found in most hardware stores.

THEN:

Practice at least three of the following knots and take photos. **I've starred the three I use most.** Don't do anything dangerous, please, lads and lasses.

NOTE: If the step-by-step text is too confusing, just follow the pics.

THE KNOT GLOSSARY—SAFE TO IGNORE

Running end: The head segment of a rope; the part most manipulated during the knot-forming process; also known as the tail end.

Standing end: The end of rope that's opposite the knot; i.e., when a rope is hitched to an object, the pull comes from the standing end.

Standing part: The inactive segment of rope around which the running end works; the length of rope between the running end and the standing end.

Turn: A single pass of a rope around or through an object.

Round turn: Two consecutive passes of a rope around an object to fully encircle it.

Hitch: A tie that secures a rope to another object (often temporary).

Bend: A knot that joins two separate ropes.

THE TIMBER HITCH

VARIOUS KNOTS WITH THE DOG

ON A BUS: THE CLOVE HITCH, MIDSHIPMAN'S HITCH, AND MY LEG

1. TIMBER HITCH

You guessed it: lumbermen use the spiraling Timber Hitch to encircle tree trunks or sections. A *hitch* is when you tie a rope to something else. Learn and test by dragging a large log or downed tree 10–20 ft. The Timber Hitch will not hold when slack, but that's not a problem for this knot's (also know as a Bowyer's Knot) other common application: stringing a long bow.

A. Pass the running end of the rope around the object and then around the standing end.

B. Wrap the end around itself three times and tighten the knot so that the three turns grip the pole snugly.

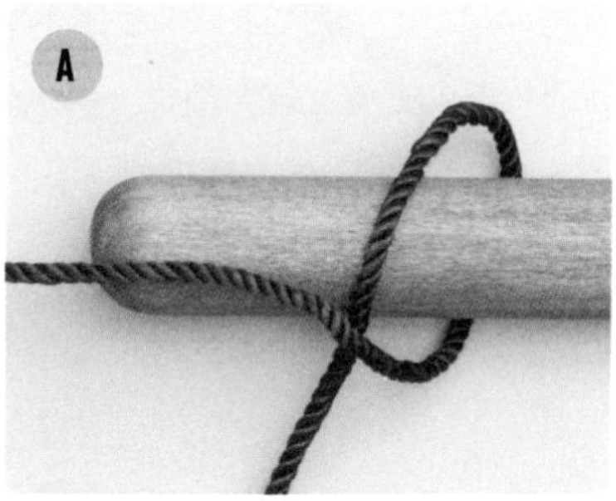
A

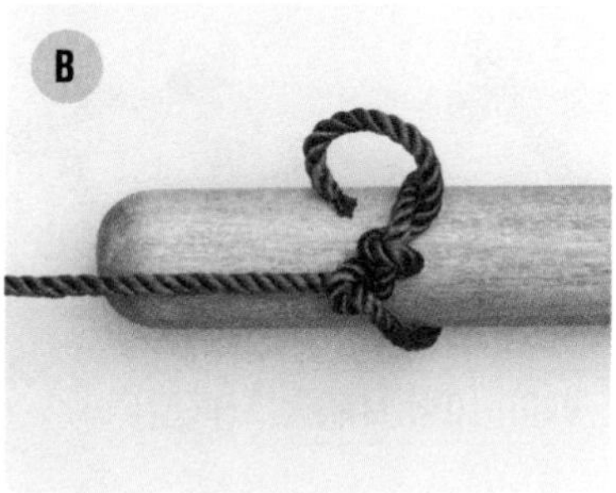
B

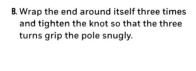

(Also see log pic, left)

2. HALF HITCH

Without the Half Hitch in your back pocket, it's going to be hell trying to form more complex knots. A Half Hitch alone is considered unstable; it's merely a building block or a finishing reinforcement for many other knots.

A. Form a loop around the object.

B. Pass the running end around the standing part and through the loop.

C. Tighten.

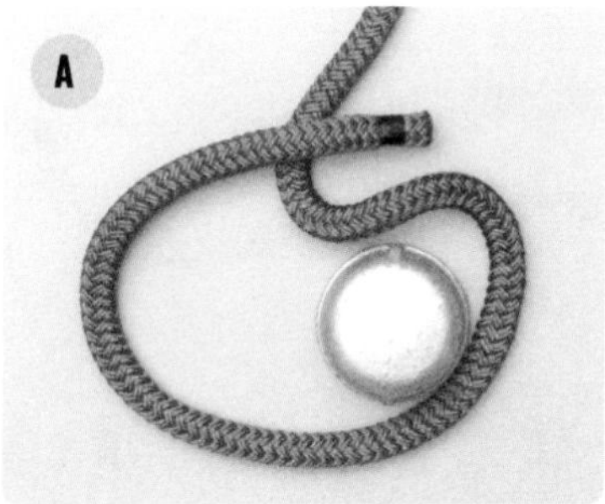
A

B

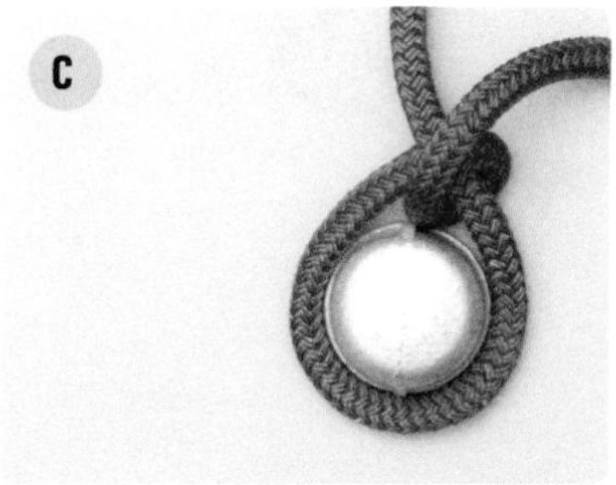
C

★ 3. CLOVE HITCH

There is some controversy about the Clove Hitch's security and its tendency to bind, which can make untying difficult. But its slip-or-bind quality gives the Clove Hitch more play than other knots, allowing for minute adjustments. You should secure the Clove Hitch by adding an extra Half Hitch or two. **It can be used to secure your tarp to a tree or (my use) hang a kettle over a fire.**

A–C. The basic Clove Hitch.

D–E. Adding a Half Hitch for security.

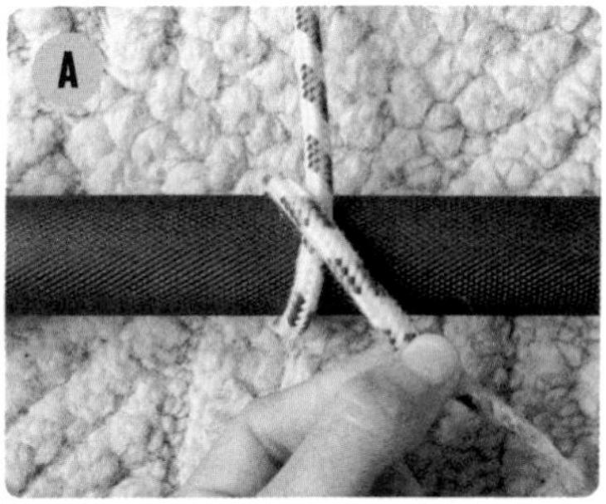
A

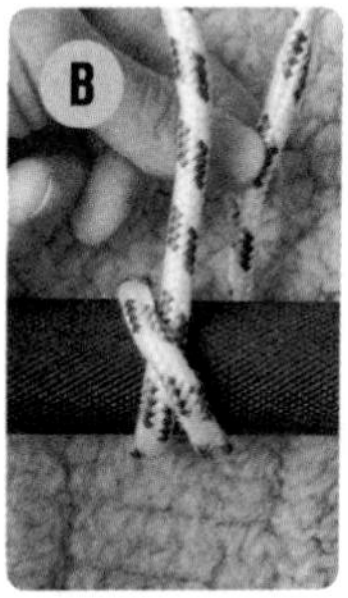
B

C

D

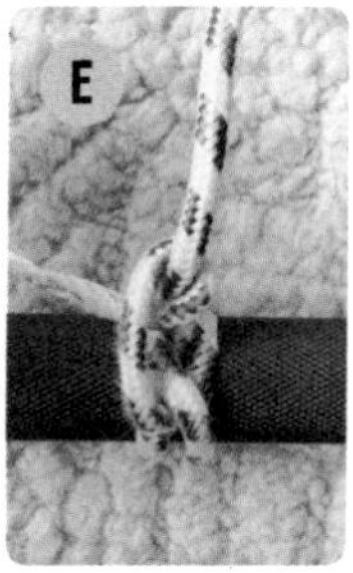
E

★ 4. BOWLINE KNOT

If you're going to learn just one knot, this is probably the one. It's the seminal "desert island survival" knot. A Bowline can withstand loads that take a rope just south of its breaking point, but it's easily undone after it serves its purpose. In an emergency, you can even tie a Bowline one-handed. **Note that you can use interlocking Bowlines to attach sections of rope, bedsheets, or other materials.**

A. Form a loop and pass the tail end through it.

B. Bring the tail end around the standing part above the small loop.

C. Thread the tail end back through the small loop and tighten.

Boy Scouts often learn this by imagining:

- a rabbit coming out of his hole...
- running around the "tree"...
- and jumping back in his hole.

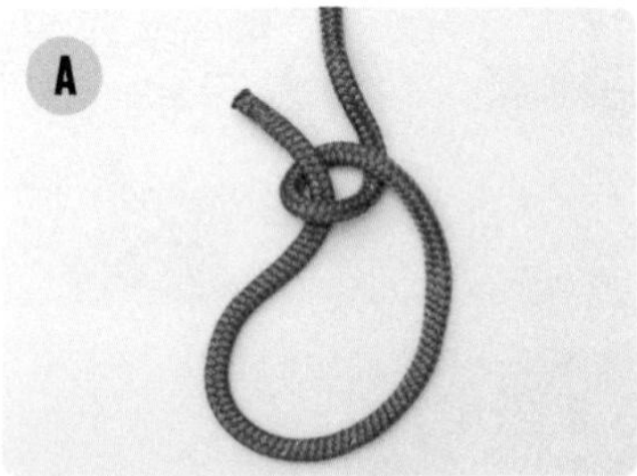
A

B

C

5. ROLLING HITCH

Bears threatening to eat your rations in the night? Employ this cousin of the Clove Hitch. First, tie a rope to a carabiner that's attached to your food-filled bear bag (use a Bowline knot for this—see left). Then throw the running end of your rope over a high tree limb. With the running end back within reach, pull it until the bag is elevated sufficiently (12–15 ft), wrap it around something, and use a Rolling Hitch to fasten it.

A. Pass the end around the main (red) rope as if to form a Half Hitch.

B. Continue around, crossing over the first turn.

C. Tuck the rope between the standing end and the first turn.

D. Tighten the knot securely.

E. Continue around in the same direction as the previous turns and add a final Half Hitch, pulling the running end up between the second and third loops.

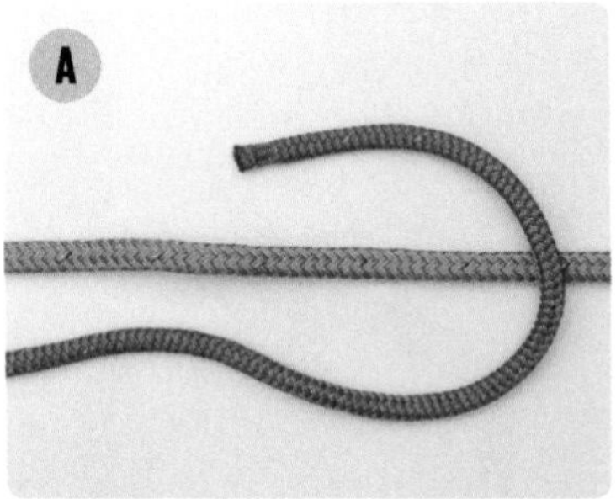
A

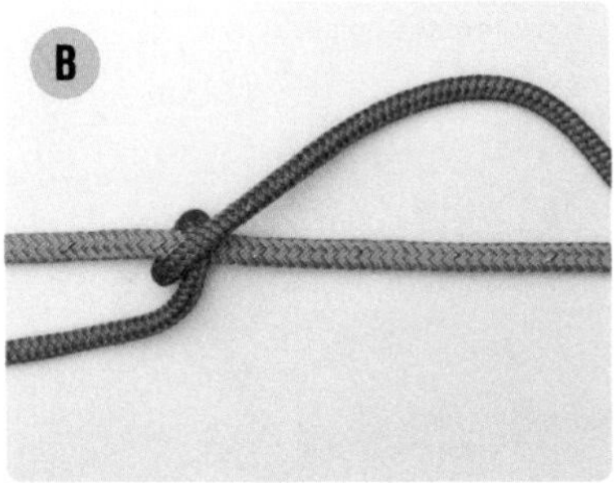
B

C

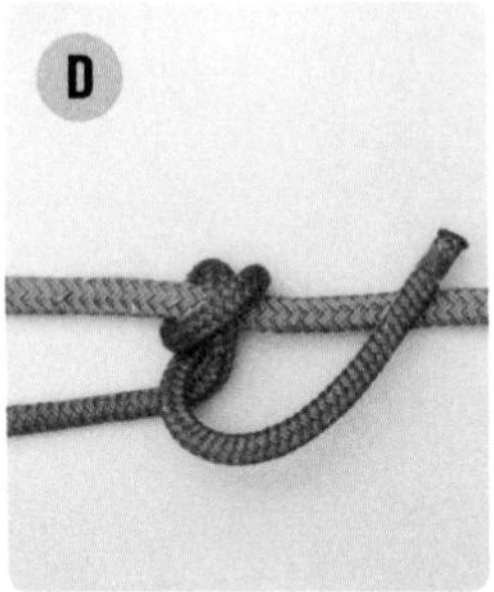
D

E

F

6. VARIATION: MAGNUS HITCH

A Rolling Hitch with a wrinkle: Reverse the direction of the Half Hitch in step E of the Rolling Hitch. According the 1944 knot bible, *The Ashley Book of Knots*, this Magnus Hitch helps eliminate twisting when binding to a rope that's slack. **Use it to attach a fishing line to a rod.**

7. SHEET BEND

A "bend" means you're joining rope to rope. Though two Bowlines can be used for this, the sheet bend is much faster, and it can unite two ropes of different thickness. You actually know one bend already: tying your shoelaces. It's technically a Short-End Sheet Bend.

A. Form a loop in the thicker rope (blue)—without crossing the running end over the standing end—and hold it in one hand.

B. Pass the thinner rope (red) through the loop and behind the (blue) running and standing ends, in that order.

C. Tuck the smaller rope under itself, finishing the knot, and tighten.

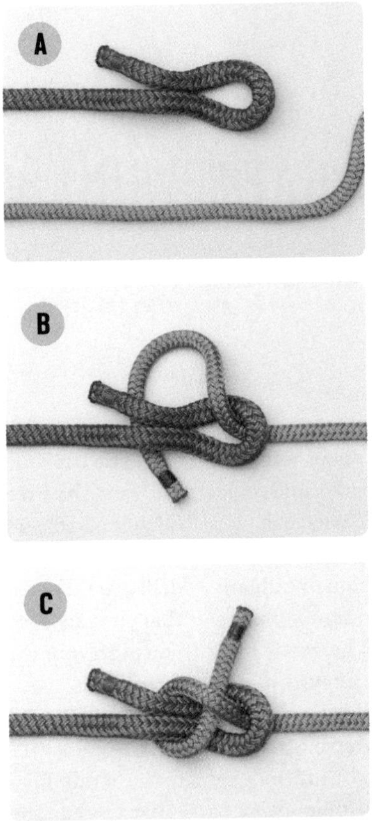
A
B
C

★ 8. MIDSHIPMAN'S HITCH

The Midshipman is useful for securing a tent or clothesline, since you can adjust tautness.

It's a Rolling Hitch (see #5) that is tied to the standing end of the same rope after the rope encircles another object, such as a stake, tree, or rock. The Midshipman's Hitch is sometimes confused with the Taut-line Hitch due to a persistent error in Boy Scouts manuals. When tying a Midshipman's Hitch, refer to the Rolling Hitch for tying directions, but note that your knot should look like this:

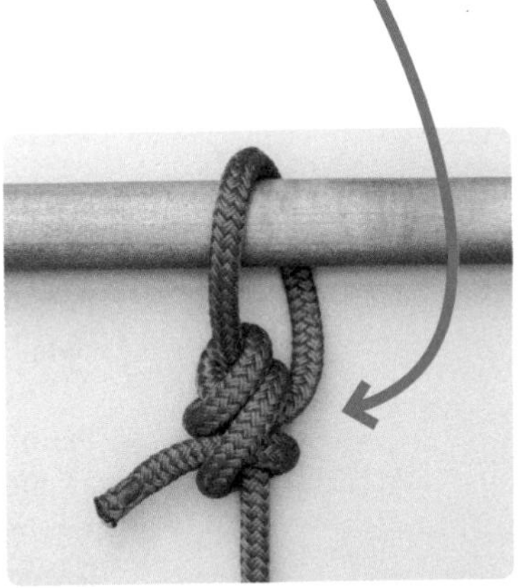

9. ROUND TURN AND TWO HALF HITCHES

A Round Turn and Two Half Hitches secures a rope to a pole or a ring. **It is a reliable hitch and is ideal for tying a hammock to a tree.** The two half hitches add security and make it useful for tying the end of a rope to any object.

A. Pass the running end around the post twice, removing the strain while you tie the rest of the knot.

B. Go around the standing end to make the first Half Hitch, and pull it tight.

C. Continue around in the same direction to make the second Half Hitch.

D. Pull tight to complete the knot.

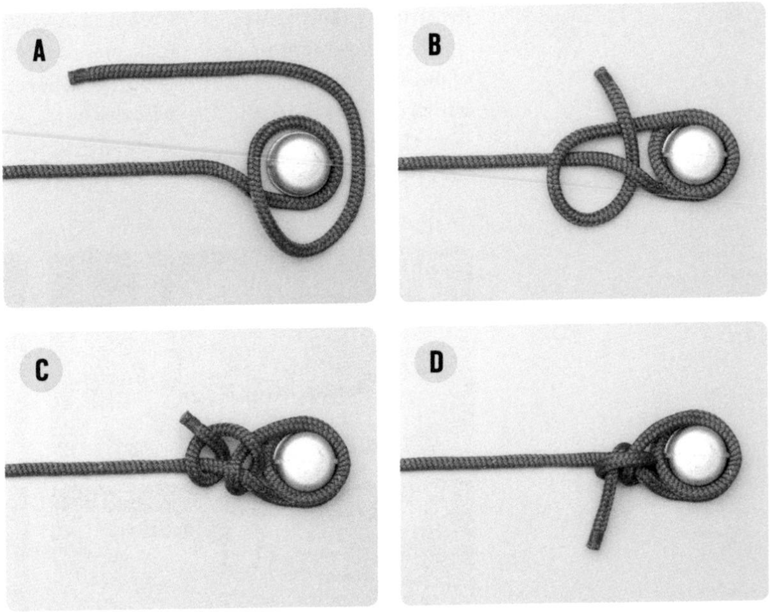
A
B
C
D

BUILDING A FIRE WITH A BOW DRILL

TOTAL TIME

1–3 hours

GEAR

- See directions

> "Education is not the filling of a pail, but the lighting of a fire."
>
> —WILLIAM BUTLER YEATS

Fire helps keep us warm, purify our water, and cook our food. It's a hell of a thing. It might also be what makes us uniquely human: Fire = big protein consumption = bigger brains.

To create a bow drill, our tool of choice, you will need a knife for whittling and carving wood. Cliff Hodges (see page 260 for more on Cliff) prefers relatively inexpensive Morakniv knives.

The constituent parts of our fire-making device, which dates back to at least the 4th or 5th century BCE, are:

1. The Drill (also "spindle") and **the Fireboard** (also "hearth"). The wood for both the fireboard and drill should be soft enough that you can leave a mark if you push your thumbnail into it.

2. The Handhold (also "bearing block"). The key to the handhold is that it is harder than the wood used for the spindle and fireboard. Any hardwood (oak, madrone, etc.) is good. Rock, bone, or antler will also work, as will a knife such as the ESEE-5 (see page 253).

3. The Bow. Slightly bowed, roughly armpit-to-wrist length. If need be, go longer instead of shorter. Ideally, find a bow with a knot or bump at one or both ends that you can tie the cordage around.

4. Cordage. Cliff recommends nylon paracord for beginners, but he uses natural cordages like pine rootlet, bark fibers, etc. In a true survival situation, use whatever will keep you alive. Shoelaces can work, as can a 1" section of a T-shirt, torn off from around the waist.

1. DRILL AND FIREBOARD

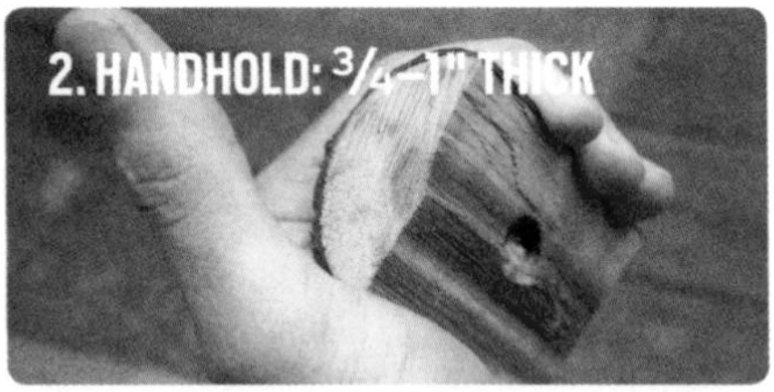
2. HANDHOLD: ¾–1" THICK

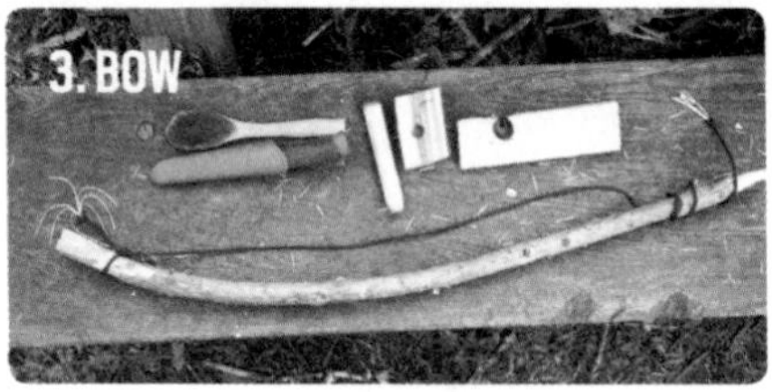
3. BOW

4. CORDAGE

WHAT IT LOOKS LIKE (INSTRUCTIONS ON NEXT PAGE)

A
B
C
D
E
F
G
H
I

THE DRILL

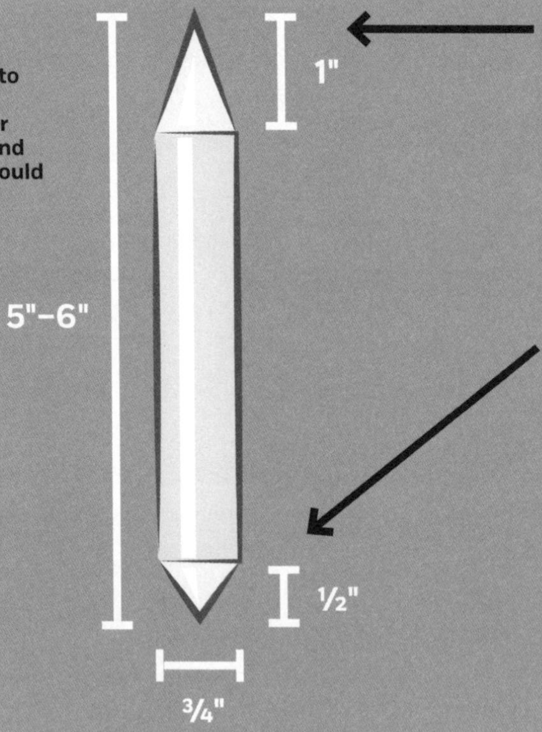
The points need to be centered, and the main cylinder should be as round as possible. It should easily roll across anything flat.
1"
5"–6"
½"
¾"
Point A
Elongated point (minimizes friction). This is where you'll be pushing down on the handhold.
Point B
Blunter end (maximizes friction).
As you wear down both the fireboard and the spindle through rotation, hot coals are kicked off into a small pile. You'll eventually put this onto wispy tinder to create your fire.

THE FIREBOARD ≈¾" THICK

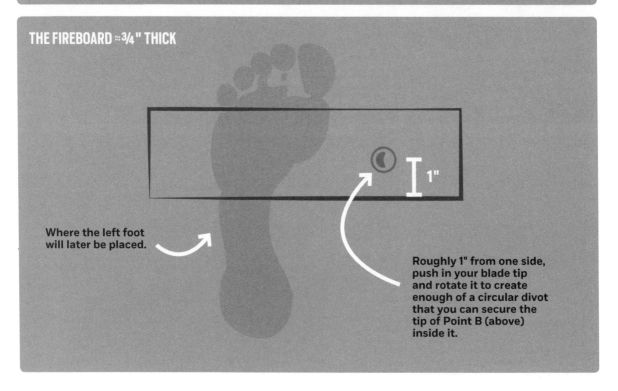

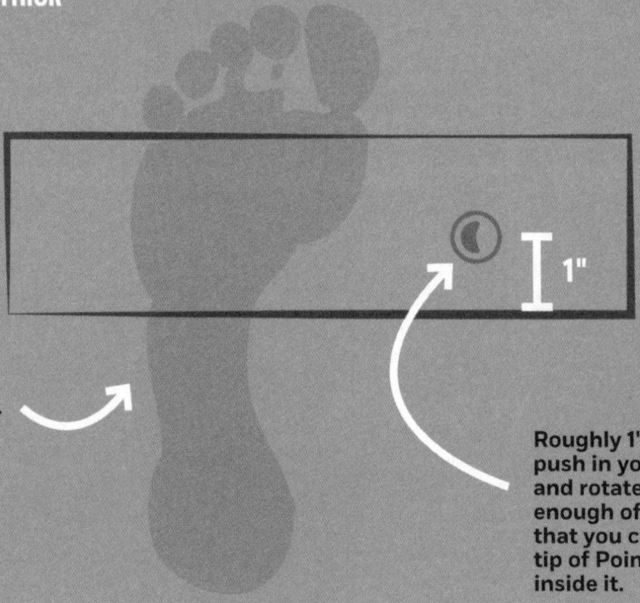
1"
Where the left foot will later be placed.
Roughly 1" from one side, push in your blade tip and rotate it to create enough of a circular divot that you can secure the tip of Point B (above) inside it.

HOW TO CARVE THE NOTCH (READ PREP STEP 02 FIRST)

A

Fireboard with the hole burned in, but no notch yet.

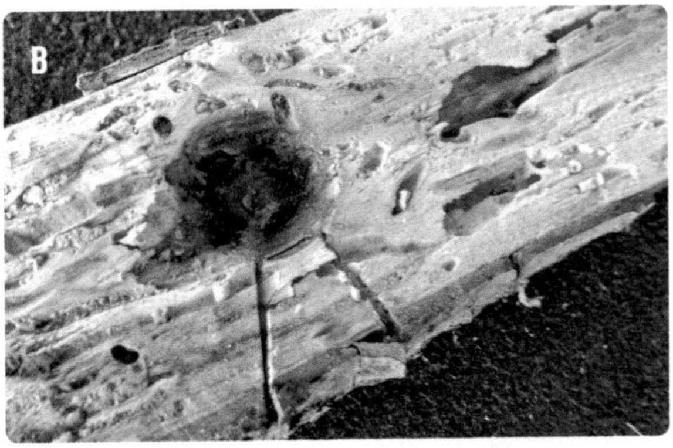
B

Guidelines carved into the fireboard to show where the notch will go.

C

Make a ⅛"–¼" cut down either side of the notch with your blade, then pop that small section out.

D

Repeat until you've chopped out the completed notch.

PREP

00 Whittle the drill per the diagram at left. Ditto with the handhold (see page 618) and fireboard (see opposite page). Create a divot in each of the latter: one per the diagram for the fireboard, and the same thing in the center of the flat, downward-facing side of the handhold.

01 Find your bow and tie your cordage to one end with a bowline knot (see page 616).

02 Drill a hole in the fireboard by performing the action of the bow drill (see pics D and E on page 619). To wrap the spindle, see the next page. You're not trying to create a coal, because there is no notch yet. You're simply burning in a hole (see pic A, above). This is what we call burnin-in your kit.

03 Once you've drilled a hole in the fireboard that is roughly the same diameter as the spindle (probably ⅛"–¼" deep), stop. The edge of your hole should still be ¼"–½" from the edge. Now you're ready to carve the V-like notch—just like a slice of pizza or pie taken out of the circle. This notch will collect your coal (see pic D, above).

04 Once that's done, it's time to go for the gold. Get your pile of tinder (a bird's nest–like collection of flammable whispy material) such as the inner portion of redwood bark, and place it next to you.

WRAPPING THE SPINDLE

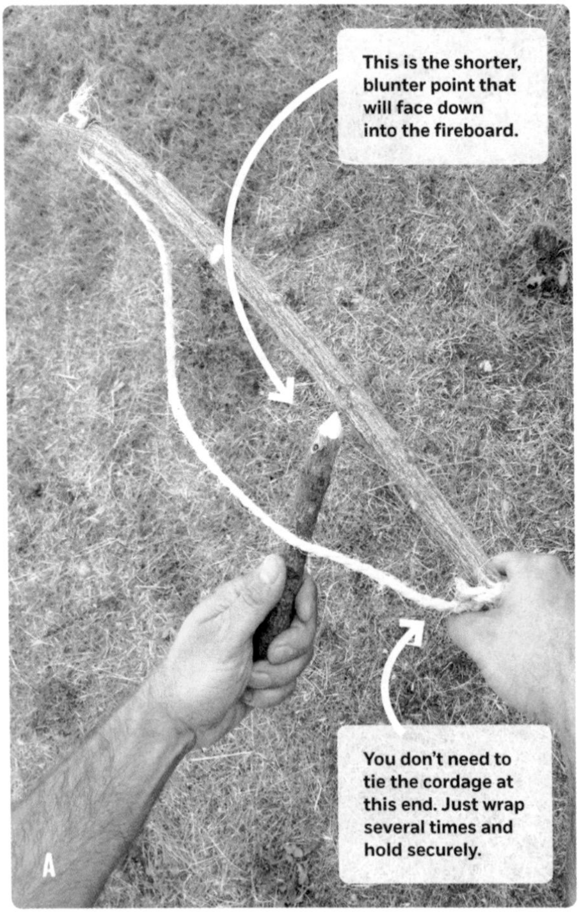
This is the shorter, blunter point that will face down into the fireboard.
You don't need to tie the cordage at this end. Just wrap several times and hold securely.
A

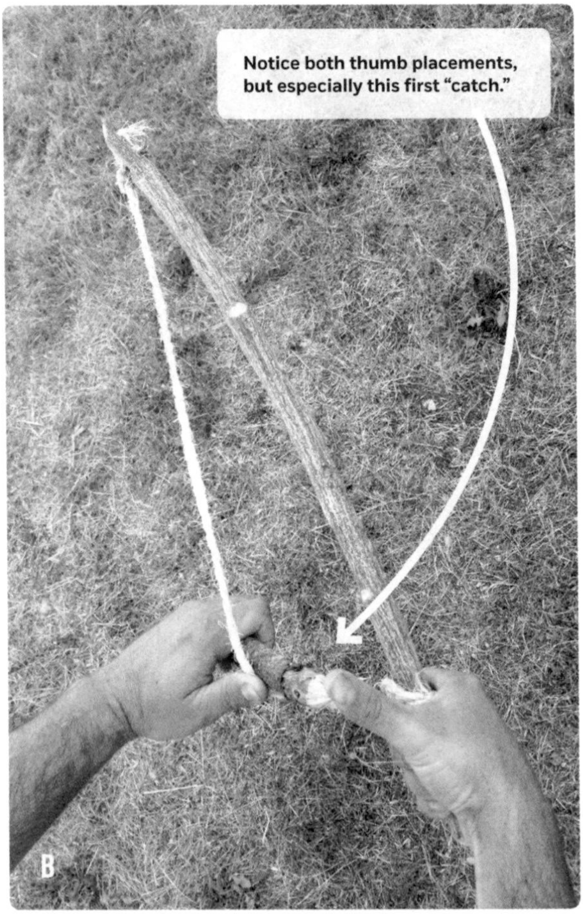
Notice both thumb placements, but especially this first "catch."
B

Now, apply pressure with your left knuckles into the rope and push your right thumb down. This will rotate the drill toward you and twist the cordage.
C

Like so.
D

Now, slide the drill (keeping it wrapped) down to your right hand so you can secure everything one-handed. Your thumb can wrap around either side of the drill.
E

PICKUP

00 Place your left foot firmly on the fireboard, about 1"–1½" (2.5–4 cm) to the left of your divot like so:

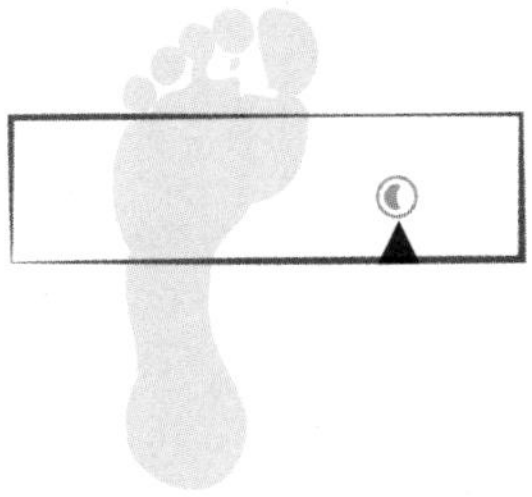

01 Place a small piece of your tinder or a dried leaf underneath your notch so there is something to catch the coal.

02 Next, wrap the cordage around the other end of your bow a few times, keeping the line *slightly* less than taut, and grab the coils to secure them.

03 Now, we tackle the part that everyone screws up a few times. Use your left hand to wrap the drill into the cordage, assisting with your right thumb (see pics, opposite page).

04 Spindle secured, insert the bottom, blunter point into the fireboard divot and secure the other point with your handhold. Looking at Cliff's position in pic E (page 619), note a critical point: his left knee is traveling over his ankle, and his left wrist is braced *against* his shin.

05 Keeping your chest weighted on your lead leg, get drilling. Don't go crazy. Start off slowly, using the full length of the bow if possible, and keep the bow parallel to the ground. It's not a muscle move. Cliff has seen 8-year-olds calmly create fire while 30-year-old marines are huffing and puffing like plow oxen.

06 When you start to see smoke, keep going. Speed up, and go as long as you are able, probably another 45–90 seconds, but possibly longer if you're forced to use hardwoods such as oak. If you stop when you first see smoke, you won't have enough coals.

07 Take your foot off, tilt and tap the fireboard to ensure all coals (probably totaling less than the glowing end of a cigarette) are on your leaf or tinder piece, and gently transfer to the middle of your tinder pile. I used a knife blade. Now, cupping your hands around the bottom of the tinder, cover the coals and raise the mass up to your face. Blow gently to turn smoke to flame.

08 It will flare up suddenly and doesn't burn long. Be ready to transfer it to your fire structure immediately. If you're not ready, I hope you have a tequila shot, since it's time to get more tinder and start over.

MORE LIVING THE GOOD LIFE

HOW TO BECOME A VIP (AND OTHER TIPS)

Sitting at Saison's "chef's table," right in the middle of the kitchen. Chef Joshua Skenes, in blue, is standing at the pass—a plate's final stop before it's sent to diners.

NOPA, in San Francisco. The woman in the striped shirt is seated next to the pass. I chose the next best seat in the house, a "two top" on the second floor, which allowed me to see everything in the kitchen.

There is always one person who rolls up to the hottest joint in town and immediately gets a table, a handshake from the maître d', and the fastest service. But how?

Unless you're a celebrity, and sometimes even then, you'll need to earn it. That's why this is called "How to Become a VIP" and not "How to Be Treated Like a VIP." In fact, I dislike the term VIP altogether and suggest a more accurate replacement: most-favored customer (MFC).

Rest assured, there are shortcuts to reaching this coveted status. Below are tips from chefs and restaurant managers in NYC, as well as lessons I learned during my own research. If you're going to eat out, you might as well do it right.

Pick and choose as you like:

THE TO-DO LIST:

- **Go from Tuesday to Thursday.** That's when restaurants cater to the foodies and experiment with their menus. For the money-making days (Friday to Sunday), they stick to the majority-pleasing safe bets.
- **Focus on density.** For you to become an MFC, restaurants have to first remember your name, so help 'em out. If possible, go for both lunch and dinner two or three nights in a row. Try everything on the menu. That will get attention. Becoming a lunch regular is a good investment and one of the shortcuts to MFC.
- **Use industry lingo.** If they ask "Table for two?" or "Table for four?" you can respond with "Yep. Any two top [two-seater] is fine" or "You got it. Do you have a four top [table for four] toward the back?"
- **Order two dishes at your first visit.** Will Schwalbe, while editor in chief of Hyperion Books, edited many of the biggest names in chefdom. He's now founder of cookstr.com and still follows advice he received long ago. In his words: "Ask your

server to ask the chef two questions: first, 'What does everyone order?' and second, 'What does almost no one order that you think everyone should?' Then order both. Chefs want to show off their popular dishes but often have an item on the menu they're really proud of, and really want people to try. I first did this at the Slanted Door in San Francisco. A cook actually came out to say hello because he thought it was so unusual."

- **For your first two or three visits, sit at the bar, if possible.** The bartender is your best friend and is beloved by all staff (can you say after-hours "shift drinks"?). If the restaurant isn't slammed, and after you've had a bunch of dishes, ask the bartender if you can thank the GM (general manager), chef, or owner, indicating that you don't want to interrupt them if they're too busy. Keep it short, big fella. Also, IMPORTANT: leave a cash tip for your bartender, even if you transfer the bill to a table.
- **For dinners, ask if you can be seated at or near "the pass,"** where the final plating is done before dishes go to tables. This might also take the form of a "chef's window/table/bar," so feel free to ask for it. Don't interrupt the chef, but go ahead and ask smart questions about the preparation of your dishes if a cook starts the conversation.
- **If you've built rapport, politely ask your server if you can get a quick tour of the kitchen** or a peek behind the scenes after dinner. Say that you admire the work of cooks and would love to see what they're able to accomplish in their kitchen.
- **Ask your server smart questions about the food.** He or she may think you're a fellow server (which earns bonus points) or a reviewer (ditto). Doing work on a notepad during your meal, especially if you're at a fancier place, also raises eyebrows. When you start to get asked, "Are you in the industry?" your service will take a quantum leap, and you might eventually get labeled "super *soigné*" (pronounced "swan-yay"), or VIP, in the restaurant booking system.
- **Don't tip dumbly.** While undertipping is a no-no, the value of overtipping is overestimated. Tipping 40% once every few weeks won't make you an MFC. C'mon, you wouldn't be that easily bought, and neither will they. Tip at least 20% at all times. If the service sucks and you feel 20% is too much, why the hell do you want to eat there in the first place? Last, if you have an outstanding experience, tip the maître d' or host/hostess. In most places, a discreet $20 in the hand for a parting handshake will go miles. DO NOT do this on the way in, young gun. That's a novice flub.
- **If you become a regular and get to know more about the chef, consider bringing him or her a small gift** relevant to his or her interests. I'm not kidding. It works for most humans, and it's a nice gesture to the person making your food. This stuff isn't rocket surgery, folks.

THE NOT-TO-DO LIST:

- **Don't eat Sunday buffets,** which are sometimes used to get rid of food that hasn't sold during the week.
- **Don't order just before closing time.** The kitchen staff doesn't like this any more than you'd like 60 minutes of surprise overtime.
- **Do not roll up with a "Do you know who I am?" vibe.** That's for DBs, which doesn't stand for databases. Asking if so-and-so is working tonight is as far as namedropping should go.
- **Do not treat servers like lackeys** if you want to be treated like a VIP. If you want to be treated like a VIP, treat all staff like they're VIPs.

YELP'S 100 BEST RESTAURANTS IN THE U.S.A.

Yelp helps people find the best things in almost any city. But what about an entire *country*?

That would be new, and that's what you see here (thanks to Mike G. and the Yelp team!). These four tables show the top 25 highest-rated restaurants in the country by price range ($ being cheapest and $$$$ being most expensive).

The top 25 restaurants were selected based on an algorithm that incorporates Yelp user feedback (star ratings) and the overall number of ratings the restaurants received. Put another way, in order to be in the top 25, a restaurant must not only receive high quality reviews, it must also receive a significant number of them.

NOTES ON METHODOLOGY FROM YELP'S ENGINEER:

As of 8 a.m. PT on August 19, 2011, we pulled a list of all businesses that had a review count greater than 20; were not inactive, removed from search, migrated, or closed; and were active members of the restaurant category.

We found the Wilson score of each of these businesses, ordered by decreasing score, then dumped the top businesses to a spreadsheet. A Wilson score (fourhourchef.com/wilson) is a way of combining both score and number of reviews into a single number. Technically, it estimates the lower bound of the 95% confidence interval around score treated as a binomial random variable. It is just a way of ranking and probably should not be displayed to users as the true score of the business.

Note that merging the lists and trying to rerank them by Wilson score overall would result in an erroneous list—these should be kept as four different lists in order to maintain accuracy.

$$$$

#	NAME	# REVIEWS	YELP STAR RATING	WILSON SCORE
1	**ALINEA** CHICAGO, IL	664	4.5	4.58
2	**GARY DANKO** SAN FRANCISCO, CA	2,767	4.5	4.531
3	**THE FRENCH LAUNDRY** YOUNTVILLE, CA	983	4.5	4.514
4	**VICTORIA & ALBERT'S** LAKE BUENA VISTA, FL	59	5	4.514
5	**PER SE** NEW YORK, NY	450	4.5	4.492
6	**JOËL ROBUCHON** LAS VEGAS, NV	278	4.5	4.463
7	**NAOE** SUNNY ISLES BEACH, FL	84	5	4.435
8	**CRAIGIE ON MAIN** CAMBRIDGE, MA	433	4.5	4.402
9	**GRAMERCY TAVERN** NEW YORK, NY	679	4.5	4.399
10	**DANIEL** NEW YORK, NY	441	4.5	4.399
11	**TOTORAKU** LOS ANGELES, CA	101	4.5	4.395
12	**MASTRO'S STEAKHOUSE** BEVERLY HILLS, CA	1,316	4.5	4.386
13	**LE BERNARDIN** NEW YORK, NY	604	4.5	4.38
14	**PROVIDENCE** LOS ANGELES, CA	926	4.5	4.37
15	**SUSHI SASABUNE** HONOLULU, HI	292	4.5	4.369
16	**KOMI** WASHINGTON, DC	268	4.5	4.368
17	**ELEVEN MADISON PARK** NEW YORK, NY	448	4.5	4.363
18	**DEL FRISCO'S DOUBLE EAGLE STEAK HOUSE** LAS VEGAS, NV	318	4.5	4.355
19	**WAKURIYA** SAN MATEO, CA	202	4.5	4.343
20	**KAGAYA** LOS ANGELES, CA	254	4.5	4.334
21	**COMMIS** OAKLAND, CA	302	4.5	4.334
22	**FORAGE** LOS ANGELES, CA	59	5	4.33
23	**CYRUS** HEALDSBURG, CA	455	4.5	4.318
24	**UCHI** AUSTIN, TX	675	4.5	4.316
25	**BLUE HILL AT STONE BARNS** POCANTICO HILLS, NY	177	4.5	4.313

$$$

#	NAME	# REVIEWS	YELP STAR RATING	WILSON SCORE
1	SYCAMORE LANSDOWNE, PA	82	5	4.528
2	SUSHI IZAKAYA GAKU HONOLULU, HI	262	4.5	4.496
3	THE BALLARD INN BALLARD, CA	87	5	4.488
4	CAFÉ MONARCH SCOTTSDALE, AZ	120	5	4.472
5	KOISO SUSHI BAR KIHEI, HI	156	4.5	4.428
6	NEPTUNE OYSTER BOSTON, MA	851	4.5	4.395
7	RAKU LAS VEGAS, NV	311	4.5	4.365
8	SUSHI OTA SAN DIEGO, CA	1034	4.5	4.357
9	NICK'S ON MAIN LOS GATOS, CA	420	4.5	4.354
10	4TH ST. BISTRO RENO, NV	85	4.5	4.353
11	KOKKARI ESTIATORIO SAN FRANCISCO, CA	1,681	4.5	4.337
12	LA SIRENE NEW YORK, NY	496	4.5	4.325
13	AD HOC YOUNTVILLE, CA	1,119	4.5	4.31
14	GIRL & THE GOAT CHICAGO, IL	1,005	4.5	4.303
15	DANTE'S KITCHEN NEW ORLEANS, LA	205	4.5	4.302
16	AU PIED DE COCHON MONTRÉAL, QC	259	4.5	4.301
17	FOGO DE CHAO CHICAGO, IL	607	4.5	4.296
18	OHSHIMA JAPANESE CUISINE ORANGE, CA	323	4.5	4.29
19	HUNGRY MOTHER CAMBRIDGE, MA	539	4.5	4.288
20	IMANAS TEI RESTAURANT HONOLULU, HI	192	4.5	4.283
21	CHAMA GAUCHA SAN ANTONIO, TX	112	4.5	4.274
22	CANOE ATLANTA, GA	211	4.5	4.268
23	CHAPEAU! SAN FRANCISCO, CA	1,348	4.5	4.267
24	USS NEMO NAPLES, FL	80	4.5	4.264
25	THE HOUSE SAN FRANCISCO, CA	1,853	4.5	4.258

$$

#	NAME	# REVIEWS	YELP STAR RATING	WILSON SCORE
1	NEW ENGLAND LOBSTER SOUTH SAN FRANCISCO, CA	98	5	4.575
2	GESTE SHRIMP TRUCK KAHULUI, HI	130	5	5.514
3	BLUDSO'S BBQ COMPTON, CA	503	4.5	4.489
4	DAMETRA CAFE CARMEL-BY-THE-SEA, CA	453	4.5	4.473
5	CHAM KOREAN BBQ BUFFET LAKEWOOD, WA	135	4.5	4.456
6	TASTE OF ETHIOPIA PFLUGERVILLE, TX	168	4.5	4.429
7	LANGER'S DELICATESSEN RESTAURANT LOS ANGELES, CA	1,234	4.5	4.408
8	LA TARASCA CENTRALIA, WA	93	4.5	4.387
9	CAFÉ ROLLE SACRAMENTO, CA	303	4.5	4.373
10	IRISH TABLE CANNON BEACH, OR	57	5	4.366
11	DISTRICT WINE LONG BEACH, CA	173	4.5	4.365
12	SOL FOOD PUERTO RICAN CUISINE SAN RAFAEL, CA	955	4.5	4.352
13	BOTTLEHOUSE SEATTLE, WA	69	5	4.348
14	PHIL'S BBQ SAN DIEGO, CA	3,262	4.5	4.343
15	OYSTER BAR LAS VEGAS, NV	268	4.5	4.341
16	MAMA D'S ITALIAN KITCHEN NEWPORT BEACH, CA	919	4.5	4.341
17	HELENA'S HAWAIIAN FOOD HONOLULU, HI	444	4.5	4.335
18	SALUMI ARTISAN CURED MEATS SEATTLE, WA	623	4.5	4.334
19	THE RIDERS CLUB CAFE SAN CLEMENTE, CA	185	4.5	4.331
20	MARUKAI MARKET GARDENA, CA	210	4.5	4.33
21	THE MARSHALL STORE MARSHALL, CA	254	4.5	4.326
22	GOOSE THE MARKET INDIANAPOLIS, IN	77	4.5	4.326
23	LA BOULANGERIE SAN FRANCISCO, CA	415	4.5	4.323
24	MRS. WILKES' DINING ROOM SAVANNAH, GA	166	4.5	4.321
25	DAVE'S FRESH PASTA SOMERVILLE, MA	354	4.5	4.319

$

#	NAME	# REVIEWS	YELP STAR RATING	WILSON SCORE
1	DA POKE SHACK KAILUA, HI	97	5	4.691
2	BIKER JIM'S GOURMET DOGS DENVER, CO	382	4.5	4.599
3	BUILT TO GRILL PORTLAND, OR	219	5	4.583
4	OKLAHOMA JOE'S BBQ & CATERING KANSAS CITY, KS	451	4.5	4.543
5	PORTO'S BAKERY BURBANK, CA	1,857	4.5	4.541
6	PASEO SEATTLE, WA	1,456	4.5	4.525
7	YOSHINO JAPANESE DELI CARLSBAD, CA	64	5	4.5
8	HOT DOUG'S CHICAGO, IL	1,791	4.5	4.496
9	GRAHAM AVENUE MEATS AND DELI BROOKLYN, NY	176	4.5	4.484
10	SWEET POTATO STALL SANTA CLARA, CA	202	4.5	4.482
11	PBJ'S PORTLAND, OR	106	5	4.481
12	PHO 95 DENVER, CO	376	4.5	4.479
13	THE CHEESEBOARD COLLECTIVE BERKELEY, CA	2,105	4.5	4.477
14	POKE EXPRESS NORTH LAS VEGAS, NV	54	4.5	4.46
15	BLUES CITY DELI SAINT LOUIS, MO	144	4.5	4.45
16	KOMEX FUSION EXPRESS LAS VEGAS, NV	79	5	4.447
17	THE CODMOTHER FISH AND CHIPS SAN FRANCISCO, CA	70	5	4.444
18	RICKY'S FISH TACOS HOLLYWOOD, CA	243	4.5	4.442
19	OPAL THAI FOOD HALEIWA, HI	148	4.5	4.434
20	ROXIE FOOD CENTER SAN FRANCISCO, CA	583	4.5	4.424
21	LITTLE LUCCA SANDWICH SHOP & DELI SOUTH SAN FRANCISCO, CA	1,170	4.5	4.471
22	ARIZMENDI BAKERY SAN FRANCISCO, CA	1,006	4.5	4.411
23	TACOS EL GORDO CHULA VISTA, CA	519	4.5	4.407
24	BAGUETTE CAFE LAS VEGAS, NV	104	4.5	4.405
25	SAL, KRIS, & CHARLIE'S DELI ASTORIA, NY	248	4.5	4.4

THE CULINARY MAPS

NEW YORK CITY (PAGE 632) AND SAN FRANCISCO (PAGE 636)

There's nothing worse than wandering around two of the world's greatest food towns (NYC and SF) and settling for a subpar meal.

These maps are the solution. Whether you want to eat slow-carb-style, cheat like it's your last day on earth, or unearth the coolest markets and supply shops, we have you covered. Just locate the neighborhood you want to explore on the map, find the corresponding color on the list, and you're in business.

For romantic couples and food marathoners alike, all of these spots are worth a trip.

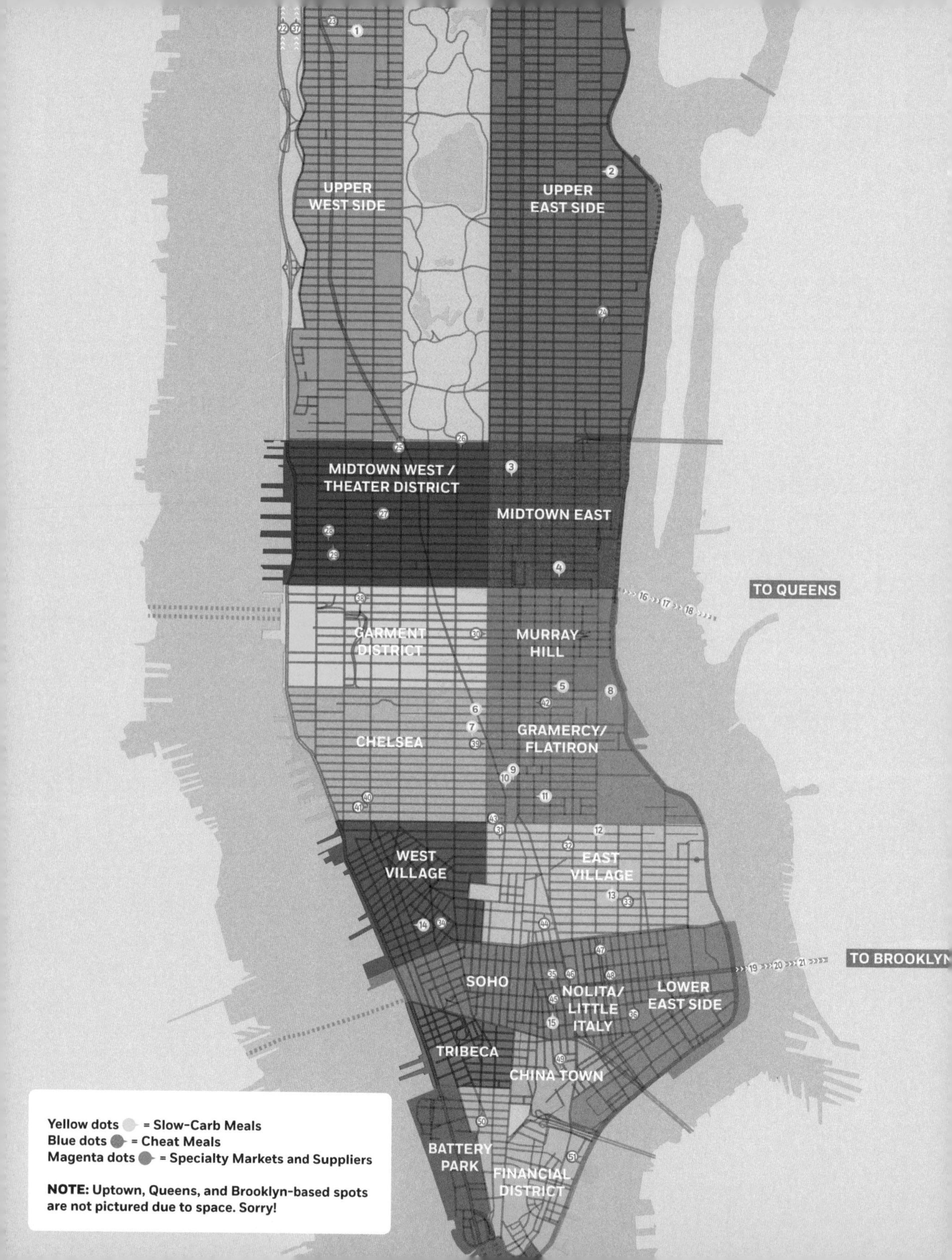

UPPER WEST SIDE
UPPER EAST SIDE
MIDTOWN WEST / THEATER DISTRICT
MIDTOWN EAST
TO QUEENS
GARMENT DISTRICT
MURRAY HILL
CHELSEA
GRAMERCY/ FLATIRON
WEST VILLAGE
EAST VILLAGE
TO BROOKLYN
SOHO
NOLITA/ LITTLE ITALY
LOWER EAST SIDE
TRIBECA
CHINA TOWN
BATTERY PARK
FINANCIAL DISTRICT
Yellow dots = Slow-Carb Meals
Blue dots = Cheat Meals
Magenta dots = Specialty Markets and Suppliers
NOTE: Uptown, Queens, and Brooklyn-based spots are not pictured due to space. Sorry!

	RESTAURANT	TYPE	ADDRESS	TEL. / WEBSITE	RECOMMENDED DISH(ES)
1.	AWASH	ETHIOPIAN	947 Amsterdam Ave.	212-961-1416 awashny.com	Special Tibs (Steak)
2.	PIO PIO	PERUVIAN	1746 1st Ave.	212-426-5800 piopio.com	Chicken Pio
3.	AQUAVIT	NORDIC	65 East 55th St.	212-307-7311 aquavit.org	Glassblower Herring, Matjes Herring
4.	SAKAGURA	JAPANESE	211 East 43rd St.	212-953-7253 sakagura.com	Buta Kakuni (Stewed Diced Pork)
5.	TERROIR	AMERICAN/ WINE BAR	439 3rd Ave.	212-481-1920 restauranthearth.com	Veal & Ricotta Meatballs
6.	ILILI	LEBANESE/ MEDITERRANEAN	236 5th Ave.	212-683-2929 ililinyc.com	Hindbeh (Dandelion Greens)
7.	JUNOON	INDIAN	27 West 24th St.	212-490-2100 junoonnyc.com	Lobster Tandoori
8.	RIVERPARK	AMERICAN	450 East 29th St.	212-729-9790 riverparknyc.com	Charcuterie Plate, Branzino
9.	CRAFT	AMERICAN	43 East 19th St.	212-780-0880 craftrestaurant.com	Braised Short Ribs, Hen of the Woods Mushrooms
10.	ABC KITCHEN	AMERICAN/ ORGANIC & LOCAL	35 East 18th St.	212-475-5829 abckitchennyc.com	Shaved Raw Summer Squash
11.	CASA MONO	SPANISH	52 Irving Pl.	212-253-2773 casamononyc.com	Razor Clams à la Plancha
12.	HEARTH	ITALIAN	403 East 12th St.	646-602-1300 restauranthearth.com	Scottish Salmon
13.	PYLOS	GREEK	128 East 7th St., #A	212-473-0220 pylosrestaurant.com	Htapothi Scharas (Grilled, Marinated Octopus)
14.	TAKASHI	JAPANESE-KOREAN BBQ	456 Hudson St.	212-414-2929 takashinyc.com	"The Tongue Experience" (Beef Tongue Three Ways)
15.	NYONYA	MALAYSIAN	199 Grand St.	212-334-3669 ilovenyonya.com	Beef Rendang
16.	AYADA THAI (not pictured)	THAI	77-08 Woodside Ave., Queens	718-424-0844 ayadathaiwoodside.com	Sauté Chinese Broccoli with Crispy Pork
17.	FU RUN (not pictured)	CHINESE	40-09 Prince St., Queens	718-321-1363	Muslim Lamb Chop
18.	HAHM JI BACH (not pictured)	KOREAN	41-08 149th Place, Queens	718-460-9289 hahmjibach.com	Sam Gyup Sal (Pork Belly)
19.	PETER LUGER STEAK HOUSE (not pictured)	AMERICAN/ STEAK HOUSE	178 Broadway, Brooklyn	718-387-7400 peterluger.com	USDA Prime Beef Steak
20.	MOMO SUSHI SHACK (not pictured)	JAPANESE	43 Bogart St., Brooklyn	718-418-6666 momosushishack.com	Pork Betty
21.	KAZ AN NOU (not pictured)	FRENCH CARIBBEAN	53 6th Ave., Brooklyn	718-938-3235 kazannou.com	Jerk Chicken

THE TOP CHEAT MEALS (NYC)

	RESTAURANT	TYPE	ADDRESS	TEL. / WEBSITE	RECOMMENDED DISH(ES)
22.	CACHAPAS Y MAS (not pictured)	VENEZUELAN/ LATIN AMERICAN	107 Dyckman St.	212-304-2224 cachapasymasnyc.com	Cubano Patacon (Fried Green Plantain Sandwich)
23.	ABSOLUTE BAGELS	BAGEL SHOP	2788 Broadway	212-932-2052	Bagel with Cream Cheese
24.	SASABUNE	JAPANESE	401 East 73rd St.	212-249-8583 sasabunenyc.com	Blue Crab Roll
25.	PER SE	FRENCH	10 Columbus Circle, #4	212-823-9335 perseny.com	Oysters & Pearls, Foie Gras
26.	QUALITY MEATS	AMERICAN	57 West 58th St.	212-371-7777 qualitymeatsnyc.com	Corn Crème Brûlée
27.	PURE THAI COOKHOUSE	THAI	766 9th Ave.	212-581-0999 purethaishophouse.com	Pork Dry Noodles
28.	SULLIVAN STREET BAKERY	BAKERY & PIZZA	533 West 47th St.	212-265-5580 sullivanstreetbakery.com	Bianca con Pecorino Pizza
29.	GUELAGUETZA	MEXICAN	526 West 47th St.	212-265-2626 guelaguetzanyc.com	Taco Guelaguetza (Rice, Egg, Potato Cake, Chorizo, and Rajas)
30.	AI FIORI	ITALIAN	400 5th Ave.	212-613-8660 aifiorinyc.com	Trofie Nero (Squid Ink Pasta)
31.	NUM PANG SANDWICHES	CAMBODIAN/ SANDWICH SHOP	21 East 12th St.	212-255-3271 numpangnyc.com	Pork Belly Sandwich
32.	MOMOFUKU SSÄM BAR	KOREAN	207 2nd Ave.	212-254-3500 momofuku.com	Bo Ssäm Pork Shoulder Meal (must reserve in advance online)
33.	LULA'S SWEET APOTHECARY	VEGAN ICE CREAM SHOP	516 East 6th St.	646-481-5852 lulassweetapothecary.com	Cake Batter Soft Serve
34.	MOLLY'S CUPCAKES	CUPCAKES	228 Bleecker St.	212-414-2253 mollyscupcakes.com	The Ron Bennington Cupcake (Chocolate Cake, Peanut Butter Filling, Chocolate Ganache, Crushed Butterscotch Topping)
35.	TARTINERY	FRENCH	209 Mulberry St.	212-300-5838 tartinery.com	Croque Madame Tartine
36.	DOUGHNUT PLANT	DOUGHNUTS/ CAFÉ	379 Grand St.	212-505-3700 doughnutplant.com	Tres Leches Doughnut, Crème Brûlée Doughnut

THE TOP SPECIALTY MARKETS AND SUPPLIERS (NYC)

	MARKET	TYPE	ADDRESS	TEL. / WEBSITE	WHAT'S UNIQUE?
37.	INWOOD GREENMARKET (not pictured)	FARMERS MARKET	Isham St. & Seaman Ave.	212-788-7476 grownyc.org/ inwoodgreenmarket	Year-round market for those who live way uptown. Get apples from Breezy Hill Orchards, plus most other foods you could possibly need from various local farms and producers.
38.	INTERNATIONAL GROCERY	INTERNATIONAL GROCERY	543 9th Ave.	212-279-1000 internationalgrocerynyc.com	International grocery specializing in Greek and Mediterranean fare with aisles of nuts, legumes, grains, olives, spices, cheeses, and olive oils.
39.	EATALY NY	GOURMET MARKET	200 5th Ave.	212-229-2560 eataly.com	There are all manner of pastas and pizzas, plus out-of-this-world gelato, for your cheat days, but you can also find an incredible selection of fish and vegetables.
40.	THE LOBSTER PLACE (CHELSEA MARKET)	FISHMONGER	75 9th Ave.	212-255-5672 lobsterplace.com	Lobster, crab, and fresh fish. And grab some clam chowder and lobster bisque to go.
41.	DICKSON'S FARMSTAND MEATS (CHELSEA MARKET)	BUTCHER & MEAT SHOP	75 9th Ave.	212-242-2630 dicksonsfarmstand.com	Grass-fed, cage-free local meat. All the meat here is outstanding. I really enjoy their homemade jerky, too. (It comes in many different flavors.)
42.	KALUSTYANS	INTERNATIONAL GROCERY	123 Lexington Ave.	212-685-3451 kalustyans.com	International bulk spices and Middle Eastern specialty items. Thirty varieties of dried whole chilies and chili powder and 180 varieties of imported tea.
43.	UNION SQUARE GREENMARKET	FARMERS MARKET	1 Union Square West	212-788-7476 grownyc.org/ unionsquaregreenmarket	It's the gold standard for farmers markets in NYC. Tons of chefs shop there. Go there especially for local fruits and vegetables and farm-fresh meats, cheeses, and milk. The selection of fall apples is particularly outstanding.
44.	JAPAN PREMIUM BEEF	BUTCHER & MEAT SHOP	57 Great Jones St.	212-260-2333	Japanese butchers are notoriously picky about quality, and this place is supposed to have some of the best. Everyone raves about the Washugyu tenderloin in particular. The most coveted and most expensive is the dry-aged version.
45.	DI PALO'S FINE FOODS	INTERNATIONAL GROCERY	200 Grand St.	212-226-1033 dipaloselects.com	A quintessential old-school Italian market in Little Italy offering cheese, *proscuitto di parma* and other cured meats, oils, vinegars, honey, and preserves.
46.	BOWERY RESTAURANT SUPPLY	RESTAURANT SUPPLY STORE	183 Bowery	212-254-9720	They've got everything for cheap. Mark Bittman says this is his favorite restaurant supply place (check out the article and video at nytimes .com/2007/05/09/dining/09mini.html).
47.	RUSS & DAUGHTERS	GOURMET MARKET	179 East Houston St.	212-475-4880 russanddaughters.com	They've been selling smoked salmon, whitefish, herring, cream cheese, and caviar since 1914.
48.	SAXELBY CHEESEMONGERS	CHEESEMONGER	120 Essex St.	212-228-8204 saxelbycheese.com	An awesome selection of cheeses curated by owner/cheesemonger Anne Saxelby (who everyone says is very helpful). They also have bread from Sullivan Street Bakery if it's your cheat day.
49.	BANGKOK CENTER GROCERY	INTERNATIONAL GROCERY	104 Mosco St.	212-349-1979 bangkokcentergrocery.com	Asian groceries, especially Thai ingredients. If you're looking for Thai basil or kaffir lime leaves, here's where to find them.
50.	KORIN	RESTAURANT SUPPLY STORE	57 Warren St.	212-587-7021 korin.com	A great kitchen begins with great knives, and this place has the most badass Japanese knives around. They'll sharpen old knives too.
51.	NEW AMSTERDAM MARKET	FARMERS MARKET	902 Peck Slip	212-766-8688 newamsterdammarket.org	Lots of great vegetables and meats from local producers. They also have hot-food vendors like Bent Spoon (ice creams), Luke's Lobster, Blue Bottle Coffee, Dickson's, and Saxelby.

NORTH BEACH
MARINA
RUSSIAN HILL
PRESIDIO
COW HOLLOW
CHINA-
TOWN
NOB HILL
FINANCIAL
DISTRICT
PACIFIC HEIGHTS
PRESIDIO
HEIGHTS
CIVIC CENTER
SEACLIFF
WESTERN ADDITION
OUTER RICHMOND
INNER RICHMOND
SOUTH OF
MARKET
HAIGHT
ASHBURY
CASTRO
MISSION
INNER SUNSET
OUTER SUNSET
POTRERO HILL
TWIN
PEAKS
NOE VALLEY
DIAMOND
HEIGHTS
BERNAL
HEIGHTS
PARKSIDE
WEST OF TWIN PEAKS
GLEN PARK
BAYVIEW
OUTER MISSION
LAKESHORE
EXCELSIOR
OCEAN VIEW
VISITACION VALLEY
CROCKER AMAZON
Yellow dots = Slow-Carb Meals
Blue dots = Cheat Meals
Magenta dots = Specialty Markets and Suppliers

THE TOP SLOW-CARB MEALS (SF)

	RESTAURANT	TYPE	ADDRESS	TEL. / WEBSITE	RECOMMENDED DISH(ES)
1.	DON PISTO'S	MEXICAN	510 Union St.	415-395-0939 donpistos.com	House-Made Chorizo Mussels
2.	SOTTO MARE	ITALIAN	552 Green St.	415-398-3181 sottomaresf.com	Cioppino
3.	KOKKARI ESTIATORIO	GREEK	200 Jackson St.	415-981-0983 kokkari.com	Octapodaki tou Yiorgou (Grilled Octopus)
4.	GITANE	SPANISH	6 Claude Lane	415-788-6686 gitanerestaurant.com	Pescado (Pan-Roasted Petrale Sole, Heirloom Tomatoes, Romano & Yellow Wax Beans, Mint, Piri Piri sauce)
5.	LERS ROS THAI	THAI	730 Larkin St.	415-931-6917 lersros.com	Pad Kra Prow Moo Krob (Stir-Fried Pork Belly with Crispy Rind and Basil Leaves)
6	ZUNI CAFE	MEDITERRANEAN	1658 Market St.	415-552-2522 zunicafe.com	Sautéed Petrale Sole (or the Chicken for Two if it's your cheat day)
7.	DOSA	INDIAN	1700 Fillmore St.	415-441-3672 dosasf.com	Chennai Chicken
8.	ASSAB ERITREAN CUISINE	EAST AFRICAN	2845 Geary Blvd.	415-441-7083	Veggie Combo
9.	ENJOY VEGETARIAN RESTAURANT	CHINESE	754 Kirkham St.	415-682-0826 enjoyveggie.com	Eggplant & Sea Bass
10.	FIREFLY	AMERICAN	4288 24th St.	415-821-7652 fireflyrestaurant.com	Brussels Sprouts
11.	LIMON ROTISSERIE	PERUVIAN	1001 South Van Ness Ave.	415-821-2134 limonrotisserie.com	Ceviche Mixto (Fish, Calamari & Tiger Shrimp)
12.	ROSAMUNDE SAUSAGE GRILL	GERMAN	2832 Mission St.	415-970-9015 rosamundesausagegrill.com	Mission Street Sausage Plate
13.	ICHI SUSHI	JAPANESE	3369 Mission St.	415-525-4750 ichisushi.com	Cucumber Salad, Scallop Sashimi
14.	LE P'TIT LAURENT	FRENCH	699 Chenery St.	415-334-3235 leptitlaurent.net	Lapin Façon Normande (Rabbit Normandy), Le Cassoulet Toulousain Maison (Home-made Cassoulet)
15.	CHEZ PANISSE (not pictured)	AMERICAN/ CALIFORNIAN CUISINE	1517 Shattuck Ave., Berkeley	510-548-5525 chezpanisse.com	Northern Halibut with Meyer Lemon and Green-Olive Sauce (or whatever fish or meat is on the menu that night)

THE TOP CHEAT MEALS (SF)

	RESTAURANT	TYPE	ADDRESS	TEL. / WEBSITE	RECOMMENDED DISH(ES)
16.	LIGURIA BAKERY	BAKERY	1700 Stockton St.	415-421-3786	Pizza or Onion Focaccia
17.	CAFFE BAONECCI	ITALIAN	516 Green St.	415-989-1806 caffebaonecci.com	Pizza Monte Biano (Parma & Mascarpone)
18.	SAIGON SANDWICH	VIETNAMESE/ SANDWICH SHOP	560 Larkin St.	415-474-5698	Pork Paté Banh Mi Sandwich
19.	M & L MARKET	SANDWICH SHOP	691 14th St.	415-431-7044	Hot Pastrami Sandwich
20.	BI-RITE CREAMERY	ICE CREAM SHOP	3692 18th St.	415-626-5600 biritecreamery.com	Salted Caramel Ice Cream
21.	TARTINE BAKERY	BAKERY/CAFÉ	600 Guerrero St.	415-487-2600 tartinebakery.com	Bread Pudding, Country Loaf
22.	SIDEWALK JUICE	SMOOTHIE & JUICE BAR	3287 21st St.	415-341-8070	Green Energy Juice (Spinach, Kale, Apple, Lemon, Ginger, Parsley, Celery, Cucumber)
23.	UDUPI PALACE	INDIAN	1007 Valencia St.	415-970-8000 udupipalaceca.com	Masala Dosa (Thin Rice Crepe with Spiced Potatoes and Onions)
24.	EL FAROLITO TAQUERIA	MEXICAN	2779 Mission St.	415-824-7877 elfarolitoinc.com	Super Quesadilla Suiza (with Chicken and Avocado)
25.	HUMPHRY SLOCOMBE	ICE CREAM SHOP	2790 Harrison St.	415-550-6971 humphryslocombe.com	Secret Breakfast Ice Cream
26.	DYNAMO DONUTS	DOUGHNUT SHOP	2760 24th St.	415-920-1978 dynamodonut.com	Saffron Chocolate Donut, Bacon Maple Apple Donut
27.	ANTHONY'S COOKIES	COOKIES	1417 Valencia St.	415-655-9834 anthonyscookies.com	Cinnamon Sugar Cookie
28.	MISSION PIE	BAKERY/CAFÉ	2901 Mission St.	415-282-1500 missionpie.com	Banana Cream Pie
29.	LA CICCIA	ITALIAN	291 30th St.	415-550-8114 laciccia.com	Fregua Cun Arrescottu e Cori de Tonnu (Fregula with Fresh Ricotta and Cured Tuna Heart)
30.	GIALINA PIZZERIA	ITALIAN	2842 Diamond St.	415-239-8500 www.gialina.com	Wild Nettles Pizza (with Pancetta, Mushrooms, Red Onions & Provolone) with Affogato dessert

THE TOP SPECIALTY MARKETS AND SUPPLIERS (SF)

	MARKET	TYPE	ADDRESS	TEL. / WEBSITE	WHAT'S UNIQUE?
31.	COWGIRL CREAMERY	CHEESEMONGER	1 Ferry Building, #17	415-362-9350 cowgirlcreamery.com	Arguably the best cheese in the Bay Area, made in Marin County. Try the Red Hawk or Mount Tam varieties.
32.	FERRY PLAZA FARMERS MARKET	FARMERS MARKET	1 Ferry Building	415-291-3276 cuesa.org	Besides all the produce, there are tons of food stalls and food trucks, the best of which are Primavera (for chilaquiles and tamales on your cheat day) and RoliRoti (for a porchetta sandwich on your cheat day).
33.	SWAN OYSTER DEPOT	FISHMONGER	1517 Polk St.	415-673-1101	An SF institution for almost 100 years, offering fresh local fish and oysters. It's also a restaurant if you want to eat there.
34.	SEAKOR POLISH DELICATESSEN AND SAUSAGE FACTORY	INTERNATIONAL GROCERY	5957 Geary Blvd.	415-387-8660	Sausages! (And if it's your cheat day, get some of the poppy seed cake.)
35.	KAMEI RESTAURANT SUPPLY	RESTAURANT SUPPLY STORE	525 Clement St.	415-666-3699	Cheap kitchen supplies—everything from plates to rice cookers.
36.	FIRST KOREAN MARKET	INTERNATIONAL GROCERY	4625 Geary Blvd.	415-221-2565	Korean grocery items and prepared foods. (Try the kimchi.)
37.	JAI HO INDIAN GROCERY	INTERNATIONAL GROCERY	1462 Fillmore St.	415-567-1070	Packaged products from India, prepared foods, and spices.
38.	OTHER AVENUES	GOURMET MARKET/ CO-OP	3930 Judah St.	415-661-7475 otheravenues.coop	A great bulk-foods section and lots of local and organic artisanal products (like milk from Straus Family Creamery) aimed at healthy eaters and dieters.
39.	SAN FRANCISCO HERB COMPANY	GOURMET MARKET	250 14th St.	415-861-7174 sfherb.com	A huge selection of essential oils, spices, and teas.
40.	RAINBOW GROCERY	GOURMET MARKET/ CO-OP	1745 Folsom St.	415-863-0620 rainbow.coop	An extensive bulk-foods section and fresh local produce, lots of it organic. It's the largest worker-owned cooperative in the city, and it's very popular with the hipsters in the Mission.
41.	BI-RITE MARKET	GOURMET MARKET	3639 18th St.	415-241-9760 biritemarket.com	A great place for local coffee beans, chocolate, wine, and cheese (and homemade ice cream for your cheat day). There's also local produce, plus organic fish and meat.
42.	SUN FAT SEAFOOD COMPANY	FISHMONGER	2687 Mission St.	415-282-9339 sunfatseafood.com	Affordable fresh fish, oysters, and fresh Dungeness crabs.
43.	DREWES BROTHERS MEATS	BUTCHER & MEAT SHOP	1706 Church St.	415-821-0515 drewesbros.com	A full-service butcher shop with all-natural, free-range meat. Try chicken from nearby Petaluma Farms and meats from Niman Ranch. If you're looking for something they don't have, they say they can get almost anything with one day's notice.
44.	AVEDANO'S HOLLY PARK MARKET	BUTCHER & MEAT SHOP	235 Cortland Ave.	415-285-6328 avedanos.com	Besides grass-fed beef, duck fat, and take-out dinners, they also offer popular butchery classes.
45.	ALEMANY SATURDAY FARMERS MARKET	FARMERS MARKET	100 Alemany Blvd.	415-647-9423 sfgsa.org	Fresh produce (less expensive than the Ferry Building) and several hot-food stands, including Salvadoran food and hummus from the Hummus Guy. If it's your cheat day, try the Bolani flatbread from the East & West Gourmet Afghan Foods stall.

ACKNOWLEDGMENTS

Note: Please also see the "On the Shoulders of Giants" thank-you list on page 14.

First, I must thank the innovative chefs, scientists, and readers whose contributions are the lifeblood of this book. Thank you so much for your generosity of spirit—you are my teachers! If I've omitted anyone by accident, I offer my sincerest apologies with hat in hand. Please reach out, and I'll make amends.

To Stephen Hanselman, the best agent in the world, I thank you for "getting" the book at first glance and helping to midwife it into existence. From negotiation to nonstop jazz, you amaze me. Next time I talk about writing a "definitive" book, please kick me in the head.

To the entire Melcher Media team, especially those whom I bother (because I love them) more than four hours a week, you were the production backbone of this book: Holly "BSD" (you asked for it!) Dolce, Jessi Rymill, Megan Worman, Nadia Bennet, David Brown, Bonnie Eldon, Kurt Andrews, Anna Wahrman, Carolyn Merriman, Shannon Fanuko, Lynne Ciccaglione, Gabriella Paiella, and—of course—Charlie Melcher.

To Amazon Publishing: thank you for believing in me and in this project. I wish more authors could have such a smooth experience. Special thanks to Julia Cheiffetz, Larry Kirschbaum, Jeff Belle, Katie Salisbury, Katie Finch Rinella, Maggie Sivon, and Kiwa Iyobe. On the PR front, I must thank my continued partner in crime, Mark Fortier.

I owe particular gratitude to Jeffrey "JZ" Zurofsky. You were a co-conspirator from the nascent stages, and you can testify to my complete culinary illiteracy on day one. I hope the end product makes you proud. The adventures are not over!

To Jack Canfield: *The 4-Hour Workweek*, which launched my writing career, was just an idea until you encouraged me to take the leap. I cannot thank you enough for your wisdom, early support, and incredible friendship. None of this would have happened without you!

To Sifu Steve Goericke and Coach John Buxton, who taught me how to act in spite of fear and fight like hell for what I believe, this book—and my life—is a product of your influence. Bless you both. The world's problems would be far fewer if young men had more mentors like the two of you.

Last but not least, this book is dedicated to my parents, Donald and Frances Ferriss, who have guided me, encouraged me, loved me, and consoled me through it all. I love you more than words can express.

ENDNOTES

NOTE:
Endnotes are indicated with a double-dagger symbol (‡) throughout the book. Please find the corresponding notes in this section.

6 REASONS TO READ THIS BOOK...

7 Joe Satran, "Cooking Survey Reveals That 28% of Americans Can't Cook," Huffington Post, September 9, 2011, http://www.huffingtonpost.com/2011/09/09/cooking-survey_n_955600.html (accessed September 16, 2012).

META-LEARNING

31 Richard J. Connors, *Warren Buffett on Business: Principles from the Sage of Omaha* (Hoboken: John Wiley & Sons, Inc., 2010).

37 David Crary, "U.S., Britain Labo(U)R For Language Hono(U)R As World Learns English," *Seattle Times,* July 21, 1996, http://community.seattletimes.nwsource.com/archive/?date=19960721&slug=2340289 (accessed September 16, 2012).

51 Marcia Levin Pelchat and Fritz Blank, "A Scientific Approach to Flavours and Olfactory Memory," *Food and the Memory: Proceedings of the Oxford Symposium on Food and Cookery 2000* (Totnes, UK: Prospect Books, 2001).

57 Oxford Dictionaries, "How Many Words Are There in the English Language?" http://oxforddictionaries.com/words/how-many-words-are-there-in-the-english-language (accessed September 16, 2012).

59 Oxford Dictionaries, "The OEC: Facts About the Language," http://oxforddictionaries.com/words/the-oec-facts-about-the-language (accessed September 16, 2012).

61 Josh Sens, "Swing School," *American Way,* September 2011, http://www.americanwaymag.com/stan-utley-golf-channel (accessed September 18, 2012).

61 Wikipedia, "Working Memory," http://en.wikipedia.org/wiki/Working_memory (accessed June 13, 2012).

64 Josh Waitzkin, *The Art of Learning: An Inner Journey to Optimal Performance* (New York: Free Press, 2008), 35.

82 Atul Gawande, "Personal Best," *New Yorker,* October 3, 2011, http://www.newyorker.com/reporting/2011/10/03/111003fa_fact_gawande (accessed September 16, 2012).

93 W. A. Johnson and others, "Attention Capture by Novel Stimuli," *Journal of Experimental Psychology*, vol. 119 (1990): 397–411.

THE DOMESTIC

107 Mark McClusky, "The Nike Experiment: How the Shoe Giant Unleashed the Power of Personal Metrics," *Wired*, June 22, 2009, http://www.wired.com/medtech/health/magazine/17-07/lbnp_nike (accessed September 16, 2012).

108 Larry Schwartz, "Montana Was Comeback King," http://espn.go.com/sportscentury/features/00016306.html (accessed September 16, 2012).

111 Louis Eguaras and Matthew Frederick, *101 Things I Learned in Culinary School* (New York: Grand Central Publishing, 2010).

111 Wikipedia, "Smoke Point," http://en.wikipedia.org/wiki/Smoke_point (accessed September 16, 2012). There are many factors that affect smoke point, so the numbers may vary, but our chart gives you an idea of the order.

117 Julia Child, Louisette Bertholle, and Simone Beck, *Mastering the Art of French Cooking*, 50th anniv. ed. (New York: Alfred A. Knopf, 2001).

123 Serious Eats, "The Food Lab," http://seriouseats.com/the-food-lab/ (accessed September 16, 2012).

126 B. J. Denny, P. W. West, and T. C. Mathew, "Antagonistic Interactions between the Flavonoids Hesperetin and Naringenin and Beta-lactam Antibiotics against *Staphylococcus aureus*," *British Journal of Biomedical Science*, vol. 65, no. 3 (2008): 145–47, http://ncbi.nlm.nih.gov/pubmed/18986103 and Jan Millehan, "Grapefruit Seed Extract and Infection," Livestrong, October 25, 2010, http://www.livestrong.com/article/288584-grapefruit-seed-extract-and-infection (both accessed September 16, 2012).

129 John T. Edge, "Green Eggs and Hamburgers," *New York Times*, July 12, 2011, http://www.nytimes.com/2011/07/13/dining/the-cult-of-the-big-green-egg-united-tastes.html (accessed September 16, 2012).

158 Jamie Oliver, *Cook with Jamie: My Guide to Making You a Better Cook* (New York: Hyperion, 2007).

176 Nathan Myhrvold, Chris Young, and Maxime Bilet, *Modernist Cuisine: The Art and Science of Cooking* (Bellevue, Washington: The Cooking Lab, 2011), 129.

192 Debora Esposito and others, "Anabolic Effect of Plant Brassinosteroid," *The FASEB Journal*, vol. 25, no. 10 (October 2011): 3708–3719. http://www.fasebj.org/content/25/10/3708.abstract (accessed September 16, 2012).

194 Harold McGee, "A Hot-Water Bath for Thawing Meats," *New York Times*, June 6, 2011, http://www.nytimes.com/2011/06/08/dining/a-hot-water-bath-for-thawing-meats-the-curious-cook.html (accessed September 16, 2012).

229 Bill Buford, *Heat: An Amateur's Adventures as Kitchen Slave, Line Cook, Pasta-Maker, and Apprentice to a Dante-Quoting Butcher in Tuscany* (New York: Alfred A. Knopf, 2006).

THE WILD

243 Seneca, "Moral Epistles," http://www.martinfrost.ws/htmlfiles/moral_epistles.html (accessed September 16, 2012).

261 Laura Read, "Going Primitive: Cliff Hodges '02, MEng '04, Revels in Early Tech," *Technology Review*, March/April 2010, http://www.technologyreview.com/mitnews/417638/going-primitive/ (accessed September 16, 2012).

264 Annette L. Adams and others, "Search

Is a Time-Critical Event: When Search and Rescue Missions May Become Futile," *Wilderness and Environmental Medicine*, vol. 8, no. 2 (June 2007): 95–101, http://www.wemjournal.org/article/S1080-6032(07)70218-1/fulltext (accessed September 18, 2012).

290 Burkhard Bilger, "Nature's Spoils," *New Yorker*, November 22, 2010, http://www.newyorker.com/reporting/2010/11/22/101122fa_fact_bilger (accessed September 16, 2012).

300 Anna Janeczko and Andrzej Skoczowski, "Mammalian Sex Hormones in Plants," *Folia Histochemica et Cytobiologica*, vol. 43, no. 2 (2005): 71–79. http://fhc.amb.edu.pl/archives/fulltxt/vol43/43_2/01_JAN.pdf (accessed September 16, 2012).

311 San Francisco Department of Public Health, "Director's Rules and Regulations for Prevention and Control of Rodents and Other Vectors, and to Promote Housing Habitability," http://www.sfdph.org/dph/files/EHSdocs/ehsPublsdocs/EHSDicrectorRules/vectorControl.pdf (accessed September 18, 2012).

330 *Food & Wine*, "2011 Best New Chef Award Profile: Joshua Skenes," http://www.foodandwine.com/best_new_chefs/joshua-skenes (accessed September 16, 2012).

342 Gayot, "Top 40 Restaurants in the U.S.," http://www.gayot.com/best-restaurants/2010/top40/commanders-palace-new-orleans.html (accessed September 18, 2012).

350 David Foster Wallace, "Consider the Lobster," *Gourmet*, August 2004, http://www.gourmet.com/magazine/2000s/2004/08/consider_the_lobster (accessed September 16, 2012).

350 Patricia Sellers, "Mark Zuckerberg's New Challenge: Eating Only What He Kills (and Yes, We Do Mean Literally...)," CNNMoney, May 26, 2011, http://postcards.blogs.fortune.cnn.com/2011/05/26/mark-zuckerbergs-new-challenge-eating-only-what-he-kills (accessed September 16, 2012).

THE SCIENTIST

368 Zagat Blog, "Sampling Nathan Myhrvold's Modernist Cuisine," February 8, 2011, http://www.zagat.com/buzz/sampling-nathan-myhrvolds-modernist-cuisine (accessed September 16, 2012).

453 Seneca, "Dialogue IX, Ad Serenum De Tranquillitate Animi," http://en.wikiquote.org/wiki/Talk:Seneca_the_Younger (accessed September 18, 2012).

THE PROFESSIONAL

499 Padma Lakshmi, "Cuisine Art," *Avenue*, July 2012, http://www.avenuemagazine.com/issue-archives/2012-archives/july-2012/ (accessed September 18, 2012).

505 The World's 50 Best Restaurants, "2011 Award Winners," (accessed September 18, 2012). http://www.theworlds50best.com/past-winners/2011-award-winners/

548 Gene Weingarten, "Pearls Before Breakfast," *Washington Post*, April 8, 2007, http://washingtonpost.com/wp-dyn/content/article/2007/04/04/AR2007040401721.html (accessed September 16, 2012).

562 Edward Tufte, "Touchscreens Have No Hand," November 9, 2011, http://www.edwardtufte.com/bboard/q-and-a-post-reply-form?topic_id=1&refers_to=0003qM (accessed September 16, 2012).

562 Thich Nhat Hanh, *The Miracle of Mindfulness: A Manual on Meditation* (Boston: Beacon Press, 1996).

INDEX

NOTE:
Page numbers in *italics* refer to illustrations; those in **bold** refer to recipes.

A

B

C

D

E

F

G

H

I

J

K

L

M

N

O

P

Q

R

S

T

U

V

W

X

Y

Z

CREDITS

PRINCIPAL PHOTOGRAPHERS

Daniel Krieger: 73, 135 (bottom), 137 (left column), 143, 145, 146, 155, 157 (bottom row), 158, 159, 160 (bottom two), 161 (top two rows), 163, 165 (sidebar), 166, 167 (top), 168, 169, 173, 174 (bottom), 175, 177, 179, 180, 181 (bottom two), 182 (top row), 183 (left and middle columns), 187 (top and bottom left), 189, 190, 191, 192, 208, 209 (bottom two, right column), 210, 213, 215, 217, 218, 219 (three bottom), 220, 222, 225, 227, 229, 230, 232, 289, 291, 293, 294, 296, 297, 317, 322, 324, 325 (bottom two), 326, 327, 329, 337, 338, 341, 436, 489, 490 (all but second row, right), 493, 582, 591 (left two)

Drew Kelly: front endpapers, first back endpaper, 16, 78, 91, 109, 170, 171, 371, 373, 481, 600 (bottom), 601 (top row and middle row, right)

Penny De Los Santos: 98, 112, 114, 115, 119 (immersion blender), 124 (cutting boards), 130 (ramekins), 136, 139, 144, 154, 156, 157 (top row), 160 (ingredients), 161 (bottom), 162, 164-165, 174 (top), 178, 181 (ingredients), 188, 195, 197 (AeroPress plunger), 207, 209 (ingredients), 211, 216, 219 (ingredients), 224 (ingredients), 228, 231, 235 (ingredients), 287, 288, 292, 295, 307, 308, 323, 325 (ingredients), 336, 339, 340, 351, 352, 391, 393, 394, 395, 397, 401, 405, 409, 413, 417, 421, 425, 433, 441, 445, 447, 485, 494, 497 (top and middle row), 511, 513, 515, 518, 519, 523, 525 (all but first top left), 529, 531, 533, 539, 542, 547

Susan Burdick: 118, 119 (all but the immersion blender), 121, 122, 124 (all but cutting boards), 125, 130 (all but ramekins), 137 (sidebar), 141, 197 (all but Chemex and AeroPress plunger), 201 (all but bottom right), 245, 246, 247, 248, 250, 251, 252, 281 (gun gear), 602 (all but bullet close-up), 604

PHOTOGRAPHERS

Alanna Hale: 193 (sidebar)

Albert Law: 193 (left column), 330

Animatedknots.com: 615 (left and middle columns), 616, 617

Barry Ross: 29

© Billy Fung: 183 (top right)

Bonnie Burke: 457, 458, 459, 460, 461, 462, 463, 469, 473 (top row, middle row, bottom left)

Chemex Brand Coffeemaker: 197

Christopher Michel: 15

Cliff Hodges: 619, 621, 622

Corey Arnold: 320, 321

Dan Bornstein: 184, 185 (right)

David Bishop, Inc.: 150

© Estate of Bob Carlos Clarke: 560 (top)

Gary Vaynerchuk: 151

Getty Images/ Hugh Turvey: 249

Harley Morenstein: 466

Hearth/Marco Canora: 476

Hillside Supper Club: 55

iStockPhoto/Alina Kurbiel: 254

iStockPhoto/David Palmer: 113

iStockPhoto/Davide Illini: 486 (left)

iStockPhoto/Fabrizio Troiani: 286

iStockPhoto/Floortje: 584

iStockPhoto/Grzegorz Slemp: 319

iStockPhoto/Jon-Erik Lido: 215

iStockPhoto/Liudmila Evdochimova: 302

iStockPhoto/Marek Mnich: 586

iStockPhoto/MKucova: back endpaper

iStockPhoto/RedHelga: 50

iStockPhoto/Shawn Hempel: 206

iStockPhoto/Zelijko Santrac: 525 (top left)

iStockPhoto/Zoran Stojkovic: 310

Jason Blalock: 429

Jean-Pierre Gabriel: 517

Jeff Potter: 451

Jeffrey Madoff: 384, 385

Jim McDonald, Supertraining.TV: 30

Jocelyn Filley: 347, 348

John Kernick, *Salt to Taste*: 483

Justin Kern: 40

Katie Swanson, NatureID.blogspot.com: 300 (male pine flowers)

Kevin Kittle & Lauren Pitts: 521

Mark Garcia: 495

Martin Lindsay: 509 (middle row, right, and bottom), 550

The Museum of the City of New York/Art Resource, NY: 583

Nick Cunard, Rex USA: 28 (bottom)

Olivia Grabowski-West: 28 (top)

Outer Cape Clambake: 359

Peak Candle Supplies: 509 (top row and middle row, left)

Reprinted with permission of Ephemera, Inc. www.ephemera-inc.com: 196

Russell James for Victoria's Secret: 530

Sex Pots...And Pans, by Munroe Howard (Paperback Library, 1970): 234

Shawn Koppenhoefer, tangopics.com: 66

Shutterstock/Anneka: 306

Shutterstock/Arid Ocean: 282–283

T. Kristian Russell: 256

Tim Ferriss: 4, 19, 20, 24, 35, 36, 44, 45, 47, 70, 75, 80, 81, 86, 92, 95, 104, 135 (top), 181 (sidebar), 182 (bottom), 187 (bottom right), 201 (bottom right), 209 (top three photos, right column), 214, 223, 235 (bottom photo), 236, 259, 261, 262 (top and bottom), 265, 268, 270, 279, 305, 309, 315, 332, 333, 343, 354, 355, 356, 361, 362, 366, 454, 473 (bottom right), 477, 479, 486 (right), 490 (second row, right), 497 (bottom), 498, 501, 503, 505, 536, 537, 541, 545, 546, 560 (bottom), 561, 564, 591 (right two columns), 593, 600 (top two), 601 (middle row, left, and bottom), 602 (bullet close-up), 614, 615 (right column), 618, 626

Tom McElroy, tommcphotography.com: 262 (middle)

Back of case: Jigoro Kano, public domain

ILLUSTRATORS

Ben Gibson: 578–579, 580–581

Betty Ho: 470, 632, 636

CALVIN AND HOBBES © 1992 Watterson. Dist. By UNIVERSAL UCLICK. Reprinted with permission. All rights reserved: 260

Gavin Aung Than: 313, 357, 387, 389, 399, 403, 407, 411, 415, 419, 423, 427, 431, 435, 439, 443, 449

Hero Design Studio/ Beth Manos & Mark Brickey: 255

Hollis Smith: 465

Jonathan Arvizu, Trapdoor Studio: front jacket and front case, 185 (illustration), 226, 241, 266, 269, 281 (bullet illustration), 314, 319 (wine bottle illustrations), 334, 335, 345, 362 (illustration), 596, 597, 598, 599, 620, 623

Margot Rogers: 167 (illustration), 299–301 (plant illustrations), 349, 360, 590

TEXT

Culinary Artistry, by Andrew Dornenburg and Karen Page (John Wiley and Sons, 1996): 23 (chart), 55 (sidebar)

The 4-Hour Body, by Timothy Ferriss (Crown Archetype, 2010): 376–385

Excerpted from *The French Laundry Cookbook*. Copyright © 1999 by Thomas Keller. Used by permission of Artisan, a division of Workman Publishing Co., Inc., New York. All Rights Reserved: 255

This book was produced by

MELCHER
MEDIA

124 West 13th Street
New York, NY 10011
www.melcher.com

PUBLISHER Charles Melcher
ASSOCIATE PUBLISHER Bonnie Eldon
EDITOR IN CHIEF Duncan Bock
SENIOR EDITOR AND PROJECT MANAGER Holly Dolce
PROJECT EDITORS Megan Worman and Nadia K. Bennet
EDITOR David E. Brown
PRODUCTION DIRECTOR Kurt Andrews
DIGITAL PRODUCER Carolyn Merriman
DIGITAL PRODUCTION ASSOCIATE Shannon Fanuko
EDITORIAL ASSISTANTS Lynne Ciccaglione and Gabriella Paiella

CREATIVE DIRECTOR Jessi Rymill
LEAD DESIGNER Liam Flanagan
DESIGNERS Chika Azuma and Lisa Maione

Recipe testing by Liana Krissoff and Leda Scheintaub
Recipe food styling by Michael Pederson
Recipe prop styling by Kate Parisian

MELCHER MEDIA WISHES TO THANK:

Don Armstrong, Jamie Beckman, Christopher Beha, Anne Calder, David Chow, Carolyn Coleman, Rachel Cutler, DC Typography, Max Dickstein, Elizabeth Drago, Alissa Faden, Marilyn Fu, Ping Furlan, Patty Gloeckler, Sallie Gmeiner, Barbara Gogan, Tara Hayes, Diane Hodges, Tracy Keshani, Jay Kim, David McAninch, Myles McDonnell, Michelle Medeiros, Jeremy Mickel, Beth Middleworth, Nancy Moy, J. D. Nasaw, Lauren Nathan, Austin O'Malley, Brian Pelletier, David J. Peterson, Blake Royer, Simon Rucker, Katharina Schmidt-Chiari, Kevin Schwartz, Andrew Shafer, Hollis Smith, Julia Sourikoff, Tetyana Sydoruk, Alfred Tam, Alex Tart, Anne Torpey, Joshua Volz, Anna Wahrman, Lee Wilcox, and Nancy Wolff.

CONVERSION CHART

EQUIVALENT MEASURES

***THE BOLDED ENTRIES ARE THOSE I USE MOST OFTEN.**

3 teaspoons = 1 tablespoon
4 tablespoons = ¼ cup
5 tablespoons + 1 teaspoon = ⅓ cup
8 tablespoons = ½ cup
10 tablespoons + 2 teaspoons = ⅔ cup
12 tablespoons = ¾ cup
16 tablespoons = 1 cup = 8 fluid ounces
2 cups = 1 pint = 16 fluid ounces
2 pints = 1 quart = 32 fluid ounces
2 quarts = ½ gallon = 64 fluid ounces
4 quarts = 1 gallon = 128 fluid ounces

Ounce measurements are for liquids only.

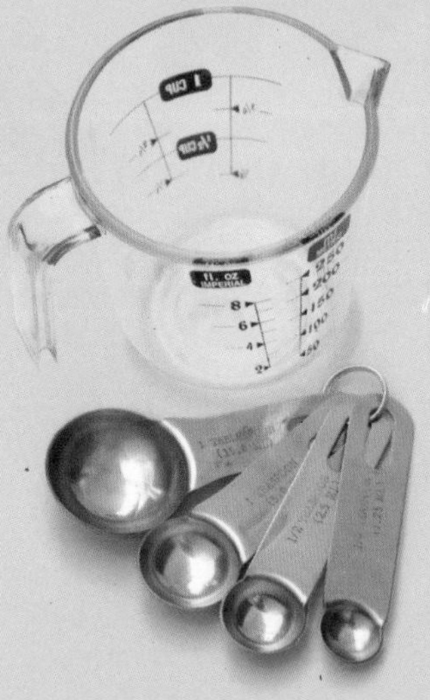

METRIC CONVERSIONS

For this book, it's safe to weigh milliliters in grams (e.g., 10 ml = 10 g).

Conversions are approximate.

VOLUME CONVERSIONS

U.S.	METRIC
1 teaspoon	**5 milliliters**
2 teaspoons	10 milliliters
1 tablespoon	**15 milliliters**
¼ cup	59 milliliters
⅓ cup	79 milliliters
1 cup	**237 milliliters**
4 cups (1 quart)	0.946 liter
1.06 quart	1 liter
4 quarts (1 gallon)	3.8 liters

WEIGHT CONVERSIONS

OUNCES (oz)	GRAMS (g)
1	**28**
4	113
8	227
16 (1 lb)	454

SUBSTITUTIONS

1 can (usually 14 oz) = almost 2 cups (16 oz) (save an empty can for pouring)

1 teaspoon kosher salt = ½ teaspoon table salt